P9-CSB-662

Clarissa

·

RIVERSIDE EDITIONS

RIVERSIDE EDITIONS

UNDER THE GENERAL EDITORSHIP OF

Gordon N. Ray

SAMUEL RICHARDSON

Clarissa

or

The History of a Young Lady

ABRIDGED AND EDITED WITH AN INTRODUCTION BY
GEORGE SHERBURN

HOUGHTON MIFFLIN COMPANY · BOSTON

Samuel Richardson: 1689–1761

Clarissa was first published in 1747–48

COPYRIGHT © 1962 BY GEORGE SHERBURN

ALL RIGHTS RESERVED

PRINTED IN THE U.S.A.

ISBN: 0-395-05164-9

INTRODUCTION

by

GEORGE SHERBURN

Much of this "large still book," as Tennyson affectionately called it, was written in the pleasant garden house at North End, on the edge of Hammersmith, where the author, Samuel Richardson (1689–1761), made his home. He was a middle-aged printer, who without much formal education had in his faithfully acquired prosperity, partly by accident, become a novelist. Two booksellers, evidently aware of Richardson's devotion to letter-writing, had asked him to prepare a manual of specimen or model letters as aid to "country readers who were unable to indite for themselves." As a confirmed moralist Richardson devised this volume, *Familiar Letters* (1741), so that his models might convey moral instruction; and it presently occurred to him that such instruction could be even better enforced in letters that told a story — and from childhood he had loved story-telling. His consequent first novel, *Pamela,* written in about ten weeks and published at the end of 1740, was received with resounding acclaim — and with scattered critical laughter. Fielding and Horace agreed *docti indoctique scribimus,* and a printer was not normally considered as among the learned. The moral teaching of *Pamela* was suspect in that, having escaped rather surprisingly from the dangers of rape, the heroine consented to reward her conscious virtue by marrying her amorous admirer. But the reception of the novel in general was enthusiastic.

Hardly was the second part of *Pamela* in print (it raised the servant girl to respectable "high life") before Richardson began work on his real masterpiece, *Clarissa.* A detailed précis of the plot was offered to the scrutiny of friends as early as 1744, and the period from 1745 to 1747 was used for revisions and particularly (we are told) for condensation. The novel was published in three sections: Volumes I and II appeared in December, 1747; III and IV came out in April, 1748. Then, after several months, Volumes V, VI, and VII were published in December, 1748. The earlier sections had whetted readers' appetites, and this last long pause kept them in suspense as to Clarissa's ultimate fate, and thus attracted attention to the story. Later editions printed by Richardson filled eight volumes.

Richardson's early biographer, Mrs. Barbauld, remarked that he dwelt "in a flower garden of ladies," and his excessive but decorous preference for female society irked even his good friend Dr. Johnson. As critics these ladies doubtless were of some assistance, but his more influential advisers in perfecting the novel in the period of revision were an ill-assorted group of male friends: Aaron Hill, a third-rate poet, dramatist and critic; Colley Cibber, a leading actor and manager, notoriously unchaste in morals; the Rev. Edward Young (whom Richardson once called his "favourite author," and who was then at work on his popular and pious *Night Thoughts*) — and doubtless others. He had many distinguished male friends, who did not frequent his "flower garden." All told, Richardson remained fairly independent of advisers or critics.

His field was "high life" or a limited aspect of such life, and he was naturally criticized as ignorant in this field. "Obscurely situated," as he calls himself, and "naturally shy and sheepish," he frankly asked his admirer Lady Bradshaigh, "How shall such a man pretend to describe and enter into the characters in upper life?" (Had he chiefly witnessed their tense emotions as seen on the theatrical stage?) All his major characters, with the exception of Pamela, are from the upper classes; but rather than the surfaces of their lives, the tensions arising from their moral problems are his central interest: he was a specialist in the emotional variations of the delicate and troubled heart. He thus augmented a trend, new in English, which was to become dominant later in his century — especially in the building up of a *distress* (almost a technical term in fiction of the time); in the dramatization of the release of pent-up emotions, which possibly tend to be similar in all classes.

Preoccupied with the depiction of psychological or moral reactions, Richardson neglected surface details of daily life. There is, however, more than one sees at first sight. We learn of the astonishingly early morning hours — busy at one's pen by 5 A.M.; breakfast (a real meal) at nine or later; dinner in the early or middle afternoon, and so on. Strange "props" such as Lovelace's costume of disguise at Hampstead, the arms on the fictitious dowager's coach, or the inscriptions on Clarissa's "house" are given in minute detail. Lovelace, sleepless in London as the silent dawn approaches, hears in the darkness the "rattling chariot wheels at a street's distance." We get glimpses of reality, but the "look" of the life of the time is not a major concern. The fit and the unfit in the behavior dominate all interest.

In treating the emotional difficulties of his persons Richardson presents an array of problems. The original title page specifies one such as "the distresses that may attend the misconduct both of parents and children in relation to marriage," and this is obviously a central theme. It may at once warn the twentieth-century reader that he must call strongly upon his historical imagination in order to achieve a sympathetic reading of the book. According to the mores of 1750 it was tyrannical, but not impossible, for parents to force a daughter to marry a man she greatly disliked. It was intolerable, however, for a daughter to marry one whom her father disliked. Clarissa is thought to wish to marry the hated Lovelace. In his early volumes Richardson lets Clarissa, unaware, hesitate about a possible love for Lovelace; but later the total incompatibility of these two is developed and dramatized.

Allied with such problems is the economic aspect of marriage. The Harlowes are "too rich to be happy," but they have an insatiable thirst for more, and, being worldly, rich, and selfish, they wish their daughter to marry so as to enhance their status as a rising family. Personal animosities lead them here to act inconsistently in preferring Solmes to Lovelace, who might well survive Lord M. and so perhaps succeed to an earldom. Clarissa stands apart from the family in that she always prefers happiness to fortune. The Harlowes think like ambitious landed gentry (though their wealth seems excessive for most of that class), and in their eye Solmes's lands complement sweetly the present family holdings.

Richardson and Clarissa prefer less selfish, softer qualities than do the inflexible, callous Harlowes; but Clarissa herself is inflexible in her devotion to virtue and decorum. To some readers in the twentieth century *decorum* seems almost an indecent word; but again historical imagination, if nothing else, should rescue them from such deprecation. Decorum is not primarily a stodgy middle-class idol. Richardson adores it because he yearns for true aristocratic quality; but he is no more devoted to decorum than was his contemporary, the *arbiter elegantiarum*, Lord Chesterfield.

For Clarissa herself, decorum is almost a religion: indeed, if religion is defined as conservation of value, decorum is certainly her religion. Her obsessive desire to avoid the unfit and to cultivate the fit is seen everywhere. And Richardson's chief study, even in the first part of *Pamela* and in *Clarissa* (where story is important), seems to be similar: the true problem always is how one ought to cope with a given delicate situation. The ultimate bewilderment of Lovelace when he asks, "Can Education have a stronger force in a woman's heart than Nature?" suggests how far in his eyes decorum, habit, training, have led the divine Clarissa. The rigid social code of the day seems to dominate her completely; but she lives by high ideals and in the end will sacrifice nothing for "appearances."

The sense of the fit is supported by orthodox religious beliefs. The relation to destiny is coupled with the doctrine of rewards and punishments in another world (a central theme in the story) and coupled also with the doctrine of divine grace. In her last days (September 7) Clarissa writes, "God Almighty would not let me depend for comfort upon any but Himself," and the weighty sentence is for emphasis printed in capitals. She is convinced that only the miracle of divine grace could change the heart of Lovelace. Her invocation of grace is perhaps frequent enough to annoy Henry Fielding, who, though he admired *Clarissa*, had plumped for "good works," and as a latitudinarian disliked appeals to the doctrine of grace. Decorum is in close alliance with religion: it almost swallows the concept of virtue — which in turn may seem wrongly at times to equate with mere chastity. The moral nature of Clarissa is not puritan: it is idealistic, and its absolutes make no concessions to circumstance.

This attitude becomes inevitably tragic. Probably no novelist has ever been under more pressure from friends than Richardson was from readers who wished *Clarissa* to have a happy ending. Firmly, Richardson held that Clarissa could not be merely a second Pamela with her virtue here rewarded: her sufferings, he held, could only be rewarded in another life. For present-day readers the necessity of a tragic ending will be felt further through the complete essential incompatibility of Clarissa and Lovelace. In 1748 readers with facile emotions did not perceive this incompatibility, which in his later volumes of the story Richardson made quite apparent. The two might have married, but without a most extreme miracle of divine grace their married life would have been hell for Clarissa: it would merely have delayed painfully her heavenly reward.

Lesser problems that Richardson touches upon are of some influence in shaping the novel: Do reformed rakes make good husbands? Does the fair sex (when not heroic) need counsel more than do men? How far is the arrogance of "men of honour" to be tolerated? This last question creeps repeatedly into Richardson's thinking. His friend Edward Young was then creating his Lorenzo in *Night Thoughts* and was to embody criticism in his less known *Centaur not Fabulous* (1754). The man of mode was fast becoming not merely a beast but rather an arrogant beast. Lovelace, though kind to his tenants, can be crudely arrogant, as he is to the Smiths in their own house. In general Lovelace is unaware that real politeness involves disinterested considerateness for the distress of another.

As a depiction of family life the story is fascinating, if not always convincing. The Harlowes, supposed to be landed gentry, are psychologically citizens, bourgeois — too rich for their own good, too little seen moving graciously among their county neighbors. Clarissa apparently has never visited London; at home, aged eighteen, she is surprisingly allowed to have a parlour of her own in which to receive her visitors — young ladies only, doubtless. For her age she has unusual liberty in the management of her dairy and even of Harlowe Place itself, where she performs the offices of a superior housekeeper. She keeps the accounts of her dairy and dutifully turns over the proceeds to her father, though legally they are her own. Her clothes seem enormously costly for a girl of her age, especially if they are to be worn only in the country. She is a great reader apparently, and has written a "little book upon the principal acting plays." (Possibly only a notebook is intended.)

The chief personalities of the story lead a reader to conclude that as characters they are less titillating than are the situations in which they commonly find themselves. Clarissa's plight is from the very beginning evocative and gripping, but Clarissa herself is too good for human use: the epithet most commonly applied to her is *divine*, closely followed by *angelic*. Realizing that perfection is inhuman, Richardson protests that he did not intend to make her perfect. Some possible flaws are occasionally seen glimmering, but they are obscured by conventional virtues. What is likely to stay in the reader's mind are her frustrating distresses and her complete and inflexible devotion to decorum and virtue. As one early critic complained, she is *methodically* virtuous.

This trait has frequently seemed to exceed common sense, and to make Clarissa almost as rigorous a tyrant in propriety as her father was in regard to filial duties. At more than one crisis decorum blocks the road to happiness. Some readers have been inclined to agree with Miss Howe, who always tends to be sensible and practical, that Clarissa should have married Lovelace at St. Albans. What stops her here, however, is largely her preference for a reconciliation with her family: she already suspects Lovelace of trickery. She is elsewhere represented as a resourceful, clear-headed young businesswoman, unable, to be sure, to devise ready ways of escape from Mrs. Sinclair's establishment. That house, however, was notorious, and to throw up the front window and cry for help was, and would naturally be, unsuccessful. When she does escape, it has been suggested that she should have gone, not to Hampstead, but to Justice Henry Fielding, who might have given protection. There were only the beginnings of a police force in London in 1750, and the status of women was then such that all Fielding could legally or actually have done would be to return the eighteen-year-old damsel to her family — who, considering her suspect condition would almost certainly have refused to receive her. Richardson has most ingeniously hemmed her in — completely!

It is difficult to predicate convincing human traits in connection with spotless near-perfection. Cordelia and Desdemona succeed; but only Shakespeare has the secret. Clarissa wins us rather more by her distresses, externally produced, than by natural personal traits. To Lady Bradshaigh, Richardson wrote (6 Oct. 1748):

> I had to shew, for example sake, a young lady struggling nobly with the greatest difficulties, and triumphing from the best motives, in the course of distresses, the tenth part of which would have sunk even manly hearts; yet tenderly educated, born to affluence, naturally meek, altho' when an exertion of spirit was necessary, manifesting herself to be a true heroine.

Although Clarissa's plight must arouse and move readers overwhelmingly, the sympathy may be somewhat lessened by the dazzlingly mixed character of Lovelace, who, whether kindly regarded or viewed with horror, steals the show. The Rosebud episode at first tips the scale for some in his favor. Later his unfeeling and brutal sexual plots, not merely against Clarissa but also against the ladies of Hampstead, and against Anna Howe and her mother, should make him either despicable or absurd. His plot against the Howes,[1] inserted first in 1751, is here omitted as an improbable fantasy designed crudely to make Lovelace blacken himself — to show that to him rape is just good fun. Clarissa often accuses him of lacking kindliness or generosity; and he himself in a passage of self-analysis tells us, "I have three passions that sway me by turns; all imperial ones. Love, revenge, ambition, or a desire of conquest." He constantly sees himself as an imperial personage.

In general, of course, he was an inveterate plotter whose early tricks succeeded to his liking. At the end Clarissa triumphs, though wronged, and his plots become somewhat childish and futile. His hardness led an early critic to say to Richardson:

> You have not been able to describe an agreeable, artful, and accomplish'd seducer, who, without raising fears and terrors could melt, surprise, or reason a woman out of her virtue.[2]

Lovelace is artful, excessively so, and accomplished; but he certainly depends on fears and terrors. In all three of his novels Richardson is far more obsessed by the idea of rape than by that of persuasive seduction.

The extremes in Lovelace's character have been thought inconsistent, but if one can imagine that his confirmed addiction to plots is here stimulated in part by his curious and passionate love of Clarissa, in part by his hatred of all other Harlowes, and in part by his imperial love of revenge, his actions seem to vary within a con-

---

[1] In the edition of 1759, vol. iv, page 494–5 (about May 25).
[2] *Critical Remarks on Sir Charles Grandison, Clarissa, and Pamela* (1754), p. 37. The pamphlet has been reproduced by A. D. McKillop for the Augustan Reprint Society.

sistent pattern. His love of Clarissa must be set against the background of his sworn aim to avenge his wrongs upon the sex. He does not believe any woman impregnably virtuous, and so enters upon his relentless psychological and physical experiment with Clarissa: how could he *know*, he asks, that she is as virtuous as she seems unless he tries. . . ? The coldness of the experiment and the depth of his genuine passion for Clarissa, can be reconciled by his subconscious separation of her chastity from her "self" — the one the object of his experiment, the other (her complete and proven "self") the object of his love and esteem. Lovelace and Clarissa lived in totally different psychological worlds: any real marriage for these two was unthinkable. As Clarissa remarks, "Mr. Lovelace's mind and mine are vastly different, different in essentials." A Victorian critic found Lovelace's dislike of marriage "unintelligible": to the eighteenth-century reader such an attitude on the part of a rake would be easily understood. In the song, such men were chanting, "I sipped each flower / I changed every hour." The attitude is morally shameful, but no less understandable than the aversions of Clarissa and Miss Howe to the subordinate state of wife. Clarissa surprises Lovelace more than once by telling him that he is deficient in politeness, good manners. Again it is a voice from without, and above, the blasé world of fashion: she is telling him that he is essentially ungenerous, that he lacks kindliness and all unselfish benevolence. With regard to Lovelace Dr. Johnson shrewdly remarked, "It was in the power of Richardson alone to teach at once esteem and detestation; to make virtuous resentment overpower all the benevolence which wit, elegance, and courage naturally excite; and to lose, at last, the hero in the villain."

If we consider the means by which Richardson accomplished his aims, we are face to face with his celebrated epistolary method, and we are at last forced to conclude that the method, while apt in producing a good moral book (we all get good moral counsel in letters!), is likely to be repetitious and slow in telling a story. So Dr. Johnson pontificated that one must not read Richardson for the story but for the "sentiment." The remark may not have convinced readers that "sentiments" are not tedious, but it truly described Richardson's emphasis: not events but psychological and moral reactions to and observations on events are his chief concern. The fact in part justifies his use of letters as a vehicle. He plays realistically with techniques of correspondence. As one of the best of modern Richardsonians, Alan McKillop,[3] has remarked: "The writing of the letters is only the beginning; they are copied, sent, received, shown about, discussed, answered, even perhaps hidden, intercepted, stolen, altered or forged." They are also by the "editor" (Richardson) cross-referenced in foot-

[3] *Samuel Richardson, Printer and Novelist* (Chapel Hill, 1936), p. 36.

notes, when a writer alludes to something written earlier. These methods are ingenious, but letters tend to dilate reactions rather than to forward the story. Richardson himself before the novel was published realized one obvious difficulty. He wrote to Aaron Hill (20 Jan. 1745/6): "length is my principal Disgust, at present. . . . The fixing of Dates has been a Task to me. I am afraid I make the Writers do too much in the Time."[4]

The varying tones of letters are admirably kept. Richardson told one lady, "Styles differ, too, as much as faces, and are indicative, generally beyond the power of disguise, of the mind of the writer." So he endeavors and usually succeeds in individualizing his correspondents by differing styles. In this way he gives distinctive character to all his persons, major or minor as they may be. His methods are more subtle and less obvious than those of another master of fictional letters, the author of *Humphry Clinker*.

It is not to be thought that Richardson is lacking in narrative skill. The famous pen-knife scene (almost on the lofty level of grand opera, without music to carry it off) and the contrived return of Clarissa to Mrs. Sinclair's from Hampstead are examples of his best narrative passages. The tea-drinking episode (May 22) is a typical example of his sense of presence.

Upon first publication Richardson's dramatic technique of "writing to the moment" was at once recognized and acclaimed. There is no emotion *recollected*: it is captured as it arises; and although the lack of any lapse between the moment and the recording of the moment is improbable, the vividness is always effective. Fielding laughed at the improbability of the method by making his Shamela exclaim (with a lewd adjectival pun on the final noun), "You see I write in the present tense."

This "writing to the moment" is certainly a large part of Richardson's contribution to novelistic technique — far more important than his use of the epistolary form. His letters are normally too long and too vividly detailed to seem like letters: they readily become journals rather than letters — most obviously in the long series written by Clarissa to Miss Howe or by Lovelace to Belford. Length aids in the development of an important added element: "big scenes" that may run for many pages and that are marked by long conversations used either to develop the story or to show the tense emotions of the characters. With these added elements of big scenes and lively conversations (much more fully developed than ever before in the novel) "writing to the moment" constitutes Richardson's very notable method that was to dominate the novel for a long time.

4 Within the period from 6 A.M. to midnight of June 10, Lovelace along with normal activities of the day is supposed to write something like 14,00€ words.

He rightly spoke of his use of "dramatic narrative," and he owes more to his acquaintance with the theater than has sometimes been recognized. He printed, so we are told,[5] plays for a dozen or more dramatists, and he printed relatively little fiction. Lovelace has been thought to be a high-finished portrait indebted to Rowe's Lothario (in *The Fair Penitent*), and the whole plot of the novel resembles that of Charles Johnson's *Caelia* (1733). Richardson is capable of giving very long scenes in dialogue with the text falling into the typographical form of a play. Words or phrases like stage directions are inserted at times to indicate the speaker's tone of voice. At the end of his early Prefaces the characters are listed as *dramatis personae*. In *Clarissa* the whole movement of rising and falling action is like a tragedy focused and followed from beginning to end. Lastly, it may be suggested that, like a good playwright, Richardson composes his conversation for the ear rather than for the eye. The sound captured is a large part of his writing to the moment. His divergent traditions, then, include that of the theater and that of moral discourse, the courtesy book, rather than that of earlier romances, though to them he does have some debts. His final achievement is that of completely capturing the reader, who though straining at a leash is yet held by the tension of the narrative situation. In 1762 Diderot summed it up by remarking that when you read a bit of *Clarissa*, you lose studious aloofness, and are a part of the story.[6]

This is true in spite of the fact that like most novelists Richardson is more interested in substance than in expression. Hazlitt thought that Richardson "had the strongest matter of fact imagination that ever existed, and wrote the oddest mixture of poetry and prose." At times the true language of passionate emotion is captured, at other times the language is as unreal and lofty as that of operatic scenes. His early editor Mangin (1811) thought a curious informality appropriate in personal letters: "Minute flippances of expression, colloquial phrases, new-coined words, and involved periods, which would be intolerable in serious history, are not merely pardonable, but perhaps expected in letter-writing." All such locutions are certainly present in Richardson's writing. It is power of conception, the strong matter-of-fact imagination, rather than power of expression that really captures the reader.

The reputation of *Clarissa* in the later eighteenth century was superlative both at home and on the Continent. Rousseau's *Nouvelle Héloise* was simply the most famous of innumerable imitations, and symbolizes the fact that above all Richardson was a moral novelist. In the nineteenth century Alfred de Musset thought it *"le premier*

---

5 W. M. Sale, *Samuel Richardson: Master Printer* (Ithaca, 1950), p. 106.
6 Diderot's *Éloge* (1762), translated, is printed in Volume I of Mangin's edition (1811) of Richardson — and elsewhere.

roman du monde," and in the twentieth century the American novelist, Ellen Glasgow, was proud to aver that annually she read through the complete *Clarissa*. It was from the first calculated for readers at leisure; for busy people, unconcerned with the life of ideals, it has to remain, what it has always been, a "large still book." For the man of "solitude and tranquillity" (Diderot's description of *Clarissa*'s best reader) the novel must always be overwhelming; and such a reader on closing the book may say with Diderot, and with reverence, "I felt I had acquired experience."

A NOTE ON THE TEXT

In Richardson's own printings of the novel (1748–59) the title-page does not carry the name of Harlowe. The heading on the opening page of the text, however, gives the family name (*The History of Clarissa Harlowe*), as does the divided running-head throughout: *The History of* on left-hand pages, and *Miss Clarissa Harlowe* on right-hand pages, with the *Miss* omitted in the edition of 1759.

In its complete form *Clarissa* runs to well over a million words. The various editions seem never to have been completely scrutinized or collated. A partial collation makes it probable that no two editions, either from Richardson's time or later, are textually identical. The first edition omitted many passages that are restored in the octavo of 1751, and the 1759 text (not printed with scrupulous care) makes perhaps final revisions and additions.

Most editions eclectically conflate passages from different texts printed by the author. Richardson's more complicated sentences seem at times to have influenced even the pressman to attempt clarification by verbal changes. The present text follows this tradition of conflation: it is based on the faulty text given in *Everyman's Library*, which has been collated with that of 1759, which in turn, chiefly for misprints, omissions of essential words, etc., has been compared with the texts of 1748 and 1751.

All insertions (clarifications or summaries) made here in the abridgment by the present editor, are placed in square brackets. For Richardson's own frequent use of these brackets or "hooks," parentheses are here substituted, according to modern usage. Footnotes not placed in brackets are by Richardson himself.

The title page of Volume I of the first edition is reproduced through the courtesy of the Houghton Library, Harvard University.

G. S.

CLARISSA.

OR, THE

HISTORY

OF A

YOUNG LADY:

Comprehending

The most Important Concerns *of* Private LIFE.

And particularly shewing,

The DISTRESSES that may attend the Misconduct
Both of PARENTS and CHILDREN,

In Relation to MARRIAGE.

Published by the EDITOR *of* PAMELA.

VOL. I.

LONDON:

Printed for S. Richardson:

And Sold by A. MILLAR, over-against *Catharine-street* in the *Strand*;
J. and JA. RIVINGTON, in *St. Paul's Church-yard*;
JOHN OSBORN, in *Pater-noster Row*.
And by J. LEAKE, at *Bath*.

M.DCC.XLVIII.

AUTHOR'S PREFACE (1759)

THE following History is given in a Series of Letters written principally in a double yet separate correspondence;

Between two young Ladies of virtue and honour, bearing an inviolable friendship for each other, and writing not merely for amusement, but upon the most *interesting* subjects; in which every private family, more or less, may find itself concerned: And,

Between two Gentlemen of free lives; one of them glorying in his talents for Stratagem and Invention, and communicating to the other, in confidence, all the secret purposes of an intriguing head and resolute heart.

But here it will be proper to observe, for the sake of such as may apprehend hurt to the morals of Youth, from the more freely written Letters, that the Gentlemen, tho' professed Libertines as to the Female Sex, and making it one of their wicked maxims, to keep no faith with any of the individuals of it, who are thrown into their power, are not, however, either Infidels or Scoffers; nor yet such as think themselves freed from the observance of those other moral duties which bind man to man.

On the contrary, it will be found, in the progress of the Work, that they very often make such reflections upon each other, and each upon himself and his own actions, as reasonable beings *must* make, who disbelieve not a Future State of Rewards and Punishments, and who one day propose to reform — One of them actually reforming, and by that means giving an opportunity to censure the freedoms which fall from the gayer pen and lighter heart of the other.

And yet that other, altho' in unbosoming himself to a select friend, he discover wickedness enough to entitle him to general detestation, preserves a decency, as well in his images, as in his language, which is not always to be found in the works of some of the most celebrated modern Writers, whose subjects and characters have less warranted the liberties they have taken.

In the Letters of the two young Ladies, it is presumed will be found not only the highest exercise of a reasonable and *practicable* Friendship, between minds endowed with the noblest principles of Virtue and Religion, but occasionally interspersed, such Delicacy of Sentiments, particularly with regard to the other Sex; such instances of Impartiality, each freely, as a fundamental principle of their friendship, blaming, praising, and setting right the other, as are strongly to be recommended to the observation of the *younger* part (more especially) of Female Readers.

The principal of the two young Ladies is proposed as an Examplar to her Sex. Nor is it any objection to her being so, that she is not in all respects a perfect character. It was not only natural, but it was necessary, that she should have some faults, were it only to shew the Reader, how laudably she could mistrust and blame herself, and carry to her own heart, divested of self-partiality, the censure which arose from her own convictions, and that even to the acquittal of those, because revered characters, whom no one else would acquit, and to whose much greater faults her errors were owing, and not to a weak or reproachable heart. As far as is consistent with human frailty, and as far as she could be perfect, considering the people she had to deal with, and those with whom she was inseparably connected, she *is* perfect. To have been impeccable, must have left nothing for the Divine Grace and a Purified State to do, and carried our idea of her from woman to angel. As such is she often esteemed by the man whose *heart* was so corrupt, that he could hardly believe human nature capable of the purity, which, on every trial or temptation, shone out in *hers*.

Besides the four principal persons, several others are introduced, whose Letters are characteristic: And it is presumed that there will be found in some of them, but more especially in those of the chief character among the men, and the second character among the women, such strokes of Gaiety, Fancy, and Humour, as will entertain and divert; and at the same time both warn and instruct.

All the Letters are written while the hearts of the writers must be supposed to be wholly engaged in their subjects (The events at the time generally dubious): So that they abound not only with critical Situations, but with what may be called *instantaneous* Descriptions and Reflections (proper to be brought home to the breast of the youthful reader); as also with affecting Conversations; many of them written in the dialogue or dramatic way.

"*Much more* lively and affecting, says one of the principal characters [Belford: Aug. 4] must be the Style of those who write in the height of a *present* distress; the mind tortured by the pangs of uncertainty (the Events then hidden in the womb of Fate); than the dry, narrative, unanimated Style of a person relating difficulties and dangers surmounted, can be; the relater perfectly at ease; and if himself unmoved by his own Story, not likely greatly to affect the Reader."

What will be found to be more particularly aimed at in the following Work, is — To warn the Inconsiderate and Thoughtless of the one Sex, against the base arts and designs of specious Contrivers of the other — To caution Parents against the undue exercise of their natural authority over their Children in the great article of Marriage — To warn Children against preferring a Man of Pleasure to a Man of Probity, upon that dangerous but too commonly-received notion, *That a reformed Rake makes the best Husband* — But above all, To investigate the highest and most important Doctrines not only of Morality, but of Christianity, by shewing them thrown into action in the conduct of the *worthy* characters; while the *unworthy*, who set those Doctrines at defiance, are condignly, and, as may be said, consequentially, punished.

From what has been said, considerate Readers will not enter upon the perusal of the Piece before them, as if it were designed *only* to divert and amuse. It will probably be thought tedious to all such as *dip* into it, expecting a *light Novel*, or *transitory Romance*; and look upon Story in it (interesting as that is generally allowed to be) as its *sole end*, rather than as a vehicle to the Instruction.

Different persons, as might be expected, have been of different opinions, in relation to the conduct of the Heroine in particular Situations; and several worthy persons have objected to the general Catastrophe, and other parts of the History. Whatever is thought material of these shall be taken notice of by way of POSTSCRIPT, at the conclusion of the History; for this Work being addressed to the Public as a History of *Life* and *Manners*, those parts of it which are proposed to carry with them the force of an Example, ought to be as unobjectionable as is consistent with the *design of the whole*, and with *human nature*.

THE HISTORY OF CLARISSA HARLOWE

Miss Anna Howe to Miss Clarissa Harlowe

Jan. 10.

I AM extremely concerned, my dearest friend, for the disturbances that have happened in your family. I know how it must hurt you to become the subject of the public talk; and yet upon an occasion so generally known, it is impossible but that whatever relates to a young lady, whose distinguished merits have made her the public care, should engage everybody's attention. I long to have the particulars from yourself; and of the usage I am told you receive upon an accident you could not help; and in which, as far as I can learn, the sufferer was the aggressor.

Mr. Diggs the surgeon, whom I sent for at the first hearing of the rencounter, to inquire, for *your* sake, how your brother was, told me that there was no danger from the wound, if there were none from the fever; which it seems has been increased by the perturbation of his spirits.

They say that Mr. Lovelace could not avoid drawing his sword: and that either your brother's unskilfulness or passion left him from the very first pass entirely in his power. This, I am told, was what Mr. Lovelace said upon it, retreating as he spoke: "Have a care, Mr. Harlowe, your violence puts you out of your defence. You give me too much advantage. For your sister's sake I will pass by everything — if ——"

But this the more provoked his rashness to lay himself open to the advantage of his adversary, who, after a slight wound given him in the arm, took away his sword.

There are people who love not your brother, because of his natural imperiousness and fierce and uncontrollable temper: these say that the young gentleman's passion was abated on seeing his blood gush plentifully down his arm; and that he received the generous offices of his adversary (who helped him off with his coat and waistcoat, and bound up his arm till the surgeon could come) with such patience, as was far from making a visit afterwards from that adversary to inquire after his health appear either insulting or improper.

Be this as it may, everybody pities you. So steady, so uniform in your conduct; so desirous, as you always said, of sliding through life to the end of it unnoted; and, as I may add, not wishing to be observed even for your silent benevolence; sufficiently happy in the noble consciousness which attends it: *Rather useful than glaring*, your deserved motto; though now, to your regret, pushed into blaze, as I may say; and yet blamed at home for the faults of others.

1

My mother and all of us, like the rest of the world, talk of nobody but you on this occasion, and of the consequences which may follow from the resentments of a man of Mr. Lovelace's spirit; who, as he gives out, has been treated with high indignity by your uncles. My mother will have it that you cannot now, with any decency, either see him or correspond with him. She is a good deal prepossessed by your uncle Antony, who occasionally calls upon us, as you know; and on this rencounter, has represented to her the crime which it would be in a sister to encourage a man who is to wade into her favour (this was his expression) through the blood of her brother.

Write to me therefore, my dear, the whole of your story from the time that Mr. Lovelace was first introduced into your family; and particularly an account of all that passed between him and your sister. You see what you draw upon yourself by excelling all your sex. Every individual of it who knows you, or has heard of you, seems to think you answerable to *her* for your conduct in points so very delicate and concerning.

MISS CLARISSA HARLOWE TO MISS HOWE

Harlowe Place, Jan. 13.

OUR family has indeed been strangely discomposed. — *Discomposed!* — It has been in *tumults* ever since the unhappy transaction; and I have borne all the blame; yet should have had too much concern from myself had I been more justly spared by everyone else.

For whether it be owing to a faulty impatience, having been too indulgently treated to be *inured* to blame, or to the regret I have to hear those censured on my account whom it is my duty to vindicate; I have sometimes wished that it had pleased God to have taken me in my last fever, when I had everybody's love and good opinion; but oftener that I had never been distinguished by my grandfather as I was since that distinction has estranged from me my brother's and sister's affections; at least, has raised a jealousy with regard to the apprehended favour of my two uncles, that now and then overshadows their love.

It was in pursuance of a conference between Lord M. and my Uncle Antony, that Mr. Lovelace (my father and mother not forbidding) paid his respects to my sister Arabella. My brother was then in Scotland, busying himself in viewing the condition of the considerable estate which was left him there by his generous godmother. I was also absent at my *Dairy-house,* as it is called,[1] busied in the accounts relating to the estate which my grandfather had the goodness

---

[1] Her grandfather, in order to invite her to him as often as her other friends would spare her, indulged her in erecting and fitting up a dairy-house in her own taste. When finished, it was so much admired for its elegant simplicity and convenience, that the whole seat (before, of old time, from its situation, called The Grove) was generally known by the name of The Dairy-House. Her grandfather in particular was fond of having it so called.

to devise to me; and which once a year are left to my inspection, although I have given the whole into my father's power.

My sister made me a visit there the day after Mr. Lovelace had been introduced, and seemed highly pleased with the gentleman. His birth, his fortune in possession — a clear two thousand pounds a year — as Lord M. had assured my uncle; presumptive heir to that nobleman's large estate; his great expectations from Lady Sarah Sadleir and Lady Betty Lawrance; who with his uncle interested themselves very warmly (he being the last of his line) to see him married.

"So handsome a man! — O her beloved Clary!" (for then she was ready to love me dearly, from the overflowings of her good humour on his account!). "He was but *too* handsome a man for *her*! — Were she but as amiable as *somebody*, there would be a probability of *holding* his affections! — For he was wild, she heard; *very* wild, very gay; loved intrigue. But he was young; *a man of sense*: would see his error, could she but have patience with his faults, if his faults were not cured by marriage."

Thus she ran on; and then wanted me "to see the charming man," as she called him. Again concerned, "that she was not handsome enough for him"; with, "a sad thing, that the man should have the advantage of the woman in that particular!" — But then, stepping to the glass she complimented herself, "That she was very *well*: that there were many women deemed passable who were inferior to herself."

I congratulated her upon her prospects. She received my compliments with a great deal of self-complacency.

She liked the gentleman still more at his next visit; and yet he made no particular address to her, although an opportunity was given him for it. This was wondered at, as my uncle had introduced him into our family declaredly as a visitor to my sister. So my sister found out a reason much to Mr. Lovelace's advantage for his not improving the opportunity that was given him. It was bashfulness, truly, in him. (Bashfulness in Mr. Lovelace, my dear!). Indeed, gay and lively as he is, he has not the look of an impudent man. But I fancy it is many, many years ago since he was bashful.

Thus, however, could my sister make it out — "Upon her word, she believed Mr. Lovelace deserved not the bad character he had as to women. He was really to *her* thinking, a modest man. He *would* have spoken out, she believed; but once or twice as he seemed to intend to do so, he was under so *agreeable* a confusion! Such a profound respect he seemed to show her! She was not one of those *flirts*, not she, who would give pain to a person that deserved to be well treated; and the more pain for the greatness of his value for her." I wish she had not somebody whom I love in her eye.)

How they managed it in their next conversation I know not. One would be tempted to think by the issue that Mr. Lovelace was ungenerous enough to seek the occasion given, and to improve it. Yet he thought fit to put the question too. But, she says, it was not till by some means or other (she knew not how) he had wrought her up to such a pitch of displeasure with him, that it was impossible for her to recover herself at the instant. Nevertheless he re-urged his question, as expecting a definitive answer, without waiting for the return of her temper, or endeavouring to mollify her; so that she was under a necessity of persisting in her denial; yet gave him reason to think she did not dislike his address, only the *manner* of it; his court being rather made to her mother than to herself, as if he were sure of *her* consent at any time.

A good encouraging denial, I must own — as was the rest of her plea, to wit: "A disinclination to change her state. Exceedingly happy as she was; she never could be happier!" And such-like *consenting negatives*, as I may call them.

Miss Clarissa Harlowe to Miss Howe

Jan. 13, 14.

And thus, as Mr. Lovelace thought fit to *take it*, had he his answer from my sister. It was with very great regret, as he pretended (I doubt the man is an hypocrite, my dear), that he acquiesced in it. "So much determinedness; such a noble firmness in my sister; that there was no hope of prevailing upon her to alter sentiments she had adopted on full consideration." He sighed, as Bella told us, when he took his leave of her: "Profoundly sighed; grasped her hand, and kissed it with *such* an ardour — withdrew with *such* an air of solemn respect — she had him then before her. She could almost find in her heart, although he had vexed her, to pity him." A good intentional preparative to love, this pity; since, at the time, she little thought that he would not renew his offer.

He waited on my mother after he had taken leave of Bella, and reported his ill success in so respectful a manner, as well with regard to my sister as to the whole family, and with so much concern that he was not accepted as a relation to it, that it left upon them all (my brother then, as I have said, in Scotland) impressions in his favour, and a belief that this matter would certainly be brought on again.

When Mr. Lovelace returned into the country, he thought fit to visit my father and mother; hoping, as he told them, that however unhappy he had been in the rejection of the wished-for-alliance, he might be allowed to keep up an acquaintance and friendship with a family which he should always respect. And then, unhappily, as I may say, was I at home and present.

It was immediately observed that his attention was fixed on me. My sister, as soon as he was gone, in a spirit of bravery, seemed desirous to promote his address, should it be tendered.

My Aunt Hervey was there, and was pleased to say we should make the finest couple in England — if my sister had no objection. — No indeed! with a haughty toss, was my sister's reply. It would be strange if she had, after the denial she had given him upon full deliberation.

My father indeed, after a long silence, being urged by my Uncle Antony to speak his mind, said that he had a letter from his son, on

4

his hearing of Mr. Lovelace's visits to his daughter Arabella; which he had not shown to anybody but my mother; that treaty being at an end when he received it; that in this letter he expressed great dislike to an alliance with Mr. Lovelace on the score of his immoralities; that he knew indeed, there was an old grudge between them; but that, being desirous to prevent all occasions of disunion and animosity in his family, he would suspend the declaration of his own mind till his son arrived, and till he had heard his further objections.

These particulars I had partly from my Aunt Hervey, and partly from my sister; for I was called out as soon as the subject was entered upon. When I returned, my Uncle Antony asked me how I should like Mr. Lovelace? Everybody saw, he was pleased to say, that I had made a conquest.

I immediately answered that I did not like him at all; he seemed to have too good an opinion of his person and parts to have any great regard to his wife, let him marry whom he would.

But the very next day Lord M. came to Harlowe Place (I was then absent), and in his nephew's name made a proposal in form, declaring that it was the ambition of all his family to be related to ours, and he hoped his kinsman would not have such an answer on the part of the younger sister, as he had had on that of the elder.

In short, Mr. Lovelace's visits were admitted as those of a man who had not deserved disrespect from our family; but as to his address to me, with a reservation, as above, on my father's part, that he would determine nothing without his son.

Mr. Lovelace received from every one those civilities which were due to his birth, and although we heard from time to time reports to his disadvantage with regard to morals, yet could we not question him upon them without giving him greater advantages in his own opinion than the situation he was in with us would justify to prudence, since it was much more likely that his address would *not* be allowed of, than that it *would*.

And thus he was admitted to converse with our family almost upon his own terms. I considered him only as a common guest when he came, and thought myself no more concerned in his visits, nor at his entrance or departure, than any other of the family.

But this indifference of my side was the means of procuring him one very great advantage; since upon it was grounded that correspondence by letters which succeeded — and which, had it been to be begun when the family-animosity broke out, would never have been entered into on my part. The occasion was this:

My Uncle Hervey has a young gentleman entrusted to his care, whom he has thoughts of sending abroad a year or two hence, to make the grand tour, as it is called; and finding Mr. Lovelace could give a good account of everything necessary for a young traveller to observe upon such an occasion, he desired him to write down a description of the courts and countries he had visited, and what was most worthy of curiosity in them.

He consented, on condition that I would *direct* his subjects, as he called it; and as every one had heard his manner of writing commended; and thought his narratives might be agreeable amusements in winter evenings; and that he could have no opportunity particularly to address me in them, since they were to be read in full assembly before they were to be given to the young gentleman, I made the less scruple to write, and to make observations and put questions for our further information. Still the less perhaps as I love writing; and those who do, are fond, you know, of occasions to use the pen; and then, having every one's consent, and my Uncle Hervey's desire that I would write, I thought that if I had been the only scrupulous person, it would have shown a particularity that a vain man would construe to his advantage, and which my sister would not fail to animadvert upon.

My sister herself allowed that the man had a tolerable knack of writing and describing; and my father, who had been abroad in his youth, said that his remarks were curious, and showed him to be a person of reading, judgment, and taste.

Thus was a kind of correspondence begun between him and me, with general approbation.

Meantime, my father kept in readiness the reports he had heard in his disfavor, to charge them upon him then, as so many objections to his address. And it was highly agreeable to me that he did so; it would have been strange if it were not, since the person who could reject Mr. Wyerley's address for the sake of his *free opinions*, must have been inexcusable, had she not rejected another's for his *freer practices*.

I had a little specimen of this temper of his upon the very occasion I have mentioned; for after he had sent me a third particular letter with the general one, he asked me the next time he came to Harlowe Place, if I had not received such a one from him? I told him I should never answer one so sent, and that I had waited for such an occasion as he had now given me to tell him so. I desired him therefore not to write again on the subject, assuring him that if he did, I would return both, and never write another line to him.

You can't imagine how saucily the man looked!

Miss CLARISSA HARLOWE TO Miss HOWE

Jan. 15.

SUCH, my dear, was the situation Mr. Lovelace and I were in when my brother arrived from Scotland.

The moment Mr. Lovelace's visits were mentioned to him, he, without hesitation or apology, expressed his disapprobation of them. He found great flaws in his character, and took the liberty to say in so many words that he wondered how it came into the heads of his uncles to encourage such a man for *either* of his sisters; at the same time returning his thanks to my father for declining his consent till *he* arrived, in such a manner, I thought, as a superior would do, when he commended an inferior for having well performed his duty in his absence.

He justified his avowed inveteracy by common fame, and by what he had known of him at college; declaring that he had ever hated him; ever should hate him, and would never own *him* for a brother, or *me* for a sister if I married him.

My brother found my sister, who waited but for the occasion, ready to join him in his resentments against the man he hated.

Now and then indeed, when I observed that their vehemence carried them beyond all bounds of probability in their charges against him, I thought it but justice to put in a word for him. But this only subjected me to reproach, as having a prepossession in his favour which I would not own. So that when I could not change the subject, I used to retire either to my music or to my closet.

Their behavior to him when they could not help seeing him, was very cold and disobliging; but as yet not directly affrontive. For they were in hopes of prevailing upon my father to forbid his visits. But as there was nothing in his behaviour that might warrant such a treatment of a man of his birth and fortune, they succeeded not; and then they were very earnest with *me* to forbid them. I asked what authority I had to take such a step in my father's house; and when my behaviour to him was so distant, that he seemed to be as much the guest of any other person of the family, themselves excepted, as mine. In revenge, they told me that it was cunning management between us, and that we both understood one another better than we pretended to do. And at last they gave such a loose to their passions, all of a sudden, as I may say, that instead of withdrawing as they used to do when he came, they threw themselves in his way purposely to affront him.

Mr. Lovelace, you may believe, very ill-brooked this; but nevertheless contented himself to complain of it to me, in high terms, however, telling me that but for my sake my brother's treatment of him was not to be borne.

My brother had just before, with the approbation of my uncles, employed a person related to a discharged bailiff or steward of Lord M. who had had the management of some part of Mr. Lovelace's affairs (from which he was also dismissed by him) to inquire into his debts, after his companions, into his amours and the like.

My Aunt Hervey, in confidence, gave me the following particulars of what the man said of him:

"That he was a generous landlord; that he spared nothing for solid and lasting improvements upon his estate; and that he looked into his own affairs, and understood them. That he had been very expensive when abroad, and contracted a large debt (for he made no secret of his affairs); yet chose to limit himself to an annual sum, and to decline equipage in order to avoid being obliged to his uncle and aunts, from whom he might have what money he pleased; but that he was very jealous of their control, had often quarrels with them, and treated them so freely that they were all afraid of him. However, that his estate was never mortgaged, as my brother had heard it was; his credit was always high; and the man believed he was by this time near upon, if not quite, clear of the world.

"He was a sad gentleman, he said, as to women. If his tenants had pretty daughters, they chose to keep them out of his sight. He believed he kept no particular mistress, for he had heard *newelty*, that was the man's word, was everything with him. But for his uncle's and aunt's teasings, the man fancied he would not think of marriage. He was never known to be disguised with liquor; but was a great plotter, and a great writer; that he lived a wild life in town, by what he had heard; had six or seven companions as bad as himself, whom now and then he brought down with him; and the country was always glad when they went back up again. He would have it, that although passionate, he was good-humoured, loved as well to take a jest as to give one; and would railly himself upon occasion the freest of any man he ever knew."

This was his character from an enemy; for, as my aunt observed, everything the man said commendably of him came grudgingly, with a *must needs say — To do him justice, etc.*, while the contrary was delivered with a free goodwill.

I doubted not that having so very little encouragement from *any*-body, his pride would soon take fire, and he would of himself discontinue his visits or go to town, where, till he came acquainted with our family, he used chiefly to reside.

But my brother's antipathy would not permit him to *wait* for such an event; and after several excesses, which Mr. Lovelace still returned with contempt and a haughtiness too much like that of the aggressor, my brother took upon himself to fill up the doorway once when he came as if to oppose his entrance; and upon his asking for me, demanded what his business was with his sister?

The other, with a challenging air, as my brother says, told him he would answer a gentleman *any* question; but he wished that Mr. James Harlowe, who had of late given himself high airs, would remember that he was not *now* at college.

Just then the good Dr. Lewen, who frequently honours me with a visit, came to the door; and hearing the words, interposed, both having their hands upon their swords; and telling Mr. Lovelace where I was, he burst by my brother to come to me, leaving him chafing, he said, like a hunted boar at bay.

This alarmed us all. My father was pleased to hint to Mr. Lovelace that he wished he would discontinue his visits for the peace-sake of the family; and I, by his command, spoke a great deal plainer.

But Mr. Lovelace is a man not easily brought to give up his purpose, especially in a point wherein he pretends his heart is so much engaged; and no absolute prohibition having been given, things went on for a little while as before; for I saw plainly that to have denied myself to his visits (which however I declined receiving as often as I could) was to bring forward some desperate issue between the two, since the offence so readily given on one side was brooked by the other only out of consideration to me.

And thus did my brother's rashness lay me under an obligation where I would least have owed it.

The intermediate proposals of Mr. Symmes and Mr. Mullins, both (in turn) encouraged by my brother, induced him to be more patient for a while; as nobody thought me over-forward in Mr. Lovelace's favour; for he hoped that he should engage my father and uncles to approve of the one or the other in opposition to the man he hated. But when he found that I had interest enough to disengage myself from the addresses of those gentlemen, as I had (before he went to Scotland and before Mr. Lovelace visited here) of Mr. Wyerley's, he then kept no measures; and first set himself to upbraid me for a supposed prepossession, which he treated as if it were criminal, and then to insult Mr. Lovelace in person at Mr. Edward Symmes's, the brother of the other Symmes, two miles off; and no good Dr. Lewen being there to interpose, the unhappy rencounter followed. My brother was disarmed, as you have heard; and on being brought home, and giving us ground to suppose he was much worse hurt than he really was, and a fever ensuing, every one flamed out; and all was laid at my door.

Mr. Lovelace for three days together sent twice each day to inquire after my brother's health, and although he received rude and even shocking returns, he thought fit on the fourth day to make in person the same inquiries, and received still greater incivilities from my two uncles who happened to be both there. My father also was held by force from going to him with his sword in his hand, although he had the gout upon him.

I fainted away with terror, seeing every one so violent, and hearing Mr. Lovelace swear that he would not depart till he had made my uncles ask his pardon for the indignities he had received at their hands, a door being held fast locked between him and them. My mother all the time was praying and struggling to withhold my father in the great parlour. Meanwhile my sister, who had treated Mr. Lovelace with virulence, came in to me and insulted me as fast as I recovered. But when Mr. Lovelace was told how ill I was he departed; nevertheless vowing revenge.

Meantime, I cannot help saying that I am exceedingly concerned to find that I am become so much the public talk as you tell me I am. Your kind, your *precautionary* regard for my fame, and the opportunity you have given me to tell my own story previous to any new accident (which Heaven avert!), is so like the warm friend I have ever found in my dear Miss Howe, that, with redoubled obligation, you bind me to be / Your ever grateful and affectionate, / CLARISSA HARLOWE.

Jan. 20.

I HAVE been hindered from prosecuting my intentions. Neither nights nor mornings have been my own. My mother has been very ill, and would have no other nurse but me.

Then the foundations laid, as she dreads, for jealousy and heart-burnings in her own family, late so happy and so united, afflict exceedingly a gentle and sensible mind, which has from the beginning, on all occasions, sacrificed its own inward satisfaction to outward peace. My brother and sister, who used very often to jar, are now so entirely one and are so much together (*caballing* was the word that dropped from my mother's lips, as if at unawares) that she is very fearful of the consequences that may follow — to my prejudice, perhaps, is her kind concern, since she sees that they behave to me every hour with more and more shyness and reserve; yet would she but exert that authority which the superiority of her fine talents gives her, all these family feuds might perhaps be extinguished in their but yet beginnings; especially as she may be assured that all fitting concessions shall be made by me, not only as my brother and sister are my elders, but for the sake of so excellent and so indulgent a mother.

But no more of this. I will prosecute my former intention in my next, which I will sit down to as soon as breakfast is over, despatching this by the messenger whom you have so kindly sent to inquire after us on my silence. Meantime, I am / Your most affectionate and obliged Friend and Servant, / CL. HARLOWE.

MISS CLARISSA HARLOWE TO MISS HOWE

Harlowe Place, Jan. 20.

I BELIEVE they all think that I receive letters from Mr. Lovelace. But Lord M. being inclined rather to support than to blame his nephew, they seem to be so much afraid of Mr. Lovelace that they do not put it to me whether I do or not, conniving on the contrary, as it should seem, at the only method left to allay the vehemence of a spirit which they have so much provoked; for he still insists upon satisfaction from my uncles, and this possibly (for he wants not art) as the best way to be introduced again with some advantage into our family. And indeed my Aunt Hervey has put it to my mother, whether it were not best to prevail upon my brother to take a turn to his Yorkshire estate (which he was intending to do before) and to stay there till all is blown over.

But this is very far from his intention; for he has already begun to hint again, that he shall never be easy or satisfied till I am married; and, finding neither Mr. Symmes nor Mr. Mullins will be accepted, has proposed Mr. Wyerley once more, on the score of his great passion for me. This I have again rejected, and but yesterday he mentioned one who has applied to him by letter, making high offers. This is Mr.

Solmes; *Rich* Solmes you know they call him. But this application has not met with the attention of one single soul.

If none of his schemes of getting me married take effect, he has thoughts, I am told, of proposing to me to go to Scotland, that, as the compliment is, I may put his house there in such order as our own is in. But this my mother intends to oppose for her own sake; because, having relieved her, as she is pleased to say, of the household cares (for which my sister, you know, has no turn) they must again devolve upon her if I go. And if *she* did not oppose it, *I* should; for, believe me, I have no mind to be his housekeeper, and I am sure, were I to go with him, I should be treated rather as a servant than a sister; perhaps, not the better because I *am* his sister. And if Mr. Lovelace should follow me, things might be worse than they are now.

But I have besought my mother, who is apprehensive of Mr. Lovelace's visits, to procure me permission to be your guest for a fortnight or so. Will your mother, think you, my dear, give me leave?

Just now, my mother has rejoiced me with the news that my requested permission is granted. Every one thinks it best that I should go, except my brother. But he was told that he must not expect to rule in everything. I am to be sent for into the great parlour, where are my two uncles and my Aunt Hervey, and to be acquainted with this concession in form.

I will acquaint you with what passed at the general leave given me to be your guest. And yet I know that you will not love my brother the better for my communication. But I am angry with him myself, and cannot help it. And besides, it is proper to let you know the terms I go upon, and their motives for permitting me to go.

Clary, said my mother, as soon as I entered the great parlour, your request to go to Miss Howe's for a few days has been taken into consideration, and granted ——

Much against my liking, I assure you, said my brother, rudely interrupting her.

Son James! said my father, and knit his brows.

He was not daunted. His arm is in a sling. He often has the mean art to look upon *that*, when anything is hinted that may be supposed to lead towards the least favour to or reconciliation with Mr. Lovelace. Let the *girl* then (I am often *the girl* with him) be prohibited seeing that vile libertine.

Nobody spoke.

Do you hear, sister Clary? taking their silence for approbation of what *he* had dictated; you are not to receive visits from Lord M.'s nephew.

Every one still remained silent.

Do you so understand the license you have, miss? interrogated he.

I would be glad, sir, said I, to understand that you are my *brother* — and that *you* would understand that you are *only* my brother.

O the fond, fond heart! with a sneer of insult, lifting up his hands.

Sir, said I to my father, to your justice I appeal. If I have deserved reflection, let me not be spared. But if I am to be answerable for the rashness ——

No more! No more of either side, said my father. You are not to receive the visits of that Lovelace, though. Nor are you, son James, to reflect upon your sister. She is a worthy child.

Sir, I have done, replied he — and yet I have *her* honour at heart, as much as the honour of the rest of the family.

And *hence*, sir, retorted I, your unbrotherly reflections upon me!

Well, but you observe, miss, said he, that it is not *I*, but your *father*, that tells you that you are not to receive the visits of that Lovelace.

Cousin Harlowe, said my Aunt Hervey, allow me to say that my cousin Clary's prudence may be confided in.

I am *convinced* it may, joined my mother.

But aunt, but madam (put in my sister), there is no hurt, I presume, in letting my sister know the condition she goes to Miss Howe upon, since, if he gets a knack of visiting her there ——

You may be sure, interrupted my Uncle Harlowe, he will endeavour to see her there.

So would such an impudent man *here*, said my Uncle Antony; and 'tis better *there* than *here*.

Better *nowhere*, said my father. I command you (turning to me), on pain of my displeasure, that you see him not at all.

I will not, sir, in any way of encouragement, I do assure you; nor at all if I can properly avoid it.

You know with what indifference, said my mother, she has hitherto seen him. Her prudence may be trusted to, as my sister Hervey says.

With what *appa* — rent indifference, drolled my brother.

Son James! said my father sternly.

I have done, sir, said he. But again, in a provoking manner, he reminded me of the prohibition.

Thus ended this conference.

Miss Clarissa Harlowe to Miss Howe

(*After her return from her*)   *Harlowe Place, Feb. 20.*

I beg your excuse for not writing sooner. Alas, my dear, I have sad prospects before me! My brother and sister have succeeded in all their views. They have found out another lover for me; an hideous one! — yet he is encouraged by everybody. No wonder that I was ordered home so suddenly. At an hour's warning! No other notice, you know, than what was brought with the chariot that was to carry me back. It was for fear, as I have been informed (an unworthy fear!), that I should have entered into any concert with Mr. Lovelace had I known their motive for commanding me home; appre-

12

hending, 'tis evident, that I should dislike the man they had to propose to me.

And well might they apprehend so; for who do you think he is? — No other than that *Solmes!* Could you have believed it? — and they are all determined too, my mother with the rest!

I was struck all of a heap as soon as I entered to see a solemnity which I had been so little used to on the like occasions in the countenance of every dear relation. They all kept their seats. I ran to my father and kneeled; then to my mother; and met from both a cold salute; from my father a blessing but half pronounced; my mother indeed called me child, but embraced me not with her usual indulgent ardour.

My unbrotherly accuser hereupon stood forth, and charged me with having received no less than *five or six visits* at Miss Howe's from the man they had all so much reason to hate (that was the expression); notwithstanding the commands I had had to the contrary. And he bid me deny it if I could.

I had never been used, I said, to deny the truth, nor would I now. I owned I had in the three weeks passed seen the person I presumed he meant *oftener* than five or six times. (Pray hear me, brother, said I, for he was going to flame out.) But he always asked for Mrs. or Miss Howe when he came.

I proceeded that I had reason to believe that both Mrs. Howe and Miss, as matters stood, would much rather have excused his visits, but they had more than once apologized that, having not the same reason my papa had to forbid him their house, his rank and fortune entitled him to civility.

You see, my dear, I made not the pleas I might have made.

My brother seemed ready to give a loose to his passion; my father put on the countenance which always portends a gathering storm; my uncles mutteringly whispered; and my sister aggravatingly held up her hands. While I begged to be heard out, and my mother said, let the *child*, that was her kind word, be heard.

I hoped, I said, there was no harm done; that it became not me to prescribe to Mrs. or Miss Howe who should be their visitors; that Mrs. Howe was always diverted with the raillery that passed between miss and him; that I had no reason to challenge *her* guest for *my* visitor, as I should seem to have done had I refused to go into their company when he was with them; that I had never seen him out of the presence of one or both of those ladies, and had signified to him once, on his urging for a few moments' private conversation with me, that unless a reconciliation were effected between my family and his, he must not expect that I would countenance his visits, much less give him an opportunity of that sort.

I told them further that Miss Howe so well understood my mind that she never left me a moment while Mr. Lovelace was there; that when he came, if I was not below in the parlour, I would not suffer myself to be called to him, although I thought it would be an affectation which would give him advantage rather than the contrary, if I had left company when he came in, or refused to enter into it when I found he would stay any time.

I was no sooner silent than my *brother* swore, although in my father's presence (swore, unchecked either by eye or countenance), that for his part he would *never* be reconciled to that libertine; and that he would renounce me for a sister if I encouraged the address of a man so obnoxious to them all.

A man who had like to have been my brother's murderer, my sister said, with a face even bursting with restraint of passion.

My father, with vehemence both of action and voice (my father has, you know, a terrible voice when he is angry!), told me, that I had met with too much indulgence in being allowed to refuse *this* gentleman, and the *other* gentleman; and it was now *his* turn to be obeyed.

Very true, my *mother* said, and hoped his will would not now be disputed by a child so favoured.

I was astonished, you must needs think. Whose addresses now, thought I, is this treatment preparative to? Mr. Wyerley's again? or whose? That it could be for Solmes, how should it enter my head?

I did not know, I said, that I had given occasion for this harshness. I hoped I should always have a just sense of every one's favour to me, superadded to the duty I owed as a daughter and a niece; but that I was so much surprised at a reception so unusual and unexpected, that I hoped my papa and mamma would give me leave to retire in order to recollect myself.

I had not recovered myself when I was sent for down to tea. I begged by my maid to be excused attending, but on the repeated command, went down with as much cheerfulness as I could assume, and had a new fault to clear myself of; for my brother charged my desire of being excused coming down to sullens, because a certain person had been spoken against, upon whom, as he supposed, my fancy ran.

I could easily answer you, sir, said I, as such a reflection deserves; but I forbear.

Pretty meekness! Bella whisperingly said, looking at my brother, and lifting up her lip in contempt.

He, with an imperious air, bid me *deserve* his love, and I should be sure to *have* it.

Mr. Solmes came in before we had done tea. My Uncle Antony presented him to me as a gentleman he had a particular friendship for. My Uncle Harlowe in terms equally favourable for him. My father said, Mr. Solmes is my friend, Clarissa Harlowe. My mother looked at him, and looked at me, now and then, as he sat near me, I thought with concern. — I at *her,* with eyes appealing for pity. At *him,* when I could glance at him, with disgust little short of affrightment. While my brother and sister Mr. *Solmes'd* him, and *sirr'd* him up at every word. So caressed, in short, by all — yet such a wretch! But I will at present only add my humble thanks and duty to your honoured mother (to whom I will particularly write, to express the

grateful sense I have of her goodness to me), and that I am / Your
ever obliged / CL. HARLOWE

MISS CLARISSA HARLOWE TO MISS HOWE

Feb. 24.

THEY drive on here at a furious rate. The man lives here, I
think. He courts them, and is more and more a favourite. Such terms,
such settlements! That's the cry.

Hitherto, I seem to be delivered over to my brother, who pretends
as great love to me as ever.

You may believe I have been very sincere with him. But he affects
to railly me, and not to believe it possible that one so dutiful and so
discreet as his sister Clary can resolve to disoblige all her friends.

I have already stood the shock of three of this man's particular
visits, besides my share in his more general ones; and find it is impossible I should ever endure him. He has but a very ordinary share
of understanding, is very illiterate, knows nothing but the value of
estates and how to improve them, and what belongs to land-jobbing
and husbandry. Yet am I as one stupid, I think. They have begun so
cruelly with me that I have not spirit enough to assert my own
negative.

My aunt likewise having said that she did not think her niece
could ever be brought to like Mr. Solmes, has been obliged to learn
another lesson.

I am to have a visit from her to-morrow. And, since I have refused so much as to hear from my brother and sister what the noble
settlements are to be, she is to acquaint me with the particulars and
to receive from me my determination.

Meantime it has been signified to me that it will be acceptable if I
do not think of going to church next Sunday.

The same signification was made me for last Sunday, and I obeyed.
They are apprehensive that Mr. Lovelace will be there with design to come home with me.

Help me, dear Miss Howe, to a little of your charming spirit; I
never more wanted it.

February 25.

I have had the expected conference with my aunt.

I have been obliged to hear the man's proposals from her, and
have been also told what their motives are for espousing his interest
with so much warmth. I am even loth to mention how equally unjust
it is for him to make such offers, or for those I am bound to reverence
to accept of them. I hate him more than before.

But here, upon my absolute refusal of him upon *any* terms, have I
had a signification made me that wounds me to the heart. How can
I tell it you? Yet I must. It is, my dear, that I must not for a month

15

to come, or till licence obtained, correspond with *anybody* out of the house.

My brother, upon my aunt's report, brought me in authoritative terms, the prohibition.

Not to Miss Howe? said I.

No, not to Miss Howe, *madam,* tauntingly; for have you not acknowledged that Lovelace is a favourite there?

See, my dear Miss Howe!

And do you think, brother, this is the way?

Do *you* look to that. But your letters will be stopped, I can tell you. And away he flung.

My sister came to me soon after: Sister Clary, you are going on in a fine way, I understand. But as there are people who are supposed to harden you against your duty, I am to tell you that it will be taken well if you avoid visits or visitings for a week or two till further order.

Can this be from those who have authority ——

Ask them, ask them, child, with a twirl of her finger. I have delivered my message. Your father will be obeyed. He is willing to hope you to be all obedience, and would prevent all *incitements* to refractoriness.

I know my duty, said I, and hope I shall not find impossible conditions annexed to it.

A pert young creature, vain and conceited, she called me.

Feb. 25.   In the evening.

What my brother and sister have said against me I cannot tell; but I am in heavy disgrace with my father.

I was sent for down to tea. I went with a very cheerful aspect; but had occasion soon to change it.

Such a solemnity in everybody's countenance! My mother's eyes were fixed upon the tea-cups, and when she looked up it was heavily, as if her eyelids had weights upon them, and then not to me. My father sat half-aside in his elbow-chair, that his head might be turned from me; his hands clasped, and waving, as it were, up and down; his fingers, poor dear gentleman! in motion, as if angry to the very ends of them. My sister sat swelling. My brother looked at me with scorn, having measured me, as I may say, with his eyes as I entered, from head to foot. My aunt was there and looked upon me as if with kindness restrained, bending coldly to my compliment to her as she sat; and then cast an eye first on my brother, then on my sister, as if to give the reason (so I am willing to construe it) of her unusual stiffness.

I took my seat. Shall I make tea, madam, to my mother? I always used, you know, my dear, to make tea.

No! A very short sentence, in one very short word, was the expressive answer. And she was pleased to take the canister in her own hand.

My brother bid the footman who attended leave the room. I, said he, will pour out the water.

My heart was up at my mouth. I did not know what to do with myself. What is to follow? thought I.

Just after the second dish, out stepped my mother. — A word with you, sister Hervey! taking her in her hand. Presently my sister dropped away. Then my brother. So I was left alone with my father.

He looked so very sternly that my heart failed me as twice or thrice I would have addressed myself to him; nothing but solemn silence on all hands having passed before.

At last, I asked, if it were his pleasure that I should pour him out another dish?

He answered me with the same angry monosyllable which I had received from my mother before, and then arose and walked about the room. I arose too, with intent to throw myself at his feet, but was too much overawed by his sternness even to make such an expression of my duty to him as my heart overflowed with.

At last, as he supported himself because of his gout on the back of a chair, I took a little more courage, and approaching him, besought him to acquaint me in what I had offended him?

He turned from me, and in a strong voice, Clarissa Harlowe, said he, know that I will be obeyed.

God forbid, sir, that you should not! I have never yet opposed your will ——.

Nor I your whimsies, Clarissa Harlowe, interrupted he. Don't let me run the fate of all who show indulgence to your sex, to be the more contradicted for mine to you.

I was going to make protestations of duty — No protestations, girl! No words! I will not be prated to! I will be obeyed! I have no child, I *will* have no child, but an obedient one.

Sir, you never had reason, I hope ——

Tell me not what I never *had*, but what I *have*, and what I *shall* have.

Good sir, be pleased to hear me. My brother and my sister, I fear ——

Your brother and sister shall not be spoken against, girl! They have a just concern for the honour of my family.

And I hope, sir ——

Hope nothing. Tell me not of *hopes*, but of *facts*. I ask nothing of you but what is in your *power* to comply with, and what it is your *duty* to comply with.

Then, sir, I *will* comply with it; but yet I hope from your goodness ——

No expostulations! No *buts*, girl! No qualifyings! I will be obeyed, I tell you; and cheerfully, too! — or you are no child of mine!

I wept.

Let me beseech you, my dear and ever honoured papa (and I dropped down on my knees), that I may have only yours and my mamma's will, and not my brother's, to obey.

I was going on, but he was pleased to withdraw, leaving me on the floor.

Feb. 26.   In the morning.

I FIND, by a few words which dropped unawares from my aunt, that they have all an absolute dependence upon what they suppose to be a meekness in my temper. But in this they may be mistaken, for I verily think, upon a strict examination of myself, that I have almost as much in me of my father's as of my mother's family.

My aunt advises me to submit for the present to the interdicts they have laid me under, and indeed to encourage Mr. Solmes's address. I have absolutely refused the latter, let what will (as I have told her) be the consequence. The visiting prohibition I will conform to. But as to that of not corresponding with you, nothing but the menace that our letters shall be intercepted can engage my observation of it.

But can you, my dear Miss Howe, condescend to carry on a private correspondence with me? If you can, there is one way I have thought of by which it may be done.

You must remember the Green Lane, as we call it, that runs by the side of the wood-house and poultry-yard where I keep my bantams, pheasants, and peahens, which generally engage my notice twice a day, the more my favourites because they were my grandfather's, and recommended to my care by him, and therefore brought hither from my dairy-house since his death.

The lane is lower than the floor of the wood-house, and in the side of the wood-house the boards are rotted away down to the floor for half an ell together in several places. Hannah can step into the lane and make a mark with chalk where a letter or parcel may be pushed in under some sticks, which may be so managed as to be an unsuspected cover for the written deposits from either.

So your faithful Robert may, without coming near the house, and as only passing through the Green Lane which leads to two or three farm-houses (out of livery, if you please) very easily take from thence my letters and deposit yours.

Try, my dear, the success of a letter this way, and give me your opinion and advice what to do in this *disgraceful* situation, as I cannot but call it, and what you think of my prospects, and what would you do in my case.

But beforehand I must tell you that your advice must not run in favour of this Solmes.

MISS HOWE TO MISS CLARISSA HARLOWE

Feb. 27.

WHAT odd heads some people have! Miss Clarissa Harlowe to be sacrificed in marriage to Mr. Roger Solmes! Astonishing!

I must not, you say, *give my advice in favour of this man!* You convince me, my dear, that you are nearer of kin than I thought you to the family that could think of so preposterous a match, or you would never have had the least notion of my advising in his favour.

You are all too rich to be happy, child. For must not each of you, by the constitutions of your family, marry to be *still* richer? People who know in what their *main* excellence consists, are not to be blamed (are they?) for cultivating and improving what they think most valuable. Is true happiness any part of your family view? So far from it that none of your family but yourself could be happy were they *not* rich. So let them fret on, grumble and grudge, and accumulate, and wondering what ails them that they have not happiness, think the cause is want of more.

That they prohibit your corresponding with *me* is a wisdom I neither wonder at, nor blame them for; since it is an evidence to me that they know their own folly; and if they do, is it strange that they should be afraid to trust another's judgment upon it?

I am glad you have found out a way to correspond with me. I approve it much. I shall *more* if this first trial of it prove successful. But should it *not,* and should it fall into their hands, it would not concern me but for your sake.

We had heard before you wrote that all was not right between your relations and you at your coming home; that Mr. Solmes visited you and that with a prospect of success. But I concluded the mistake lay in the person, and that his address was to Miss Arabella. I could not believe that the absurdest people in England could be so absurd as to think of this man for you.

My mother takes very kindly your compliments in your letter to her. Her words upon reading it were: "Miss Clarissa Harlowe is an admirable young lady. Wherever she goes, she confers a favour; whomever she leaves, she fills with regret." And then a little comparative reflection: "O my Nancy, that you had a little of her sweet obligingness!"

The result is this: that I am fitter for *this* world than you; you for the *next* than me — that's the difference.

You are pleased to say, and *upon your word too*! that your *regards* (a mighty quaint word for *affections*) *are not so much engaged, as some of your friends suppose, to another person.* What need you give one to imagine, my dear, that the last month or two has been a period extremely favourable to that *other* person — whom it has made an obliger of the niece for his patience with the uncles.

But, to pass that by — *so much* engaged! *How much,* my dear? Shall I infer? *Some of your friends* suppose *a great deal.* You seem to own *a little.*

Don't be angry. It is all fair; because you have not acknowledged to me that *little.* People, I have heard you say, who affect secrets. always excite curiosity.

But, O my friend, depend upon it you are in danger. Depend upon it, whether you know it or not, you are a little in for 't.

In short, my dear, it is my opinion, and that from the easiness of his heart and behaviour, that he has seen more than *I* have seen, more than you think *could* be seen; more than I believe you *yourself* know, or else you would have let *me* know it.

Already, in order to restrain him from resenting the indignities he has received, and which are daily offered him, he has prevailed upon you to correspond with him privately. I know he has nothing to boast of from *what* you have written; but is not his inducing you to receive his letters, and to answer them, a great point gained? By your insisting that he should keep this correspondence private, it appears that there is *one secret* which you do not wish the world should know; and *he* is master of that secret. He is indeed *himself*, as I may say, that secret! What an intimacy does this beget for the lover! How is it distancing the parent!

It is my humble opinion, I tell you frankly, that on inquiry it will come out to be LOVE — don't start, my dear! To be sure, Lovelace is a charming fellow. And were he only — but I will not make you *glow*, as you read — upon *my word* I will not. Yet, my dear, don't you find at your heart somewhat unusual make it go throb, throb, throb, as you read just here! If you do, don't be ashamed to own it. It is your *generosity*, my love, that's all.

Adieu, my dearest friend. Forgive, and very speedily, by the new-found expedient, tell me that you forgive, / Your ever affectionate, / ANNA HOWE.

MISS CLARISSA HARLOWE TO MISS HOWE

Wednesday, March 1.

You both nettled and alarmed me, my dearest Miss Howe, by the concluding part of your last. At first reading it I did not think it necessary, said I to myself, to guard against a critic when I was writing to so dear a friend. But then recollecting myself, is there not more in it, said I, than the result of a vein so naturally lively? Surely I must have been guilty of an inadvertence. Let me enter into the close examination of myself which my beloved friend advises.

I did so, and cannot own any of the *glow*, any of the *throbs* you mention. *Upon my word* I will repeat, I cannot.

Mr. Lovelace, for instance, I may be allowed to say, is a man to be preferred to Mr. Solmes, and that I *do* prefer him to that man; but surely, this may be said without its being a necessary consequence that I must be in love with him.

Indeed I would not be *in love* with him, as it is called, for the world: first, because I have no opinion of his morals, and think it a fault in which our whole family (my brother excepted) has had a share, that he was permitted to visit us with a hope, which however, being distant, did not, as I have observed heretofore, entitle any of us to call him to account for such of his immoralities as came to our ears. Next because I think him to be a vain man, capable of triumphing (secretly at least) over a person whose heart he thinks he has engaged. And thirdly, because the assiduities and veneration which you impute to him seem to carry an haughtiness in them, as if he thought his address had a merit in it that would be more than an equivalent to a woman's love.

Indeed, my dear THIS man is not THE man. I have great objections to him. My heart *throbs* not after him. I *glow* not but with indignation against myself for having given room for such an imputation. But you must not, my dearest friend, construe common gratitude into love. I cannot bear that you should. But if ever I should have the misfortune to think it love, I promise you, *upon my word,* which is the same as *upon my honour,* that I will acquaint you with it.

MISS HOWE TO MISS CLARISSA HARLOWE

Thursday morn.   March 2.

Indeed you would not be in love with him for the world! — Your servant, my dear. Nor would I have you; and this opinion I give as well from the reasons you mention (which I cannot but confirm), as from what I have heard of him but a few hours ago from Mrs. Fortescue, a favourite of Lady Betty Lawrance, who knows him well.

A hundred wild stories she tells of him from childhood to manhood; for, as she observes, having never been subject to contradiction, he was always as mischievous as a monkey.

Mrs. Fortescue owns, what everybody knows, "that he is notoriously, nay, avowedly, a man of pleasure, yet says that in anything he sets his heart upon or undertakes, he is the most industrious and persevering mortal under the sun. He rests, it seems, not above six hours in the twenty-four — any more than you. He delights in writing. Whether at Lord M.'s, or at Lady Betty's, or Lady Sarah's, he has always a pen in his fingers when he retires. One of his companions (confirming his love of writing) has told her that his thoughts flow rapidly to his pen."

Mrs. Fortescue says, "that he is a complete master of shorthand writing." By the way, what inducements could such a swift writer as he have to learn shorthand?

"She says (and we know it as well as she) that he has a surprising memory, and a very lively imagination."

Whatever his other vices are, all the world, as well as Mrs. Fortescue, says "he is a sober man. And among all his bad qualities, *gaming,* that great waster of time as well as fortune, is not his vice." So that he must have his head as cool, and his reason as clear, as the prime of youth and his natural gaiety will permit, and by his early morning hours, a great portion of time upon his hands, to employ in writing, or worse.

A person willing to think favourably of him would hope that a *brave,* a *learned,* and a *diligent* man, cannot be *naturally* a *bad* man. But if he be better than his enemies say he is (and if worse, he is bad indeed), he is guilty of an inexcusable fault in being so careless as he is of his reputation. I think a man can be so but from one of these two reasons: either that he is conscious he deserves the evil spoken of him; or, that he takes a pride in being thought worse than he is.

Upon the whole, and upon all that I could gather from Mrs.

Fortescue, Mr. Lovelace is a very faulty man. You and I have thought him too gay, too inconsiderate, too rash, too little an hypocrite to be *deep*. You see he never would disguise his natural temper (haughty as it certainly is) with respect to your brother's behavior to him. Where he thinks a contempt due, he pays it to the uttermost. Nor has he complaisance enough to spare your uncles.

But were he deep, and ever so deep, you would soon penetrate him, if they would leave you to yourself. His vanity would be your clue. Never man had more. Yet, as Mrs. Fortescue observed, "never did man carry it off so happily." There is a strange mixture in it of humorous vivacity, since but for one half of what he says of himself, when he is in the vein, any other man would be insufferable.

Talk *of the devil* is an old saying. The lively wretch has made me a visit and is but just gone away. He is all impatience and resentment at the treatment you meet with, and full of apprehensions, too, that they will carry their point with you.

I told him my opinion that you will never be brought to think of such a man as Solmes; but that it will probably end in a composition never to have either.

No man, he said, whose fortunes and alliances are so considerable, ever had so little favour from a woman for whose sake he had borne so much.

I told him my mind as freely as I used to do. But whoever was in fault, self being judge? He complained of spies set upon his conduct, and to pry into his life and morals, and this by your brother and uncles.

I told him that this was very hard upon him, and the more so as neither his life nor morals perhaps would stand a fair inquiry.

He smiled, and called himself *my servant*. The occasion was too fair, he said, for Miss Howe, who never spared him, to let it pass. But, Lord help the shallow souls of the Harlowes! Would I believe it? they were for turning plotters upon *him*.

The object so meritorious, who can doubt the reality of his professions?

Adieu, my dearest, my noble friend! I love and admire you for the generous conclusion of your last more than I can express. Though I began this letter with impertinent raillery, knowing that you always loved to indulge my mad vein, yet never was there a heart that more glowed with friendly love than that of / Your own / ANNA HOWE.

MISS CLARISSA HARLOWE TO MISS HOWE

Wedn., March 1.

I NOW take up my pen to lay before you the inducements and motives which my friends have to espouse so earnestly the address of this Mr. Solmes.

Now it comes out that this *sudden* vehemence on my brother's and sister's parts, was owing to stronger reasons than to the college-begun

antipathy on his side or to slighted love on hers: to wit, to an apprehension that my uncles intended to follow my grandfather's example
in my favour at least in a higher degree than they wish they should.

I have more than once mentioned to you the darling view some of
us have long had of *raising a family,* as it is called; a reflection, as I
have often thought, upon our own, which is no inconsiderable or up-
start one on either side; of my mother's especially. A view too frequently, it seems, entertained by families which having great substance, cannot be satisfied without rank and title.

My uncles had once extended this view to each of us three children,
urging, that as they themselves intended not to marry, we each of us
might be so portioned, and so advantageously matched, as that our
posterity, if not ourselves, might make a first figure in our country.
While my brother, as the only son, thought the two girls might be
very well provided for by ten or fifteen thousand pounds apiece; and
that all the real estates in the family: to wit, my grandfather's, father's,
and two uncles', and the remainder of their respective personal estates, together with what he had an expectation of from his godmother, would make such a noble fortune, and give him such an interest, as might entitle him to hope for a peerage. Nothing less would
satisfy his ambition.

But when my grandfather's will (of the purport of which in my
particular favour, until it was opened, I was as ignorant as they) had
lopped off one branch of my brother's expectation, he was extremely
dissatisfied with me. Nobody indeed was pleased.

To obviate therefore every one's jealousy, I gave up to my father's
management, as you know, not only the estate, but the money bequeathed me (which was a moiety of what my grandfather had by him
at his death, the other moiety being bequeathed to my sister), contenting myself to take as from his bounty what he was pleased to
allow me, without desiring the least addition to my annual stipend.
And then I hoped I had laid all envy asleep.

My brother's acquisition then took place. This made us all very
happy, and he went down to take possession of it; and his absence
(on so good an account too) made us still happier.

My brother then returned, and we were all wrong again; and
Bella, as I observed in my letters above-mentioned, had an opportunity to give herself the credit of having refused Mr. Lovelace on
the score of his reputed faulty morals. This united my brother and
sister in one cause.

They were bitterly inveighing against him in their usual way,
strengthening their invectives with some new stories in his disfavour,
when my Uncle Antony, having given them a patient hearing, declared, "that he thought the gentleman behaved like a gentleman, his
niece Clary with prudence, and that a more honourable alliance for
the family, *as he had often told them,* could not be wished for; since
Mr. Lovelace had a very good paternal estate, and that, by the evidence of an enemy, all clear."

My Uncle Harlowe, it seems, far from disapproving of what his brother had said, declared that there was but one objection to an alliance with Mr. Lovelace: to wit, his faulty morals; especially as so much could be done for Miss Bella and for my brother, too, by my father, and as my brother was actually possessed of a considerable estate by virtue of the Deed of Gift and will of his godmother Lovell.

You may easily guess how much this conversation affected my brother at the time. He could not, you know, but be very uneasy to hear *two of his stewards* talk at this rate to his face.

"See, Sister Bella," said he in an indecent passion before my uncles on the occasion I have mentioned, "See how it is! You and I ought to look about us! This little siren is in a fair way to *out-uncle* us, as she already has *out-grandfathered* us both!"

Mr. Lovelace was received more and more coldly by all; but not being to be put out of his course by slights *only*, personal affronts succeeded; defiances next, then the rencounter. That, as you have heard, did the business; and now, if I do not oblige them, my grandfather's estate is to be litigated with me.

But if I will suffer myself to be prevailed upon, how happy (as they lay out) shall we all be! Such presents am I to have, such jewels, and I cannot tell what from every one of the family! Then Mr. Solmes's fortunes are so great, and his proposals so very advantageous (no relation whom he values) that there will be abundant room to raise mine upon them, were the high-intended favours of my own relations to be quite out of the question.

This is the bright side that is turned to my father and uncles to captivate *them*; but I am afraid that my brother's and sister's design is to ruin me with them at any rate. Were it otherwise, would they not on my return from you have rather sought to *court* than *frighten* me into measures their hearts are so much bent to carry? A method they have followed ever since.

Noble is the word used to enforce the offers of a man who is mean enough avowedly to *hate,* and wicked enough to propose to *rob* of their just expectations, his own family (every one of which at the same time stands in too much need of his favour) in order to settle all he is worth upon me, and if I die without children, and he has none by any other marriage, upon a family which already abounds.

Hatred to Lovelace, family aggrandisement, and this great motive, *paternal authority*! What a force *united* must they be supposed to have, when *singly* each consideration is sufficient to carry all before it.

This is the formidable appearance which the address of this disagreeable man wears at present. My BROTHER and my SISTER triumph. *They have got me down,* as Hannah overheard them exult.

MISS CLARISSA HARLOWE TO MISS HOWE

Thursday evening, March 2.

I MUST take or seek the occasion to apply to my mother for her mediation; for I am in danger of having a day fixed, and antipathy taken for bashfulness. Should not sisters *be* sisters to each other? Should they not make a common cause of it, as I may say, a cause of sex, on such occasions as the present? Yet mine, in support of my brother's selfishness, and no doubt in concert with him, has been urging in full assembly, it seems, (and that with an earnestness peculiar to herself when she sets upon anything), that an absolute day be given me, and if I comply not, to be told, that it shall be to the forfeiture of all my fortunes, and of all their love.

What the discharged steward reported of him is surely bad enough; what Mrs. Fortescue said, not only confirms that bad, but gives room to think him still worse. And yet the *something further* which my friends have come at, is of so heinous a nature (as Betty Barnes tells Hannah) that it proves him to be the worst of men. But hang the man, I had almost said, what is he to me? What *would* he be — were not this Mr. Sol—— O my dear, how I hate that man in the light he is proposed to me!

MISS HOWE TO MISS CLARISSA HARLOWE

Friday, March 3.

I HAVE both your letters at once. It is very unhappy, my dear, since your friends will have you marry, that a person of your merit should be addressed by a succession of worthless creatures, who have nothing but their presumption for their excuse.

That these presumers appear not in this very unworthy light to some of your friends is because their defects are not so striking to *them* as to *others*. And why? Shall I venture to tell you? Because they are nearer their own standard. *Modesty,* after all, perhaps has a concern in it; for how should they think, that a *niece* or a *sister* of *theirs* (I will not go higher for fear of incurring your displeasure) should be an angel?

But where indeed is the man to be found (who has the least share of due diffidence) that dares to look up to Miss Clarissa Harlowe with hope, or with anything but wishes?

Yet I am afraid all opposition will be in vain. You must, you will, I doubt, be sacrificed to this odious man. I know your family. There will be no resisting such baits as he has thrown out. Oh, my dear, my beloved friend! and are such charming qualities, is such exalted merit, to be sunk in such a marriage!

Wonder not, however, at your Bell's unsisterly behaviour in this affair: I have a particular to add to the inducements your insolent brother is governed by, which will account for all her driving. You have already owned that her *outward* eye was from *the first* struck with the figure and address of the man whom she pretends to despise, and who, 'tis certain, thoroughly despises her: but you have not told me that *still* she loves him of all men. Bell has a meanness in her very pride; that meanness rises with her pride, and goes hand in hand with it, and no one is so proud as Bell. She has owned her love, her uneasy days and sleepless nights, and her revenge grafted upon her love to her favourite Betty Barnes. To lay herself in the power of a servant's tongue! Poor creature —

What a sweet revenge will she take, as well upon Lovelace as upon you, if she can procure her rival sister to be married to the man that sister hates; and so prevent her having the man whom she herself loves (whether *she* have hope of him or not) and whom she suspects her sister loves!

O my dear, how will you be able to maintain your ground? I am sure, alas! I am *too* sure, that they will subdue such a fine spirit as yours, unused to opposition; and (*tell it not in Gath*) you *must* be Mrs. Solmes!

Miss Clarissa Harlowe to Miss Howe
(*Her preceding not at the time received*)   *Friday, March 3.*

O my dear friend, I have had a sad conflict! Trial upon trial; conference upon conference! But what law, what ceremony, can give a man a right to a heart which abhors him more than it does any living creature?

I went down this morning when breakfast was ready with a very uneasy heart, from what Hannah had informed me of yesterday afternoon; wishing for an opportunity, however, to appeal to my mother, in hopes to engage her interest in my behalf, and purposing to try to find one when she retired to her own apartment after breakfast: but, unluckily, there was the odious Solmes sitting asquat between my mother and sister, with *so much* assurance in his looks!

Had the wretch kept his seat, it might have been well enough: but the bent and broad-shouldered creature must needs rise and stalk towards a chair; which was just by that which was set for me.

I removed it to a distance, as if to make way to my own: And down I sat, abruptly I believe; what I had heard all in my head.

But this was not enough to daunt him. The man is a very confident, he is a very bold, staring man! Indeed, my dear, the man is very confident!

He took the removed chair and drew it so near mine, squatting in it with his ugly weight, that he pressed upon my hoop. I was so offended that I removed to another chair. I own I had too little command of myself. It gave my brother and sister too much advantage. I dare say they took it. But I did it involuntarily, I think. I could not help it.

I saw that my father was excessively displeased. Clarissa Harlowe! said he with a big voice — and there he stopped. Sir! said I, trembling and curtsying (for I *had* not then sat down again): and put my chair nearer the wretch, and sat down — my face, as I could feel, all in a glow.

Make tea, child, said my kind mamma: sit by me, love, and make tea.

I removed with pleasure to the seat the man had quitted; and being thus indulgently put into employment, soon recovered myself; and in the course of the breakfasting officiously asked two or three questions of Mr. Solmes, which I would not have done, but to make up with my father. *Proud spirits may be brought to!* whisperingly spoke my sister to me over her shoulder, with an air of triumph and scorn: but I did not mind her.

Before the usual breakfast-time was over my father withdrew with my mother, telling her he wanted to speak to her. Then my sister and next my aunt (who was with us) dropped away.

My brother gave himself some airs of insult, which I understood well enough; but which Mr. Solmes could make nothing of: and at last he arose from *his* seat. Sister, said he, I have a curiosity to show you. I will fetch it. And away he went; shutting the door close after him.

I saw what all this was for. I arose; the man hemming up for a speech, rising and beginning to set his splay feet (indeed, my dear, the man in all his ways is hateful to me!) in an approaching posture. I will save my brother the trouble of bringing to me his curiosity, said I. I curtsied — your servant, sir. The man cried, madam, madam, twice, and looked like a fool. But away I went — to find my brother to save my word. But my brother, indifferent as the weather was, was gone to walk in the garden with my sister. A plain case that he had left his *curiosity* with me, and designed to show me no other.

I had but just got into my own apartment, and began to think of sending Hannah to beg an audience of my mother (the more encouraged by her condescending goodness at breakfast), when Shorey, her woman, brought me her commands to attend her in her closet.

My father, Hannah told me, was just gone out of it with a positive angry countenance. Then I as much dreaded the audience as I had wished for it before.

She saw my concern. Holding out her kind arms as she sat, Come kiss me, my dear, said she, with a smile like a sunbeam breaking through the cloud that overshadowed her naturally benign aspect. Why flutters my jewel so?

This preparative sweetness, with her goodness just before, confirmed my apprehensions. My mother saw the bitter pill wanted gilding.

O my mamma! was all I could say; and I clasped my arms round her neck, and my face sunk into her bosom.

My child! my child! restrain, said she, your powers of moving! I dare not else trust myself with you.

Then rising, she drew a chair near her own and made me sit down by her, overwhelmed as I was with tears of apprehension of what she had to say, and of gratitude for her truly maternal goodness to me — sobs still my only language.

And drawing her chair still nearer to mine, she put her arms round my neck, and my glowing cheek, wet with my tears, close to her own: Let me talk to you, my child.

You know, my dear, what I every day forgo, and undergo, for the sake of peace. Your papa is a very good man and means well; but he will not be controlled, nor yet persuaded. Obedience is better than sacrifice. O my Clary Harlowe, rejoice my heart, by telling me I have apprehended too much! I see your concern! I see your perplexity!

Look up to me, my Clary Harlowe — no sullenness, I hope!

No, indeed, my ever-to-be-revered mamma — and I arose. I bent my knee.

She raised me. No kneeling to me but with knees of duty and compliance. Your heart, not your knees, must bend. It is absolutely determined — prepare yourself, therefore, to receive your *father*, when he visits you by and by, as he would wish to receive *you*. But on this one quarter of an hour depends the peace of my future life, the satisfaction of all the family, and your own security from a man of violence; and I charge you *besides*, on my blessing, that you think of being Mrs. Solmes.

There went the dagger to my heart, and down I sunk: and when I recovered, found myself in the arms of my Hannah, my sister's Betty holding open my reluctantly-opened palm, my laces cut, my linen scented with hartshorn; and my mother gone.

Shorey came in with a message (delivered in her solemn way). Your mamma, miss, is concerned for your disorder: she expects you down again in an hour; and bid me say that she then hopes everything from your duty.

I made no reply; for what could I say? And leaning upon my Hannah's arm, withdrew to my own apartment.

Within that time my mother came up to *me*.

I love, she was pleased to say, to come into *this* apartment! — No emotions, child! No flutters! Am I not your mother! Am I not your fond, your indulgent mother! Do not discompose *me* by discomposing *yourself*! Do not occasion *me* uneasiness, when I would give *you* nothing but pleasure.

She was pleased to tell me that my father and she, in order to spare my natural modesty, had taken the whole affair upon themselves ——

Hear me out; and then speak, for I was going to expostulate. You are no stranger to the end of Mr. Solmes's visits ——

O madam! ——

Hear me out, and then speak. He is not indeed everything I wish him to be: but he is a man of probity, and has no vices ——

No vices, madam! ——

Hear me out, child. You have not behaved much amiss to him: we have seen with pleasure that you have not ——

O madam, must I not now speak!

I shall have done presently — a young creature of your virtuous and *pious* turn, she was pleased to say, cannot surely love a profligate: you love your brother too well to wish to marry one who had like to have killed him, and who threatened your uncles and defies us all. You have had your own way six or seven times: we want to secure you against a man so vile. Tell me (I have a *right* to know) whether you prefer this man to all others? Yet God forbid that I should know you do! for such a declaration would make us all miserable. Yet tell me, are your affections engaged to this man?

I knew what the inference would be if I had said they were not. You hesitate — you answer me not —— you cannot answer me. *Rising* — never more will I look upon you with an eye of favour ——

O madam, madam! Kill me not with your displeasure — I would not, I *need* not, hesitate one moment did I not dread the inference, if I answer you as you wish. Yet be that inference what it will, your threatened displeasure will make me speak. And I declare to you that I know not my own heart, if it be not absolutely free.

Well then, Clary (passing over the force of my plea), if your heart be free ——

O my beloved mamma, let the usual generosity of your dear heart operate in my favour. Urge not upon me the inference that made me hesitate.

Again, Clary Harlowe! ——

Dearest madam, forgive me: it was always my pride and my pleasure to obey you. But look upon that man — see but the disagreeableness of his person ——

Now, Clary, do I see whose person you have in your eye! Now is Mr. Solmes, I see, but *comparatively* disagreeable; disagreeable only as another man has a much more specious person.

But, madam, are not his manners equally so? Is not his person the true representative of his mind? That other man is not, shall not, be anything to me, release me but from this one man, whom my heart, unbidden, resists.

Condition thus with your father. Will *he* bear, do you think, to be thus dialogued with?

And saying this, she arose, and went from me. But at the chamber door stopped and turned back; I will not say below in what a disposition I leave you. Consider of everything. The matter is resolved upon. As you value your father's blessing and mine, and the satisfaction of all the family, resolve to comply. I will leave you for a few moments. I will come up to you again: see that I find you as I wish to find you; and since *your heart is free* let your duty govern it.

In about half an hour my mother returned. She found me in tears. She took my hand: it is my part evermore, said she, to be of the acknowledging side. I believe I have needlessly exposed myself to your opposition by the method I have taken with you. I first began as if I *expected* a denial, and by my indulgence, brought it upon myself.

Do not, my dearest mamma! do not say so!

When I came to you a second time, proceeded she, knowing that your opposition would avail you nothing, I refused to hear your reasons, and in this I was wrong: I now, therefore, this third time, see you, and am come resolved to hear all you have to say; but with this intimation, that say what you will, it will be of no avail elsewhere.

What a dreadful saying is that! But could I engage your pity, madam, it would be somewhat.

You have as much of my pity as of my love. But what is person, Clary, with one of your prudence, and *your heart disengaged?*

Should the eye be disgusted when the heart is to be engaged? O madam, who can think of marrying when the heart is shocked at the first appearance, and where the disgust must be confirmed by every conversation afterwards?

This, Clary, is owing to your prepossession. Let me not have cause to regret that noble firmness of mind in so young a creature which I thought your glory, and which was my boast in your character. In this instance it would be obstinacy, and want of duty. Have you not made objections to several ——

That was to their *minds,* to their *principles,* madam — but this man ——

Is an honest man, Clary Harlowe. He has a good mind. He is a virtuous man.

He an honest man! *His* a good mind, madam! *He* a virtuous man! Nobody denies him these qualities.

Can *he* be an honest man who offers terms that will rob all his own relations of their just expectations? Can *his* mind be good ——

You, Clary Harlowe, for whose sake he offers so much, are the last person that should make this observation.

Give me leave to say, madam, that a person preferring happiness to fortune, as I do; that want not even what I *have,* and can give up the use of *that,* as an instance of duty ——

Just then, up came my father, with a sternness in his looks that made me tremble. He took two or three turns about my chamber, though pained by his gout. And then said to my mother, who was silent as soon as she saw him:

My dear, you are long absent. Dinner is near ready. What you had to say lay in a very little compass. Surely, you have nothing to do but to declare *your* will, and *my* will — but perhaps you may be talking of the preparations. Let us have you soon down — your daughter in your hand, if worthy of the name.

And down he went casting his eye upon me with a look so stern that I was unable to say one word to him, or even for a few minutes to my mother.

Was not this very intimidating, my dear?

My mother, seeing my concern, seemed to pity me. She called me her good child, and kissed me; and told me that my father should not know I had made such opposition. He has kindly furnished us with an excuse for being so long together, said she. Come, my dear, dinner will be upon table presently; shall we go down? — and took my hand.

This made me start: what, madam, go down to let it be supposed we were talking of *preparations!* O my beloved mamma, command me not down upon such a supposition.

You see, child, that to stay longer together, will be owning that you are debating about an absolute duty: and that will not be borne. Did not your father himself some days ago tell you he would be obeyed? I will a third time leave you. I must say something by way of excuse for you: and that you desire not to go down to dinner — that your modesty on the occasion ——

O madam! say not my modesty on *such* an occasion: for that will be to give hope ——

And design you *not* to give hope? Perverse girl! *Rising, and flinging from me*; take more time for consideration!

My mother on her return, which was as soon as she had dined, was pleased to inform me, that she told my father, on his questioning her about my *cheerful* compliance (for it seems, the *cheerful* was all that was doubted), that she was willing, on so material a point, to give a child whom she had so *much reason to love* (as she condescended to acknowledge were her words), liberty to say all that was in her heart to say, that her compliance might be the freer; letting him know, that when he came up, she was attending to my pleas; for that she found I had rather not marry at all.

She told me that to this my father angrily said, let her take care — let her take care — that she give me not ground to suspect her of a preference somewhere else. But, if it be to ease *her* heart, and not to dispute *my* will, you may hear her out.

But, why, dearest madam, why am I, the *youngest*, to be precipitated into a state, that I am very far from wishing to enter into with anybody?

You are going to question me, I suppose, why your sister is not thought of for Mr. Solmes?

I hope, madam, it will not displease you if I were?

I might refer you for an answer to your *father*. — Mr. Solmes has reasons for preferring *you* ——

And I have reasons, madam, for disliking *him*. And why am I ——

If you mean to show your duty and your obedience, Clary, you must show it in *our* way; not in *your own*.

I hope, madam, that I have not so behaved hitherto, as to render such a trial of my obedience necessary.

Yes, Clary, I cannot but say that you have hitherto behaved extremely well: but you have had no trials till now: and I hope, that now you are called to one you will not fail in it.

Thus are my imputed good qualities to be made my punishment; and I am to be wedded to a *monster* ——

Astonishing! — Can this, Clarissa, be from you?

The man, madam, person and mind, is a monster in my eye.

Now, Clary, I suppose you will allow *me* to speak. You know your father has made it a point; and did he ever give up one he thought he had a right to carry?

Too true, thought I to myself! And now my brother has engaged my father, his fine scheme will *walk alone*, without needing his leading strings; and it is become my *father's will* that I oppose; not my brother's grasping views.

I was silent. To say the truth, I was just then sullenly silent. My heart was too big. I thought it was hard to be thus given up by my mother; and that she should make a will so uncontrollable as my brother's, her will. My mother, my dear, though I must not say so, was not obliged to marry against *her* liking. My mother loved my father.

My silence availed me still less.

I see, my dear, said she, that you are convinced. Now, my good child, now, my Clary, do I love you! It shall not be known that you have argued with me at all. All shall be imputed to that modesty which has ever so much distinguished you. You shall have the full merit of your resignation.

I wept.

O my dear mamma, said I, forgive me! But surely you cannot believe I can ever think of having that man!

I, said she, in a milder accent, have early said all that I thought could be said against the present proposal, on a supposition that you, who have refused several others (whom I own to be preferable as to person) would *not* approve of it; and could I have succeeded, you, Clary, had never heard of it. But if *I* could not, how can *you* expect to prevail? And well you know, that were Mr. Lovelace an angel, and your father made it a point that you should not have him, it would be in vain to dispute his will. As to the prohibition laid upon you, (much as I will own against *my* liking, that is owing to the belief that you corresponded by Miss Howe's means with that man; nor do I doubt that you did so.

I sighed. I wept. I was silent.

Shall I, Clary, said she, shall I tell your father that these prohibitions are as unnecessary as I hoped they would be? That you know your *duty*, and will not offer to controvert his will? What say you, my love?

O madam, what can I say to questions so indulgently put? I do indeed *know* my duty: no creature in the world is more willing to *practise* it: but, pardon me, dearest madam, if I say that I must bear these prohibitions, if I am to pay so dear to have them taken off.

Determined and perverse, my dear mamma called me: and after walking twice or thrice in anger about the room, she turned to me; your heart *free*, Clarissa! How can you tell me your heart is free? Such extraordinary antipathies to a particular person must be owing to extraordinary prepossessions in another's favour! Tell me, Clary, and tell me truly — do you not continue to correspond with Mr. Lovelace?

Dearest madam, replied I, you know my motives: to prevent mischief, I answered his letters. The reasons for our apprehensions of this sort are not over.

Be pleased, madam, only to advise me how to break it off with safety to my brother and uncles; and it is all I wish for.

You have made offers, Clary, if you might be obliged in the point in question — are you really earnest, were you to be complied with, to break off all correspondence with Mr. Lovelace? Let me know this.

Indeed, I am; and I will. You, madam, shall see all the letters that have passed between us. You shall see I have given him no encouragement independent of my duty. And when you have seen them, you will be better able to direct me how, on the condition I have offered, to break entirely with him.

I take you at your word, Clarissa — give me *his* letters; and the copies of *yours*.

I am sure, madam, you will keep the knowledge that I write, and what I write ———

No conditions with your mother — surely my prudence may be trusted to.

I begged her pardon; and besought her to take the key of the private drawer in my escritoire, where they lay, that she herself might see that I had no reserves to my mother.

She did; and took all his letters and the copies of mine. Unconditioned with, she was pleased to say, they shall be yours again, unseen by anybody else.

I thanked her; and she withdrew to read them, saying she would return them when she had.

You, my dear, have seen all the letters that passed between Mr. Lovelace and me till my last return from you. Three others I have received since by the private conveyance *I told you of*: the last I have not yet answered. He earnestly insists (upon what he has so often proposed) that I will give him leave, in company with Lord M., to wait upon my uncles, and even upon my father — and he promises patience, if new provocations, absolutely beneath a man to bear, be not given: which by the way I am far from being able to engage for.

In my answer, I absolutely declare, as I tell him I have often done, that he is to expect no favour from me against the approbation of my friends: that I am sure their consents for his visiting any of them will never be obtained: that I will not be either so undutiful, or so indiscreet, as to suffer my interests to be separated from the interests of my family, for any man upon earth: that I do not think myself *obliged* to him for the forbearance I desire one flaming spirit to have with others; that in this desire I require nothing of him, but what prudence, justice, and the laws of his country require: that if he has any expectations of favour from me on that account, he deceives himself: that I have no inclination, as I have often told him, to change my condition: that I cannot allow myself to correspond with him any longer in this clandestine manner: it is mean, low, undutiful, I tell him; and has a giddy appearance which cannot be excused: that therefore he is not to expect that I *will* continue it.

To this, in his last, among other things, he replies, that if I am actually determined to break off all correspondence with him, he must conclude that it is with a view to become the wife of a man whom no woman of honour and fortune can think tolerable. But that nevertheless he will not threaten either his own life or that of any other man. He must take his resolutions as such a dreaded event shall impel him at the time. If he shall know that it will have my consent, he must endeavour to resign to his destiny: but if it be brought about by compulsion, he shall not be able to answer for the consequence.

In about an hour my mother returned. Take your letters, Clary: I have nothing, she was pleased to say, to tax your discretion with, as to the wording of yours to him: you have even kept up a proper dignity, as well as observed all the rules of decorum; and you have resented, as you ought to resent, his menacing invectives. Your heart, you *say*, is *free*: you own, that you cannot think, as matters are circumstanced, that a match with a man so obnoxious as he now is to us all, is proper to be thought of; what do you propose to do? What, Clary, are your own thoughts of the matter?

Without hesitation thus I answered — what I humbly propose is this: That I will write to Mr. Lovelace (for I have not answered his last) that he has nothing to do between my father and me: that I neither *ask* his advice nor *need* it: but that since he thinks he has some pretence for interfering, because of my brother's avowal of the interest of Mr. Solmes in displeasure to him, I will assure him (without giving him any reason to impute the assurance to be in the least favourable to himself) that I never will be that man's.

Ah! my love! But what shall we do about the *terms* Mr. Solmes offers? Those are the inducements with everybody. He has even given hopes to your brother that he will make exchanges of estates; or at least that he will purchase the northern one; for you know it must be entirely consistent with the family views, that we increase our interest in this county. Your brother, in short, has given in a plan that captivates us all: and a family so rich in all its branches, and that has its views to honour, must be pleased to see a very great probability of taking rank one day among the principal in the kingdom.

And for the sake of these views, for the sake of this plan of my brother's, am I, madam, to be given in marriage to a man I never can endure! O my dear mamma, save me, save me if you can, from this heavy evil! I had rather be buried alive, indeed I had, than have that man!

She went down to tea, and kindly undertook to excuse my attendance at supper.

MISS CLARISSA HARLOWE TO MISS HOWE

Sat., March 4.   12 o'clock.

HANNAH has just now brought me from the usual place your favour of yesterday. The contents of it have made me very thoughtful.

34

As to what you say of my giving up to my father's control the estate devised me, my motives at the time, as you acknowledge, were not blameable. Your advice to me on the subject was grounded, as I remember, on your good opinion of me; believing that I should not make a bad use of the power willed me: neither you nor I, my dear, although you now assume the air of a diviner (pardon me), could have believed *that* would have happened which has happened, as to my *father's* part particularly.

You think I must of necessity, as matters are circumstanced, be Solmes's wife. I will not be very rash, my dear, in protesting to the contrary: but I think it never can, and what is still more, never *ought* to be! My temper, I know, is depended upon. But I have hitherto said that I have something in me of my father's family, as well as of my mother's.

Surely I ought not to be the instrument of depriving Mr. Solmes's relations of their natural rights and reversionary prospects, for the sake of further aggrandising a family (although *that* I am of), which already lives in great affluence and splendour. The less, surely, ought I to give into these grasping views of my brother, as I myself heartily despise the end aimed at; as I wish not either to change my state, or better my fortunes; and as I am fully persuaded that happiness and riches are two things and very seldom meet together.

As only my sister dines with my mother, I thought I should have been commanded down: but she sent me up a plate from her table. I continued my writing. I could not touch a morsel. I ordered Hannah however to eat of it, that I might not be thought sullen.

MISS CLARISSA HARLOWE TO MISS HOWE

Sat. Afternoon.

THE expected conference is over: but my difficulties are increased. This, as my mother was pleased to tell me, being the last *persuasory* effort that is to be attempted, I will be as particular in the account of it as my head and my heart will allow me to be.

I have made, said she, as she entered my room, a *short* as well as *early* dinner, on purpose to confer with you.

Your father both dines and sups at your uncle's, on purpose to give us this opportunity; and according to the report I shall make on his return (which I have promised shall be a very faithful one), he will take his measures with you.

I was offering to speak — hear, Clarissa, what I have to tell you, said she, before you speak, unless what you have to say will signify to me your compliance — say — *will* it? If it will, you may speak.

I was silent.

She looked with concern and anger upon me — no compliance, I find! — such a dutiful young creature hitherto! Your *father* is determined. Have I not told you there is no receding; that the honour as well as the interest of the family is concerned? Take notice, that there are flaws in your grandfather's will: not a shilling of that estate will be yours if you do not yield. Your grandfather left it to you as a reward of your duty to *him* and to *us*. You will *justly* forfeit it, if ——

Permit me, good madam, to say that, if it were *unjustly* bequeathed me, I ought not to wish to have it. But I hope Mr. Solmes will be apprised of these flaws.

This is very pertly said, Clarissa: but, reflect, that the forfeiture of that estate through your opposition will be attended with the total loss of your father's favour; and then how destitute must you be; how unable to support yourself; and how many benevolent designs and good actions must you give up!

I must accommodate myself, madam, in the latter case, to my circumstances: *much* only is *required* where *much is given*. It becomes me to be thankful for what I have had.

All this, Clarissa, makes your prepossession in a certain man's favour the more evident. Indeed your brother and sister cannot go any whither but they hear of these prepossessions.

I received her rebukes in silence.

You are sullen, Clarissa: I see you are *sullen*. And she walked about the room in anger.

I now tell you, that the settlements are actually drawn; and that you will be called down in a very few days to hear them read and to sign them: for it is impossible, if your heart be free, that you can make the least objection to them; except it will be an objection with you, that they are so much in your favour and in the favour of all our family.

I was speechless, absolutely speechless. Although my heart was ready to burst, yet could I neither weep nor speak.

I am sorry, said she, for your averseness to this match (*match* she was pleased to call it); but there is no help. The honour and interest of the family, as your aunt has told you, and as I have told you, are concerned; and you must comply.

I was still speechless.

Your father is resolved not to see you till he sees you as obedient a child as you used to be. You have never been put to a test till now, that deserved to be called a test. This *is*, this *must* be, my last effort with you. Give me hope, my dear child: my peace is concerned: I will compound with you but for *hope*; and yet your father will not be satisfied without an implicit, and even a cheerful obedience — give me but hope, my child!

To give you hope, my dearest, my most indulgent mamma, is to give you everything. Can I be honest, if I give a hope that I cannot confirm?

She was very angry.

Your father's heart, I tell you once more, is in it: he has declared that he had rather have no daughter in you, than one he cannot dispose of for your own good: especially as you have owned, that *your heart is free*; and as the general good of his whole family is to be promoted by your obedience. He has pleaded, poor man! that his frequent gouty paroxysms (every fit more threatening than the former) give him no extraordinary prospects, either of worldly happiness, or of long days: and he hopes that you, who have been supposed to have contributed to the lengthening of your *grandfather's* life, will not, by your disobedience, shorten your *father's*.

This was a most affecting plea, my dear. I wept in silence upon it. I could not speak to it. And my mother proceeded: Your father has declared that your unexpected opposition (*unexpected she was pleased to call it*), and Mr. Lovelace's continued menaces and insults, more and more convince him that a short day is necessary in order to put an end to all that man's hopes, and to his own apprehensions resulting from the disobedience of a child so favoured. He has, therefore, actually ordered patterns of the richest silks to be sent for from London ——

I started — I was out of breath — I gasped at this frightful precipitance. I was going to open with warmth against it. I knew whose the *happy* expedient must be: female minds, I once heard my brother say, that could but be brought to *balance* on the change of their state, might easily be *determined* by the glare and splendour of the nuptial preparations and the pride of becoming the mistress of a family. But she was pleased to hurry on, that I might not have time to express my disgusts at such a communication — to this effect:

Your father at his going out, told me what he expected from me, in case I found that I had not the requisite influence upon you. It was this — that I should directly separate myself from you, and leave you singly to take the consequence of your double disobedience.

I then, half-franticly I believe, laid hold of her gown. Have patience with me, dearest madam! said I. Do not *you* renounce me totally! If you *must* separate yourself from your child, let it not be with *absolute* reprobation on *your own* part! My uncles may be hard-hearted — my father may be immovable. I may suffer from my brother's ambition, and from my sister's envy! But let me not lose my mamma's love; at least her pity.

She turned to me with benigner rays. You *have* my love! You *have* my *pity*! But, O my dearest girl — I have not *yours*. You forget that I must separate myself from you, if you will not comply. You do not remember that your father will take you up, where I leave you. Once more, however, I will put it to you: are you determined to brave your father's displeasure? Are you determined to defy your uncles? Do you choose to break with us all, rather than encourage Mr. Solmes? Rather than give me hope?

Dear, dear madam, how can I give hope, and not intend to be this man's?

Ah, girl, never say your *heart is free*! You deceive yourself if you think it is.

But here, run away with my pen, I suffer my mother to be angry with me on her own account. She hinted to me, indeed, that I must seek *her* if my mind *changed;* which is a condition that amounts to a prohibition of attending her: but, as she left me in displeasure, will it not have a very obstinate appearance, and look like a kind of renunciation of her mediation in my favour, if I go down before my father returns, to supplicate her pity, and her kind report to him?

I will attend her. I had rather all the world should be angry with me than my mamma!

MISS CLARISSA HARLOWE TO MISS HOWE

Sat. Night.

I FOUND mother and sister together in my sister's parlour. My mother, I fear, by the glow in her fine face (and as the browner, sullener glow in my sister's confirmed) had been expressing herself with warmth, against her *unhappier* child: perhaps giving such an account of what had passed, as should clear herself, and convince Bella, and through *her*, my brother and uncles, of the sincere pains she had taken with me.

I entered like a dejected criminal; and besought the favour of a private audience. My mother's return, both looks and words, gave but too much reason for my above surmise.

I come down, madam, said I, to beg of you to forgive me for anything you may have taken amiss in what passed above respecting your honoured self; and that you will be pleased to use your endeavours to soften my papa's displeasure against me on his return.

Such aggravating looks; such lifting up of hands and eyes; such a furrowed forehead in my sister!

My mother was angry enough without all that; and asked me to what purpose I came down, if I were still so untractable?

She had hardly spoken the words when Shorey came in to tell her that Mr. Solmes was in the hall, and desired admittance.

The man stalked in, and first paid his clumsy respects to my mother; then to my sister; next to me, as if I were already his wife, and therefore to be last in his notice; and sitting down by me, told us in general what weather it was. Very cold he made it; but I was warm enough. Then addressing himself to me; and how do *you* find it, miss? was his question; and would have taken my hand.

I withdrew it, I believe with disdain enough. My mother frowned. My sister bit her lip.

I could not contain myself: I never was so bold in my life; for I went on with my plea as if Mr. Solmes had not been there.

My mother coloured, and looked at him, at my sister, and at me. My sister's eyes were opener and bigger than ever I saw them before.

The man understood me. He hemmed, and removed from one chair to another.

I went on, supplicating for my mother's favourable report: Nothing but invincible dislike, said I ——

What would the girl be at, interrupted my mother? Why, Clary!

Is this a subject! Is this! — is this! — is this a time — and again she looked upon Mr. Solmes.

I am sorry, on reflection, that I put my mamma into so much confusion. To be sure it was very saucy in me.

I beg pardon, madam, said I. But my papa will soon return. And since I am not permitted to withdraw, it is not necessary, I humbly presume, that Mr. Solmes's presence should deprive me of this opportunity to implore your favourable report; and at the same time, if he still visit on my account (looking at him) to convince him, that it cannot possibly be to any purpose ——

Is the girl mad? said my mother, interrupting me.

My mother came to me, and angrily taking my hand, led me out of that parlour into my own; which, you know, is next to it. Is not this behaviour very bold, very provoking, think you, Clary?

I beg your pardon, madam, if it has that appearance to you. But indeed, my dear mamma, there seem to be snares laying for me. Too well I know my brother's drift. With a good word he shall have my consent for all he wishes to worm me out of. Neither he, nor my sister, shall need to take half this pains.

My mother was about to leave me in high displeasure.

I besought her to stay: one favour, but one favour, dearest madam, said I, give me leave to beg of you ——

What would the girl?

I see how everything is working about. I never, never can think of Mr. Solmes. My papa will be in tumults when he is told I cannot. They will judge of the tenderness of your heart to a poor child who seems devoted by every one else, from the willingness you have already shown to hearken to my prayers. There will be endeavours used to confine me, and keep me out of your presence, and out of the presence of every one who used to love me (*this, my dear Miss Howe, is threatened*). If this be effected; if it be put out of my power to plead my own cause, and to appeal to you, and to my Uncle Harlowe, of whom only I have hope; then will every ear be opened against me, and every tale encouraged — it is, therefore, my humble request, that, added to the disgraceful prohibitions I now suffer under, you will not, if you can help it, give way to my being denied *your* ear.

Your listening Hannah has given you this intelligence, as she does many others.

My Hannah, madam, listens not — my Hannah ——

No more in Hannah's behalf — Hannah is known to make mischief — Hannah is known — but no more of that bold intermeddler. 'Tis true your father threatened to confine you to your chamber if you complied not, in order the more assuredly to deprive you of the opportunity of corresponding with those who harden your heart against his will. He bid me tell you so, when he went out, if I found you refractory. But I was loth to deliver so harsh a declaration; being still in hope that you would come down to us in a compliant temper. And I now assure you, that you will be confined, and prohibited making teasing appeals to any of us: and we shall see who is to submit, you to us, or everybody to you.

And this, said I, is all I have to hope for from my mamma?

It is. But, Clary, this one further opportunity I give you: go in again to Mr. Solmes, and behave discreetly to him; and let your father find you together, upon *civil* terms at least.

My feet moved (of *themselves*, I think) farther from the parlour where he was, and towards the stairs; and there I stopped and paused.

If, proceeded she, you are determined to stand in defiance of us all — then indeed may you go up to your chamber (as you are ready to do) — and God help you!

My father is come home, and my brother with him. Late as it is they are all shut up together. Not a door opens; not a soul stirs. Hannah, as she moves up and down, is shunned as a person infected.

The angry assembly is broken up. My two uncles and my Aunt Hervey are sent for, it seems, to be here in the morning to breakfast. I shall then, I suppose, know my doom. 'Tis past eleven, and I am ordered not to go to bed.

Twelve o'clock.

This moment the keys of everything are taken from me. It was proposed to send for me down: but my father said he could not bear to look upon me. Strange alteration in a few weeks! Shorey was the messenger. The tears stood in her eyes when she delivered her message.

You, my dear, are happy — may you always be so — and then I can never be wholly miserable. Adieu, my beloved friend! / CL. HARLOWE.

MISS CLARISSA HARLOWE TO MISS HOWE

Saturday Morning, March 4.

HANNAH has just brought me, from the private place in the garden wall, a letter from Mr. Lovelace, deposited last night, signed also by Lord M.

He tells me in it, That Mr. Solmes makes it his boast that he is to be married in a few days to one of the shyest women in England: that my brother explains his meaning; this shy creature, he says, is me; and he assures every one that his younger sister is very soon to be Mr. Solmes's wife. He tells of the patterns bespoken which my mother mentioned to me.

Not one thing escapes him that is done or said in this house.

He knows not, he says, what my relations' inducements can be to prefer such a man as Solmes to him. If advantageous settlements be the motive, Solmes shall not offer what he will refuse to comply with.

As to his estate and family; the first cannot be excepted against:

and for the second, he will not disgrace himself by a comparison so odious. He appeals to Lord M. for the regularity of his life and manners ever since he has made his addresses to me, or had hope of my favour.

I suppose he would have his lordship's signing to this letter to be taken as a voucher for him.

He desires my leave (in company with my lord, in a pacific manner) to attend my father or uncles, in order to make proposals that *must* be accepted, if they will but see him and hear what they are: and tells me, that he will submit to any measures that I shall prescribe, in order to bring about a reconciliation.

He presumes to be very earnest with me, to give him a private meeting some night in my father's garden, attended by whom I please.

Really, my dear, were you to see his letter, you would think I had given him great encouragement, and that I am in direct treaty with him; or that he is sure that my friends will drive me into a foreign protection; for he has the boldness to offer, in my lord's name, an asylum to me should I be tyrannically treated in Solmes's behalf.

For my own part, I am very uneasy to think how I have been *drawn* on the one hand, and *driven* on the other, into a clandestine, in short, into a mere lover-like correspondence which my heart condemns. It is easy to see, if I do not break it off, that Mr. Lovelace's advantages, by reason of my unhappy situation, will every day increase, and I shall be more and more entangled. Yet if I do put an end to it, without making it a condition of being freed from Mr. Solmes's address ——

All my relations are met. They are at breakfast together. Mr. Solmes is expected. I am excessively uneasy. I must lay down my pen.

Sunday Noon.

I desired to speak with Shorey. I directed her to carry to my mother my request for permission to go to church this afternoon. What do you think was the return? Tell her that she must direct herself to her brother for any favour she has to ask.

I was resolved, however, to ask of *him* this favour. Accordingly, when they sent me up my solitary dinner, I gave the messenger a billet, in which I made my humble request through him to my father, to be permitted to go to church this afternoon.

This was the contemptuous answer: "Tell her that her request will be taken into consideration *tomorrow*." On recollection I thought it best to renew my request. I did. The following is a copy of what I wrote, and what follows that of the answer sent me.

SIR, — I know not what to make of the answer brought to my request of being permitted to go to church this afternoon. If you designed to show your pleasantry by it, I hope that will continue, and then my request will be granted.

I will solemnly engage only to go thither and back again. My disgraces, if they are to have an end, need not to be proclaimed to the whole world. I ask this favour, therefore, for my reputation's sake, that I may be able to hold up my head in the neighbourhood if I live to see an end to the unmerited severities which seem to be designed for / Your unhappy sister, / CL. HARLOWE.

To Miss Clarissa Harlowe

FOR a girl to lay so much stress upon going to church, and yet resolve to defy her parents in an article of the greatest consequence to them, and to the whole family, is an absurdity. The *intention* is, I tell you plainly, to mortify you into a sense of your duty. The neighbours you are so solicitous to appear well with, already know that you defy *that*. So, miss, if you have a real value for your reputation, show it as you ought. It is yet in your power to establish or impair it. / JA. HARLOWE.

MISS CLARISSA HARLOWE TO MISS HOWE

Monday Morning, March 6.

THEY are resolved to break my heart. My poor Hannah is discharged — disgracefully discharged! Thus it was:

Within half an hour after I had sent the poor girl down for my breakfast, that bold creature Betty Barnes, my sister's confident and servant (if a favourite maid and confident can be deemed a *servant*), came up.

What, miss, will you please to have for breakfast?

I was surprised. What will I have for breakfast, Betty! How! — what! — how comes it! Then I named Hannah. I could not tell what to say.

Don't be surprised, miss: but you'll see Hannah no more in this house.

God forbid; Is any harm come to Hannah? What! What is the matter with Hannah?

Why, miss, the short and the long is this: your papa and mamma think Hannah has stayed long enough in the house to do mischief; and so she is ordered to *troop* (that was the confident creature's word); and I am directed to wait upon you in her stead.

I burst into tears. I have no service for you, Betty Barnes; none at all. But where is Hannah? Cannot I speak with the poor girl? I owe her half a year's wages. May I not see the honest creature, and pay her her wages?

The worthy creature was as earnest to see me; and the favour was granted in presence of Shorey and Betty.

I gave her instead of four pounds which were due to her, ten guineas: and said, if ever I were again allowed to be my own mistress, I would think of *her* in the first place.

Betty enviously whispered Shorey upon it.

Hannah told me, before their faces, having no other opportunity, that she had been examined about letters *to* me and *from* me: and that she had given her pockets to Miss Harlowe, who looked into them, and put her fingers in her stays, to satisfy herself that she had not any.

She gave me an account of the number of my pheasants and bantams; and I said they should be my own care twice or thrice a day.

We wept over each other at parting. The girl prayed for all the family.

To have so good a servant so disgracefully dismissed, is very cruel: and I could not help saying that these methods might break my heart, but not any other way answer the end of the authors of my disgraces.

Betty, with a very saucy leer, said to Shorey, there would be a trial of skill about that, she fancied.

MISS CLARISSA HARLOWE TO MISS HOWE

Monday near 12 o'clock.

THE enclosed letter was just now delivered to me. My brother has carried all his points.

I send you also the copy of my answer. No more at this time can I write!

MISS CLARY, — By command of your father and mother I write expressly to forbid you to come into their presence or into the garden when *they* are there: nor when they are *not* there, but with Betty Barnes to attend you; except by particular licence or command.

On their blessings, you are forbidden likewise to correspond with the vile Lovelace; as it is well known you did by means of your sly Hannah. Whence her sudden discharge. As was fit.

Neither are you to correspond with Miss Howe; who has given herself high airs of late; and might possibly help on your correspondence with that detested libertine. Nor, in short, with anybody without leave.

You are not to enter into the presence of either of your uncles without their leave first obtained. It is in *mercy* to you, after such a behaviour to your mother, that your father refuses to see you.

You are not to be seen in any apartment of the house you so lately governed as you pleased, unless you are commanded down.

In short, you are strictly to confine yourself to your chamber, except now and then you take a turn in the garden.

If anything I have written appear severe or harsh, it is still in your power (but perhaps will not always be so) to remedy it, and that by a single word. / JA HARLOWE.

To James Harlowe, junior, Esq.

SIR, — I will only say that you may congratulate yourself on having *so far* succeeded in all your views, that you may report what you please of me, and I can no more defend myself than if I were dead.

Yet one favour, nevertheless, I will beg of you. It is this: that you will not occasion more severities, more disgraces, than are necessary for carrying into execution your further designs, whatever they be, against / Your unhappy sister, / CLARISSA HARLOWE.

MISS CLARISSA HARLOWE TO MISS HOWE

Tuesday, March 7.

BY my last deposit you will see how I am driven, and what a poor prisoner I am. No regard had to my reputation. The whole matter is now before you. Can *such* measures be supposed to soften? But surely they can only mean to try to frighten me into my brother's views! All my hope is to be able to weather this point till my Cousin Morden comes from Florence; and he is soon expected: yet, if they are determined upon a short day, I doubt he will not be here time enough to save me.

I asked Mrs. Betty if she had any orders to watch or attend me; or whether I was to ask *her* leave whenever I should be disposed to walk in the garden or to go to feed my bantams? Lord bless her! what could I mean by such a question! Yet she owned that she had heard that I was not to go into the garden when my father, mother, or uncles were there.

However, as it behoved me to be assured on this head, I went down directly, and stayed an hour without question or impediment; and yet a good part of the time I walked under and in *sight*, as I may say, of my brother's study window, where both he and my sister happened to be.

So this part of my restraint was doubtless a stretch of the authority given him. The enforcing of that may, perhaps, come next. But I hope not.

Tuesday Night.

Since I wrote the above, I ventured to send a letter by Shorey to my mother:

HONOURED MADAM, — Having acknowledged to you that I had received letters from Mr. Lovelace full of resentment, and that I answered them purely to prevent further mischief; I think it my duty to acquaint you that another letter from him has since come to my hand, in which he is very earnest with me to permit him to wait upon my papa, or you, or my two uncles, in a pacific way, accompanied by Lord M.: on which I beg your commands.

I own to you, madam, that had not the prohibition been renewed, and had not Hannah been so suddenly dismissed my service, I should have made the less scruple to have written an answer and to have commanded her to convey it to him with all speed, in order to dissuade him from these visits, lest anything should happen on the occasion that my heart aches but to think of.

If I do *not* answer him, he will be made desperate, and think himself justified (though I shall not think him so) in resenting the treatment he complains of: if I *do*, and if, in compliment to me, he forbears to resent what he thinks himself entitled to resent; be pleased, madam, to consider the obligation he will suppose he lays me under. And so leaving the whole to your own wisdom, and whether you choose to consult my papa and uncles upon this humble application, or not; or whether I shall be allowed to write an answer to Mr. Lovelace or not (and if allowed so to do, I beg your direction by whom to send it); I remain, Honoured Madam, / Your unhappy, but ever dutiful daughter, / CL. HARLOWE.

Wednesday Morning.

I have just received an answer to the enclosed letter.

CLARISSA, — I don't know what to write about your answering that man of violence. What can you think of it, that such a family as ours, should have such a rod held over it? For my part, I have not owned that I know you *have* corresponded: by your last boldness to me (an astonishing one it was, to pursue before Mr. Solmes the subject that I was forced to break from above stairs!) you may, as far as I know, plead, that you had my countenance for your correspondence with him; and so add to the uneasiness between your father and me. You were once all my comfort, Clarissa: you made all my hardships tolerable: but now! However, nothing, it is plain, can move you; and I will say no more on that head: for you are under your father's discipline now; and he will neither be prescribed to nor entreated.

I should have been glad to see the letter you tell me of; but it is not for me to see it if you would *choose* to show it me. I will not be in your secret. I will not know that you did correspond. And as to an answer, take your own methods. But let him know it will be the last you will write. And if you do write, I won't see it: so seal it up (if you do) and give it to Shorey; and she — yet do not think I give you licence to write.

Your father takes upon himself to be answerable for all consequences. You must not, therefore, apply to me for favour. I shall endeavour to be only an observer; happy, if I could be an unconcerned one! While I had power, you would not let me use it as I *would* have used it.

Write not another letter to me. I can do nothing for you. But you can do everything for yourself.

After this letter, you will believe, that I could have very little hopes, that an application directly to my father would stand me in my stead: but I thought it became me to write, were it but to acquit myself *to* myself, that I have left nothing unattempted that has the least likelihood to restore me to his favour. Accordingly I wrote to the following effect:

"I presume not, I say, to argue with my papa; I only beg his mercy and indulgence in this *one* point, on which depends my present and

45

perhaps my *future* happiness; and beseech him not to reprobate his child for an aversion which it is not in her power to conquer. I beg that I may not be sacrificed to projects and remote contingencies. I complain of the disgraces I suffer in this banishment from his presence, and in being confined to my chamber. In everything but this *one* point, I promise implicit duty and resignation to his will. I repeat my offers of a single life; and appeal to him, whether I have ever given him cause to doubt my word."

This is the answer, sent without superscription, and unsealed, although by Betty Barnes, who delivered it with an air, as if she knew the contents.

Wednesday.

I WRITE, perverse girl; but with all the indignation that your disobedience deserves. To desire to be forgiven a fault you own, and yet resolve to persevere in, is a boldness, no more to be equalled, than passed over. It is *my* authority you defy. Your behaviour to your too indulgent, and too fond mother — but, I have no patience — continue banished from my presence, undutiful as you are, till you know how to conform to my will. / A JUSTLY-INCENSED FATHER.

MISS CLARISSA HARLOWE TO MISS HOWE

Thursday Morn., Mar. 9.

I HAVE another letter from Mr. Lovelace, although I had not answered his former.

This man, somehow or other, knows everything that passes in our family. My confinement; Hannah's dismission; and more of the resentments and resolutions of my father, uncles, and brother than I can possibly know, and almost as soon as the things happen which he tells me of. He cannot come at these intelligences fairly.

He is excessively uneasy upon what he hears; and his expressions both of love to me, and resentment to them, are very fervent. He solicits me to engage my honour to him, never to have Mr. Solmes.

I think I may fairly promise him that I will not.

He begs, that I will not think he is endeavouring to make to himself a *merit* at any man's expense, since he hopes to obtain my favour on the foot of his *own*; nor that he seeks to *intimidate* me into a consideration for him. But declares that the treatment he meets with from my family is of such a nature that he is perpetually reproached for not resenting it; and that as well by Lord M. and Lady Sarah and Lady Betty, as by all his other friends: and if he must have no hope from me, he cannot answer for what his despair will make him do.

You see, my dear, that my mother seems as apprehensive of mischief as myself; and has *indirectly* offered to let Shorey carry my answer to the letter he sent me before.

I have answered his letters. If he take me at my word I shall need to be the less solicitous for the opinions of his relations in my favour: and yet one would be glad to be well thought of by the worthy.

This is the substance of my letter:

I express my surprise at his knowing (and so early) all that passes here.

I assure him that were there not such a man in the world as himself I would not have Mr. Solmes.

I tell him that to return, as I understand he does, defiances for defiances to my relations, is far from being a proof with me, either of his politeness or of the consideration he pretends to have for me.

That the moment I hear he visits any of my friends without their consent, I will make a resolution never to see him more if I can help it.

This last I put in that he may not be quite desperate. But if he take me at my word I shall be rid of one of my tormentors.

But enough for the present of a creature so very various.

Miss Howe to Miss Clarissa Harlowe

Thursday Night, March 9.

I HAVE no patience with any of the people you are with. I know not what to advise you to do.

Your insolent brother — what has *he* to do to control you? Were it me (I wish it were for one month, and no more) I'd show him the difference. I would be in my own mansion, pursuing my charming schemes and making all around me happy. I would set up my own chariot. I would visit them when they deserved it. But when my brother and sister gave themselves airs, I would let them know that I was their sister, and not their servant: and, if that did not do, I would shut my gates against them; and bid them go and be company for each other.

Here my mother broke in upon me. She wanted to see what I had written. I was chidden for setting you against complying with your father's will. Then followed a lecture upon the preference to be given in favour of a man who took care to discharge all his obligations to the world and to keep all together, in opposition to a spendthrift or profligate. A fruitful subject you know, whether any particular person be meant by it, or not.

Why will these wise parents, by saying too much against the persons they dislike, put one upon defending them?

It is proper to acquaint you that I was obliged to comply with my mother's *curiosity* (my mother has her share, her full share, of *curiosity*, my dear) and to let her see here and there some passages in your letters.

I must needs say that I think duty to parents is a very meritorious excellence: but I bless God I have not your trials. We can all be good when we have no temptation nor provocation to the contrary: but few young persons (who can help themselves too as you can) would bear what you bear.

I will not mention all that is upon my mind in relation to the behaviour of your father and uncles *and the rest of them,* because I would not offend you: but I have now a higher opinion of my own sagacity than ever I had, in that I could never cordially love any one of your family but yourself. I am not *born* to like them. But it is my *duty* to be sincere to my *friend*: and this will excuse her Anna Howe to Miss Clarissa Harlowe.

Mr. Hickman is expected from London this evening. I have desired him to inquire after Lovelace's life and conversation in town. If he has not inquired, I shall be very angry with him. Don't expect a very good account of either. He is certainly an intriguing wretch and full of inventions.

If I have not been clear enough in my advice about what you shall do, let me say that I can give it in one word: it is only by re-urging you to RESUME. If you do all the rest will follow.

RESUME, my dear. And that is all I will give myself time to say further, lest I offend you when I cannot serve you — only this, that I am / Your truly affectionate friend and servant / ANNA HOWE.

MISS CLARISSA HARLOWE TO MISS HOWE

Friday, March 10.

You will permit me, my dear, to touch upon a few passages in your last letter that affect me sensibly.

In the first place, you must allow me to say, low as I am in spirits, that I am very angry with you for your reflections on my relations, particularly on my father and mother, and on the memory of my grandfather.

If then you would avoid my highest displeasure, you must spare my mother; and, surely, you will allow me, with her, to pity, as well as to love and honour my father.

I should be very blameable to endeavour to hide any the least bias upon my mind, from you: and I cannot but say that this man — this Lovelace — is a man that might be liked well enough, if he bore such a character as Mr. Hickman bears; and even if there were hopes of reclaiming him. And further still, I will acknowledge that I believe it possible that one might be driven, by violent measures, step by step as it were, into something that might be called — I don't know what to call it — a *conditional kind of liking,* or so. But as to the word LOVE justifiable and charming as it is in some cases (that is to say, in all the *relative,* in all the *social,* and, what is still beyond *both,* in all our *superior* duties, in which it may be properly called *divine*); it has, methinks, in the narrow, circumscribed, selfish, peculiar sense in which you apply it to me (the man, too, so little to be approved of for his morals, if all that report says of him be true) no pretty sound with it.

MISS CLARISSA HARLOWE TO MISS HOWE

Saturday, March 11.

I HAVE had such taunting messages, and such repeated avowals of ill-offices, brought me from my brother and sister, if I do not comply with their will (delivered, too, with provoking sauciness by Betty Barnes) that I have thought it proper, before I entered upon my intended address to my uncles, in pursuance of the hint given me in my mother's letter, to expostulate a little with *them*. But I have done it in such a manner, as will give you (if you please to take it as you have done some parts of my former letters) great advantage over me. In short, you will have more cause than ever to declare me far gone in love, if my *reasons* for the change of my style in these letters, with regard to Mr. Lovelace, do not engage your more favourable opinion. — For I have thought proper to give them their own way; and, since they will have it, that I have preferable regard for Mr. Lovelace, I give them cause rather to confirm their opinion than doubt it.

MISS CLARISSA HARLOWE TO MISS HOWE

Sunday Night, March 12.

THIS man, this Lovelace, gives me great uneasiness. He is extremely bold and rash. He was this afternoon at our church — in hopes to see me, I suppose: and yet, if he had such hopes, his usual intelligence must have failed him.

Shorey was at church; and a principal part of her observation was upon his haughty and proud behaviour when he turned round in the pew where he sat to our family pew. My father and both my uncles were there; so were my mother and sister. My brother happily was not. They all came home in disorder. Nor did the congregation mind anybody but him; it being his first appearance there since the unhappy rencounter.

Shorey says that Mr. Lovelace watched my mother's eye, and bowed to her: and she returned the compliment. He always admired my mother. She would not, I believe, have hated *him* had she not been *bid* to hate him; and had it not been for the rencounter between him and her only son.

Dr. Lewen was at church; and observing, as every one else did, the disorder into which Mr. Lovelace's appearance had put all our family, was so good as to engage him in conversation, when the service was over, till they were all gone to their coaches.

MR. LOVELACE TO JOHN BELFORD, ESQ.

Monday, March 13.

IN vain dost thou[1] and thy compeers press me to go to town,

[1] These gentlemen affected what they called the Roman style (to wit, the *thee* and the *thou* in their letters); and it was an agreed rule with them, to take in good part whatever freedoms they treated each other with, if the passages were written in that style.

while I am in such an uncertainty as I am in at present with this proud beauty. All the ground I have hitherto gained with her, is entirely owing to her concern for the safety of people whom I have reason to hate.

The lady's malevolent brother has now, as I told thee at M. Hall, introduced another man; the most unpromising in his person and qualities, the most formidable in his offers, that has yet appeared.

This man has by his proposals captivated every soul of the Harlowes — *soul!* did I say — there is not a soul among them but my charmer's: and she, withstanding them all, is actually confined, and otherwise maltreated by a father the most gloomy and positive; at the instigation of a brother the most arrogant and selfish — but thou knowest their characters; and I will not therefore sully my paper with them.

Thou knowest my heart, if any man living does. As far as I know it myself, thou knowest it. But 'tis a cursed deceiver; for it has many and many a time imposed upon its master — *master*, did I say? That am I not now; nor have I been from the moment I beheld this angel of a woman. Prepared indeed as I was by her character before I saw her: for what a mind must that be, which though not virtuous itself, admires not virtue in another? My visit to Arabella, owing to a mistake of the sisters, into which, as thou hast heard me say, I was led by the blundering uncle; who was to introduce *me* (but lately come from abroad) to the *divinity* as I thought; but, instead of her, carried me to a *mere mortal*. And much difficulty had I, so fond and so forward my lady! to get off without forfeiting all with a family that I intended should give me a goddess.

I have boasted that I was once in love before: and indeed I thought I was. It was in my early manhood — with that quality-jilt, whose infidelity I have vowed to revenge upon as many of the sex as shall come into my power. I believe, in different climes, I have already sacrificed an hecatomb to my Nemesis, in pursuance of this vow. But upon recollecting what I was *then*, and comparing it with what I find in myself *now*, I cannot say that I was ever in love before.

But now am I *indeed* in love. I can think of nothing, of nobody, but the divine Clarissa Harlowe. *Harlowe!* How that hated word sticks in my throat — but I shall give her for it the name of love.[1]

And what my motive, dost thou ask? No less than this, that my beloved shall find no protection out of my family; for, if I know *hers*, fly she must or have the man she hates. This, therefore, if I take my measures right, and my familiar fail me not, will secure her mine in spite of them all; in spite of her own inflexible heart: mine, without condition; without reformation promises; without the necessity of a siege of years, perhaps; and to be even then, after wearing the guise of a merit-doubting hypocrisy, at an uncertainty, upon a probation unapproved of. Then shall I have all the rascals and rascalesses of the family come creeping to me: I prescribing to them; and bringing that sordidly-imperious brother to kneel at the footstool of my throne.

[1] Lovelace.

How my heart rises at her preference of them to me, when she is convinced of their injustice to me! But how much more will my heart rise with indignation against her, if I find she hesitates but one moment (however persecuted) about preferring me to the man she avowedly hates! That her indifference to me is not owing to the superior liking she has for *any* other man, is what rivets my chains: but take care, fair one; take care, O thou most exalted of female minds, and loveliest of persons, how thou debasest thyself, by encouraging such a competition as thy sordid relations have set on foot in mere malice to me! Thou wilt say I rave. And so I do:

> Perdition catch my soul, but I *do* love her.

By the advices I have this moment received, I have reason to think that I shall have occasion for thee here. Hold thyself in readiness to come down upon the first summons.

Let Belton, and Mowbray, and Tourville, likewise prepare themselves. The reinforced orders for this hostile apparatus are owing it seems to a visit I made yesterday to their church — a good place I thought to begin a reconciliation in; supposing the heads of the family to be Christians, and that they meant something by their prayers. My hopes were to have an invitation (or, at least, to gain a pretence) to accompany home the gloomy sire; and so get an opportunity to see my goddess: for I believed they durst not but be *civil* to me, at least.

Such faces never could four men show — Mowbray's so fierce and so fighting: Belton's so pert and so pimply: Tourville's so fair and so foppish: thine so rough and so resolute: and *I* your leader!

Thus, Jack, as thou desirest, have I written. Written upon something; upon nothing; upon REVENGE, which I love; upon LOVE, which I hate, *heartily* hate, because 'tis my master: and upon the devil knows what besides.

MISS CLARISSA HARLOWE TO MISS HOWE
Thursday, March 16.

[*Clarissa writes to tell Miss Howe of her lack of success in applications to her relations — here omitted — and to tell her of her desperate appeal to Solmes himself. She enclosed to Miss Howe her letter to Solmes and his reply, both here following:*]

To Roger Solmes, Esq.
Wednesday, Mar. 15.

SIR, — When you first came acquainted with our family, you found the writer of this one of the happiest creatures in the world; beloved by the best and most indulgent of parents, and rejoicing in the kind favour of two affectionate uncles, and in the esteem of every one.

But how is this happy scene now changed! You was pleased to cast a favourable eye upon me. You addressed yourself to my friends: your proposals were approved of by them — approved of without consulting me; as if my choice and happiness were of the least signification. Those who had a right to all reasonable obedience from me, insisted upon it without reserve.

The consequence of all is too grievous for me to repeat: you, who have such free access to the rest of the family, know it too well — too well you know it, either for the credit of your own generosity or for my reputation.

Thus distressed and made unhappy, and all for your sake, and through your cruel perseverance, I write, sir, to demand of you the peace of mind you have robbed me of: to demand of you the love of so many dear friends of which you have deprived me; and, if you have the generosity that should distinguish a man, and a gentleman, to adjure you not to continue an address that has been attended with such cruel effects to the creature you profess to esteem.

Your compliance with this request will lay me under the highest obligation to your generosity, and make me ever / Your well-wisher and humble servant, / CLARISSA HARLOWE.

To Miss Clarissa Harlowe

These most humbly present.

DEAREST MISS, — Your letter has had a very contrary effect upon me, to what you seem to have expected from it. It has doubly convinced me of the excellency of your mind and of the honour of your disposition. Call it *selfish,* or what you please, I must persist in my suit; and happy shall I be, if by patience and perseverance and a steady and unalterable devoir, I may at last overcome the difficulty laid in my way.

As your good parents, your uncles, and other friends, are absolutely determined you shall never have Mr. Lovelace if they can help it; and as I presume no other person is in the way; I will contentedly wait the issue of this matter.

Pardon me, dear miss, but I must persevere, though I am sorry you suffer on my account, as you are pleased to think; for I never before saw the woman I could love; and while there is any hope, and that you remain undisposed of to some happier man, I must and will be / Your faithful and obsequious admirer / ROGER SOLMES.
March 16.

Mr. James Harlowe to Miss Cl. Harlowe

March 16.

WHAT a fine whim you took into your head to write a letter to Mr. Solmes!

But to say nothing of what fires us all with indignation against you (your owning your prepossession in a villain's favour, and your impertinence to me and your sister and your uncles); how can you lay at Mr. Solmes's door the usage you bitterly complain of? You know, little fool as you are, that it is your fondness for Lovelace that has brought upon you all these things; and which would have happened whether Mr. Solmes had honoured you with his addresses or not. Depend upon it, whether you have Mr. Solmes or not, you shall never have your heart's delight, the vile rake Lovelace, if our parents, if our uncles, if I can hinder it. / Your brother, / JAMES HARLOWE.

P.S. — I know your knack of letter-writing. If you send me an answer to this, I will return it unopened; for I will not argue with your perverseness in so plain a case.

MR. LOVELACE TO JOHN BELFORD, ESQ.

Friday, March 17.

THOU wilt find me at at little alehouse; they call it an inn: the White Hart; most terribly wounded (but by the weather only) the sign: — in a sorry village; five miles from Harlowe Place.

The people here at the Hart are poor but honest; and have gotten it into their heads that I am a man of quality in disguise; and there is no reigning-in their officious respect. Here is a pretty little smirking daughter; seventeen six days ago. I call her my Rosebud. Her grandmother (for there is no mother) a good neat old woman, as ever filled a wicker-chair in a chimney corner, has besought me to be merciful to her.

This is the right way with me. Many and many a pretty rogue had I spared, whom I did *not* spare, had my power been acknowledged, and my mercy in time implored. But the *debellare superbos* should be my motto, were I to have a new one.

But I charge thee, that thou do not (what I would not permit myself to do for the world — I charge thee, that thou do not) crop my Rosebud.

Unsuspicious of her danger, the lamb's throat will hardly shun thy knife! O be not thou the butcher of my lambkin!

The less be thou so for the reason I am going to give thee — the gentle heart is touched by love: her soft bosom heaves with a passion she has not yet found a name for. I once caught her eye following a young carpenter, a widow neighbour's son, living (to speak in her dialect) *at the little white house over the way.*

I have examined the little heart. She has made me her confidante. She owns she could love Johnny Barton very well: and Johnny Barton has told her he could love her better than any maiden he ever saw. But, alas! it must not be thought of. Why not be thought of? She don't know! And then she sighed: but Johnny has an aunt who will give him a hundred pounds when his time is out: and her father cannot give her but a few things, or so, to set her out with: and though Johnny's mother says she knows not where Johnny would have a prettier or notabler wife, yet — and then she sighed again — what signifies talking? I would not have Johnny be unhappy and poor for me! For what good would that do *me*, you know, sir!

Meantime, as I make it my rule, whenever I have committed a very capital enormity, to do some good by way of atonement; and as I believe I am a pretty deal indebted on that score, I intend, before I leave these parts, to join an hundred pounds to Johnny's aunt's hundred pounds, to make one innocent couple happy. I repeat therefore, and for half a dozen *therefores,* spare thou my Rosebud.

MR. LOVELACE TO JOHN BELFORD, ESQ.

I HAVE found out by my *watchful spy* almost as many of my charmer's motions, as of those of the rest of her relations. It delights me to think how the rascal is caressed by the uncles and nephew; and let into *their* secrets; yet proceeds all the time by *my* line of direction.

The dear creature has tempted him, he told *them,* with a bribe (*which she never offered*) to convey a letter (*which she never wrote*) to Miss Howe; *he believes,* with one enclosed (*perhaps to me*): but he declined it, and he begged they would take no notice of it to *her.* This brought him a stingy shilling, and about an hour after an order was given him to throw himself in her way; and (expressing his concern for denying her request) to tender his service to her, and to bring them her letter: which it will be *proper for him to report* that she has refused to give him.

Now seest thou not how many good ends this contrivance answers?

In the first place, the lady is secured by it, against her own knowledge, in the liberty allowed her of taking her private walks in the garden: for *this attempt* has confirmed them in their belief, that now they have turned off her maid, she has no way to send a letter out of the house.

In the next place, it will perhaps afford me an opportunity of a private interview with her, which I am meditating, let her take it as she will; having found out by my *spy* (who can keep off everybody else) that she goes every morning and evening to a woodhouse remote from the dwelling house, under pretence of visiting and feeding a set of bantam poultry, which were produced from a breed that was her grandfather's, and of which for that reason she is very fond; as also of some other curious fowls brought from the same place. I have an account of all her motions here. And as she has owned to me in one of her letters that she corresponds privately with Miss Howe, I presume it is by this way.

The interview I am meditating, will produce her consent I hope, to other favours of the like kind: for, should she not choose the place in which I am expecting to see her, I can attend her anywhere in the rambling, Dutch-taste garden, whenever she will permit me that honour: for my implement, *hight Joseph Leman,* has procured me the opportunity of getting two keys made to the garden door (one of which I have given him, for reasons good); which door opens to the haunted coppice, as tradition has made the servants think it; a man having been found hanging in it about twenty years ago; and Joseph, upon proper notice, will leave it unbolted.

Sat. Night, Mar. 18.

I HAVE been frighted out of my wits — still am in a manner out of breath. Thus occasioned, I went down under the usual pretence, in hopes to find something from you. Concerned at my disappointment, I was returning from the woodhouse, when I heard a rustling as of somebody behind a stack of wood. I was extremely surprised: but still more to behold a man coming from behind the furthermost stack — and who should it be but Mr. Lovelace! I could not scream out (yet attempted to scream the moment I saw a man; and again, when I saw who it was) for I had no voice: and had I not caught hold of a prop which supported the old roof, I should have sunk.

His respectful behaviour soon dissipated these fears, and gave me others, lest we should be seen together; and information of it be given to my brother: the consequences of which, I could readily think, would be, if not further mischief, an imputed assignation, a stricter confinement, a forfeited correspondence with you, my beloved friend, and a pretence for the most violent compulsion: and neither the one set of reflections, nor the other, acquitted him to me for his bold intrusion.

As soon, therefore, as I could speak, I expressed with the greatest warmth my displeasure; and told him that he cared not how much he exposed me to the resentment of all my friends, provided he could gratify his own impetuous humour. I then commanded him to leave the place that moment; and was hurrying from him when he threw himself in the way at my feet, beseeching my stay for one moment; declaring that he suffered himself to be guilty of this rashness, as I thought it, to avoid one much greater: for, in short, he could not bear the hourly insults he received from my family, with the thoughts of having so little interest in my favour, that he could not promise himself that his patience and forbearance would be attended with any other issue than to lose me for ever, and be triumphed over and insulted upon it.

I told him he might be assured that the severity and ill-usage I met with would be far from effecting the proposed end: that although I could, with great sincerity, declare for a single life (which had always been my choice); and particularly, that if ever I married, if they would not insist upon the man I had an aversion to, it should not be with the man they disliked ———

He interrupted me here: he hoped I would forgive him for it; but he could not help expressing his great concern, that, after so many instances of his passionate and obsequious devotion ———

And pray, sir, said I, let me interrupt you in my turn: why don't you assert, in still plainer words, the obligation you have laid me under by this your boasted devotion? Why don't you let me know, in terms as high as your implication, that a perseverance I have not wished for, which has set all my relations at variance with me, is a merit that throws upon me the guilt of ingratitude for not answering it as you seem to expect?

He took the liberty to say, that my favour to him, far from increasing those difficulties, would be the readiest way to extricate me from them. They had made it impossible (he told me, with too much truth) to oblige them any way but by sacrificing myself to Solmes.

How comes this man to know so well all our foibles? But I more wonder how he came to have a notion of meeting me in this place.

I was very uneasy to be gone; and the more as the night came on apace. But there was no getting from him till I had heard a great deal more of what he had to say.

He asked me if I would receive a letter from Lady Betty Lawrance, on this occasion: for Lady Sarah Sadlier, he said, having lately lost her only child, hardly looked into the world or thought of it farther than to wish him married, and preferably to all the women in the world, with me.

To be sure, my dear, there is a great deal in what the man said — I may be allowed to say this, without an imputed *glow* or *throb*. But I told him nevertheless, that although I had great honour for the ladies he was related to, yet I should not choose to receive a letter on a subject that had a tendency to promote an end I was far from intending to promote: that it became me, ill as I was treated at present, to *hope* everything, to *bear* everything, and to *try* everything. When my father saw my steadfastness and that I would die rather than have Mr. Solmes, he would perhaps recede.

He appealed to me, whether ever I knew my father recede from any resolution he had once fixed; especially if he thought either his prerogative or his authority concerned in the question.

How unhappy, my dear, that there is but too much reason for these observations and for this inference; made likewise with more coolness and respect to my family than one would have apprehended from a man so much provoked, and of passions so high, and generally thought uncontrollable!

He then again pressed me to receive a letter of offered protection from Lady Betty. He said that people of birth stood a little too much upon punctilio; as people of virtue also did (but indeed birth, worthily lived up to, was virtue: virtue, birth; the inducements to a decent punctilio the same; the origin of both, one [how came this notion from him!]): else, Lady Betty would write to *me*: but she would be willing to be first apprised that her offer would be well received — as it would have the appearance of being made against the liking of one part of my family; and which nothing would induce her to make but the degree of unworthy persecution which I actually laboured under, and had reason further to apprehend.

The man's vehemence frightened me: yet, in resentment, I would have left him; but throwing himself at my feet again, Leave me not thus — I beseech you, dearest madam, leave me not thus in despair. I kneel not, repenting of what I have vowed in such a case as that I have supposed. I re-vow it, at your feet! *And so he did.*

I said I would try every method that either my duty or my influence upon any of them should suggest, before I would put myself into any other protection. And if nothing else would do, would resign the envied estate: and that I dared to say *would*.

He was contented, he said, to abide that issue. He should be far from wishing me to embrace any other protection, but, as he had frequently said, in the last necessity. But, dearest creature, said he, catching my hand with ardour and pressing it to his lips, if the yielding up that estate will do — resign it and be mine; and I will corroborate, with all my soul, your resignation!

This was not ungenerously said: but what will not these men say to obtain belief and a power over one?

I got back without observation: but the apprehension that I should not, gave me great uneasiness; and made me begin my letter in a greater flutter than he gave me cause to be in, except at the first seeing him; for then indeed my spirits failed me; and it was a particular felicity, that, in such a place, in such a fright, and alone with him, I fainted not away.

MISS HOWE TO MISS CLARISSA HARLOWE

Sunday, March 19.

I BEG your pardon, my dearest friend, for having given you occasion to remind me of the date of my last. I was willing to have before me as much of the workings of your *wise* relations as possible; being verily persuaded that one side or the other would have yielded by this time: and then I should have had some degree of certainty to found my observations upon. And indeed what can I write that I have not already written? You know that I can do nothing but rave at your stupid persecutors; and that you don't like. I think you must be either the one man's or the other's. Let us see what their *next* step will be.

As to Lovelace, while he tells his own story (having also behaved so handsomely on his intrusion in the wood-house; and intended so well at church) who can say that the man is in the *least* blameworthy?

Before the malady you wot of, yet wot *not* of, grows so importunate, as that you must be obliged to sweat it out, let me advise you to mind how it comes on. For I am persuaded, as surely as that I am now writing to *you*, that the indiscreet violence of your friends on one hand, and the insinuating address of Lovelace on the other (if the man be not a greater fool than anybody thinks him) will effectually bring it to this, and do all his work for him.

Why, my Anna Howe, I hope you don't think that I am already in love!

No, to be sure! How can your Anna Howe have such a thought? What then shall we call it? You have helped me to a phrase. A *conditional kind of liking*! — that's it. O my friend! Did I not know how much you despise prudery; and that you are too young, and too lovely, to be a prude —

Let me add, that if you would clearly and explicitly tell me, how far Lovelace *has*, or has *not*, a hold on your affections, I could better advise you what to do, than at present I can.

MISS CLARISSA HARLOWE TO MISS HOWE
Monday, March 20.

IF I have in *fifty passages* of my letters given you such *un-doubted* proofs of my value for Mr. Lovelace, that you have spared me for the sake of my *explicitness*, it is acting by me with a generosity worthy of yourself.

I am not conscious that I have written anything of this man, that has not been more in his dispraise than in his favour. Such *is* the man, that I think I must have been faulty, and ought to take myself to account, if I had not: but if you think otherwise, I will put not you upon *labouring the proof*, as you call it. My conduct must then have a faulty *appearance* at least, and I will endeavour to rectify it.

O my dear, I must here break off!

MISS CLARISSA HARLOWE TO MISS HOWE
Monday, March 20.

THIS letter will account to you, my dear, for my abrupt break-ing off. What I am now to give you are the particulars of another effort made by my friends, through the good Mrs. Norton.

It seems they had sent to her yesterday, to be here this day, to take their instructions, and to try what *she* could do with me. She found assembled my father and mother, my brother and sister, my two uncles, and my Aunt Hervey.

My brother acquainted her with all that had passed since she was last permitted to see me; with the contents of my letters avowing my regard to Mr. Lovelace (as they all interpreted them); with the sub-stance of their answers to them; and with their resolutions.

My mother spoke next; and delivered herself to this effect, as the good woman told me.

After reciting how many times I had been indulged in my refusals of different men, and the pains she had taken with me, to induce me to oblige my whole family in one instance out of five or six, and my obstinacy upon it; "O my good Mrs. Norton," said the dear lady, "could you have thought, that *my* Clarissa and *your* Clarissa was capable of so determined an opposition to the will of parents so in-dulgent to her? But see what *you* can do with her. The matter is gone too far to be receded from on our parts. Her father had con-cluded everything with Mr. Solmes, not doubting her compliance. Such noble settlements, Mrs. Norton, and such advantages to the whole family! In short, she has it in her power to lay an obligation upon us all. Mr. Solmes, knowing she has good principles, and hoping by his patience *now*, and good treatment *hereafter*, to engage her gratitude, and by degrees her love, is willing to overlook all!"

(*Overlook* all, my dear! Mr. Solmes to *overlook* all! There's a word!)

"So, Mrs. Norton, if you are convinced that it is a child's duty to submit to her parents' authority in the most important point as well as in the least, I beg you will try *your* influence over her: *I* have none. Her *father* has none: her *uncles* neither. Although it is her apparent interest to oblige us all for, on that condition, her grandfather's estate is not half of what, living and dying, is purposed to be done for her. If anybody can prevail with her, it is *you*; and I hope you will *heartily* enter upon this task."

That good woman asked whether she was permitted to expostulate with them upon the occasion, before she came up to me?

My arrogant brother told her she was sent for to expostulate with his *sister*, and not with *them*. And *this*, Goody Norton (she is always *Goody* with him!) you may tell her, that the treaty with Mr. Solmes is concluded: that nothing but her compliance with her duty is wanting; of consequence, that there is no room for *your* expostulation, or *hers* either.

Be assured of this, Mrs. Norton, said my father, in an angry tone, that we will not be baffled by her. We will not appear like fools in this matter, and as if we had no authority over our own daughter.

Thus instructed, the good woman came up to me. She was very earnest with me to comply; but when she saw what an immovable aversion I had to the man, she lamented their determined resolution, and then examined into the sincerity of my declaration, that I would gladly compound with them by living single. Of this being satisfied, she was so convinced that this offer *ought* to be accepted, that she would go down (although I told her it was what I had tendered over and over to no purpose) and undertake to be guaranty for me on that score.

She went accordingly, but soon returned in tears; being used harshly for urging this alternative: they had a *right* to my obedience upon their own terms, they said; and they *would* be obeyed, or I never should be restored to their favour, let the consequence be what it would.

Adieu, my dear. Be you happy!

Miss Clarissa Harlowe to Miss Howe

Situated as I am, thus persecuted, and driven, I own to you that I have now and then had a little more difficulty than I wished for, in passing by Mr. Lovelace's tolerable qualities, to keep up my dislike to him for his others.

You say, I must have argued with myself in his favour, and in his disfavour, on a supposition that I might possibly be one day his. I own that I have: and thus called upon by my dearest friend, I will set before you both parts of the argument.

And first, *what occurred to me in his favour.*

His fortunes in possession are handsome; in expectation, splendid: so nothing need be said on that subject.

But it is impossible, say some, that he should make a tender or kind husband. Those who are for imposing upon me such a man as Mr. Solmes, and by methods so violent, are not entitled to make this objection.

At worst, will he confine me prisoner to my chamber? Will he deny me the visits of my dearest friend, and forbid me to correspond with her? Will he take from me the mistressly management, which I had not faultily discharged? Will he set a servant over me with licence to insult me? Will he, as he has not a *sister*, permit his cousins Montague, or would either of those ladies *accept* of a permission, to insult and tyrannize over me? It cannot be. Why then, think I often, do you tempt me, O my cruel friends, to try the difference?

And then has the secret pleasure intruded itself, to be able to re-claim such a man to the paths of virtue and honour: to be a *secondary* means, if I were to be his, of saving him, and preventing the mis-chiefs so enterprising a creature might otherwise be guilty of if he be such a one.

When I have thought of him in these lights (and that as a man of sense he will sooner see his errors, than another) I own to you, that I have had some difficulty to avoid taking the path they so violently endeavour to make me shun.

And let me add, that the favour of his relations (all but himself unexceptionable) has made a good deal of additional weight, thrown into the same scale.

But now, in his disfavour. When I have reflected that there is no manner of likelihood that ever the animosity will be got over: that I must therefore be at perpetual variance with all my own family: that I must go to *him*, and to *his*, as an obliged and half-fortuned person: that his aversion to them all is as strong as theirs to him: that his whole family are hated for his sake; they hating ours in return: that he has a very immoral character as to women: that knowing this, it is a high degree of impurity, to think of joining in wedlock with such a man: that he is young, unbroken, his passions unsubdued: that he is violent in his temper; yet artful: I am afraid vindictive too: that such a husband might unsettle me in all my own principles, and hazard my future hopes.

I will proceed by and by.

Sometimes we have both thought him one of the most undesigning *merely* witty men we ever knew; at other times one of the deepest creatures we ever conversed with. So that when in one visit we have imagined we fathomed him, in the next he has made us ready to give him up as impenetrable.

But I used to say then, and I still am of opinion, that he wants a *heart*: and if he does, he wants everything. A wrong *head* may be convinced, may have a right turn given it: but who is able to give a *heart*, if a heart be wanting? Divine grace working a miracle, or next to a miracle, can only change a bad heart.

I have said that I think Mr. Lovelace a vindictive man: upon my word, I have sometimes doubted, whether his perseverance in his addresses to me has not been more obstinate since he found himself so disagreeable to my friends.

From these considerations; from these *over-balances*; it was, that I said in a former, that I would not be in love with this man for the world: and it was going further than prudence would warrant, when I was for compounding with you, by the words *conditional liking*; which you so humorously railly.

MISS CLARISSA HARLOWE TO MISS HOWE

Tuesday, March 21.

How willingly would my dear mother show kindness to me, were she permitted! Whether owing to her, or to my aunt, or to both, that a new trial was to be made upon me, I cannot tell; but this morning her Shorey delivered into my hand the following condescending letter.

MY DEAR GIRL — for so I must still call you; since *dear* you may be to me, in every sense of the word. We have taken into particular consideration some hints that fell yesterday from your good Norton, as if we had not, at Mr. Solmes's first application, treated you with that condescension, wherewith we have in all other instances treated you. If it even *had been so,* my dear, you were not excusable to be wanting in *your* part, and to set yourself to oppose your father's will in a point into which he had entered too far, to recede with honour. But all yet may be well. On your single will, my child, depends all our happiness.

I hinted to you, you must remember, that patterns of the richest silks were sent for. They are come: and as they *are* come, your father, to show how much he is determined, will have me send them up to you. These are the newest, as well as richest, that we could procure; answerable to our station in the world; answerable to the fortune, additional to your grandfather's estate, designed you; and to the noble settlements agreed upon.

The draft of the settlements you may see whenever you will. We think there can be no room for objection to any of the articles. There is still more in them in our family's favour than was stipulated at first. Do, my dear girl, send to me within this day or two, or rather *ask* me for the perusal of them.

As a certain person's appearance at church so lately, and what he gives out everywhere, makes us extremely uneasy, and as that uneasiness will continue while you are single, you must not wonder that a short day is intended. This day fortnight we design it to be, if you have no objection to make that I shall approve of. But if you determine as we would have you, and signify it to us, we shall not stand with you for a week or so.

Signify to us, now, therefore, your compliance with our wishes. And then there is an end of your confinement. An act of oblivion, as I may call it, shall pass upon all your former refractoriness: and you will once more make us happy in you, and in one another. You may, in this case, directly come down to your father and me in his study; where we will give you our opinions of the patterns, with our hearty forgiveness and blessings. I shall then, as I said, give you the most tender proofs, how much I am / YOUR TRULY AFFECTIONATE MOTHER.

Think for me, my dearest friend, how I must be affected by this letter; the contents of it so surprisingly terrifying, yet so sweetly urged!

Upon the whole, it was not possible for me to go down upon the prescribed condition. Do you think it was?

I walked backward and forward. I knew not what to do! And while I was in this suspense, having again taken up the letter to reperuse it, Betty came in, reminding me, by order, that my papa and mama waited for me in my father's study.

Tell my mamma, said I, that I beg the favour of seeing her here for one moment; or to permit me to attend her anywhere by herself.

I listened at the stairs-head — You see, my dear, how it is, cried my father, very angrily: all your condescension (as your indulgence heretofore) is thrown away.

At last Betty brought me these lines from my father.

UNDUTIFUL AND PERVERSE CLARISSA, — No condescension, I see, will move you. Your mother shall *not* see you; nor will I. Prepare however to obey. You know our pleasure. Your Uncle Antony, your brother, and your sister, and your favourite Mrs. Norton, shall see the ceremony performed privately at your uncle's chapel. And when Mr. Solmes can introduce you to us, in the temper we wish to behold you in, we may perhaps forgive *his* wife, although we never can, in any *other* character, our perverse daughter. As it will be so privately performed, clothes and equipage may be provided afterwards. So prepare to go to your uncle's for an early day in next week. We will not see you till all is over: and we will have it over the sooner in order to shorten the time of your deserved confinement, and our own trouble in contending with such a rebel, as you have been of late. I will hear no pleas. I will receive no letter, nor expostulation. Nor shall you hear from me any more till you have changed your name to my liking. This from / YOUR INCENSED FATHER.

If this resolution be adhered to, then will my father never see me more! For I will never be the wife of that Solmes — I will die first!

Tuesday Evening.

He, this Solmes, came hither soon after I had received my father's

62

letter. He sent up to beg leave to wait upon me — I wonder at his assurance!

I said to Betty, who brought me his message, let him restore an unhappy creature to her father and mother, and then I may hear what he has to say. But, if my friends will not see *me* on *his* account, I will not see *him* upon his *own*.

I hope, miss, said Betty, you will not send me down with this answer. He is with your papa and mamma.

I am driven to despair, said I. I cannot be used worse. I will not see him.

Down she went with my answer.

Oh how I heard my father storm!

They were all together, it seems, in his study. My brother was for having me turned out of the house that moment, to Lovelace, and my evil destiny.

My mother was pleased, however, to blame Betty, as the wench owned, for giving my answer its full force. But my father praised her for it.

The wench says that he would have come up in his wrath, at my refusing to see Mr. Solmes, had not my brother and sister prevailed upon him to the contrary.

I wish he had! And, were it not for his own sake, that he had killed me!

They are all in tumults! How it will end, I know not.

Miss Clarissa Harlowe to Miss Howe

An angry dialogue, a scolding-bout rather, has passed between my sister and me.

She was sent up to me, upon my refusal to see Mr. Solmes — let loose upon me, I think! No intention on their parts to conciliate! It seems evident that I am given up to my brother and her, by general consent. She reflected upon my Norton, as if she encouraged me in my perverseness. She ridiculed me for my supposed esteem for Mr. Lovelace. Was surprised that the *witty*, the *prudent*, nay, the *dutiful* and *pi — ous* (so she sneeringly pronounced the word) Clarissa Harlowe, should be so strangely fond of a profligate man, that her parents were forced to lock her up, in order to hinder her from running into his arms.

I vindicated the good Mrs. Norton with a warmth that was due to her merit. With equal warmth I resented her reflections upon me on Mr. Lovelace's account.

O child, says she, methinks you are as pleasant to the full as I am: I begin to have some hopes for you now. But do you think I will rob my sister of her humble servant? Had he first addressed himself to me, proceeded she, something might have been said: but to take my younger sister's refusal! No, no, child; it is not come to that neither!

63

Besides, that would be to leave the door open in your heart for you know who, child; and we would fain bar him out, if possible. In short (and then she changed both her tone, and her looks) had I been as forward as somebody, to throw myself into the arms of one of the greatest profligates in England —

Alas! for my poor sister! said I! The man was not *always* so great a profligate. How true is the observation, *that unrequited love turns to deepest hate*!

I thought she would have beat me. But I proceeded: I have heard often of my brothers' danger, and my brother's murderer. When so little ceremony is made with me, why should I not speak out? Did he not seek to kill the *other*, if he could have done it? Would my brother have given Lovelace *his* life, had it been in his power? The *aggressor* should not *complain*.

Then did she pour upon me with greater violence; considering my gentleness as a triumph of temper over her. She was resolved, she said, to let everybody know how I took the wicked Lovelace's part against my brother.

I replied that her pleasantry was much more agreeable than her anger. But I wished she would let me know the end of a visit that had hitherto (*between* us) been so unsisterly.

She desired to be informed, in the name of *everybody*, was her word, what I was determined upon? And whether to comply or not — one word for all: my friends were not to have patience with so perverse a creature for ever.

This then I told her I would do: absolutely break with the man they were all so determined against: upon condition, however, that neither Mr. Solmes, nor any other, were urged to me with the force of a command.

If I knew what other proposals I could make, I told her, that would be acceptable to them all, and free me from the address of a man so disagreeable to me, I *would* make them. I had indeed before offered, never to marry without my father's consent.

You are *indeed* a very artful one for that matter, interrupted she in a passion: one of the artfullest I ever knew! And then followed an accusation so low! so unsisterly! That I half-bewitched people by my insinuating address: that nobody could be valued or respected, but must stand like cyphers wherever I came. How often, said she, have I and my brother been talking upon a subject, and had everybody's attention till *you* came in with your bewitching *meek* pride, and *humble* significance; and then have we either been stopped by references to Miss Clary's opinion, forsooth; or been forced to stop ourselves, or must have talked on unattended to by everybody.

She paused. Dear Bella, proceed!

She indeed seemed only gathering breath.

And so I *will*, said she. Did you not bewitch my grandfather? Could anything be pleasing to him that *you* did not say or do? How did he use to hang, till he slabbered again, poor doting old man! on your silver tongue! Yet what did *you* say, that *we* could not have said? What did *you* do that *we* did not endeavour to do? And what was all this for? Why, truly, his last will showed what effect your *smooth* obligingness had upon him!

Hence my misfortune, Bella, in your envy, I doubt! But have I not given up that possession in the best manner I could ——

Yes, interrupting me; she hated me for that *best manner*. Specious little witch! she called me: your *best manner*, so full of art and design, had never been seen through, if you, with your blandishing ways, had not been put out of sight, and reduced to positive declarations! Hindered from playing your little, whining tricks; curling, like a serpent, about your mamma; and making her cry to deny you anything your little obstinate heart was set upon! O Clary! Clary! Thou wert always a *two-faced* girl!

Nobody thought I had two faces when I gave up all into my father's management; taking from his bounty, as before, all my little pocket-money, without a shilling addition to my stipend, or desiring it ——

Yes, cunning creature! And that was another of your *fetches*!

Poor Bella! I believe I smiled a little too contemptuously for a sister to a sister.

None of your saucy contempts (rising in her voice): None of your *poor Bella's*, with that air of superiority in a younger sister!

Well then, *rich* Bella! curtseying — that will please you better. And it is due likewise to the hoards you boast of.

Look ye, Clary, holding up her hand, if you are not a little more *abject* in your *meekness*, a little more *mean* in your *humility*, and treat me with the respect due to an elder sister — you shall find ——

Not that you will treat me worse than you *have done*, Bella! That cannot be; unless you were to let fall your uplifted hand upon me, and that would less become you to *do*, than me to *bear*.

Good, meek creature! But you were upon your overtures just now! I shall surprise everybody by tarrying so long. They will think some good may be done with you, and supper will be ready.

She asked me, upon turning from her, if she should say anything *below* of my *compliances*?

You may say that I will do everything they would have me do, if they will free me from Mr. Solmes's address. And say further that I will by any means I can in the law, or otherwise, make over to my father, to my uncles, or even to my brother, all I am entitled to by my grandfather's will, as a security for the performance of my promises. And as I shall have no reason to expect any favour from my father, if I break them, I shall not be worth anybody's having. And further still, unkindly as my brother has used me, I will go down to Scotland privately as his housekeeper (I now see I may be spared here) if he will promise to treat me no worse than he would a hired one. Or I will go to Florence to my Cousin Morden, if his stay in Italy will admit of it. In *either case*, it may be given out that I am gone to the *other;* or to the world's end. I care not whither it is said I am gone, or do go.

So down she went.

MISS HOWE TO MISS CLARISSA HARLOWE

Tuesday Morn., 7 o'clock.

I MUST begin with blaming you, my dear, for your resolution not to litigate for your right, if occasion were to be given you. Justice is due to ourselves, as well as to everybody else. Still more must I blame you for declaring to your aunt and sister, that you will *not*: since (as they will tell it to your father and brother) the declaration must needs give advantage to spirits who have so little of that generosity for which you are so much distinguished.

MISS HOWE TO MISS CLARISSA HARLOWE

Thursday Morn., 10 o'clock (Mar. 23).

MR. HICKMAN, when in London, found an opportunity to inquire after Mr. Lovelace's town life and conversation.

At the Cocoa Tree in Pall Mall he fell in with two of his intimates, the one named Belton, the other Mowbray; both very free of speech, and probably as free in their lives: but the waiters paid them great respect, and on Mr. Hickman's inquiry after their characters, called them men of fortune and honour.

They began to talk of Mr. Lovelace of their own accord; and upon some gentlemen in the room asking when they expected him in town, answered, that very day. Mr. Hickman (as they both went on praising Lovelace) said, he had indeed heard that Mr. Lovelace was a very fine gentleman — and was proceeding, when one of them interrupting him, said — only, sir, the finest gentleman in the world; that's all.

And so he led them on to expatiate more particularly on his qualities; which they were very fond of doing: but said not one single word in behalf of his morals — *mind that* also, in your uncle's style.

Mr. Hickman said that Mr. Lovelace was very happy, as he understood in the esteem of the ladies; and, smiling, to make them believe he did not think amiss of it, that he pushed his good fortune as far as it would go.

Well put, Mr. Hickman! thought I; equally grave and sage — thou seemest not to be a stranger to their dialect, as I suppose this is. But I said nothing; for I have often tried to find out this *mighty* sober man of my mother's: but hitherto have only to say that he is either very moral or very cunning.

No doubt of it, replied one of them; and out came an oath, with a who would not? That he did as every young fellow would do.

Mr. Hickman, upon the whole, professed to me upon his *second recovery*, that he had no reason to think well of Mr. Lovelace's morals, from what he heard of him in town: yet his two intimates talked of his being *more regular* than he *used to be*: that he had made a very good resolution, *that* of old Tom Wharton, was the expression, that he would never *give* a challenge, nor *refuse* one; which they praised in him highly: that, in short, he was a very brave fellow, and the most agreeable companion in the world: and would one day make a **great figure** in his country; since there was nothing he was not capable of.

I am afraid that this last assertion is too true. And this my dear, is all that Mr. Hickman could pick up about him: and is it not enough to determine such a mind as yours, if not *already* determined?

Miss Howe to Miss Clarissa Harlowe
Thursday Afternoon, March 23.

An unexpected visitor has turned the course of my thoughts, and changed the subject I had intended to pursue. It was your too agreeable rake. Our sex is said to love to trade in surprises: yet have I, by my promptitude, surprised myself out of mine. I had intended, you must know, to run twice the length, before I had suffered you so much as to guess, who, and whether man or woman, my visitor was: but since you have the discovery at so cheap a rate, you are welcome to it.

The end of his coming was to engage my interest with my *charming friend*; and as he was sure that I knew all your mind, to acquaint him with what he had to trust to.

He gave me fresh instances of indignities cast upon himself by your uncles and brother; and declared that if you suffered yourself to be forced into the arms of the man for whose sake he was loaded with undeserved abuses, you should be one of the youngest, as you would be one of the loveliest widows in England: and that he would moreover call your brother to account for the liberties he takes with his character to every one he meets with.

He proposed several schemes for you to choose some one of them, in order to enable you to avoid the persecutions you labour under: one I will mention: that you will resume your estate; and if you find difficulties that can be no otherwise surmounted, that you will, either avowedly or privately, as he had proposed to you, accept of Lady Betty Lawrance's or Lord M.'s assistance to instate you in it. He declared that if you did he would leave it absolutely to your own pleasure afterwards, and to the advice which your Cousin Morden on his arrival should give you, whether to encourage his address or not, as you should be convinced of the sincerity of the reformation which his enemies make him so much want.

I had now a good opportunity to sound him, as you wished Mr. Hickman would Lord M. as to the continued or diminished favour of the ladies, and of his lordship, towards you, upon their being acquainted with the animosity of your relations to them, as well as to their kinsman.

I told him, as you yourself I knew had done, that you were extremely averse to Mr. Solmes; and that, might you be left to your own choice, it would be the single life. As to himself, I plainly said that you had great and just objections to him on the score of his careless morals: that it was surprising that men who gave themselves the liberties he was said to take, should presume to think that whenever they took it into their heads to marry, the most virtuous and worthy of the sex were to fall to their lot.

I told him that with regard to the mischief he threatened, neither the act nor the menace could serve any end but theirs who persecuted you; as it would give them a pretence for carrying into effect their compulsatory projects; and that with the approbation of all the world; since he must not think the public would give its voice in favour of a violent young man, of no extraordinary character as to morals, who should seek to rob a family of eminence of a child so valuable; and who threatened, if he could not obtain her in preference to a man chosen by themselves, that he would avenge himself upon them all by acts of violence.

I added that he was very much mistaken if he thought to intimidate *you* by such menaces: for that, though your disposition was all sweetness, yet I knew not a steadier temper in the world than yours; nor one more inflexible.

He was so very far from intending to intimidate you, he said, that he besought me not to mention one word to you of what had passed between us: that what he hinted at, which carried the air of a menace, was owing to the fervour of his spirits, raised by his apprehensions of losing all hope of you for ever; and on a supposition that you were to be actually forced into the arms of a man you hated.

He added, that all the countries in the world were alike to him, but on your account: so that whatever he should think fit to do, were you lost to *him*, he should have nothing to apprehend from the laws of this.

I did not like the determined air he spoke this with: he is certainly capable of great rashness.

He palliated a little this fierceness (which by the way I warmly censured) by saying that while you remain single, he will bear all the indignities that shall be cast upon him by your family. But would you throw yourself, if you were still further driven, into any *other* protection, if not Lord M.'s, or that of the ladies of his family, into my mother's,[1] suppose; or would you go to London to private lodgings, where he would never visit you, unless he had your leave (and from whence you might make your own terms with your relations); he would be entirely satisfied; and would, as he had said before, wait the effect of your cousin's arrival, and your free determination as to his own fate. — Adding, that he knew the family so well, and how much fixed they were upon their measures, as well as the absolute dependence they had upon your temper and principles, that he could not but

[1] Perhaps it will be unnecessary to remind the reader, that although Mr. Lovelace proposes (as above) to Miss Howe, that her fair friend should have recourse to the protection of Mrs. Howe, if farther driven; yet he had artfully taken care, by means of his agent in the Harlowe family, not only to influence the family against her, but to deprive her of Mrs. Howe's, and of every other protection, being from the first resolved to reduce her to an absolute dependence upon himself.

apprehend the worst, while you remained in their power, and under the influence of their persuasion and menaces.

And now, my dear, upon the whole, I think it behoves you to make yourself independent: all then will fall right. This man is a violent man. I should wish, methinks, that you should not have either him or Solmes. You will find, if you get out of your brother's and sister's way, what you *can* or *cannot do,* with regard to either. If your relations persist in their foolish scheme, I think I will take his hint, and, at a proper opportunity, sound my mother.

MISS CLARISSA HARLOWE TO MISS HOWE

Wedn. Night, March 22.

ON THE report made by my aunt and sister of my *obstinacy,* my assembled relations have taken an *unanimous* resolution (as Betty tells me it is) against me. This resolution you will find signified to me in the enclosed letter from my brother, just now brought me. Be pleased to return it, when perused. I may have occasion for it in the altercations between my relations and me.

MISS CLARY, — It is resolved that you shall go to your Uncle Antony's: and you must accordingly prepare yourself so to do. You will have but short notice of the day, for obvious reasons.

I will honestly tell you the motive for your going: it is a double one; first, that they may be sure that you shall not correspond with anybody they do not like (for they find from Mrs. Howe, that, by some means or other, you *do* correspond with her daughter; and, through her, perhaps with somebody else): and next, that you may receive the visits of Mr. Solmes; which you have thought fit to refuse to do here; by which means you have deprived yourself of the opportunity of knowing *whom* and *what* you have hitherto refused.

It is hoped, that as you *must* go, you will go cheerfully. Your Uncle Antony will make everything at his house agreeable to you. But indeed he won't promise, that he will not, *at proper times,* draw up the bridge.

Your visitors, besides Mr. Solmes, will be myself, if you permit me that honour, Miss Clary; your sister; and, as you behave to Mr. Solmes, your Aunt Hervey, and your Uncle Harlowe; and yet the two latter will hardly come neither, if they think it will be to hear your *whining vocatives.* Betty Barnes will be your attendant: and, I must needs tell you, miss, that we none of us think the worse of the faithful maid, for your dislike of her: although Betty Barnes, who would be glad to oblige you, laments it as a misfortune.

Your answer is required whether you *cheerfully* consent to go? And your indulgent mother bids me remind you from her, that a fortnight's visits from Mr. Solmes are all that is meant at present.

I am, as you shall be pleased to deserve, / Yours, etc., / JAMES HARLOWE, JUN.

So here is the master-stroke of my brother's policy! Called upon to consent to go to my Uncle Antony's, *avowedly* to receive Mr. Solmes's visits! A chapel! A moated house! Deprived of the opportunity of corresponding with you! — or of any possibility of escape should violence be used to compel me to be that odious man's![1]

Late as it was when I received this insolent letter, I wrote an answer to it directly, that it might be ready for the writer's time of rising. I enclose the rough draft of it.

You might have told me, brother, in three lines, what the determination of my friends was. The time is indeed come that I can no longer bear those contempts and reflections which a brother, least of all men, is entitled to give. And let me beg of you one favour, officious sir: it is this, that you will not give yourself any concern about a husband for *me*, till I shall have the forwardness to propose a wife for *you*. Pardon me, sir, but I cannot help thinking that could I have the art to *get my father* of my side, I should have as much right to prescribe for you, as you have for me.

As to the communication you make me, I must take upon me to say, that although I will receive, as becomes me, any of my father's commands; yet, as this signification is made by a brother, who has shown of late so much of an unbrotherly animosity to me (for no reason in the world that I know of, but that he believes he has, in me, *one* sister too many for his interest) I think myself entitled to conclude, that such a letter as you have sent me is all your own — and of course to declare that, while I *so* think it, I will not, willingly, nor even without violence, go to any place, avowedly to receive Mr. Solmes's visits.

One more word, provoked as I am, I will add: that had I been thought as really obstinate and perverse as of late I am said to be, I should not have been so disgracefully treated as I have been. Lay your hand upon your heart, brother, and say, by whose instigations — and examine what I have done to deserve to be made thus unhappy, and to be obliged to style myself / Your injured sister, / CL. HARLOWE.

When, my dear, you have read my answer to my brother's letter, tell me, what you think of me? It *shall* go!

[*With two letters — here omitted — Clarissa forwards to Miss Howe further letters that passed between her and the family as represented by her brother. They concern the project to remove her to her Uncle Antony's moated mansion.*]

---

[1] These violent measures, and the obstinate perseverance of the whole family in them, will be the less wondered at, when it is considered, that all the time they were but as so many puppets danced upon Mr. Lovelace's wires, as he boasts.

Friday Morning, Six o'clock.

MRS. BETTY tells me there is now nothing talked of but of my going to my Uncle Antony's. She has been ordered, she says, to get ready to attend me thither: and, upon my expressing my averseness to go, had the confidence to say that having heard me often praise the *romanticness* of the place, she was *astonished* (her hands and eyes lifted up) that I should set myself against going to a house so much in *my taste.*

As the wench looked as if she really thought she had said a good thing, without knowing the boldness of it, I let it pass. But, to say the truth, this creature has surprised me on many occasions with her smartness: for, since she has been employed in this controlling office, I have discovered a great deal of wit in her assurance, which I never suspected before. This shows that insolence is her talent; and that fortune, in placing her as a servant to my sister, had not done so kindly by her as nature; for that she would make a better figure as her *companion.* And indeed I can't help thinking sometimes, that I myself was better fitted by *nature* to be the servant of *both*, than the *mistress* of the *one*, or the *sister* of the *other.* And within these few months past, *fortune* has acted by me, as if she were of the same mind.

Friday, Ten o'clock.

Going down to my poultry-yard just now, I heard my brother and sister and that Solmes laughing and triumphing together. The high yew hedge between us, which divides the yard from the garden, hindered them from seeing me.

My brother, as I found, had been reading part, or the whole perhaps, of the copy of his last letter. Mighty prudent, and consistent, you'll say, with their views to make me the wife of a man from whom they conceal not what, were I to be such, it would be kind in them to endeavour to conceal, out of regard to my future peace! But I have no doubt but that they hate me heartily.

Never fear, Mr. Solmes, said my brother, but we'll carry our point, if she do not tire *you* out first. We have gone too far in this method to recede. Her Cousin Morden will soon be here: so all must be over before that time, or she'll be made independent of us all.

There, Miss Howe, is the reason given for their Jehu-driving!

Mr. Solmes declared that he was determined to persevere while my brother gave him any hopes, and while my father stood firm.

If you think, my dear, that what I have related did not again fire me, you will find yourself mistaken when you read at this place the enclosed copy of my letter to my brother; struck off while the iron was red hot.

No more call me meek and gentle, I beseech you.

To Mr. James Harlowe

SIR, — If, notwithstanding your prohibition, I should be silent on occasion of your last, you would perhaps conclude that I was consenting to go to my Uncle Antony's upon the condition you mention. My father must do as he pleases with his child. He may turn me out of his doors, if he think fit, or give *you* leave to do it; but (loth as I am to say it) I should think it very hard to be carried by force to anybody's house when I have one of *my own* to go to.

Far be it from me, notwithstanding yours and my sister's provocations, to think of taking my estate into my own hands, without my father's leave: but why, if I must not stay any longer here, may I not be permitted to go thither? I will engage to see nobody they would not have me see, if this favour be permitted. *Favour* I call it, and am ready to receive and acknowledge it as such, although my grandfather's will has made it a matter of right.

You ask me, in a very unbrotherly manner, in the postscript to your letter, if I have not some new proposals to make? I HAVE (since you put the question) three or four; *new ones* all, I think; though I will be bold to say, that, submitting the case to any one person whom *you* have not set against me, my *old* ones ought not to have been rejected. I *think* this; why then should I not *write* it? Nor have you any more reason to storm at your *sister* for telling it you (since you seem in your letter to make it your boast how you turned my mother and my Aunt Hervey against me) than I have to be angry with my *brother,* for treating me as no brother ought to treat a sister.

These, then, are my new proposals:

That, as above, I may not be hindered from going to reside (under such conditions as shall be prescribed to me, which I will most religiously observe) at my grandfather's late house. I will not again in this place call it *mine.* I have reason to think it a great misfortune that ever it was so — *indeed* I have.

If this be not permitted, I desire leave to go for a month, or for what time shall be thought fit, to Miss Howe's. I dare say her mother will consent to it, if I have my father's permission to go.

If this, neither, be allowed, and I *am* to be turned out of my father's house, I beg I may be suffered to go to my Aunt Hervey's, where I will inviolably observe her commands, and those of my father and mother.

But if this, neither, is to be granted, it is my humble request, that I may be sent to Uncle Harlowe's, instead of my Uncle Antony's. I mean not by this any disrespect to my Uncle Antony: but his moat, with his bridge threatened to be drawn up, and perhaps the chapel there, terrify me beyond expression, notwithstanding your *witty* ridicule upon me for that apprehension.

If this likewise be refused, and if I *must* be carried to the moated house, which used to be a delightful one to me, let it be promised me, that I shall not be compelled to receive Mr. Solmes's visits there; and then I will as cheerfully go as ever I did.

And now, sir, if I have seemed to show some spirit, not quite foreign to the relation I have the honour to bear to *you* and to my *sister*; and which may be deemed not altogether of a piece with that part of my character which once, it seems, gained me every one's love; be pleased to consider to *whom*, and to *what* it is owing; and that this part of that character was not dispensed with till it subjected me to that scorn and to those insults which a brother, who has been *so tenacious of an independence voluntarily* given up by me, and who has appeared *so exalted* upon it, ought not to have shown to *any-body*, much less to a *weak* and *defenceless* sister: who is, notwith-standing, an affectionate and respectful one, and would be glad to show herself to be so upon all future occasions; as she has in every action of her past life, although of late she has met with such unkind returns. / CL. HARLOWE.

See, my dear, the force and volubility, as I may say, of passion for the letter I send you, is my first draft, struck off without a blot or erasure.

Friday, Three o'clock.

As soon as I had transcribed it, I sent it down to my brother by Mrs. Betty.

The wench came up soon after, all aghast, with a *Laud, miss*! What *have* you done? What *have* you written? For you have set them all in a *joyful* uproar!

· · · · · · · · · · ·

As it is but too probable that I may be hurried away to my uncle's without being able to give you previous notice, I beg that as soon as you shall hear of such a violence, you would send to the usual place to take back such of your letters as may not have reached my hands, or to fetch any of mine that may be there.

May you, my dear, be always happy, prays your / CLARISSA HAR-LOWE.

MISS CLARISSA HARLOWE TO MISS HOWE

Friday Midnight.

You again insist (strengthened by Mr. Lovelace's opinion) upon my *assuming* my own estate (I cannot call it *resuming*, having never been in possession of it): and I have given you room to expect that I will consider this subject more closely than I have done before. I must however own, that the reasons which I had to offer against taking your advice, were so obvious, that I thought you would have seen them yourself, and been determined by them, against your own hastier counsel. But since this has not been so, and that both you and Mr. Lovelace call upon me to assume my own estate, I will enter briefly into the subject.

In the first place, let me ask you, my dear, supposing I were *inclined* to follow your advice, whom have I to support me in my demand? My Uncle Harlowe is one of my trustees — he is against me. My Cousin Morden is the other — he is in Italy, and very probably may be set against me too.

My brother sometimes talks of going to reside at *The Grove*: I suppose, with a design to make ejectments necessary, were I to offer at assuming; or were I to marry Mr. Lovelace, in order to give him all the opposition and difficulty the law would help him to give.

These cases I have put to myself for argument sake: but they are all out of the question; for I do assure you, I would sooner beg my bread than litigate for my right with my father: since I am convinced that whether the parent do his duty by the child or not, the child cannot be excused from doing hers to him.

How willingly would I run away from myself, and what most concerns myself, if I could! This digression brings me back again to the occasion of it — and that to the impatience I was in, when I ended my last letter; for my situation is not altered. I renew therefore my former earnestness, as the new day approaches, and will bring with it perhaps new trials, that you will (as undivestedly as possible of favour or resentment) tell me what you would have me do; for, if I am obliged to go to my Uncle Antony's, all, I doubt, will be over with me. Yet how to avoid it — that's the difficulty!

I shall deposit this the first thing. When you have it, lose no time, I pray you, to advise (lest it be too late).

Miss Howe to Miss Clarissa Harlowe

Sat., March 25.

WHAT *can* I advise you to do, my noble creature? Your merit is your crime. You can no more change *your* nature than your persecutors can *theirs*. Your distress is owing to the vast disparity between you and them. What would you have of them? Do they not act in character? And to whom? To an alien. You are not one of them. They have two dependencies in their hope to move you to compliance: upon their *impenetrableness* one (I'd give it a more proper name, if I dared); the other, on the regard you have always had for your *character* (have they not heretofore owned as much?) and upon your apprehensions from *that* of Lovelace, which would discredit you, should you take any step by his means to extricate yourself.

As to that wretch's perseverance, those only who know not the man, will wonder at it. He has not the least delicacy. His principal view in marriage is not to the mind. How shall those beauties be valued, which cannot be comprehended? Were you to be his, and show a visible want of tenderness to him, it is my opinion, he would not be much concerned at it.

I'll give you the substance of a conversation (no fear you can be

74

made to like him worse than you do already) that passed between Sir Harry Downeton and this Solmes, but three days ago, as Sir Harry told it but yesterday to my mother and me. It will confirm to you that what your sister's insolent Betty reported he should say, of governing by *fear*, was not of her own head.

Sir Harry told him, he wondered he should wish to obtain you so much against your inclination as everybody knew it would be if he did.

Fear and terror, the wretch (the horrid wretch) said, looked pretty in a bride as well as in a wife: and, laughing (yes, my dear, the hideous wretch laughed immoderately, as Sir Harry told us, when he said it) it should be his care to perpetuate the occasion for that *fear*, if he could not think he had the *love*. And, truly, he was of opinion, that if LOVE and FEAR must be separated in matrimony, the man who made himself *feared*, fared best.

I will lay down my pen and think.

My mother will have it that after they have tried their utmost efforts to bring you into their measures, and find them ineffectual, they will recede. But I cannot say I am of her mind.

You must, if possible, avoid being carried to that uncle's. The man, the parson, your brother and sister present — they'll certainly there marry you to the wretch. Nor will your newly-raised spirit support you in your resistance on such an occasion. Your meekness will return; and you will have nothing for it but tears (tears despised by them all) and ineffectual appeals and lamentations: and *these*, when the ceremony is *profaned*, you must suddenly dry up, and endeavour to dispose yourself to such an humble frame of mind as may induce your new-made lord to forgive all your past declarations of aversion.

In short, my dear, you must then blandish him over with a confession that all your past behaviour was maidenly reserve only.

Miss Clarissa Harlowe to Miss Howe
Sunday Morning, March 26.

Most heartily I thank you for the kind dispatch of your last favour. How much am I indebted to you! and even to your honest servant! Under what obligations does my unhappy situation lay me!

But let me answer the kind contents of it, as well as I may.

As to getting over my disgusts to Mr. Solmes, it is impossible to be done; while he wants generosity, frankness of heart, benevolence, manners, and every qualification that distinguishes the worthy man. O my dear! what a degree of patience, what a greatness of soul is required in the wife, not to despise a husband who is more ignorant, more illiterate, more low-minded, than herself?

I have received two letters from Mr. Lovelace, since his visit to you; which make three that I have not answered. I doubt not his being very uneasy; but in his last he complains in high terms of my silence; not in the still small voice, or, rather, style of an humble lover, but in a style like that which would probably be used by a slighted protector. And his pride is again touched, that like a *thief* or *eaves-dropper*, he is forced to dodge about in hopes of a letter, and return five miles (and then to an inconvenient lodging) without any.

His letters, and the copy of mine to him, shall soon attend you: till when, I will give you the substance of what I wrote to him yesterday.

I take him severely to task, for his freedom in threatening me, through you, with a visit to Mr. Solmes, or to my brother.

As to the solemn vows and protestations he is so ready, upon all occasions, to make, they have the less weight with me, I tell him, as they give a kind of demonstration, that he himself, from his own character, thinks there is *reason* to make them. *Deeds* are to me the only evidences of *intentions*. And I am more and more convinced of the necessity of breaking-off a correspondence with a person, whose addresses I see it is impossible either to expect my friends to encourage, or him to deserve that they should.

This is the substance of the letter I have written to him.

The man, to be sure, must have the penetration to observe that my correspondence with him hitherto is owing more to the severity I meet with, than to a very high value for him. And so I would have him think. What a *worse* than Moloch deity is that, which expects an offering of reason, duty, and discretion, to be made to its shrine!

Your mother is of opinion, you say, that *at last* my friends will relent. Heaven grant that they may! But my brother and sister have such an influence over everybody, and are so determined; so pique themselves upon subduing me, and carrying their point; that I despair that they will: and yet, if they do not, I frankly own, I would not scruple to throw myself upon any not disreputable protection, by which I might avoid my present persecutions, on one hand, and not give Mr. Lovelace advantage over me, on the other. That is to say, were there manifestly *no other* way left me: for, if there *were*, I should think the leaving my father's house, without his consent, one of the most inexcusable actions I could be guilty of, were the protection to be ever so unexceptionable; and this notwithstanding the independent fortune willed me by my grandfather. And indeed I have often reflected with a degree of indignation and disdain, upon the thought of what a low, selfish creature that child must be, who is to be reined in only by what a parent can or will do for her.

But, upon the whole, this I do repeat — that nothing but the *last* extremity shall make me abandon my father's house, if they will permit me to stay; and if I can, by any means, by any honest pretences, but keep off my evil destiny in it till my Cousin Morden arrives. As one of my trustees, *his* is a protection into which I may without discredit throw myself, if my other friends should remain determined.

MISS HOWE TO MISS CLARISSA HARLOWE

Sat., March 25.

MY MOTHER argues upon this case in a most discouraging

manner for all such of our sex as look forward for happiness in marriage with the *man of their choice*.

Only, that I know, she has a side-view to her daughter; who, at the same time that she now prefers no one to another, values not the man her mother most regards of one farthing; or I should lay it more to heart.

What is there in it, says she, that all this bustle is about? Is it such a mighty matter for a young woman to give up her inclinations to oblige her friends?

Very well, my mamma, thought I! Now, may you ask this. At FORTY, you may — but what would you have said at EIGHTEEN is the question?

Either, said she, the lady must be thought to have very violent inclinations (and what nice young creature would have that supposed?) which she *could* not give up; or a very stubborn will, which she *would* not; or, thirdly, have parents she was indifferent about obliging.

You know my mother now and then argues very notably; always very warmly at least. I happen often to differ from her; and we both think so well of our own arguments, that we very seldom are so happy as to convince one another. A pretty common case, I believe, in all *vehement* debatings. She says I am *too witty*; Anglicè, *too pert*; I, that she is *too wise*; that is to say, being likewise put into English, *not so young as she has been*: in short, is grown so much into *mother*, that she had forgotten she ever was a *daughter*. So, generally, we call another cause by consent — yet fall into the old one half a dozen times over, *without* consent — quitting and resuming, with half-angry faces, forced into a smile, that there might be some room to piece together again: but go to bed, if bedtime, a little sullen nevertheless; or, if we speak, her silence is broken, with an Ah! Nancy! You are so lively! so quick! I wish you were less like your papa, child!

I told my mother that if *you* were to take any rash step, it would be owing to the indiscreet violence of your friends.

I insisted upon the extraordinary circumstances in your case; particularizing them. I took notice, that Mr. Lovelace's morals were at one time no objection with your relations for Arabella: that then much was built upon his family, and more upon his parts and learning, which made it out of doubt, that he might be reclaimed by a woman of virtue and prudence: and (pray forgive me for mentioning it) I ventured to add, that although your family might be good sort of folks, as the world went, yet nobody imputed to any of them but you, a *very* punctilious concern for religion or piety. Therefore were they the less entitled to object to defects of that kind in others. Then, what an odious man, said I, have they picked out, to supplant in a lady's affections one of the finest figures of a man, and one noted for his brilliant parts and other accomplishments, whatever his morals may be!

I said I did not believe, had they left you to your own way, and treated you generously, that you would have had the thought of encouraging any man whom they disliked.

Then, Nancy, catching me up, the excuse is less; for, if so, must there not be more of *contradiction* than *love*, in the case?

Not so, neither, madam: for I know Miss Clarissa Harlowe would prefer Mr. Lovelace to all men, if morals ——

IF, Nancy! That *if* is everything. Do you really think she loves Mr. Lovelace?

What would you have had me to say, my dear? I won't tell you what I *did* say: but had I *not* said what I *did*, who would have believed me?

Besides, I *know* you love him! Excuse me, my dear: yet, if you deny it, what do you but reflect upon yourself, as if you thought you *ought* not to allow yourself in what you cannot help doing?

Indeed, madam, said I, the man is worthy of any woman's love (*If,* again, I *could* say) — but her parents ——

Her parents, Nancy — (you know, my dear, how my mother, who accuses her daughter of quickness, is evermore interrupting one!)

May take wrong measures, said I ——

Cannot do wrong. They have reason, I'll warrant, said she —

By which they may provoke a young woman, said I, to do rash things, which otherwise she would not do.

MISS CLARISSA HARLOWE TO MISS HOWE

Sunday Afternoon.

I HAD reason to fear, as I mentioned in mine of this morning, that a storm was brewing. Mr. Solmes came home from church this afternoon with my brother. Soon after, Betty brought me up a letter, without saying from whom. It was in a cover, and directed by a hand I never saw before; as if it were supposed that I would not receive and open it, had I known from whom it came. These are the contents:

To Miss Clarissa Harlowe.

Sunday, March 26.

DEAREST MADAM, I think myself a most unhappy man, in that I have never yet been able to pay my respects to you with youre consent, for one halfe-hour. I have something to communicat to you that concernes you much, if you be pleased to admit me to youre speech. Youre honour is concerned in it, and the honour of all youre familly. It relates to the designes of one whom you are sed to valew more than he desarves; and to some of his reprobat actions; which I am reddie to give you convincing proofes of the truth of. I may appear to be interested in it: But nevertheless, I am reddie to make oathe, that every tittle is true: And you will see what a man you are sed to favour. But I hope not so, for your owne honour.

Pray, Madam, vouchsafe me a hearing, as you valew your honour and familly: Which will oblidge, dearest Miss, / *Your most humble and most faithful Servant,* / ROGER SOLMES.

I waite below *for* the hope of admittance.[1]

[1 The misspellings in Solmes's letter are not found in the first edition: they occur in the 4th ed. (1759). — Ed.]

I have no manner of doubt that this is a poor device to get this man into my company. I would have sent down a verbal answer; but Betty refused to carry any message, which should prohibit his visiting me. So I was obliged either to see him, or to write to him. I wrote therefore an answer, of which I shall send you the rough draft. And now my heart aches for what may follow from it; for I hear a great hurry below.

To Roger Solmes, Esq.

SIR, — Whatever you have to communicate to me, which concerns my honour, may as well be done by writing as by word of mouth. If Mr. Lovelace is any of *my* concern, I know not that *therefore* he ought to be *yours*: for the usage I receive on *your* account (I *must* think it so!) is so harsh, that were there not such a man in the world as Mr. *Lovelace,* I would not wish to see Mr. *Solmes,* no, not for one half-hour, in the way he is pleased to be desirous to see me. I never can be in any danger from Mr. Lovelace (and of consequence, cannot be affected by any of your discoveries) if the proposal I made be accepted. You have been acquainted with it, no doubt. If not, be pleased to let my friends know, that if they rid *me* of my apprehensions of one gentleman, I will rid them of *theirs* of another: and then, of what consequence to *them,* or to *me,* will it be, whether Mr. Lovelace be a good man, or a bad? And if not to *them* nor to *me,* I see not how it can be of any to *you.* But if *you* do, I have nothing to say to that; and it will be a Christian part, if you will expostulate with him upon the errors you have discovered, and endeavour to make him as good a man, as, no doubt, you are *yourself,* or you would not be so ready to detect and expose *him.* / CL. HARLOWE.

Sunday Night.

My father was for coming up to me in great wrath it seems; but was persuaded to the contrary. My Aunt Hervey was permitted to send me this that follows. Quick work, my dear!

To Miss Clarissa Harlowe

NIECE, — Everybody is now convinced that nothing is to be done with you by way of gentleness or persuasion. Your mother will not permit you to stay in the house; for your father is so incensed by your strange letter to his friend, that she knows not what will be the consequence if you do. So you are commanded to get ready to go to your Uncle Antony's out of hand.

You must not answer me. There will be no end of that.

You know not the affliction you give to everybody; but to none more than to / Your affectionate aunt, / DOROTHY HERVEY.

[*Clarissa in desperation addresses written entreaties to her father, and then to her mother: both notes are returned unread. She then writes to her Uncle Harlowe, who in a kind reply reproaches her for her rebelliousness and expects her cheerful compliance. With a comment to Miss Howe (March 27) on her uncle's letter Clarissa sends to him again:*]

In about an hour after this letter was given me, my uncle sent up to know if he should be a welcome visitor upon the terms mentioned in his letter? He bid Betty bring him down a verbal answer: a written one, he said, would be a bad sign: and he bid her therefore not bring a letter. But I had just finished the enclosed transcription of one I had been writing. She made a difficulty to carry it; but was prevailed upon to oblige me by a token which these Mrs. Bettys cannot withstand.

DEAR AND HONOURED SIR, — How you rejoice me by your condescending goodness! So kind, so paternal a letter! so soothing to a wounded heart; and of late what I have been so little used to! How am I affected with it! Tell me not, dear sir, of my way of writing: your letter has more moved *me* than I have been able of writing *anybody*! It has made me wish with all my heart that I could entitle myself to be visited upon your own terms; and to be led down to my father and mother by so good and so kind an uncle.

I will tell you, dearest sir, what I will do to make my peace. I have a doubt that Mr. Solmes, upon consideration, would greatly prefer my sister to such a strange averse creature as me. His chief, or one of his chief motives in his address to me, is, as I have reason to believe, the contiguity of my grandfather's estate to his own. I will resign it; for ever I will resign it: and the resignation must be good, because I will never marry at all. I will make it over to my sister, and her heirs for ever. I shall have no heirs but my brother and her; and I will receive, as of my father's bounty, such an annuity (not in lieu of the estate, but as *of* his bounty) as he shall be pleased to grant me, if it be ever so small: and whenever I disoblige him, he to withdraw it, at his pleasure.

Will not this be accepted? Surely it must. Surely it will!

If this be accepted, grant me, sir, the honour of a visit; and do me then the inexpressible pleasure of leading me down to the feet of my honoured parents, and they shall find me the most dutiful of children; and to the arms of my brother and sister, and they shall find me the most obliging and most affectionate of sisters.

I wait, sir, for your answer to this proposal, made with the whole heart of / Your dutiful and most obliged niece, / CL. HARLOWE.

Monday Noon.

I hope this will be accepted: for Betty tells me that my Uncle Antony and my Aunt Hervey are sent for; and not Mr. Solmes; which I look upon as a favourable circumstance. With what cheerfulness will I assign over this envied estate! What a much more valuable consideration shall I part with it for! The love and favour of all my relations! That love and favour which I used for eighteen years to-gether to rejoice in, and be distinguished by! And what a charming pretence will this afford me of breaking with Mr. Lovelace! And how easy will it possibly make him to part with *me*!

I found this morning in the usual place, a letter from him. But I have not opened it; nor will I, till I see what effect this new offer will have.

MISS CLARISSA HARLOWE TO MISS HOWE

Monday Afternoon, March 27.

THEY HAVE been all assembled some time, and are in close debate I believe: but can there be room for debate upon a proposal, which, if accepted, will so effectually answer all their views?

Monday Evening

Would you believe it? Betty, by anticipation, tells me that I am to be refused. I am "a vile, artful creature. Everybody is too good to me. My Uncle Harlowe has been *taken in*," that's the phrase.

The result of their debate, I suppose, will somehow or other be communicated to me by and by. But let me tell you, my dear. that I am made so desperate, that I am afraid to open Mr. Lovelace's letter, lest, in the humour I am in, I should do something (if I find it not exceptionable) that may give me repentance as long as I live.

Monday Night.

This moment the following letter is brought me by Betty.

Monday, 5 o'clock.

MISS CUNNING-ONES, — Your fine new proposal is thought unworthy of a particular answer. Your Uncle Harlowe is ashamed to be so taken in. Tomorrow you go to my Uncle Antony's. That's all, child. / JAMES HARLOWE.

Having so little ground to hope for either favour or mercy, I opened Mr. Lovelace's letter.

He says he has more reason than ever, from the contents of my last, to apprehend, that I shall be prevailed upon by force, if not by fair means, to fall in with my brother's measures; and sees but too plainly that I am preparing him to expect it.

He begs, in the most earnest and humble manner, for one half-hour's interview; undertaking by a key, which he owns he has to the garden door, leading into the *coppice*, as we call it (if I will but un-bolt the door) to come into the garden at night, and wait till I have an opportunity to come to him, that he may reassure me of the truth of all he writes, and of the affection, and, if needful, protection, of all his family.

He apprises me (it is still my wonder how he comes by his intelligence!) that my friends have written to my Cousin Morden to represent matters to him in their own partial way; nor doubt they to influence him on their side of the question.

That all this shows I have but *one* way; if none of my own friends or intimates will receive me.

If I will transport him with the honour of my choice of this *one* way, settlements shall be drawn, with proper blanks, which I shall fill up as I please. Let him but have my commands from my own mouth; all my doubts and scruples from my own lips; and only a repetition, that I will not, on any consideration, be Solmes's wife; and he shall be easy. But, after such a letter as I have written, nothing but an interview can make him so. He beseeches me therefore, to unbolt the door, *as that very night*; or, if I receive not this time enough, *this night*; and he will in a disguise that shall not give a suspicion who he is, if he should be seen, come to the garden door, in hopes to open it with his key; nor will he have any other lodging than in the coppice both nights: watching every wakeful hour for the propitious unbolting, unless he has a letter with my orders to the contrary, or to make some other appointment.

This letter was dated yesterday: so he was there last night, I suppose; and will be there this night; and I have not written a line to him: and now it is too late, were I determined *what* to write.

MISS CLARISSA HARLOWE TO MISS HOWE

Tuesday Morning, 7 o'clock.

MY UNCLE has vouchsafed to answer me. These that follow are the contents of his letter; but just now brought me, although written last night — late, I suppose.

MISS CLARY, — Nobody wants your estate from you. Are *you*, who refuse everybody's advice, to prescribe a husband to your *sister?* Your parents *will* be obeyed. It is fit they *should*. Your mother has nevertheless prevailed to have your going to your Uncle Antony's put off till Thursday: yet owns you deserve not that, or any other favour from her. I will receive no more of your letters. You are too artful for me. You are an ungrateful and unreasonable child: must you have your will paramount to everybody's? How are you altered! / Your displeased uncle, / JOHN HARLOWE.

To be carried away on Thursday — to the moated house — to the chapel — to Solmes! How can I think of this! They will make me desperate.

Tuesday Morning, Eight o'clock.

I have another letter from Mr. Lovelace.

He says he had been in different disguises loitering about our garden and park wall, all the day on Sunday last; and all Sunday night was wandering about the coppice, and near the back door. It rained; and he has got a great cold, attended with feverishness, and so hoarse, that he has almost lost his voice.

His letter is dated last night at eight: and indisposed as he is, he tells me that he will watch till ten, in hopes of my giving him the meeting he so earnestly requests. And after that, he has a mile to walk to his horse and servant; and four miles then to ride to his inn.

He owns that he has an intelligencer in our family; who has failed him for a day or two past: and not knowing how I do, or how I may be treated, his anxiety is increased.

This circumstance gives me to guess who this intelligencer is: Joseph Leman: the very creature employed and confided in, more than any other, by my brother.

I have been often jealous of this Leman in my little airings and poultry visits. Doubly obsequious as he was always to me, I have thought him my brother's spy upon me; and although he obliged me by his hastening out of the garden and poultry yard, whenever I came into either, have wondered, that from *his reports* my liberties of those kinds have not been abridged. So, possibly, this man may be bribed by both, and yet betray both.

He presses with the utmost earnestness for an interview. He would not presume, he says, to disobey my last personal commands, that he should not endeavour to attend me again in the wood-house. But says he can give me such reasons for my permitting him to wait upon my father or uncles, as he hopes will be approved by me: for he cannot help observing that it is no more suitable to my own spirit than to his, that he, a man of fortune and family, should be obliged to pursue such a clandestine address as would only become a vile fortune-hunter. But, if I will give my consent for his visiting me like a man and a gentleman, no ill-treatment shall provoke him to forfeit his temper.

Lord M. will accompany him, if I please: or Lady Betty Lawrance will first make the visit to my mother, or to my Aunt Hervey, or even to my uncles, if I choose it. And such terms shall be offered as *shall* have weight upon them.

I cannot but say, I am sorry the man is not well.

I am afraid to ask you dear, what *you* would have done, thus situated. But what I *have* done, I *have* done. In a word, I wrote, that I would, if possible, give him a meeting to-morrow night, between the hours of nine and twelve, by the ivy summer house, or in it, or near the great cascade, at the bottom of the garden; and would unbolt the door, that he might come in by his own key. But that, if I found the meeting impracticable, or should change my mind, I would signify as much by another line; which he must wait for until it were dark.

Tuesday, Eleven o'clock.

I am just returned from depositing my billet. How diligent is this man! It is plain he was in waiting: for I had walked but a few paces, after I had deposited it, when, my heart misgiving me, I returned, to have taken it back, in order to reconsider it as I walked, and whether I should, or should not, let it go. But I found it gone.

In all probability there was but a brick wall, of a few inches thick, between Mr. Lovelace and me, at the very time I put the letter under the brick!

I am come back dissatisfied with myself. But I think, my dear, there can be no harm in meeting him. If I do *not*, he may take some violent measures. What he knows of the treatment I meet with in malice to him, and with a view to frustrate all his hopes, may make him desperate. What he requires is not unreasonable, and cannot affect my future choice and determination: it is only to assure him from my own lips, that I will never be the wife of a man I hate. All his trouble, and mine too, is owing to his faulty character. This, although I hate tyranny and arrogance in all shapes, makes me think less of the risks he runs, and the fatigues he undergoes, than otherwise I should do; and still less, as my sufferings (derived from the same source) are greater than his.

Betty confirms the intimation, that I must go to my uncle's on Thursday.

MISS CLARISSA HARLOWE TO MISS HOWE

Tuesday, Three o'clock, March 28.

[*After detailing a long conversation with the impudent Betty, Clarissa continues*:]

I retired to my closet, and wrote a few lines to my Uncle Harlowe, notwithstanding his prohibition; in order to get a reprieve from being carried away so soon as Thursday next, if I must go. And this, that I might, if complied with, suspend the appointment I have made with Mr. Lovelace; for my heart misgives me as to meeting him; and that more and more; I know not why. Under the superscription of the letter, I wrote these words: "Pray, dear sir, be pleased to give this a reading."

This is the copy of what I wrote:

Tuesday Afternoon.

HONOURED SIR, — Let me this once be heard with patience, and have my petition granted. It is only that I may not be hurried away so soon as next Thursday.

Why should the poor girl be turned out of doors so suddenly, so disgracefully? Procure for me, sir, one fortnight's respite. In that space of time I hope you will all relent. My mamma shall not need to shut her door in apprehension of seeing her disgraced child. / Your dutiful, though greatly afflicted niece, / CL. HARLOWE.

I sent this down: my uncle was not gone: and he now stays to know the result of the question put to me in the enclosed answer which he has given to mine.

Your going to your uncle's was absolutely concluded upon for next Thursday. Nevertheless, your mother, seconded by Mr. Solmes, pleaded so strongly to have you indulged, that your request for a delay will be complied with, upon one condition; and whether for a fortnight, or a shorter time, that will depend upon yourself. If you refuse this condition, your mother declares, she will give over all further intercession for you. Nor do you deserve this favour, as you put it upon our yielding to you, not you to us.

This condition is, that you admit of a visit from Mr. Solmes, for one hour, in company of your brother, your sister, or your Uncle Antony, choose which you will.

If you comply not, you go next Thursday to a house which is become strangely odious to you of late, whether you get ready to go or not. Answer therefore directly to the point. No evasion. Name your day and hour. Mr. Solmes will neither eat you, nor drink you. Let us see whether *we* are to be complied with *in anything* or not. John Harlowe.

After a very little deliberation, I resolved to comply with this condition. All I fear is that Mr. Lovelace's intelligencer may inform him of it; and that his apprehensions upon it may make him take some desperate resolution: especially as now (having more time given me here) I think to write to him to suspend the interview he is possibly so sure of. I sent down the following to my uncle:

Honoured Sir, — Although I see not what end the proposed condition can answer, I comply with it. I wish I could with everything expected of me. If I must name one, in whose company I am to see the gentleman, and that one *not* my mamma, whose presence I could wish to be honoured by on the occasion, let my uncle, if he pleases, be the *person*. If I must name the *day* (a long day, I doubt, will not be permitted me) let it be next Tuesday. The *hour,* four in the afternoon. The *place* either the ivy summer-house, or in the little parlour I used to be permitted to call mine.

Be pleased, sir, nevertheless, to prevail upon my mamma to vouchsafe me her presence on the occasion. I am, sir, / Your ever dutiful / Cl. Harlowe.

A reply is just sent me. I thought it became my averseness to this meeting, to name a distant day: but I did not expect they would have complied with it. So here is one week gained!

This is the reply:

You have done well to comply. We are willing to think the best of every slight instance of duty from you. Yet have you seemed to consider the day as an evil day, and so put it far off. This nevertheless is granted you, as no time need to be lost, if you are as generous *after* the day as we are condescending *before* it. Let me advise you not to harden your mind; nor take up your resolution beforehand. Mr. Solmes has more awe, and even terror, at the thoughts of seeing you than you can have at the thoughts of seeing him. *His* motive is *love*; let not yours be *hatred*. My brother, Antony, will be present, in hopes you will deserve well of *him*, by behaving well to the friend of the family.

One hint I am to give you meantime. It is this: *to make a discreet use of your pen and ink.* Methinks a young creature of niceness should be less ready to write to one man, when she is designed to be another's. / Your loving uncle, / JOHN HARLOWE.

Repenting of my appointment with Mr. Lovelace *before* I had this favour granted me, you may believe I hesitated not a moment to revoke it *now* that I had gained such a respite. Accordingly I wrote that I found it inconvenient to meet him as I had intended: that the risk I should run of a discovery, and the mischiefs that might flow from it, could not be justified by any end that such a meeting could answer; that things drawing towards a crisis between my friends and me, an interview could avail nothing; especially as the method by which this correspondence was carried on was not suspected, and he could write all that was in his mind to write: that I expected to be at liberty to judge of what was proper and fit upon this occasion: especially as he might be assured that I would sooner choose death than Mr. Solmes.

Tuesday Night.

I have deposited my letter to Mr. Lovelace.

MISS CLARISSA HARLOWE TO MISS HOWE

Wednesday Morning, Nine o'clock.

I AM just returned from my morning walk, and already have received a letter from Mr. Lovelace in answer to mine deposited last night. He must have had pen, ink, and paper with him; for it was written in the coppice; with this circumstance; on one knee, kneeling with the other. *Not* from reverence to the written to, however, as you'll find!

I so much to suffer *through* him; yet, to be treated as if I were obliged to bear insults *from* him!

But here you will be pleased to read his letter; which I shall enclose.

To Miss Clarissa Harlowe

Good God!

What is *now* to become of me! How shall I support this disappointment! No new cause! On one knee, kneeling with the other, I write! my feet benumbed with midnight wanderings through the heaviest dews that ever fell: my wig and my linen dripping with the hoar frost dissolving on them! Day but just breaking — sun not risen to exhale.

And *are things drawing towards a crisis between your friends and*

86

you? Is not this a reason for me to expect, the *rather* to expect, the promised interview?

Can *I write all that is in my mind, say you?* Impossible! Not the hundredth part of what is in my mind, and in my apprehension, can I write!

Oh, the wavering, the changeable sex! But can Miss Clarissa Harlowe ——

Forgive me, madam! I know not what I write!

Yet, I must, I do, insist upon your promise.

You would sooner choose death than Solmes (How my soul spurns the competition!) O my beloved creature, what are these but *words!* *Whose* words? Sweet and ever adorable — what? Promise-breaker must I call you?

Forgive me, dearest creature, forgive me! I know I have written in too much anguish of mind! Writing this in the same moment that the just-dawning light has imparted to me the heavy disappointment.

But if, exerting your usual generosity, you will excuse and *reappoint,* may that God, whom you profess to serve, and who is the God of *truth* and of *promises,* protect and bless you, for both; and for restoring to Himself, and to hope, / Your ever-adoring, / yet almost desponding / LOVELACE.

Ivy-Cavern in the Coppice — Day but just breaking.

This is the answer I shall return.

> *Wednesday Morning.*

I AM amazed, sir, at the freedom of your reproaches. Pressed and teased, against convenience and inclination, to give you a private meeting, am *I* to be thus challenged and upbraided, and my sex reflected upon, because I thought it prudent to change my mind? A liberty I had reserved to myself, when I made the *appointment,* as you call it. Two motives you must be governed by in this excess. The one *my easiness;* the other *your own presumption.* Since you think you have found out the *first,* and have shown so much for the *last* upon it, I am too much alarmed, not to wish and desire, that your letter of this day may conclude all the trouble you have had from, or for, / Your humble servant, / CL. HARLOWE.

> *Wednesday Noon, March 29.*

We cannot always answer for what we *can* do: but to convince you that I can keep my above resolution, with regard to Mr. Lovelace, angry as my letter is, and three hours as it is since it was written, I assure you, that I repent it not, nor will soften it, although I find it is not taken away. And yet I hardly ever before did anything in anger, that I did not repent in half an hour; and question myself in *less* than that time, whether I were right or wrong.

In this respite till Tuesday, I have a little time to look about me, as I may say, and to consider of what I *have* to do, and *can* do. And Mr. Lovelace's insolence will make me go very home with myself. Not that I think I can conquer my aversion to Mr. Solmes. I am sure I cannot. But, if I absolutely break with Mr. Lovelace, and give my friends convincing proofs of it, who knows but they will restore me to their favour, and let their views in relation to the other man go off by degrees?

But, with all my courage, I am exceedingly apprehensive about the Tuesday next, and about what may result from my stedfastness; for stedfast I am sure I shall be. They are resolved, I am told, to try every means to induce me to comply with what they are determined upon. I am resolved to do the like, to avoid what they would force me to do. A dreadful contention between parents and child! Each hoping to leave the other without excuse, whatever the consequence may be.

MISS HOWE TO MISS CLARISSA HARLOWE

Thursday morning.

YOUR resolution not to leave your father's house is right — if you can stay in it and avoid being Solmes's wife.

I think you answered Solmes's letter as *I* should have answered it. Will you not compliment me and yourself at once by saying that *that* was right?

You have, in your letters to your uncle and the rest, done all that you ought to do.

The deuce take the man, I was going to say, for not having had so much regard to his character and morals, as would have entirely justified such a step in a CLARISSA, persecuted as she is!

I shall be all impatience to know how this matter ends between you and him. But a *few inches of brick wall* between you so lately; and such *mountains*! And you think to hold it? May be so!

You see, you say, that the temper he showed in his preceding letter was not *natural to him*. And did you before think it *was*? Wretched creepers and insinuators! Yet when opportunity serves as insolent encroachers! This very Hickman, I make no doubt, would be as saucy as your Lovelace, if he dared. He has not half the arrogant bravery of the other, and can better hide his horns; that's all. But whenever he has the power, depend upon it, he will *butt* at one as valiantly as the other.

But if two persons of discretion, you'll say, come together —

Ay, my dear, that's true: but if none but persons of discretion were to marry — and would it not surprise you if I were to advance, that the persons of discretion are generally single? Such persons are apt to consider too much, to resolve. Are not you and I complimented as such? And would either of us marry if the fellows, and our friends, would let us alone?

How artfully has Lovelace, in the abstract you give me of one of his letters, calculated to your meridian; *generous spirits* hate compulsion! He is certainly a deeper creature by much than once we thought him He knows, as you intimate, that his own wild pranks cannot be concealed; and so owns just enough to palliate (because it teaches you not to be surprised at) any new one, that may come to your ears; and then, truly, he is, however faulty, a mighty *ingenious* man; and by no means an hypocrite.

But, upon the whole, I have no patience to see you thus made the sport of your brother's and sister's cruelty: for what, after *so much steadiness* on your part, in *so many trials,* can be their hope? *Except indeed it be to drive you to extremity, and to ruin you in the opinion of your uncles, as well as father.*

I urge you by all means to send out of their reach all the letters and papers you would not have them see. Methinks, I would wish you to deposit likewise a parcel of clothes, linen, and the like, before your interview with Solmes; lest you should not have an opportunity for it afterwards. Robin shall fetch it away on the first orders, by day or by night.

I am in hopes to procure from my mother, if things come to extremity, leave for you to be privately with us.

This alternative has been a good while in my head. But as your foolish uncle has so strangely attached my mother to their views, I cannot promise that I shall succeed as I wish.

Miss Clarissa Harlowe to Miss Howe

Friday, March 31.

You have very kindly accounted for your silence. People in misfortune are always in doubt. They are too apt to turn even unavoidable accidents into slights and neglects; especially in those whose favourable opinion they wish to preserve.

You have taught me what to say to, and what to think of, Mr. Lovelace. You have, by agreeable anticipation, let me know how it is probable he will apply to me to be excused. I will lay everything before you that shall pass on the occasion, if he *do* apply, that I may take your advice, when it can come in time; and when it cannot, that I may receive your correction, or approbation, as I may happen to merit either. Only one thing must be allowed for me; that whatever course I shall be *permitted* or be *forced* to steer, I must be considered as a person out of her own direction. Tossed to and fro by the high winds of passionate control (and, as I think, unreasonable severity) I behold the desired port, the *single state,* into which I would fain steer; but am kept off by the foaming billows of a brother's and sister's envy, and by the raging winds of a supposed invaded authority; while I see in Lovelace the rocks on one hand, and in Solmes, the sands on the other; and tremble lest I should split upon the former or strike upon the latter.

I am afraid I must not venture to take the hint you give me, to deposit some of my clothes; although I will some of my linen as well as papers.

I will tell you why: Betty had for some time been very curious about my wardrobe, whenever I took out any of my things before her.

Observing this, I once, on taking one of my garden-airings, left my keys in the locks; and on my return surprised the creature with her hand upon the keys as if shutting the door.

She was confounded at my sudden coming back. I took no notice: but, on her retiring, I found my clothes were not in the usual order.

I doubted not, upon this, that her curiosity was owing to the orders she had received; and being afraid they would abridge me of my airings, if their suspicions were not obviated, it has ever since been my custom (among other contrivances) not only to leave my keys in the locks; but to employ the wench now and then, in taking out my clothes, suit by suit, on pretence of preventing their being rumpled or creased, and to see that the flowered silver suit did not tarnish; sometimes declaredly to give myself employment, having little else to do: with which employment (superadded to the delight taken by the low as well as by the high of our sex in seeing fine clothes) she seemed always, I thought, as well pleased as if it answered one of the offices she had in charge.

If therefore such a step should become necessary (which I yet hope will not) I must be contented to go away with the clothes I shall have on at the time. My custom to be dressed for the day, as soon as breakfast is over, when I have had no household employments to prevent me, will make such a step (if I am forced to take it) less suspected. And the linen I shall deposit, in pursuance of your kind hint, cannot be missed.

Friday Morning, Eleven o'Clock

I have already made up my parcel of linen. My heart ached all the time I was employed about it; and still aches, at the thoughts of its being a necessary precaution.

When the parcel comes to your hands, as I hope it safely will, you will be pleased to open it. You will find in it two parcels sealed up; one of which contains the letters you have not yet seen; being those written since I left you: in the other are all the letters and copies of letters that have passed between you and me since I was last with you; with some other papers on subjects so much above me, that I cannot wish them to be seen by anybody whose indulgence I am not so sure of as I am of yours. If my judgment ripen with my years, perhaps I may review them.

In a third division, folded up separately, are all Mr. Lovelace's letters written to me since he was forbidden this house, and copies of my answers to them. I expect that you will break the seals of this parcel, and when you have perused them all, give me your free opinion of my conduct.

By the way, not a line from that man! — not *one* line! — Wednesday I deposited mine. It remained there on Wednesday night.

I was going to put up what little money I have, and some of my ornaments; but they are portable, and I cannot forget them. Besides, should they (suspecting me) desire to see any of the jewels, and were

I not able to produce them, it would amount to a demonstration of an intention which would have a guilty appearance to them.

Friday, One o'Clock, in the Wood-house

No letter yet from this man! I have luckily deposited my parcel, and have your letter of last night. If Robert take this without the parcel, pray let him return immediately for it. But he cannot miss it, I think; and must conclude that it is put there for him to take away. You may believe, from the contents of yours that I shall immediately write again.

MISS HOWE TO MISS CLARISSA HARLOWE

Thursday Night, March 30

THE fruits of my inquiry after your abominable wretch's behaviour and baseness at the paltry alehouse, which he calls an inn, prepare to hear.

Wrens and sparrows are not too ignoble a quarry for this villainous goshawk! His assiduities; his watchings; his nightly risks; the inclement weather he journeys in; must not be all placed to *your* account. He has opportunities of making everything light to him of that sort. A sweet pretty girl, I am told — innocent till he went hither — now (Ah! poor girl!) who knows what?

But just turned of seventeen! His friend and brother rake (a man of humour and intrigue) as I am told, to share the social bottle with. And sometimes another disguised rake or two. No sorrow comes near their hearts. Be not disturbed, my dear, at his *hoarsenesses*! His pretty Betsy, his Rosebud, as the vile wretch calls her, can *hear* all he says.

He is very fond of her. They say she is innocent even yet — her father, her grandmother, believe her to be so. He is to fortune her out to a young lover! Ah! the poor young lover! Ah! the poor simple girl!

. . . .

I have sent for this girl and her father; and am just now informed that I shall see them. I will sift them thoroughly. I shall soon find out such a simple thing as this, if he has not corrupted her already — and if he has, I shall soon find that out too. If more art than nature appear either in her or her father, I shall give them both up; but depend upon it, the girl's undone.

He is said to be fond of her. He places her at the upper end of his table. He sets her a-prattling. He keeps his friend at a distance from her. She prates away. He admires for nature all she says. Once was heard to call her charming little creature! An hundred has he called so no doubt. He puts her upon singing. He praises her wild note. O my dear, the girl's undone! — must be undone! The man, you know, is LOVELACE.

Let 'em bring Wyerley to you, if they will have you married — anybody but Solmes and Lovelace be yours! So advises / Your / ANNA HOWE.

My dearest friend, consider this alehouse as his garrison. Him as an enemy. His brother-rakes as his assistants and abetters: would not your brother, would not your uncles, tremble, if they knew how near them he is, as they pass to and fro? I am told, he is resolved you shall not be carried to your Uncle Antony's. What can you do, *with* or *without* such an enterprising ——? Fill up the blank I leave — I cannot find a word bad enough.

MISS CLARISSA HARLOWE TO MISS HOWE

Friday, Three o'Clock

YOU incense, alarm, and terrify me, at the same time. Hasten, my dearest friend, hasten to me, what further intelligence you can gather about this vilest of men.

But never talk of innocence, of simplicity, and this unhappy girl, together! Would her father and grandmother, if honest people, and careful of their simple girl, permit such freedoms?

Warn, my dear, if not too late, the unthinking father, of his child's danger. There cannot be a father in the world who would sell his child's virtue. No mother! — the poor thing!

And now, my dear, I will tell you, how I came to put you upon this inquiry.

This vile *Joseph Leman* had given a hint to *Betty*, and she to *me*, as if Lovelace would be found out to be a very bad man, at a place where he had been lately seen in disguise. But he would see further, he said, before he told her more; and she promised *secrecy*, in hope to get at *further intelligence*. I thought it could be no harm, to get you to inform yourself, and me, of what could be gathered.[1] And now I

---

[1] It will be seen that Mr. Lovelace's motive for sparing his Rosebud was twofold. First: because his pride was gratified by the grandmother's desiring him to spare her grand-daughter. *Many a pretty rogue,* says he, *had I spared, whom I did not spare, had my power been acknowledged, and my mercy in time implored. But the* debellare superbos *should be my motto, were I to have a new one.*

His other motive will be explained in the following passage in the same Letter: *I never was so honest for a long time together,* says he, *since my matriculation. It behoves me so to be. Some way or other my recess* (at this little inn) *may be found out! and it will then be thought that my Rosebud has attracted me. A report in my favour from simplicities so amiable, may establish me, etc.*

Accordingly, as the reader will here after see, Mr. Lovelace finds by the *effects,* his expectations from the contrivance he set on foot by means of his agent Joseph Leman (who plays, as above, upon Betty Barnes) fully answered, though he could not know what passed on the occasion between the two ladies.

This explanation is the more necessary to be given, as several of our readers (through want of due attention) have attributed to Mr. Lovelace, on his behaviour to his Rosebud, a greater merit than was due to him; and moreover imagined that it was improbable that a man who was capable of acting so

see, his enemies are but too well warranted in their reports of him: and, if the ruin of this poor young creature be his aim, and if he had not known her but for his visits to Harlowe Place, I shall have reason to be doubly concerned for her; and doubly incensed against so vile a man.

I think I hate him worse than I do Solmes himself.

But I will not add one other word about him; after I have told you, that I wish to know, as soon as possible, what further occurs from your inquiry. I have a letter from him; but shall not open it till I do: and then, if it come out as I dare say it will, I will directly put the letter unopened into the place I took it from, and never trouble myself more about him. Adieu, my dearest friend.

MISS HOWE TO MISS CLARISSA HARLOWE
Friday Noon, March 31.

JUSTICE obliges me to forward this after my last on the wings of the wind, as I may say. I really believe the man is innocent. Of this *one* accusation, I think, he must be acquitted; and I am sorry I was so forward in dispatching away my intelligence by halves.

I have seen the girl. She is really a very pretty, a very neat, and, what is still a greater beauty, a very innocent young creature. He who could have ruined such an undesigning home-bred, must have been indeed infernally wicked. Her father is an honest simple man: entirely satisfied with his child, and with her new acquaintance.

I am almost afraid for your heart, when I tell you, that I find, now I have got to the bottom of this inquiry, something noble come out in this Lovelace's favour.

The girl is to be married next week; and this promoted and brought about by him. He is resolved, her father says, to make one couple happy, and wishes he could make more so (*There's for you, my dear!*): and having taken a liking also to the young fellow whom she professes to love, he has given her an hundred pounds: the grandmother actually has it in her hands, to answer to the like sum given to the youth by one of his own relations: while Mr. Lovelace's companion, attracted by the example, has given twenty-five guineas to the father, who is poor, towards clothes to equip the pretty rustic.

Mr. Lovelace and his friend, the poor man says, when they first came to this house, affected to appear as *persons of low degree;* but now he knows the one (but mentioned it in confidence) to be Colonel Barrow, the other Capt. Sloane. The colonel he owns was at first very *sweet upon his girl*: but upon her grandmother's begging of him to spare her innocence, he vowed, that he never would offer anything but good counsel to her. He kept his word; and the pretty fool ac-

generously (as they supposed) in *this* instance, should be guilty of any *atrocious* vileness. Not considering that Love, Pride, and Revenge, as he owns, were ingredients of equal force in his composition; and that resistance was a *stimulus* to him. [1759].

knowledged that she never could have been better instructed by the minister himself from the *Bible-book!* The girl pleased me so well, that I made her visit to me worth her while.

But what, my dear, will become of us now? Lovelace not only reformed, but turned preacher! What will become of us now? Why, my sweet friend, your *generosity* is now engaged in his favour! Fie upon this *generosity!* I think in my heart that it does as much mischief to the noble-minded, as *love* to the ignobler. — What before was only a *conditional liking*, I am now afraid will turn to *liking unconditional.*

Upon the whole, Mr. Lovelace comes out with so much advantage from this inquiry, that were there the least room for it, I should suspect the whole to be *a plot set on foot to wash a blackmoor white.* Adieu, my dear.

MISS CLARISSA HARLOWE TO MISS HOWE

Saturday, April 1.

MR. LOVELACE has faults enow to deserve very severe censure, although he be not guilty of this. If I were upon such terms with him as he would wish me to be, I should give him a hint, that this treacherous Joseph Leman cannot be *so much* attached to him, as perhaps he thinks him to be. If he were, he would not have been so ready to report to his disadvantage (and to Betty Barnes too) this slight affair of the pretty rustic.

You may believe I made no scruple to open his letter, after the receipt of your second on this subject: nor shall I of answering it, as I have no reason to find fault with it. An article in his favour, procured him, however, so much the easier (as I must own) by way of amends for the undue displeasure I took against him; though he knows it not.

When I send you this letter of his you will see how very humble he is: what *acknowledgments* of *natural* impatience: what confession of faults, as you prognosticated.

A very different appearance, I must own, all these make, now the story of the pretty rustic is cleared up, to what they would have made, had it not.

But you will see, in this very letter, an haughtiness even in his submissions. 'Tis true, I know not where to find fault as to the expression; yet cannot I be satisfied, that his humility *is* humility; or even an humility upon such conviction as one should be pleased with.

To be sure, he is far from being a polite man: yet is not directly and characteristically as I may say, *unpolite.* But *his* is such a sort of politeness, as has by a carelessness founded on a very early indulgence built upon both, grown into assuredness, and, of course, as I may say, into delicacy.

He complains heavily of my readiness to take mortal offence at him, and to dismiss him for ever: it is a *high* conduct, he says he must be frank enough to tell me; a conduct that must be very far from contributing to allay his apprehensions of the possibility that I may be persecuted into my relations' measures in behalf of Mr. Solmes.

You will see, that he has already heard of the interview I am to have with Mr. Solmes; and with what vehemence and anguish he expresses himself on the occasion. I intend to take proper notice of the ignoble means he stoops to, to come at his early intelligence out of our family. If persons pretending to principle bear not their testimony against unprincipled actions, what check can they have?

You will see how passionately he presses me to oblige him with a few lines, before the interview between Mr. Solmes and me takes place (if, as he says, it *must* take place) to confirm his hope, that I have no view, in my present displeasure against *him*, to give encouragement to *Solmes*. An apprehension, he says, that he must be excused for repeating: especially as the interview is a favour granted to that man, which I have refused to him; since, as he infers, were it not with such an expectation, why should my *friends* press it?

. . . .

I have written; and to this effect: That I had never intended to write another line to a man, who could take upon himself to reflect upon my sex and myself, for having thought fit to make use of my own judgment.

I tell him, that I have submitted to this interview with Mr. Solmes, purely as an act of duty, to show my friends, that I will comply with their commands as far as I can; and that I hope, when Mr. Solmes himself shall see how determined I am, he will cease to prosecute a suit, in which it is impossible he should succeed with my consent.

I assure him, that my aversion to Mr. Solmes is too sincere to permit me to doubt myself on this occasion. But, nevertheless, he must not imagine that my rejecting of Mr. Solmes is in favour to him. That I value my freedom and independency too much, if my friends will but leave me to my own judgment, to give them up to a man so uncontrollable, and who shows me beforehand what I have to expect from him, were I in his power.

I express my high disapprobation of the methods he takes to come at what passes in a private family: the pretence of corrupting other people's servants by way of reprisal for the spies they have set upon him, I tell him, is a very poor excuse; and no other than an attempt to justify one meanness by another.

I tell him, that if I am obliged to go to my Uncle Antony's, it is not to be inferred, that I must therefore *necessarily* be Mr. Solmes's wife: since I may not be so sure perhaps that the same exceptions lie so strongly against my quitting a house to which I shall be forcibly carried, as if I left my father's house: and, at the worst, I may be able to keep them in suspense till my Cousin Morden comes, who will have a right to put me in possession of my grandfather's estate, if I insist upon it.

I see not any of my family, nor hear from them in any way of kindness. This looks as if they themselves expected no great matters from that Tuesday's conference which makes my heart flutter every time I think of it.

My Uncle Antony's presence on the occasion I do not much like; but I had rather meet him than my brother or sister: yet my uncle is very impetuous. I can't think Mr. Lovelace can be much more so; at least he cannot *look* anger, as my uncle, with his harder features, can.

MISS HOWE TO MISS CLARISSA HARLOWE

Sunday, April 2.

I OUGHT yesterday to have acknowledged the receipt of your parcel: Robin tells me, that the Joseph Leman whom you mention as the traitor, saw him. He was in the poultry-yard, and spoke to Robin over the bank which divides that from the Green Lane. "What brings you hither, Mr. Robert? But I can tell. Hie away, as fast as you can."

I read to my mother several passages of your letters. And while her fit of gratitude for it lasted, I was thinking to make my proposal, and to press it with all the earnestness I could give it, when Hickman came in, making his legs, and stroking his cravat and ruffles.

I choose not to mention my proposal before him, till I know how it will be relished by my mother. If it be not well received, perhaps I may employ *him* on the occasion. Yet I don't like to owe him an obligation, if I could help it. For men who have his views in their heads, do so parade it, so strut about, if a woman condescend to employ them in her affairs, that one has no patience with them.

However, if I *find* not an opportunity this day, I will *make* one to-morrow.

I shall not open either of your sealed-up parcels, but in *your* presence. There is no need. Your conduct is out of all question with me: and by the extracts you have given me from his letters and your own, I know all that relates to the present situation of things between you.

I MUST *give you your way in these things,* you say. And I know there is no contradicting you: for you were ever putting too great a value upon little offices done for *you,* and too little upon the great ones you do for *others.* The satisfaction you have in doing so, I grant it, repays you. But why should you, by the nobleness of your mind, throw reproaches upon the rest of the world? Particularly, upon your own family — and upon ours too?

Heaven direct you, in your own arduous trials, is all I have room to add; and make you as happy as you think to be.

MISS CLARISSA HARLOWE TO MISS HOWE

Sunday Night, April 2.

I HAVE many new particulars to acquaint you with that show a great change in the behaviour of my friends to me. I did not think we had so much art among us, as I find we have. I will give these particulars to you as they offered.

All the family was at church in the morning. They brought good Dr. Lewen with them, in pursuance of a previous invitation. And the doctor sent up to desire my permission to attend me in my own apartment.

You may believe it was easily granted.

So the doctor came up.

We had a conversation of near an hour before dinner: but, to my surprise, he waived everything that would have led to the subject I supposed he wanted to talk about.

I was prodigiously disappointed: but supposing that he was thought too just a man to be made a judge of in this cause; I led no more to it: nor, when he was called down to dinner, did he take the least notice of leaving me behind him there.

In the afternoon, all but my brother and sister went to church with the good doctor; who left his compliments for me. I took a walk in the garden: my brother and sister walked in it too, and kept me in their eye a good while, on purpose, as I thought, that I might see how gay and good-humoured they were together. At last they came down the walk that I was coming up, hand in hand, lover-like.

Your servant, miss — your servant, sir — passed between my brother and me.

Is it not coldish, Sister Clary? in a kinder voice than usual, said my sister, and stopped. I stopped, and curtsied low to her half-curtsey. I think not, sister, said I.

She went on. I curtsied without return; and proceeded; turning to my poultry-yard.

By a shorter run, arm-in-arm, they were there before me.

I think, Clary, said my brother, you must present me with some of this breed, for Scotland.

If you please, brother.

I'll choose for you, said my sister.

And while I fed them, they pointed to half a dozen: yet intending nothing by it, I believe, but to show a deal of love and good-humour to each other before me.

My uncles next (at their return from church) were to do me the honour of *their* notice. They bid Betty tell me, they would drink tea with me in my own apartment.

Now, thought I, shall I have the subject of next Tuesday enforced upon me.

But they contradicted the order for tea, and only my Uncle Harlowe came up to me.

Half-distant, half-affectionate, at his entering my chamber, was the air he put on to his *daughter-niece*, as he used to call me; and I threw myself at his feet, and besought his favour.

None of these discomposures, child. None of these apprehensions. You will now have everybody's favour. All is coming about, my dear.

I was impatient to see you. I could no longer deny myself this satisfaction.

O my cunning brother! This is *his* contrivance. And then my anger made me recollect the triumph in his and my sister's fondness for each other, as practised before me; and the mingled indignation flashing from their eyes, as arm in arm they spoke to me, and the forced condescension playing upon their lips, when they called me Clary, and sister.

At his going away — You are not expected down indeed; but I protest I had a good mind to surprise your father and mother! If I thought nothing would arise that would be disagreeable. What say you? Will you give me your hand? Will you see your father? Can you stand his displeasure, on first seeing the dear creature who has given him and all of us so much disturbance? Can you promise future ——

He saw me rising in my temper. Nay, my dear, interrupting himself, if you cannot be all resignation, I would not have you think of it.

My heart, struggling between duty and warmth of temper, was full. You know, my dear, I never could bear to be dealt meanly with! How — how *can* you, sir! You, my papa-uncle. How *can* you, sir! The poor girl! For I could not speak with connection.

Nay, my dear, if you cannot be all duty, all resignation — better stay where you are. But after the instance you have given ——

Instance I have given! What instance, sir?

Well, well, child, better stay where you are, if your past confinement hangs so heavy upon you. But now there will be a sudden end to it. Adieu, my dear! Three words only. Let your compliance be sincere! And love me, as you used to love me. Your grandfather did not do so much for you, as I will do for you.

Without suffering me to reply he hurried away, as I thought, like one who had been employed to act a part against his will, and was glad it was over.

Don't you see, my dear Miss Howe, how they are all determined? Have I not reason to dread next Tuesday?

I found in the afternoon a reply to my answer to Mr. Lovelace's letter. It is full of promises, full of vows of gratitude, of *eternal* gratitude, is his word, among others still more hyperbolic. He regrets my indifference to him; which puts all the hope he has in my favour upon the shocking usage I receive from my friends.

As to my charge upon him of unpoliteness and uncontrollableness. What (he asks) can he say? Since being unable absolutely to vindicate himself, he has too much ingenuousness to attempt to do so: yet is struck dumb by my harsh construction that his acknowledging temper is owing more to his carelessness to defend himself, than to his inclination to amend. He had never *before* met with the objections against his morals which I had raised, *justly* raised: and he was resolved to obviate them. What is it, he asks, that he has promised, but reformation by my example?

He gives me up, as absolutely lost, if I go to my Uncle Antony's:

the close confinement; the moated house; the chapel, the implacableness of my brother and sister, and their power over the rest of my family, he sets forth in strong lights; and plainly says that he must have a struggle to prevent my being carried thither.

Your kind, your generous endeavours to interest your mother in my behalf, will, I hope, prevent those harsher extremities to which I might be otherwise driven. And to you I will fly, if permitted, and keep all my promises, of not corresponding with anybody, not seeing anybody, but by your mother's direction and yours.

I will close and deposit at this place.

MISS CLARISSA HARLOWE TO MISS HOWE

I AM glad my papers are safe in your hands.

I have another letter from Mr. Lovelace. He is extremely apprehensive of the meeting I am to have with Mr. Solmes tomorrow. He assures me that Solmes has actually talked with tradesmen of new equipages, and names the people in town with whom he has treated: that he has even (was there ever such a horrid wretch!) allotted this and that apartment in his house, for a nursery, and other offices.

How shall I bear to hear such a creature talk of love to me? I shall be out of all patience with him. Besides, I thought that he did not dare to make or talk of these impudent preparations — so inconsistent as such are with my brother's views — but I fly the subject.

You will see how he threatens to watch and waylay them, and to *rescue* me as he calls it, by an armed force of friends and servants, if they attempt to carry me against my will to my uncle's; and this, whether I give my consent to the enterprise, or not; since he shall have no hopes if I am once there.

O my dear friend! Who can think of these things, and not be extremely miserable in her apprehensions!

I have deposited a letter for Mr. Lovelace: in which I charge him, as he would not disoblige me for ever, to avoid any rash step, any visit to Mr. Solmes, which may be followed by acts of violence.

To-morrow is Tuesday! How soon comes upon us the day we dread!

MISS CLARISSA HARLOWE TO MISS HOWE

Tuesday, Eleven o'clock.

I HAVE had a visit from my Aunt Hervey.

I never found myself so fretful in all my life: and so I told my aunt; and begged her pardon for it. But she said it was well disguised then; for she saw nothing but little tremors, which were usual with young ladies when they were to see their admirers for the *first* time; and this might be called so, with respect to me; since it was the first time I had consented to see Mr. Solmes in that light. But that the *next* ——

How, madam, interrupted I, is it then imagined that I give this meeting on that foot?

To be sure it is, child.

To be sure it is, madam! Then do I yet desire to decline it. I will not, I cannot, see him if he expects me to see him upon those terms.

Indeed, he *has* this hope; and justly founded too.

She told me it signified nothing to talk: I knew the expectation of every one.

Indeed I did not. It was impossible I could think of such a strange expectation, upon a compliance made only to show I would comply in all that was in my power to comply with.

Again my aunt told me, that talking and invective, now I had given the expectation, would signify nothing. She hoped I would not show every one that they had been too forward in their constructions of my desire to oblige them. She could assure me that it would be worse for me, if *now* I receded, than if I had never advanced.

Advanced, madam! How can you say *advanced?* Why, this is a trick upon me! A poor low trick! Pardon me, madam, I don't say you have a hand in it — but, my dearest aunt, tell me, tell me, will not my mother be present at this dreaded interview? Will she not so far favour me? Were it but to qualify ——

Qualify, my dear, interrupted she — your mother, and your Uncle Harlowe would not be present on this occasion, for the world ——

O then, madam, how can they look upon my consent — to this interview as an *advance?*

My aunt was displeased at this home push.

Miss Clarissa Harlowe to Miss Howe   *Tuesday Evening,*
                                          and continued thro' the Night.

WELL, my dear, I am alive, and here! But how long I shall be either here, or alive, I cannot say. I must tell you how the saucy Betty again discomposed me, when she came up with this Solmes's message.

Miss! Miss! cried she, as fast as she could speak, with her arms spread abroad, and all her fingers distended and held up, will you be pleased to walk down into your own parlour? There is everybody, I will assure you, in full *congregation!* And there is Mr. Solmes, as fine as a lord, with a charming white peruke, fine laced shirt and ruffles, coat trimmed with silver, and a waistcoat standing on end with lace! Quite handsome, believe me! You never saw such an alteration! Ah! miss, shaking her head, 'tis pity you have said so much against him! But you know how to come off, for all that! I hope it will not be too late!

Everybody there, do you say? Who do you call everybody?

Why, miss, holding out her left palm opened, and with a flourish, and a saucy leer, patting it with the forefinger of the other, at every mentioned person, there is your papa! There is your mamma! There is your Uncle Harlowe! There is your Uncle Antony! Your Aunt Hervey! *My* young lady! And my young master! And Mr. Solmes, with the air of a great courtier, standing up, because he named you: Mrs. Betty, said he (then the ape of a wench bowed and scraped as awkwardly as I suppose the person did whom she endeavoured to imitate) pray give my humble service to miss, and tell her I wait her commands.

Say you, *all* my friends are below with him? And am I to *appear* before them *all*?

I can't tell if they'll stay when you come. I think they seemed to be moving when Mr. Solmes gave me his orders. But what answer shall I carry to the squire?

Say, I can't go! But yet when 'tis over, 'tis over! Say, I'll wait upon — I'll attend — I'll come presently — say anything; I care not what — but give me my fan, and fetch me a glass of water.

There are two doors to *my* parlour, as I used to call it. As I entered at one, my friends hurried out at the other. I saw just the gown of my sister, the last who slid away. My Uncle Antony went out with them; but he stayed not long, as you shall hear: and they all remained in the next parlour, a wainscot partition only parting the two. I remember them both in one: but they were separated in favour of us girls, for each to receive her visitors in at her pleasure.

Mr. Solmes approached me as soon as I entered, cringing to the ground, a visible confusion in every feature of his face. After half a dozen choked-up madams — he was very sorry — he was very much concerned — it was his misfortune — and there he stopped, being unable presently to complete a sentence.

This gave me a little more presence of mind.

I turned from him, and seated myself in one of the fireside chairs, fanning myself. I have since recollected that I must have looked saucily.

He hemmed five or six times, as I had done above; and these produced a sentence — that I could not but see his confusion. This sentence produced two or three more.

I do indeed see you under some confusion, sir; and this gives me hope, that although I have been compelled, as I may call it, to give way to this interview, it may be attended with happier effects than I had apprehended from it.

He had hemmed himself into more courage.

You could not, madam, imagine any creature so blind to your merits, and so little attracted by them, as easily to forego the interest and approbation he was honoured with by your worthy family, while he had any hope given him, that one day he might, by his perseverance and zeal, expect your favour.

I am but too much aware, sir, that it is upon the interest and approbation you mention, that you build such hope.

He had seen many instances, he told me, and had heard of more, where ladies had seemed as averse, and yet had been induced, some by motives of compassion, others by persuasion of friends, to change their minds; and had been very happy afterwards: and he hoped this might be the case here.

I have no notion, sir, of compliment, in an article of such importance as this: yet am I sorry to be obliged to speak my mind so plainly, as I am going to do. Know then that I have invincible objections, sir, to your address. I have avowed them with an earnestness that I believe is without example: and why? Because I believe it is without example that any young creature, circumstanced as I am, was ever treated as I have been treated on your account.

I am sorry, madam, to hear this. I am sure you should not tell me of any fault, that I would be unwilling to correct in myself.

Then, sir, correct this fault — do not wish to have a young creature compelled in the most material article of her life, in behalf of a person she cannot value.

He paused and seemed a little at a loss; and I was going to give him still stronger and more personal instances of my plain-dealing, when in came my Uncle Antony.

So, niece, so! Sitting in state like a queen, giving audience! *haughty* audience! Mr. Solmes, why stand you thus humbly? Why this distance, man? I hope to see you upon a more intimate footing before we part.

I arose, as soon as he entered — and approached him with a bent knee: let me, sir, reverence my uncle, whom I have not for so long a time seen! Let me, sir, bespeak your favour and compassion!

You'll have the favour of everybody, niece, when you know how to deserve it.

Why, dear good sir, am I to be made unhappy in a point so concerning to my happiness? I will engage never to marry any man, without my father's consent, and yours, sir, and everybody's. Did I ever give you cause to doubt my word? And here I will take the solemnest oath that can be offered me ——

That is the matrimonial one, interrupted he, with a big voice — and to this gentleman. It shall, it shall, Cousin Clary! And the more you oppose it the worse it shall be for you.

This, and before the man, who seemed to assume courage upon it, highly provoked me.

Then, sir, you shall sooner follow me to the grave *indeed*. I will undergo the cruellest death — I will even consent to enter into the awful vault of my ancestors, and to have that bricked up upon me, rather than consent to be miserable for life. And, Mr. Solmes, turning to him, take notice of what I say: *This* or *any* death, I will sooner undergo (that will quickly be over) than be yours, and for *ever* unhappy!

How could I avoid making these strong declarations, the man in presence?

I was going out at the door I came in at, and whom should I meet at the door but my brother, who had heard all that had passed!

He bolted upon me so unexpectedly, that I was surprised. He

took my hand, and grasped it with violence. Return, pretty miss, said he; return, if you please. You shall not yet be *bricked up.* Your *instigating* brother shall save you from that!

He had led me up to meet Mr. Solmes, whose hand he took, as he held mine. Here, sir, said he, take the rebel daughter's hand: I give it you now: she shall confirm the gift in a week's time; or will have neither father, mother, nor uncles, to boast of.

I snatched my hand away.

How now, miss!

And how now, sir! What right have *you* to dispose of my hand? If you govern everybody else, you shall not govern me; especially in a point so immediately relative to myself, and in which you neither have, nor ever shall have, anything to do.

I would have broken from him; but he held my hand too fast.

Let me go, sir! Why am I thus treated? You *design,* I doubt not, with your unmanly grippings, to hurt me, as you do: but again I ask, wherefore is it that I am to be thus treated by *you?*

He tossed my hand from him with a whirl, that pained my very shoulder. I wept, and held my other hand to the part.

Mr. Solmes blamed him. So did my uncle.

How generous in you, Mr. Solmes, said my brother, to interpose so kindly in behalf of such an immovable spirit! I beg of you to persist in your address! The unnatural brother called it *address!* For all our family's sake, and for *her* sake too, if you love her, persist! Let us save her, if possible, from ruining herself. Look at her person (and he gazed at me, from head to foot, pointing at me, as he referred to Mr. Solmes) think of her fine qualities! All the world confesses them, and we all gloried in her till now. She is worth saving; and, after two or three more struggles, she will be yours, and, take my word for it, will reward your patience. Talk not, therefore, of giving up your hopes, for a little whining folly.

Mr. Solmes, with a self-satisfied air, presumptuously said he would suffer everything to *oblige* my family and to *save* me: and doubted not to be amply rewarded, could he be so happy as to succeed at last.

I had put myself by this time into great disorder: they were silent, and seemed by their looks to want to talk to one another, walking about (in violent disorders too) between whiles. I sat down fanning myself (as it happened, against the glass) and I could perceive my colour go and come; and being sick to the very heart, and apprehensive of fainting, I rung.

Betty came in. — Permit me, sir, said I, to withdraw.

Whither go you, niece? said my uncle: we have not done with you yet. I charge you depart not. Mr. Solmes has something to open to you, that will astonish you — and you *shall* hear it.

Only, sir, by your leave, for a few minutes into the air. I will return, if you command it. I will hear all that I am to hear; that it may be over *now* and *for ever.* You will go with me, Betty?

And so, without any further prohibition, I retired into the garden. It was near an hour before I was sent for in again. The messenger was my Cousin Dolly Hervey, who, with an eye of compassion and respect (for Miss Hervey always loved me, and calls herself my scholar, as you know) told me, my company was desired.

Betty left us.

Who commands my attendance, miss? said I. Have you not been in tears, my dear?

Who can forbear tears, said she.

Why, what is the matter, Cousin Dolly? Surely nobody is entitled to weep in this family, but *me*!

Yes, I am, madam, said she, because I love you.

She said, Mr. Solmes would have given up his claim to you; for he said, you hated him, and there were no hopes; and your mamma was willing he should; and to have you taken at your word, to renounce Mr. Lovelace, and to live single: my mamma was for it too; for they heard all that passed between you and Uncle Antony, and Cousin James; saying it was impossible to think of prevailing upon you to have Mr. Solmes. Uncle Harlowe seemed in the same way of thinking; at least, my mamma says he did not say anything to the contrary. But your papa was immovable, and was angry at your mamma and mine upon it: and hereupon your brother, your sister, and my Uncle Antony joined in, and changed the scene entirely.

I asked her what *she* would do, were she in my case?

Without hesitation she replied, Have Mr. Lovelace, out-of-hand, and take up her own estate, if she were me; and there would be an end of it — and Mr. Lovelace, she said, was a fine gentleman; Mr. Solmes was not worthy to *buckle his shoes*.

By this time we entered the house. Miss Hervey accompanied me into the parlour, and left me, as a person devoted, I then thought.

Nobody was there. I sat down, and had leisure to weep; reflecting upon what my Cousin Dolly had told me.

They were all in my sister's parlour adjoining: for I heard a confused mixture of voices, some louder than others, which drowned the more compassionating accents.

I believe I was above a quarter of an hour enjoying my own comfortless contemplations, before anybody came in to me; for they seemed to be in full debate. My aunt looked in first; O my dear, said she, are you there? and withdrew hastily to apprise them of it.

And then (as agreed upon, I suppose) in came my Uncle Antony, crediting Mr. Solmes with the words, *Let me lead you in, my dear friend*, having hold of his hand.

I stood up. My uncle looked very surly. Sit down! sit down, girl, said he — and drawing a chair near me, he placed his *dear* friend in it, whether he would or not, I having taken my seat. And my uncle sat on the other side of me.

Well, niece, taking my hand, we shall have very little more to say to you than we have already said, as to the subject that is so distasteful to you — unless, indeed you have better considered the matter — and first, let me know if you have?

The matter wants no consideration, sir.

Very well, very well, *madam*! said my uncle, withdrawing his hands from mine: could I ever have thought of this from you?

For God's sake, dearest madam, said Mr. Solmes, folding his hands — and there he stopped.

For God's sake, *what*, sir? How came God's sake and your sake, I pray you, to be the same?

This silenced *him*. My uncle could only be angry; and that he was before.

Well, well, well, Mr. Solmes, said my uncle, no more of supplication. You have not *confidence* enough to expect a woman's favour.

. . . .

But both being silent, I was sorry, I added, that I had too much reason to say a very harsh thing, as it might be thought; which was, that if he would but be pleased to convince my brother and sister, that he was absolutely determined to alter his generous purposes towards me, it might possibly procure me better treatment from both than I was otherwise likely to have.

My uncle was very much displeased. But he had not the opportunity to express his displeasure, as he seemed preparing to do; for in came my brother in exceeding great wrath; and called me several vile names. His success hitherto, in his devices against me, had set him above keeping even decent measures.

Was this my spiteful construction? he asked — was this the interpretation I put upon his brotherly care of me, and concern for me, in order to prevent my ruining myself?

It *is*, indeed it *is*, said I: I know no other way to account for your late behaviour to me.

How they all gazed upon one another! — but could I be less peremptory before the man?

How, niece! And is a brother, an *only* brother, of so little consideration with you as this comes to? And ought he to have no concern for his sister's honour and the family's honour?

My honour, sir! I desire none of his concern for that!

Then was Mr. Solmes told that I was unworthy of his pursuit.

But Mr. Solmes warmly took my part: he could not bear, he said, that I should be treated so roughly.

And so very much did he exert himself on this occasion, and so patiently was his warmth received by my brother, that I began to suspect that it was a contrivance to make me think myself obliged to him; and that this might perhaps be one end of the pressed-for interview.

The very suspicion of this low artifice, violent as I was thought to be before, put me still more out of patience; and my uncle and my brother again praising his wonderful generosity and his noble return of good for evil, You are a happy man, Mr. Solmes, said I, that you can so *easily* confer obligations upon a whole family, except upon one ungrateful person of it, whom you seem to intend *most* to oblige; but who being made unhappy by your favour, desires not to owe to *you* any protection from the violence of a brother.

Then was I a rude, an ungrateful, an unworthy creature.

Instantly almost came in Betty, in a great hurry, looking at me as spitefully as if she were my *sister*: Sir, said she to my brother, my master desires to speak with you this moment at the door.

He went to that which led into my sister's parlour; and this sentence I heard thundered from the mouth of one who had a right to all my reverence: Son James, let the rebel be this moment carried away to my brother's — this very moment — she shall not stay one hour more under my roof!

I trembled; I was ready to sink. Yet, not knowing what I did or said, I flew to the door, and would have opened it: but my brother pulled it to, and held it close by the key. O my papa! — my dear papa, said I, falling upon my knees at the door — admit your child to your presence! Let me but plead my cause at your feet! Oh, reprobate not thus your distressed daughter!

The door was endeavoured to be opened on the inside, which made my brother let go the key on a sudden; and I pressing against it (all the time remaining on my knees) fell flat on my face into the other parlour; however without hurting myself. But everybody was gone, except Betty, and when I was on my feet, I threw myself into the chair which I had sat in before; and my eyes overflowed, to my great relief: while my Uncle Antony, my brother, and Mr. Solmes left me, and went to my other relations.

What passed among them I know not: but my brother came in by the time I had tolerably recovered myself, with a settled and haughty gloom upon his brow. Your father and mother command you instantly to prepare for your Uncle Antony's. You need not be solicitous about what you shall take with you. You may give Betty your keys — take them, Betty, if the perverse one has them about her, and carry them to her mother. She will take care to send everything after you that you shall want — but another night you will not be permitted to stay in this house.

You see how much I am disordered. It may cost me my life, to be hurried away so suddenly. I beg to be indulged till next Monday at least.

That will not be granted you. So prepare for this very night. And give up your keys. Give them to *me*, miss. I'll carry them to your mother.

Excuse me, brother. Indeed, I won't.

Indeed you must. Have you anything you are afraid should be seen by your mother?

Not if I be permitted to attend her.

I'll make a report accordingly.

He went out.

In came Miss Dolly Hervey: I am sorry, madam, to be the messenger

— but your mamma insists upon your sending up all the keys of your cabinet, library, and drawers.

Tell my mother that I yield them up to her commands: tell her I make no conditions with my mother: but if she find nothing she shall disapprove of, I beg that she will permit me to tarry here a few days longer. Try, my Dolly (the dear girl sobbing with grief); try if your gentleness cannot prevail for me.

She wept still more, and said, It is sad, very sad, to see matters thus carried!

She took the keys, and wrapped her arms about me; and begged me to excuse her for her message; and would have said more; but Betty's presence awed her, as I saw.

Don't pity me, my dear, said I. It will be imputed to you as a fault. You see who is by.

The insolent wench scornfully smiled. It soon appeared for what she stayed; for I offering to go upstairs to my apartment when my cousin went from me with the keys, she told me she was commanded (to her very great regret, she must own) to desire me not to go up at present.

Such a bold face as she, I told her, should not hinder me. She instantly rang the bell, and in came my brother, meeting me at the door.

Return, return, miss — no going up yet.

I desired several times, while he stayed, to have leave to retire to my apartment; but was denied. The search, I suppose, was not over.

. . . .

My Aunt Hervey accosted me thus: O my dear child, what troubles do you give to your parents, and to everybody! I wonder at you!

I am sorry for it, madam.

Sorry for it, child! *Why* then so very obstinate! Come, sit down, my dear. I will sit next you; taking my hand.

My uncle placed Mr. Solmes on the other side of me: himself over against me, almost close to me. Was I not finely beset, my dear?

Your brother, child, said my aunt, is too passionate — his zeal for *your* welfare pushes him on a little too vehemently.

Very true, said my uncle: but no more of this. We would now be glad to see if milder means will do with you. Though, indeed, they were tried before.

I asked my aunt if it were necessary that that gentleman should be present?

There is a reason that he should, said my aunt, as you will hear by and by. I am to tell you, said my aunt, that the sending up your keys, without making any conditions, has wrought for you what nothing else could have done. That, and the not finding anything that could give them umbrage, together with Mr. Solmes's interposition ——

O madam, let me not owe an obligation to Mr. Solmes. I cannot repay it, except by my *thanks*; and *those* only on condition that he will decline his suit.

Your mother and Mr. Solmes, replied my aunt, have prevailed, that your request to stay here till Monday next shall be granted, if you promise to go cheerfully then.

Let me but choose my own visitors, and I will go to my uncle's house with pleasure.

Well, niece, said my aunt, we must waive this subject, I find. We will now proceed to another, which will require your utmost attention. It will give you the reason why Mr. Solmes's presence is requisite ——

Ay, said my uncle, and show you what sort of man somebody is. Mr. Solmes, pray favour us, in the first place, with the letter you received from your anonymous friend.

I will, sir. And out he pulled a letter-case, and, taking out a letter: It is written in answer to one sent to the person. It is superscribed, *To Roger Solmes, Esq.* It begins thus: *Honoured Sir* ——

I beg your pardon, sir, said I: but what, pray, is the intent of reading this letter to me?

To let you know what a vile man you are thought to have set your heart upon, said my uncle in an audible whisper.

If, sir, it be suspected, that I have set my heart upon any other, why is Mr. Solmes to give himself any further trouble about me?

Only hear, niece, said my aunt; only hear what Mr. Solmes has to read and to say to you on this head.

He began to read; and there seemed to be a heavy load of charges in this letter against the poor criminal: but I stopped the reading of it, and said: It will not be *my* fault, if this vilified man be not as indifferent to me as one whom I never saw.

Still — Proceed, Mr. Solmes — hear it out, niece, was my uncle's cry.

But to what purpose, sir? said I. Has not Mr. Solmes a *view* in this? And, besides, can anything worse be said of Mr. Lovelace, than I have heard said for several months past?

But this, said my uncle, and what Mr. Solmes can tell you besides, amounts to the *fullest proof* ——

Was the unhappy man, then, so freely treated in his character before, *without* full proof?

Permit me to observe further, that Mr. Solmes himself may not be absolutely faultless. I never heard of his virtues. Some vices I have heard of. Excuse me, Mr. Solmes, I speak to your face. The text about *casting the first stone* affords an excellent lesson.

What must be the man who *hates his own flesh*?

You know not, madam; ⎫
You know not, niece; ⎬ all in one breath.
You know not, Clary; ⎭

I may not, nor do I desire to know Mr. Solmes's reasons. It *concerns* not me to know them: but the world, even the impartial part of it, accuses him. If the world is unjust, or rash, in *one* man's case, why may it not be so in *another's*?

I should have absolutely silenced both gentlemen, had not my brother come in again to their assistance.

108

This was the strange speech he made at his entrance, his eyes flaming with anger: This prating girl has struck you all dumb, I perceive. Persevere, however, Mr. Solmes. I have heard every word she has said: and I know no other method of being even with her, than, after she is yours, to make her as sensible of your power as she now makes you of her insolence.

Fie, Cousin Harlowe! said my aunt. Could I have thought a *brother* would have said this to a gentleman, of a *sister*?

Not more unbrotherly than all the rest of his conduct to me, of late, madam, said I. I see by this specimen of his violence, how everybody has been brought into his measures.

I disclaim Mr. Harlowe's violence, madam, with all my soul. I will never remind you ——

Silence, worthy sir! said I; I will take care you never shall have the opportunity.

.   .   .   .

Mr. Solmes, after a little while, came in again by himself, to take leave of me: full of scrapes and compliments; but too well tutored and encouraged, to give me hope of his declining his suit. He begged me not to impute to him any of the severe things to which he had been a sorrowful witness. He besought my compassion, as he called it.

Am I to be cruel to myself, to show mercy to you? Take my estate, with all my heart, since you are such a favourite in this house! Only leave me *myself*. The mercy you ask for, do *you* show to others.

If you mean to my relations, madam — unworthy as they are, all shall be done that you shall prescribe.

Who, I, sir, to find you bowels you naturally have not? I to purchase *their* happiness by the forfeiture of *my own*? What I ask you for is mercy to myself.

I will risk all consequences, said the fell wretch, rising, with a countenance whitened over, as if with malice, his hollow eyes flashing fire, and biting his underlip, to show he could be *manly*. Your hatred, madam, shall be no objection with me: and I doubt not a few days to have it in my power to show you ——

You have it in your power, sir ——

He came well off. *To show you* more generosity than, noble as you are said to be to others, you show to me.

The man's face became his anger: it seems formed to express the passion.

I flung from him with high disdain: and he withdrew, bowing and cringing; self-satisfied, and enjoying, as I thought, the confusion he saw me in.

Upon his withdrawing, Betty brought me word that I was permitted to go up to my own chamber: and was bid to consider of everything: for my time was short. Nevertheless, she believed I might be permitted to stay till Saturday.

How lucky it was that I had got away my papers! They made a strict search for them

Wednesday, Eleven o'clock, April 5.

I must write as I have opportunity; making use of my concealed stores: for my pens and ink (all of each that they could find) are taken from me; as I shall tell you more particularly by and by.

About an hour ago, I deposited my long letter to you; as also, in the usual place, a billet to Mr. Lovelace, lest his impatience should put him upon some rashness; signifying, in four lines, that the interview was over; and that I hoped my steady refusal of Mr. Solmes would discourage any further applications to me in his favour.

My aunt, who (as well as Mr. Solmes and my two uncles) lives here, I think, came up to me, and said she would fain have me hear what Mr. Solmes had to say of Mr. Lovelace — only that what a vile man he is, and what a wretched husband he must make. I might give them what degree of credit I pleased; and take them with abatement for Mr. Solmes's interestedness, if I thought fit. But it might be of use to me, were it but to question Mr. Lovelace indirectly upon some of them that related to *myself*.

I was indifferent, I said, about what he could say of me; as I was sure it could not be to my disadvantage; and as *he* had no reason to impute to me the forwardness which my unkind friends had so causelessly taxed me with.

Well, but still, my dear, there can be no harm to let Mr. Solmes tell you what Mr. Lovelace has said of *you*. Severely as you have treated Mr. Solmes, he is fond of attending you once more: he begs to be heard on this head.

If it be proper for me to hear it, madam ——

It *is*, eagerly interrupted she, very proper.

Has what he has said of *me*, madam, convinced *you* of Mr. Lovelace's baseness?

It has, my dear: and that you ought to abhor him for it.

Then, dear madam, be pleased to let me hear it from *your* mouth: there is no need that I should see Mr. *Solmes*, when it will have double the weight from *you*. What, madam, has the man dared to say of *me*?

My aunt was quite at a loss.

At last: Well, said she, I see how you are attached. I am sorry for it, miss. For I do assure you it will signify nothing. You must be Mrs. Solmes; and that in a very few days.

I had scarcely recovered myself from this attack, when up came Betty. Miss, said she, your company is desired belowstairs in your own parlour.

Down I went: and to whom should I be sent for, but to my brother and Mr. Solmes? The latter standing sneaking behind the door, so that I saw him not, till I was mockingly led by the hand into the room by my brother. And then I started as if I had beheld a ghost.

You are to sit down, Clary.

And what then, brother?

Why then, you are to put off that scornful look, and hear what Mr. Solmes has to say to you.

Sent for to be baited again, thought I?

Madam, said Mr. Solmes, as if in haste to speak, lest he should not have opportunity given him (and indeed he judged right) Mr. Lovelace is a declared *marriage-hater*, and has a design upon your honour, if ever ——

Base accuser! said I, in a passion, snatching my hand from my brother, who was insolently motioning to give it to Mr. Solmes; he has not! he dares not! But *you* have, if endeavouring to force a free mind be to dishonour it!

O thou violent creature! said my brother. But not gone yet — for I was rushing away.

What mean you, sir (struggling vehemently to get away), to detain me thus against my will?

You shall not go, Violence; clasping his unbrotherly arms about me.

Then let not Mr. Solmes stay. Why hold you me thus? He shall not, for *your own* sake, if I can help it, see how barbarously a brother can treat a sister who deserves not evil treatment.

And I struggled so vehemently to get from him, that he was forced to quit my hand; which he did with these words: Begone then, Fury! How strong is will! There is no holding her.

And up I flew to my chamber, and locked myself in, trembling, and out of breath.

In less than a quarter of an hour, up came Betty.

Don't be angry with me, miss. But I must carry down your pen and ink: and that, this moment.

By whose order?

By your papa's and mamma's.

How shall I know that?

She offered to go to my closet: I stepped in before her: Touch it, if you dare.

Up came my Cousin Dolly. Madam! — madam! said the poor weeping good-natured creature, in broken sentences — you must — indeed you must — deliver to Betty — or to me — your pen and ink.

Must I, my sweet cousin? Then I will to you; but not to this bold body. And so I gave my standish to her.

I am sorry, very sorry, said miss, to be the messenger; but your papa will not have you in the same house with him: he is resolved you shall be carried away to-morrow, or Saturday at furthest. And therefore your pen and ink are taken away, that you may give nobody notice of it.

And away went the dear girl, very sorrowful, carrying down with her my standish, and all its furniture, and a little parcel of pens beside, which having been seen when the great search was made, she was bid to ask for.

All my dependence, all my hopes, are in your mother's favour. But for that, I know not *what* I might do: for who can tell what will come next?

Wednesday, Four o'clock in the Afternoon.

I FOUND in the usual place another letter from this diligent man: and by its contents, a confirmation that nothing passes in this house but he knows it.

He assures me that they are more and more determined to subdue me. But he repeats that, in all events, he will oppose my being carried to my uncle's; being well assured that I shall be lost to him for ever if once I enter into that house.

What a dangerous enterpriser, however, is this man!

Would but your mother permit you to send her chariot, or chaise, to the by-place where Mr. Lovelace proposes Lord M.'s shall come (provoked, intimidated, and apprehensive as I am) I would not hesitate a moment what to do. Place me anywhere, as I have said before — in a cot, in a garret; anywhere — disguised as a servant — or let me pass as a servant's sister — so that I may but escape Mr. Solmes on one hand, and the disgrace of refuging with the family of a man at enmity with my own on the other; and I shall be in some measure happy! Should your good mother refuse me, what refuge, or whose, can I fly to? Dearest creature, advise your distressed friend.

Wednesday Night.

All is in a hurry below-stairs. Betty is in and out like a spy. Something is working, I know not what. I am really a good deal disordered in body as well as mind. Indeed I am quite heartsick.

I will go down, though 'tis almost dark, on pretence of getting a little air and composure. Robert has my two former, I hope, before now: and I will deposit this, with Lovelace's enclosed, if I can, for fear of another search.

More dark hints thrown out by this saucy creature. Probably they arise from the information Mr. Lovelace says he has secretly permitted them to have of his resolution to prevent my being carried to my uncle's. / Your ever-affectionate and grateful / Cl. Harlowe.

Under the superscription, written with a pencil, after she went down: "My two former are not yet taken away — I am surprised — I hope you are well — I hope all is right betwixt your mother and you."

Thursday Morning, April 6.

I HAVE your three letters. Never was there a creature more impatient on the most interesting uncertainty than I was, to know the event of the interview between you and Solmes.

As to going to your uncle's, that you must not do if you can help it. Nor must you have Solmes, that's certain. For your reputation's sake therefore, as well as to prevent mischief, you must either live single or have Lovelace.

If you think of going to London, let me know; and I hope you will have *time* to allow me a further concert as to the manner of your getting away, and thither, and how to procure proper lodgings for you.

To obtain this *time* you must palliate a little, and come into some seeming compromise, if you cannot do otherwise. Driven as you are driven, it will be strange if you are not obliged to part with a few of your admirable punctilios.

You will observe from what I have written, that I have not succeeded with my mother.

I am extremely mortified and disappointed. We have had very strong debates upon it. But, besides the narrow argument of *embroiling ourselves with other people's affairs.* as above mentioned, she will have it that it is your duty to comply.

I think you should have written to your Cousin Morden the moment they had begun to treat you disgracefully. I shall be impatient to hear whether they will attempt to carry you to your uncle's.

. . . .

We have just now had another pull. Upon my word she is *excessively* — what shall I say? — *unpersuadable* — I must let her off with that soft word.

I think in my conscience you must take one of these two alternatives: either to consent to let us go to London together privately (in which case I will procure a vehicle and meet you at your appointment at the stile to which Lovelace proposes to bring his uncle's chariot); or to put yourself into the protection of Lord M. and the ladies of his family.

You have another, indeed, and that is, if you are absolutely resolved against Solmes, to meet and marry Lovelace directly.

Miss Clarissa Harlowe to Miss Howe

Thursday, April 6.

This kind protection was raised by my despair of other refuge, rather than by a reasonable hope: for why indeed should anybody embroil themselves for others when they can avoid it?

All my consolation is, as I have frequently said, that I have not, by my own inadvertence or folly, brought myself into this sad situation. Much less have you a right to be displeased with so prudent a mother; for not engaging herself so warmly in my favour as you wished she would.

Indeed, my dearest love (permit me to be very serious) I am afraid I am singled out (either for my own faults, or for the faults of my

113

family) to be a very unhappy creature! — *signally* unhappy! For see you not how irresistibly the waves of affliction come tumbling down upon me? Who knows what the justice of Heaven may inflict, in order to convince us that we are not out of the reach of misfortune; and to reduce us to a better reliance than we have hitherto presumptuously made?

．　．　．　．　．　．　．　．　．　．　．

I will return to a subject which I cannot fly from for ten minutes together — called upon especially as I am by your three alternatives stated in the conclusion of your last.

What appears to me upon the fullest deliberation, the most eligible, if I *must* be thus driven, is the escaping to London. But I would forfeit all my hopes of happiness in this life, rather than you should go away with me, as you rashly, though with the kindest intention, propose. If I could get safely thither, and be private, methinks I might remain absolutely independent of Mr. Lovelace, and at liberty either to make proposals to my friends, or, should they renounce me (and I had no other or better way) to make terms with him; supposing my Cousin Morden, on his arrival, were to join with my other relations. But they would *then* perhaps indulge me in my choice of a single life, on giving him up: the renewing to them this offer, when at my own liberty, will at least convince them that I was in earnest when I made it first: and, upon my word, I *would* stand to it, dear as you seem to think, when you are disposed to rally me, it would cost me, *to* stand to it.

But, alas! my dear, this, even *this* alternative, is not without difficulties which, to a spirit so little enterprising as mine, seem in a manner insuperable. These are my reflections upon it.

I am afraid, in the first place, that I shall not have time for the requisite preparations for an escape.

But were I even to get safely to London, I know nobody there but by name; and those the tradesmen to our family; who no doubt would be the first wrote to and engaged to find me out. And should Mr. Lovelace discover where I was, and he and my brother meet, what mischiefs might ensue between them, whether I were willing or not to return to Harlowe Place!

You say I should have written my Cousin Morden the moment I was treated disgracefully: but could I have believed that my friends would not have softened by degrees when they saw my antipathy to their Solmes?

MISS CLARISSA HARLOWE TO MISS HOWE

Thursday Night.

THE alarming hurry I mentioned under my date of last night, and Betty's saucy dark hints, come out to be owing to what I guessed they were; that is to say, to the private intimation Mr. Lovelace contrived our family should have of his insolent resolution (*insolent* I must call it) to prevent my being carried to my uncle's.

About six o'clock this evening, my aunt tapped at my door; for l was writing, and had locked myself in. I opened it; and she entering, thus delivered herself:

I come once more to visit you, my dear, to impart to you matters of the utmost concern to you, and to the whole family.

What, madam, is now to be done with me? said I, wholly attentive.

You will not be hurried away to your uncle's, child; let that comfort you. They see your aversion to go. You will not be obliged to go to your Uncle Antony's.

Hold, niece, said she. You must not give yourself too much joy upon the occasion neither. Don't be surprised, my dear. Why look you upon me, child, with so affecting an earnestness? But you must be Mrs. Solmes, for all that.

I was dumb.

She then told me that they had had undoubted information, that a certain desperate *ruffian* (I must excuse her that word, she said) had prepared armed men to waylay my brother and uncles, and seize me, and carry me off. Surely, she said, I was not consenting to a violence that might be followed by murder on one side or the other; perhaps on both.

I was still silent.

That therefore my father (still more exasperated than before) had changed his resolution as to my going to my uncle's; and was determined next Tuesday to set out thither *himself* with my mother; and that (for it was to no purpose to conceal a resolution so soon to be put in execution) — I must not dispute it any longer — on Wednesday I must give my hand — as they would have me.

She proceeded, that orders were already given for a licence: that the ceremony was to be performed in my own chamber, in presence of all my friends, except my father and mother; who would not return, nor see me, till all was over, and till they had a good account of my behaviour.

I was still dumb — only sighing, as if my heart would break.

Observing this, and that I only sat weeping, my handkerchief covering my face, and my bosom heaving ready to burst: What! no answer, my dear? Why so much *silent* grief?

My dear, you must have Mr. Solmes: indeed you must.

Indeed I never will! This, as I have said over and over, is not originally my father's will. Indeed I never will — and that is all I will say!

[*Wednesday is the day set for her marriage to Solmes. Clarissa begs for deferment, but is refused, her aunt bringing the decision.*]

Did I want, was the answer, to give the vilest of men an opportunity to put his murderous schemes into execution? It was time for them to put an end to my obstinacy (they were tired out with me) and to his hopes at once. And an end *should* be put on Tuesday or Wednesday next, at furthest; unless I would give my honour to comply with the condition upon which my aunt had been so good as to allow me a longer time.

I even stamped with impatience! I called upon her to witness, that I was guiltless of the consequence of this compulsion; this *barbarous* compulsion, I called it; let that consequence be what it would!

Having shaken off the impertinent Betty, I wrote to Mr. Lovelace, to let him know: That all that was threatened at my Uncle Antony's, was intended to be executed *here*. That I had come to a resolution to throw myself upon the protection *of either of his two aunts*, who would afford it me — in short, that my endeavouring to obtain leave on Monday to dine in the ivy summer-house, I would, if possible, meet him without the garden door, at two, three, four, or five o'clock on Monday afternoon, as I should be able. That in the meantime he should acquaint me, *whether I should hope for either of those ladies' protection*: and if I might, I absolutely insisted that *he should leave me with either, and go to London himself*, or *remain at Lord M.'s; nor offer to visit me, till I was satisfied that nothing could be done with my friends in an amicable way; and that I could not obtain possession of my own estate*, and leave to live upon it: and particularly, *that he should not hint marriage to me, till I consented to hear him upon that subject*. I added, that if he could prevail upon one of the Misses Montague to *favour me with her company on the road*, it would make me abundantly more easy in the thoughts of carrying into effect a resolution which I had not come to, although so driven, but with the utmost reluctance and concern; and which would throw such a slur upon my reputation in the eye of the world, as perhaps I should never be able to wipe off.

But, solicitous for your advice, and approbation too, if I *can* have it, I will put an end to this letter.

Adieu, my dearest friend, adieu!

MISS CLARISSA HARLOWE TO MISS HOWE

Friday Morning, Seven o'clock (*April* 7).

I UNHAPPILY overslept myself. I went to bed at about half an hour after two. I told the quarters till five; after which I dropped asleep, and awaked not till past six.

Eight o'clock.

The man, my dear, has got the letter! What a strange diligence! I wish he mean me well, that he takes so much pains! Yet, to be ingenuous, I must own that I should be displeased if he took less. I wish, however, he had been a hundred miles off! What an advantage have I given him over me!

Now the letter is out of my power, I have more uneasiness and regret than I had before. For, till now, I had a doubt whether it should or should not go: and now I think it ought *not* to have gone. And yet is there any other way than to do as I have done, if I would avoid Solmes? But what a giddy creature shall I be thought if I pursue the course to which this letter must lead me?

Friday, Eleven o'clock.

My aunt has made me another visit. She began what she had to say with letting me know that my friends are all persuaded that I still correspond with Mr. Lovelace; as is plain, she said, by hints and menaces he throws out, which show that he is apprised of several things that have passed between my relations and me, sometimes within a very little while after they have happened.

Although I approve not of the method he stoops to take to come at his intelligence, yet it is not prudent in me to clear myself by the ruin of the corrupted servant (although his vileness has neither my connivance nor approbation), since my doing so might occasion the detection of my own correspondence; and so frustrate all the hopes I have to avoid this Solmes. Yet it is not at all unlikely that this very agent of Mr. Lovelace acts a double part between my brother and him: how else can *our* family know (so *soon* too) his menaces upon the passages they hint at?

It was but too natural, my aunt said, for my friends to suppose that he had his intelligence (part of it at least) from me; who, thinking myself hardly treated, might complain of it, if not to him, to Miss Howe; which, perhaps, might be the same thing; for they knew Miss Howe spoke as freely of them as they could do of Mr. Lovelace; and must have the particulars she spoke of from somebody who knew what was done here. That this determined my father to bring the whole matter to a speedy issue, lest fatal consequences should ensue.

I perceive you are going to speak with warmth, proceeded she (*and so I was*). For my own part I am sure, you would not write anything, if you *do* write, to inflame so violent a spirit.

Friday, One o'clock.

I HAVE a letter from Mr. Lovelace, full of transports, vows, and promises. I will send it to you enclosed. You'll see how he engages in it for Lady Betty's protection, and for Miss Charlotte Montague's accompanying me. I have nothing to do but to persevere, he says, and prepare to receive the personal congratulations of his whole family.

But you'll see how he presumes upon my being *his*, as the consequence of throwing myself into that lady's protection.

However, I have replied to the following effect: That although I had given him room to expect, that I would put myself into the *protection of one of the ladies of his family*, yet as I have three days to come, between this and Monday, and as I still hope that my friends will relent, or that Mr. Solmes will give up a point they will find it impossible to carry; I shall not look upon myself as *absolutely bound by the appointment*: and expect therefore, if I recede, that I shall not again be called to account for it by him.

Friday, Six o'clock.

My aunt, who again stays all night, has just left me. She came to tell me the result of my friends' deliberations about me. It is this.

Next Wednesday morning they are all to be assembled: to wit, my father, mother, my uncles, herself, and my Uncle Hervey; my brother and sister of course: my good Mrs. Norton is likewise to be admitted: and Dr. Lewen is to be at hand, to exhort me, it seems, if there be occasion: but my aunt is not certain whether he is to be among them, or to tarry till called in.

What is hoped from me, she says, is that I will cheerfully, on Tuesday night, if not before, sign the articles; and so turn the succeeding day's solemn convention into a day of activity. I am to have the licence sent up, however, and once more the settlements, that I may see how much in earnest they are.

My dear, you will not offer any violence to your health? I hope God has given you more grace than to do that.

I hope he has, madam. But there is violence enough offered, and threatened, to affect my health; and so it will be found, without my needing to have recourse to any other, or to *artifice* either.

I'll only tell you one thing, my dear: and that is; ill or well, the ceremony will probably be performed before Wednesday night.

Friday, Nine o'clock.

I have been down, and already have another letter from Mr. Lovelace (*the man lives upon the spot, I think*) and I must write to him, either that I will or will not stand to my first resolution of escaping hence on Monday next. If I let him know that I will not (appearances so strong *against* him, and *for* Solmes, even stronger than when I made the appointment) will it not be justly deemed my own fault, if I am compelled to marry their odious man? And if any mischief ensue from Mr. Lovelace's rage and disappointment, will it not lie at my door? Yet he offers so fair!

He offers *to attend me directly to Lady Betty's*; or, if I had rather, *to my own estate*; and that my Lord M. shall protect me there. (He knows not, my dear, my reasons for rejecting this inconsiderate advice.) In either case, as soon as he sees me safe, he will go up to London, or whither I please; and not come near me, but by my own permission; and till I am satisfied in everything I am doubtful of, as well with regard to his reformation, as to settlements, etc.

To *conduct me to you,* my dear, is another of his proposals; not doubting, he says, but your mother will receive me.

Again, if it be more agreeable, he proposes *to attend me privately to London,* where he will procure handsome lodgings for me, and *both his Cousins Montague to receive me in them, and to accompany me till all should be adjusted to my mind*; and *till a reconciliation shall be effected*; which he assures me nothing shall be wanting in him to facilitate; greatly as he has been insulted by all my family.

These several measures he proposes to my choice; as it was unlikely, he says, that he could procure, *in the time,* a letter from Lady Betty, under her own hand, to invite me in form to her house, unless he had been himself to go to that lady for it; which, at this critical conjuncture, while he is attending my commands, is impossible.

In short, he solemnly vows that his *whole* view at present is to free me from my imprisonment; and to restore me to my own free will, in a point so absolutely necessary to my future happiness. He declares that neither the hopes he has of my future favour, nor the consideration of his own and family's honour, will permit him to propose anything *that shall be inconsistent with my own most scrupulous notions.*

Miss Clarissa Harlowe to Miss Howe
                                    Sat. Morn, 8 o'clock (April 8).

I HAVE deposited a letter confirming my resolution to leave this house on Monday next, within the hours mentioned in my former, if possible.

I tell him that I have no way to avoid the determined resolution of my friends in behalf of Mr. Solmes, but by abandoning this house by his assistance.

I have not pretended to make a merit with him on this score; for I plainly tell him: That could I, *without an unpardonable sin,* die when I *would,* I would sooner make death my choice than take a step which all the world, if not my own heart, will condemn me for taking.

I tell him that I shall not try to bring any other clothes with me than those I shall have on; and those but my common wearing apparel; lest I should be suspected. That I must expect to be denied the possession of my estate: but that I am determined never to consent to a litigation with my father, were I to be reduced to ever so low a state: so that the protection I am to be obliged for to any one must be alone for the distress sake. That, therefore, he will have nothing to hope for from this step, *that he had not before*: and that, in every light, I reserve to myself to *accept or refuse his address, as his behaviour and circumspection shall appear to me to deserve.*

I tell him: That I think it best to go into a private lodging, in the neighbourhood of Lady Betty Lawrance; and not to her ladyships' house; that it may not appear to the world, *that I have refuged myself in his family*; and that a reconciliation with my friends may not, on that account, be made impracticable: that I will send for thither my faithful Hannah; and apprise only Miss Howe where I am: that *he shall instantly leave me,* and go to London, or to one of Lord M.'s seats; and (as he had promised) not come near me, but by my leave; contenting himself with a correspondence by letter only.

That if I find myself in danger of being discovered, and carried back by violence, I will then throw myself directly into the protection either of Lady Betty or Lady Sarah: but *this is only in case of absolute necessity*; for that it will be more to my reputation, for me, by the best means I can (taking advantage of my privacy) to enter by a second or third hand *into a treaty of reconciliation with my friends.*

That I must, however, plainly tell him that if, in this treaty, my friends *insist upon my resolving against marrying him, I will engage to comply with them*; provided they will allow me to promise him *that I will never be the wife of any other man while he remains single, or is living*: that this is a compliment I am willing to pay him in return for the trouble and pains he has taken, and the usage he has met with on my account: Although I intimate that he may, in a great measure, thank himself (by reason of the little regard he has paid to his reputation) for the slights he has met with.

I added, by way of postscript: That their suspicions seeming to increase, I advise him to contrive to send or come to the usual place, as frequently as possible, in the interval of time till Monday morning ten or eleven o'clock; as something may possibly happen to make me alter my mind.

Saturday, Ten o'clock.

Mr. Solmes is here. He is to dine with his new relations, as Betty tells me he already calls them.

He would have thrown himself in my way once more: but I hurried up to my prison, in my return from my garden-walk, to avoid him.

I had, when in the garden, the curiosity to see if my letter were gone: I cannot say with an intention to take it back again if it were not, because I see not how I could do otherwise than I have done; yet, what a caprice! when I found it gone, I began (as yesterday morning) to wish it had not: for no other reason, I believe, than because it was out of my power.

A strange diligence in this man! He *says* he almost lives upon the place; and I think so too.

MISS HOWE TO MISS CLARISSA HARLOWE

Sat. Afternoon.

BY YOUR last date of ten o'clock in your letter of this day, you could not long have deposited it before Robin took it. He rode hard, and brought it to me just as I had risen from table.

I had been inquiring privately how to procure you a conveyance from Harlowe Place. I found more difficulty than I expected (as the time was confined, and secrecy required, and as you so earnestly forbid me to accompany you in your enterprise) in procuring you a vehicle. Had you not obliged me to keep measures with my mother, I could have managed it with ease. I could even have taken our own chariot, on one pretence or other, and put two horses extraordinary to it, if I had thought fit; and I could when we had got to London, have sent it back, and nobody the wiser as to the lodgings we might have taken.

I wish to the Lord you had permitted this. Indeed, I think you are too punctilious a great deal for your situation. Would you expect to enjoy yourself with your usual placidness, and not be ruffled, in a hurricane which every moment threatens to blow your house down?

You are angry with me for proposing such a step. Only be so good as to encourage me to resume it, if, upon further consideration, and upon weighing matters well (and in *this* light, whether best to go off with *me* or with *Lovelace*), you can get over your punctilious regard for my reputation. A woman going away with a *woman* is not so discreditable a thing, surely! and with no view but to *avoid the fellows!*

But one thing, in your present situation and prospects, let me advise: it is this: That if you *do* go off with Mr. Lovelace, you take the first opportunity to marry. Why should you *not,* when everybody will know by *whose* assistance, and in *whose* company, you leave your father's house, go whithersoever you will? You may indeed keep him at a distance until settlements are drawn, and such-like matters are adjusted to your mind: but even these are matters of less consideration in your particular case than they would be in that of most others.

It is therefore my absolute opinion that, if you *do* withdraw with him (and in that case you must let *him* be judge, when he can leave you with safety, *you'll observe that*) you should not postpone the ceremony.

Give this matter your most serious consideration. Punctilio is out of doors the moment you are out of your father's house.

I hurried myself in writing this; and I hurry Robin away with it, that in a situation so very critical, you may have all the time possible to consider what I have written upon two points so very important. I will repeat them in a very few words:

"Whether you choose not rather to go off with one of *your own sex*; with your ANNA HOWE — than with one of the *other*; with Mr. LOVELACE?"

And if *not,*

"Whether you should not marry him as soon as possible?"

MISS CLARISSA HARLOWE TO MISS HOWE

(*The preceding letter not received*)   *Saturday afternoon.*

ALREADY have I an ecstatic answer, as I may call it, to my letter.

He promises compliance with my will in every article: approves of all I propose; particularly of the private lodging: and thinks it a happy expedient to obviate the censures of the busy and the unreflecting: and yet he hopes that the putting myself into the protection of either of his aunts (treated as I am treated) would be far from being looked upon by anybody in a disreputable light.

He is afraid that the time will hardly allow of his procuring Miss Charlotte Montague's attendance upon me at St. Albans, as he had proposed she should; because, he understands, she keeps her chamber with a violent cold and sore throat. But both she and her sister, the first moment she is able to go abroad, shall visit me at my private lodgings; and introduce me to Lady Sarah and Lady Betty, or those ladies to me, as I shall choose; and accompany me to town, if I please; and stay as long in it with me as I shall think fit to stay there.

. . . .

After all, far as I have gone, I know not but I may still recede: and if I do, a mortal quarrel I suppose will ensue. And what if it does? Could there be any way to escape this Solmes, a breach with Lovelace might make way for the single life to take place, which I so much prefer.

What to do I know not. The more I think, the more I am embarrassed — and the stronger will be my doubts as the appointed time draws near.

MISS CLARISSA HARLOWE TO MISS HOWE

Sunday Morning, April 9.

Do NOT think, my beloved friend, although you have given me in yours of yesterday a *severer* instance of what, nevertheless, I must call your *impartial* love, than ever yet I received from you, that I will be displeased with you for it. That would be to put myself into the inconvenient situation of royalty: that is to say, *out of the way* of ever being told of my faults; of ever mending them; and *in the way* of making the sincerest and warmest friendship useless to me.

But now I come to the two points in your letter which most sensibly concern me: thus you put them:

"Whether I choose not rather to go off (shocking words!) with one of my *own sex*; with my ANNA HOWE — than with one of the *other*; with Mr. LOVELACE?"

And if *not*,

"Whether I should not marry him as soon as possible?"

You know, my dear, my reasons for rejecting your proposal, and even for being earnest that you should not be *known* to be assisting me in an enterprise in which a cruel necessity induced *me* to think of engaging; and for which *you* have not the same plea. At this rate, *well* might your mother be uneasy at our correspondence, not knowing to what inconveniences it might subject her and you!

But, my dearest, kindest friend, let me tell you that we will *neither* of us take such a step. The manner of putting your questions abundantly convinces me that I ought not, in *your* opinion, to *attempt* it. You no doubt *intend* that I shall *so* take it; and I thank you for the equally polite and forcible conviction.

It is some satisfaction to me (taking the matter in this light) that

I had begun to waver before I received your last. And now I tell you that it has absolutely determined me *not* to go off; at least, not to-morrow.

But how, on this revocation of my appointment, shall I be able to pacify him?

How? Why assert the privilege of my sex! Surely, on *this* side of the solemnity he has no *right* to be displeased. Besides, did I not reserve a power of receding if I saw fit?

I resolve then, upon the whole, to stand this one trial of Wednesday next — or, perhaps I should rather say, of Tuesday evening, if my father hold his purpose of endeavouring, in person, to make me *read*, or *hear* read, and then *sign*, the settlements. *That, that* must be the greatest trial of all.

Forgive these indigested self-reasonings. I will close here: and instantly set about a letter of revocation to Mr. Lovelace; take it as he will. It will only be another trial of temper to *him*. To *me* of infinite importance. And has he not promised temper and acquiescence on the supposition of a change in my mind?

MISS CLARISSA HARLOWE TO MISS HOWE

Sunday Morning, April 9.

NOBODY, it seems, will go to church this day. No blessing to be expected perhaps upon views so worldly, and in some so cruel.

They have a mistrust that I have some device in my head. Betty has been looking among my clothes. I found her, on coming up from depositing my letter to Lovelace(for I *have* written!) peering among them; for I had left the key in the lock. She coloured, and was confounded to be caught. But I only said I should be accustomed to *any* sort of treatment in time. If she had her orders — those were enough for her.

She owned, in her confusion, that a motion had been made to abridge me of my airings; and the report *she* should make, would be of no disadvantage to me. One of my friends, she told me, urged in my behalf that there was no need of laying me under greater restraint, since Mr. Lovelace's threatening to *rescue* me by violence, were I to have been carried to my uncle's, was a conviction that I had no design to go to him voluntarily; and that if I *had,* I should have made preparations of that kind *before now*; and, most probably, been detected in them. *Hence,* it was also inferred that there was no room to doubt but I would at last comply.

This is the substance of my letter to Mr. Lovelace:

That I have reasons of the greatest consequence to *myself* (and which, when known, must satisfy *him*) to suspend, for the present, my intention of leaving my father's house: that I have hopes that matters may be brought to a happy conclusion without taking a step which nothing but the last necessity could justify: and that he may depend upon my promise that I will die rather than consent to marry Mr. Solmes.

Sunday Evening, Seven o'clock.

There remains my letter still! He is busied, I suppose, in his preparations for to-morrow. But then he has servants. Does the man think he is so *secure* of me, that having appointed he need not give himself any further concern about me till the very moment? He knows how I am beset. He knows not what may happen. I *might* be ill, or still more closely watched or confined than before. The correspondence *might* be discovered. It *might* be necessary to vary the scheme. I *might* be forced into measures which might entirely frustrate my purpose. I *might* have new doubts. I *might* suggest something more convenient for anything he knew. What can the man mean, I wonder!

Monday Morn., April 10, Seven o'clock.

O my dear! There yet lies the letter, just as I left it!

Does he think he is so sure of me?

I was half inclined to resume my former intention; especially as my countermanding letter was not taken away; and as my heart ached at the thoughts of the conflict I must expect to have with him on my refusal. For see him for a few moments I doubt I must, lest he should take some rash resolutions; especially as he has reason to expect I will see him. But here your words, *that all punctilio is at an end the moment I am out of my father's house,* added to the still more cogent considerations of duty and reputation, determined me once more against taking the rash step.

Miss Clarissa Harlowe to Miss Howe

Ivy Summer-house, Eleven o'clock.

He has not yet got my letter: and while I was contriving here how to send my officious jaileress from me, that I might have time for the intended reviewer, and had hit upon an expedient which I believe would have done, came my aunt, and furnished me with a much better. She saw my little table covered, preparative to my solitary dinner; and hoped, she told me, that this would be the last day that my friends would be deprived of my company at table.

I am come, I doubt, upon a very unwelcome errand. Some things that have been told us yesterday, which came from the mouth of one of the most desperate and insolent men in the world, convince your father, and all of us, that you still find means to write out of the house. Mr. Lovelace knows everything that is done here; and that as soon as done; and great mischief is apprehended from him, which you are as much concerned as anybody to prevent. Your mother cannot be easy, nor will be permitted to be easy, if she would, unless (while you remain here in the garden or in this summer-house) you give her the opportunity once more of looking into your closet, your cabinet, and drawers. It will be the better taken if you give me cheerfully your keys. I hope, my dear, you won't dispute it. Your desire of dining in this place was the more readily complied with for the sake of such an opportunity.

Some papers they will find, I doubt: but I must take consequences. My brother and sister will be at hand with their good-natured constructions. I am made desperate, and care not what is found.

I hope, I *earnestly* hope, said she, that nothing can be found that will impeach your discretion; and then — but I may say too much ——

And away she went, having added to my perplexity.

But I now can think of nothing but this interview. Would to Heaven it were over! To meet to quarrel — but, let him take what measures he will, I will not stay a *moment* with him if he be not quite calm and resigned.

But, after all, should I, *ought* I, to meet him? How have I taken it for granted that I should!

Here comes Betty Barnes with my dinner.

· · · · · · · · · ·

The wench is gone. The time of meeting is at hand. Oh, that he may not come! But should I, or should I not, meet him? How I question, without possibility of a timely answer!

Betty, according to my leading hint to my aunt, boasted to me that she was to be *employed*, as she called it, after she had eat her own dinner.

She should be sorry, she told me, to have me found out. Yet 'twould be all for my good. She begged my excuse — but — but — and then the saucy creature laughed again, she could not help it; to think how I had drawn myself in by my summer-house dinnering; since it had given so fine an opportunity, by way of surprise, to look into all my private hoards. She thought *something was in the wind* when my brother came in to my dining here so readily. Her young master was too hard for everybody. Squire Lovelace himself was nothing at all at a quick thought to her young master.

I dare say we shall be all to pieces. But I don't care for that. It would be hard if I, who have held it out so sturdily to my father and uncles, should not — but he is at the garden door ——

· · · · · · · · · ·

I was mistaken! How may noises *unlike* be made *like* what one fears! Why flutters the fool so!

· · · · · · · · · ·

I will hasten to deposit this. Then I will, for the last time, go to the usual place, in hopes to find that he has got my letter. If he *has,* I will not meet him. If he has *not* I will take it back, and show him that I have written. That will break the ice, as I may say, and save me much circumlocution and reasoning: and a steadfast adherence to that my written mind is all that will be necessary. The interview must be as short as possible; for should it be discovered it would furnish a new and strong pretence for the intended evil of Wednesday next.

Perhaps I shall not be able to write again one while. Perhaps not, till I am the miserable property of that Solmes! But that shall never, never be while I have my senses.

If your servant find nothing from me by Wednesday morning, you may conclude that I can then neither write to you nor receive your favours.

In that case pity and pray for me, my beloved friend, and continue to me that place in your affection which is the pride of my life and the only concern left to / Your / CL. HARLOWE.

MISS CLARISSA HARLOWE TO MISS HOWE

St. Albans, Tuesday Morn., past One.

O MY DEAREST FRIEND! — After what I had resolved upon, as by my former, what shall I write? What *can* I? With what consciousness, even by *letter,* do I approach you! You will soon hear (if already you have not heard from the mouth of common fame) that your Clarissa Harlowe is gone off with a man!

I am busying myself to give you the particulars at large. The whole twenty-four hours of each day (to begin the moment I can fix) shall be employed in it till it is finished: every one of the hours, I mean, that will be spared me by this interrupting man, to whom I have made myself so foolishly accountable for too many of them. Rest is departed from me. I have no call for that: and that has no balm for the wounds of my mind. So you'll have all those hours without interruption till the account is ended.

But will you receive, shall you be *permitted* to receive, my letters after what I have done?

O, my dearest friend! But I must make the best of it. I hope that will not be very bad! Yet am I convinced that I did a rash and inexcusable thing in meeting him; and all his tenderness, all his vows, cannot pacify my inward reproaches on that account.

The bearer comes to you, my dear, for the little parcel of linen which I sent you with far better and more agreeable hopes.

Send not my letters. Send the linen only: except you will favour me with one line, to tell me you love me still; and that you will suspend your censures till you have the whole before you. I am the readier to send thus early because if you have deposited anything for me you may cause it to be taken back, or withhold anything you had but intended to send.

MISS HOWE TO MISS CLARISSA HARLOWE

Tuesday, Nine o'clock.

I WRITE because you enjoin me to do so. Love you still! — how can I help it if I would? You may believe how I stand aghast, your letter communicating the first news. Good God of heaven and earth! — but what shall I say? I am all impatience for particulars.

My mother will *indeed* be astonished! How can I tell it her? It was but last night that I assured her, and this upon the strength of your *own* assurances, that neither man nor devil would be able to induce you to take a step that was in the least derogatory to the most punctilious honour.

Let nothing escape you in your letters. Direct them for me, however, to Mrs. Knollys's, till further notice.

.   .   .   .

Observe, my dear, that I don't blame *you* by all this — your relations only are in fault! Yet how you came to change your mind is the surprising thing.

How to break it to my mother I know not. Yet, if she hear it first from any other, and find I knew it before, she will believe it to be by my connivance! Yet, as I hope to live, I know not how to break it to her.

But this is teasing you. I am sure without intention.

Let me now repeat my former advice. If you are *not* married by this time, be sure delay not the ceremony. Since things are as they are, I wish it were thought that you were privately married before you went away.

.   .   .   .

Miss Lloyd and Miss Biddulph this moment send up their names. They are out of breath, Kitty says, to speak to me — easy to guess their errand! I must see my mother before I see them. I have no way to show her your letter to clear myself. I shall not be able to say a word till she has run herself out of her first breath.

I send what you write for. If there be anything else you want that is in my power, command without reserve / You ever affectionate / ANNA HOWE.

MISS CLARISSA HARLOWE TO MISS HOWE

Tuesday Night.

I THINK myself obliged to thank you, my dear Miss Howe, for your condescension in taking notice of a creature who has occasioned you so much scandal.

.   .   .   .

After I had deposited my letter to you, written down to the last hour, as I may say, I returned to the ivy summer-house; first taking back my letter from the loose bricks. I began to hope that I needed not to be so very apprehensive as I have been of next Wednesday. And thus I argued with myself:

Wednesday cannot possibly be the day they intend, although to intimidate me they may wish me to think it is: for the settlements are unsigned: nor have they been offered me to sign. I can choose whether I will or will not put my hand to them; hard as it will be to refuse if my father tender them to me — besides, did not my father and mother propose, if I made compulsion necessary, to go to my uncle's themselves, in order to be out of the way of my appeals? Whereas they intend to be present on Wednesday. And however affecting to me the thought of meeting them and all my friends in full assembly is, perhaps it is the very thing I ought to wish for: since my brother and sister had such an opinion of my interest in them that they got me excluded from their presence, as a measure which they thought previously necessary to carry on their designs.

Then, supposing the very worst, challenging the minister as I shall challenge him, he will not presume to proceed: nor surely will Mr. Solmes dare to accept my refusing and struggling hand. And finally, if nothing else will do, nor procure me delay, I can plead scruples of conscience, and even pretend prior obligation; for, my dear, I have given Mr. Lovelace room to hope (as you will see in one of my letters in your hands) that I will be no other man's while he is single, and gives me not wilful and premeditated cause of offence against him; and this in order to rein in his resentments on the declared animosity of my brother and uncles to him. And as I shall appeal, or refer my scruples on this head, to the good Dr. Lewen, it is impossible but that my mother and aunt (if nobody else) must be affected with this plea.

Revolving cursorily these things, I congratulated myself that I had resolved against going away with Mr. Lovelace.

As the above kind of reasoning had lessened my apprehensions as to the Wednesday, it added to those I had of meeting Mr. Lovelace — now, as it seemed, not only the nearest but the heaviest evil; principally indeed because *nearest*; for little did I dream (foolish creature that I was, and every way beset!) of the event proving what it has proved.

On what a point of time may one's worldly happiness depend! Had I had but two hours more to consider of the matter, and to attend to and improve upon these new lights, as I may call them. But even then, perhaps, I might have given him a meeting. Fool that I was! what had I to do to give him hope that I would *personally* acquaint him with the reason for my change of mind, if I did change it?

When the bell rang to call the servants to dinner, Betty came to me and asked if I had any commands before she went to hers; repeating her hint that she should be *employed*; adding that she believed it was expected that I should not come up till she came down, or till I saw my aunt or Miss Hervey.

I asked her some questions about the cascade, which had been out of order, and lately mended; and expressed a curiosity to see how it played, in order to induce her (how cunning to cheat myself, as it proved!) to go thither if she found me not where she left me; it being at a part of the garden most distant from the ivy summer-house.

She could hardly have got into the house when I heard the first signal — Oh, how my heart fluttered! But no time was to be lost. I stepped to the garden door; and seeing a clear coast, unbolted the already unlocked door. And there was he, all impatience, waiting for me.

Fear nothing, dearest creature, said he. Let us hasten away — the chariot is at hand and, by this sweet condescension, you have obliged me beyond expression or return.

Recovering my spirits a little, as he kept drawing me after him, O Mr. Lovelace, said I, I cannot go with you — *indeed* I cannot — I wrote you word so — let go my hand and you shall see my letter. It has lain there from yesterday morning till within this half-hour. I bid you watch to the last for a letter from me, lest I should be obliged to revoke the appointment; and had you followed the direction you would have found it.

I have been watched, my dearest life, said he, half out of breath — I have been watched in every step I took: and my trusty servant has been watched too, ever since Saturday; and dared not to come near your wall. And here we shall be discovered in a moment. Speed away, my charmer — this is the moment of your deliverance — if you neglect this opportunity you *never* can have such another.

What is it you mean, sir? Let go my hand: for I tell you (struggling vehemently) that I will sooner die than go with you.

Good God! said he, with a look of wildness and surprise, what is it I hear! But (still drawing me after him as he retreated farther from the door) it is no time to argue — by all that's good you must go. Surely you cannot doubt my honour, nor give me cause to question your own.

As you value me, Mr. Lovelace, urge me no farther. I come fixed and resolved. Let me give you the letter I had written. My further reasons shall follow; and they will convince you that I ought not to go.

Nothing, madam, can convince me. By all that's sacred I will not leave you. To leave you now would be to lose you for ever ——

Am I to be thus compelled? interrupted I, with equal indignation and vehemence. Let go my hands. I am resolved not to go with you — and I will convince you that I *ought* not.

All my friends expect you, madam — all your own are determined against you. Wednesday next is the day, the important, perhaps the fatal day! Would you stay to be Solmes's wife? Can this be your determination at last?

No, never, never, will I be that man's — but I will not go with you! (Draw me not thus — how dare you, sir? I would not have seen you but to tell you so.) I had not met you but for fear you would have been guilty of some rashness. And, once more, I will *not* go. What mean you! — striving with all my force to get from him.

I see how it is, said he, with a dejected but passionate air. What a severe fate is mine! At length your spirit is subdued! Your brother and sister have prevailed; and I must give up all my hopes to a wretch so *truly* despicable ——

Once more I tell you, interrupted I, I never will be his. All may end on Wednesday differently from what you expect ——

And it may *not*. And then, good Heaven! ——

It is to be their last effort, as I have reason to believe ——

And I have reason to believe so too — since, if you stay, you will inevitably be Solmes's wife.

Not so, interrupted I. I have obliged them in one point. They will be in good humour with me. I shall gain time at least. I am sure I shall. I have several ways to gain time.

And what, madam, will gaining time do? It is plain you have not a hope beyond that. It is plain you have not, by putting all upon that precarious issue. O my dearest, dearest life! let me beseech you not to run a risk of this consequence. I can convince you that it will be *more* than a risk if you go back, that you will on Wednesday's next be Solmes's wife. Prevent therefore, now that it is in your power to prevent, the fatal mischiefs that will allow such a dreadful certainty.

While I have any room for hope it concerns *your* honour, Mr. Lovelace, as well as mine (if you have the value for me you pretend, and wish me to believe you), that my conduct in this great point should justify my prudence.

Your prudence, madam! When has that been questionable? Yet what stead has either your prudence or your duty stood you in with people so strangely determined?

Urge me no more, Mr. Lovelace, I conjure you. You yourself have given me a hint, which I will speak plainer to than prudence, perhaps, on any other occasion, would allow. I am convinced that Wednesday next (if I had time I would give you my reasons) is not intended to be the day we had both so much dreaded: and if after that day shall be over I find my friends determined in Mr. Solmes's favour, I will then contrive some way to meet you with Miss Howe, who is not your enemy: and when the solemnity has passed I shall think that step a duty which *till* then will be criminal to take: since now my father's authority is unimpeached by any greater.

Dearest madam ——

Nay, Mr. Lovelace, if you now dispute — if, after this more favourable declaration than I had the thought of making, you are not satisfied, I shall know what to think both of your gratitude and generosity.

The case, madam, admits not of this alternative. I am all gratitude upon it. I cannot express how much I should be delighted with the charming hope you have given me, were you not next Wednesday, if you stay, to be another man's. Think, dearest creature! what an heightening of my anguish the distant hope you bid me look up to is, taken in this light!

Depend, depend upon it, I will die sooner than be Mr. Solmes's. If you would have me rely upon *your* honour, why should you doubt of *mine*?

I doubt not your *honour*, madam; your *power* is all I doubt. You

130

never, never can have such another opportunity. Dearest creature, permit me. And he was again drawing me after him.

Whither, sir, do you draw me? Leave me this moment. Do you seek to keep me till my return shall grow dangerous or impracticable? This moment let me go if you would have me think tolerably of you.

My happiness, madam, both here and hereafter, and the safety of all your implacable family, depend upon this moment.

To Providence, Mr. Lovelace, and to the law, will I leave the safety of my friends. You shall not threaten me into a rashness that my heart condemns! Shall *I*, to promote your happiness, as you call it, destroy all my future peace of mind?

I will obey you, my dearest creature! — and quitted my hand with a look full of tender despondency, that, knowing the violence of his temper, half-concerned me for him. Yet I was hastening from him when, with a solemn air, looking upon his sword, but catching, as it were, his hand from it, he folded both his arms, as if a sudden thought had recovered him from an intended rashness.

Stay one moment — but one moment stay, O best beloved of my soul! Your retreat is secure, if you *will* go: the key lies down at the door. But, O madam, next *Wednesday*, and you are Mr. Solmes's! Fly me not so eagerly — hear me but a few words.

When near the garden door I stopped; and was the more satisfied, as I saw the key there, by which I could let myself in again at pleasure. But, being uneasy lest I should be missed, I told him I could stay no longer. I had already stayed too long. I would write to him all my reasons. And depend upon it, Mr. Lovelace, said I (just upon the point of stooping for the key, in order to return) I will die rather than have that man. You know what I have promised if I find myself in danger.

One word, madam, however; one word more (approaching me, his arms still folded, as if, I thought, he would not be tempted to mischief). Remember only that I come at your appointment, to redeem you, at the hazard of my life, from your jailers and persecutors, with a resolution, God is my witness, or may He for ever blast me! (that was his shocking imprecation) to be a father, uncle, brother, and, as I humbly hoped, in your own good time, a *husband* to you, all in one. But since I find you are so ready to cry out for help against me, which must bring down upon me the vengeance of all your family, I am contented to run all risks. I will not ask you to retreat with *me*; I will attend you into the garden, and into the *house*, if I am not intercepted. Nay, be not surprised, madam. The help you would have called for, I will attend you to; for I will face them all: but not as a revenger, if they provoke me not too much. You shall see what I can further bear for your sake. And let us both see if expostulation, and the behaviour of a gentleman *to* them, will not procure me the treatment due to a gentleman *from* them.

Had he offered to draw his sword upon himself I was prepared to have despised him for supposing me such a poor novice as to be intimidated by an artifice so common. But this resolution, uttered with so serious an air, of accompanying me in to my friends, made me gasp with terror.

What mean you, Mr. Lovelace? said I: I beseech you leave me — leave me, sir, I beseech you.

Excuse me, madam! I beg you to excuse me. I have long enough skulked like a thief about these lonely walls. Long, too long, have I borne the insults of your brother, and other of your relations. Absence but heightens malice. I am desperate. I have but this one chance for it; for is not the day after to-morrow *Wednesday*? I have encouraged virulence by my tameness. Yet *tame* I will still be. You shall see, madam, what I will bear for your sake. My sword shall be put sheathed into your hands (and he offered it to me in the scabbard). My heart, if you please, clapping one hand upon his breast, shall afford a sheath to your brother's sword. Life is nothing if I lose you. Be pleased, madam, to show me the way into the garden; (moving towards the door). I will attend you, though to my fate! But too happy, be it what it will, if I receive it in your presence. Lead on, dear creature! (putting his sword into his belt) — you shall see what I can bear for you. And he stooped and took up the key; and offered it to the lock; but dropped it again, without opening the door, upon my earnest expostulations.

What can you mean, Mr. Lovelace? said I. Would you thus expose *yourself*? Would you thus expose *me*? Is this your generosity? Is everybody to take advantage thus of the weakness of my temper? And I wept. I could not help it.

He threw himself upon his knees at my feet. Who can bear, said he (with an ardour that could not be feigned, his own eyes glistening), who can bear to behold such sweet emotion? O charmer of my heart (and, respectfully still kneeling, he took my hand with both his, pressing it to his lips), command me *with* you, command me *from* you; in every way I am all implicit obedience. O my beloved creature! pressing my hand once more to his lips, let not such an opportunity slip. You never, never, will have such another.

I bid him rise. He arose; and I told him that were I not thus unaccountably hurried by his impatience, I doubted not to convince him that both he and I had looked upon next Wednesday with greater apprehension than was necessary. I was proceeding to give him my reasons; but he broke in upon me ——

Had I, madam, but the shadow of a probability to hope what *you* hope, I would be all obedience and resignation. But the licence is actually got: the parson is provided: the pedant Brand is the man. O my dearest creature, do these preparations mean only a trial?

You know not, sir, were the worst to be intended, and weak as you think me, what a spirit I have: you know not what I can do, and how I can resist when I think myself meanly or unreasonably dealt with: nor do you know what I have already suffered, what I have already borne, knowing to whose unbrotherly instigations all is to be ascribed ——

I may expect all things, madam, interrupted he, from the nobleness of your mind.

I was sure, I said, of procuring a delay at least. Many ways I had to procure delay. Nothing could be so fatal to us both as for me now to be found with him. My apprehensions on this score, I told him, grew too strong for my heart. I should think very hardly of him if he sought to detain me longer. But his acquiescence should engage my gratitude.

And then stooping to take up the key to let myself into the garden, he started, and looked as if he had heard somebody near the door, on the inside; clapping his hand on his sword.

This frightened me so that I thought I should have sunk down at his feet. But he instantly reassured me: he thought, he said, he had heard a rustling against the door: but *had* it been so the noise would have been stronger. It was only the effect of his apprehension for me.

And then taking up the key, he presented it to me. If you *will* go, madam — yet I cannot, cannot leave you! I must enter the garden with you — forgive me, but I *must* enter the garden with you.

And will you, will you thus ungenerously, Mr. Lovelace, take advantage of my fears? — of my wishes to prevent mischief? I, vain fool, to be concerned for every one: nobody for me!

Dearest creature! interrupted he, holding my hand as I tremblingly offered to put the key to the lock. Let *me*, if you *will go*, open the door. But once more consider, could you possibly obtain that delay which seems to be your only dependence, whether you may not be closer confined? I know they have already had *that* in consideration. Will you not, in this case, be prevented from corresponding either with Miss Howe or with me? Who then shall assist you in your escape, if escape you would? From your chamber window only permitted to view the garden you must not enter into, how will you wish for the opportunity you now have, if your hatred to Solmes continue? But, alas! that cannot continue. If you go back it must be from the impulses of a yielding (which you'll call a dutiful) heart, tired and teased out of your own will.

And then, freeing my hand, I again offered the key to the door.

Down the ready kneeler dropped between me and that: And can you, can you, madam, once more on my knees let me ask you, look with an indifferent eye upon the evils that may follow? Provoked as I have been, and triumphed over as I shall be if your brother succeeds, my *own* heart shudders, at times, at the thoughts of what *must* happen; and can *yours* be unconcerned?

I was once more offering the key to the lock when, starting from his knees, with a voice of affrightment, loudly whispering, as if out of breath, *They are at the door, my beloved creature!* And taking the key from me, he fluttered with it, as if he would double-lock it. And instantly a voice from within cried out, bursting against the door, as if to break it open, the person repeating his violent pushes: *Are you there? Come up this moment! — this moment! Here they are — here they are both together! Your pistol this moment! — your gun!*

Then another push, and another. He at the same moment drew his sword, and clapping it naked under his arm, took both my trembling hands in his; and, drawing me swiftly after him: Fly, fly, my charmer; this moment is all you have for it, said he. Your brother! — your uncles! — or this Solmes! They will instantly burst the door. Fly, my dearest life, if you would not be more cruelly used than ever — if you would not see two or three murders committed at your feet, fly, fly, I beseech you.

Now behind me, now before me, now on this side, now on that, turned I my affrighted face in the same moment; expecting a furious brother here, armed servants there, an enraged sister screaming, and a father armed with terror in his countenance more dreadful than even the drawn sword which I saw, or those I apprehended. I ran as fast as he; yet knew not that I ran; my fears adding wings to my feet, at the same time that they took all power of thinking from me. My fears, which probably would not have suffered me to know what course to take, had I not had him to urge and draw me after him: especially as I beheld a man, who must have come out of the door, keeping us in his eye, running now towards us; then back to the garden; beckoning and calling to others, whom I supposed *he* saw, although the turning of the wall hindered *me* from seeing them; and whom I imagined to be my brother, my father, and their servants.

Thus terrified, I was got out of sight of the door in a very few minutes: and then, although quite breathless between running and apprehension, he put my arm under his, his drawn sword in the other hand, and hurried me on still faster: my voice, however, contradicting my action; crying, No, no, no, all the while, straining my neck to look back, as long as the walls of the garden and park were within sight, and till he brought me to the chariot: where, attending, were two armed servants of his own, and two of Lord M.'s, on horseback.

Here I must suspend my relation for a while: for now I am come to this sad period of it my indiscretion stares me in the face; and my shame and my grief give me a compunction that is more poignant methinks than if I had a dagger in my heart. To have it to reflect, that I should so inconsiderately give in to an interview which, had I known either myself or him, or in the least considered the circumstances of the case, I might have supposed would put me into the power of his resolution, and out of that of my own reason.

For, might I not have believed that *he*, who thought he had cause to apprehend that he was on the point of losing a person who had cost him so much pains and trouble, would not hinder her, if possible, from returning? That he, who knew I had promised to give him up for ever if insisted on as a condition of reconciliation, would not endeavour to put it out of my power to do so?

But if it shall come out that the person within the garden was his corrupted implement, employed to frighten me away with him, do you think, my dear, that I shall not have reason to hate him and myself still more? I hope his heart cannot be so deep and so vile a one: I hope it cannot! But how came it to pass that one man could get out at the garden door, and no more? How that that man kept aloof, as it were, and pursued us not; nor ran back to alarm the house? My fright and my distance would not let me be certain; but really this man, as I now recollect, had the air of that vile Joseph Leman.

. . . .

You know, my dear, that your Clarissa's mind was ever above justifying her own failings by those of others. God forgive those of my friends who have acted cruelly by me! But their faults *are* their own, and not excuses for mine. And mine began early: for I ought not to have corresponded with him.

O the vile encroacher! how my indignation, at times, rises at him! Thus to lead a young creature (too much indeed relying upon her own strength) from evil to evil! This last evil, although the *remote* yet *sure* consequence of my first — my prohibited correspondence! by a father *early* prohibited.

How much more properly had I acted, with regard to that correspondence, had I, once for all, when he was forbidden to visit me, and I to receive his visits, pleaded the authority by which I ought to have been bound, and denied to write to him!

As to this last rashness; now that it is too late I plainly see how I ought to have conducted myself. I should not have been solicitous whether he had got my letter or not; when he had come, and found I did not answer his signal, he would presently have resorted to the loose bricks, and there been satisfied by the date of my letter that it was his own fault he had it not before. But, *governed by the same pragmatical motives* which induced me to correspond with him at first, I was again afraid, truly, with my foolish and busy prescience, that the disappointment would have thrown him into the way of receiving fresh insults from the same persons; which might have made him guilty of some violence to them. And so, to save him an *apprehended* rashness, I have rushed into a *real* one myself. And what vexes me more is, that it is plain to me now, by all his behaviour, that he had as great a confidence in my weakness as I had in my own strength. And so, in a point entirely relative to my honour, he has triumphed; for he has not been mistaken in me, while I have in myself!

Tell me, my dear Miss Howe, tell me truly, if your unbiased heart does not despise me? It must! for your mind and mine were ever *one*; and I despise *myself*! — and well I may; for could the giddiest and most inconsiderate girl in England have done worse than I shall appear to have done in the eye of the world? Since my crime will be known without the provocations, and without the artifices of the betrayer too; while it will be a high aggravation, that better things were expected from me than from many others.

You charge me *to marry the first opportunity*. Ah! my dear! *another* of the blessed effects of my folly. That's as much in my power now as — as I am myself! And can I besides give a sanction immediately to his deluding arts? Can I *avoid* being angry with him for tricking me thus, as I may say (and as I have called it to him) out of *myself*?

For compelling me to take a step so contrary to all my resolutions and assurances given to you; a step so disgracefully inconvenient to myself; so disgraceful and so grievous (as it must be) to my dear mother, were I to be less regardful of any other of my family or friends. You don't know, nor can you imagine, my dear, how I am mortified! — how much I am sunk in my own opinion — I that was proposed for an example, truly, to others! Oh, that I were again in my father's house, stealing down with a letter *to* you; my heart beating with expectation of finding one *from* you!

. . . .

This is the Wednesday morning I dreaded so much, that I once thought of it as the day of my doom: but of the Monday, it is plain, I ought to have been most apprehensive. Had I stayed, and had the worst I dreaded happened, my friends would then have been answerable for the consequences, if any bad ones had followed: but now I have this *only* consolation left me (a very poor one, you'll say!), that I have cleared *them* of blame and taken it all upon *myself!*

Only thus much I will say, that he is extremely respectful (even obsequiously so) at present, though I am so much dissatisfied with him and myself that he has hitherto had no great cause to praise my complaisance to him. Indeed I can hardly, at times, bear the seducer in my sight.

The lodgings I am in are inconvenient. I shall not stay in them: so it signifies nothing to tell you how to direct to me hither. And where my next may be as yet I know not.

He knows that I am writing to you; and has offered to send my letter, when finished, by a servant of his. But I thought I could not be too cautious, as I am now situated, in having a letter of this importance conveyed to you. Who knows what such a man may do? So very wicked a contriver!

MR. LOVELACE TO JOSEPH LEMAN

Sat., April 8.

HONEST JOSEPH, — At length your beloved young lady has consented to free herself from the cruel treatment she has so long borne. She is to meet me without the garden door at about four o'clock on Monday afternoon.

I shall have a chariot-and-six ready in the by-road fronting the private path to Harlowe Paddock; and several of my friends and servants not far off, armed to protect her if there be occasion: but every one charged to avoid mischief.

Be very mindful therefore of the following directions: take them into your heart.

Contrive to be in the garden, in *disguise* if possible, and unseen by your young lady. If you find the garden door unbolted you will know that she and I are together, although you should not see her go out at it. It will be locked, but my key shall be on the ground just without the door, that you may open it with yours as it may be needful.

If you hear our voices parleying, keep at the door till I cry Ahem, ahem, twice: but be watchful for this signal, for I must not ahem very loud, lest she should take it for a signal. Perhaps, in struggling to prevail upon the dear creature, I may have an opportunity to strike the door hard with my elbow, or heel, to confirm you. Then you are to make a violent burst against the door, as if you would break it open, drawing backward and forward the bolt in a hurry: then, with another push, but with more noise than strength, lest the lock give way, cry out (as if you saw some of the family): Come up, come up instantly! Here they are! Here they are! — hasten! This instant hasten! And mention swords, pistols, guns, with as terrible a voice as you can cry out with. Then shall I prevail upon her no doubt, if loath before, to fly. If I cannot, I will enter the garden with her, and the house too, be the consequence what it will. But so affrighted, there is no question but she will fly.

When you think us at a sufficient distance (and I shall raise my voice urging her swifter flight, that you may guess at *that*), then open the door with your key: but you must be sure to open it very cautiously, lest we should not be far enough off. I would not have her know you have a hand in this matter, out of my great regard to you.

When you have opened the door, take your key out of the lock, and put it in your pocket: then, stooping for mine, put it in the lock on the *inside*, that it may appear as if the door was opened by herself, with a key which they will suppose of my procuring (it being new), and left open by us.

They *should* conclude she is gone off by her own consent, that they may not pursue us.

But you must take notice, that you are only to open the door with your key, in case none of the family come up to interrupt us, and before we are quite gone: for, if they do, you'll find by what follows that you must not open the door at all. Let them, on breaking it open, or by getting over the fall, find my key on the ground, if they will.

If they do not come to interrupt us, and if you, by help of your key, come out, follow us at a distance; and, with uplifted hands and wild and impatient gestures (running backward and forward, for fear you should come too near us; and as if you saw somebody coming to your assistance), cry out for Help, help, and to hasten. Then shall we be soon at the chariot.

Tell the family that you saw me enter a chariot with her: a dozen or more men on horseback attending us; all armed; some with blunderbusses, as you believe; and that we took the quite contrary way to that we shall take.

You see, honest Joseph, how careful I am, as well as you, to avoid mischief.

To Robert Lovelace, Esquier. His Honner

Sunday Morning, April 9.

Honnered Sir, — I must confesse I am infinitely obliged to your honner's bounty. But this last command! — it seems so intricket! Lord be merciful to me, how have I been led from little stepps to grate stepps! And if I should be found out! But your honner says you will take me into your honner's sarvise, and proteckt me, if as I should at any time be found out; and raise my wages besides; or set me upp in a good inne; which is my ambishion. And you will be honnerable and kind to my dearest young lady, God love her. But who can be unkind to she?

I will do the best I am able, since your honner will be apt to lose her, as your honner says, if I do not; and a man so stingie will be apt to gain her. But mayhap my dearest younge lady will not make all this troubble needful. If she has promised, she will stand to it, I dare to say.

I love your honner for contriveing to save mischiff so well. I thought till I knowed your honner, that you was verry mischevous, and plese your honner. But find it to be clene contrary. Your honner, it is plane, means mighty well by everybody, as far as I see. As I am sure I do myself; for I am, althoff a very plane man, and all that, a very honnest one, I thank my God. And have good principels, and have kept my young lady's pressepts always in mind: for she goes nowhere, but saves a soul or two, more or less.

Be pleased, howsomever, if it like your honner, not to call me *honnest Joseph,* and *honnest Joseph* so often. For, althoff I think myself very honnest, and all that; yet I am touched a little, for fear I should not do the quite right thing: and too besides, your honner has such a fesseshious way with you, as that I hardly know whether you are in jest or earnest when your honner calls me honnest so often.

As to Mrs. Betty; I tho'te, indede, she looked above me. But she comes on very well, nathelesse. I could like her better iff she was better to my young lady. But she has too much wit for so plane a man. Natheless, if she was to angre me, althoff it is a shame to bete a woman; yet I colde make shift to throe my hat at her, or so, your honner.

But I shall grow impartient to such a grate man — and *hereafter* may do for that, as she turnes out: for one mought be loath to part with her, mayhap, so *verry* soon too; espessially if she was to make the notable lanlady your honner put into my head.

Butt wonce moer, beging your honer's parden, and promissing all dilligence and exsacknesse, I reste, / Your honner's dewtifull sarvant to commande, / Joseph Leman.

Mr. Lovelace to John Belford, Esq.

St. Albans, Monday night.

I snatch a few moments while my beloved is retired (as I hope, to rest) to perform my promise No pursuit — nor have I apprehensions of any; though I must make my charmer dread that there will be one.

I knew that the whole stupid family were in a combination to do my business for me. I told thee that they were all working for me like so many underground moles; and still more blind than the moles are said to be, unknowing that they did so. I myself, the director of their principal motions; which falling in with the malice of their little hearts they took to be all their own.

But did I say my joy was perfect? Oh, no! It receives some abatement from my disgusted pride. For how can I endure to think that I owe more to her relations' persecutions than to her favour for me? Or even, as far as I know, to her preference of me to another man?

But let me not indulge this thought. Were I to do so it might cost my charmer dear. Let me rejoice that she has passed the Rubicon: that she cannot return: that, as I have ordered it, the flight will appear to the implacables to be altogether with her own consent: and that, if I doubt her love, I can put her to trials as mortifying to her niceness as glorious to my pride. For, let me tell thee, dearly as I love her, if I thought there was but the shadow of a doubt in her mind, whether she preferred me to any man living, I would show her no mercy.

But why, as in the chariot, as in the inn, at alighting, all heart-bursting grief, my dearest creature? So persecuted, as thou wert persecuted! So much in danger of the most abhorred compulsion! Yet grief so *unsuspectably* sincere for an escape so critical! Take care — take care, O beloved of my soul! for jealous is the heart in which love has erected a temple to thee.

Yet it must be allowed that such a sudden transition must affect her; must ice her over. When a little more used to her new situation; when her hurries are at an end; when she sees how religiously I shall observe all her INJUNCTIONS, she will undoubtedly have the gratitude to distinguish between the confinement she has escaped from and the liberty she has reason to rejoice in.

MISS CLARISSA HARLOWE TO MISS HOWE

Wednesday, April 12.

I WILL pursue my melancholy story.

Being thus hurried to the chariot, it would have been to no purpose to have refused entering into it, had he not in my fright lifted me in as he did: and instantly drove away at full gallop, and stopped not till it brought us to St. Albans; which was just as the day shut in.

I have reason to think there were other horsemen at his devotion; three or four different persons, above the rank of servants, galloping by us now and then on each side of the chariot: but he took no notice of them; and I had too much grief, mingled with indignation, notwithstanding all his blandishments, to ask any questions about them or anything else.

Think, my dear, what were my thoughts on alighting from the chariot; having no attendant of my own sex; no clothes but what I had on, and those little suited for such a journey as I had *already* taken, and was *still* to take: neither hood nor hat, nor anything but a handkerchief about my neck and shoulders: fatigued to death: my mind still more fatigued than my body: and in such a foam the horses that every one in the inn we put up at guessed (they could not otherwise) that I was a young giddy creature who had run away from her friends. This it was easy to see by their whispering and gaping; more of the people of the house also coming in by turns than were necessary for the attendance.

The mistress of the house, whom he sent in to me, showed me another apartment; and, seeing me ready to faint, brought me hartshorn and water; and then, upon my desiring to be left alone for half an hour, retired: for I found my heart ready to burst, on revolving everything in my thoughts: and the moment she was gone, fastening the door, I threw myself into an old great chair, and gave way to a violent flood of tears; which a little relieved me.

Mr. Lovelace, sooner than I wished, sent up the gentlewoman, who pressed me, in his name, to admit my brother or to come down to to him: for he had told her I was his sister; and that he had brought me, against my will and without warning, from a friend's house, where I had been all the winter, in order to prevent my marrying against the consent of my friends; to whom he was now conducting me.

The room I was in being a bedchamber, I chose to go down, at his repeated message, attended by the mistress of the house, to that in which he was.

When we were alone, he besought me (I cannot say but with all the tokens of a passionate and respectful tenderness) to be better reconciled to myself, and to him: he repeated all the vows of honour and inviolable affection that he ever made me: he promised to be wholly governed by me in every future step: he asked me to give him leave to propose, whether I chose to set out next day to either of his aunts?

I was silent. I knew not what to say, nor what to do.

Whether I chose to have private lodgings procured for me in either of those ladies' neighbourhood, as were once my thoughts?

I was still silent.

Whether I chose to go to either of Lord M.'s seats; that of Berks, or that in the county we were in?

In lodgings, I said, anywhere, where he was not to be.

He had *promised this*, he owned; and he would religiously keep to his word as soon as he found all danger of pursuit over; and that I was settled to my mind. But, if the place were indifferent to me, London was the safest, and the most private: and his relations should all visit me there.

I told him, I wished not to go to any of his relations: that my reputation was concerned to have *him* absent from me: that, if I were in some private lodging, it would be most suitable both to my mind and to my situation.

If he might deliver his opinion, he said, it was that, since I declined going to any of his relations, London was the only place in the world to be private in. Every new-comer in a country town or village excited a curiosity: a person of my figure (and many compliments he made me) would excite more. Even messages and letters, where none used to be brought, would occasion inquiry.

Only that I were safe was all he was solicitous about. He had lodgings in town; but he did not offer to propose them. He knew I would have more objection to go to them than I could have to go to Lord M.'s or to Lady Betty's.

I was too peevish, and too much afflicted, and indeed to much incensed against him to take well anything he said.

I thought myself, I said, extremely unhappy. I know not what to determine upon; my reputation now, no doubt, utterly ruined: destitute of clothes; unfit to be seen by anybody: my very indigence, as I might call it, proclaiming my folly to every one who saw me; who would suppose that I had been taken at advantage, or had given an undue one; and had no power over either my will or my actions: that I could not but think I had been dealt artfully with.

He was very attentive to all I said.

As to my *reputation* (he must be very sincere with me), that could not suffer half so much by the step I so greatly regretted to have taken, as by the confinement, and equally foolish and unjust treatment I had met with from my relations: that every mouth was full of blame of them, of my brother and sister particularly; and of wonder at my patience: that he must repeat what he had written to me he believed more than once, that my friends themselves expected that I should take a proper opportunity to free myself from their persecutions; why else did they confine me? that my exalted character, as he called it, would still bear me out with those who knew *me*; who knew my *brother's* and *sister's* motives; and who knew the wretch they were for compelling me to have.

With regard to *clothes*; who, as matters were circumstanced, could expect that I should be able to bring away any others than those I had on at the time? For *present* use or wear all the ladies of his family would take a pride to supply me: for *future*, the product of the best looms, not only in England, but throughout the world, were at my command.

If I wanted *money*, as no doubt I must, he should be proud to supply me: would to heaven, he might presume to hope, there were but one interest between us!

And then he would fain have had me to accept of a bank-note of a hundred pounds; which, unawares to me, he put into my hand: but which, you may be sure, I refused with warmth.

He was inexpressibly grieved and surprised, he said, to hear me say he had acted *artfully* by me. He came provided, according to my *confirmed* appointment (*a wretch, to upbraid me thus!*) to redeem me from my persecutors; and little expected a change of sentiment, and that he should have so much difficulty to prevail upon me as he had met with.

As to what further remained for him to say, in answer to what I had said, he hoped I would pardon him; but, upon his soul, he was concerned, infinitely concerned, he repeated (his colour and his voice rising) that it was *necessary* for him to observe how much I chose rather to have run the risk of being Solmes's wife than to have it in my power to reward a man who; I must forgive him, had been as much insulted on *my* account as *I* had been on *his* — who had watched my commands and (pardon me, madam) every *changeable* motion of your pen, all hours, in all weathers, and with a cheerfulness and ardour that nothing but the most faithful and obsequious passion could inspire.

I now, my dear, began to revive into a little more warmth of attention.

And all, madam, for what? How I stared! for he stopped then a moment or two. *Only*, went he on, to prevail upon you to free yourself from ungenerous and base oppression ——

Indeed, my dear, I have since thought that his anger was not owing to that sudden *impetus* which cannot be easily bridled; but rather was a sort of *manageable* anger, let loose to intimidate me.

Forgive me, madam — I have just done. Have I not, in your own opinion, hazarded my life to redeem you from oppression? Yet is not my reward, after all, precarious? For, madam, *have you not conditioned with me* (and, hard as the condition is, *most sacredly will I observe it*) *that all my hope must be remote?* That you are determined to have it in your power *to favour or reject me totally*, as you please?

See, my dear! In every respect my condition changed for the worse! Is it in *my power* to take your advice, if I should think it ever so right to take it?[1]

And have you not furthermore declared, proceeded he, *that you will engage to renounce me for ever, if your friends insist upon that cruel renunciation as the terms of being reconciled to you?*

But nevertheless, madam, all the merit of having saved you from an odious compulsion shall be mine. I glory in it, though I were to lose you for ever — *as I see I am but too likely to do*, from your present displeasure; and especially *if your friends insist upon the terms you are ready to comply with*.

That you are *your own mistress*, through *my* means, is, I repeat, my boast. *As such*, I humbly implore your favour — and *that only upon the conditions I have yielded to hope for it*. As I do now *thus humbly*

[1] Clarissa has been censured as behaving to Mr. Lovelace, in their first conversation at St. Albans, and afterwards with too much reserve, and even with haughtiness. Surely those who have thought her to blame on this account, have not paid a due attention to the story. How early, as above, and in what immediately follows, does he remind her of the terms of distance which she prescribed to him, before she was in his power, *in hopes to leave a door open for the reconciliation with her friends* which her heart was set upon! And how artfully does he (unrequired) promise to observe the conditions, which she, in her present circumstances and situation (in pursuance of Miss Howe's advice) would gladly have dispensed with! — To say nothing of the resentment which she was under a *necessity* to show, at the manner of his getting her away, in order to justify to him *the sincerity of her refusal to go off with him*.

(the proud wretch falling on one knee) your forgiveness for so long detaining your ear, and for all the plain-dealing that my undesigning heart would not be denied to utter by my lips.

O sir, pray rise! Let the *obliged* kneel if one of us must kneel!

But here, sir, like the first pair (I, at least, driven out of my paradise), are we recriminating. No more shall you need to tell me of your *sufferings* and your *merits*! — your *all hours* and *all weathers*! For I will bear them in memory as long as I live; and if it be impossible for me to *reward* them, be ever ready to *own* the obligation. All that I desire of you now is to leave it to myself to seek for some private abode: to take the chariot with you to London or elsewhere: and, if I have any further occasion for your assistance and protection I will signify it to you, and be still *further* obliged to you.

You are warm, my dearest life! But indeed there is no occasion for it. Had I any views unworthy of my faithful love for you I should not have been so honest in my declarations.

Then he began again to vow the sincerity of his intentions.

You are absolutely your own mistress. It were very strange if you were not. *The moment you are in a place of safety* I will leave you. To one condition only, give me leave to beg your consent: it is this: that you will be pleased, now you are so entirely in your own power, to renew a promise *voluntarily* made before; *voluntarily,* or I would not *now* presume to request it; for although I would not be thought capable of growing upon concession, yet I cannot bear to think of losing the ground your goodness had given me room to hope I had gained; "That, make up how you please with your relations, you will never marry any other man while I am living and single, unless I should be so wicked as to give new cause for high displeasure."

I hesitate not to confirm this promise, sir, upon your *own* condition. In what manner do you expect me to confirm it?

Only, madam, by your word.

Then I never will.

He had the assurance (*I was now in his power*) to salute me as a sealing of my promise, as he called it. His motion was so sudden that I was not aware of it. It would have looked *affected* to be very angry; yet I could not be pleased, considering this as a *leading freedom* from a spirit so audacious and encroaching: and he might see what I was not.

I broke from him to write to you my preceding letter; but refused to send it by his servant, as I told you.

I looked over my little stock of money; and found it to be no more than seven guineas and some silver: the rest of my stock was but fifty guineas, and that five more than I thought it was, when my sister challenged me as to the sum I had by me: and those I left in my escritoire, little intending to go away with him.

Indeed my case abounds with a shocking number of indelicate circumstances. Among the rest, I was forced to account to *him,* who knew I could have no clothes but what I had on, how I came to have linen with you (for he could not but know I sent for it); lest he should imagine I had an early design to go away with him, and made that a *part of the preparation.*

. . . .

Before five o'clock (Tuesday morning) the maidservant came up to tell me my *brother* was ready, and that breakfast also waited for me in the parlour. I went down with a heart as heavy as my eyes, and received great acknowledgments and compliments from him on being so soon dressed, and ready (as he interpreted it) to continue our journey.

He had the thought, which I had not (for what had I to do with thinking, who had it not when I stood most in need of it?) to purchase for me a velvet hood, and a short cloak, trimmed with silver, without saying anything to me.

How could I be complaisant, my dear, to such a man as this?

When we had got into the chariot, and it began to move, he asked me whether I had any objection to go to Lord M.'s Hertfordshire seat? His lordship, he said, was at his Berkshire one.

I told him I chose not to go, *as yet*, to any of his relations; for that would indicate a plain defiance to my own. My choice was to go to a private lodging, and for him to be at a distance from me: at least till I heard how things were taken by my friends.

I should govern him as I pleased, he solemnly assured me, in everything. But he still thought *London* was the best place for me; and if I were once safe there, and in a lodging to my liking, he would go to M. Hall. But, as I approved not of London, he would urge it no further.

He proposed, and I consented, to put up at an inn in the neighbourhood of *The Lawn* (as he called Lord M.'s seat in this county), since I chose not to go thither. And here I got two hours to myself: which I told him I should pass in writing another letter to you (meaning my narrative, which, though greatly fatigued, I had begun at St. Albans), and in one to my sister, to apprise the family (whether they were solicitous about it or not) that I was well; and to beg that my clothes, some particular books, and the fifty guineas I had left in my escritoire, might be sent me.

He asked if I had considered whither to have them directed?

Indeed not I, I told him: I was a stranger to ——

So was he, he interrupted me; but it struck him by chance ——

Wicked story-teller!

But, added he, I will tell you, madam, how it shall be managed. If you don't choose to go to London, it is, nevertheless, best that your relations should *think* you there; for then they will absolutely despair of fiinding you. If you write, be pleased to direct: To be left for you at Mr. Osgood's, near Soho Square. Mr. Osgood is a man of reputation: and this will effectually amuse them.

Amuse them, my dear! Amuse whom? My father! — my uncles! But it must be so! *All his expedients ready, you see!*

I had no objection to this: and I have written accordingly. But what answer I shall have, or whether any, that is what gives me no small anxiety.

Mrs. Greme[1] came to pay her *duty* to me, as Mr. Lovelace called it; and was very urgent with me to go to her lord's house; letting me know what handsome things she had heard her lord, and his two nieces, and all the family, say of me; and what wishes for several months past they had put up for the honour she now hoped would soon be done them all.

This gave me some satisfaction, as it confirmed from the mouth of a very good sort of woman all that Mr. Lovelace had told me.

Upon inquiry about a private lodging, she recommended me to a sister-in-law of hers, eight miles from thence — where I now am. And what pleased me the better was that Mr. Lovelace (of whom I could see she was infinitely observant) obliged her, of his own motion, to accompany me in the chaise; himself riding on horseback, with his two servants and one of Lord M.'s. And here we arrived about four o'clock.

Mrs. Greme and I had a good deal of talk in the chaise about him: she was very easy and free in her answers to all I asked; and has, I find, a very serious turn.

This, indifferent as it is, is better than my brother says of him.

The people of the house here are very honest-looking industrious folks: Mrs. Sorlings is the gentlewoman's name. The farm seems well stocked and thriving. She is a widow; has two sons, men grown, who vie with each other which shall take most pains in promoting the common good; and they are both of them, I already see, more respectful to two modest young women their sisters than my brother was to his sister.

I believe I must stay here longer than at first I thought I should.

Fie upon me! for *meeting the seducer!* Let all end as happily as it now may, I have laid up for myself *remorse for my whole life.*

What still more concerns me is, that every time I see this man I am still at a greater loss than before what to make of him. I watch every turn of his countenance: and I think I see very deep lines in it. He looks with more meaning, I verily think, than he used to look; yet not more serious; not less gay — I don't know how he looks — but with more confidence a great deal than formerly; and yet he never wanted that.

But here is the thing: I behold him with *fear* now, as conscious of the power my indiscretion has given him over me. And well may *he* look more elate, when he sees me deprived of all the self-supposed significance which adorns and exalts a person who has been accustomed to respect; and who now, by a *conscious inferiority,* allows herself *to be overcome,* and in a state of *obligation,* as I may say, to a man who, from an humble suitor to her for her favour, assumes the consequence and airs of a protector.

[1 Housekeeper at Lord M.'s Hertfordshire seat.]

I shall send this, as my former, by a poor man, who travels every day with pedlary matters. He will leave it at Mrs. Knollys's, as you direct.

MR. LOVELACE TO JOHN BELFORD, ESQ.

Tuesday, Wedn., April 11, 12.

You claim my promise that I will be as particular as possible in all that passes between me and my goddess.

I told thee my reasons for not going in search of a letter of countermand. I was right; for, if I had, I should have found such a one; and had I received it she would not have met me. Did she think that, after I had been more than once disappointed, I would not keep her to her promise; that I would not hold her to it, when I had got her in so deeply?

The moment I heard the door unbolt I was sure of her. That motion made my heart bound to my throat. But when that was followed with the presence of my charmer, flashing upon me all at once in a flood of brightness, sweetly dressed, though all unprepared for a journey, I trod air, and hardly thought myself a mortal.

I have told thee what were *my* transports, when the undrawn bolt presented to me my long-expected goddess. *Her* emotions were more sweetly feminine after the first moments; for then the fire of her starry eyes began to sink into a less dazzling languor. She trembled: nor knew she how to support the agitations of a heart she had never found so ungovernable. She was even fainting, when I clasped her in my supporting arms. What a precious moment that! How near, how sweetly near, the throbbing partners!

By her dress I saw, as I observed before, how unprepared she was for a journey; and not doubting her intention once more to disappoint me, I would have drawn her after me. Then began a contention the most vehement that ever I had with woman. It would pain thy friendly heart to be told the infinite trouble I had with her. I begged, I prayed; on my knees, yet in vain, I begged and prayed her to answer her own appointment: and had I not happily provided for such a struggle, knowing whom I had to deal with, I had certainly failed in my design; and as certainly would have accompanied her in without thee and thy brethren: and who knows what might have been the consequence?

But my honest agent answering my signal, *though not quite so soon as I expected*, in the manner thou knowest I had prescribed, They are coming! They are coming! Fly, fly, my beloved creature, cried I, drawing my sword with a flourish, as if I would have slain half an hundred of the supposed intruders; and, seizing her trembling hands, I drew her after me so swiftly that *my* feet, winged by love, could hardly keep pace with *her* feet, agitated by fear. And so I became her emperor.

I'll tell thee all when I see thee: and thou shalt then judge of *my* difficulties and of *her* perverseness. And thou wilt rejoice with me at my conquest over such a watchful and open-eyed charmer.

But seest thou not now (as I think I do) the wind-outstripping fair one flying *from* her love *to* her love? Is there not such a game? Nay, flying from friends she was resolved not to abandon to the man she was determined not to go off with? *The sex! the sex all over!* — charming contradiction! Ha, ha, ha, ha! I must here — I must here lay down my pen to hold my sides; for I must have my laugh out now the fit is upon me.

. . . .

But O my best-beloved fair one, repine not thou at the arts by which thou suspectest thy fruitless vigilance has been overwatched, Take care that thou provokest not new ones that may be still more worthy of thee. If once thy emperor decrees thy fall, thou shalt greatly fall.

Thou wilt not dare, methinks I hear thee say, to attempt to reduce such a goddess as this to a standard unworthy of her excellences. It is impossible, Lovelace, that thou shouldst intend to break through oaths and protestations so solemn.

That I did *not* intend it is certain. That I *do* intend it I cannot (my heart, my reverence for her, will not let me) say. But knowest thou not my aversion to the state of shackles? And is she not IN MY POWER?

And wilt thou, Lovelace, abuse that power, which ——

Which what, Belford? — which I obtained not by her own consent, but *against* it.

But which thou never hadst obtained had she not esteemed thee above all men.

And which I had never taken so much pains to obtain had I not loved her above all women.

Then thou knowest what a *false* little rogue she has been. How little conscience she has made of disappointing me. Hast thou not been a witness of my ravings on this score? Have I not, in the height of them, vowed revenge upon the faithless charmer? And, if I *must* be forsworn, whether I answer her expectations or follow my own inclinations; and if the option be in my own power; can I hesitate a moment which to choose?

Then, I fancy, by her circumspection and her continual grief, that she *expects* some mischief from me. I don't care to disappoint anybody I have a value for.

But I resolve not *any way*. I will see how *her* will works; and how *my* will leads me on. I will give the combatants fair play. And yet, every time I attend her, I find that she is less in *my* power; I more in *hers*.

Yet a foolish little rogue! to forbid me to think of marriage till I am a reformed man! Till the implacables of her family change their natures and become placable!

It is true, when she was for making those conditions, she did not think that, without *any*, she should *be cheated out of herself*; for so the dear soul, as I may tell thee in its place, phrases it.

In short, my whole soul is joy. When I go to bed I laugh myself asleep: and I awake either laughing or singing. Yet nothing *nearly* in view, neither. For why? *I am not yet reformed enough!*

O my charmer, look to it! Abate of thy haughty airs! Value not thyself upon thy sincerity if thou *art* indifferent to me! I will not bear it *now*. *Art thou not in my* POWER? Nor, if thou lovest me, think that the female affectation of denying thy love will avail thee *now*, with a heart so proud and so jealous as mine? Remember, moreover, that all thy family's sins are upon thy head!

But, ah! Jack, when I see my angel, when I am admitted to the presence of this radiant beauty, what will become of all this vapouring?

But, be my end what it may, I am obliged, by thy penetration, fair one, to proceed by the sap. *Fair and softly. A wife at any time!* Marriage will be always in my power.

MISS HOWE TO MISS CLARISSA HARLOWE

Wednesday Night, April 12.

I HAVE your narrative, my dear. You are the same noble creature you ever were.

Forgive me, my dear — here is that stupid Uncle Antony of yours. My mother was dressing. His errand was to set her against you, and to show their determined rage on your going away. The issue proved too evidently that this was the principal end of his visit. The issue showed what the errand was. Its first appearance was a rigorous prohibition of correspondence.

Mr. Hickman, who greatly honors you, has, unknown to me, interposed so warmly in your favour with my mother that it makes for him no small merit with me.

. . . .

The man's a fool, my dear, with all his pride, and with all his complaisance, and *affected regards to your injunctions.* Yet his ready inventions ——

Sometimes I think you should go to Lady Betty's. I know not what to advise you to. I *should,* if you were not so intent upon reconciling yourself to your relations. Yet they are implacable. You can have no hopes from them. Your uncle's errand to my mother may convince you of that; and if you have an answer to your letter to your sister, that will confirm you, I dare say.

I think, your *provocations* and *inducements* considered, you are free from blame: at least the freest that ever young creature was who took such a step.

But *you took it not*. You were *driven on one side,* and, possibly, *tricked on the other.* If any woman on earth shall be circumstanced as you were, and shall hold out so long as you did against her persecutors on one hand, and her seducer on the other, I will forgive her for all the rest of her conduct, be it what it will.

Your father is all rage and violence. He ought, I am sure, to turn his rage inward. All your family accuse you of acting with *deep art*; and are put upon supposing that you are actually *every hour exulting over them*, with your man, in the success of it.

They all pretend now, that your trial of Wednesday was to be the last.

They own, however, that a minister was to be present. Mr. Solmes was to be at hand. And your father was previously to try his authority over you, in order to make you sign the settlements. All of it a romantic contrivance of your wild headed foolish brother, I make no doubt. Is it likely that he and Bell would have given way to your restoration to favour, supposing it in their power to hinder it, on any other terms than those their hearts had been so long set upon? How they took your flight, when they found it out, may be better supposed than described.

Your Aunt Hervey, it seems, was the first that went down to the ivy summer-house in order to acquaint you that their search was over. Betty followed her; and they not finding you there, went on towards the cascade, according to a hint of yours.

Returning by the garden door, they met a servant (*they don't say it was that Joseph Leman; but it is very likely that it was he*) running, as he said, from pursuing Mr. Lovelace (a great hedge-stake in his hand, and out of breath) to alarm the family.

If it were this fellow, and if he were employed in the double agency of cheating them and cheating you, what shall we think of the wretch you are with? Run away from him, my dear, if so — no matter to whom — or marry him, if you cannot.

Your aunt and all your family were accordingly alarmed by this fellow — *evidently when too late for pursuit.*

Your brother, at first, ordered horses and armed men to be got ready for a pursuit. Solmes and your Uncle *Tony* were to be of the party. But your mother and your Aunt Hervey dissuaded them from it, for fear of adding evil to evil; not doubting but Lovelace had taken measures to support himself in what he had done.

.   .   .   .

My mother's absence was owing to her suspicion that the Knollys's were to assist in our correspondence. She made them a visit upon it. *She does everything at once.* And they have promised that no more letters shall be left there without her knowledge.

But Mr. Hickman has engaged one Filmer, a husbandman, in the lane we call Finch Lane, near us, to receive them. Thither you will be pleased to direct yours, under cover, to Mr. John Soberton; and Mr. Hickman himself will call for them there; and there shall leave mine. It goes against me too, to make him so useful to me. He looks already so proud upon it! I shall have him (who knows?) give himself airs.

If you think not of marrying soon, I approve of your resolution to fix somewhere out of his reach: and if he know not where to find you, so much the better. Yet I verily believe they would force you back, could they but come at you, if they were not afraid of *him*.

I think, by all means, you should demand of both your trustees to be put in possession of your own estate. Meantime I have sixty guineas at your service. I beg you will command them.

As they believe you went away by your own consent, they are, it seems, equally surprised and glad that you have left your jewels and money behind you, and have contrived for clothes so ill. Very little likelihood this shows of their answering your requests.

Indeed every one who knows not what I *now* know, must be at a loss to account for your *flight*, as they call it. And how, my dear, can one report it with any tolerable advantage to you? To say you *did not intend it* when you met him, who will believe it? To say that a person of your known steadiness and punctilio was *over-persuaded* when you gave him the meeting, how will that sound? To say you were *tricked out of yourself*, and people were to give credit to it, how disreputable! And while *unmarried*, and *yet with him*, the man a man of such a character, what would it not lead a censuring world to think?

I want to see how you put it in your letter for your clothes.

Upon the whole, I do not think it is in your power to dismiss him when you please. I apprised you beforehand that it would not. I repeat therefore, that were I you, I would at least *seem* to place some confidence in him. So long as he is decent, you may. Very visibly observable, to such delicacy as yours, must be that behaviour in him which will make him unworthy of *some* confidence.

MISS CLARISSA HARLOWE TO MISS HOWE

Thursday Afternoon, April 13.

I AM infinitely concerned, my ever dear and ever kind friend, that I am the sad occasion of the displeasure between your mother and you. How many persons have I made unhappy!

I think, however, that you should obey your mother; and decline a correspondence with me; at least for the present. I thank you, my dear, most cordially I thank you, for your kind offers. I am willing to hope (notwithstanding what you write) that my friends will send me my little money, together with my clothes.

Small hopes indeed of a reconciliation from your account of my uncle's visit to your mother, in order to set her against an almost friendless creature whom once he loved! *But is it not my duty to try for it?*

These considerations make me waver about following your advice in relation to marriage; and the rather, as he is so full of complaisance with regard to my former conditions, which he calls my *injunctions*. Meanwhile, to what censures, as you remind me, do I expose myself

150

while he and I are together and unmarried! Yet (can I with patience ask the question?) *is it in my power?* O my dear Miss Howe! And am I so reduced, as that, to save the poor remains of my reputation in the world's eye, I must *watch the gracious motion* from this man's lips?

Were my Cousin Morden in England, all might still perhaps be determined happily. If my situation with Mr. Lovelace alter not in the interim, I must endeavour to keep myself in a state of independence till he arrive, that I may be at liberty to govern myself by his advice and direction.

I will acquaint you, as you desire, with all that passes between Mr. Lovelace and me. He has doubtless an arrogant and encroaching spirit.

Indeed, indeed, my dear, I could tear my hair, on reconsidering what you write (as to the probability that the dreaded Wednesday was more dreaded than it needed to be), to think that I should be thus tricked by this man; and that, in all likelihood, through his vile agent Joseph Leman. So premeditated and elaborate a wickedness as it must be!

I enclose the copy of my letter to my sister, which you are desirous to see. You will observe that, although I have not demanded my estate in form, and of my trustees, yet that I have hinted at leave to retire to it. How joyfully would I keep my word if they would accept of the offer I renew! It was not proper, I believe you will think, on many accounts, to own that I was carried off against my inclination. I am, my dearest friend, / Your ever obliged and affectionate / CL. HARLOWE.

TO MISS ARABELLA HARLOWE

(*Enclosed to Miss Howe in the preceding*)   *St. Albans. Apr. 11.*

MY DEAR SISTER, — I have, I confess, been guilty of an action which carried with it a rash and undutiful appearance. And I should have thought it an inexcusable one had I been used with less severity than I have been of late; and had I not had too great reason to apprehend that I was to be made a sacrifice to a man I could not bear to think of. But what is done, is done — perhaps I could wish it had not; and that I had trusted to the relenting of my dear and honoured parents. Yet this from no other motives but those of duty to them. To whom I am ready to return (if I may not be permitted to retire to *The Grove*) on conditions which I before offered to comply with.

Nor shall I be in any sort of dependence upon the person by whose means I have taken this *truly reluctant step,* inconsistent with any reasonable engagement I shall enter into if I am not further precipitated.

For your own sake therefore, for my brother's sake, by whom (I *must* say) I have been thus precipitated, and for all the family's sake, aggravate not my fault, if, on recollecting everything, you think it

one; nor by widening the unhappy difference, expose a sister for ever
— prays / Your affectionate / CL. HARLOWE.

I shall take it for a very great favour to have my clothes directly
sent me, together with fifty guineas, which you will find in my escritoire (of which I enclose the key); as also the divinity and miscellany
classes of my little library; and, if it be thought fit, my jewels — directed for *me*, to be left till called for, at Mr. Osgood's, near Soho
Square.

MR. LOVELACE TO JOHN BELFORD, ESQ.

*Mr. Lovelace, in continuation of his last letter, gives an account to
his friend (pretty much to the same effect with the lady's) of all that
passed between them at the inns, in the journey, and till their fixing
at Mrs. Sorlings's. To avoid repetition, those passages in his narrative
are only extracted which will serve to embellish hers; to open his
views; or to display the humorous talent he was noted for.*

*At their alighting at the inn at St. Albans on Monday night, thus he
writes:*

Ovid was not a greater master of metamorphoses than thy friend.
To the mistress of the house I instantly changed her into a sister,
brought off by surprise from a near relation's (where she had wintered)
to prevent her marrying a confounded rake (I love always to go as
near the truth as I can), whom her father and mother, her elder sister,
and all her loving uncles, aunts, and cousins abhorred.

*To that part where she tells him of the difficulty she made to corre-
spond with him at first, thus he writes:*

Very true, my precious! And innumerable have been the difficulties
thou hast made me struggle with. But one day thou mayest wish that
thou hadst spared this boast; as well as those other pretty haughti-
nesses: "That thou didst not reject Solmes for *my* sake: that *my* glory,
if I valued myself upon carrying thee off, was *thy* shame: that I have
more merit with *myself* than with thee or anybody else (*what a coxcomb she makes me, Jack!*): that thou wished thyself in thy father's
house again, *whatever were to be the consequence.*" If I forgive
thee, charmer, for these hints, for these reflections, for these wishes,
for these contempts, I am not the Lovelace I have been reputed to be;
and that thy treatment of me shows that thou thinkest I am.

Thou hast heard me often expatiate upon the pitiful figure a man
must make, whose wife *has*, or *believes* she has, more sense than himself. A thousand reasons could I give why I ought not to think of
marrying Miss Clarissa Harlowe: at least till I can be sure that she
loves me with the preference I must expect from a wife.

But there lie before me such charming difficulties, such scenery
for intrigue, for stratagem, for enterprise. What a horrible thing that

152

my talents point all that way — when I know what is honourable and just; and would almost wish to be honest! *Almost*, I say; for such a varlet am I, that I cannot altogether wish it, for the soul of me! Such a triumph over the whole sex, if I can subdue this lady! My maiden vow, as I may call it! For did not the sex begin with me? And does this lady spare me?

Why, why will the dear creature take such pains to appear all ice to me? Why will she, by *her* pride, awaken *mine*? Hast thou not seen, in the above, how contemptibly she treats me? What have I not suffered for her, and even *from* her? Ought I to bear being told that she will despise me, if I value myself above that odious Solmes?

And now, Belford, I am only afraid that I shall be *too* cunning; for she does not at present *talk* enough for me. I hardly know what to make of the dear creature yet.

I hope I shall be honest, I once more say: but as we frail mortals are not our own masters at all times, I must endeavour to keep the dear creature unapprehensive until I can get her to *our acquaintance's in London, or to some other safe place there.*

I would not be so barbarous as to permit old Antony to set Mrs. Howe against her, did I not dread the consequence of the correspondence between the two young ladies. So lively the one, so vigilant, so prudent both, who would not wish to outwit such girls, and to be able to twirl them round his finger?

This is Wednesday; the day that I was to have lost my charmer for ever to the hideous Solmes! With what high satisfaction and heart's ease can I now sit down and triumph over my men of straw at Harlowe Place! Yet 'tis perhaps best for them that she got off as she did. Who knows what consequences might have followed upon my attending her in; or (if she had not met me) upon my projected visit, followed by my myrmidons?

Miss Clarissa Harlowe to Miss Howe

Thursday Night, April 13.

I HAVE had another very warm debate with Mr. Lovelace. It brought on the subject which you advised me not to decline when it handsomely offered. And I want to have either your acquittal or blame for having suffered it to go off without effect.

He told me that he had, upon this occasion, been entering into himself, and had found a great deal of reason to blame himself for an impatience and inconsideration which, although he meant nothing by it, must be very disagreeable to one of my delicacy. But, from this time forth, I should find such an alteration in his whole behaviour as might be expected from a man who knew himself to be honoured with the presence and conversation of a person *who had the most delicate mind in the world* — that was his flourish.

I said that he might perhaps expect congratulation upon the discovery he had just now made, to wit, that *true politeness* and *sincerity* were reconcilable: but that I, who had, by a perverse fate, been thrown into his company, had abundant reason to regret that he had not sooner found this out: since, I believed, very few men of *birth* and *education* were strangers to it.

He knew not, *neither,* he said, that he had so badly behaved himself as to deserve so very severe a rebuke.

I told him *that I desired his absence,* of all things. I saw not, I said, that my friends thought it worth their while to give me disturbance: therefore, if he would set out for London, or Berkshire, or whither he pleased, it would be most agreeable to me, and most reputable too.

He would do so, he said, he *intended to do so,* the moment I was in a place to my liking — in a place convenient for me.

He wished, he said, he were at liberty, without giving me offence, or being thought to intend to *infringe the articles I had stipulated and insisted upon,* to make one humble proposal to me. But the *sacred regard* he was determined *to pay to all my injunctions* (reluctantly as I had on Monday last put it into his power to serve me) would not permit him to make it, unless I would promise to excuse him if I did not approve of it.

I asked, in some confusion, what he would say?

He prefaced and paraded on; and then out came, with great diffidence, and many apologies, and a bashfulness which sat very awkwardly upon him, a proposal of speedy solemnization: which, he said, would put all right; and make my first three or four months (which otherwise must be passed in obscurity and apprehension) a round of visits and visitings to and from all his relations; to Miss Howe; to whom I pleased: and would pave the way to the reconciliation I had so much at heart.

Your advice had great weight with me just then, as well as *his reasons,* and the consideration of my *unhappy situation*: but what could I say? I wanted somebody to speak for me.

The man saw I was not angry at his motion. I only blushed; and that I am sure I did up to the ears; and looked silly, and like a fool.

He wants not courage. Would he have had me catch at his first, at his *very* first word? I was *silent* too — and do not the bold sex take silence for a mark of favour? Then, *so lately* in my father's house! Having also declared to him in my letters, before I had your advice, that I would not think of marriage till he had passed through a state of probation, as I may call it. How was it possible I could encourage, with *very* ready signs of approbation, such an early proposal? especially so soon after the free treatment he had provoked from me. If I were to die, I could not.

He looked at me with great confidence; as if (notwithstanding his contradictory bashfulness) he would look me through; while my eye but now and then could glance at him. He begged my pardon with great humility: he was *afraid* I would think he deserved no other answer but that of a *contemptuous silence.* True love was fearful of offending. (Take care, Mr. Lovelace, thought I, how yours is tried

154

by that rule.) Indeed so *sacred a regard* (foolish man!) would he have *to all my declarations made before I honoured him* —

I would hear him no further; but withdrew in a confusion *too visible*, and left him to make his nonsensical flourishes to himself.

I will only add that, if he really wishes for a speedy solemnization, he never could have had a luckier time to press for my consent to it. But he let it go off; and indignation has taken place of it: and now it shall be a point with me to get him at a distance from me.

I am, my dearest friend, /Your ever faithful and obliged / CL. H.

MR. LOVELACE TO JOHN BELFORD, ESQ.

Thursday, Apr. 13.

WHY, Jack, thou needst not make such a *wonderment*, as the girls say, if I should have taken large strides already towards reformation; for dost thou not see, that while I have been so assiduously, night and day, pursuing this single charmer, I have infinitely less to answer for than otherwise I should have had? But reformation for my stalking-horse, I hope, will be a sure, though a slow method to effect all my purposes.

.   .   .   .

What can be done with a woman who is above flattery, and despises all praise but that which flows from the approbation of her own heart?

Well, Jack, thou seest it is high time to change my measures. I must run into the *pious* a little faster than I had designed.

What a sad thing would it be, were I, after all, to lose her person as well as her opinion! The only time that further acquaintance, and no blow struck, nor suspicion given, ever lessened me in a lady's favour — a cursed mortification! 'Tis certain I can have no pretence for holding her, if she will go. No such thing as force to be used, or so much as hinted at; Lord send us safe at London! That's all I have for it now; and yet it must be the least part of my speech.

But why will this admirable creature urge her destiny? Why will she defy the power she is absolutely dependent upon? Why will she still wish to my face that she had never left her father's house?

Is it prudent, thinkest thou, in *her* circumstances, to tell me, *repeatedly* to tell me, that she is every hour more and more dissatisfied with herself and me? That I am not one who improve upon her in my conversation and address? (Couldst *thou*, Jack, bear this from a captive!) That she shall not be easy while she is with me? That she was thrown upon me by a perverse fate?

.   .   .   .

And do I not see that I shall need nothing but patience in order to have all power with me? For what shall we say, if all these complaints of a character wounded; these declarations of increasing regrets for meeting me; of resentments never to be got over for my *seducing* her away; these angry commands to leave her: — What shall we say if all were to mean nothing but MATRIMONY? And what if my forbearing to enter upon that subject come out to be the true cause of her petulance and uneasiness? I spoke out upon the subject, and offered reasons, although with infinite doubt and hesitation (*lest she should be offended at me*, Belford!), why she should assent to the legal tie and and make me the happiest of men. And oh, how the mantled cheek, the downcast eye, the silent, yet trembling lip, and the heaving bosom, a sweet collection of heightened beauties, gave evidence that the tender was not mortally offensive!

Charming creature! thought I (*but I charge thee, that thou let not any of thy sex know my exultation*), is it so *soon* come to this? Am I *already* lord of the destiny of a Clarissa Harlowe? Am I already the reformed man thou resolvedst I *should* be, before I had the least encouragement given me?

Then what a triumph would it be to the *Harlowe pride* were I now to marry this lady! A family beneath my own! No one in it worthy of an alliance with, but her! My own estate not contemptible! Living within the bounds of it to avoid dependence upon *their* betters, and obliged to no man living! To be forced to *steal* her away, not only from *them*, but from *herself*! And must I be brought to implore forgiveness and reconciliation from the Harlowes? Forbid it the blood of the Lovelaces, that your last, and let me say, not the *meanest* of your stock, should thus creep, thus fawn, thus lick the dust, for a WIFE! —

.   .   .   .

But is it not the divine Clarissa (*Harlowe* let me not say; my soul spurns them all but her) whom I am thus by implication threatening? If virtue be the true nobility, how is she ennobled.

And what! (methinks thou askest with surprise): Dost thou question this most admirable of women? — The virtue of a Clarissa dost thou question?

I do not, I dare not question it. My reverence for her will not let me *directly* question it. But let me, in my turn, ask thee: Is not, may not, her virtue be founded rather in *pride* than in *principle*? Whose daughter is she? And is she not a *daughter*? If impeccable how came she by her impeccability? The pride of setting an example to her sex has run away with her hitherto, and may have made her till *now* invincible.

Then who says Miss Clarissa Harlowe is the paragon of virtue? — is Virtue itself? Has her virtue ever been *proved*? Who has dared to try her virtue? To the test then, since now I have the question brought home to me whether I am to have a wife? And whether she be to be a wife at the *first* or at the *second* hand?

I will proceed fairly. I will do the dear creature not only strict, but generous justice; for I will try her by her own judgment, as well as by our principles.

She blames herself for having corresponded with me, a man of free character, and one indeed whose *first* view it was to draw her into this correspondence, and who succeeded in it by means unknown to herself.

Well, but it will be said that her principal view was to prevent mischief between her brother and her other friends, and the man vilely insulted by them all.

Shall we suppose another motive? — And that is LOVE; a motive which all the world will excuse her for. But let me tell all the world that do, *not* because they *ought,* but because all the world is apt to be misled by it.

Let LOVE, then, be the motive: — Love of *whom?*

A *Lovelace,* is the answer.

But has she had the candour, the openness, to *acknowledge* that love?

She has not.

And what results? Is then the divine Clarissa capable of loving a man whom she ought *not* to love? And is she capable of *affectation?* And is her virtue founded in *pride?* And, if the answer to these questions be affirmative, must she not then be a woman?

Shun not, therefore, my dear soul, further trials, nor hate me for making them. "For what woman can be said to be virtuous till she has been tried?"

Nor is *one* effort, *one* trial, to be sufficient. Why? Because a woman's heart may be at one time *adamant,* at another *wax* — as I have often experienced. And so, no doubt, hast thou.

But what, methinks, thou askest, is to become of the lady if she fail? What? — Why will she not, *"if once subdued, be always subdued?"* Another of our libertine maxims. And what an immense pleasure to a marriage-hater, what rapture to thought, to be able to prevail upon such a woman as Miss Clarissa Harlowe to live with him without *real* change of name!

But if she resist — if nobly she stand her trial?

Why then I will marry her, and bless my stars for such an angel of a wife.

Nobody doubts that she is to be my wife. Let her pass for such when I give the word. Meantime reformation shall be my stalking-horse; some of the women in London, if I can get her thither, my bird. And so much for this time.

MISS HOWE TO MISS CLARISSA HARLOWE

DON'T advise me, my dear, to subscribe to my mother's prohibition of correspondence with you. If your talent is *scribbling,* as you call it, so is mine — and I will scribble on at all opportunities, and to you, let 'em say what they will.

I will say nothing upon your letter to your sister till I see the effect it will have. You hope, you tell me, that you shall have your money and clothes sent you, notwithstanding my opinion to the contrary.

I am sorry to have it to acquaint you that I have just now heard that they have sat in council upon your letter; and that your mother was the only person who was for sending you your things, and was over-ruled. I charge you, therefore, to accept of my offer as by my last, and give me particular directions for what you want, that I can supply you with besides.

Don't set your thought so much upon a reconciliation as to prevent your having hold of any handsome opportunity to give yourself a pro-tector; such a one as the man will be who, I imagine, husband-like, will let nobody insult you but himself.

He is naturally proud and saucy. I doubt you must engage his *pride*, which he calls his *honour*; and that you must throw off a little more of the veil. And I would have you restrain your wishes before him, that you had not met him and the like. What signifies wishing, my dear? He will not bear it. You can hardly expect that he will.

Methinks I see the man hesitating, and looking like the fool you paint him, under your corrective superiority! But he is not a fool. Don't put him upon mingling resentment with his love.

Miss Clarissa Harlowe to Miss Howe

You tell me, my dear, that my clothes and the little sum of money I left behind me will not be sent me — but I will still hope. It is yet early days. When their passions subside, they will better con-sider of the matter; and especially as I have my ever dear and excellent mother for my friend in this request. Oh, the sweet indulgence! How has my heart bled, and how does it still bleed for her!

You advise me not to depend upon a reconciliation. I do not, I cannot depend upon it. But nevertheless it is the wish next my heart. And as to this man, what can I do? You see *that marriage is not absolutely in my own power*, if I were *inclined* to prefer it to the trial which I think I ought to have principally in view to make for a reconciliation.

But I hope, as I am out of all other protection, that he is not ca-pable of mean or *low* resentments. If he has had any extraordinary trouble on my account, may he not thank himself for it? He may; and lay it, if he pleases, to his *character*; which, as I have told him, gave at least a *pretence* to my brother against him. And then, did I ever make him any promises? Did I ever profess a love for him? Did I ever wish for the continuance of his address? Had not my brother's violence precipitated matters, would not my indifference to him in all likelihood (as I designed it should) have tired out his proud spirit, and made him set out for London, where he used chiefly to reside? And if he *had*, would there not have been an end of all his pretensions and hopes? For no encouragement had I given him; nor did I then correspond with him.

You may believe, my dear Miss Howe, that the circumstance of the noise and outcry within the garden door on Monday last gave me no small uneasiness, to think that I was in the hands of a man who could, by such vile premeditation, lay a snare to trick me out of myself, as I have so frequently called it.

I was resolved to task him upon this subject, the first time I could have patience to enter upon it with him. I have had the opportunity I waited for, and will lay before you the result.

He was making his court to my good opinion in very polite terms, and with great seriousness lamenting that he had lost it; declaring that he knew not how he had deserved to do so; attributing to me an indifference to him that seemed, to his infinite concern, hourly to increase. And he besought me to let him know my whole mind, that he might have an opportunity either to confess his faults and amend them, or clear his conduct to my satisfaction, and thereby entitle himself to a greater share of my confidence.

I answered him with quickness: Then Mr. Lovelace, I will tell you one thing with a frankness that is, perhaps, more suitable to *my* character than to *yours* (*He hoped not, he said*) which gives me a very bad opinion of you as a designing, artful man.

I am all attention, madam.

I never can think tolerably of you, while the noise and voice I heard at the garden door, which put me into the terror you took so much advantage of, remains unaccounted for. Tell me fairly, tell me candidly, the whole of that circumstance, and of your dealings with that wicked Joseph Leman; and according to your explicitness ·in this particular, I shall form a judgment of your future professions.

I knew nothing, *said he*, of this man — this Leman, and should have scorned a resort to so low a method as bribing the servant of any family to let me into the secrets of that family, if I had not detected him in attempting to corrupt a servant of mine, to inform him of all my motions, of all my supposed intrigues, and, in short, of every action of my private life, as well as of my circumstances and engagements; and this for motives too obvious to be dwelt upon.

My servant told me of his offers, and I ordered him, unknown to the fellow, to let me hear a conversation that was to pass between them. In the midst of it, and just as he had made an offer of money for a particular piece of intelligence, promising more when procured, I broke in upon them, and by bluster, calling for a knife to cut off his ears (one of which I took hold of) in order to make a present of it, as I said, to his employers, I obliged him to tell me who they were.

Your brother, madam, and your Uncle Antony he named.

It was not difficult to prevail upon him, by a larger reward, to serve me; since at the same time he might preserve the favour of your uncle and brother, as I desired to know nothing but what related to myself and to you, in order to guard us both against the effects of an ill-will, which all his fellow-servants, as well as himself, as he acknowledged, thought undeserved.

I sat in astonishment, and thus he went on:

As to the circumstance for which you think so hardly of me, I do freely confess, that having a suspicion that you would revoke your intention of getting away, and in that case apprehending that we should not have the time together that was necessary for that purpose; I had ordered him to keep off everybody he *could* keep off, and to be himself within view of the garden door, for I was determined, if possible, to induce you to adhere to your resolution.

I ordered the fellow, as I told you, madam, said he, to keep within view of the garden door; and if he found any parley between us, and anybody coming (before you could retreat undiscovered) whose coming might be attended with violent effects, he would cry out; and this not only in order to save himself from their suspicions of him, but to give me warning to make off, and, if possible, to induce you (I own it, madam) to go off with me, according to your own appointment. And I hope, all circumstances considered, and the danger I was in of losing you for ever, that the acknowledgment of *this* contrivance, or if you had *not* met me, *that* upon Solmes, will not procure me your hatred; for had they come as *I* expected as well as *you*, what a despicable wretch had I been, could I have left you to the insults of a brother and others of your family, whose mercy was cruelty when they had *not* the pretence with which this detected interview would have furnished them!"

What a wretch, said I! But if, sir, taking your *own* account of this strange matter to be fact, anybody were coming, how happened it that I saw only that man Leman (I *thought* it was he) out of the door, and at a distance, look after us?

Very lucky! said he, putting his hand first in one pocket, then in another — I hope I have not thrown it away — it is, perhaps, in the coat I had on yesterday — little did I think it would be necessary to be produced — but I love to come to a demonstration whenever I can — I *may* be giddy — I *may* be heedless. I *am* indeed — but no man, as to *you*, madam, ever had a sincerer heart.

He then, stepping to the parlour door, called his servant to bring him the coat he had on yesterday.

The servant did. And in the pocket, rumpled up as a paper he regarded not, he pulled out a letter written by that Joseph, dated Monday night; in which he begs pardon for crying out so soon — says that his fears of being discovered to act on both sides, had made him take the rushing of a little dog (that always follows him) through the phyllirea-hedge, for Betty's being at hand, or some of his masters; and that when he found his mistake, he opened the door by his own key (which the contriving wretch confessed he had furnished him with) and inconsiderately ran out in a hurry, to have apprised him that his crying-out was owing to his fright only: and he added: that they were upon the hunt for me by the time he returned.

I shook my head. Deep! deep! deep! said I, at the best! O Mr.

Lovelace! God forgive and reform you! But you are, I see plainly (upon the whole of your own account), a very artful, a very designing man.

Love, my dearest life, is ingenious. Night and day have I racked my stupid brain (*O sir, thought I, not stupid! 'Twere well perhaps if it were*) to contrive methods to prevent the sacrifice designed to be made of you, and the mischief that must have ensued upon it; so little hold in your affections; such undeserved antipathy from your friends; so much danger of losing you for ever from *both* causes.

Again I blamed myself for meeting him; and justly, for there were many chances to one that I had *not* met him. And if I had not, all his fortnight's contrivances as to me would have come to nothing; and perhaps I might nevertheless have escaped Solmes.

I asked him if he thought such enormities as these, such defiances of the laws of society, would have passed unpunished?

He had the assurance to say, with one of his usual gay airs, that he should by this means have disappointed his enemies, and saved me from a forced marriage. He had no pleasure in such desperate pushes. Solmes he would not have *personally* hurt.

What a wicked schemer are you, sir! Who shall avenge upon you the still greater evils which you have been guilty of?

I had no patience with him. I told him so. I see, sir, said I, I see what a man I am with. Your *rattle* warns me of the *snake*. And away I flung, leaving him seemingly vexed and in confusion.

MISS CLARISSA HARLOWE TO MISS HOWE

Friday, April 14.

I WILL now give you the particulars of a conversation that has just passed between Mr. Lovelace and me, which I must call agreeable.

It began with his telling me that he had just received intelligence that my friends were on a sudden come to a resolution to lay aside all thoughts of pursuing me, or of getting me back; and that therefore he attended me to know my pleasure, and what *I* would do or have *him* do?

I told him that I would have him leave me directly; and that when it was known to everybody that I was absolutely independent of him, it would pass that I had left my father's house because of my brother's ill-usage of me; which was a plea that I might make with justice, and to the excuse of my father as well as of myself.

He mildly replied that if he could be certain that my relations would *adhere* to this their new resolution, he could have no objection, since such was my pleasure; but as he was well assured that they had taken it only from apprehensions that a more *active* one might involve my brother (who had breathed nothing but revenge) in some fatal misfortune, there was too much reason to believe that they would resume their former purpose the moment they should think they *safely* might.

This, madam, said he, is a risk I cannot run. You would think it strange if I could. And yet, as soon as I knew they had so given out, I thought it proper to apprise you of it, and to take your commands upon it.

Let me hear, said I, willing to try if he had any particular view, what *you* think most advisable?

'Tis very easy to say that, if I durst — *if I might not offend you* — if it were not to *break conditions that shall be inviolable with me.*

Say, then, sir, what you *would* say. I can approve or disapprove as I think fit.

Had not the man a fine opportunity here to speak out? He had. And thus he used it.

To waive, madam, what I *would* say till I have more courage to speak out — (*more courage* — *Mr. Lovelace more courage, my dear!*) — I will only propose what I think will be most agreeable to *you* — suppose, *if you choose not to go to Lady Betty's*, that you take a turn cross the country to Windsor?

Why to Windsor?

Because it is a pleasant place; because it lies in the way either to Berkshire, to Oxford, or to London. *Berkshire,* where Lord M. is at present; *London,* whither you may retire at your pleasure; or, if you will *have* it so, whither I may go, you staying at Windsor; and yet be within an easy distance of you, if anything should happen, or if your friends should change their new-taken resolution.

This proposal, however, displeased me not. But I said my only objection was the distance of Windsor from Miss Howe, of whom I should be glad to be always within two or three hours' reach by a messenger, if possible.

If I had thoughts of any other place than Windsor, or nearer to Miss Howe, he wanted but my commands, and would seek for proper accommodations; but, fix as I pleased, farther or nearer, he had servants, and they had nothing else to do but to obey me.

A grateful thing then he named to me: to send for my Hannah as soon as I should be fixed; unless I would choose one of the young gentlewomen *here* to attend me; both of whom, as I had acknowledged, were very obliging; and he knew I had generosity enough to make it worth their while.

This of Hannah, he might see, I took very well. I said I had thoughts of sending for her as soon as I got to more convenient lodgings.

Upon the whole, I told him that I thought his proposal of Windsor not amiss; and that I would remove thither, if I could get a lodging only for myself, and an upper chamber for Hannah;

This conversation was to be, all of it, in the main agreeable. He asked whether I would choose to lodge in the town of Windsor, or out of it?

As near the castle, I said, as possible, for the convenience of going constantly to the public worship; an opportunity I had been long deprived of.

162

He should be very glad, he told me, if he could procure me accommodations in any one of the canon's houses; which he imagined would be more agreeable to me than any other on many accounts. And as he could depend upon my promise, never to have any other man but himself, on the condition to which he had so cheerfully subscribed, he should be easy; since it was now his part, *in earnest*, to set about recommending himself to my favour by the *only* way he knew it could be done. Adding, with a very serious air, I am but a young man, madam; but I have run a long course; let not your purity of mind incline you to despise me for the acknowledgment. It is high time to be weary of it, and to reform.

I was agreeably surprised. I looked at him, I believe, as if I doubted my ears and my eyes. His aspect, however, became his words. Surely, my dear, the man *must* be in earnest. He could not have *said* this, he could not have *thought* it, had he not.

The divine grace or favour, Mr. Lovelace, must do all, and confirm all. You know not how much you please me that I can talk to you in this dialect.

Yet, madam, be pleased to remember one thing: reformation cannot be a sudden work. I have infinite vivacity; it is that which runs away with me.

.   .   .   .

Mr. Lovelace is gone to Windsor, having left two servants to attend me. He purposes to be back to-morrow.

I have written to my Aunt Hervey to supplicate her interest in my behalf, for my clothes, books, and money, signifying to her that, if I may be restored to the favour of my family, and allowed a negative only as to any man who may be proposed to me, and be used like a daughter, a niece, a sister, I will stand by my offer to live single, and submit as I ought to a negative from my father. Intimating, nevertheless, that it were perhaps better, after the usage I have received from my brother and sister, that I may be allowed to be distant from them, as well for their sakes as for my own (meaning, as I suppose it will be taken, at my Dairy-house) — offering "to take my father's directions as to the manner I shall live in, the servants I shall have, and in everything that shall show the dutiful subordination to which I am willing to conform."

MR. LOVELACE TO JOHN BELFORD, ESQ.

Friday, April 14.

SHE is very apprehensive of me, I see. I have studied before her and Miss Howe, as often as I have been with them, to pass for a giddy thoughtless creature. What a folly, then, to be so *expatiatingly* sincere in my answer to her home-put upon the noises within the garden! But such success having attended that contrivance (success, Jack, has blown many a man up!) my cursed *vanity* got uppermost, and kept down my *caution*. The menace to have secreted Solmes, and that other, that I had thoughts to run away with her foolish brother, and of my project to revenge her upon the two servants, so much terrified the dear creature that I was forced to sit down to muse after means to put myself right in her opinion.

Some favourable incidents, at the time, tumbled in from my agent in her family; at least such as I was determined to *make* favourable; and therefore I desired admittance, and this before she could resolve anything against me; that is to say, while her admiration of my intrepidity kept resolution in suspense.

He then acquaints his friend with what passed between him and the lady, in relation to his advices from Harlowe Place, and to his proposal about lodgings, pretty much to the same purpose as in her preceding letter.

When he comes to mention his proposal of the Windsor lodgings, thus he expresses himself:

Now, Belford, can it enter into thy leaden head what I meant by this proposal? I know it cannot. And so I'll tell thee.

To leave her for a day or two, with a view *to serve her by my absence*, would, as I thought, look like confiding in her favour. I could not think of leaving her, thou knowest, while I had reason to believe her friends would pursue us; and I began to apprehend that she would suspect that I made a pretence of that intentional pursuit to keep about her and with her. But now that they had declared against it, and that they would *not* receive her if she went back (a declaration she had better hear first from me than from Miss Howe or any other), what should hinder me from giving her this mark of my obedience; especially as I could leave Will, who is a clever fellow, and can do anything but write and spell, and Lord M.'s Jonas (not as guards, to be sure, but as attendants only); the latter to be dispatched to me occasionally by the former, whom I could acquaint with my motions?

As to Windsor, I had no design to carry her particularly thither; but somewhere it was proper to name, as she condescended to ask my advice about it. London, I durst not, but very cautiously, and so as to make it her own option; for I must tell thee that there is such a perverseness in the sex, that when they ask your advice, they do it only to know your opinion, that they may oppose it; though had not the thing in question been *your* choice, perhaps it had been *theirs*.

.   .   .   .

But is it not a confounded thing that I cannot fasten an obligation upon this proud beauty? I have two motives in endeavouring to prevail upon her to accept of money and raiment from me; one, the real pleasure I should have in the accommodating of the haughty maid; and to think there was something near her, and upon her, that I could call *mine*; the other, in order to abate her severity and humble her a little.

Nothing sooner brings down a proud spirit than a sense of lying under pecuniary obligations. No more could I do it than I could borrow of an insolent uncle, or inquisitive aunt, who would thence think themselves entitled to have an account of all my life and actions laid before them for their review and censure.

My charmer, I see, has a pride like my own; but she has no *distinction* in her pride; nor knows the pretty fool that there is nothing nobler, nothing more delightful, than for lovers to be conferring and receiving obligations from each other.

Now, Belford, canst thou imagine what I meant by proposing Hannah, or one of the girls here, for an attendant?

Believing she would certainly propose to have that favourite wench about her as soon as she was a little settled, I had caused the girl to be inquired after, with an intent to make interest, somehow or other, that a month's warning should be insisted on by her master or mistress, or by some other means which I had not determined upon, to prevent her coming to her. But fortune fights for me. The wench is luckily ill; a violent rheumatic disorder, which has obliged her to leave her place, confines her to her chamber. Poor Hannah! How I pity the girl! These things are very hard upon industrious servants! I intend to make the poor wench a small present on the occasion — I know it will oblige my charmer.

And so, Jack, *pretending not to know anything of the matter*, I pressed her to send for Hannah. She knew I had always a regard for this servant, because of her honest love to her lady; but *now* I have a greater regard for her than ever.

He gives an account of the serious part of their conversation, with no great variation from the lady's account of it; and when he comes to that part of it where he bids her remember that reformation cannot be a sudden thing, he asks his friend:

Is not this fair play? Is it not dealing ingenuously? Then the observation, I will be bold to say, is founded in *truth* and *nature*. But there was a little touch of *policy* in it besides; that the lady, if I should fly out again, should not think me too gross an hypocrite, for, as I plainly told her, I was afraid that my fits of reformation were *but* fits and sallies; but I hoped her example would fix them into habits.

Miss Howe to Miss Clarissa Harlowe

Saturday, April 15.

I will write a few lines upon the new light that has broke in upon your gentleman; and send it by a particular hand.

His ingenuousness is the thing that staggers me; yet is he cunning enough to know that whoever accuses himself first, blunts the edge of an adversary's accusation.

He is certainly a man of sense; there is more hope of such a one than of a fool; and there must be a *beginning* to a reformation. These I will allow in his favour.

But this that follows, I think, is the only way to judge of his specious confessions and self-accusations. Does he confess anything that you knew not before, or that you are not likely to find out from others? If nothing else, what does he confess to his own disadvantage? You have heard of his duels; you have heard of his seductions — all the world has. He *owns*, therefore, what it would be to no purpose to *conceal*; and his ingenuousness is a salvo — "Why, this, madam, is no more than Mr. Lovelace *himself* acknowledges."

MISS CLARISSA HARLOWE TO MISS HOWE

Sat. Afternoon.

You dishearten me a good deal about Mr. Lovelace. I may be too willing from my sad circumstances to think the best of him. If his pretences to reformation are *but* pretences, what must be his intent? But can the heart of man be so very vile? Can he, *dare* he, mock the Almighty? But may I not, from one very sad reflection, think better of him; that I am thrown too much into his power to make it *necessary* for him (except he were to intend the *very utmost* villainy by me) to be such a shocking hypocrite? He must, at least, be in earnest at the *time* he gives the better hopes. Surely he must. You yourself must join with me in this hope, or you could not wish me to be so dreadfully yoked.

Mrs. Sorlings showed me a letter this morning which she had received from her sister Greme last night; in which Mrs. Greme (hoping I will forgive her forward zeal if her sister thinks fit to show her letter to me) wishes (and that for all the noble family's sake, and she hopes she may say for my own) that I will be pleased to yield to make his honour, as she calls him, happy. She grounds her *officiousness*, as she calls it, upon what he was so *condescending* (her word also) to say to her yesterday in his way to Windsor, on her *presuming* to ask if she might soon give him joy: that no man ever loved a woman as he loves me; that no woman ever so well deserved to be beloved; that in every conversation he admires me still more; that he loves me with such a purity as he had never believed himself capable of, or that a mortal creature could have inspired him with; looking upon me as all *soul*; as an angel sent down to save *his*; and a great deal more of this sort: but that he apprehends my consent to make him happy is at a greater distance than he wishes. And complained of the too severe restrictions I had laid upon him before I honoured him with my *confidence*; which restrictions *must be as sacred to him as if they were parts of the marriage contract*, etc.

What, my dear, shall I say to this? How shall I take it? Mrs. Greme is a good woman. Mrs. Sorlings is a good woman. And this letter agrees with the conversation between Mr. Lovelace and me, which I thought, and still think, so agreeable. Yet what means the man by *foregoing the opportunities he has had to declare himself?* What mean his *complaints of my restrictions* to Mrs. Greme? He is not a bashful man. But you say I inspire people with an awe of me. An awe, my dear! As how?

Forgive me, my dear, and love me as you used to do. For although my fortunes are changed, my heart is not; nor ever will, but while it bids my pen tell you that it must cease to beat when it is not as much yours as / Your / CLARISSA HARLOWE's.

MISS CLARISSA HARLOWE TO MISS HOWE

Saturday Evening.

MR. LOVELACE has seen divers apartments at Windsor, but not one, he says, that he thought fit for me, and which at the same time answered my description.

He has been very solicitous to keep to the letter of my instructions; which looks well; and the better I liked him, as, although he proposed that town, he came back dissuading me from it; for he said that in his journey from thence he had thought Windsor, although of his own proposal, a wrong choice; because I coveted privacy, and that was a place generally visited and admired.

I told him that if Mrs. Sorlings thought me not an encumbrance I would be willing to stay here a little longer; provided he would leave me and go to Lord M.'s or to London, whichever he thought best.

He hoped, he said, that he might suppose me absolutely safe from the insults or attempts of my brother; and therefore, if it would make me easier, he would obey, for a few days at least.

He hinted to me that he had received a letter from Lady Betty, and another (as I understood him) from one of the Miss Montagues. If they take notice of *me* in them, I wonder that he did not acquaint me with the contents. I am afraid, my dear, that his relations are among those who think I have taken a rash and inexcusable step. It is not to my *credit* to let *even them* know how I have been *frighted out of myself*; and yet perhaps they would hold me unworthy of their alliance if they were to think my flight a voluntary one. O my dear, how uneasy to us are our reflections upon every doubtful occurrence, when we know we have been prevailed upon to do a wrong thing!

Sunday Morning.

Ah! this man, my dear! We have had warmer dialogues than ever yet we have had. At fair argument I find I need not fear him; but he is such a wild, such an ungovernable creature (*he* reformed!), that I am half afraid of him.

He again, on my declaring myself uneasy at his stay with me here, proposed that I would put myself in Lady Betty's protection, assuring me that he thought he could not leave me at Mrs. Sorlings's with safety to myself. And upon my declining to do that, for the reason I gave you in my last, he urged me to make a demand of my estate.

He knew it, I told him, to be my resolution not to litigate with my father.

Nor would he put me upon it, he replied, but as the *last* thing. But if my spirit would not permit me to be *obliged,* as I called it, to anybody, and yet if my relations would refuse me my own, he knew not how I could keep up that spirit without being put to inconveniences which would give him infinite concern — unless — unless — unless, he said hesitating, as if afraid to speak out — unless I would take the only method I *could* take to obtain the possession of my own.

What is *that*, sir?

Sure the man saw by my looks, when he came with his creeping *unlesses,* that I guessed what he meant.

Ah, madam! can you be at a loss to know what that method is? They will not dispute with a *man* that right which they would contest with *you.*

Why said he with a *man*, instead of with *him?* Yet he looked as if he wanted to be encouraged to say more.

So, sir, you would have me employ a lawyer, would you, notwithstanding what I have ever declared as to litigating with my papa?

No, I would not, my dearest creature, snatching my hand, and pressing it with his lips — except you would make *me* the lawyer.

Had he said *me* at first, I should have been above the affectation of mentioning a lawyer.

I blushed. The man pursued not the subject so ardently, but that it was more easy as well as more natural to avoid it than to fall into it.

Would to Heaven he might, without offending! But I *so* overawed him! (*Overawed* him — *your* notion, my dear.) And so the overawed, bashful man went off from the subject, repeating his proposal that I would demand my own estate, or empower some man of the law to demand it, if I *would not* (he put in) empower a happier man to demand it. But it could not be amiss, he thought, to acquaint my two trustees that I intended to assume it.

I should know better what to do, I told him, when he was at a distance from me and *known* to be so. I suppose, sir, that if my father propose my return, and engage never to mention Solmes to me, nor any other man, but by *my consent,* and I agree, upon that condition, to think no more of *you,* you will acquiesce.

I was willing to try whether he had the regard to *all* my previous declarations which he pretended to have to *some* of them.

He was struck all of a heap.

What say you, Mr. Lovelace? You know, all you mean is for my good. Surely I am my own mistress; surely I need not ask your leave to make what terms I please for myself, *so long as I break none with you?*

He hemm'd twice or thrice. Why, madam — why, madam, I cannot say — then pausing, and rising from his seat with petulance: I see plainly enough, said he, the reason why none of my proposals can be accepted; at *last* I am to be a sacrifice to your reconciliation with your implacable family.

It has always been your respectful way, Mr. Lovelace, to treat my family in this free manner. But pray, sir, when you call *others* implacable, see that you deserve not the same censure *yourself*.

He must needs say there was no love lost between some of my family and him, but he had not deserved of *them* what they had of *him*.

Yourself being judge, I suppose, sir?

All the world, you yourself, madam, being judge.

Then, sir, let me tell you, had you been less upon your defiances, they would not have been irritated so much against you. But nobody ever heard that avowed despite to the relations of a person was a proper courtship either to that person or to her friends.

Well, madam, all that I know is, that their malice against me is such that, if you determine to sacrifice *me*, you may be reconciled when you please.

And all that I know, sir, is, that if I do give my father the power of a negative, and he will be contented with *that*, it will be but my *duty* to give it him; and if I preserve one to myself, I shall break through no obligation to *you*.

Your duty to your capricious *brother*, not to your *father*, you mean, madam.

If the dispute lay between my brother and me at *first*, surely, sir, a father may choose which party he will take.

He *may*, madam — but that exempts him not from blame for all that, if he take the wrong ——

Your hope, sir, had been better grounded if you had had my consent to my abandoning of my father's house ——

Always, madam, and for ever to be reminded of the choice you would have made of that damned Solmes — rather than ——

Not so hasty! Not so rash, Mr. Lovelace! I am convinced that there was no intention to marry me to that Solmes on Wednesday.

So I am told they now give out, in order to justify themselves at your expense. Everybody living, madam, is obliged to you for your kind thoughts but I.

Excuse me, *good* Mr. Lovelace (waving my hand and bowing), that I am willing to think the best of my father.

Charming creature! said he, with what a bewitching air is that said! — And with a vehemence in his manner, would have snatched my hand. But I withdrew it, being offended with him.

I think, madam, my sufferings for your sake might have entitled me to some favour.

My sufferings, sir, for *your* impetuous temper, set against *your* sufferings for *my sake*, I humbly conceive, leave me very little your debtor.

Lord! Madam (assuming a drolling air), what have *you* suffered! Nothing but what you can easily forgive. You have been *only* made a prisoner in your father's house by the way of doing credit to your judgment! You have *only* had an innocent and faithful servant turned out of your service because you loved her. You have *only* had your sister's confident servant set over you, with leave to tease and affront you!

Very well, sir!

You have *only* had an insolent brother take upon him to treat you like a slave, and as insolent a sister to undermine you in everybody's favour, on pretence to keep you out of hands which, if as vile as they vilely report, are not, however, half so vile and cruel as their own!

Go on, sir, if you please!

You have *only* been persecuted in order to oblige you to have a sordid fellow whom you have professed to hate, and whom everybody despises! The licence has been *only* got! The parson has *only* been held in readiness! The day, a near, a *very* near day, has been *only* fixed! And you were *only* to be searched for your correspondences, and still closer confined till the day came, in order to deprive you of all means of escaping the snare laid for you! But all this you can forgive! You can wish you had stood all this, inevitable as the compulsion must have been! And the man who, at the hazard of his life, has delivered you from all these mortifications, is the only person you *cannot* forgive!

Can't you go on, sir? You see I have patience to hear you. Can't you go on, sir?"

I can, madam, with *my* sufferings; which I confess ought not to be mentioned, were I at last to be rewarded in the manner I hoped.

Your *sufferings*, then, if you please, sir?

Affrontingly forbidden your father's house, after encouragement given, without any reasons they knew not before, to justify the prohibition; forced upon a rencounter I wished to avoid: the first I ever, so provoked, wished to avoid; and that, because the wretch was your brother!

Wretch, sir! — and my brother! This could be from no man breathing but from him before me!

Pardon me, madam! But oh! how unworthy to be your brother! The quarrel grafted upon an old one when at college; he universally known to be the aggressor; and revived for views equally sordid and injurious both to yourself and me — giving life to him who would have taken away mine!

Your *generosity* THIS, sir, not your sufferings; a little more of your *sufferings*, if you please! I hope you do not repent that you did not murder my brother!

Menaces every day and defiances put into every one's mouth against me! Forced to creep about in disguises — and to watch *all hours* ——

And in *all weathers*, I suppose, sir — that, I remember, was once your grievance! *In all weathers*, sir! And all these hardships arising from yourself, not imposed by me.

— Like a thief, or an eavesdropper, proceeded he; and yet neither by birth nor alliances unworthy of *their* relation, whatever I may be and am of their admirable daughter; of whom they, every one of them, are at least *as* unworthy! These, madam, I call sufferings; *justly* call so; if at last I am to be sacrificed to an imperfect reconciliation —

imperfect, I say; for can you expect to live so much as *tolerably* under the same roof, after all that is passed, with that brother and sister?

O sir, sir! What sufferings have yours been! And all for my sake, I warrant! I can never reward you for them! Never think of me more, I beseech you. How can you have patience with me? Nothing has been owing to your own behaviour, I presume; nothing to your defiances for defiances; nothing to your resolution declared more than once, that you *would* be related to a family which, nevertheless, you would not stoop to ask a relation of; nothing, in short, to courses which everybody blamed you for, you not thinking it worth your while to justify yourself. Had I not thought you used in an ungentlemanly manner as I have heretofore told you, you had not had my notice by pen and ink. That notice gave you a supposed security, and you generously defied my friends the more for it; and this brought upon me (perhaps not undeservedly) my father's displeasure; without which my brother's private pique and selfish views would have wanted a foundation to build upon; so that all that followed of my treatment, and your redundant *onlys*, I might thank you principally, as you may yourself for all your *sufferings*, your *mighty* sufferings! And if, voluble sir, you have founded any merit upon them, be so good as to revoke it; and look upon *me*, with my forfeited reputation, as the only sufferer. For what — pray hear me out, sir (for he was going to speak), have you suffered in, but your pride? Your reputation *could not* suffer; *that* it was beneath you to be solicitous about.

Darkness, light; light, darkness; by my soul! — just as you please to have it. O charmer of my heart! snatching my hand, and pressing it between both his, to his lips, in a strange wild way, take me, take me to yourself; mould me as you please; I am wax in your hands; give me your own impression, and seal me for ever yours. We were born for each other! — you to make me happy, and save a soul — I am all error, all crime. I see what I ought to have done. But do you think, madam, I can willingly consent to be sacrificed to a partial reconciliation in which I shall be so great, so irreparable a sufferer? — Anything but *that*. Include me in your terms; prescribe to me; promise for me as you please; put a halter about my neck and lead me by it, upon condition of forgiveness on that disgraceful penance, and of a prostration as servile, to your father's presence (your brother absent), and I will beg his consent at his feet, and bear anything but spurning from him, because he is your father. But to give you up upon *cold* conditions, d—n me (said the shocking wretch), if I either will or can!

These were his words as near as I can remember them; for his behaviour was so strangely wild and fervent that I was perfectly frighted. I thought he would have devoured my hand. I wished myself a thousand miles distant from him.

I told him I by no means approved of his violent temper; he was too boisterous a man for my liking. I saw *now*, by the conversation that had passed, what was his boasted regard to my *injunctions*; and should take my measures accordingly, as he should *soon* find. And with a half-frighted earnestness I desired him to withdraw and leave me to myself.

He obeyed; and that with extreme complaisance in his manner, but with his complexion greatly heightened, and a countenance as greatly dissatisfied.

But on recollecting all that passed, I plainly see that he means not, if he can help it, to leave me to the liberty of refusing him; which I had nevertheless preserved a *right* to do; but looks upon me as *his*, by a strange sort of obligation, for having run away with me *against my will*.

What to do about going from this place, I cannot tell. I could stay here with all my heart.

Miss Clarissa Harlowe to Miss Howe

Sunday Night (April 16).

I AM strangely at a loss what to think of this man. He is a perfect Proteus. I can but write according to the shape he assumes at the time. Don't think *me* the changeable person, I beseech you, if m one letter I contradict what I said in the same letter; for he is a perfect chameleon.

Before I could finish my last to you, he sent up twice more to beg admittance. I have a letter, madam, said he, from Lady Betty Lawrance, and another from my Cousin Charlotte. But of these more by and by. I came now to make my humble acknowledgments to you, upon the arguments that passed between us so lately.

I was silent, wondering what he was driving at.

He then read to me part of Lady Betty's letter; turning down the beginning, which was a little too severe upon him, he said. She hopes I will not too long delay the ceremony, because that performed will be to her, and to Lord M. and Lady Sarah, a sure pledge of her nephew's merits and good behaviour.

She says she was always sorry to hear of the hardships I had met with on his account. That he will be the most ingrateful of men if he make not *all up* to me; and that she thinks it incumbent upon all their family to supply to me the lost favour of my own; and for her part, nothing of that kind, she bids him assure me, shall be wanting.

She concludes with desiring to be informed of our nuptials the moment they are celebrated, that she may be with the earliest in felicitating me on the happy occasion. But her ladyship gives me no direct invitation to attend her before marriage; which I might have expected from what he had told me.

He then showed me part of Miss Montague's more sprightly letter, congratulating him upon the honour he had obtained, of the *confidence of so admirable a lady*. Those are her words. *Confidence*, my dear! She also wishes for his speedy nuptials, and to see her new cousin at M. Hall; as do Lord M., she tells him, and her sister; and in general all the well-wishers of their family.

This young lady says nothing in excuse for not meeting me on the road, or at St. Albans, as he had made me expect she would; yet mentions *her having been indisposed.* Mr. Lovelace had also told me that Lord M. *was ill of the gout,* which Miss Montague's letter confirms.

Miss Clarissa Harlowe to Miss Howe

You may believe, my dear, that these letters put me in good humour with him. He saw in it my countenance and congratulated himself upon it. Yet I cannot but repeat my wonder that I could not have the contents of them communicated to me last night.

He then urged me to go directly to Lady Betty's, on the strength of her letter.

But how, said I, can I do that, were I even out of all hope of a reconciliation with my friends (which yet, however unlikely to be effected, is my duty to *attempt*), as her ladyship has given me no particular invitation?

That, he was sure, was owing to her doubt that it would be accepted — else she had done it with the greatest pleasure in the world.

That doubt itself, I said, was enough to deter me; since her ladyship, who knew so well the boundaries of the fit and the unfit, by her not expecting I would accept of an invitation, had she given it, would have reason to think me very forward if I *had* accepted it; and much more forward to go without it.

He wished he knew but my mind — that should direct him in his proposals, and it would be his delight to observe it, whatever it were.

My mind is, that you, sir, should leave me out of hand. How often must I tell you so?

He seemed a little disconcerted.

You know, Mr. Lovelace, proceeded I, why I am so earnest for your absence. It is that I may appear to the world independent of you; and in hopes, by that means, to find it less difficult to set on foot a reconciliation with my friends.

Charming reasoning! And let him tell me that the assurance I had given him was *all he wished for*. It was *more* than he could ask. What a happiness to have a woman of honour and generosity to depend upon! Had he, on his first entrance into the world, met with such a one, he had never been other than a man of strict virtue. But all, he hoped, was for the best; since, in that case, he had never perhaps had the happiness he had now in view; because his relations had been always urging him to marry, and that before he had the honour to know me. And now, as he had not been so bad as some people's malice reported him to be, he hoped he should have near as much merit in his repentance as if he had never erred. A fine rakish notion and hope! And too much encouraged, I doubt, my dear, by the generality of our sex!

This brought on a more serious question or two. You'll see by it what a creature an unmortified libertine is.

I asked him if he knew what he had said alluded to a sentence in the best of books: *That there was more joy in heaven* ——

He took the words out of my mouth,

Over one sinner that repenteth, than over ninety-and-nine just persons which need no repentance,[1] were his words.

Yes, madam, I thought of it as soon as I said it, but not before. I have read the story of the Prodigal Son, I'll assure you; and one day, when I am settled as I hope to be, will write a dramatic piece on the subject. I have at times had it in my head, and you will be too ready, perhaps, to allow me to be qualified for it.

O sir, do you want to be complimented into repentance and salvation?

Dearest madam, forbear for the present: I am but in my noviciate. Your foundation must be laid brick by brick. You'll hinder the progress of the good work you would promote, if you tumble in a whole wagon-load at once upon me.

I asked him what he really, and in his most deliberate mind, would advise me to do in my present situation? He must needs see, I said, that I was at a great loss what to resolve upon, entirely a stranger to London, having no adviser, no protector at present: himself, he must give me leave to tell him, greatly deficient in *practice,* if not in the *knowledge,* of those decorums which, I had supposed, were always to be found in a man of birth, fortune, and education.

He imagines himself, I find, to be a very polite man, and cannot bear to be thought otherwise. He put up his lip — I am sorry for it, madam — a man of breeding, a man of politeness, give me leave to say (colouring), is much more of a black swan with *you,* than with any lady I ever met with.

Then that is your misfortune, Mr. Lovelace, as well as mine, at present.

O Lord! O Lord! Poor I! — was the light, yet the half-angry wretch's self-pitying expression.

I proceeded: Upon my word, sir, you are not the accomplished man which your talents and opportunities would have led one to expect you to be. You are indeed in your noviciate as to every laudable attainment.

·　·　·　·　·　·　·　·　·　·　·

I remember, my dear, in one of your former letters you mentioned London as the most private place to be in; and I said that since he made such pretences against leaving me here, as showed he had no intention to do so; and since he engaged to go from me, and to leave me to pursue my own measures, if I were elsewhere; and since his presence made these lodgings inconvenient to me, I should not be disinclined to go to London, did I know anybody there.

As he had several times proposed London to me, I expected that

[1] Luke xv, 7. The parable is concerning the Ninety-nine Sheep, not the Prodigal Son, as Mr. Lovelace erroneously imagines.

he would eagerly have embraced that motion from me. But he took not ready hold of it; yet I thought his eye approved of it.

We are both great watchers of each other's eyes; and indeed seem to be more than half afraid of each other.

He then made a grateful proposal to me, that I would send for my Norton to attend me.

He saw by my eyes, he said, that he had at last been happy in an expedient which would answer the wishes of us both. Why, says he, did not I think of it before? And snatching my hand: Shall I write, madam? Shall I send? Shall I go and fetch the worthy woman myself?

More coolly than perhaps his generosity deserved, I told him it was impossible but I must soon hear from my friends. I should not, meantime, embroil anybody with them. Not Mrs. Norton especially, from whose interest in, and mediation with my mother, I might expect some good, were she to keep herself in a neutral state; that besides, the good woman had a mind above her fortune; and would sooner want than be beholden to anybody improperly.

Improperly! said he. Have not persons of merit a *right* to all the benefits conferred upon them?

Give me leave, sir, said I, to tell you there is a strange mixture in your mind. You must have taken *pains* to suppress many good motions and reflections as they arose, or levity must have been surprisingly predominant in it. But as to the subject we were upon, there is no taking any resolutions till I hear from my friends.

Well, madam, I can only say I would find out some expedient, if I could, that should be agreeable to you.

I am quite at a loss, said I, what to do or whither to go. Would you, Mr. Lovelace, in earnest advise me to think of going to London?

And I looked at him with steadfastness. But nothing could I gather from his looks.

At first, madam, said he, I was for proposing London, as I was then more apprehensive of pursuit. But as your relations seem cooler on that head, I am the more indifferent about the place you go to. So as *you* are pleased, so as *you* are easy, I shall be happy.

This indifference of his to London, I cannot but say, made me incline the more to go thither. I asked him (to hear what he would say) if he could recommend me to any *particular place* in London?

No, he said; none that was fit for me or that I should like. His friend Belford, indeed, had very handsome lodgings near Soho Square, at a relation's, whose wife was a woman of virtue and honour. These, as Mr. Belford was generally in the country, he could borrow till I were better accommodated.

Well, sir, said I (rising to leave him), something must be resolved upon; but I will postpone this subject till to-morrow morning.

He would fain have engaged me longer; but I said I would see him as early as he pleased in the morning. He might think of any convenient place in London, or near it, meantime.

And so I retired from him. As I do from my pen; hoping for better rest for the few hours that remain of this night than I have had of a long time.

(*In continuation*)   *Monday Morning, April 17.*

Mr. Lovelace, who is an early riser as well as I, joined me in the garden about six, and after the usual salutations, asked me to resume our last night's subject. It was upon lodgings at London, he said.

I think you mentioned one to me, sir — did you not?

Yes, madam, but (watching the turn of my countenance) rather as what you would be welcome to than perhaps approve of.

I believe so too. To go to town upon an *uncertainty*, I own, is not agreeable; but to be obliged to any persons of your acquaintance, when I want to be thought independent of you, is an absurd thing to mention.

He did not mention it as what he imagined I would accept, but only to confirm to me what he had said, that he himself knew of none fit for me.

Has not your family, madam, some one tradesman they deal with who has convenience of this kind?

My father's tradesmen, I said, would no doubt be the first employed to find me out.

We had a good deal of discourse upon the same topic. But at last the result was this: he wrote a letter to one Mr. Doleman, a married man of fortune and character (I excepting to Mr. Belford), desiring him to provide decent apartments ready furnished for a single woman; consisting of a bed-chamber, another for a maid-servant, with the use of a dining-room or parlour. This letter he gave me to peruse; and then sealed it up and dispatched it away in my presence by one of his own servants, who, having business in town, is to bring back an answer.

I attend the issue of it.

MR. LOVELACE TO JOHN BELFORD, ESQ.

                                                     Sat., Sunday, Monday.

UPON such good terms when we parted, I was surprised to find so solemn a brow upon my return, and her charming eyes red with weeping. But when I had understood she had received letters from Miss Howe, it was natural to imagine that that little devil had put her out of humour with me.

It is easy for me to perceive that my charmer is more sullen when she receives a letter from that vixen than at other times. I must contrive some way or other to get at their correspondence — only to see the turn of it, that's all. But no attempt of this kind must be made yet. A detected invasion in an article so sacred would ruin me beyond retrieve.

.   .   .   .

I wanted her to propose London herself. This made me again mention Windsor. If you would have a woman do one thing you must always propose another, and that the very contrary. The sex! the very sex! as I hope to be saved! Why, Jack, they lay a man under a necessity to deal doubly with them! And when they find themselves outwitted, they cry out upon an honest fellow who has been too hard for them at their own weapons.

I could hardly contain myself. My heart was at my throat. Down, down, said I to myself, exuberant exultation! A sudden cough befriended me; I again turned to her, all is *indifferenced over* as a girl at the first long-expected question, who waits for two more. I heard out the rest of her speech; and when she had done, instead of saying anything to her of London, I advised her *to send for Mrs. Norton.*

. . . .

I am in the right train now. Every hour, I doubt not, will give me an increasing interest in the affections of this proud beauty. I have just carried *unpoliteness* far enough to *make her afraid of me*, and to show her that I am *no whiner*. Every instance of politeness *now* will give me a double credit with her. My next point will be to make her acknowledge a *lambent* flame, a preference of me to all other men at least; and then my happy hour is not far off. An *acknowledged* reciprocality of love sanctifies every little freedom; and little freedoms beget greater. And if she call me *ungenerous*, I can call her *cruel*. The sex love to be called cruel. Many a time I complained of cruelty, even in the act of yielding, because I knew it gratified the fair one's pride.

I had a view, moreover, to give her an high opinion of her own sagacity. I love, when I dig a pit, to have my prey tumble in with secure feet and open eyes; then a man can look down upon her, with an *O-ho, charmer, how came you there?*

MISS HOWE TO MISS CLARISSA HARLOWE
Tuesday, April 18.

You ASK me if I would treat Mr. Lovelace, were he to be in Mr. Hickman's place, as I do Mr. Hickman? Why really, my dear, I believe I should not. I have been very sagely considering this point of behaviour (in general) on both sides in courtship, and I will very candidly tell you the result. I have concluded that politeness, even to excess, is necessary on the men's part, to bring us to listen to their first addresses, in order to induce us to bow our necks to a yoke so unequal. But upon my conscience, I very much doubt whether a little intermingled insolence is not requisite from them, to keep up that interest when once it has got footing. Men must not let us see that we can make fools of them.

Your frequent quarrels and reconciliations verify this observation; and I really believe that could Hickman have kept my attention alive after the Lovelace manner, only that he had preserved his morals, I should have married the man by this time.

I am pleased with the contents of these ladies' letters. And the more as I have caused the family to be again sounded, and find that they are all as desirous as ever of your alliance.

They really are (every one of them) your very great admirers. And as for Lord M., he is so much pleased with you, and with the confidence, as he calls it, which you have reposed in his nephew, that he vows he will disinherit him if he reward it not as he ought. You must take care that you lose not both families.

Your handsome husbands, my dear, make a wife's heart ache very often; and though you are as fine a person of a woman, at the least, as he is of a man, he will take too much delight in *himself* to think himself more indebted to your favour than you are to his distinction and preference of you. But no man, take your finer mind with your very fine person, can deserve you. So you must be contented should your merit be underrated; since that *must* be so, marry whom you will. Perhaps you will think I indulge these sort of reflections against your Narcissuses of men, to keep my mother's choice for me of Hickman in countenance with myself — I don't know but there is something in it; at least enough to have given birth to the reflection.

I think there can be no objection to your going to London. There, as in the centre, you will be in the way of hearing from everybody and sending to anybody. And then you will put all his sincerity to the test, *as to his promised absence* and such like.

But indeed, my dear, I think you have nothing for it but marriage. All the world, in short, expect you to have this man. They think that you left your father's house for this very purpose. The longer the ceremony is delayed, the worse appearance it will have in the world's eye. And it will not be the fault of some of your relations if a slur be not thrown upon your reputation while you continue unmarried.

Your Hannah, cannot attend you. The poor girl left her place about a fortnight ago on account of a rheumatic disorder, which has confined her to her room ever since. She burst into tears when Kitty carried to her your desire of having her with you, and called herself doubly unhappy that she could not wait upon a mistress whom she so dearly loved.

My mother has vexed me a little very lately by some instances of her jealous narrowness. I will mention one of them, though I did not intend it. She wanted to borrow thirty guineas of me; *only* while she changed a note. I said I could lend her but eight or ten. Eight or ten would not do; she thought I was much richer. I could have told her I was much cunninger than to let her know my stock; which, on a review, I find ninety-five guineas, and all of them most heartily at your service.

I believe your Uncle Tony put her upon this wise project for she was *out of cash* in an hour after he left her. If he did, you will judge that they intend to distress you. If it will provoke *you* to demand your own in a legal way, I wish they would; since their putting you upon that course will justify the necessity of your leaving them.

Your next, I suppose, will be from London. Pray direct it, and your future letters till further notice, to Mr. Hickman at his own house. He is entirely devoted to you. Don't take so heavily my mother's partiality and prejudices. I hope I am past a baby.

MISS CLARISSA HARLOWE TO MISS HOWE

Wedn. Morn., April 19.

I AM glad, my dear friend, that you approve of my removal to London.

I am unhappy that I cannot have my worthy Hannah. I am as sorry for the poor creature's illness as for my own disappointment by it. Come, my dear Miss Howe, since you press me to be beholden to you, and would think me proud if I absolutely refused your favour, pray be so good as to send her two guineas in my name.

If I have nothing for it, as you say, but matrimony, it yields a little comfort that his relations do not despise the *fugitive*, as persons of their rank and quality-pride might be supposed to do, for having *been* a fugitive.

Thursday, April 20.

Mr. Lovelace's servant is already returned with an answer from his friend Mr. Doleman. You will see that his friends in town have a notion that we are actually married.

To Robert Lovelace, Esq.

Tuesday Night, April 18.

DEAR SIR, — I have been in town for this week past to get help, if I could, from my paralytic complaints, and am in a course for them. Which nevertheless did not prevent me from making the desired inquiries. This is the result.

You may have a first floor, well furnished, at a mercer's in Bedford Street, Covent Garden, with conveniences for servants: and these either by the quarter or month. The terms according to the conveniences required.

Mrs. Doleman has seen lodgings in Norfolk Street and others in Cecil Street; but though the prospects to the Thames and Surrey hills look inviting from both these streets, yet I suppose they are too near the city.

You may have good accommodations in Dover Street, at a widow's, the relict of an officer in the guards, who dying soon after he had purchased his commission (to which he had a good title by service, and which cost him the most part of what he had), she *was obliged to let lodgings.*

She rents two good houses, distant from each other, only joined by a *large handsome passage.* The *inner house* is the genteelest and is very elegantly furnished; but you may have the use of a very handsome parlour in the *outer house* if you choose to look into the street. A little garden belongs to the inner house.

As these lodgings seemed to me the most likely to please you, I was more particular in my inquiries about them. A *dignified clergyman,* his *wife,* and maiden *daughter,* were the last who lived in them. They have but lately quitted them on his being presented to a considerable church preferment in Ireland.

I had some knowledge of the colonel, who was always looked upon as a man of honour. His relict I never saw before. I think she has a *masculine air,* and is a *little forbidding at first.*

If these, or any other of the lodgings I have mentioned, be not altogether to your lady's mind, she may continue in them *the less while* and *choose others for herself.*

As we *suppose you married,* but that you have reason, from family differences, to keep it private for the present, I thought it not amiss to hint as much to the widow (but as *uncertainty,* however), and asked her if she could in that case accommodate you and your servants, as well as the lady and hers? She said she could, and wished, by all means, it were to be so; since the circumstance of a person's *being single,* if not as well recommended as this lady, was *one of her usual exceptions.*

If none of these lodgings please, you need not doubt very handsome ones in or near Hanover Square, Soho Square, Golden Square, or in some of the new streets about Grosvenor Square.

Your sincere and affectionate friend and servant, / THO. DOLEMAN.

You will easily guess, my dear, when you have read the letter, *which* lodgings I made choice of. But first, to try him (as in so material a point I thought I could not be too circumspect), I seemed to prefer those in Norfolk Street. Then seeming to incline to the lodgings in Cecil Street — then to the mercer's. But he made no visible preference; and when I asked his opinion of the widow-gentlewoman's, he said he thought those the most to my taste and convenience; but as he hoped that I would think lodgings necessary but for a very little while, he knew not which to give his vote for.

I then fixed upon the widow's; and he has written accordingly to Mr. Doleman, making my compliments to his lady and sister for their kind offer.

MR. LOVELACE TO JOHN BELFORD, ESQ.

Thursday, April 20.

He begins with communicating to him the letter he wrote to Mr. Doleman, and then gives him a copy of the answer to it, upon which he thus expresses himself:

Thou knowest the widow; thou knowest her nieces; thou knowest the lodgings. And didst thou ever read a letter more artfully couched than this of Tom Doleman? Every possible objection anticipated! Every accident provided against! Every tittle of it plot-proof!

But, Belford, didst thou not mind that sly rogue Doleman's naming *Dover Street* for the widow's place of abode? — What dost think could be meant by that. 'Tis impossible thou shouldst guess, so, not to puzzle thee about it, suppose the *widow Sinclair's in Dover Street* should be inquired after by some officious person in order to come at characters (Miss Howe is as *sly* as the devil, and as *busy* to the full), and neither such a name, nor such a house, can be found in that street, nor a house to answer the description; then will not the keenest hunter in England be at a fault?

Widow SINCLAIR! didst thou not say, Lovelace?

Ay, SINCLAIR, Jack. Remember the name! SINCLAIR, I repeat. She *has* no other. And her features being broad and full blown, I will suppose her to be of Highland extraction; as her husband the colonel (*mind that too*) was a Scot, as brave, as honest.

I never forget the *minutiae* in my contrivances.

MISS HOWE TO MISS CLARISSA HARLOWE
Wednesday, April 19.

I HAVE a piece of intelligence to give you which concerns you much to know.

Your brother having been assured that you are not married, has taken a resolution to find you out, waylay you, and carry you off. A friend of his, a captain of a ship, undertakes to get you on shipboard, and to sail away with you, either to Hull or Leith, in the way to one of your brother's houses.

They are very wicked; for in spite of your virtue they conclude you to be *ruined*. But if they can be assured when they have you that you are not, they will secure you till they can bring you out Mrs. Solmes. Meantime, in order to give Mr. Lovelace full employment, they talk of a prosecution which will be set up against him for some crime they have got a notion of, which they think, if it do not cost him his life, will make him fly his country.

If you can engage Mr. Lovelace to keep his temper upon it, I think you should acquaint him with it.

MISS CLARISSA HARLOWE TO MISS HOWE
Thursday, April 20.

YOU command me not to attempt to dissuade you from this correspondence; and you tell me how kindly Mr. Hickman approves of it, and how obliging he is to me to permit it to be carried on under cover to him; but this does not quite satisfy me.

I am a very bad casuist, and the pleasure I take in writing to you may make me very partial to my own wishes. Indeed, my dear, I know not how to *forbear* writing. I have now no other employment or diversion.

But why, if your mother will permit our correspondence on communicating to her all that passes in it, and if she will condescend to one only condition, may it not be complied with?

Would she not, do you think, my dear, be prevailed upon to have the communication made to her *in confidence?*

Miss Howe to Miss Clarissa Harlowe
Friday Morn., April 21.

MY mother will not comply with your condition, my dear. I hinted it to her as from myself. But the *Harlowes* (excuse me) have got her entirely in with them. It is a scheme of mine, she told me, formed to draw her into your party against your parents. Which, for her own sake, she is very careful about.

Miss Clarissa Harlowe to Miss Howe
Friday, April 21.

MR. LOVELACE communicated to me this morning early, from his intelligencer, the news of my brother's scheme. I like him the better for making very light of it, and for his treating it with contempt. And indeed, had I not had the hint of it from you, I should have suspected it to be some contrivance of his, in order to hasten me to town, where he has long wished to be himself.

Lord bless me! said I, to what has this fatal step that I have been betrayed into ——

You condescended, dearest creature, said he, to ask my advice. It is very easy, give me leave to say, to advise you what to do. I hope I may, in this *new* occasion, speak without offence, *notwithstanding your former injunctions.* You see that there can be no hope of reconciliation with your relations. Can you, madam, consent to honour with your hand a wretch whom you have never yet obliged with one *voluntary* favour?

What a *recriminating* what a *reproachful way,* my dear, was this of putting a question of this nature! I expected not from him at the time, and just as I was very angry with him, either the question or the manner. I burst into tears, and was going from him in high disgust, when, throwing his arms about me, with an air, however, the most tenderly respectful, he gave a *stupid* turn to the subject.

He only besought me to suffer his *future actions* to speak for him; and if I saw him worthy of any favour, that I would not let him be the *only* person without my knowledge who was not entitled to my consideration.

He would be very sincere with me, he said; this project of my brother's had changed the face of things.

Do you propose, sir, said I, to take up your lodgings in the house where I lodge?

He did *not,* he said, as he knew the use I intended to make of his absence, and my punctilio. He could go to his friend Belford's in Soho, or perhaps overnight to Edgeware, but to no greater distance should he care to venture.

The result of all was, to set out on Monday next for town. I hope it will be in a happy hour.

MR. LOVELACE TO JOHN BELFORD, ESQ.

Friday, April 21.

AND NOW, Belford, I had like to have singed the silken wings of my liberty. Never was man in greater danger of being caught in his own snares; all my views anticipated; all my schemes untried; the admirable creature not brought to town; nor one effort made to know if she be really Angel or Woman.

I offered myself to her acceptance with a suddenness, 'tis true, that gave her no time to wrap herself in reserves; and in terms less *tender* than *fervent*, tending to upbraid her for her past indifference, and to remind her of her injunctions; for it was the fear of her brother, not her love of me, that had inclined her to dispense with those injunctions.

I never beheld so sweet a confusion. She spoke, but with vexation: I am — I am — *very* unhappy.

Didst thou ever before hear of a man uttering solemn things by an involuntary impulse, in defiance of premeditation, and of all his own proud schemes? But this sweet creature is able to make a man forego every purpose of his heart that is not favourable to her.

Well, but what was the result of this voluntary impulse on my part? Wouldst thou not think I was taken at my offer? — an offer so solemnly made, and on one knee too?

No such thing! The pretty trifler let me off as easily as I could have wished.

I re-urged her to make me happy; but I was to be postponed to her Cousin Morden's arrival. On him are now placed all her hopes.

I raved; but to no purpose.

Another letter was to be sent, or had been sent, to her Aunt Hervey, to which she hoped an answer.

Yet sometimes I think that fainter and fainter would have been her procastinations, had I been a man of courage — *but so fearful was I of offending!*

A confounded thing! The man to be so bashful; the woman to want so much courting! — How shall two such come together, no kind mediatress in the way?

MISS CLARISSA HARLOWE TO MRS. HERVEY

(*Enclosed in her last to Miss Howe*)   *Thursday, April 20.*

HONOURED MADAM, — Having not had the favour of an answer to a letter I took the liberty to write to you on the 14th, I am in some hopes that it may have miscarried; for I had much rather it should, than to have the mortification to think that my Aunt Hervey deemed me unworthy of the honour of her notice.

Hitherto it is in my power to perform what I undertake for in this letter; and it would be very grievous to me to be precipitated upon measures which may render the desirable reconciliation more difficult.

At least, my dear aunt, procure for me the justice of my wearing apparel, and the little money and other things which I wrote to my sister for, and mention in the enclosed to you; that I may not be destitute of common conveniences, or be under a necessity to owe an obligation for such where (at present, however) I would least of all owe it.

Allow me to say that had I *designed* what happened, I might (as to the money and jewels at least) have saved myself some of the mortifications which I have suffered, and which I still further apprehend, if my request be not complied with.

I am, my dearest aunt, / Your ever dutiful / CL. HARLOWE.

Be pleased to direct to me, if I am to be favoured with a few lines, to be left at Mr. Osgood's near Soho Square; and nobody shall ever know of your goodness to me if you desire it to be kept a secret.

MISS HOWE TO MISS CLARISSA HARLOWE

Sat., April 22.

I CANNOT for my life account for your wretch's teasing ways. But he certainly doubts your love of him.

I have been looking back on the whole of his conduct, and comparing it with his general character; and find that he is more *consistently*, more *uniformly* mean, revengeful, and proud than either of us once imagined.

Well, but what in such a situation is to be done? Why, you must despise him; you must hate him — if you can — and run away from him. But whither? Whither indeed, now that your brother is laying foolish plots to put you in a still worse condition, as it may happen!

But if you cannot despise and hate him; if you care not to break with him, you must part with some punctilios; and if the so doing bring not on the solemnity, you must put yourself into the protection of the ladies of his family.

This, you'll say, will be as good as *declaring* yourself to be his. *And so let it.* You ought not now to think of anything else but to be *his*. Does not your brother's project convince you more and more of this?

What a wretch to be so easily answered by your reference to the arrival of your Cousin Morden! But I am afraid that you was too scrupulous; for did he not resent that reference?

Could we have *his* account of the matter, I fancy, my dear, I should think you over-nice, over-delicate.[1]

---

[1] The reader who has seen his account, which Miss Howe could not have seen when she wrote thus, will observe that it was not possible for a person of her true delicacy of mind to act otherwise than she did, to a man so cruelly and so insolently artful.

I grant that it gives a worthy mind some satisfaction in having borne its testimony against the immoralities of a bad one; but that correction which is unseasonably given, is more likely either to harden or make an hypocrite, than to reclaim. I am pleased, however, as well as you, with his making light of your brother's *wise* project.

I expect nothing from your letter to your aunt. I hope Lovelace will never know the contents of it. In every one of yours I see that he as warmly resents as he dares the little confidence you have in him. I should resent it too were I he, and knew I deserved better.

I know you won't demand possession of your estate. But give *him* a right to demand it for you, and that will be still better.

MR. BELFORD TO ROBERT LOVELACE, ESQ.

Friday, April 21.

Now that I find thou hast so far succeeded as to induce her to come to town, and to choose her lodgings in a house, the people of which will too probably damp and suppress any honourable motions which may arise in thy mind in her favour, I cannot help writing; and that professedly in her behalf.

My inducements to this are not owing to virtue.

What then is my motive? What, but the true friendship that I bear thee, Lovelace; which makes me plead *thy own sake,* and *thy family's sake,* in the justice thou owest to this incomparable creature; who, however, so well deserves to have *her sake* to be mentioned as the principal consideration.

By what I have heard of this lady's perfections from every mouth, as well as from thine, and from every letter thou hast written, where wilt thou find such another woman? And why shouldst thou tempt her virtue? Why shouldst thou wish to try where there is no reason to doubt?

But let me touch upon thy predominant passion, *revenge*; for *love* is but second to that, as I have often told thee, though it has set thee into raving at me: what poor pretences for revenge are the difficulties thou hadst in getting her off? If these are other than pretences, why thankest thou not those who threw her into thy power?

As thou art the last of thy name; as thy family is of note and figure in thy country; and as thou thyself thinkest that thou shalt one day marry; is it possible, let me ask thee, that thou canst have such another opportunity as thou now hast, if thou lettest this slip? A woman in her family and fortune not unworthy of thine own (though thou art so apt, from pride of ancestry and pride of heart, to speak slightly of the families thou dislikest); so celebrated for beauty; and so noted at the same time for prudence, for *soul* (I will say, instead of *sense*), and for virtue?

And shall this admirable woman suffer for her generous endeavours to set on foot thy reformation, and for insisting upon proofs of the sincerity of thy professions before she will be thine?

I suppose you will soon be in town. Without the lady, I hope. Farewell. / Be honest and be happy. / J. BELFORD, /

MRS. HERVEY TO MISS CLARISSA HARLOWE

DEAR NIECE, — It would be hard not to write a few lines, so much pressed to write, to one I ever loved. Your former letter I received, yet was not at liberty to answer it. I break my word to answer you now.

But you want to clear up things — *what* can you clear up? Are you not gone off? — With a Lovelace, too? *What*, my dear, would you clear up?

You did not design to go, you say. Why did you meet him then, chariot and six, horsemen, all prepared by him? Oh, my dear, how art produces art! — Will it be believed? If it *would*, what power will he be thought to have had over you! He! — Who? *Lovelace!* — the vilest of libertines! Over whom? — A *Clarissa!* Was your love for such a man above your reason? Above your resolution? What credit would a belief of this, *if* believed, bring you? How mend the matter?

I am sorry for it, but am afraid nothing you ask will be complied with. I dare not open my lips in your favour. Nobody dare. Your letter must stand by itself. This has caused me to send it to Harlowe Place. Expect therefore great severity. May you be enabled to support the lot you have drawn!

At *present*, if *ever*, there can be no thought of reconciliation. The *upshot* of your precipitation must first be seen. There may be murder yet, as far as we know. Will the man you are with part willingly with you? If *not*, what may be the consequence? If he *will* — Lord bless me! what shall we think of his reasons for it? I will fly this thought. I know your purity — but, my dear, are you not out of all protection? Are you not unmarried? Have you not (making your daily prayers useless) thrown yourself into temptation? And is not the man the most wicked of plotters?

No answer, I beseech you. I hope your messenger will not tell anybody that I have written to you. And I dare say you will not show what I have written to Mr. Lovelace — for I have written with the less reserve, depending upon your prudence.

You have my prayers.

My Dolly knows not that I write. Nobody does[1]; not even Mr. Hervey.

You have the poor girl's hourly prayers, I will, however, tell you, though she knows not what I do, as well as those of / Your truly afflicted aunt, / D. HERVEY.

Friday, April 21.

[1] Notwithstanding what Mrs. Hervey here says, it will be hereafter seen that this severe letter of hers was written in private concert with the implacable Arabella.

MISS CLARISSA HARLOWE TO MISS HOWE
(*With the preceding*)   *Sat. Morn., April 22.*

I HAVE just now received the enclosed from my Aunt Hervey.
Be pleased, my dear, to keep her secret of having written to the unhappy wretch her niece.

I may go to London, I see, or where I will. No matter what becomes of me.

I was the willinger to suspend my journey thither till I heard from
Harlowe Place. I thought if I could be encouraged to hope for a
reconciliation, I would let this man see that he should not have me
in his power, but upon my own terms, if at all.

But I find I must be *his*, whether I will or not; and perhaps through
still greater mortifications than those great ones which I have already
met with — and must I be so absolutely thrown upon a man with
whom I am not at all satisfied?

There may be murder, my aunt says. This looks as if she knew
of Singleton's rash plot. Such an *upshot*, as *she* calls it, of this unhappy
affair, Heaven avert!

She flies a thought that I can *less* dwell upon — a *cruel* thought —
but she has a poor opinion of the purity she compliments me with, if
she thinks that I am not, by GOD'S grace, above temptation from this
sex. Although I never saw a man, whose *person* I could like, before
this man, yet his faulty character allowed me but little merit from the
indifference I pretended to on his account. But now I see him *in
nearer lights*, I like him less than ever. Unpolite, cruel, insolent! Un-
wise! A trifler with his own happiness; the destroyer of mine! His
last treatment — *my fate too visibly in his power* — *master of his
own wishes* (shame to say it) — *if he knew what to wish for*. Indeed
I never liked him so little as now. Upon my word, I think I could
hate him (if I do not already hate him) sooner than any man I ever
thought tolerably of.

I intended to have returned after the interview; and then perhaps
she would have explained herself. O this artful, this designing Lovelace! Yet I must repeat, that most I ought to blame myself for meeting
him.

TO MISS CLARISSA HARLOWE
(*To be left at Mr.* Osgood's, *near* Soho Square)   *Friday, April 21.*

IT WAS expected that you would send again to me or to my
Aunt Hervey. The enclosed has lain ready for you therefore by direction. You will have no answer from anybody, write to *whom* you
will, and as *often* as you will, and *what* you will.

It was designed to bring you back by proper authority, or to send
you whither the disgraces you have brought upon us all should be in
the likeliest way, after a while, to be forgotten. But I believe that
design is over; so you may *range* securely — nobody will think it

worth while to give themselves any trouble about you. Yet my mother has obtained leave to send you your clothes of all sorts; but your clothes only. This is a favour you'll see by the within letter not *designed* you; and *now* not granted for *your* sake, but because my poor mother cannot bear in her sight anything you used to wear. Read the enclosed and tremble. / ARABELLA HARLOWE.

To the Most Ungrateful and Undutiful of Daughters

Harlowe Place, April 15.

SISTER THAT WAS! — For I know not what name you are *permitted* or *choose* to go by.

You have filled us with distraction. My father, in the first agitations of his mind, on discovering your wicked, your shameful elopement, imprecated on his knees a fearful curse upon you. Tremble at the recital of it! No less than that you may meet your punishment, both *here* and *hereafter*, by means of the very wretch in whom you have chosen to place your wicked confidence.

Your clothes will not be sent you. You seem, by leaving them behind you, to have been secure of them whenever you demanded them. But perhaps you could think of nothing but meeting your fellow — nothing but how to get off your forward self!

Was there ever a giddier creature? Yet this is the celebrated, the blazing Clarissa — Clarissa *what*? *Harlowe,* no doubt! — And Harlowe it will be, to the disgrace of us all!

Your drawings and your pieces are all taken down; as is also your own whole-length picture, in the Vandyke taste, from your late parlour; they are taken down and thrown into your closet, which will be nailed up, as if it were not a part of the house, there to perish together; for who can bear to see them?

My brother vows revenge upon your libertine — for the *family's* sake he vows it; not for *yours*! For he will treat you, he declares, like a common creature, if ever he sees you; and doubts not that this will be your fate.

My Uncle Harlowe renounces you for ever.

So does my Uncle Antony.

So does my Aunt Hervey.

So do *I*, base unworthy creature! the disgrace of a good family, and the property of an infamous rake, as questionless you will soon find yourself, if you are not already.

Your books, since they have not taught you what belongs to your family, to your sex, and to your education, will not be sent you. Your money neither. Nor yet the jewels so undeservedly made yours. For it is wished you may be seen a beggar along London streets.

If all this is heavy, lay your hand to your heart and ask yourself why you have deserved it?

Everybody, in short, is ashamed of you; but none more than / ARABELLA HARLOWE.

MISS HOWE TO MISS CLARISSA HARLOWE

Tuesday, April 25.

BE comforted; be not dejected; do not despond, my dearest and best beloved friend. God Almighty is just and gracious, and gives not His assent to rash and inhuman curses. Can you think that Heaven will seal to the black passions of its depraved creatures?

This outrageousness shows only what manner of spirit they are of, and how much their sordid views exceed their parental love. 'Tis all owing to rage and disappointment — disappointment in designs proper to be frustrated.

My mother blames them for this wicked letter of your sister, and she pities you, and, of her own accord, wished me to write to comfort you for this once; for she says, it is pity your heart, which was so noble (and when the sense of your fault and the weight of a parent's curse are so strong upon you), should be quite broken.

But do not mind their after-pretences, my dear — all of them serve but for tacit confessions of their vile usage of you. I will keep your aunt's secret, never fear. I would not, on any consideration, that my mother should see her letter.

You will now see that you have nothing left but to overcome all scrupulousness and marry as soon as you have opportunity. Determine so to do, my dear.

I would show Lovelace your sister's abominable letter were it to me. I enclose it. It shall not have a place in this house. This will enter him, of course, into the subject which now you ought to have most in view. Let him see what you suffer for him. He cannot prove base to such an excellence. I should never enjoy my head or my senses should this man prove a villain to you! With a merit so exalted, you may have punishment more than enough for your involuntary fault in that husband.

Come, my dear, when things are at worst they will mend. Good often comes when evil is expected. But if you despond, there can be no hopes of cure. Don't let them break your heart; for that, it is plain to me, is now what some people have in view to do.

How poor to withhold from you your books, your jewels, and your money! As money is all you can at present want, since they will vouchsafe to send your clothes, I send fifty guineas by the bearer, enclosed in single papers in my *Norris's Miscellanies.* I charge you, as you love me, return them not.

MISS CLARISSA HARLOWE TO MISS HOWE

Wednesday Morning, April 26.

YOUR messenger finds me just setting out for London; the chaise at the door. Already I have taken leave of the good widow. I received my sister's dreadful letter on Sunday when Mr. Lovelace was out. He saw on his return my *extreme anguish* and *dejection,* and he was told *how much worse I had been*; for I had fainted away more than once.

I think the contents of it have touched my head as well as my heart.

He would fain have seen it. But I would not permit that, because of the threatenings he would have found in it against himself. As it *was*, the effect it had upon me made him break out into execrations and menaces. I was so ill that he himself advised me to delay going to town on Monday, as I proposed to do.

He is extremely regardful and tender of me. All that you supposed *would* follow this violent letter *has* followed it. He has offered himself to my acceptance in so unreserved a manner, that I am concerned I have written so freely and so diffidently of him. Pray, my dearest friend, keep to yourself everything that may appear disreputable of him from me.

I must acquaint you with one thing more, notwithstanding my hurry, and that is that Mr. Lovelace offered either to attend me to Lord M.'s, or to send for his chaplain, yesterday. He pressed me to consent to this proposal most earnestly, and even seemed desirous to have the ceremony pass here than in London. But this dreadful letter *has unhinged my whole frame.* Then some *little* punctilio surely is necessary. No preparation made. No articles drawn. No licence ready. Grief so extreme; no pleasure in prospect, nor so much as in wish — oh, my dear, who could think of entering into so solemn an engagement! Who, *so* unprepared, could seem to be *so* ready!

If I could flatter myself that my indifference to all the joys of this life proceeded from *proper* motives, and not rather from the disappointments and mortifications my pride has met with, how much rather, I think, should I choose to be wedded to my shroud than to any man on earth!

Miss Howe to Miss Clarissa Harlowe

Thursday, April 27.

I am sorry you sent back my Norris. But you must be allowed to do as you please.

I am most heartily rejoiced that your prospects are so much mended; and that, as I hoped, good has been produced out of evil.

You *know best* your *motives* for suspending; but I wish you *could* have taken him at offers so earnest. Why should you not have permitted him to send for Lord M.'s chaplain? If punctilio only was in the way, and want of a licence and of proper preparations and suchlike, my service to you, my dear; and there is ceremony tantamount to your ceremony.

Mr. Lovelace to John Belford, Esq.

Monday, April 24.

Fate is weaving a whimsical web for thy friend, and I see not but I shall be inevitably manacled.

Here have I been at work, dig, dig, dig, like a cunning miner, at one time, and spreading my snares, like an artful fowler, at another, and exulting in my contrivances to get this inimitable creature absolutely into my power. Everything made for me, and just as all this was completed, wouldst thou believe that I should be my own enemy and her friend? That I should be so totally diverted from all my favourite purposes, as to propose to marry her before I went to town, in order to put it out of my own power to resume them?

Thou wilt be still the more surprised when I tell thee that there seems to be a coalition going forward between the black angels and the white ones; for here has hers induced her in one hour, and by one retrograde accident, to *acknowledge*, what the charming creature never before acknowledged, a preferable favour for me. She even avows an intention to be mine — mine, without reformation conditions! She permits me to talk of love to her: of the irrevocable ceremony: yet, another extraordinary! postpones that ceremony; chooses to set out for London; and even to go to the widow's in town.

This, in short, was the case: While she was refusing all manner of obligation to me, keeping me at haughty distance, in hopes that her Cousin Morden's arrival would soon fix her in a full and absolute independence of me — disgusted likewise at her adorer, for holding himself the reins of his own passions, instead of giving them up to her control — she writes a letter, urging an answer to a letter before sent, for her apparel, her jewels, and some gold, which she had left behind her; all which was to save her pride from obligation, and to promote the independence her heart was set upon. And what followed but a shocking answer, made still more shocking by the communication of a father's curse upon a daughter deserving only blessings? A curse upon the curser's heart, and a double one upon the transmitter's, the spiteful, the envious Arabella!

Absent when it came; on my return I found her recovering from fits, again to fall into stronger fits; and nobody expecting her life; half a dozen messengers dispatched to find me out. Nor wonder at her being so affected; she, whose filial piety gave her dreadful faith in a father's curses; and the curse of this gloomy tyrant extending (to use her own words, when she could speak) *to both worlds.* Oh, that it had turned, in the moment of its utterance, to a mortal quinsey, and, sticking in his gullet, had choked the old execrator, as a warning to all such unnatural fathers!

What a miscreant had I been, not to have endeavoured to bring her back, by all the endearments, by all the vows, by all the offers that I could make her!

I *did* bring her back. More than a father to her; for I have given her a life her unnatural father had well-nigh taken away: shall I not cherish the fruits of my own benefaction? I was in earnest in my vows to marry; and my ardour to urge the present time was a *real* ardour. But extreme dejection, with a mingled delicacy, that in her dying moments I doubt not she will preserve, have caused her to refuse me the *time*, though not the solemnity; for she has told me that now she must be wholly in my protection (*being destitute of every other!*). More indebted, still, thy friend, as thou seest, to her cruel relations, than to herself for her favour!

Low, very low, she remains; yet, dreading her stupid brother's enterprise, she wants to be in London; where, but for *this* accident, and (wouldst thou have believed it?) for *my* persuasions, seeing her so very ill, she would have been this night; and we shall actually set out on Wednesday morning if she be not worse.

MR. LOVELACE TO JOHN BELFORD, ESQ.
Tuesday, April 25.

ALL hands at work in preparation for London. What makes my heart beat so strong? Why rises it to my throat in such half-choking flutters, when I think of what this removal may do for me? I am hitherto to be honest; and that increases my wonder at these involuntary commotions. 'Tis a plotting villain of a heart: it ever was; and ever will be, I doubt. Such a joy when any roguery is going forward! — I so little its master!

But after all, so low, so dejected continues she to be, that I am terribly afraid I shall have a vapourish wife; if I *do* marry. I should then be doubly undone. Not that I shall be *much at home with her, perhaps, after the first fortnight or so.* But when a man has been ranging, like the painful bee, from flower to flower, perhaps for a month together, and the thoughts of home and a wife begin to have their charms with him, to be received by a Niobe, who, like a wounded vine, weeps her vitals away, while she but involuntarily curls about him; how shall I be able to bear that?

It is infinitely better for her and for me that we should not marry. What a delightful manner of life (oh, that I could persuade her to it!) would the life of honour be with such a woman! The fears, the inquietudes, the uneasy days, the restless nights; all arising from doubts of having disobliged me! Every absence dreaded to be an absence for ever! And then how amply rewarded, and rewarding, by the rapture-causing return! Such a passion as this keeps love in a continual fervour; makes it all alive. The happy pair, instead of sitting dozing and nodding at each other in opposite chimney-corners in a winter evening, and over a wintry love, always new to each other, and having always something to say.

MR. LOVELACE TO JOHN BELFORD, ESQ.
Wedn., Apr. 26.

AT LAST my lucky star has directed us into the desired port, and we are safely landed.

Things already appear with a very different face *now that I have got her here.* Already have our mother and her daughters been about me: "Charming lady! What a complexion! What eyes! What majesty in her person! O Mr. Lovelace, you are a happy man! *You owe us such a lady!*" Then they remind me of my revenge, and of my hatred to her whole family.

In so many ways will it be now in my power to have the dear creature, that I shall not know which of them to choose!

It would be a miracle, as thou sayest, if this lady can save herself — and having gone so far, how can I recede? Then my revenge upon the Harlowes! To have run away with a daughter of theirs, to make her a Lovelace — to make her one of a family so superior to her own — what a triumph, as I have heretofore observed, to *them*! But to run away with her, and to bring her to my lure in the *other* light, what a mortification of their pride! What a gratification of my own!

And now, why dost thou not wish me joy, Jack?

Joy of what?

Why, joy of my nuptials. Know then, that *said* is *done* with me, when I have a mind to have it so; and that we are actually man and wife! Only that consummation has not passed: bound down to the contrary of that by a solemn vow, till a reconciliation with her family take place. The women here are told so. They know it before my beloved knows it; and that, thou wilt say, is odd.

But how shall I do to make my fair one keep her temper on the intimation? *Why, is she not here?* — at Mrs. Sinclair's? But if she will hear reason, I doubt not to convince her that she ought to acquiesce.

She will insist, I suppose, upon my leaving her, and that I shall not take up my lodgings under the same roof. But circumstances are changed since I first made her that promise. I have taken all the vacant apartments, and must carry this point also.

Miss Clarissa Harlowe to Miss Howe

Wedn. Afternoon, Apr. 26.

At length, my dearest Miss Howe, I am in London, and in my new lodgings. They are neatly furnished, and the situation, for the town, is pleasant. But I think you must not ask me how I like the old gentlewoman. Yet she seems courteous and obliging. Her kinswomen just appeared to welcome me at my alighting. They seem to be genteel young women. But more of their aunt and of them, as I shall see more.

.   .   .   .

Here I was broken in upon by Mr. Lovelace; introducing the widow leading in a kinswoman of hers to attend me, if I approved of her, till my Hannah should come, or till I had provided myself with some other servant. The widow gave her many good qualities; but said that she had one great defect; which was that she could not write, nor read writing; that part of her education having been neglected when she was young: but for discretion, fidelity, obligingness, she was not to be outdone by anybody. She commended her likewise for her skill at the needle.

As for *her defect,* I can easily forgive that. She is very likely and genteel; too genteel indeed, I think, for a servant. But, what I like least of all in her, she has a strange sly eye. I never saw such an eye — half-confident, I think.

I accepted her: how could I do otherwise? But upon their leaving me, I told *him* (who seemed inclinable to begin a conversation with me) that I desired that this apartment might be considered as my retirement: that when I saw him it might be in the dining-room (which is up a few stairs; for this back house being once two, the rooms do not all of them very conveniently communicate with each other); and that I might be as little broken in upon as possible when I am here. He withdrew very respectfully to the door; but there stopped; and asked for my company *then* in the dining-room. If he were about setting out for other lodgings, I would go with him now, I told him: but if he did not just then go, I would first finish my letter to Miss Howe.

I see he has no mind to leave me if he can help it. My brother's scheme may give him a pretence to try to engage me to dispense with his promise. But if I *now do,* I must acquit him of it entirely.

While we were talking at the door, my new servant came up with an invitation to us both to tea. I said *he* might accept of it, if he pleased; but I must pursue my writing; and not choosing either tea or supper, I desired him to make my excuses below as to both; and inform them of my choice to be retired as much as possible; yet to promise for me my attendance on the widow and her nieces at breakfast in the morning.

He objected particularity in the eyes of strangers as to avoiding supper.

You know, said I, and you can tell them, that I seldom eat suppers. My spirits are low. You must never urge me against a declared choice. Pray, Mr. Lovelace, inform them of all my particularities. If they are obliging they will allow for them. I come not hither to make new acquaintance.

I have turned over the books I have in my closet; and am not a little pleased with them; and think the better of the people of the house for their sakes.

Stanhope's *Gospels;* Sharp's, Tillotson's, and South's *Sermons;* Nelson's *Feasts and Fasts;* a sacramental piece of the Bishop of Man, and another of Dr. Gauden, Bishop of Exeter; and Inett's *Devotions,* are among the devout books: and among those of lighter turn, the following not ill-chosen ones; a Telemachus in French, another in English; Steele's, Rowe's, and Shakespeare's plays; that genteel comedy of Mr. Cibber, *The Careless Husband,* and others of the same author. Dryden's *Miscellanies;* the *Tatlers, Spectators,* and *Guardians;* Pope's, and Swift's, and Addison's works.

. . . .

I am exceedingly out of humour with Mr. Lovelace: and have great reason to be so.

He began with letting me know that he had been out to inquire after the character of the widow; which was the more necessary, he said, as he supposed that I would *expect his frequent absence.*

I *did*, I said; and that he would not think of taking up his lodging in the same house with me. But what, said *I*, is the result of your inquiry?

Why, indeed, the widow's character was, in the main, what he liked well enough. But as it was Miss Howe's opinion, as I had told him, that my brother had not given over his scheme; as the widow lived by letting lodgings; and had others to let in the same part of the house, which might be taken by an enemy; he knew no better way than for him to take them all, as it could not be for a long time — *unless I would think of removing to others.*

So far was well enough: but as it was easy for me to see that he spoke the slighter of the widow in order to have a pretence to lodge here himself, I asked him his intention in that respect. And he frankly owned, that if I chose to stay here, he could not, as matters stood, think of leaving me for six hours together; and he had prepared the widow to expect that we should be here but for a few days; only till we could fix ourselves in a house suitable to our condition; and this, that I might be under the less embarrass if I pleased to remove.

Fix *ourselves* in a house, and *we* and *our*, Mr. Lovelace — pray, *in* what light ——

He interrupted me: Why, my dearest life, if you will hear me with patience — yet I am half afraid, that I have been too forward, as I have not consulted you upon it — but as my friends in town, according to what Mr. Doleman has written in the letter, you have seen, conclude us to be married ——

Surely, sir, you have not presumed ——

Hear me out, dearest creature: you have received with favour my addresses; you have made me hope for the honour of your consenting hand: yet, by declining my most fervent tender of myself to you at Mrs. Sorlings's, have given me apprehensions of delay: I would not for the world be thought so ungenerous a wretch, now you have honoured me with your confidence, *as to wish to precipitate you.* Yet your brother's schemes are not given up. The widow's character may be as worthy *as it is said to be*, but if she believes us married, her good character will stand us in stead, and she will be of our party. Then I have taken care to give her a reason why two apartments are requisite to us at the hour of retirement.

I perfectly raved at him. I would have flung from him in resentment; but he would not let me: and what could I do? Whither go, the evening advanced?

I am astonished at you! said I. If you are a man of honour, what need of all this strange obliquity! You delight in crooked ways. Let me know, since I *must* stay in your company (for he held my hand), let me know all you have said to the people below. Indeed, indeed, Mr. Lovelace, you are a very unaccountable man.

My dearest creature, need I to have mentioned anything of this? and could I not have taken up my lodgings in this house unknown to you, if I had not intended to make you the judge of all my proceedings? But *this* is what I have told the widow before her kinswomen, and before your new servant — That indeed we were privately married at Hertford; but that you had preliminarily bound me under a solemn vow, which I am most religiously resolved to keep, to be contented with separate apartments, and even not to lodge under the same roof, till a certain reconciliation shall take place, which is of high consequence to both. And further, that I might convince you of the purity of my intentions, and that my whole view in this was to prevent mischief, I have acquainted them, that I have solemnly promised to behave to you before everybody, as if we were only betrothed and not married; not even offering to take any of those innocent freedoms which are not refused in the most punctilious loves.

And then he solemnly vowed to me the strictest observance of the same respectful behaviour to me.

I said that I was not by any means satisfied with the tale he had told, nor with the necessity he wanted to lay me under of appearing what I was not; that every step he took was a wry one, a needless wry one: and since he thought it necessary to tell the people below anything about me, I insisted that he should unsay all he had said and tell them the truth.

What he had told them, he said, was with so many circumstances that he should sooner die than contradict it. And still he insisted upon the propriety of appearing to be married, for the reasons he had given before.

'Tis true I should have consulted you first, and had your leave. But since you dislike what I have said, let me implore you, dearest madam, to give the only proper sanction to it, by naming an early day. Would to Heaven that were to be to-morrow! For God's sake, let it be to-morrow! But if not (was it his business, my dear, before I spoke (yet he seemed to be afraid of me) to say, *if not?*), let me beseech you, madam, if my behaviour shall not be to your dislike, that you will not to-morrow at breakfast-time discredit what I have told them.

. . . .

Alas! my dear, how vain a thing to say what we will or what we will not do, when we have put ourselves into the power of this sex! He besought my leave to stay that one night, promising to set out either for Lord M.'s, or for Edgware to his friend Belford's in the morning after breakfast. But if I were against it, he said, he would not stay supper; and would attend me about eight next day.

I thought, notwithstanding my resolution above-mentioned, that it would seem too punctilious to deny him, under the circumstances he had mentioned; having, besides, no reason to think he would obey me; for he looked as if he were determined to debate the matter with me. And now, as I see no likelihood of a reconciliation with my friends, and as I have actually received his addresses, I thought I would not quarrel with him, if I could help it, especially as he asked to stay but for one night.

This was what I said: What you *will* do, you *must* do, I think. You are very ready to promise; very ready to depart from your promise. You say, however, that you will set out to-morrow for the country. You know how ill I have been. I am not well enough now to debate with you upon your encroaching ways. I am utterly dissatisfied with the tale you have told below. Nor will I promise to appear to the people of the house to-morrow what I am not.

We withdrew in the most respectful manner, beseeching me only to favour him with such a meeting in the morning as might not make the widow and her nieces think he had given me reason to be offended with him.

I retired to my own apartment, and Dorcas came to me soon after to take my commands. I told her that I required very little attendance, and always dressed and undressed myself.

If, my dear, you *will* write against prohibition, be pleased to direct, *To Miss Lætitia Beaumont; to be left till called for, at Mr. Wilson's in Pall Mall.*

Mr. Lovelace proposed this direction to me, not *knowing* of your desire that our letters should pass by a third hand.

Mr. Lovelace is so full of his contrivances and expedients, that I think it may not be amiss to desire you to look carefully to the seals of my letters, as I shall to those of yours. If I find him base in this particular, I shall think him capable of any evil; and will fly him as my worst enemy.

MISS HOWE TO MISS CLARISSA HARLOWE
(*With her two last letters enclosed*)   *Thursday Night, April 27.*

I CONGRATULATE you on your arrival in town, so much amended in spirits. I must be brief. I hope you'll have no cause to repent returning my Norris. It is forthcoming on demand.

I know not what to write upon his reporting to them that you are actually married. His reasons for it are plausible. But he delights in odd expedients and inventions.

Whether you like the people or not, do not, by your noble sincerity and plain-dealing, make yourself enemies. You are in the *world* now, you know.

I am glad you had thoughts of taking him at his offer, if he had re-urged it. I wonder he did not. But if he do not soon, and in such a way as you *can* accept of it, don't think of staying with him.

Depend upon it, my dear, he will not leave you, either night or day, if he can help it, now he has got footing.

I should have abhorred him for his report of your marriage, had he not made it with such circumstances as leave it still in your power

197

to keep him at a distance. If once he offer the *least* familiarity —
but this is needless to say to you. He can have, I think, no other
design but what he professes; because he must needs think that his
report of being married to you must increase your vigilance.

MISS CLARISSA HARLOWE TO MISS HOWE

Thursday Morning, Eight o'clock.

I AM more and more displeased with Mr. Lovelace, on reflection, for his boldness in hoping to make me, though but *passively*, as
I may say, testify to his great untruth. He has sent me his compliments
by Dorcas, with a request that I will permit him to attend me in the
dining-room — perhaps, that he may guess from thence whether I
will meet him in good humour or not; but I have answered, that as I
shall see him at breakfast-time, I desire to be excused.

Ten o'clock.

I tried to adjust my countenance, before I went down, to an easier
air than I had a heart, and was received with the highest tokens of
respect by the widow and her two nieces: agreeable young women
enough in their persons; but they seemed to put on an air of reserve;
while Mr. Lovelace was easy and free to all, as if he were of long
acquaintance with them: gracefully enough, I cannot but say; an
advantage which travelled gentlemen have over other people.

Only that circumstances, and what passed in conversation, encouraged not the notion; or I should have been apt to think that the
young ladies and Mr. Lovelace were of longer acquaintance than of
yesterday. For he, by stealth, as it were, cast glances sometimes at
them, which they returned; and on my ocular notice their eyes fell,
as I may say, under my eye, as if they could not stand its examination.

The widow directed all her talk to me as to Mrs. Lovelace; and I,
with a very ill grace, bore it.

I asked after the nearest church; for I have been too long a stranger
to the sacred worship. They named St. James's, St. Anne's, and another in Bloomsbury; and the two nieces said they oftenest went to
St. James's Church, because of the good company, as well as for the
excellent preaching.

I left him with them, and retired to my closet and my pen.

Just as I have written thus far, I am interrupted by a message from
him, that he is setting out on a journey, and desires to take my commands. So here I will leave off to give him a meeting in the dining-
room.

He hoped, he said, that on his *return* I would name his happy day;
and the rather as I might be convinced, by my brother's projects,
that no reconciliation was to be expected.

I told him that perhaps I might write one letter to my Uncle
Harlowe. He once loved me. I should be easier when I had made one

direct application. I might possibly propose such terms, in relation to my grandfather's estate, as might procure me their attention; and I hoped he would be long enough absent to give me time to write to him, and receive an answer from him.

May you, my dear friend, be always happy in your reflections, prays / Your ever affectionate / CL. HARLOWE.

Mr. Lovelace in his next letter triumphs on his having carried his two great points of making the lady yield to pass for his wife to the people of the house, and to his taking up his lodging in it, though but for one night. He is now, *he says,* in a fair way, and doubts not but that he shall soon prevail, if not by persuasion, by surprise. *Yet he pretends to have some little remorse, and* censures himself as acting the part of the grand tempter. But having succeeded thus far, he cannot, *he says,* forbear trying, according to the resolution he had before made, whether he cannot go farther.

He takes notice of the jealousy, pride, and vanity of Sally Martin and Polly Horton, on his respectful behaviour to the lady: *creatures who, brought up too high for their fortunes, and to a taste of pleasure, and the public diversions, had fallen an easy prey to his seducing arts: and who, as he observes,* "had not yet got over that distinction in their love, which makes a woman prefer one man to another."

He mentions what his meaning was in making the lady the compliment of his absence.

As to leaving her; if I go but for *one* night, I have fulfilled my promise: and if she think not, I can mutter and grumble, and yield again, and make a merit of it; and then, unable to live out of her presence, soon return. Nor are women ever angry at bottom for being disobeyed through excess of love. They like an uncontrollable passion.

MISS CLARISSA HARLOWE TO MISS HOWE

Friday, April 28.

MR. LOVELACE is returned already. My brother's projects were his pretence. I could not but look upon this short absence as an evasion of his promise. I cannot bear to be dealt meanly with, and angrily insisted that he should directly set out for Berkshire, in order to engage his cousin, as he had promised.

O my dearest life, said he, why will you banish me from your presence? I cannot leave you for so long a time as you seem to expect I should. I have been hovering about town ever since I left you. Edgware was the farthest place I went to; and there I was not able to stay two hours, for fear, at this crisis, anything should happen.

Why will you not give the man who has brought you into difficulties, and who so honourably wishes to extricate you from them, the happiness of doing so?

He was silent. My voice failed to second the inclination. I had to say something not wholly discouraging to a point so warmly pressed.

I'll tell you, my angel, resumed he, what I propose to do, if you approve of it. I will instantly go out to view some of the handsome new squares, or fine streets round them, and make a report to you of any suitable house I find to be let. You shall direct the whole. And on some early day, either before or after we fix (it must be at your own choice), be pleased to make me the happiest of men. O my angel, take me to you, instead of banishing me from you, and make me yours for ever.

You see, my dear, that here was no *day* pressed for. I was not uneasy about that; and the sooner recovered myself, as there was not. But, however, I gave him no reason to upbraid me for refusing his offer of going in search of a house.

He is accordingly gone out for this purpose. But I find that he intends to take up his lodging here to-night; and if to-night, no doubt on other nights, while he is in town. As the doors and windows of my apartment have good fastenings; as he has not, in all this time, given me cause for apprehension; as he has the pretence of my brother's schemes to plead; as the people below are very courteous and obliging, I imagine it would look particular to them all, and bring me into a debate with a man who (let him be set upon what he will) has always a great deal to say for himself, if I were to insist upon his promise: on all these accounts, I think, I will take no notice of his lodging here, if he don't.

Saturday Morning.

He has made his inquiries, and actually seen the house he was told of last night. The owner of it is a young widow lady, who is inconsolable for the death of her husband; *Fretchville* her name.

The lady sees nobody; nor are the best apartments above-stairs to be viewed till she is either absent, or gone into the country; which she talks of doing in a fortnight, or three weeks, at farthest; and to live there retired.

He now does nothing but talk of the *ceremony*; but not indeed of the *day.* I don't want to urge that — but I wonder he does not. Which is the *more extraordinary*, as he was so pressing for marriage before we came to town.

He was very earnest with me to give him, and four of his friends, my company on Monday evening at a little collation. Miss Martin and Miss Horton cannot, he says, be there, being engaged in a party of their own. But Mrs. Sinclair will be present, and she gave him hope of the company of a young lady of very great fortune and merit (Miss *Partington*), an heiress to whom Colonel Sinclair, it seems, in his lifetime was guardian, and who therefore calls Mrs. Sinclair mamma.

I desired to be excused. He had laid me, I said, under a most disagreeable necessity of appearing as a married person; and I would see as few people as possible who were to think me so.

He would not urge it, he said, if I were *much* averse: but they were his select friends; men of birth and fortune, who longed to see me. It was true, he added, that they, as well as his friend Doleman, believed we were married: but they thought him under the restrictions that he had mentioned to the people below. I might be assured, he told me, that his politeness before them should be carried into the highest degree of reverence.

When he is set upon anything, there is no knowing, as I have said heretofore, what one *can* do. But I will not, if I can help it, be made a show of; especially to men of whose characters and principles I have no good opinion.

Mr. Lovelace in his next letter glories in the story of the house, and of the young widow possessor of it, and leaves it doubtful to Mr. Belford whether it be a real or fictitious story.

He mentions his different proposals in relation to the ceremony, which he so earnestly pressed for; and owns his artful intention in avoiding to name the day.

Mowbray, Belton, and Tourville long to see my angel, and will be there. She has *refused* me; but *must be present* notwithstanding. And thou must come. And then will I show thee the pride and glory of the Harlowe family, my implacable enemies; and thou shalt join with me in my triumph over them all.

I know not what may still be the perverse beauty's fate; I want thee, therefore, to see and admire her while she is serene and full of hope: while yet her charming face is surrounded with all its virgin glories; and before the plough of disappointment has thrown up furrows of distress upon every lovely feature.

I will now give you the instructions I have drawn up for your and your companions' behaviour on Monday night.

Ye must be sure to let it sink deep into your heavy heads, that there is no such lady in the world as Miss Clarissa Harlowe; and that she is neither more nor less than Mrs. Lovelace, though at present, to my shame be it spoken, a virgin.

Mowbray and Tourville, the two greatest blunderers of the four, I allow to be acquainted with the widow and nieces, from the knowledge they had of the colonel.

Priscilla Partington (for her looks so innocent, and discretion so deep, yet seeming so softly) may be greatly relied upon. She will accompany the mother, gorgeously dressed, with all her Jew's extravagance flaming out upon her. She has her cue, and I hope will make her acquaintance coveted by my charmer. She is just come to pass a day or two, and then to return to her surviving guardian's at Barnet.

Be it principally thy part, Jack, who art a parading fellow, and aimest at wisdom, to keep thy brother-varlets from blundering; for, as thou must have observed from what I have written, we have the most watchful and most penetrating lady in the world to deal with: a lady worth deceiving! but whose eyes will pierce to the bottom of your shallow souls the moment she hears you open. Do thou, therefore, place thyself between Mowbray and Tourville: their toes to be played upon and commanded by thine, if they go wrong: thy elbows to be the ministers of approbation.

As to your general behaviour; no hypocrisy! I hate it: so does my charmer. If I had studied for it, I believe I *could* have been an hypocrite: but my general character is so well known, that I should have been suspected at once, had I aimed at making myself too white.

And now, methinks, thou art curious to know what can be my view in risking the displeasure of my fair one, and alarming her fears, after four or five halcyon days have gone over our heads? I'll satisfy thee.

The visitors of the two nieces will crowd the house. Beds will be scarce. Miss Partington, a sweet, modest, genteel girl, will be prodigiously taken with my charmer; will want to begin a friendship with her. A share in her bed, for one night only, will be requested. Who knows but on that very Monday night I may be so unhappy as to give *mortal offence* to my beloved? *The shiest birds may be caught napping.* Should she *attempt to fly me* upon it, cannot I *detain her?* Should she *actually fly,* cannot I *bring her back* by authority civil or uncivil, if I have evidence upon evidence that she acknowledged, though but tacitly, her marriage? And *should I, or should I not* succeed, and she *forgive me,* or if she but descend to *expostulate,* or if she *bear me in her sight;* then will she be all my own. All delicacy is my charmer. I long to see how such a delicacy, on *any* of these occasions, will behave. And in my situation it behooves me to provide against every accident.

Well then, here are — let me see — how many persons are there who, after Monday night, will be able to swear that she has gone by my name, answered to my name, had no other view in leaving her friends, but to go by my name? Her own relations neither able nor willing to deny it.

And here's a faint sketch of my plot. Stand by, varlets — Tantara-ra-ra! Veil your bonnets, and confess your master!

Sunday.

Have been at church, Jack — behaved admirably well too! My charmer is pleased with me now: for I was exceedingly attentive to the discourse, and very ready in the auditor's part of the service. Eyes did not much wander. How could they, when the loveliest object, infinitely the loveliest, in the whole church, was in my view?

But let me tell thee what passed between us in my first visit of this morning; and then I will acquaint thee more largely with my good behaviour at church.

I could not be admitted till after eight. I found her ready prepared to go out. I pretended to be ignorant of her intention, having charged Dorcas not to own that she had told me of it.

Going abroad, madam? — with an air of indifference.

Yes, sir; I intend to go to church.

I hope, madam, I shall have the honour to attend you.

No: she designed to take a chair, and go to the next church.

This startled me: a chair to carry her to the next church from Mrs. Sinclair's, her right name not Sinclair, and to bring her back hither, in the face of people who might not think well of the house! There was no permitting that. Yet I was to appear indifferent. But said, I should take it for a favour if she would permit me to attend her in a coach, as there was time for it, to St. Paul's.

She made objections to the gaiety of my dress; and told me, that, if she went to St. Paul's, she could go in a coach without *me*.

She made some further objections: but at last permitted me the honour of attending her.

Sunday Evening.

We all dined together in Mrs. Sinclair's parlour. All *excessively* right! The two nieces have topped their parts; Mrs. Sinclair hers. Never so easy as now! She really thought a little oddly of these people at first, she said: Mrs. Sinclair seemed very forbidding! Her nieces were persons with whom she could not wish to be acquainted. But really we should not be too hasty in our censures. Some people improve upon us. The widow seems *tolerable*. She went no farther than *tolerable*. Miss Martin and Miss Horton are young people of good sense, and have read a great deal. What Miss Martin particularly said of marriage, and of her humble servant, was very solid. She believes, with such notions, she cannot make a bad wife. I have said, Sally's humble servant is a woollen draper of great reputation; and she is soon to be married.

The house is to be taken in three weeks: all will be over in three weeks, or bad will be my luck! Who knows but in three days? Have I not carried that great point of making her pass for my wife to the people below? And that other great one of fixing myself here night and day? What woman ever escaped me, who lodged under one roof with me? The house too, THE house; the people, people after my own heart: her servants, Will and Dorcas, both *my* servants. *Three days*, did I say! Pho! pho! pho! *Three hours!*

.   .   .   .

I have carried my third point; but so extremely to the dislike of my charmer, that I have been threatened, for suffering Miss Partington to be introduced to her without her leave.

But the point thus so much against her will carried, I doubt thou wilt see in her more of a sullen than of an obliging charmer. For when Miss Partington was withdrawn, What was Miss Partington to her? In her situation she wanted no new acquaintance. And what were my four friends to her in her present circumstances? She would assure me, if ever again —— And there she stopped, with a twirl of her hand.

When we meet, I will, in her presence, tipping thee a wink, show thee the motion; for it was a very pretty one. Quite new. Yet have I seen an hundred pretty passionate twirls too, in my time, from other fair ones.

Adieu, varlets four At six on Monday evening, I expect ye all.

MISS CLARISSA HARLOWE TO MISS HOWE

Sunday, April 30.

I AM still well pleased with Mr. Lovelace's behaviour. We have had a good deal of serious discourse together. The man has really just and good notions. He confesses how much he is pleased with this day, and hopes for many such. Nevertheless, he ingenuously warned me that his unlucky vivacity might return: but he doubted not that he should be fixed at last by my example and conversation.

He has given me an entertaining account of the four gentlemen he is to meet to-morrow night: *entertaining,* I mean, for his humorous description of their persons, manners, etc., but such a description as is far from being to their praise: yet he seemed rather to design to divert my melancholy by it, than to degrade them. I think at bottom, my dear, that he must be a good-natured man; but that he was spoiled young for want of check or control.

I cannot but call this, my circumstances considered, a happy day to the end of it. Indeed, my dear, I think I could prefer him to all the men I ever knew, were he but to be always what he has been this day.

She dates again on Monday, and declares herself highly displeased at Miss Partington's being introduced to her: and still more for being obliged to promise to be present at Mr. Lovelace's collation. She foresees, she says, a murdered evening.

MISS CLARISSA HARLOWE TO MISS HOWE

Monday Night, May 1.

I HAVE just escaped from the very disagreeable company I was obliged, so much against my will, to be in.

The names of the gentlemen are Belton, Mowbray, Tourville, and Belford. These four, with Mrs. Sinclair, Miss Partington, the great heiress mentioned in my last, Mr. Lovelace, and myself, made up the company.

I gave you before the favourable side of Miss Partington's character, such as it was given me by Mrs. Sinclair and her nieces. I will now add a few words from my own observation upon her behaviour in *this* company.

204

In *better* company perhaps she would have appeared to less disadvantage: but, notwithstanding her *innocent looks,* which Mr. Lovelace highly praised, he is the last person whose judgment I would take upon real modesty. For I observed, that, upon some talk from the gentlemen, not free enough to be openly censured, yet too indecent in its implication to come from well-bred persons, in the company of virtuous people, this young lady was very ready to apprehend; and yet, by smiles and simperings, to encourage, rather than discourage, the culpable freedoms of persons, who, in what they went out of their way to say, must either be guilty of absurdity, meaning *nothing*; or, meaning *something*, of rudeness.

Mr. Belford is the fourth gentleman, and one of whom Mr. Lovelace seems more fond than of any of the rest; for he is a man of tried bravery, it seems; and this pair of friends came acquainted upon occasion of a quarrel (possibly about a woman) which brought on a challenge, and a meeting at Kensington Gravel-pits; which ended without unhappy consequences, by the mediation of three gentlemen strangers, just as each had made a pass at the other.

Mr. Belford, it seems, is about seven- or eight-and-twenty. He is the youngest of the five, except Mr. Lovelace: and they are perhaps the wickedest; for they seem to lead the other three as they please. Mr. Belford, as the others, dresses gaily: but has not those advantages of person, nor from his dress, which Mr. Lovelace is too proud of. He has, however, the appearance and air of a gentleman. He is well read in classical authors, and in the best English poets and writers: and, by his means, the conversation took now and then a more agreeable turn.

Mr. Belford seems good-natured and obliging; and, although very complaisant, not so fulsomely so as Mr. Tourville; and has a polite and easy manner of expressing his sentiments on all occasions. He seems to delight in a logical way of argumentation, as also does Mr. Belton. These two attacked each other in this way; and both looked at us women, as if to observe whether we did not admire their learning, or, when they had said a smart thing, their wit. But Mr. Belford had visibly the advantage of the other, having quicker parts, and, by taking the worst sides of the argument, seemed to *think* he had.

I could not but observe often, how much Mr. Lovelace excelled all his four friends in everything they seemed desirous to excel in. But as to wit and vivacity, he had no equal there. All the others gave up to him, when his lips began to open.

Mr. Belford, to my no small vexation and confusion, with the forwardness of a favoured and entrusted friend, singled me out, on Mr. Lovelace's being sent for down, to make me congratulatory compliments on my supposed nuptials; which he did with a caution not to insist too long on the rigorous vow I had imposed upon a man so universally admired ——

"See him among twenty men," said he, "all of distinction, and nobody is regarded but Mr. Lovelace."

MISS CLARISSA HARLOWE TO MISS HOWE

Monday Midnight.

I AM very much vexed and disturbed at an odd incident.

Mrs. Sinclair has just now left me; I believe in displeasure, on my declining to comply with a request she made me: which was to admit Miss Partington to a share in my bed; her house being crowded by her nieces' guests and by their attendants, as well as by those of Miss Partington.

There might be nothing in it; and my denial carried a stiff ill-natured appearance. To deny, thought I, can carry only an appearance of singularity to people who already think me singular. To consent may possibly, if not probably, be attended with inconveniences. The consequences of the alternative so very disproportionate, I thought it more prudent to incur the censure, than to risk the inconvenience.

I told her that I was writing a long letter: that I should choose to write till I was sleepy: and that a companion would be a restraint upon me, and I upon her.

She was loath, she said, that so delicate a young creature and so great a fortune as Miss Partington should be put to lie with Dorcas in a press-bed. She should be very sorry, if she had asked an improper thing. She had never been so put to it before. And Miss would stay up with *her* till I had done writing.

Alarmed at this urgency, and it being easier to persist in a denial *given,* than to give it at *first,* I said, Miss Partington should be welcome to my whole bed, and I would retire into the dining-room, and there, locking myself in, write all the night.

The poor thing, she said, was afraid to lie alone. To be sure Miss Partington would not put me to such an inconvenience.

She then withdrew: but returned; begged my pardon for returning: but the poor child, she said, was in tears. Miss Partington had never seen a young lady she so much admired, and so much wished to imitate, as me. The dear girl hoped that nothing had passed in her behaviour to give me dislike to her. Should she bring her to me?

I was very busy, I said. The letter I was writing was upon a very important subject. I hoped to see the young lady in the morning; when I would apologize to her for my particularity. And then Mrs. Sinclair hesitating, and moving towards the door (though she turned round to me again), I desired her (*lighting her*) to take care how she went down.

Now, my dear, is not this a particular incident, either as I have made it, or as it was designed? I don't love to do an uncivil thing. And if nothing were meant by the request, my refusal deserves to be called uncivil. Then I have shown a suspicion of foul usage by it, which surely dare not be meant.

I am now out of humour with him, with myself, with all the world, but you. His companions are shocking creatures. Why, again I repeat, should he have been desirous to bring me into such company? Once more, I like him not. Indeed I do not like him!

MISS CLARISSA HARLOWE TO MISS HOWE

Tuesday, May 2.

WITH infinite regret I am obliged to tell you, that I can no longer write to you, or receive letters from you. Your mother has sent me a letter enclosed in a cover to Mr. Lovelace, directed for him at Lord M.'s (and which was brought him just now), reproaching me on this subject in very angry terms, and forbidding me, "as I would not be thought to intend to make her and you unhappy, to write to you without her leave."

This, therefore, is the last you must receive from me, till happier days: and as my prospects are not very bad, I presume we shall soon have leave to write again; and even to see each other: since an alliance with a family so honourable as Mr. Lovelace's is, will not be a disgrace.

These circumstances I mention (as you will suppose) that your kind heart may be at ease about me; that you may be induced by them to acquiesce with your mother's commands (*cheerfully* acquiesce), and that for *my sake*, lest I should be thought an *inflamer*; who am, with very contrary intentions, my dearest and best-beloved friend, / Your ever obliged and affectionate, / CLARISSA HARLOWE.

MISS HOWE TO MISS CLARISSA HARLOWE

Wedn., May 3.

I AM astonished that my mother should take such a step — purely to exercise an unreasonable act of authority; and to oblige the most remorseless hearts in the world. If I find that I can be of use to you, either by advice or information, do you think I will not give it? Were it to any other person, much *less* dear to me than you are, do you think, in such a case, I would forbear giving it?

This I will come into, if it will make you easy — I will forbear to write to *you* for a few days, if nothing extraordinary happen; and till the rigour of her prohibition is abated. But be assured that I will not dispense with your writing to *me*. My heart, my conscience, my honour, will not permit it.

You have brought an inconvenience upon yourself, as you observe, by your refusal of Miss Partington for your bedfellow. Pity you had not admitted her. Watchful as *you* are, what *could* have happened? If violence were intended, he would not stay for the *night*. You might have sat up after her, or not gone to bed. Mrs. Sinclair pressed it too far. You was over-scrupulous.

If anything happen to delay your nuptials, I would advise you to remove: but if you marry, perhaps you may think it no great matter to stay where you are till you take possession of your own estate.

MISS CLARISSA HARLOWE TO MISS HOWE

Thursday, May 4.

I FOREGO every other engagement, I suspend every wish, I banish every other fear, to take up my pen, to beg of you that you will not think of being *guilty* of such an act of love as I can never thank you for; but must for ever regret. If I *must* continue to write to you, I must. I know full well your impatience of control, when you have the least imagination that your generosity or friendship is likely to be wounded by it.

If I write, as I find I must, I insist upon *your* forbearing to write. Your silence to *this* shall be the sign to me that you will not think of the rashness you threaten me with; and that you will obey your mother as to *your own* part of the correspondence, however; especially as you can inform or advise me in every weighty case by Mr. Hickman's pen.

My clothes were brought to me just now. But you have so much discomposed me, that I have no heart to look into the trunks. Why, why, my dear, will you frighten me with your flaming love? Discomposure gives distress to a weak heart, whether it arise from friendship or enmity.

MR. LOVELACE TO JOHN BELFORD, ESQ.

Tuesday, May 2.

A THOUSAND pounds wouldst thou give for the good opinion of this single lady — to be only thought tolerably of, and not quite unworthy of her conversation, would make thee happy. And at parting last night, or rather this morning, thou madest me promise a few lines to Edgware, to let thee know what she thinks of thee and of thy brethren.

Thy thousand pounds, Jack, is all thy own: for most heartily does she dislike ye all — thee as much as any of the rest.

I saw not, I said, begging her pardon, that she liked *anybody* (*Plain dealing for plain dealing, Jack! Why then did she abuse my friends?*). However, let me but know whom and what she did or did not like; and, if possible, I would like and dislike the very same persons and things.

She bid me then, in a pet, *dislike myself.*

Cursed severe! Does she think she must not pay for it one day, or one night? And if one, many; that's my comfort.

I had like to have been blasted by two or three flashes of lightning from her indignant eyes; and she turned scornfully from me, and retired to her own apartment.

And now, dost thou not think that I owe my charmer some revenge for her cruelty in obliging such a fine young creature and so vast a fortune, as Miss Partington, to crowd into a press-bed with Dorcas the maidservant of the proud refuser? Thinkest thou that I could not guess at her dishonourable fears of me? — that she apprehended that the supposed *husband* would endeavour to take possession of *his own?* — and that Miss Partington would be willing to contribute to such a piece of justice?

Thus, then, thou both remindest and defiest me, charmer! And since thou reliest more on thy own precaution than upon my honour, be it unto thee, fair one, as thou apprehendest!

MR. BELFORD TO ROBERT LOVELACE, ESQ.

Edgware, Tuesday Night, May 2.

WITHOUT staying for the promised letter from you to inform us what the lady says of *us*, I write to tell you that we are all of *one* opinion with regard to *her*; which is, that there is not of her age a finer woman in the world, as to her understanding. As for her person, she is at the age of bloom, and an admirable creature; a perfect beauty: but this *poorer* praise, a man, who has been honoured with her conversation, can hardly descend to give; and yet she was brought amongst us contrary to her will.

Permit me, dear Lovelace, to be a means of saving this excellent creature from the dangers she hourly runs from the most plotting heart in the world. In a former, I pleaded your own family, Lord M.'s wishes particularly; and then I had not seen her: but now, I join *her* sake, *honour's* sake, motives of justice, generosity, gratitude, and humanity, which are all concerned in the preservation of so fine a woman. Thou knowest not the anguish I should have had (whence arising, I cannot devise), had I not known before I set out this morning, that the incomparable creature had disappointed thee in thy cursed view of getting her to admit the specious Partington for a bedfellow.

I have done nothing but talk of this lady ever since I saw her. There is something *so awful*, and yet *so sweet*, in her aspect, that were I to have the virtues and the graces all drawn in one piece, they should be taken, every one of them, from different airs and attitudes in her. She was born to adorn the age she was given to, and would be an ornament to the first dignity. What a piercing, yet gentle eye; every glance, I thought, mingled with love and fear of you! What a sweet smile darting through the cloud that overspread her fair face; demonstrating that she had more apprehensions and grief at her heart than she cared to express!

Our companions consented that I should withdraw to write to the above effect. They can make nothing of the characters we write in; so I read this to them. They approve of it; and of their own motion each man would set his name to it. I would not delay sending it, for fear of some detestable scheme taking place.

THOMAS BELTON.
RICHARD MOWBRAY.
JAMES TOURVILLE.

Just now are brought me both yours. I vary not my opinion, nor forbear my earnest prayers to you in her behalf, notwithstanding her dislike of me.

MR. LOVELACE TO JOHN BELFORD, ESQ.

Wednesday, May 3.

I OWN with thee, and with the poet, *that sweet are the joys that come with willingness* — but is it to be expected that a *woman of education,* and a *lover of forms,* will yield before she is attacked? And have I so much as summoned This to surrender? I doubt not but I shall meet with difficulty. I must, therefore, make my first effort by surprise. There may possibly be some *cruelty* necessary: but there may be *consent in struggle;* there may be *yielding in resistance.* But the first conflict over, whether the following may not be weaker and weaker, till *willingness* ensue, is the point to be tried. I will illustrate what I have said by the simile of a bird new-caught. We begin, when boys, with birds, and, when grown up, go on to women; and both, perhaps, in turn, experience our sportive cruelty.

Now let me tell thee, that I have known a bird actually starve itself, and die with grief, at its being caught and caged. But never did I meet with a woman who was so silly. Yet have I heard the dear souls most vehemently threaten their own lives on such an occasion.

Now, Belford, were I to go no further than I have gone with my beloved Miss Harlowe, how shall I know the difference between *her* and *another* bird? To let her fly now, what a pretty jest would that be! How do I know, except I try, whether she may not be brought to sing me a fine song, and to be as well contented as I have brought other birds to be, and very shy ones too?

But I guess at thy principal motive in this thy earnestness in behalf of this charming creature. I know that thou correspendeth with Lord M., who is impatient, and has long been desirous, to see me shackled. And thou wantest to make a merit with the uncle, with a view to one of his nieces. But knowest thou not, that *my consent* will be wanting to complete thy wishes? And what a commendation will it be of thee to such a girl as Charlotte, when I shall acquaint her with the affront thou puttest upon the whole sex, by asking, *Whether I think my reward, when I have subdued the most charming woman in the world, will be equal to my trouble?* Which, thinkest thou, a woman of spirit will soonest forgive: the undervaluing varlet who *can put such a question;* or him who *prefers the pursuit and conquest of a fine woman to all the joys of life?* Have I not known even a *virtuous woman,* as she would be thought, vow everlasting antipathy to a man who gave out that she was *too old for him to attempt?*

Learn of thy master, for the future, to treat more respectfully a sex that yields us our principal diversions and delights.

. . . .

Well sayest thou, that mine is the *most plotting heart in the world.* Thou dost me honour, and I thank thee heartily.

She is, thou sayest, *all mind*. So say I. But why shouldst thou imagine that such a mind as hers, meeting with such a one as mine, and, to dwell upon the word, *meeting* with an inclination in hers, should not propagate minds like her own?

Were I to take thy stupid advice, and marry what a figure should I make in rakish annals! The lady in my power: yet not having *intended* to put herself in my power: declaring against love, and a rebel to it: so much open-eyed caution: no confidence in my honour: her family expecting the worst *hath* passed; herself seeming to expect that the worst *will* be attempted. What! wouldst thou not have me act in character?

And when I think I can keep the marriage vow, then will it be time to marry. Take ye that thistle to mumble upon.

. . . .

And now imagine (the charmer overcome) thou seest me sitting supinely cross-kneed, reclining on my sofa, the god of love dancing in my eyes, and rejoicing in every mantling feature; the sweet rogue, late such a proud rogue, wholly in my power, moving up slowly to me, at my beck, with heaving sighs, half-pronounced upbraidings from murmuring lips, her finger in her eye, and quickening her pace at my *Come hither, dearest!*

If I could bring my charmer to this, would it not be the eligible of eligibles? Is it not worth trying for? As I said, I can marry her when I will. She *can* be nobody's but mine, neither for shame, nor by choice, nor yet by address: for who, that knows my character, believes that the worst she dreads is *now* to be dreaded?

I have the highest opinion that man can have (thou knowest I have) of the merit and perfections of this admirable woman; of her virtue and honour too; although thou, in a former, art of opinion that she *may be overcome*. Am I not therefore obliged to go further, in order to contradict thee, and, as I have often urged, to be *sure* that she is what I really think her to be, and, if I am ever to marry her, hope to find her?

But to return to thy objections — Thou wilt perhaps tell me, in the names of thy brethren, as well as in thy own name, that among all the objects of your respective attempts, there was not one of the rank and merit of my charming Miss Harlowe.

And will ye not now all join to say, that it is more manly to attack a lion than a sheep? Thou knowest that I always illustrated my eagle-ship, by aiming at the noblest quarries; and by disdaining to make a stoop at wrens, phyl-tits,[1] and wagtails.

Be convinced then, that *I* (according to *our* principles) am right, *thou* wrong; or, at least, be silent. But I *command thee to be convinced*. And in thy next be sure to tell me that thou art.

---

[1] *Phyl-tits,* q.d. *Phyllis-tits,* in opposition to *Tom-tits.* It need not now be observed, that Mr. Lovelace, in the wanton gaiety of his heart, often takes liberties of coining words and phrases in his letters to this his familiar friend.

MR. BELFORD TO ROBERT LOVELACE, ESQ.

Edgware, Thursday, May 4.

I KNOW that thou art so abandoned a man, that to give thee the best reasons in the world against what thou hast once resolved upon, will be but acting the madman whom once we saw trying to buffet down a hurricane with his hat. I hope, however, that the lady's merit will still avail her with thee.

Upon my faith, Lovelace, the subject sticks with me, notwithstanding I find I have not the honour of the lady's good opinion. And, O Lovelace, I conjure thee, if thou art a *man*, let not the specious devils thou hast brought her among be suffered to triumph over her; nor make her the victim of *unmanly artifices*. If she yield to *fair seduction*, if I may so express myself; if thou canst raise a weakness in her by love, or by arts not inhuman; I shall the less pity her: and shall then conclude that there is not a woman in the world who can resist a bold and resolute lover.

MISS CLARISSA HARLOWE TO MISS HOWE

HE IS constantly accusing me of over-scrupulousness. He says, I am always out of humour with him. That I could not have behaved more reservedly to Mr. Solmes: and that it is contrary to all his hopes and notions, that he should not, in so long a time, find himself able to inspire the person whom he hoped so soon to have the honour to call his, with the least distinguishing tenderness for him beforehand.

You will say that I am very grave: and so I am. Mr. Lovelace is extremely sunk in my opinion since Monday night: nor see I before me anything that can afford me a pleasing hope. For what, with a mind *so unequal as his*, can be my *best* hope?

I think I mentioned to you, in my former, that my clothes were brought me. They were brought me on Thursday; but neither my few guineas with them, nor any of my books, except a *Drexelius on Eternity*, the good old *Practice of Piety*, and a *Francis Spira*. My brother's wit, I suppose. He thinks he does well to point out death and despair to me.

You will the less wonder at my being so very solemn, when, added to the above, and to my uncertain situation, I tell you that they have sent me with these books a letter from my Cousin Morden. It has set my heart against Mr. Lovelace. Against myself too. I send it enclosed. If you please, my dear, you may read it here.

Col. Morden to Miss Clarissa Harlowe

Florence, April 13.

I AM extremely concerned to hear of a difference betwixt the rest of a family so near and dear to me, and *you* still dearer to me than any of the rest.

My Cousin James has acquainted me with the offers you have had, and with your refusals. I wonder not at either. I know very little of either of the gentlemen; but of Mr. Lovelace I know more than of Mr. Solmes. I wish I could say more to his advantage than I can.

If your parents and you differ in sentiment on this important occasion, let me ask you, my dear cousin, who ought to give way? I own to you, that I should have thought there could not anywhere have been a more suitable match for you than with Mr. Lovelace, had he been a moral man. I should have very little to say against a man, of whose actions I am not to set up myself as a judge, did he not address my cousin. But, on this occasion, let me tell you, my dear Clarissa, that Mr. Lovelace cannot possibly deserve you. He *may* reform, you'll say: but he may *not*. Habit is not soon shaken off. Libertines, who are libertines in defiance of talents, of superior lights, of conviction, hardly ever reform but by miracle, or by incapacity. Well do I know mine own sex.

A libertine, my dear cousin, a *plotting*, an *intriguing* libertine, must be generally *remorseless* — *unjust* he must always be. The noble rule of doing to others what he would have done to himself, is the first rule he breaks; and every day he breaks it; the oftener, the greater his triumph. He has great contempt for your sex. He believes no woman chaste, because he is a profligate. Every woman who *favours him, confirms him* in his wicked incredulity.

You have an opportunity offered you to give the highest instance that can be given of filial duty. Embrace it. It is worthy *of* you. It is expected *from* you; however, for your inclination sake, we may be sorry that you are called upon to give it.

I am, with the greatest respect, my dearest cousin, / Your most affectionate and faithful servant, / WM. MORDEN.

I will suppose, my dear Miss Howe, that you have read my cousin's letter. It is now in vain to wish it had come sooner. But if it *had*, I might perhaps have been so rash as to give Mr. Lovelace the *fatal meeting*, as I little thought of going away with him.

That a man of a character which ever was my abhorrence should fall to my lot! But depending on my own strength; having no reason to apprehend danger from headstrong and disgraceful impulses; I too little perhaps cast up my eyes to the Supreme Director; in whom, mistrusting myself, I ought to have placed my whole confidence — and the more when I saw myself so perseveringly addressed by a man of this character.

I had begun a letter to my cousin; but laid it by, because of the uncertainty of my situation, and expecting every day for several days past to be at a greater certainty. You bid me write to him some time ago, you know. I had begun a letter, but now I can never end it. You will *believe* I cannot: for how shall I tell him that all his compliments are misbestowed? that all his advice is thrown away? and that even my highest expectation is to be the wife of that free-liver, whom he so pathetically warns me to shun?

Sunday Night, May 7.

She tells Miss Howe that Mr. Lovelace is continually teasing her to go abroad with him in a coach, attended by whom she pleases of her own sex, either for the air, or to the public diversions.

Now, my dear, I cannot bear the life I live. I would be glad at my heart to be out of his reach. If I were, he should soon *find the difference*. If I must be humbled, it had better be by those to whom I owe duty, than by him. My aunt writes that SHE dare not propose anything in my favour.

I can but try, my dear. It is my duty to try all *probable* methods to restore the poor outcast to favour. I will give up all right and title to my grandfather's devises and bequests, with all my heart and soul, to whom they please, in order to make my proposal palatable to my brother. And that my surrender may be effectual, I will engage never to marry.

What, therefore, I am thinking of, is this: Suppose Mr. Hickman, whose good character has gained him everybody's respect, should put himself in my Uncle Harlowe's way? And (as if from your knowledge of the state of things between Mr. Lovelace and me) assure him not only of the above particulars but that I am under no obligations that shall hinder me from taking his directions?

I submit the whole to your discretion, whether to pursue it at all, or in what manner.

Mr. Lovelace to John Belford, Esq.

Monday Night.

THIS perverse lady keeps me at such distance that I am sure something is going on between her and Miss Howe, notwithstanding the prohibition from Mrs. Howe to both; and as I have thought it some degree of merit in myself to punish others for their transgressions, I am of opinion that both these girls are punishable for their breach of parental injunctions.

But if I could find out that the dear creature carried any of her letters in her pockets, I can get her to a play or to a concert, and she may have the misfortune to lose her pockets.

But how shall I find this out; since her Dorcas knows no more of her dressing or undressing than her Lovelace? For she is dressed for the day before she appears even to her servant. Vilely suspicious! Upon my soul, Jack, a suspicious temper is a punishable temper. If a woman suspects a rogue in an honest man, is it not enough to make the honest man who knows it a rogue?

But as to her pockets, I think my mind hankers after them, as the less mischievous attempt. But they cannot hold all the letters that I should wish to see. And yet a woman's pockets are half as deep as she is high.

I have ordered Dorcas to cultivate by all means her lady's favour; to lament her incapacity as to writing and reading; to show letters to her lady, as from pretended country relations; to beg her advice how to answer them, and to get them answered; and to be always aiming at scrawling with a pen, lest inky fingers should give suspicion. I have moreover given the wench an ivory-leafed pocket-book, with a silver pencil, that she may make memoranda on occasion.

And let me tell thee that the lady has already (at Mrs. Sinclair's motion) removed her clothes out of the trunks they came in, into an ample mahogany repository, where they will lie at full length, and which has drawers in it for linen.

A master-key which will open every lock in this chest, is put into Dorcas's hands; and she is to take care, when she searches for papers, before she removes anything, to observe how it lies, that she may replace all to a hair. Sally and Polly can occasionally help to transcribe.

So far, so good. I shall never rest till I have discovered, in the first place, where the dear creature puts her letters; and in the next, till I have got her to a play, to a concert, or to take an airing with me out of town for a day or two.

I must, I must come at them. This difficulty augments my curiosity. Strange, so much as she writes, and at all hours, that not one sleepy or forgetful moment has offered in our favour.

Tuesday, May 9.

I am a very unhappy man. This lady is said to be one of the sweetest-tempered creatures in the world: and so I thought her. But to *me*, she is one of the most perverse. I imagined, for a long while, that we were born to make each other happy: but, quite the contrary, we really seem to be sent to plague each other.

But I will lead to the occasion of this preamble.

I had been out. On my return, meeting Dorcas on the stairs — Your lady in her chamber, Dorcas? In the dining-room, sir: and if ever you hope for an opportunity to come at a letter, it must be now. For at her feet I saw one lie, which, as may be seen by its open folds, she has been reading, with a little parcel of others she is now busied with — all pulled out of her pocket, as I believe: so, sir, you'll know where to find them another time.

I was ready to leap for joy, and instantly resolved to bring forward an expedient which I had held *in petto*; and entering into the dining-room with an air of transport, I boldly clasped my arms about her, as she sat; she huddling up her papers in her handkerchief all the time; the dropped paper unseen. Oh, my dearest life, a lucky expedient have Mr. Mennell and I hit upon just now. In order to hasten Mrs. Fretchville to quit the house, I have agreed, if you approve of it, to entertain her cook, her housemaid and two menservants (about whom she was very solicitous), till you are provided to your mind.

O my beloved creature, will not this be agreeable to you? I am sure it will — it must — and clasping her closer to me, I gave her a more fervent kiss than ever I had dared to give her before. I permitted not my ardour to overcome my discretion, however; for I took care to set my foot upon the letter, and scraped it farther from her, as it were behind her chair.

She was in a passion at the liberty I took. Bowing low, I begged her pardon; and stooping still lower, in the same motion took up the letter, and whipped it into my bosom.

Up she flew in a moment: Traitor! Judas! her eyes flashing lightning, and a perturbation in her eager countenance, so charming! What have you taken up? And then, what for both my ears I durst not have done to her, she made no scruple to seize the stolen letter, though in my bosom.

What was to be done on so palpable a detection? I clasped her hand, which had hold of the ravished paper, between mine: O my beloved creature! said I, can you think I have not *some* curiosity?

Let go my hand! — stamping with her pretty foot. How dare you, sir! At this rate, I see — too plainly I see — and more she could not say: but, gasping, was ready to faint with passion and affright; the devil a bit of her accustomed gentleness to be seen in her charming face, or to be heard in her musical voice.

And now is my charmer shut up from me: refusing to see me; refusing her meals. She resolves *not* to see me; that's more: never again, if she can help it; and *in the mind she is in* — I hope she has said.

Wednesday Morning.

I must keep a good look-out. She is not now afraid of her brother's plot. I shan't be at all surprised if Singleton calls upon Miss Howe, as the only person who *knows*, or is *likely to know*, where Miss Harlowe is; pretending to have affairs of importance, and of particular service to her, if he can but be admitted to her speech. Of compromise, who knows, from her brother?

Well, then, I will find a Singleton; that's all I have to do. But to own the truth, I have overplotted myself.

I am very unwilling to have recourse to measures which these demons below are continually urging me to take; because I am sure that, at last, I shall be brought to make her legally mine.

One complete trial over, and I think I will do her noble justice. She must be mine, let me do or offer what I will. Courage whenever I assume, all is over: for should she think of escaping from hence, whither can she fly to avoid me? Her parents will not receive her. Her uncles will not entertain her. Her beloved Norton is in their direction, and cannot. Miss Howe dare not. She has not one friend in town but me — is entirely a stranger to the town. And what then is the matter with me, that I should be thus unaccounably overawed and tyrannized over by a dear creature who wants only to know how impossible it is that she should escape me, in order to be as humble to me as she is to her persecuting relations!

Should I even make the grand attempt, and fail, and should she hate me for it, her hatred can be but temporary. She has already incurred the censure of the world. She must therefore choose to be mine, for the sake of soldering up her reputation in the eye of that impudent world. For who that knows me, and knows that she has been in my power, though but for twenty-four hours; will think her spotless as to fact, let her inclination be what it will?

MISS CLARISSA HARLOWE TO MISS HOWE

Tuesday, May 9.

WE ARE quite out again.

I am more and more convinced that I am too much in his power to make it prudent to stay with him. And if my friends *will* but give me hope, I will resolve to abandon him forever.

Till I can know whether my friends will give me hope or not, I must do what I never studied to do before in any case; that is, try to keep this difference open: and yet it will make me look *little in my own eyes;* because I shall mean by it more than I can own. But this is one of the consequences of a step I shall ever deplore! The natural fruits of all engagements, where the minds are unpaired — *dispaired*, in my case, may I say.

But you must not, my dear, suppose my heart to be still a confederate with my eye. That deluded eye now clearly sees its fault, and the misled heart despises it for it.

MISS HOWE TO MISS CLARISSA HARLOWE

Wednesday, May 10.

I MUCH approve of your resolution to leave this wretch, if you can make up with your uncle. I hate the man — most heartily do I hate him, for his teasing ways.

I am sorry to tell you that I have reason to think that your brother has not laid aside his foolish plot. A sunburnt, sailor-looking fellow was with me just now, pretending great service to you from Captain Singleton, could he be admitted to your speech. I pleaded ignorance as to the place of your abode. The fellow was too well instructed for me to get anything out of him.

MISS CLARISSA HARLOWE TO MISS HOWE

Friday, May 12.

WHATEVER, my dearest creature, is *my* shining-time, the adversity of a friend is *yours*. I am sorry you have reason to think Singleton's projects are not at an end. But who knows what the sailor had to propose? Yet had any good been intended me, this method would hardly have been fallen upon.

Shnday, May 14.

I have not been able to avoid a short debate with Mr. Lovelace. I had ordered a coach to the door. When I had notice that it was come, I went out of my chamber to go to it; but met him dressed on the stairs head, with a book in his hand, but without his hat and sword. He asked with an air very solemn, yet respectful, if I were going abroad. I told him I was. He desired leave to attend me, if I were going to church. I refused him. And then he complained heavily of my treatment of him; and declared that he would not live such another week as the past, for the world.

I owned to him very frankly, that I had made an application to my friends; and that I was resolved to keep myself to myself till I knew the issue of it.

He coloured, and seemed surprised. But checking himself in something he was going to say, he pleaded my danger from Singleton, and again desired to attend me.

And then he told me that Mrs. Fretchville had desired to continue a fortnight longer in the house. She found, said he, that I was unable to determine about entering upon it; and now who knows *when* such a vapourish creature will come to a resolution? This, madam, has been an unhappy week; for had I not stood upon such bad terms with you, *you might have been now mistress of that house*; and probably had my Cousin Montague, if not Lady Betty, actually with you.

And so, sir, taking all you say for granted, your Cousin Montague cannot come to Mrs. Sinclair's? What, pray, is her objection to Mrs. Sinclair's? Is this house fit for me to live in a month or two, and not fit for any of your relations for a few days? And Mrs. Fretchville has *taken more time too!* Then, pushing by him, I hurried downstairs.

He called to Dorcas to bring him his sword and hat; and following me down into the passage, placed himself between me and the door; and again desired leave to attend me.

Then turning to him, I asked if he kept me there his prisoner?

Dorcas just then bringing him his sword and hat, he opened the street door, and taking my reluctant hand, led me, in a very obsequious manner, to the coach. People passing by, stopped, stared, and whispered — but he is so graceful in his person and dress, that he generally takes every eye.

I was uneasy to be so gazed at; and he stepped in after me, and the coachman drove to St. Paul's.

Miss Howe to Miss Clarissa Harlowe

Sunday, May 14.

How it is now, my dear, between you and Mr. Lovelace, I cannot tell. But wicked as the man is, I am afraid he must be your lord and master.

By the time you have read to this place, you will have no doubt of what has been the issue of the conference between the *two gentlemen*.[1] I am equally shocked, and enraged against them all. Against them *all*, I say; for I have tried your good Norton's weight with your

[1 Mr. Hickman and Mr. John Harlowe.]

mother (though at first I did not intend to tell you so), to the same purpose as the gentleman sounded your uncle. Never were there such determined brutes in the world! Why should I mince the matter? Yet would I fain, methinks, make an exception for your mother.

Your uncle will have it that you are ruined. "He can believe everything bad of a creature, he says, who could run away with a man; with such a one especially as Lovelace. They *expected* applications from you, when some heavy distress had fallen upon you. But they are all resolved not to stir an inch in your favour; no, not to save your life!"

My dearest soul! resolve to assert your right. Claim your own, and go and live upon it, as you ought. Then, if you marry not, how will the wretches creep to you for your reversionary dispositions!

Upon the whole, it is now evident to me, and so it must be to you, when you read this letter, that you must be his. And the sooner you are so, the better. Shall we suppose that marriage is not in your power? I cannot have patience to suppose that.

As your evil destiny has thrown you out of all other protection and mediation, you must be father, mother, uncle to yourself; and enter upon the requisite points for yourself. It is hard upon you, but indeed you must. *What room for delicacy now?* No delays on your side, I beseech you. Give him the day. Let it be a short one.

This is my advice: mend it as circumstances offer, and follow *your own*. But indeed, my dear, this, or something like it, would I do. And let him tell me afterwards, if he dared or would, that he humbled down to his shoe-buckles the person it would have been his glory to exalt.

MISS CLARISSA HARLOWE TO MISS HOWE

Monday Afternoon, May 15.

Now indeed it is evident, my best, my only friend, that I have but one choice to make. And now do I find that I have carried my resentment against this man too far. O my dear, to be cast upon a man that is not a *generous man*; that is indeed a *cruel* man! A man that is capable of creating a distress to a young creature, who by her evil destiny is thrown into his power; and then of *enjoying* it, as I may say! (I verily think I may say so of this savage!) What a fate is mine!

Tuesday, May 16.

I heard him in the dining-room at five in the morning. I had rested very ill, and was up too. But not opened my door till six: when Dorcas brought me his request for my company.

He approached me, and taking my hand as I entered the dining-room, I went not to bed, madam, till two, said he; yet slept not a wink. For God's sake, torment me not, as you have done for a week past.

I acknowledge that I have a *proud heart*, madam. I cannot but hope for some instances of previous and preferable favour from the lady I am ambitious to call mine; and that her choice of me should not appear, not *flagrantly* appear, directed by the perverseness of her selfish persecutors, who are my irreconcilable enemies.

More to the same purpose he said. You know, my dear, the room he had given me to recriminate upon him in twenty instances. I did not spare him.

Let me, my dearest creature, ask you, What sort of pride must *his* be, which can dispense with inclination and preference in the lady whom he adores? What must be that love —

Love, sir! who talks of *love*? Was not *merit* the thing we were talking of? Have *I* ever professed, have *I* ever required of *you* professions of a passion of that nature? But there is no end of these debatings; each *so* faultless, each *so* full of self —

I do not think myself *faultless*, madam — but —

But what, sir! Would you evermore argue with me, as if you were a child? Seeking palliations, and making promises? Promises of what, sir? Of being in future the man it is a shame a gentleman is not? Of being the man —

Good God! interrupted he, with eyes lifted up, if *thou* wert to be thus severe —

Well, well, sir (impatiently), I need only to observe, that all this vast difference in sentiments shows how unpaired our minds are — so let us —

Let us *what*, madam! He looked so wildly, that I was a good deal terrified.

Why, sir, let us resolve to quit every regard for each other — nay, flame not out — I am a poor weak-minded creature in some things: but where what I *should be*, or not deserve to live, if I *am not* is in the question, I have a great and invincible spirit, or my own conceit betrays me — let us resolve to quit every regard for each other that is more than civil. *This* you may depend upon: I will never marry any other man. I have seen enough of your sex; at least of *you*. A single life shall ever be *my* choice — while I will leave you at liberty to persue *your own*.

Indifference, *worse* than indifference! said he, in a passion ——

Interrupting him: Indifference let it be — you have not (in *my* opinion at least) deserved that it should be other: if you have in *your own*, you have cause (at least your *pride* has) to hate me for misjudging you.

By my soul, said he, and grasped my hand with an eagerness that hurt it, we *were* born for one another: you *must* be mine — you *shall* be mine (and put his other arm round me), although my damnation were to be the purchase!

I was still more terrified. Let me leave you, Mr. Lovelace.

You must not go, madam! You must not leave me in anger —

I will return — I will return — when you can be less violent — less shocking. And he let me go.

In half an hour, he sent a little billet, expressing his concern for the vehemence of his behaviour, and praying to see me.

I went. Because I could not help myself, I went.

He was full of his excuses.

It was very possible for him now, he said, to account for the work-ings of a beginning frenzy. For his part, he was near distraction. All last week to suffer as he had suffered; and now to talk of *civil regards* only, when he had hoped from the nobleness of my mind —

Hope what you will, interrupted I; I must insist upon it, that our minds are by no means suited to each other. You have brought me into difficulties. I am deserted by every friend but Miss Howe. If you leave me, I will privately retire to some one of the neighbouring villages, and there wait my Cousin Morden's arrival with patience.

I presume, madam, replied he, from what you have said, that your application to Harlowe Place has proved unsuccessful; I therefore hope that you will now give me leave to mention the terms in the nature of settlements, which I have long intended to propose to you; and which having till now delayed to do, through accidents not pro-ceeding from myself, I had thoughts of urging to you *the moment you entered upon your new house*; and upon your finding yourself as inde-pendent in *appearance* as you are in *fact*. Permit me, madam, to pro-pose these matters to you — not with an expectation of your *immediate answer*; but for your *consideration*.

Were not hesitation a self-felt glow, a downcast eye, encourage-ment more than enough? And yet you will observe (as I now do on recollection) that he was in no great hurry to solicit for a *day*.

He seemed to think it enough that he had asked my *leave* to propose his settlements. He took no advantage of my silence, as I presume men *as modest* as Mr. Lovelace would have done in a like case: yet, gazing in my face very confidently, and seeming to expect my an-swer, I thought myself obliged to give the subject a more diffuse turn, in order to save myself the mortification of appearing too ready in my compliance, after such a distance as had been between us.

You talk of *generosity*, Mr. Lovelace, said I. Let me tell you what *generosity* is, in my sense of the word: TRUE GENEROSITY is not con-fined to pecuniary instances: it is *more* than politeness: it is *more* than good faith: it is *more* than honor: it is *more* than *justice*: since all these are but duties, and what a worthy mind cannot dispense with. But TRUE GENEROSITY is greatness of soul. It incites us to do more by a fellow-creature than can be strictly. required of us. It obliges us to hasten to the relief of an object that wants relief; anticipating even such a one's hope or expectation. Generosity, sir, will not surely permit a worthy mind to doubt of its honourable and beneficent intentions: much less will it allow itself to shock, to offend any one; and, least of all, a person thrown by adversity, mishap, or accident, into its protection.

What an opportunity had he to clear his intentions, had he been so disposed, from the *latter part* of this home observation! But he ran away with the first, and kept to that.

Admirably defined! he said. But who, at this rate, madam, can be said to be *generous* to *you*?

His divine monitress, he called me. But he hoped I would now permit him to mention briefly the *justice* he proposed to do me, in the terms of settlements: a subject so proper, *before now*, to have been entered upon; and which would have been entered upon long ago had not my *frequent displeasure* (*I am ever in fault, my dear!*) taken from him the *opportunity* he had often wished for.

I have no spirits just now, sir, to attend to such weighty points. What you have in mind to propose, write to me; and I shall know what answer to return.

． ． ． ． ． ． ． ． ． ． ．

In this way are we now: a sort of calm, as I said, succeeding a storm.

Although circumstances have so offered that I could not take your advice as to the *manner* of dealing with him; yet you gave me so much courage by it, as has enabled me to conduct things to this issue; as well as determined me against leaving him: which, *before*, I was thinking to do, at all adventures. Whether, when it came to the point, I *should* have done so, or not, I cannot say, because it would have depended upon his behaviour at the time.

But let his behaviour be what it will, I am afraid (with you), that should anything offer at last to oblige me to leave him. I shall not mend my situation in the world's eye; but the contrary. And yet I will not be treated by him with indignity while I have any power to help myself.

You, my dear, have accused me of having *modestied away*, as you phrase it, several opportunities of being — being what, my dear? Why, the wife of a libertine: and what a libertine and his wife are, my Cousin Morden's letter tells us.

Miss Clarissa Harlowe to Miss Howe

Tuesday Night, May 16.

Mr. Lovelace has sent me, by Dorcas, his proposals, as follows:

"To spare a delicacy so extreme, and to obey you, I write: and the rather that you may communicate this paper to Miss Howe, who may consult any of her friends you shall think proper to have entrusted on this occasion. I say, *entrusted*; because, as you know, I have given it out to several persons that we are actually married.

"In the first place, madam, I offer to settle upon you, by way of jointure, your whole estate: and moreover to vest in trustees such a part of mine in Lancashire, as shall produce a clear four hundred pounds a year, to be paid to your sole and separate use quarterly.

"My own estate is a clear not nominal £2,000 *per annum*. Lord M. proposes to give me possession either of that which he has in Lancashire (to which, by the way, I think I have a better title than he has himself), or that we call *The Lawn* in Hertfordshire, upon my nuptials with a lady whom he so greatly admires; and to make that I shall choose a clear £1,000 *per annum*.

"If, as your own estate is at present in your father's hands, you rather choose that I should make a jointure out of mine, tantamount to yours, be it what it will, it shall be done.

"To show the beloved daughter the consideration I have for her, I will consent that she shall prescribe the terms of agreement in relation to the large sums, which must be in her father's hands, arising from her grandfather's estate.

"I will only add, that if I have omitted anything that would have given you further satisfaction; or if the above terms be short of what you would wish; you will be pleased to supply them as you think fit. And when I know your pleasure, I will instantly order articles to be drawn up conformably, that nothing in my power may be wanting to make you happy.

"You will now, dearest madam, judge how far all the rest depends upon yourself."

MISS CLARISSA HARLOWE TO MISS HOWE

Wednesday Morning, May 17.

ABOUT seven o'clock we met in the dining-room.

I find he was full of expectation that I should meet him with a very favourable, who knows but with a *thankful aspect*? And I immediately found by his sullen countenance, that he was under no small disappointment that I did not.

My dearest love, are you well? Why look you so solemn upon me? Will your indifference never be over? If I have proposed terms in any respect *short* of your expectation —

He asked me then, if I would so far permit him to touch upon the happy day, as to request the presence of Lord M. on the occasion, and to be my father.

Father had a sweet and venerable sound with it, I said. I should be glad to have a father who would own me.

I am but a very young creature, Mr. Lovelace, said I (and wiped my eyes as I turned away my face), although you have *kindly*, and in *love to me*, introduced so much sorrow to me already: so you must not wonder that the word *father* strikes so sensibly upon the heart of a child ever dutiful till she knew you, and whose tender years still require the paternal wing.

For his own part, he said, as Lord M. was so subject to the gout, he was afraid that the compliment he had just proposed to make him, might, if made, occasion a *longer suspension* than he could bear to think of: and if it did, it would vex him to the heart that he had made it.

I could not say a single word to this, you know, my dear. But you will guess at my thoughts of what he said — so much passionate love, *lip-deep*! So prudent, and so dutifully patient *at heart* to a relation he had till now so undutifully despised! Why, why, am I thrown upon such a man, thought I!

He hesitated, as if contending with himself; and after taking a turn or two about the room, he was at a great loss what to determine upon, he said, because he had not the honour of knowing when he was to be made the happiest of men. Would to God it might that very instant be resolved upon!

To be sure, Mr. Lovelace, if this matter be *ever to be,* it must be agreeable to me to have the full approbation of *one* side, since I cannot have that of the *other.*

If this matter be ever to be! Good God! what words are those at this time of day! And full *approbation* of one side! Why that word *approbation?* when the greatest pride of all my family is that of having the honour of so dear a creature for their relation? Would to Heaven, my dearest life, added he, that, without complimenting *any*body, to-morrow might be the happiest day of my life! What say you, my angel? with a trembling impatience, that *seemed* not affected. What say you for *to-morrow?*

It was likely, my dear, I could say much to it, or name another day, had I been disposed to the latter, with such an *hinted delay from him.*

I was silent.

Next day, madam, if not to-morrow?

Had he given me *time* to answer, it could not have been in the affirmative, you must think — but, *in the same breath,* he went on: Or the *day after that?* And taking both my hands in his, he stared me into a half-confusion. Would *you* have had patience with him, my dear?

No, no, said I, as calmly as possible, you cannot think that I should imagine there can be reason for such a hurry. It will be most agreeable, to be sure, for my lord to be present.

I am all obedience and resignation, returned the wretch, with a self-pluming air, as if he had acquiesced to a proposal *made by me*, and had complimented me with a great piece of *self-denial.*

But when he would have *rewarded himself*, as he had heretofore called it, for this self-supposed concession, with a kiss, I repulsed him with a just and very sincere disdain.

He seemed both vexed and surprised, as one who had made the most agreeable proposals and concessions, and thought them ungratefully returned. He plainly said, that he thought our situation would entitle him to such an innocent freedom: and he was both amazed and grieved to be thus scornfully repulsed.

No reply could be made by me on such a subject. I abruptly broke from him. I recollect, as I passed by one of the pier-glasses, that I saw in it his clenched hand offered in wrath to his forehead: the words, *Indifference, by his soul, next to hatred,* I heard him speak: and something of *ice* he mentioned: I heard not what.

And after all, since I *must* take him as I find him, I *must*: that is to say, as a man so vain, and so accustomed to be admired, that, not being conscious of internal defect, he has taken no pains to polish more than his outside: and as his proposals are higher than my expectations; and as, in his own opinion, he has a great deal to bear. from *me*; I *will* (no new offence preventing) sit down to answer them: and if possible, in terms as unobjectionable to him, as his are to me.

But after all, see you not, my dear, more and more, the mismatch that there is in our minds?

And so much at present for Mr. Lovelace's proposals: of which I desire your opinion.[1]

MR. LOVELACE TO JOHN BELFORD, ESQ.

AFTER her haughty treatment of me, I am resolved she shall speak out.

I'll tell thee beforehand, how it will be with my charmer in this case. She will be about it, and about it, several times: but I will not understand her: at last, after half a dozen hem—ings, she will be obliged to speak out: *I think, Mr. Lovelace — I think, sir — I think you were saying some days ago* — Still I will be all silence — her eyes fixed upon my shoe-buckles, as I sit over against her. Ladies, when put to it thus, always admire a man's shoe-buckles, or perhaps some particular beauties in the carpet. *I think you said that Mrs. Fretchville* — then a crystal tear trickles down each crimson cheek, vexed to have her virgin pride so little assisted. But, come, my meaning dear, cry I to myself, remember what I have suffered *for* thee, and what I have suffered *by* thee! Thy tearful pausings shall not be helped out by me. Speak out, love! O the sweet confusion! Can I rob myself of so many conflicting beauties by the precipitate charmer-pitying folly, by which a *politer* man (thou *knowest*, lovely, that I am no polite man!), betrayed by his own tenderness, and *unused* to female tears, would have been overcome? I will feign an irresolution of mind on the occasion, that she may not *quite* abhor me — that her reflections on the scene in my absence may bring to her remembrance some beauties in *my* part of it: an irresolution that will be owing to awe,

[1] We cannot forbear observing in this place that the lady has been particularly censured, even by some of her own sex, as *over-nice* in her part of the above conversations. But surely this must be owing to want of attention to the *circumstances* she was in, and to her *character*, as well as to the *character of the man she had to deal with:* for although she could not be supposed to know so much of his designs as the reader does by means of his letters to Belford, yet she was but too well convinced of his faulty morals, and of the necessity there was, from the whole of his behaviour to her, to keep such an encroacher, as she frequently calls him, at a distance.

But the reader perhaps is too apt to form a judgment of Clarissa's conduct in critical cases by *Lovelace's complaints of her coldness;* not considering his views upon her; and that she is proposed as an *example;* and therefore in her trials and distresses must not be allowed to dispense with those rules which perhaps some others of her sex, in her delicate situation, would not have thought themselves so strictly bound to observe; although, if she had *not* observed them, a *Lovelace* would have carried all his points.

to reverence, to profound veneration; and that will have more eloquence in it than words *can* have. Speak out then, love, and spare not.

I am in earnest as to the terms. If I marry her (and I have no doubt but that I shall, after my pride, my ambition, my *revenge*, if thou wilt, is gratified) I will do her noble justice. The more I do for such a prudent, such an excellent economist, the more shall I do for myself. But, by my soul, Belford, her haughtiness shall be brought down to own both love and obligation to me.

I more than half regretted that I could not permit her to enjoy a triumph which she so well deserved to glory in — her youth, her beauty, her artless innocence, and her manner, equally beyond comparison or description. But her *indifference*, Belford! That she could resolve to sacrifice me to the malice of my enemies; and carry on the design in so clandestine a manner — yet love her, as I do, to frenzy! — revere her, as I do, to adoration! These were the recollections with which I fortified my recreant heart against her! Yet, after all, if she persevere, she must conquer! Coward, as she has made me, that never was a coward before!

The women below say she hates me; she despises me! And 'tis true: she does; she must. And why cannot I take their advice? I will not long, my fair one, be despised, by *thee*, and laughed at by *them*!

Let me acquaint thee, Jack, that this effort of hers to leave me, if she could have been received; her sending for a coach on Sunday; no doubt, resolving not to return, if she had gone out without me (for did she not declare that she had thoughts to retire to some of the villages about town, where she could be safe and private?), have, all together, so much alarmed me, that I have been adding to the written instructions for my fellow and the people below how to act in case she should elope in my absence: particularly letting Will know what he shall report to strangers in case she shall throw herself upon any such with a resolution to abandon me.

These instructions I shall further add to as circumstances offer.

MISS HOWE TO MISS CLARISSA HARLOWE

Thursday, May 18.

I HAVE neither time nor patience, my dear friend, to answer every material article in your last letters just now received. Mr. Lovelace's proposals are all I like of him. And yet (as you do) I think that he concludes them not with that warmth and earnestness which we might naturally have expected from him. Never in my life did I hear or read of so patient a man, with such a blessing in his reach.

Would to Heaven to-morrow, without complimenting anybody, might be his happy day! Villain! After he had himself suggested the compliment! And I think he accuses YOU of delaying! Fellow, that he is! How my heart is wrung!

I will endeavour to think of some method, of some scheme, to get you from him, and to fix you safely somewhere till your Cousin Morden arrives — a scheme to lie by you, and to be pursued as occasion may be given. You are sure that you can go abroad when you please? and that our correspondence is safe? I cannot, however (for the reasons heretofore mentioned respecting your own reputation), wish you to leave him while he gives you not cause to suspect his honour. But your heart I know would be the easier, if you were sure of some asylum in case of necessity.

And what is the result of all I have written, but this? Either marry, my dear, or get from them all, and from him too.

MR. BELFORD TO ROBERT LOVELACE, ESQ.

Wednesday, May 17.

I CANNOT conceal from you anything that relates to yourself so much as the enclosed does. You will see what the noble writer apprehends from you, and wishes of you, with regard to Miss Harlowe, and how much at heart all your relations have it that you do honourably by her. They compliment me with an influence over you, which I wish with all my soul you would let me have in this article.

Let me once more entreat thee, Lovelace, to reflect, before it be too late (before the mortal offence be given), upon the graces and merits of this lady. Let thy frequent remorses at last end in one effectual remorse. Let not pride and wantonness of heart ruin thy fairer prospects.

We all know what an inventive genius thou art master of: we are all sensible that thou hast *a head to contrive, and a heart to execute.* Have I not called thine *the plottingest heart in the universe?* I called it so upon knowledge. What wouldst thou *more?* Why should it be the most *villainous,* as well as the most *able?*

And what, Lovelace, all the time is thy pride? what art thou more, or better, than the instrument even of her implacable brother, and envious sister, to perpetuate the disgrace of the most excellent of sisters, which they are moved to by vilely low and sordid motives? Canst thou bear, Lovelace, to be thought the machine of thy inveterate enemy James Harlowe? Nay, art thou not the cully of that still viler Joseph Leman, who serves himself as much by thy money, as he does thee by the double part he acts by thy direction? And further still, art thou not the devil's agent, who only can, and who certainly will, suitably reward thee, if thou proceedest, and if thou effectest thy wicked purpose?

Thou knowest that I have no interest, that I can have no view, in wishing thee to do justice to this admirable creature. For thy own sake, once more I conjure thee, for thy family's sake, and for the sake of our *common humanity,* let me beseech thee to be just to Miss Clarissa Harlowe.

MR. LOVELACE TO JOHN BELFORD, ESQ.

Friday Night, May 19.

I AM amazed at the repetition of thy wambling nonsense. I do *not* intend *to let this matchless creature slide through my fingers.*

An instrument of the vile James Harlowe, dost thou call me? O Jack! how I could curse thee! *I* an *instrument* of that brother! of that sister! But mark the end — and thou shalt see what will become of that brother, and of that sister!

I do intend to endeavour to overcome *myself*; but I must first try if I cannot overcome *this lady*. Have I not said that the honour of her sex is concerned that I should try?

Let my lord know that thou *hast* scribbled to me. But give him not the contents of thy epistle. Let us leave old saws to old men.

MR. BELFORD TO ROBERT LOVELACE, ESQ.

Saturday, May 20.

Not one word will I reply to such an abandoned wretch as thou hast shown thyself to be in thine of last night. I will leave the lady to the protection of that Power who only can work miracles; and to her own merits. I have hopes that these will save her.

· · · · · · · · · ·

I leave this as a lesson upon thy heart, without making any application: only with this remark, "That after we libertines have indulged our licentious appetites, reflecting (in the conceit of our vain hearts), both with our lips and by our lives, upon our ancestors, and the good old ways, we find out, when we come to years of discretion, that those good old ways would have been best for *us*, as well as for the rest of the world; and that in every step we have deviated from them, we have only exposed our vanity, and our ignorance at the same time."

MR. LOVELACE TO JOHN BELFORD, ESQ.

How stands it between thyself and the lady, methinks thou askest, since her abrupt departure from thee, and undutiful repulse of Wednesday morning?

Why pretty well in the main. Nay, *very* well. For why? The dear saucy-face knows not how to help herself. Can fly to no other protection. And has, besides, overheard a conversation (who would have thought she had been so near?) which passed between Mrs. Sinclair, Miss Martin, and myself, that very Wednesday afternoon; which has set her heart at ease with respect to several doubtful points.

Such as, particularly, Mrs. Fretchville's unhappy state of mind — most humanely pitied by Miss Martin, who knows her very well.

My Lord M.'s gout his only hindrance from visiting my spouse. Lady Betty and Miss Montague soon expected in town.

My earnest desire signified to have my spouse receive those ladies in her own house, if Mrs. Fretchville would but know her own mind; and I pathetically lamented the delay occasioned by her not knowing it.

My intention to stay at Mrs. Sinclair's, *as I said I had told them before*, while my spouse resides in her own house (when Mrs. Fretchville could be brought to quit it), in order to gratify her utmost punctilio.

My passion for my beloved (which, as I told them in a high and fervent accent, was the truest that man could have for woman) I boasted of. It was, in short, I said, of the *true platonic kind*; or I had no notion of what platonic love was.

So it is, Jack; and must end as platonic love generally does end.

Sally and Mrs. Sinclair next praised, *but not grossly*, my beloved. Sally particularly admired her purity; but nevertheless she applauded me for the strict observation I made of my vow.

I more freely blamed her reserves to me; called her cruel; inveighed against her relations; doubted her love. Every favour I asked of her denied me. Yet my behaviour to her as pure and delicate when alone, as when before them — hinted at something that had passed between us that very day, that showed her indifference to me in so strong a light, that I could not bear it. But that I would ask her for her company to the play of *Venice Preserved*, given out for Saturday night as a benefit play; the prime actors to be in it; and this, to see if I were to be denied every favour. Yet, for my own part, I *loved not tragedies*; though she did, for the sake of the instruction, the warning, and the example generally given in them.

I had too much *feeling*, I said. There was enough in the world to make our hearts sad, without carrying grief into our diversions, and making the distress of others our own.

I then, from a letter just before received from one of her father's family, warned them of a person who had undertaken to find us out, and whom I thus in writing (having called for pen and ink) described, that they might arm all the family against him: "A sun-burnt, pock-fretten sailor, ill-looking, big-boned; his stature about six foot; an heavy eye, an overhanging brow, a deck-treading stride in his walk; a couteau generally by his side; lips parched from his gums, as if by staring at the sun in hot climates; a brown coat; a coloured handkerchief about his neck; an oaken plant in his hand, near as long as himself, and proportionably thick."

No questions asked by this fellow must be answered. They should call *me* to him. But not let my beloved know a tittle of this, so long as it could be helped. And I added, that if her brother or Singleton came, and if they behaved civilly, I would, for *her sake*, be civil to *them*: and in this case, she had nothing to do but to own her marriage, and there could be no pretence for violence on either side. But most fervently I swore, that if she were *conveyed away*, either by *persuasion* or *force*, I would directly, *on missing her but one day*, go to demand her at Harlowe Place, whether she were there or not; and if I recovered not a sister, I would have a brother; and should find out a captain of a ship as well as he.

And now, Jack, dost thou think she'll attempt to get from me, do what I will?

.   .   .   .

And what must necessarily be the consequence of all this with regard to my beloved's behaviour to me? Canst thou doubt that it was all complaisance next time she admitted me into her presence?

Thursday we were very happy. All the morning *extremely* happy. I kissed her charming hand — I need not describe to thee her hand and arm. When thou sawest her, I took notice that thy eyes dwelt upon them whenever thou couldst spare them from that beauty-spot of wonders, her face — fifty times kissed her hand, I believe; once her cheek, intending her lip, but so rapturously, that she could not help seeming angry.

Had she not thus kept me at arm's length; had she not denied me those innocent liberties which our sex, from step to step, aspire to; could I but have gained access to her in her hours of heedlessness and dishabille (for full dress creates dignity, augments consciousness, and compels distance); we had been familiarized to each other long ago. But keep her up ever so late; meet her ever so early; by breakfast she is dressed for the day; and at her *earliest hour*, as nice as others dressed.

I dined out. Returning, I talked of the house, and of Mrs. Fretchville — had seen Mennell — had pressed him to get the widow to quit: she pitied Mrs. Fretchville (another good effect of the overheard conversation) — had written to Lord M.; expected an answer soon from him. I was admitted to sup with her. I urged for her approbation or correction of my written terms. She again promised an answer as soon as she had heard from Miss Howe.

Then I pressed for her company to the play on Saturday night. She made objections, as I had foreseen: her brother's projects, warmth of the weather, etc; but in such a manner, as if half afraid to disoblige me (another happy effect of the overheard conversation). I soon got over these, therefore; and she consented to favour me.

Friday passed as the day before.

Here were two happy days to both. Why cannot I make every day equally happy? It looks *as if it were in my power to do so.* Strange, I should thus delight in teasing a woman I so dearly love!

Saturday is half over. We are equally happy — preparing for the play. Polly has offered her company, and is accepted. The woes of others, so well represented as those of Belvidera particularly will be, must, I hope, unlock and open my charmer's heart.

Indeed, I have no hope of such an effect here; but I have more than one end to answer by getting her to a play. To name but one — Dorcas has a *master-key*, as I have told thee. But it were worth while to carry her to the play of *Venice Preserved*, were it but to show her that there have been, and may be, much deeper distresses than she can possibly know.

MISS CLARISSA HARLOWE TO MISS HOWE

Friday, May 19.

LET ME give you my *reflections* on my more hopeful prospects.

I am now, in the first place, better able to account for the delays about the house than I was before. Poor Mrs. Fretchville! Though I know her not, I pity her! Next, it looks well, that he had apprised the women (before this conversation with them) of his intention to stay in this house, after I was removed to the other. By the tone of his voice he seemed concerned for the appearance this new delay would have with me.

So handsomely did Miss Martin express herself of me, that I am sorry, methinks, that I judged so hardly of her, when I first came hither.

His reason for declining to go in person to bring up the ladies of his family, while my brother and Singleton continue their machinations, carries no bad face with it; and one may the rather allow for *their* expectations, that so proud a spirit as his should attend them for this purpose, as he speaks of them sometimes as persons of punctilio.

Other reasons I will mention for my being easier in my mind than I was before I overheard this conversation.

Such as the advice he has received in relation to Singleton's mate; which agrees but too well with what you, my dear, wrote to me in yours of May the 10th.

His not intending to acquaint *me* with it.

His cautions to the servants about the sailor, if he should come and make inquiries about us.

His resolution to avoid violence, were he to fall in either with my brother or this Singleton.

I think myself obliged, from what passed between Mr. Lovelace and me on Wednesday, and from what I overheard him say, to consent to go with him to the play; and the rather, as he had the discretion to propose one of the nieces to accompany me.

I cannot but acknowledge that I am pleased to find that he has actually written to Lord M.

I have promised to give Mr. Lovelace an answer to his proposals as soon as I have heard from you, my dear, on the subject.

I hope, that in the trial which you hint may happen between *me* and *myself* (as you express it), if he should so behave as to oblige me to leave him, I shall be able to act in such a manner as to bring no discredit upon myself in your eye; and that is all now that I have to wish for. But if I value him so much as you are pleased to suppose I do, the trial, which you imagine will be so difficult to me, will not, I conceive, be upon getting from him, when the means to effect my escape are lent me; but how I shall behave when got from him; and, if, like the Israelites of old, I shall be so weak as to wish to return to my Egyptian bondage.

I think it will not be amiss, notwithstanding the present favourable appearances, that you should perfect the scheme (whatever it be) you have thought of, in order to procure for me an asylum, in case of necessity. Mr. Lovelace is certainly a deep and dangerous man; and it is therefore but prudence to be watchful, and to be provided against the worst. Lord bless me, my dear, how am I reduced! Could

I ever have thought to be in such a situation, as to be obliged to stay with a man, of whose honour by me I could have but the *shadow* of a doubt! But I will look forward, and hope the best.

I am certain that your letters are safe. Be perfectly easy, therefore, on that head.

Mr. Lovelace will never be out out of my company by his good-will; otherwise I have no doubt that I am mistress of my goings-out and comings-in; and did I think it needful, and were I not afraid of my brother, and Captain Singleton, I would oftener put it to trial.

MISS HOWE TO MISS CLARISSA HARLOWE

Saturday, May 20.

THE SCHEME I think of is this:

There is a person whom I believe you have seen with me, her name Townsend, who is a great dealer in Indian silks, Brussels and French laces, cambrics, linen, and other valuable goods; which she has a way of coming at duty-free; and has a great vend for them (and for other curiosities which she imports) in the private families of the gentry round us.

I am sure I can engage her to give you protection at her house at Deptford; which she says is a populous village, and one of the last, I should think, in which you would be sought for. She is not much there, you will believe, by the course of her dealings; but, no doubt, must have somebody in the spot, in whom she can confide; and there perhaps you might be safe till your cousin comes. And I should not think it amiss that you write to him out of hand. I cannot suggest to you *what* you should write. That must be left to your own discretion. For you will be afraid, no doubt, of the consequence of a variance between the two men.

Mrs. Townsend, as I have recollected, has two brothers, each a master of a vessel; and who knows, as she and they have concerns together, but that, in case of need, you may have a whole ship's crew at your devotion? If Lovelace give you cause to leave him, take no thought for the people at Harlowe Place. Let *them* take care of one another. It is a care they are *used to*. The law will help to secure *them*. The wretch is no assassin, no night-murderer. He is an *open*, because a *fearless* enemy; and should he attempt anything that would make him obnoxious to the laws of society, you might have a fair riddance of him either by flight or the gallows; no matter which.

Had you not been so minute in your account of the circumstances that attended the opportunity you had of overhearing the dialogue between Mr. Lovelace and two of the women, I should have thought the conference contrived on purpose for your ear.

But, my dear, let the articles be drawn up, and engrossed, and solemnize upon them; and there's no more to be said.

MR. LOVELACE TO JOHN BELFORD, ESQ.

Sunday, May 21.

WHAT'S the matter *now*, thou'lt ask?

Matter enough; for while we were at the play, Dorcas, who had her orders, and a key to her lady's chamber, as well as a master-key to her drawers and mahogany chest, closet-key and all, found means to come at some of Miss Howe's last written letters. The vigilant wench was directed to them by seeing her lady take a letter out of her stays, and put it to the others, before she went out with me — afraid, as the women upbraidingly tell me, that I should find it *there*.

Dorcas no sooner found them, than she assembled three ready writers of the *non-apparents*; and *Sally*, and *she*, and *they* employed themselves with the utmost diligence, in making extracts, according to former directions, from these cursed letters, for my use. *Cursed,* I may well call them — such abuses! such virulence! O this little fury Miss Howe! Well might her saucy friend (who has been equally free with me, or the occasion could not have been given) be so violent as she lately was, at my endeavouring to come at one of these letters.

I have been denied breakfasting with her. Indeed she was a little displeased with me last night; because, on our return from the play, I obliged her to pass the rest of the night with the women and me, in their parlour, and to stay till near one. She told me at *parting,* that she expected to have the whole next day to herself.

.   .   .   .

She is gone. Slipped down before I was aware. She had ordered a chair, on purpose to exclude my personal attendance. But I had taken proper precautions. Will attended her by consent; Peter, the house-servant, was within Will's call.

But she would not be so careless of obliging me, if she knew what I have already come at, and how the women urge me on; for they are continually complaining of *the restraint they lie under,* in their behaviour; in their attendance; *neglecting all their concerns in the front house;* and *keeping this elegant back one entirely free from company,* that she may have no suspicion of them. They doubt not my generosity, they say: but *why* for my own sake, in Lord M.'s style, *should I make so long a harvest of so little corn?*

Women, ye reason well. I think I will begin my operations the moment she comes in.

.   .   .   .

I have come at the letter brought her from Miss Howe to-day. Plot, conjuration, sorcery, witchcraft, all going forward! I shall not be able to see this *Miss Harlowe* with patience. As the nymphs below ask, so do I, Why is *night* necessary? And Sally and Polly upbraidingly remind me of my first attempts upon themselves. Yet *force* answers not my end — and yet it may, if there be truth in that part of the libertine's creed, *That once subdued, is always subdued!* And what woman answers *affirmatively* to the question?

. . . .

She is returned: but refuses to admit me; and insists upon having the day to herself. Dorcas tells me, that she believes her denial is from motives of piety — Oons, Jack, is there impiety in seeing me! Would it not be the highest act of piety to reclaim me? And is this to be done by her refusing to see me, when she is in a devouter frame than usual? But I hate her, hate her heartily! She is old, ugly, and deformed. But oh, the blasphemy! Yet she is a Harlowe: and I do and *can* hate her for that.

[*Lovelace here, in several pages, comments on the letters from Miss Howe that the "nieces" have found and transcribed for him. He meets with extreme criticism of himself in the letters, and learns of the project of engaging Mrs. Townsend's aid in an escape. He says, in extreme understatement, "My resentments are warm."*]

MISS CLARISSA HARLOWE TO MISS HOWE
Sunday Morning, Seven o'clock.

I WAS at the play last night with Mr. Lovelace and Miss Horton. It is, you know, a deep and most affecting tragedy in the reading. You have my remarks upon it in the little book you made me write upon the principal acting plays. You will not wonder that I was greatly moved at the representation, when I tell you, and have some pleasure in telling you, that Mr. Lovelace himself was very sensibly touched with some of the most affecting scenes. I mention this in praise of the author's performance; for I take Mr. Lovelace to be one of the most hard-hearted men in the world. Upon my word, my dear, I do.

His behaviour, however, on this occasion, and on our return, was unexceptionable; only that he would oblige me to stay to supper with the women below, when we came back, and to sit up with him and them till near one o'clock this morning. I was resolved to be even with him; and indeed I am not very sorry to have the pretence; for I love to pass the Sundays by myself.

To have the better excuse to avoid his teasing, I am ready dressed to go to church this morning. I will go only to St. James's Church, and in a *chair*; that I may be sure I can go out and come in when I please, without being intruded upon by him, as I was twice before.

Near Nine o'clock.

He is very importunate to see me. He has desired to attend me to church. He is angry that I have declined to breakfast with him. I am sure that I should not have been at my own liberty if I had. I bid Dorcas tell him, that I desired to have this day to myself. I would see him in the morning, as early as he pleased. She says, she knows not what ails him, but he is out of humour with everybody.

I did not see him as I went down. He is, it seems, excessively out of humour. Dorcas says, not with me neither, she believes: but something has vexed him. This is put on perhaps to make me dine with him. But I will not, if I can help it. I shan't get rid of him for the rest of the day, if I do.

. . . .

He was very earnest to dine with me. But I was resolved to carry this one small point; and so denied to dine myself. And indeed I was endeavouring to write to my Cousin Morden; and had begun three different times, without being able to please myself.

. . . .

While I was considering, he came up, and, tapping at my door, told me, in a very angry tone, he must see me this night. He could not rest till he had been told what he had done to deserve the treatment I gave him.

Treatment I give him! A wretch! Yet perhaps he has nothing new to say to me. I shall be very angry with him.

Mr. Lovelace to John Belford, Esq.

As the lady could not know what Mr. Lovelace's designs were, nor the cause of his ill humour, it will not be improper to pursue the subject from this letter.

Having described his angry manner of demanding, in person, her company at supper; he proceeds as follows:

'Tis hard, answered the fair perverse, that I am to be so little my own mistress. I will meet you in the dining-room half an hour hence.

With an erect mien she entered, her face averted, her lovely bosom swelling, and the more charmingly protuberant for the erectness of her mien. O Jack! that sullenness and reserve should add to the charms of this haughty maid! But in every attitude, in every humour, in every gesture, is beauty beautiful. By her averted face, and indignant aspect, I saw the dear insolent was disposed to be angry — but by the fierceness of mine, as my trembling hands seized hers, I soon made fear her predominant passion. And yet the moment I beheld her, my heart was dastardized; and my reverence for the virgin purity so visible in her whole deportment, again took place. Surely, Belford, this is an angel. And yet, had she not been known to be a female, they would not from *babyhood* have dressed her as such, nor would she, but upon that conviction, have continued the dress.

This I have to say, madam, that I cannot bear to be kept at this distance from you under the same roof.

Under the same roof, sir! How came you ——

Hear me out, madam (letting go her trembling hands, and snatching them back again with an eagerness that made her start) — I have a thousand things to say, to talk of, relating to our present and future prospects; but when I want to open my whole soul to you, you are always contriving to keep me at a distance. You make me inconsistent with myself. Your heart is set upon delays. You must have views that you will not own. Tell me, madam, I conjure you to tell me, this moment, without subterfuge or reserve, in what light am I to appear to you in future? I cannot bear this distance. The suspense you hold me in I cannot bear.

In what light, Mr. Lovelace! (visibly terrified). In no bad light, I hope. Pray, Mr. Lovelace, do not grasp my hands so hard (endeavouring to withdraw them). Pray let me go.

You *hate* me, madam.

I hate nobody, sir.

You *hate* me, madam, repeated I.

You come up in no good temper, I see, Mr. Lovelace — but pray be not violent — *I have done you no hurt* — pray be not violent ——

Sweet creature! And I clasped one arm about her, holding one hand in my other. *You have done me no hurt!* I could have devoured her — but restraining myself — You have done me the greatest hurt! In what have I deserved the distance you keep me at? I knew not what to say.

She struggled to disengage herself. Pray, Mr. Lovelace, let me withdraw. I know not why this is. I know not what I have done to offend you. I see you are come with a *design to quarrel with me.*

Night, *mid*night, *is* necessary, Belford. Surprise, terror, *must* be necessary to the ultimate trial of this charming creature, say the women below what they will. I could not hold my purposes. This was not the first time that I had *intended* to try if she could forgive.

I kissed her hand with a fervour, as if I would have left my lips upon it. Withdraw then, dearest and ever-dear creature. Indeed I entered in a very ill-humour.

And so saying, I conducted her to the door, and left her there. But instead of going down to the women, I went into my own chamber, and locked myself in; ashamed of being awed by her majestic loveliness, and apprehensive virtue, into so great a change of purpose, notwithstanding I had such just provocations from the letters of her saucy friend, founded on her own representations of facts and situations between herself and me.

The lady (dating Sunday night) thus describes her terrors, and Mr. Lovelace's behaviour, on the occasion:

On my entering the dining room, he took my hands in his, in such a humour, as I saw plainly he was resolved to quarrel with me. *And for what? What had I done to him?* I never in my life beheld in anybody such wild, such angry, such impatient airs. I was terrified; and instead of being angry as I intended to be, I was forced to be all mildness. I can hardly remember what were his first words, I was so

236

frightened. But, *You hate me, madam! You hate me, madam!* were some of them — with such a fierceness — I wished myself a thousand miles distant from him. I hate nobody, said I; I thank God I hate nobody. You terrify me, Mr. Lovelace — let me leave you. The man, my dear, looked *quite ugly* — I never saw a man look so ugly as passion made him look. *And for what?* And he so grasped my hands! fierce creature! He so grasped my hands! In short, he seemed by his looks, and by his words (once putting his arms about me), to wish me to provoke him. So that I had nothing to do but to beg of him (which I did repeatedly) to permit me to withdraw; and to promise to meet him at his own time in the morning.

It was with a very ill grace that he complied, on that condition; and at parting he kissed my hand with such a savageness, that a redness remains upon it still.

Do you not think, my dear, that I have reason to be incensed at him, my situation considered? Am I not under a *necessity*, as it were, of quarrelling with him; at least every other time I see him? No prudery, no coquetry, no tyranny in my heart, or in my behaviour to him, that I know of. No affected procrastination. Aiming at nothing but decorum.

Perfect for me, my dearest Miss Howe, perfect for me, I beseech you, your kind scheme with Mrs. Townsend; and I will then leave this man.

. . . .

I was so disgusted with him, as well as frighted by him, that, on my return to my chamber, in a fit of passionate despair, I tore almost in two the answer I had written to his proposals.

I will see him in the morning, because I promised I would. But I will go out, and that without him, or any attendant. If he account not tolerably for his sudden change of behaviour, and a proper opportunity offer of a private lodging in some credible house, I will not any more return to this: at present I think so. And there will I either attend the perfecting of your scheme; or, by your epistolary mediation, make my own terms with the wretch; since it is your opinion, that I must be his, and cannot help myself: or, perhaps, take a resolution to throw myself at once into Lady Betty's protection; and this will hinder him from making his insolently threatened visit to Harlowe Place.

MR. LOVELACE TO JOHN BELFORD, ESQ.
Monday Morn., May 22.

I WAS in the dining-room before six, expecting her. She opened not her door. I was astonished when (following the wench as she did at the first invitation) I saw her enter dressed all but her gloves, and those and her fan in her hand; in the same moment bidding Dorcas direct Will to get her a chair to the door.

Cruel creature, thought I, to expose me thus to the derision of the women below!

Going abroad, madam?

I am, sir.

I looked cursed silly, I am sure. You will breakfast first, I hope, madam; in a very humble strain; yet with a hundred tenter-hooks in my heart.

Yes, she would drink one dish; and then laid her gloves and fan in the window just by.

I was perfectly disconcerted. I hemmed, and was going to speak several times; but knew not in what key. Who's modest now, thought I! Who's insolent now! How a tyrant of a woman confounds a bashful man! She was acting Miss Howe, I thought; and I the spiritless Hickman.

At last, I *will* begin, thought I.

She a dish — I a dish.

Sip, her eyes her own, she; like a haughty and imperious sovereign, conscious of dignity, every look a favour.

Sip, like her vassal, I; lips and hands trembling, and not knowing that I sipped or tasted.

I was — I was — I sipped — (drawing in my breath and the liquor together, though I scalded my mouth with it) I was in hopes, madam ——

Dorcas came in just then. Dorcas, said she, is a chair gone for?

Damned impertinence, thought I, thus to put me out in my speech! And I was forced to wait for the servant's answer to the insolent mistress's question.

William is gone for one, madam.

This cost me a minute's silence before I could begin again. And then it was with my hopes, and my hopes, and my hopes, that I should have been early admitted to ——

What weather is it, Dorcas? said she, as regardless of me as if I had not been present.

A little lowering, madam. The sun is gone in. It was very fine half an hour ago.

I had no patience. Up I rose. Down went the tea-cup, saucer and all. Confound the weather, the sunshine, and the wench! Begone for a devil, when I am speaking to your lady, and have so little opportunity given me.

Up rose the saucy-face, half-frighted; and snatched from the window her gloves and fan.

You must not go, madam! — seizing her hand — by my soul you must not ——

Must not, sir! But I must. You can curse your maid in my absence, as well as if I were present — except — except — you intend for *me,* what you direct to *her.*

Dearest creature, you must not go — you must not leave me. Such determined scorn! Such contempts! Questions asked your servant of no meaning but to break in upon me — I cannot bear it!

238

Detain me not (struggling). I will not be withheld. I like you not, nor your ways. You sought to quarrel with me yesterday, *for no reason in the world I can think of, but because I was too obliging.* You are an ungrateful man; and I hate you with my whole heart, Mr. Lovelace.

She would have flung from me: I will *not* be detained, Mr. Lovelace. I *will* go out.

Indeed you must not, madam, in this humour. And I placed myself between her and the door. And then, fanning, she threw herself into a chair, her sweet face all crimsoned over with passion.

I cast myself at her feet. Begone, Mr. Lovelace, said she, with a rejecting motion, her fan in her hand; for your own sake leave me! My soul is above thee, man! with both her hands pushing me from her! Urge me not to tell thee, how sincerely I think my soul above thee! Thou hast, in mine, a proud, a too proud heart to contend with! Leave me, and leave me for ever! Thou hast a proud heart to contend with!

Her air, her manner, her voice, were bewitchingly noble, though her words were so severe.

Let me worship an angel, said I, no woman. Forgive me, dearest creature! Creature if you be, forgive me! Forgive my inadvertencies! Forgive my inequalities! Pity my infirmities! Who is equal to my Clarissa?

But free as my clasping emotion might appear to her apprehensive heart, I had not, at the instant, any thought but what reverence inspired. And till she had actually withdrawn (which I permitted under promise of a speedy return, and on her consent to dismiss the chair) all the motions of my heart were as pure as her own.

She kept not her word. An hour I waited before I sent to claim her promise. She could not possibly see me yet, was the answer. As soon as she could, she would.

Dorcas says she still excessively trembled; and ordered her to give her hartshorn and water.

A strange apprehensive creature! Her terror is too great for the occasion. Evils in apprehension are often greater than evils in reality.

Dear creature! Did she never romp? Oh, the consecrated beauty! how can she think to be a wife!

But how do I know till I try, whether she may not by a less alarming treatment be prevailed upon, or whether (*day,* I have done with thee!) she may not yield to *nightly surprises?* This is still the burden of my song, I can marry her when I will. And if I do, after prevailing (whether by *surprise,* or by *reluctant consent*), whom but myself shall I have injured?

Monday, Two o'clock.

Not yet visible! My beloved is not well. What *expectations* had she from my ardent admiration of her! More rudeness than revenge apprehended. Yet, how my soul thirsts for revenge upon both these ladies! I must have recourse to my *master-strokes.* This cursed project of Miss Howe and her Mrs. Townsend (if I cannot contrive to render it abortive) will be always a sword hanging over my head.

I will discard all my boisterous inventions; and if I can oblige my sweet traveller to throw aside, *but for one moment*, the cloak of her rigid virtue, I shall have nothing to do but, like the sun, to bless new objects with my rays. But my chosen hours of conversation and repose, after all my peregrinations, will be devoted to my goddess.

Monday Evening.

At my repeated request she condescended to meet me in the dining-room to afternoon tea, and not before.

She entered with bashfulness, as I thought; in a pretty confusion, for having carried her apprehensions too far. Sullen and slow moved she towards the tea-table. Dorcas present, busy in tea-cup preparations. I took her reluctant hand, and pressed it to my lips. Dearest, loveliest of creatures, why this distance? Why this displeasure? How can you thus torture the faithfullest heart in the world?

She looked steadily upon me for a moment, and with her other hand, not withdrawing that I held, pulled her handkerchief out of her pocket; and by a twinkling motion urged forward a tear or two, which having arisen in each sweet eye, it was plain by that motion, she would rather have dissipated: but answered me only with a sigh, and an averted face.

I urged her to speak; to look up at me; to bless me with an eye more favourable.

I had reason, she told me, for my complaint of her indifference. She saw nothing in my mind that was generous. I was not a man to be obliged or favoured. My strange behaviour to her since Saturday night, *for no cause at all that she knew of*, convinced her of this. Whatever hopes she had conceived of me, were utterly dissipated: all my ways were disgustful to her.

I re-acknowledged the pride of my heart, which could not bear the thought of that want of preference in the heart of a lady whom I hoped to call mine, which she had always manifested. Marriage, I said, was a state that was not to be entered upon with indifference on either side.

It is insolence, interrupted she, it is presumption, sir, to expect tokens of value, without resolving to deserve them. You have no whining creature before you, Mr. Lovelace, overcome by weak motives, to love where there is no merit.

I was guilty, it seems, of going to church, said the indignant charmer; and without the company of a man, whose choice it would not have been to go, had I not gone — I was guilty of desiring to have the whole Sunday to myself, after I had obliged you, against my will, at a play; and after you had detained me (equally to my dislike) to a very late hour over-night. These were my faults: for these I was to be punished; I was to be compelled to see you, and to be terrified when I did see you, by the most shocking ill humour that was ever shown to a creature in my circumstances, and not bound to bear it. You have pretended to find free fault with my father's temper, Mr. Lovelace: but the worst that he ever showed *after* marriage, was not in the least to be compared to what you have shown twenty times *beforehand*.

O Mr. Lovelace, we have been long enough together to be tired of each other's humours and ways; ways and humours so different, that perhaps you ought to dislike *me*, as much as I do *you*. I think, I think, that I cannot make an answerable return to the value you profess for me.

She paused. I was silent. By my soul, thought I, this sweet creature will at last undo me!

She proceeded. What now remains, but that you pronounce me free of all obligation to you? And that you hinder me not from pursuing the destiny that shall be allotted me?

She went on: Propitious to me be your silence, Mr. Lovelace! Tell me that I am free of all obligation to you. You know I never made *you* promises. You know that you are not under any to *me*. My broken fortunes I matter not ——

She was proceeding. My dearest life, said I, I have been all this time, though you fill me with doubts of your favour, busy in the nuptial preparations. I am actually in treaty for equipage.

Equipage, sir! Trappings, tinsel! What is equipage; what is life; what is anything; to a creature sunk so low as I am in my own opinion! Labouring under a father's curse! Unable to look backward without reproach, or forward without terror! These reflections strengthened by every cross accident! And what but cross accidents befall me! All my darling schemes dashed in pieces; all my hopes at an end; deny me not the liberty to refuge myself in some obscure corner, where neither the enemies you have made me, nor the few friends you have left me, may ever hear of the supposed rash one, till those happy moments are at hand, which shall expiate for all!

I had certainly been a lost man, had not Dorcas come seasonably in with a letter. On the superscription written, *Be pleased to open it now.*

I retired to the window — opened it. It was from Dorcas herself. These the contents. "Be pleased to detain my lady: a paper of importance to transcribe. I will cough when I have done."

I put the paper in my pocket, and turned to my charmer, less disconcerted, as she, by that time, had also a little recovered herself. Indeed, my beloved creature, you were *very* vehement. Do you think it must not be matter of high regret to me, to find my wishes so often delayed and postponed in favour of your predominant view to a reconciliation with relations who will not be reconciled to you? To this was owing your declining to celebrate our nuptials before we came to town, though you were so atrociously treated by your sister, and your whole family; and though so ardently pressed to celebrate by me — to this was owing the ready offence you took at my four friends; and at the unavailing attempt I made to see a dropped letter; little imagining, from what two such ladies could write to each other that there could be room for mortal displeasure. To this was owing the week's distance you held me at, till you knew the issue of another application. But when they had rejected that; when you had sent my coldly-received proposals to Miss Howe for her approbation or advice, as indeed I advised; and had honoured me with your company at the play on Saturday night (my whole behaviour unobjectionable to the last hour); must not, madam, the sudden change in your conduct, the very next morning, astonish and distress me? And this persisted in with still stronger declarations, after you had received the impatiently-expected letter from Miss Howe. And now, dearest creature, let me know, I once more ask you, what is Miss Howe's opinion of my proposals?

Were I disposed to debate with you, Mr. Lovelace, I could very easily answer your fine harangue. But at present, I shall only say, that your ways have been very unaccountable. You seem to me, if your meanings were always just, to have taken pains to embarrass them. Whether owing in you to the want of a clear head, or a sound heart, I cannot determine; but it is to the want of one of them, I verily think, that I am to ascribe the greatest part of your strange conduct.

Curse upon the heart of the little devil, said I, who instigates you to think so hardly of the faithfullest heart in the world!

How dare you, sir? And there she stopped; having almost over-shot herself; as I designed she should.

How dare I *what*, madam? And I looked with meaning. How dare I *what*?

Vile man! And do you —— and there again she stopped.

Do I *what*, madam? And why *vile man*?

How dare you to curse *anybody* in my presence?

O the sweet receder! But that was not to go off so with a Lovelace. Why then, dearest creature, is there *anybody* that instigates you? If there be, again I curse them, be they whom they will.

She was in a charming pretty passion. And this was the first time that I had the odds in my favour.

Artful wretch! And is it thus you would entrap me? But know, sir, that I receive letters from nobody but Miss Howe. Miss Howe likes some of your ways as little as I do; for I have set everything before her. Yet she is thus far *your* enemy, as she is *mine* — she thinks I should not refuse your offers; but endeavour to make the best of my lot. And now you have the truth. Would to Heaven you were capable of dealing with equal sincerity!

I *am*, madam. And here, on my knee, I renew my vows, and my supplication, that you will make me yours — yours for ever. And let me have cause to bless you and Miss Howe in the same breath.

Rise, sir, from your too-ready knees; and mock me not.

Mock you, madam! And I arose, and re-urged her for the day. I blamed myself at the same time, for the invitation I had given to Lord M., as it might subject me to delay from his infirmities: but told her, that I would write to him to excuse me, if she had no objection;

242

or to give the day she would give me, and not wait for him, if he could not come in time.

My day, sir, said she, is never. Be not surprised. A person of politeness judging between us, would not be surprised that I say so. But indeed, Mr. Lovelace (and wept through impatience), you either know not how to treat with a mind of the least degree of delicacy, notwithstanding your birth and education, or you are an ungrateful man; and (after a pause) a *worse* than ungrateful one. But I will retire. I will see you again to-morrow. I cannot before. I think I hate you — you *may* look — indeed I think I hate you. And if, upon a re-examination of my heart, I find I do, I would not for the world that matters should go on farther between us.

But I see, I see, she does not *hate* me! The moment the rough covering that my teasing behaviour has thrown over her affections is quite removed, I doubt not to find all silk and silver at bottom, all soft, bright, and charming.

I was, however, too much vexed, disconcerted, mortified to hinder her from retiring — and yet she had not gone, if Dorcas had not coughed.

The wench came in, as soon as her lady had retired, and gave me the copy she had taken. And what should it be but of the answer the truly admirable creature had intended to give to my written proposals in relation to settlements?

MR. LOVELACE TO JOHN BELFORD, ESQ.
Tuesday Morning, May 23.

READ here, if thou wilt, the paper transcribed by Dorcas. It is impossible that I should proceed with my project against this admirable woman, were it not that I am resolved, after a few trials more, if as nobly sustained as those she has already passed through, to make her (if she really hate me not) legally mine.

To Mr. Lovelace

"When a woman is married, that supreme earthly obligation requires that in all instances where her husband's real honour is concerned, she should yield her own will to his. But, beforehand, I could be glad, conformably to what I have always signified, to have the most explicit assurances, that every possible way should be tried to avoid litigation with my father. Time and patience will subdue all things. My prospects of happiness are extremely contracted. In my lifetime I could wish nothing to be done of this sort.

"This article, then, I urge to your serious consideration, as what lies next my heart. I enter not here minutely into the fatal misunderstanding between them and you: the fault may be in both.

"But this may lead into hateful recrimination. Let it be remembered, I will only say, in this place, that, in *their* eye, you have robbed them of a daughter they doted upon; and that their resentments on this occasion rise but in proportion to their love and their disappointment. If they were faulty in some of the measures they took, while they themselves did not think so, who shall judge for *them*? You, sir, who will judge everybody as you please, and will let nobody judge you, in *your own* particular, must not be *their* judge. It may therefore be expected that they will stand out.

"As for *myself*, sir, I must leave it (so seems it to be destined) to your justice, to treat me as you shall think I deserve.

"Let me only then, on this subject, further observe, that condescension is not meanness. There is a glory in yielding, that hardly any violent spirit can judge of. My brother perhaps is no more sensible of *this* than you.

"This article being considered as I wish, all the rest will be easy. Were I to accept of the handsome separate provision you seem to intend me; added to the considerable sums arisen from my grandfather's estate since his death (more considerable than perhaps you may suppose from your offer); I should think it my duty to lay up for the family good, and for unforeseen events, out of it.

"As to your complaints of my diffidences, and the like, I appeal to your own heart, if it be possible for you to make my case your own for one moment, and to retrospect some parts of your behaviour, words, and actions, whether I am not rather to be justified than censured: and whether, of all men in the world, *avowing what you avow*, you ought not to think so. If you do not, let me admonish you, sir, from the very great *mismatch* that then must appear to be in our minds, never to seek, nor so much as wish, to bring about the *most intimate* union of interests between yourself and / CLARISSA HARLOWE.
"May 20."

The original of this charming paper, as Dorcas tells me, was torn almost in two. In one of her pets, I suppose! What business have the sex, whose principal glory is meekness, and patience, and resignation, to be in a passion, I trow? Will not she, who allows herself such liberties as a maiden, take greater when married?

I had better not to have had a copy of it, as far as I know: for determined as I was before upon my operations, it instantly turned all my resolutions in her favour. After all, I am sorry, *almost* sorry (for how shall I do to be *quite* sorry, when it is not *given* to me to be so?) that I cannot, until I have made further trials, resolve upon wedlock.

I have just read over again this intended answer to my proposals: and how I adore her for it!

But yet; another *yet*! She has not given it or sent it to me. It is not therefore *her* answer. It is not written *for* me, though to me.

Then again, remember thy recent discoveries, Lovelace! Remember her indifference, attended with all the appearance of contempt and hatred. View her, even *now*, wrapped up in reserve and mystery; meditating plots, as far as thou knowest, against the sovereignty thou hast, by right of conquest, obtained over her. Remember, in short, all thou hast *threatened* to remember against this insolent beauty, who is a rebel to the power she has listed under.

And must, think I, O creature so divinely excellent, and so beloved of my soul, those arms, those encircling arms, that would make a monarch happy, be used to repel brutal force; all their strength, unavailingly perhaps, exerted to repel it, and to defend a person so delicately framed? Can violence enter into the heart of a wretch, who might entitle himself to all her willing, yet virtuous love, and make the blessings he aspirest after, her *duty* to confer? Begone, villain-purposes! Sink ye all to the hell that could only inspire ye! And I am then ready to throw myself at her feet, to confess my villainous designs, to avow my repentance, and to put it out of my power to act unworthily by such an excellence.

How then comes it, that all these compassionate, and, as some would call them, *honest* sensibilities go off? Why, Miss Howe will tell thee: she says, I am the *devil*. By my conscience, I think he has at present a great share in me.

O Belford, Belford! I cannot, cannot (at least *at present* I cannot) marry.

.   .   .   .

Mennell has, though with some reluctance, consented to write me a letter, provided I will allow it to be the last step he shall take in this affair.

This letter is directed, *To Robert Lovelace, Esq.; or, in his absence, to his lady.* She had refused dining with me, or seeing me; and I was out when it came. She opened it: so is my lady by her own consent, proud and saucy as she is.

I came in to dinner. She sent me down the letter, desiring my excuse for opening it. Did it before she was aware. Lady pride, Belford! Recollection, then retrogradation!

I requested to see her upon it that moment. But she desires to suspend our interview till morning. I will bring her to own, before I have done with her, that she can't see me too often.

My impatience was so great, on an occasion so *unexpected*, that I could not help writing to tell her, "how much vexed I was at the accident: but that it need not delay my happy day, as that did not depend upon the house (*she knew that before, she'll think; and so did I*): and as Mrs. Fretchville, by Mr. Mennell, so handsomely expressed her concern upon it, and her wishes that it could suit us to bear with the unavoidable delay, I hoped, that going down to the Lawn for two or three of the summer months, when I was made the happiest of men, would be favourable to all round."

Can see her but once a day now, Jack!

Did I tell thee that I wrote a letter to my Cousin Montague, wondering that I heard not from Lord M. as the subject was so very interesting? In it I acquainted her with the house I was about taking; and with Mrs. Fretchville's vapourish delays.

I have received just now an answer from Charlotte.

Charlotte isn't well. A stomach disorder!

Poor Charlotte! But I *heard* she was not well: that encouraged me to write to her; and to express myself a little concerned, that she had not of her own accord thought of a visit in town to my charmer.

Here follows a copy of her letter. Thou wilt see by it that every little monkey is to catechize *me*. They all depend upon my good nature.

M. Hall, May 22.

DEAR COUSIN, — We have been in daily hope for a long time, I must call it, of hearing that the happy knot was tied. My lord has been very much out of order; and yet nothing would serve him, but he would himself write an answer to your letter. It was the only opportunity he should ever have, perhaps, to throw in a little good advice to you, with the hope of its being of any signification; and he has been several hours in a day, as his gout would let him, busied in it. It wants now only his last revisal. He hopes it will have the greater weight with you, if it appear all in his own handwriting.

His lordship has been very busy, at the times he could not write, in consulting Pritchard about those estates which he proposes to transfer to you on the happy occasion, that he may answer your letter in the most acceptable manner; and show, by effects, how kindly he takes your invitation. I assure you, he is mighty proud of it.

As for myself, I am not at all well, and have not been for some weeks past, with my old stomach disorder. I had certainly else before now have done myself the honour you wonder I have *not* done myself. Lady Betty, who would have accompanied me (for we had laid it all out), has been exceedingly busy in her law affair; her antagonist, who is actually on the spot, having been making proposals for an accommodation.

My best compliments, and sister's, to the most deserving lady in the world, conclude me / Your affectionate cousin and servant, / CHARL. MONTAGUE.

The lady in her next letter gives Miss Howe an account of what has passed between Mr. Lovelace and herself. She resents his behaviour with her usual dignity: but when she comes to mention Mr. Mennell's letter, she re-urges Miss Howe to perfect her scheme for her deliverance; being resolved to leave him. But, dating again, on his sending up to her Miss Montague's letter, she alters her mind, and desires her to suspend for the present her application to Mrs. Townsend.

MR. LOVELACE TO JOHN BELFORD, ESQ.

Wednesday, May 24.

I REGRETTED the illness of Mrs. Fretchville; as the intention I had to fix her dear self in the house before the happy knot was tied, would have set her in that independence in *appearance*, as well as *fact*, which was necessary to show to all the world that her choice was free; and as the ladies of my family would have been proud to make their court to her there; while the settlements and our equipages were preparing. But on any other account, there was no great matter in it; since when my happy day was over, we could, with so much convenience, go down to the Lawn, to my Lord M.'s, and to Lady Sarah's or Lady Betty's, in turn; which would give full time to provide ourselves with servants, and other accommodations.

How sweetly the charmer listened!

. . . .

The devil take this uncle of mine! He has at last sent me a letter which I cannot show, without exposing the head of our family for a fool. A confounded parcel of pop-guns has he let off upon me. I was in hopes he had exhausted his whole stock of this sort in his letter to you. To keep it back, to delay sending it, till he had recollected all this *farrago* of nonsense — confound his *wisdom of nations*, if so much of it is to be scraped together, in disgrace of itself, to make one egregious simpleton! But I am glad I am fortified with this piece of flagrant folly, however; since, in all human affairs, the *convenient* and *inconvenient*, the *good* and the *bad*, are so mingled, that there is no having the one without the other.

All that makes for me in it, I will transcribe for her. Yet hang it, she shall have the letter, and my soul with it, for one consenting kiss.

. . . .

She has got the letter from me without the reward. Deuce take me, if I had the courage to propose the condition. A new character this of bashfulness in thy friend. I *see that a truly modest woman may make even a confident man keep his distance.* By my soul, Belford, I believe that nine women in ten, who fall, fall either *from their own vanity or levity,* or for want of *circumspection* and *proper reserves.*

LORD M. TO ROBERT LOVELACE, ESQ.

Tuesday, May 23.

It is a long lane that has no turning. Do not despise me for my proverbs. You know I was always fond of them; and if you had been so too, it would have been the better for you, let me tell you. I dare swear, the fine lady you are so likely to be soon happy with, will be far from despising them; for I am told that she writes well, and that all her letters are full of sentences. God convert you! for nobody but He and this lady can.

Pray let her know as that I will present HER (not *you*) either my Lancashire seat, or *The Lawn* in Hertfordshire; and settle upon her a thousand pounds a year penny-rents.

I am still very bad with my gout; but will come in a litter, as soon

247

as the day is fixed: it would be the joy of my heart to join your hands. And, let me tell you, if you do not make the best of husbands to so good a young lady, and one who has had so much courage for your sake, I will renounce you; and settle all I can upon her and hers by you, and leave you out of the question.

If anything be wanting for your further security, I am ready to give it; though you know that my word has always been looked upon as my bond. And when the Harlowes know all this, let us see whether they are able to blush, and take shame to themselves.

Lady Sarah and Lady Betty want only to know the day, to make all the country round them blaze, and all their tenants mad. And, if any one of mine be sober upon the occasion, Pritchard shall eject him. And, on the birth of the first child, if a son, I will do something more for you, and repeat all our rejoicings.

[*Lord M. gives Lovelace advice as to good conduct in both public and private life. He sketches a career for his nephew in parliament, and then continues:*]

You may come in for the title when I am dead and gone — God help me! So I would have you keep an equilibrium. If once you get the name of being a fine speaker, you may have anything: and, to be sure, you have naturally a great deal of elocution; a tongue that would delude an angel, as the women say — to their sorrow, some of them, poor creatures! A leading man in the House of Commons is a very important character; because that House has the giving of money: and *money makes the mare to go*; ay, and queens and kings too, sometimes, to go in a manner very different from what they might otherwise choose to go, let me tell you.

MR. LOVELACE TO JOHN BELFORD, ESQ.

Thursday, May 25.

THOU seest, Belford, how we now drive before the wind. The dear creature now comes almost at the first word, whenever I desire the honour of her company.

Now, Belford, I have actually deposited these writings with Counsellor Williams; and I expect the drafts in a week at furthest. So shall be doubly armed. For if I *attempt*, and *fail*, these will be ready to throw in, to make her have patience with me *till I can try again*.

Everything of this nature, the dear creature answered (with a downcast eye, and a blushing cheek), she left to me.

I proposed my lord's chapel for the celebration, where we might have the presence of Lady Betty, Lady Sarah, and my two cousins Montague.

She seemed not to favour a public celebration; and waived this subject for the present. I doubted not but she would be as willing as I to decline a public wedding; so I pressed not this matter further just then.

But what a pretty fellow of an uncle is this foolish peer, to think of making a wife independent of her emperor, and a rebel of course; yet smarter himself for an error of this kind.

But yet, what mortifies my pride is, that this exalted creature, if I *were* to marry her, would not be governed in her behaviour to me by love, but by generosity merely, or by blind duty; and had rather live single, than be mine.

I cannot bear this. I would have the woman whom I honour with my name forego even her *superior duties* for me. I would have her look after me when I go out, as far as she can see me. I would be the subject of her dreams, as well as of her waking thoughts. I would have her think every moment lost, that is not passed with me: sing to me, read to me, play to me when I pleased; no joy so great as in obeying me.

. . . .

Another agreeable conversation. The Day of days the subject. As to fixing a particular one, that need not be done, my charmer says, till the settlements are completed.

I cannot, said she, endure the thoughts of a public day. It will carry with it an air of insult upon my whole family. And for my part, if my lord will not take it amiss (and perhaps he will not, as the motion came not from himself, but from you, Mr. Lovelace), I will very willingly dispense with his lordship's presence; the rather, as dress and appearance then will be unnecessary; for I cannot bear to think of decking my person while my parents are in tears.

How excellent this! Yet do not her parents richly deserve to be in tears.

All obedience, all resignation — no will but hers. I withdrew, and wrote directly to my lord; and she not disapproving of it, I sent it away. The purport as follows; for I took no copy.

That I was much obliged to his lordship for his intended goodness to me, on an occasion the most solemn of my life. That the admirable lady, whom he so justly praised, thought his lordship's proposals in her favour too high. That she chose not to make a public appearance, if, without disobliging my friends, she could avoid it, till a reconciliation with her own could be effected. That although she expressed a grateful sense of his lordship's consent to give her to me with his own hand; yet presuming that the motive to this kind intention was rather to do her honour, than it otherwise would have been his own choice (especially as travelling would be at this time so inconvenient to him), she thought it advisable to save his lordship trouble on this occasion; and hoped he would take as meant her declining the favour.

That the Lawn will be most acceptable to us both to retire to; and the rather, as it is so to his lordship.

*The lady, after having given to Miss Howe the particulars con-
tained in Mr. Lovelace's last letter, thus expresses herself:*

A principal consolation arising from these favourable appearances,
is, that I, who have now but one only friend, shall most probably, and,
if it be not my own fault, have as many new ones as there are persons
in Mr. Lovelace's family; and this whether Mr. Lovelace treat me
kindly or not. And who knows, but that by degrees, those new friends,
by their rank and merit, may have weight enough to get me restored
to the favour of my relations? Till which can be effected, I shall not
be tolerably easy. Happy I never expect to be. Mr. Lovelace's mind
and mine are vastly different: different in *essentials*.

But as matters are at present circumstanced, I pray you, my dear
friend, to keep to yourself everything that might bring discredit to
him, if revealed. Better anybody expose a man than a wife, if I *am*
to be his; and what is said by you will be thought to come from me.

MR. LOVELACE TO JOHN BELFORD, ESQ.

AND NOW, Belford, what dost think?

That thou art a cursed fellow, if ——

If — no if's. But I shall be very sick to-morrow. I shall, faith.

Sick! Why sick? What a-devil shouldst thou be sick for?

For more good reasons than one, Jack.

I should be glad to hear but one. Sick, quotha! Of all thy roguish
inventions I should not have thought of this.

I'll condescend to make thee as wise as myself. I am excessively
disturbed about this smuggling scheme of Miss Howe. I have no
doubt that my fair one, were I to make an attempt, and miscarry, will
fly from me, if she can. I once believed she loved me: but now I
doubt whether she does or not: at least, that it is with such an *ardour*,
as Miss Howe calls it, as will make her overlook a premeditated fault,
should I be guilty of one.

And what will being sick do for thee?

Have patience. I don't intend to be so very bad as Dorcas shall
represent me to be. But yet I know I shall retch confoundedly, and
bring up some clotted blood. To be sure, I shall break a vessel; there's
no doubt of that: and a bottle of Eaton's Styptic shall be sent for; but
no doctor. If she has *humanity*, she will be concerned. But if she has
love, let it have been pushed ever so far back, it will, on this occasion,
come forward and show itself; not only in her eye, but in every line
of her sweet face.

Well, methinks thou sayest, I begin to think tolerably of this device.

Well but, Lovelace, how the deuce wilt thou, with that full health
and vigour of constitution, and with that bloom in thy face, make
anybody believe thou art sick?

How! Why, take a few grains of ipecacuanha; enough to make me
retch like a fury.

250

Good! But how wilt thou manage to bring up blood, and not hurt thyself?

Foolish fellow! Are there not pigeons and chickens in every poulterer's shop?

Cry thy mercy.

Then I will have a chair called, and be carried to the park; where I will try to walk half the length of the Mall, or so; and in my return, amuse myself at White's or the Cocoa.

And will this do?

Shall I not see whether she receives me with tenderness at my return? But this is not all: *I have a foreboding that something affecting will happen while I am out.* But of this more in its place.

MR. LOVELACE TO JOHN BELFORD, ESQ.

Friday Evening.

JUST returned from an airing with my charmer, complied with after great importunity. She was attended by the two nymphs. They both topped their parts; kept their eyes within bounds; made moral reflections now and then. O Jack! what devils are women, when all tests are got over, and we have completely ruined them!

The coach carried us to Hampstead, to Highgate, to Muswell Hill; back to Hampstead to the Upper Flask; there, in compliment to the nymphs, my beloved consented to alight, and take a little repast. Then home early by Kentish Town.

Delightfully easy she: and so respectful and obliging I, all the way, and as we walked out upon the heath, to view the variegated prospects which that agreeable elevation affords, that she promised to take now and then a little excursion with me. I think, Miss Howe, I *think*, said I to myself, every now and then as we walked, that thy wicked devices are superseded.

Cocoa Tree, Saturday, May 27.

This ipecacuanha is a most disagreeable medicine. Two hours it held me. I had forbid Dorcas to let her lady know anything of the matter; out of tenderness to her; being willing, when she knew my prohibition, to let her see that I *expected* her to be concerned for me.

Well, but Dorcas was nevertheless a *woman,* and she can *whisper* to her lady the secret she is enjoined to keep!

Come hither, toad!

There! Begone! Be in a plaguy hurry running upstairs and down, to fetch from the dining-room what you carry up on purpose to fetch, till motion extraordinary put you out of breath, and give you the sigh natural.

What's the matter, Dorcas?

Nothing, madam.

I must not tell you, madam. My master ordered me not to tell you

— but he is in a worse way than he thinks for! But he would not have you frighted.

High concern took possession of every sweet feature. She pitied me! By my soul, she pitied me!

Where is he?

Out she darts. As how! as how, Dorcas!

O madam, a vomiting of blood! A vessel broke, to be sure!

Down she hastens; finds every one as busy over my blood in the entry, as if it were that of the Neapolitan saint.

In steps my charmer, with a face of sweet concern.

How do you, Mr. Lovelace?

O my best love! Very well! Very well! Nothing at all! Nothing of consequence! I shall be well in an instant! Straining again! for I was indeed plaguy sick, though no more blood came.

In short, Belford, I have gained my end. I see the dear soul loves me. I see she forgives me all that's past. I see I have credit for a new score.

Miss Howe, I defy thee, my dear. Mrs. Townsend! Who the devil are you? Troop away with your contrabands. No smuggling! Nor smuggler, but myself! Nor will the choicest of my fair one's favours be long prohibited goods to me!

Miss Clarissa Harlowe to Miss Howe

Saturday, May 27.

MR. LOVELACE, my dear, has been very ill. Suddenly taken. With a vomiting of blood in great quantities. Some vessel broken. He complained of a disorder in his stomach over-night. I was the more affected with it, *as I am afraid it was occasioned by the violent contentions between us.* But was I in fault?

How lately did I think I hated him! But hatred and anger, I see, are but temporary passions with me. One cannot, my dear, hate people in danger of death, or who are in distress or affliction. My heart, I find, is not proof against kindness, and acknowledgment of errors committed.

He is gone out in a chair. I advised him to do so. I fear that my advice was wrong; since quiet in such a disorder must needs be best.

I am really very uneasy. For I have, I doubt, exposed myself to him, and to the women below. *They* indeed will excuse me, as they think us married. But if he be not generous, I shall have cause to regret this surprise; which (as I had reason to think myself unaccountably treated by him) has taught me more than I knew of myself.

Mr. Lovelace to John Belford, Esq.

Sat. Evening.

I HAD a charming airing. No return of my malady. My heart perfectly easy, how could my stomach be otherwise?

But when I came home, I found that my sweet soul had been alarmed by a *new incident.* The inquiry after us both, in a very suspicious manner, and that by description of our persons, and not by names, by a servant in a blue livery turned up and trimmed with yellow.

Dorcas bid the man come forward. Well, friend, what is your business with Mr. or Mrs. Lovelace? Whom came you from?

From a gentleman who ordered me to say, if I was *made* to tell, it was from a friend of Mr. John Harlowe, Mrs. Lovelace's eldest uncle.

What is his name?

His name is Captain Tomlinson, sir.

I don't know such a one.

Do you know such a man as Captain Tomlinson, my dearest life (*aside*), your uncle's friend?

No; but my uncle may have acquaintance, no doubt, that I don't know. But I hope (trembling) this is not a trick.

Well, friend, if your master has anything to say to Mr. Lovelace, you may tell him that Mr. Lovelace is here; and will see him whenever he pleases.

. . . .

Sunday, May 28.

Dorcas, desire the gentleman to walk up.

Enter Captain Tomlinson, in a riding-dress, whip in hand.

Your servant, sir. Mr. Lovelace, I presume?

My name is Lovelace, sir.

Sir, I have no interest in the affair I come about. I may appear officious; and if I thought I should, I would decline any concern in it, after I have just hinted what it is.

And pray, sir, what is it?

May I ask you, sir, without offence, whether you wish to be reconciled, and to co-operate upon honourable terms, with *one* gentleman of the name of Harlowe; preparative, as it may be hoped, to a general reconciliation?

O how my heart fluttered! cried my charmer.

Lovel. Well but, sir, have you then any commission to me from Mr. John Harlowe?

Capt. Sir, I will tell you, as briefly as I can, the whole of what I have to say; but you'll excuse *me* also a previous question, for which curiosity is not my motive; but it is necessary to be answered before I can proceed; as you will judge when you hear it.

Lovel. What, pray, sir, is your question?

Capt. Briefly, Whether you are actually, and *bona fide*, married to Miss Clarissa Harlowe?

I started, and, in a haughty tone, Is this, sir, a question that *must* be answered before you can proceed in the business you have undertaken?

I mean no offence, Mr. Lovelace. Mr. Harlowe sought to me to

253

undertake this office. I have daughters and nieces of my own. I thought it a good office, or I, who have many considerable affairs upon my hands, had not accepted of it. I know the world; and will take the liberty to say, that if that young lady ——

Enter Dorcas, in a hurry.

A *gentleman*, this minute, sir, desires to speak with your honour. (*My lady, sir! — Aside.*)

Dorcas's message staggered me. And yet I was upon one of my master-strokes, which was, to take advantage of the captain's inquiries, and to make her *own her marriage before him*, as she had done to the people below; and if she had been brought to that, to induce her, for her uncle's satisfaction, to write him a letter of gratitude; which of course must have been signed *Clarissa Lovelace*.

Capt. I hope, Mr. Lovelace, I make no mischief. Mr. John Harlowe desired my advice how to act. He told me that no father ever loved a daughter as he loved this niece of his; whom, indeed, he used to call his *daughter-niece*. He said she had really been unkindly treated by her brother and sister: and as your alliance, sir, was far from being a discredit to their family, he would do his endeavour to reconcile all parties, if he could be sure that ye were actually man and wife. Mr. Harlowe, having still doubts, and being willing to proceed on some grounds in so important a point, besought me to undertake this matter.

Enter Dorcas again, out of breath.

Sir, the gentleman will step up to you. (*My lady is impatient. She wonders at your honour's delay. Aside.*)

Excuse me, captain, for one moment.

I have stayed my full time, Mr. Lovelace. Will you permit me to attend you in the morning, before I set out on my return?

You will then breakfast with me, captain?

It must be early if I do.

It shall be by seven o'clock, if you please, captain.

Sunday Night.

After I had attended the captain down to the very passage, I returned to the dining-room, and put on a joyful air, on my beloved's entrance into it. O my dearest creature, said I, let me congratulate you on a prospect so agreeable to your wishes! And I snatched her hand and smothered it with kisses.

I was going on; when, interrupting me, You see, Mr. Lovelace, said she, how you have embarrassed yourself by your obliquities! You see that you have not been able to return a direct answer to a plain and honest question, though upon it depends all the happiness on the prospect of which you congratulate me.

You know, my best love, what my prudent, and I will say, my *kind* motives were, for giving out that we were married. You see that I have taken no advantage of it; and, that no inconvenience has followed it. You see that your uncle wants only to be assured from ourselves *that it is so* ——

I would have you appear, sir, as *you are*! I am resolved that I will appear to my uncle's friend, and to my uncle, as *I am*.

What, my dear, would you have me say to the captain to-morrow morning? I have given him room to think ——

Then put him right, Mr. Lovelace. Tell the truth. Tell him what you please of the favour of your relations to me: tell him what you will about the settlements: and if, when drawn, you will submit them to his perusal and approbation, it will show him how much you are in earnest.

My dearest life — do you think that he would disapprove of the terms I have offered?

No.

Then may I be accursed, if I willingly submit to be trampled under foot by my enemies!

And may I, Mr. Lovelace, never be happy in this life, if I submit to the passing upon my Uncle Harlowe a wilful and premeditated falsehood for truth! I have too long laboured under the affliction which the rejection of all my friends has given me, to purchase my reconciliation with them now at so dear a price as that of my veracity.

The women below, my dear ——

What are the women below to me? I want not to establish myself with them. Urge this point no farther, Mr. Lovelace. If *you* will not tell the truth, *I* will to-morrow morning (if I see Captain Tomlinson) tell it myself. Indeed I will.

I saw there was no help. I saw that the inflexible Harlowe spirit was all up in her. A little witch! A little — Forgive me Love, for calling her names! And so I said, with an air, We have had too many misunderstandings, madam, for me to wish for new ones: I will obey you without reserve.

And then, clasping my arms about her, I gave her averted cheek (her charming lip designed) a fervent kiss. And your forgiveness of this sweet freedom (bowing) is that condition.

She was not mortally offended. And now must I make out the rest as well as I can.

Shall I now not see (since I must be for ever unhappy, if I marry her, and leave any trial unessayed) what I can make of her love and her newly-raised confidence? Will it not be to my glory to succeed? And to hers, and to the honour of her sex, if I cannot? Where then will be the hurt to either, to make the trial? And cannot I, as I have often said, reward her when I will by marriage?

'Tis late, or rather early. Good night to me!

MR. LOVELACE TO JOHN BELFORD, ESQ.

Monday, May 29.

Now have I established myself for ever in my charmer's heart. The captain came at seven, as promised, and ready equipped for his journey. My beloved chose not to give us her company till our first conversation was over.

I told the captain that I would prevent his question; and accordingly (after I had enjoined the strictest secrecy, that no advantage might be given to James Harlowe; and which he answered for as well on Mr. Harlowe's part as his own) I acknowledged nakedly and fairly the whole truth — to wit, that we were not yet married. I gave him hints of the causes of procrastination. Some of them owing to unhappy misunderstandings: but chiefly to the lady's desire of previous reconciliation with her friends; and to a delicacy that had no example.

When I returned from attending the captain downstairs, which I did to the outward door, my beloved met me as I entered the dining-room; complacency reigning in every lovely feature.

You see me already, *said she,* another creature. You know not, Mr. Lovelace, how near my heart this hoped-for reconciliation is. I am now willing to banish every disagreeable remembrance. You know not, sir, how much you have obliged me. And oh, Mr. Lovelace, how happy shall I be, when my heart is lightened from the all-sinking weight of a father's curse! When my dear mamma (you don't know, sir, half the excellences of my dear mamma! and what a kind heart she has, when it is left to follow its own impulses — when this blessed mamma) shall once more fold me to her indulgent bosom! When I shall again have uncles and aunts, and a brother and sister, all striving who shall show most kindness and favour to the poor outcast, then *no more* an outcast! And you, Mr. Lovelace, to behold all this, and to be received into a family so dear to me, with welcome — what though a little cold at first? when they come to know you better, and to see you oftener, no fresh causes of disgust occurring, and you, as I hope, having entered upon a new course, all will be warmer and warmer love on both sides, till every one perhaps will wonder how they came to set themselves against you.

Then drying her tears with her handkerchief, after a few moments pausing, on a sudden, as if recollecting that she had been led by her joy to an expression of it which she had not intended I should see, she retired to her chamber with precipitation; leaving me almost as unable to stand it as herself.

This effect of her joy on such an occasion gives me a high notion of what that virtue must be (what other name can I call it?), which in a mind so capable of delicate transport, should be able to make so charming a creature, in her very bloom, all frost and snow to every advance of love from the man she hates not. This must be all from education too — must it not, Belford? Can *education* have stronger force in a woman's heart than *nature?* Sure it cannot.

· · · · · · · · · · · ·

And now it is time to confess (and yet I know that thy conjectures are aforehand with my exposition) that this Captain Tomlinson, who is so great a favourite with my charmer, and who takes so much delight in healing breaches, and reconciling differences, is neither a greater man nor a less than honest Patrick McDonald, attended by a discarded footman of his own finding out.

Wednesday, May 31.

All still happier and happier. A very high honour done me: a chariot, instead of a coach, permitted, purposely to indulge me in the subject of subjects.

Our discourse in this sweet airing turned upon our future manner of life. The day is bashfully promised me. *Soon*, was the answer to my repeated urgency. Our equipage, our servants, our liveries, were parts of the delightful subject. A desire that the wretch who had given me intelligence out of the family (honest Joseph Leman) might not be one of our menials; and her resolution to have her faithful Hannah, whether recovered or not; were signified; and both as readily assented to.

Mrs. Sinclair and the nymphs are all of opinion that I am now so much a favourite, and have such a visible share in her confidence, and even in her affections, that I may do what I will, and plead for excuse violence of *passion*; which, they will have it, makes violence of *action* pardonable with their sex; as well as an *allowed extenuation* with the *unconcerned of both sexes*; and they all offer their helping hands. Why not? they say: has she not passed for my wife before them all? And is she not in a fine way of being reconciled to her friends? And was not the want of that reconciliation the pretence for postponing consummation?

MR. LOVELACE TO JOHN BELFORD, ESQ.

Friday, June 2.

NOTWITHSTANDING my studied-for politeness and complaisance for some days past; and though I have wanted courage to throw the mask quite aside; yet I have made the dear creature more than once look about her, by the warm, though decent expression of my passion. I have brought her to own that I am *more* than indifferent with her: but as to LOVE, which I pressed her to acknowledge, *what need of acknowledgments of that sort, when a woman consents to marry?* And once repulsing me with displeasure, *the proof of the true love I was vowing for her was* RESPECT, *not* FREEDOM. And offering to defend myself, she told me that all the conception she had been able to form of a faulty passion was that it must demonstrate itself as mine sought to do.

I have just now been called to account for some innocent liberties which I thought myself entitled to take before the women; as they suppose us to be married, and now within view of consummation.

I took the lecture very hardly; and with impatience wished for the happy day and hour when I might call her all my own, and meet with no check from a niceness that had no example.

257

MR. LOVELACE TO JOHN BELFORD, ESQ.

Monday, June 5.

NEVER, I believe, was there so true, so delicate a modesty in the human mind as in that of this lady. And this has been my security all along; and, in spite of Miss Howe's advice to her, will be so still; since, if her delicacy be a fault, she can no more overcome it than I can my aversion to matrimony. Habit, habit, Jack, seest thou not? may subject us both to weaknesses. And should she not have charity for me, as I have for her?

I have now at this instant wrought myself up, for the dozenth time, to a half-resolution. A thousand agreeable things I have to say to her. She is in the dining-room. Just gone up. She always expects me when there.

. . . .

High displeasure! followed by an abrupt departure.

The Lawn I proposed to retire to as soon as the happy ceremony was over. This day and that day I proposed.

It was time enough to name the day when the settlements were completed and the licence obtained. Happy should she be, could the kind Captain Tomlinson obtain her *uncle's presence privately.*

A good hint! It may perhaps be improved upon — either for a *delay* or a *pacifier.*

No new delays, for Heaven's sake, I besought her; and reproached her gently for the past. Name but the day (an *early* day, I hoped it would be, in the following week), that I might hail its approach and number the tardy hours.

My cheek reclined on her shoulder — kissing her hands by turns. Rather bashfully than angrily reluctant, her hands sought to be withdrawn; her shoulder avoiding my reclined cheek — apparently loath, and more loath, to quarrel with me; her downcast eye confessing more than her lips could utter. Now surely, thought I, is my time to try if she can forgive a still bolder freedom than I had ever yet taken.

I then gave her struggling hands liberty. I put one arm round her waist: I imprinted a kiss on her sweet lips, with a *Be quiet* only, and an averted face, as if she feared another.

Encouraged by so gentle a repulse, the tenderest things I said; and then, with my other hand, drew aside the handkerchief that concealed the beauty of beauties, and pressed with my burning lips the most charming breast that ever my ravished eyes beheld.

A very contrary passion to that which gave her bosom so delightful a swell immediately took place. She struggled out of my encircling arms with indignation. I detained her reluctant hand. Let me go, said she. *I see there is no keeping terms with you.* Base encroacher! Is this the design of your flattering speeches? Far as matters have gone, I will for ever renounce you. You have an odious heart. Let me go, I tell you.

I was forced to obey, and she flung from me, repeating *base,* and adding *flattering,* encroacher.

And should not my beloved, for her own sake, desecend by *degrees* from *goddess-hood* into *humanity?* If it be *pride* that restrains her, ought not that pride to be punished? If, as in the Eastern emperors, it be *art* as well as *pride, art* is what she of all women need not use. If *shame,* what a shame to be ashamed to communicate to her adorer's sight the most admirable of her personal graces?

Let me perish, Belford, if I would not forego the brightest diadem in the world for the pleasure of seeing a twin Lovelace at each charming breast, drawing from it his first sustenance; the pious task, for physical reasons, continued for one month and no more!

Monday Afternoon.

A letter received from the worthy Captain Tomlinson has introduced me into the presence of my charmer sooner than perhaps I should otherwise have been admitted.

The captain, after letting me know that he chose not to write till he had the promised draft of the settlements, acquaints me that his friend Mr. John Harlowe, in their first conference (which was held as soon as he got down), was extremely surprised, and even grieved (*as he feared he would be*), to hear that we were not married. The world, he said, who knew my character, would be very censorious, were it owned that we had lived so long together unmarried in the same lodgings; although our marriage were now to be ever so publicly celebrated.

And then, the captain says, his dear friend made a proposal: it was this: *That we should marry out of hand, but as privately as possible, as indeed he found we intended* (for he could have no objection to the drafts) — *but yet, he expected to have present one trusty friend of his own, for his better satisfaction* ———

Here I stopped, with a design to be angry; but she desiring me to read on, I obeyed.

But that it should pass to every one living, except to that trusty person, to himself, and to the captain, that we were married from the time that we had lived together in one house; and that this time should be made to agree with that of Mr. Hickman's application to him from Miss Howe.

This, my dearest life, said I, is a very considerate proposal. Shall I write to the captain and acquaint him that we have no objection to it?

She was silent for a few minutes. At last, with a sigh: See, Mr. Lovelace, said she, what you have brought me to, by treading after you in such crooked paths! See what disgrace I have incurred! Indeed you have not acted like a wise man.

My beloved creature, do you not remember how earnestly I besought the honour of your hand before we came to town? Had I been *then* favoured ———

Well, well, sir, there has been much amiss somewhere; that's all I will say at present. And since what's past cannot be recalled, my uncle must be obeyed, I think.

I withdrew, and wrote to the captain to the following effect: I desired that he would be so good as to acquaint his dear friend that we entirely acquiesced with what he had proposed; and had already *properly* cautioned the gentlewomen of the house, and their servants, as well as our own: and to tell him that, if he would in person give me the blessing of his dear niece's hand, it would crown the wishes of both. In this case I consented that his own day, *as I presumed it would be a short one*, should be ours.

I showed this letter to my fair one. She was not displeased with it. So, Jack, we cannot now move too fast as to settlements and licence: the day is her *uncle's day*, or Captain *Tomlinson's* perhaps, as shall best suit the occasion.

And now for a little mine which I am getting ready to spring. The *first* that I have sprung, and at the rate I go on (now a *resolution*, and now a *remorse*) perhaps the *last* that I shall attempt to spring.

A *little* mine, I call it. But it may be attended with great effects. I shall not, however, absolutely depend upon the success of it, having much more effectual ones in reserve. And yet great engines are often moved by small springs.

MR. BELFORD TO ROBERT LOVELACE, ESQ.

Tuesday, June 6.

UNSUCCESSFUL as hitherto my application to you has been, I cannot for the heart of me forbear writing once more in behalf of this admirable woman: and yet am unable to account for the zeal which impels me to take her part with an earnestness so sincere.

Yet, as it is not too late, and thou art nevertheless upon the crisis, I am resolved to try what another letter will do. It is but my writing in vain, if it do no good; and if thou wilt let me prevail, I know thou wilt hereafter think me richly entitled to thy thanks.

If thou proceedest, I have no doubt that this affair will end tragically. And will not the remembrance of thy *ever-during* guilt, and *transitory* triumph, be a torment of torments to thee?

But whatever be thy determination on this head; and if I write not in time, but that thou hast actually pulled off the mask; let it not be one of thy devices, if thou wouldest avoid the curses of every heart, and hereafter of thy own, to give her, no, not for one hour (be her resentment ever so great), into the power of that villainous woman, who has, if possible, less remorse than thyself; and whose *trade* it is to break the resisting spirit, and utterly to ruin the heart unpractised in evil. O Lovelace, Lovelace, how many dreadful stories could this horrid woman tell the sex! And shall that of a Clarissa swell the guilty list?

But this I might have spared. Of this, devil as thou art, thou canst not be capable. Thou couldst not enjoy a triumph so disgraceful to thy wicked pride, as well as to humanity.

MR. LOVELACE TO JOHN BELFORD, ESQ.

Tuesday Afternoon, June 6.

ABUNDANCE of impertinent things thou tellest me in this letter; some of which thou hadst from myself; others that I knew before.

What of uncommon would there be in this case, but for her watchfulness? Dost think I had not rather have gained my end with less trouble and less guilt?

In what, then, am I so *singularly* vile?

In my *contrivances*, thou wilt say (for thou art my echo), if not in my proposed *end* of them.

How difficult does every man find it, as well as I, to forego a predominant passion! I have three passions that sway me by turns; all imperial ones. Love, revenge, ambition, or a desire of conquest.

Enough, sayest thou, *have I tried this paragon of virtue.* Not so; for I have not tried her at all. All I have been doing is but *preparation to a trial.*

. . . .

I threatened to refrain writing to thee. But take it not to heart, Jack — I must write on, and cannot help it.

MR. LOVELACE TO JOHN BELFORD, ESQ.

Wednesday Night 11 o'clock.

FAITH, Jack, thou hadst half undone me with thy nonsense, though I would not own it in my yesterday's letter: my conscience of thy party before. But I think I am my own man again.

So near to execution my plot; so near springing my mine; all agreed upon between the women and me; or I believe thou hadst overthrown me.

I have time for a few lines preparative to what is to happen in an hour or two; and I love to write to the *moment.*

MR. LOVELACE TO JOHN BELFORD, ESQ.   *Thursday Morning,*
Five o'clock (June 8).

AT A LITTLE after two, when the whole house was still, or seemed to be so, and, as it proved, my Clarissa in bed and fast asleep; I also in a manner undressed (as indeed I was for an hour before), and in my gown and slippers, I was alarmed by a trampling noise overhead, and a confused buzz of mixed voices, some louder than others, like scolding, and little short of screaming. While I was wondering what could be the matter, downstairs ran Dorcas, and at my door, in an accent rather frightedly and hoarsely inward, than shrilly clamorous, she cried out: Fire! Fire! And this the more alarmed me, as she seemed to endeavour to cry out louder, but could not.

My pen dropped from my fingers; and up started I; and making but three steps to the door, opening it, I cried out, Where? Where? almost as much terrified as the wench: while she, more than half-undressed, her petticoats in her hand, unable to speak distinctly, pointed upstairs.

I was there in a moment, and found all owing to the carelessness of Mrs. Sinclair's cook-maid, who, having sat up to read the simple *History of Dorastus and Faunia* when she should have been in bed, had set fire to an old pair of calico window-curtains.

She had had the presence of mind, in her fright, to tear down the half-burnt valance, as well as curtains, and had got them, though blazing, into the chimney, by the time I came up; so that I had the satisfaction to find the danger happily over.

Meantime Dorcas, after she had directed me upstairs, not knowing the worst was over, and expecting every minute the house would be in a blaze, out of tender regard for her lady (*I shall for ever love the wench for it*), ran to her door, and rapping loudly at it, in a recovered voice cried out, with a shrillness equal to her love: *Fire! Fire! The house is on fire! Rise, madam! — this instant rise — if you would not be burnt in your bed!*

No sooner had she made this dreadful outcry, but I heard her lady's door, with hasty violence, unbar, unbolt, unlock, and open, and my charmers' voice sounding like that of one going into a fit.

Thou mayest believe that I was greatly affected. I trembled with concern for her, and hastened down faster than the alarm of fire had made me run up, in order to satisfy her that all the danger was over.

When I had *flown down* to her chamber door, there I beheld the most charming creature in the world, supporting herself on the arm of the gasping Dorcas, sighing, trembling, and ready to faint, with nothing on but an under-petticoat, her lovely bosom half open, and her feet just slipped into her shoes. As soon as she saw me she panted, and struggled to speak; but could only say, O Mr. Lovelace! and down was ready to sink.

I clasped her in my arms with an ardour she never felt before: My dearest life! fear nothing: I have been up — the danger is over — the fire is got under. And how, foolish devil! (to Dorcas) could you thus, by your hideous yell, alarm and frighten my angel!

O Jack! how her sweet bosom, as I clasped her to mine, heaved and panted! I could even distinguish her dear heart flutter, flutter, flutter against mine; and for a few minutes I feared she would go into fits.

Lest the half-lifeless charmer should catch cold in this undress, I lifted her to her bed, and sat down by her upon the side of it, endeavouring with the utmost tenderness, as well of action as expression, to dissipate her terrors.

But what did I get by this my generous care of her, and by my *successful* endeavour to bring her to herself? Nothing (ungrateful as she was!) but the most passionate exclamations: I never saw a bitterer, or more moving grief, when she came fully to herself.

She appealed to Heaven against my *treachery*, as she called it;

262

while I, by the most solemn vows, pleaded my own equal fright, and the reality of the danger that had alarmed us both.

She conjured me, in the most solemn and affecting manner, by turns threatening and soothing, to quit her apartment and permit her to hide herself from the light, and from every human eye.

I besought her pardon; yet could not avoid offending; and repeatedly vowed that the next morning's sun should witness our espousals: but taking, I suppose, all my protestations of this kind as an indication that I intended to proceed to the last extremity, she would hear nothing that I said; but, redoubling her struggles to get from me, in broken accents, and exclamations the most vehement, she protested that she would not survive what she called a treatment so disgraceful and villainous; and, looking all wildly round her, as if for some instrument of mischief, she espied a pair of sharp-pointed scissors on a chair by the bedside, and endeavoured to catch them up, with design to make her words good on the spot.

Seeing her desperation, I begged her to be pacified; that she would hear me speak but one word; declaring that I intended no dishonour to her: and having seized the scissors, I threw them into the chimney; and she still insisting vehemently upon my distance, I permitted her to take the chair.

But, oh, the sweet discomposure! Her bared shoulders and arms, so inimitably fair and lovely: her spread hands crossed over her charming neck; yet not half concealing its glossy beauties: the scanty coat, as she rose from me, giving the whole of her admirable shape, and fine-turned limbs: her eyes running over, yet seeming to threaten future vengeance: and at last her lips uttering what every indignant look and glowing feature portended; exclaiming as if I had done the worst I could do, and vowing never to forgive me; wilt thou wonder if I resumed the incensed, the already too much provoked fair one?

I did; and clasped her once more to my bosom: but, considering the delicacy of her frame, her force was amazing, and showed how much in earnest she was in her resentment; for it was with the utmost difficulty that I was able to hold her: nor could I prevent her sliding through my arms, to fall upon her knees: which she did at my feet: and there, in anguish of her soul, her streaming eyes lifted up to my face with supplicating softness, hands folded, dishevelled hair; for her night head-dress having fallen off in her struggling, her charming tresses fell down in naturally shining ringlets, as if officious to conceal the dazzling beauties of her neck and shoulders; her lovely bosom too heaving with sighs and broken sobs, as if to aid her quivering lips in pleading for her — in this manner, but when her grief gave way to her speech, in words pronounced with that emphatical propriety which distinguishes this admirable creature in her elocution from all the women I ever heard speak, did she implore my compassion and my honour.

"Consider me, *dear* Lovelace" (*dear* was her charming word!), "on my knees I beg you to consider me, as a poor creature who has no protector but you; who has no defence but your honour: by that honour! by your humanity! by all you have vowed! I conjure you not to make me abhor myself! — not to make me vile in my own eyes!"

I mentioned the morrow as the happiest day of my life.

Tell me not of to-morrow. If indeed you mean me honourably, *now*, this very instant NOW! you must show it, and be gone! You can never in a whole long life repair the evils you may NOW make me suffer.

Wicked wretch! Insolent villain! — Yes, she called me insolent villain, although so much in my power! And for what? — only for kissing (*with passion indeed*) her inimitable neck, her lips, her cheeks, her forehead, and her streaming eyes, as this assemblage of beauties offered itself at once to my ravished sight; she continuing kneeling at my feet, as I sat.

If I *am* a villain, madam — And then my grasping, but trembling hand — I hope I did not hurt the tenderest and loveliest of all her beauties — If I *am* a villain, madam ——

She tore my ruffle, shrunk from my happy hand with amazing force and agility, as with my other arm I would have encircled her waist.

Indeed you are! The worst of villains! Help! dear blessed people! and screamed. No help for a poor creature!

Am I then a villain, madam? *Am* I then a villain, say you? and clasped both my arms about her, offering to raise her to my bounding heart.

Oh, no — and yet you are! And again I was her *dear* Lovelace! — her hands again clasped over her charming bosom. Kill me! kill me! if I am odious enough in your eyes to deserve this treatment; and I will thank you! Too long, much too long, has my life been a burden to me! Or (wildly looking all around her), give me but the means, and I will instantly convince you that my honour is dearer to me than my life!

I sat suspended for a moment. By my soul, thought I, thou art, upon full proof, an angel and no woman! Still, however, close clasping her to my bosom, as I had raised her from her knees, she again slid through my arms and dropped upon them:

"See, Mr. Lovelace! — Good God! that I should live to see this hour, and to bear this treatment! — See at your feet a poor creature, imploring your pity, who, for your sake, is abandoned of all the world! Let not my father's curse thus dreadfully operate! Be not *you* the inflicter, who have been the *cause* of it: but spare me, I beseech you, spare me! For how have I deserved this treatment from you? For *your own sake*, if not for *my sake*, and as you would that God Almighty, in your last hour, should have mercy upon *you*, spare me!"

What heart but must have been penetrated?

I would again have raised the dear suppliant from her knees; but she would not be raised, till my softened mind, she said, had yielded to her prayer, and bid her rise to be innocent.

Rise then, my angel! Rise, and be what you are, and all you wish to be!

Impute not everything, my best beloved, to design; for design it was not ——

O Mr. Lovelace!

Upon my soul, madam, the fire was real. (*And so it was, Jack!*) The house, my dearest life, might have been consumed by it, as you will be convinced in the morning by ocular demonstration.

O Mr. Lovelace!

Let my passion for you, madam, and the unexpected meeting of you at your chamber door, in an attitude so charming ——

Leave me, leave me, this moment! I beseech you, leave me; looking wildly and in confusion about her, and upon herself.

Excuse me, dearest creature, for those liberties which, innocent as they were, your too great delicacy may make you take amiss ——

No more! no more! Leave me, I beseech you! Again looking upon herself, and around her, in a sweet confusion. Begone! Begone!

Then weeping, she struggled vehemently to withdraw her hands, which all the while I held between mine. Her struggles! Oh, what additional charms, as I now reflect, did her struggles give to every feature, every limb, of a person so sweetly elegant and lovely!

Impossible, my dearest life, till you pronounce my pardon! Say but you forgive me! — say but you forgive me!

I beseech you, begone! Leave me to myself, that I may think what I *can* do, and what I *ought* to do.

That, my dearest creature, is not enough. You must tell me that I am forgiven; that you will see me to-morrow as if nothing had happened.

And then I clasped her again in my arms, hoping she would not forgive me.

I will — I do forgive you — wretch that you are!

Nay, my Clarissa! And is it such a reluctant pardon, mingled with a word so upbraiding, that I am to be put off with, when you are thus (clasping her close to me) in my power?

I do, I *do* forgive you!

Heartily?

Yes, heartily!

And freely?

Freely!

And will you look upon me to-morrow as if nothing had passed?

Yes, yes!

I cannot take these peevish affirmatives, so much like intentional negatives! Say you will, upon your honour.

Upon my honour, then. Oh, now begone! And never — never ——

What, never, my angel! Is this forgiveness?

Never, said she, let what has passed be remembered more!

I insisted upon one kiss to seal my pardon — and retired like a fool, a woman's fool, as I was! I sneakingly retired! Couldst thou have believed it?

But I had no sooner entered my own apartment than, reflecting upon the opportunity I had lost, and that all I had gained was but an increase of my own difficulties; and upon the ridicule I should meet with below upon a weakness so much out of my usual character; I repented, and hastened back, in hope that through the distress of mind which I left her in, she had not so soon fastened her door; and I was fully resolved to execute all my purposes, be the consequence what it would; for, thought I, I have already sinned beyond *cordial* forgiveness, I doubt; and if fits and desperation ensue, I can but marry at last, and then I shall make her amends.

But I was justly punished; for her door was fast: and hearing her sigh and sob, as if her heart would burst: My beloved creature, said I, rapping gently (her sobbings then ceasing), I want but to say three words to you, which must be the most acceptable you ever heard from me. Let me see you but for one moment.

I thought I heard her coming to open the door, and my heart leaped in that hope; but it was only to draw another bolt, to make it still the faster; and she either could not or would not answer me, but retired to the farther end of her apartment, to her closet probably: and more like a fool than before, again I sneaked away.

This was my mine, my plot! And this was all I made of it!

Thursday Morning, Eight o'clock.

Her chamber door has not yet been opened. I must not expect she will breakfast with me. Nor dine with me. I doubt. A little silly soul, what troubles does she make to herself by her over-niceness! All I have done to her would have been looked upon as a *frolic* only, a *romping-bout*, and laughed off by nine parts in ten of the sex accordingly. The more she makes of it, the more painful to herself, as well as to me.

Past Ten o'clock.

I never longed in my life for anything with so much impatience as to see my charmer. She has been stirring, it seems, these two hours. Dorcas just now tapped at her door, to take her morning commands. *She had none for her*, was the answer.
She desired to know if she would not breakfast?
A sullen and low-voiced *negative* received Dorcas.
I will go myself.

.   .   .   .

Three different times tapped I at the door; but had no answer.
Permit me, dearest creature, to inquire after your health. As you have not been seen to-day, I am impatient to know how you do?
Not a word of answer; but a deep sigh, even to sobbing.
Let me beg of you, madam, to accompany me up another pair of stairs — you'll rejoice to see what a happy escape we have all had.
A happy escape indeed, Jack! For the fire had scorched the window-board, singed the hangings, and burnt through the slit-deal lining of the window-jambs.
No answer, madam! Am I not worthy of one word? Is it thus you keep your promise with me? Shall I not have the favour of your company for two minutes (only for two minutes) in the dining-room?
Ahem! and a deep sigh! were all the answer.

Answer me but how you do! Answer me but that you are well! Is this the forgiveness that was the condition of my obedience?

Then, in a faintish, but angry voice: Begone from my door! Wretch, inhuman, barbarous, and all that is base and treacherous! begone from my door! Nor tease thus a poor creature, entitled to protection, not outrage.

I see, madam, how you keep your word with me! *If* a sudden impulse, the effects of an unthought-of accident, cannot be forgiven ——

Oh, the dreadful weight of a father's curse, thus in the very letter of it ——

And then her voice dying away in murmurs inarticulate, I looked through the keyhole, and saw her on her knees, her face, though not towards me, lifted up, as well as hands, and these folded, deprecating, I suppose, that gloomy tyrant's curse.

I could not help being moved.

Past Eleven o'clock.

She rung her bell for Dorcas; and, with her door in her hand, only half opened, gave her a billet for me.

How did the dear creature look, Dorcas?

She was dressed. She turned her face quite from me; and sighed, as if her heart would break.

Sweet creature! I kissed the wet wafer, and drew it from the paper with my breath.

These are the contents. No inscriptive Sir! No Mr. Lovelace!

I CANNOT see you: nor will I, if I can help it. Words cannot express the anguish of my soul on your baseness and ingratitude.

If the circumstances of things are such, that I can have no way for reconciliation with those who would have been my natural protectors from such outrages, but through *you* (the only inducement I can have to stay a moment longer in your knowledge), pen and ink must be, at present, the only means of communication between us.

Vilest of men! and most detestable of plotters! how have I deserved from you the shocking indignities — But no more — only for your own sake, wish not, at least for a week to come, to see / The undeservedly injured and insulted / CLARISSA HARLOWE.

So thou seest, nothing could have stood me in stead but this plot of Tomlinson and her uncle! To what a pretty pass, nevertheless, have I brought myself!

But not to see her for a week! Dear pretty soul! how she anticipates me in everything! The counsellor will have finished the writings to-day or to-morrow, at furthest: the license with the parson, or the parson without the licence, must be also procured within the next four-and-twenty hours; Pritchard is as good as ready with his indentures tripartite: Tomlinson is at hand with a favourable answer from her uncle. *Yet not to see her for a week! Dear sweet soul!* Her good angel is gone a journey: is truanting at least. But nevertheless, in thy week's time, or in much less, my charmer, I doubt not to complete my triumph!

MR. LOVELACE TO JOHN BELFORD, ESQ.

King's Arms, Pallmall, Thursday, Two o'clock.

SEVERAL billets passed between us before I went out, by the *internuncioship* of Dorcas: for which reason mine are superscribed by her married name. She would not open her door to receive them; lest I should be near it, I suppose: so Dorcas was forced to put them under the door (after copying them for thee); and thence to take the answers. Read them, if thou wilt, at this place.

To Mrs. Lovelace

INDEED my dearest life, you carry this matter too far. What will the people below, who suppose us one as to the ceremony, think of so great a niceness? Liberties so innocent! the occasion so accidental! You will expose *yourself* as well *as me*.

If you step up another pair of stairs you will be convinced that however *detestable* I may be to you, I am no plotter in this affair.

I beg your presence in the dining-room for one quarter of an hour, and I will then leave you for the day. I am, / My dearest life, / Your ever-adoring and truly penitent, / LOVELACE.

To Mr. Lovelace

I WILL not see you. I cannot see you. I have no directions to give you. Let Providence decide for me as it pleases. 'Tis grievous to me to write, or even to *think* of you at present. Urge me no more then. Once more, I will *not* see you. Nor care I, now you have made me vile to myself, what other people think of me.

To Mrs. Lovelace

AGAIN, madam, I remind you of your promise: and beg leave to say, I insist upon the performance of it.

I own that the violence of my passion for you might have carried me beyond fit bounds. But that your commands and adjurations had power over me at *such* a moment, I humbly presume to say, deserves some consideration.

You enjoin me not to see you for a week. If I have not your pardon before Captain Tomlinson comes to town, what shall I say to *him*?

I beg once more your presence in the dining-room. By my soul, madam, I *must* see you.

To Mr. Lovelace

THE MORE you tease me, the worse will it be for you.

Time is wanted to consider whether I ever should think of you at all.

At *present*, it is my sincere wish that I may never more see your face.

All that can afford you the least shadow of favour from me, arises from the hoped-for reconciliation with my real friends, not my *Judas*-protector.

To Mrs. Lovelace

MADAM, — I will go to the Commons, and proceed in every particular as if I had not the misfortune to be under your displeasure.

I hope to find you in a kinder and, I will say, *juster* disposition on my return. Whether I get the licence or not, let me beg you to make the *soon* you have been pleased to bid me hope for, to-morrow morning. This will reconcile everything, and make me the happiest of men.

The settlements are ready to sign, or will be by night.

I looked through the keyhole at my going by her door, and saw her on her knees, at her bed's feet, and in an agony she seemed to be, sobbing, as I heard at that distance, as if her heart would break. Divine excellence: she is purity itself. And why, after all, should I thus torment —

Yet, to have taken such bold steps, as with Tomlinson and her uncle — to have made such a progress — O Belford, Belford, how have I puzzled myself, as well as her! This cursed aversion to wedlock how has it entangled me! The dear creature herself once told me that there was a strange mixture in my mind.

MR. LOVELACE TO JOHN BELFORD, ESQ.

Thursday Evening, June 8.

Oh, for a curse to kill with! Ruined! Undone! Outwitted! Tricked! Zounds, man, the lady is gone off! Absolutely gone off! Escaped!

How she could effect this her wicked escape, is my astonishment; the whole sisterhood having charge of her: for, as yet, I have not patience enough to inquire into the particulars, nor to let a soul of them approach me.

To what purpose brought I this angel (angel I must yet call her) to this hellish house? And was I not meditating to do her deserved honour? By my soul, Belford, I was resolved. But thou knowest what I had *conditionally* resolved. And now, who can tell into what hands she may have fallen?

Going home, as I did, with resolutions favourable to her, judge thou of my distraction, when her escape was first hinted to me, although but in broken sentences. I knew not what I said, nor what I did. I wanted to kill somebody. I flew out of one room into another, while all avoided me but the veteran Betty Carberry, who broke the matter to me.

This is the substance of the old wretch's account.

She told me that I had no sooner left the vile house than Dorcas acquainted her lady with it; and that I had left word that I was gone to Doctor's Commons, and should not return till late. She then urged her to take some refreshment.

Being resolved to see me for not a week at least, she ordered her to bring her up three or four French rolls, with a little butter and a decanter of water; telling her she would dispense with her attendance; and that should be all she would live upon in the interim. So, artful creature! pretending to lay up for a week's siege.

Dorcas consulted the old wretch about obeying her: Oh, yes, by all means: for Mr. Lovelace knew how to come at her at any time; and directed a bottle of sherry to be added.

This cheerful compliance so obliged her that she was prevailed upon to go up, and look at the damage done by the fire; and seemed not only shocked at it, but, as they thought, satisfied it was no trick; as she owned she had at first apprehended it to be. All this made them secure; and they laughed in their sleeves, to think what a childish way of showing her resentment she had found out; Sally throwing out her witticisms that Mrs. Lovelace was right, however, *not to quarrel with her bread and butter*.

Now this very childishness, as *they* imagined it, in such a genius, would have made *me* suspect either her head, after what had happened the night before; or her purpose, when the marriage was (so far as she knew) to be completed within the week in which she was resolved to secrete herself from me in the same house.

She sent Will with a letter to Wilson's, directed to Miss Howe, ordering him to inquire if there were not one for her there.

He only pretended to go, and brought word there was none; and put her letter in his pocket for me.

She then ordered him to carry another (which she gave him) to the Horn Tavern to me. All this done without any seeming hurry; yet she appeared to be very solemn; and put her handkerchief frequently to her eyes.

Will pretended to come to me with this letter. But though the dog had the sagacity to mistrust something on her sending him out a second time (and to *me*, whom she had refused to see); which he thought extraordinary; and mentioned his mistrusts to Sally, Polly, and Dorcas; yet they made light of his suspicions; Dorcas assuring them all that her lady seemed more stupid with her grief, than active; and that she really believed she was a little turned in her head, and knew not what she did.

Will went out, pretending to bring the letter to me; but quickly returned; his heart still misgiving him, on recollecting my frequent cautions, that he was not to judge for himself, when he had *positive* orders; but if any doubt occurred, from circumstances I could not foresee, literally to follow them, as the only way to avoid blame.

But it must have been in this little interval that she escaped; for soon after his return they made fast the street door and hatch, the mother and the two nymphs, taking a little turn into the garden; Dorcas going upstairs, and Will (to avoid being seen, by his lady, or his voice heard) down into the kitchen.

About half an hour after, Dorcas, who had planted herself where she could see her lady's door open, had the curiosity to go to look through the keyhole, having a misgiving, as she said, that her lady might offer some violence to herself, in the mood she had been in all day; and finding the key in the door, which was not very usual, she tapped at it three or four times, and having no answer, opened it, with Madam, madam, did you call? Supposing her in her closet.

Having no answer she stepped forward, and was astonished to find she was not there. She hastily ran into the dining-room, then into my apartments, searched every closet; dreading all the time to behold some sad catastrophe.

Not finding her anywhere, she ran down to the old creature and her nymphs, with a Have you seen my lady? — Then she's gone! She's nowhere above!

They were sure she could not be gone out.

The whole house was in an uproar in an instant; some running upstairs, some down, from the upper room to the lower; and all screaming, How should they look *me* in the face

When they had searched the whole house, and every closet in it, ten times over, to no purpose, they took it into their heads to send to all the porters, chairmen, and hackney-coachmen, that had been near the house for two hours past, to inquire if any of them saw such a young lady; describing her.

This brought them some light: the only dawning for hope that I can have, and which keeps me from absolute despair. One of the chairmen gave them this account: That he saw such a one come out of the house a little before four (in a great hurry, and as if frighted) with a little parcel tied up in an handkerchief, in her hand: that he took notice to his fellow, who plied her without her answering, that she was a fine young lady: that he'd warrant she had either a bad husband, or very cross parents; for that her eyes seemed swelled with crying. Upon which, a third fellow replied that it might be a doe escaped from Mother *Damnable's* park.

From these appearances the fellow who gave this information had the curiosity to follow her, unperceived. She often looked back. Everybody who passed her, turned to look after her; passing their verdicts upon her tears, her hurry, and her charming person; till coming to a stand of coaches, a coachman plied her; was accepted; alighted; opened the coach door in a hurry, seeing *her* hurry; and in it she stumbled for haste; and, as the fellow believed, hurt her shins with the stumble.

The fellow heard her say, Drive fast! Very fast! Where, madam? To Holborn Bars, answered she; repeating, Drive very fast! And up she pulled both the windows: and he lost sight of the coach in a minute.

Will, as soon as he had this intelligence, speeded away in hopes to trace her out; declaring, that he would never think of seeing me till he had heard some tidings of his lady.

And now, Belford, all my hope is, that this fellow (who attended us in our airing to Hampstead, to Highgate, to Muswell Hill, to Kentish Town) will hear of her at some one or other of those places. And on this I the rather build, as I remember she was once, after our return, very inquisitive about the stages, and their prices; praising the convenience to passengers in their going off every hour; and this in Will's hearing, who was then in attendance. Woe be to the villain, if he recollect not this!

If ever ——

Here Mr. Lovelace lays himself under a curse, too shocking to be repeated, if he revenge not himself upon the lady, should he once more get her into his hands.

. . . .

Fresh cause of aggravation! But for this scribbling vein, or I should still run mad.

Again going into her chamber, because it *was* hers, and sighing over the bed, and every piece of furniture in it, I cast my eye towards the drawers of the dressing-glass, and saw peep out, as it were, in one of the half-drawn drawers, the corner of a letter. I snatched it out, and found it superscribed by her, *To Mr. Lovelace.* The sight of it made my heart leap, and I trembled so, that I could hardly open the seal.

I will not give thee a copy of this letter. I owe her not so much service.

But if ever again I get her into my hands, *art*, and more *art*, and *compulsion* too, if she make it necessary (*and 'tis plain that nothing else will do*), shall she experience from the man whose fear *of* her has been above even his passion *for* her; and whose gentleness and forbearance she has thus *perfidiously* triumphed over.

MR. LOVELACE TO JOHN BELFORD, ESQ.

A LETTER from Miss Howe to her cruel friend! I made no scruple to open it.

It is a miracle that I fell not into fits at the reading of it; and at the thought of what *might* have been the consequence had it come into the hands of *this Clarissa Harlowe.* Let my justly excited rage excuse my irreverence.

Thou wilt see the margin of this cursed letter crowded with indices [*]. I put them to mark the places which call for vengeance upon the vixen writer, or which require animadversion. Return thou it to me the moment thou hast perused it.

Read it here, and avoid trembling for me if thou canst.

To Miss Lætitia Beaumont
Wednesday, June 7.

MY DEAREST FRIEND, — You will perhaps think that I have been too long silent. But I had begun two letters at different times since my

last, and written a great deal each time, and with spirit enough I
*assure you, incensed as I was against the abominable wretch you
are with, particularly on reading yours of the twenty-first of the past
month.

* The *first* I intended to keep open till I could give you some account
of my proceedings with Mrs. Townsend. It was some days before
I saw her; and this intervenient space giving me time to reperuse
what I had written, I thought it proper to lay that aside and to write
*in a style a little less fervent, for you would have blamed me, I know,
*for the freedom of some of my expressions (*execrations,* if you
please). And when I had gone a good way in the *second,* the change
in your prospects, on his communicating to you Miss Montague's
letter, and his better behaviour, occasioning a change in your mind,
I laid that aside also. And in this uncertainty thought I would wait
to see the issue of affairs between you before I wrote again, believing
all would soon be decided one way or other.

The women of the house where you are — O my dear the women
of the house — but you never thought highly of them, so it cannot
*be very surprising — nor would you ave *stayed so long with them,
had not the notion of removing to one of your own,* made you less
uneasy, and less curious about their characters and behaviour. Yet
*I *now* wish that you had been less reserved among them — but I
*tease you. In short, my dear, you are certainly in a devilish house!
Be assured that the woman is one of the vilest of women — nor does
she go to you by her right name. — Very true! Her name is *not*
Sinclair, nor is the street she lives in, Dover Street.

The wretch might indeed have held out these false lights a little
more excusably had the house been an honest house, and had his
end only been to prevent mischief from your brother. But this contrivance was antecedent, as I think, to your brother's project; so that
no excuse can be made for his intentions at the *time* — the man,
*whatever he may *now* intend, was certainly then, even *then,* a villain
in his heart.

But I will tell you how I came by my intelligence. *That* being a
fact and requiring the less attention, I will try to account to you for
that.

Thus then it came about: Miss Lardner (whom you have seen at
her Cousin Biddulph's) saw you at St. James's Church on Sunday
was fortnight. She kept you in her eye during the whole time, but
could not once obtain the notice of yours, though she curtsied to you
twice. She thought to pay her compliments to you when the service
*was over, for she doubted not but you were married; and for an odd
reason — *Because you came to church by yourself.* Every eye (as
usual, wherever you are, she said) was upon you; and this seeming
to give you hurry, and you being nearer the door than she, you slid
out before she could get to you. But she ordered her servant to
follow you till you were housed. This servant saw you step into a
chair which waited for you, and you ordered the men to carry you
to the place where they took you up.

The next day Miss Lardner sent the same servant, out of mere curiosity, to make private inquiry whether Mr. Lovelace were, or were not, with you there. And this inquiry brought out, from *different* people, that the house was suspected to be one of those genteel wicked houses which receive and accommodate *fashionable people* of both sexes.

Miss Lardner, confounded at this strange intelligence, made further inquiry, enjoining secrecy to the servant she had sent, as well as to the gentleman whom she employed; who had it confirmed from a rakish friend who knew the house, and told him that there were two houses; the one *in which all decent appearances were preserved, and guests rarely admitted;* the other, the receptacle of those who were absolutely engaged, and broken to the vile yoke.

Miss Lardner kept this to herself some days, not knowing what to do; for she loves you, and admires you of all women. At last she revealed it, but in confidence, to Miss Biddulph by letter. Miss Biddulph, in like confidence, being afraid it would distract *me* were I to know it, communicated to Miss Lloyd; and so, like a whispered scandal, it passed through several canals; and then it came to me. Which was not till last Monday.

I thought I should have fainted upon the surprising communication. But rage taking place, it blew away the sudden illness. I besought Miss Lloyd to re-enjoin secrecy to every one. I told her that °I would not for the world that my mother, or any of your family, should know it. And I instantly caused a trusty friend to make what inquiries he could about Tomlinson.

° I had thoughts to have done it before I had this intelligence; but not imagining it to be needful, and little thinking that you could be in such a house, and as you were pleased with your changed °prospects, I forbore. And the rather forbore, as the matter is so laid, that Mrs. Hodges is supposed to know nothing of the projected treaty of accommodation; but, on the contrary, that it was designed to be a secret to her, and to everybody but immediate parties, and it was Mrs. Hodges that I had proposed to sound by a *second* hand.

° Now, my dear, it is certain, without applying to that too much favoured housekeeper, that there is not such a man within ten miles of your uncle. Very true! One *Tomkins* there is, about four miles off, but he is a day-labourer; and one *Thompson*, about five miles distant the other way, but he is a parish schoolmaster, poor, and about seventy.

° A man, though but of eight hundred pounds a year, cannot come from one county to settle in another but everybody in both must know it and talk of it.

° Mrs. Hodges may yet be sounded at a distance, if you will.

° Yet, methinks, the story is so plausible; Tomlinson, as you describe him, is so good a man, and so much of a gentleman; the end to be answered by his being an impostor, so much *more than necessary* if Lovelace has villainy in his head — *These things make me willing to try for a tolerable construction to be made of all;* though I am *so much puzzled by what occurs on both sides of the question, that I cannot but abhor the devilish wretch, whose inventions and con-*trivances are for ever employing an inquisitive head, as mine is, without affording the means of absolute detection.

But this is what I am ready to conjecture, that Tomlinson, specious as he is, is a machine of Lovelace; and that he is employed for some *end, which has not yet been answered. This is certain, that not only Tomlinson, but Mennell, who, I think, attended you more than once at this vile house, must know it to *be* a vile house.

What can you then think of Tomlinson's declaring himself in *favour* of it, upon inquiry?

Lovelace too must know it to be so; if not before he brought you to it, soon after.

* Perhaps the *company he found there* may be the most probable way of accounting for his bearing with the house, and for his strange suspensions of marriage, when it was in his power to call such an angel of a woman his.

* O my dear, the man is a villain! the greatest of villains, in every light! I am convinced that he is. And this Doleman must be another of his implements!

* But can I think (you will ask with indignant astonishment) that Lovelace can have designs upon your honour?

* That such designs he *has had*, if he *still* hold them not, I can have no doubt, now that I know the house he has brought you to, to be a vile one. This is a clue that has led me to account for all his behaviour to you ever since you have been in his hands.

And now may not all the rest be naturally accounted for? His delays — his teasing ways — his bringing you to bear with his lodging in the same house — his making you pass to the people of it as his wife; *though restrictively so*, yet with hope, no doubt (vilest *of villains as he is!), to take you at advantage — his bringing you *into the company of his libertine companions —the attempt of imposing upon you that Miss Partington for a bedfellow, very probably his own invention for the worst of purposes — his terrifying you at many different times — his obtruding himself upon you when you went out to church, no doubt to prevent your finding out what the people of the house were — the advantages he made of your brother's foolish project with Singleton.

But if this be so, what (it would be asked by an indifferent person) has hitherto saved you? Glorious creature! What, morally speaking, but your watchfulness!

I took time for inquiries of different natures, as I knew by the train you are in, that whatever his designs are, they cannot ripen *either for good or evil till something shall result from this new device of his about Tomlinson and your uncle.

Device I have no doubt that it is, whatever this dark, this impenetrable spirit intends by it.

* And yet I find it to be true that Counsellor Williams (whom Mr. Hickman knows to be a man of eminence in his profession) has actu-

*ally as good as finished the settlements; that two drafts of them have been made; one avowedly to be sent to one Captain Tomlinson, as the clerk says: — and I find that a licence has been actually been more than once endeavoured to be obtained! and that difficulties have *hitherto been made, equally to Lovelace's vexation and disappointment.

I fear nothing (as I know who has said) that devil carnate or incarnate can fairly do against a virtue so established. But surprises, *my dear, in such a house as that you are in, and in such circumstances as I have mentioned, I greatly fear! The man, one who has *already triumphed over persons worthy of his alliance.

* What then have you to do but to fly this house, this infernal house! O that your heart would let you fly the *man!*

* If you should be disposed so to do, Mrs. Townsend shall be ready at your command. But if you meet with no impediments, no new causes of doubt, I think your reputation in the eye of the world, though not your happiness. is concerned, that you should be his. *And yet I cannot bear that these libertines should be rewarded for their villainy with the best of the sex, when the worst of it are too good for them.

But if you meet with the least ground for suspicion; if he would detain you at the odious house, or wish you to stay, now you know *what the people are; fly *him*, whatever your prospects are, as well as *them.*

* One word more. Command me up, if I can be of the least service or pleasure to you. I value not fame; I value not censure; nor even life itself, I verily think, as I do your honour and your friendship — for is not your honour my honour? And is not your friendship the pride of my life?

May Heaven preserve you, my dearest creature, in honour and safety, is the prayer, the hourly prayer, of / Your ever faithful and affectionate / ANNA HOWE.

Thursday Morn. 5. I have written all night.

To Miss Howe

MY DEAREST CREATURE, — How you have shocked, confounded, surprised, astonished me, by your dreadful communication! My *heart is too weak* to bear up against such a stroke as this! — When all hope was with me! When my prospects were so much mended! But can there be such villainy in men as in this vile principal, and equally vile agent?

I am really ill — very ill. Grief and surprise, and *now* I will say despair, have overcome me! All, all, you have laid down as conjecture, appears to *me now* to be *more* than conjecture!

O that your mother would have the goodness to permit me the presence of the only comforter that my afflicted, my half-broken heart, could be raised by! But I charge you, think not of coming up without her indulgent permission. I am too ill at present, my dear, to think

276

of combating with this dreadful man; and of flying from this horrid house! — *My bad writing will show you this.* / CLARISSA HOWE.

Well, Jack! And what thinkest thou of this last letter? Miss Howe values not either *fame* or *censure*; and thinkest thou that this letter will not bring the little fury up, though she could procure no other conveyance than her higgler's panniers, one for herself, the other for her maid? She knows where to come now. Many a little villain have I punished for knowing more than I would have her know; and that by adding to her knowledge and experience. What thinkest thou, Belford, if, by getting hither this virago, and giving *cause* for a lamentable letter from her to the fair fugitive, I should be able to recover *her*? Would she not visit that friend in *her* distress, thinkest thou, whose intended visit to her in *hers* brought her into the condition from which she herself had so perfidiously escaped?

Let me enjoy the thought!

Shall I send this letter? Thou seest I have left room, if I fail in the exact imitation of so charming a hand, to avoid too strict a scrutiny. Do they not both deserve it of me?

But the principal reason that withholds me (for 'tis a tempting project!) is, for fear of being utterly blown up, if I should not be quick enough with my letter, or if Miss Howe should deliberate on setting out, or try her mother's consent first; in which time a letter from my frighted beauty might reach her; for I have no doubt, wherever she has refuged, but her first work was to write to her vixen friend. I will therefore go on patiently, and take my revenge upon the little fury at my leisure.

I am loath to reproach *myself*, now the cruel creature has escaped me; for what would that do but add to my torment? Since evils self-caused, and avoidable, admit not of palliation or comfort. And yet, if *thou* tellest me that all *her* strength was owing to *my* weakness, and that I have been a cursed coward in this whole affair; why then, Jack, I may blush, and be vexed; but, by my soul, I cannot contradict thee.

But this, Belford, I hope — that if I can turn the poison of the enclosed letter into wholesome aliment; that is to say, if I can make use of it to my advantage; I shall have *thy* free consent to do it.

I am always careful to open covers cautiously, and to preserve seals entire. I will draw out from this cursed letter an alphabet. Nor was Nick Rowe ever half so diligent to learn Spanish, at the Quixote recommendation of a certain peer, as I will be to gain a mastery of this vixen's hand.

MISS CLARISSA HARLOWE TO MISS HOWE
Thursday Evening, June 8.

AFTER my last, so full of other hopes, the contents of this will surprise you. O my dearest friend, the man has at last proved himself to be a villain!

It was with the utmost difficulty last night that I preserved myself

277

from the vilest dishonour. He extorted from me a promise of forgiveness, and that I would see him next day as if nothing had happened; but if it were possible to escape from a wretch, who, as I have too much reason to believe, formed a plot to fire the house, to frighten me, almost naked, into his arms, how could I see him next day?

I have escaped — Heaven be praised that I have! — And have now no other concern than that I fly from the only hope that could have made such an husband tolerable to me: the reconciliation with my friends, so agreeably undertaken by my uncle.

All my present hope is to find some reputable family, or person of my own sex, who is obliged to go beyond sea, or who lives abroad; I care not whither; but if I might choose, in some one of our American colonies — never to be heard of more by my relations, whom I have so grievously offended.

I am at present at one Mrs. Moore's at Hampstead. My heart misgave me at coming to this village, because I had been here with him more than once; but the coach hither was so ready a conveniency that I knew not what to do better. Then I shall stay here no longer than till I can receive your answer to this; in which you will be pleased to let me know if I cannot be hid, according to your former contrivance (happy, had I given into it at the time!), by Mrs. Townsend's assistance, till the heat of the search be over. The Deptford road, I imagine, will be the right direction to hear of a passage and to get safely aboard.

I am sure you will approve of my escape — the rather, as the people of the house must be very vile; for they, and that Dorcas too, did hear me (I know they did) cry out for help; if the fire had been other than a villainous plot (although in the morning, to blind them, I pretended to think it otherwise) they would have been alarmed as much as I; and have run in, hearing me scream, to *comfort me*, supposing my terror was the fire; to *relieve me*, supposing it were anything else. But the vile Dorcas went away as soon as she saw the wretch throw his arms about me! — Bless me, my dear, I had only my slippers and an under-petticoat on. I was frighted out of my bed by her cries of fire; and that I should be burnt to ashes in a moment — and she to go away, and never to return, nor anybody else! And yet I heard women's voices in the next room; indeed I did. — An evident contrivance of them all: — God be praised, I am out of their house!

I know you will expedite an answer. A man and horse will be procured me to-morrow early, to carry this. To be sure, you cannot return an answer by the same man, because you must see Mrs. Townsend first; nevertheless, I shall wait with impatience till you *can*; having no friend but you to apply to; and being such a stranger to this part of the world, that I know not which way to turn myself; whither to go; nor what to do. — What a dreadful hand have I made of it!

I will not set my foot out of doors till I have your direction; and I am the more secure, having dropped words to the people of the house where the coach set me down, as if I expected a chariot to meet me in my way to Hendon, a village a little distance from this. And when I left their house, I walked backward and forward upon the hill; at first, not knowing what to do; and afterwards, to be certain that I was not watched before I ventured to inquire after a lodging.

You will direct for me, my dear, by the name of Mrs. Harriot Lucas.

Had I not made my escape when I did, I was resolved to attempt it again and again. He was gone to the Commons for a licence, as he wrote me word; for I refused to see him, notwithstanding the promise he extorted from me.

MR. LOVELACE TO JOHN BELFORD, ESQ.
Friday Morning, past Two o'clock.

Io Triumphe! Io Clarissa, sing! — Once more, what a happy man thy friend! — A silly dear novice, to be heard to tell the coachman whither to carry her! — And to go to *Hampstead*, of all the villages about London! — The place where we had been together more than once!

Methinks I am sorry she managed no better!

Well, but after all this exultation, thou wilt ask, "If I have already got back my charmer?" I have not; but knowing where she is, is almost the same thing as having her in my power.

But thou wilt be impatient to know how I came by my lights. Read the enclosed here, and remember the instructions which from time to time, as I have told thee, I have given my fellow, in apprehension of such an elopement; and that will tell thee all, and what I may reasonably expect from the rascal's diligence and management, if he wishes ever to see my face again.

I received it about half an hour ago, just as I was going to lie down in my clothes; and it has made me so much alive, that, midnight as it is, I have sent for a Blunt's chariot to attend me here by day-peep, with *my usual coachman,* if possible; and knowing not else what to do with myself, I sat down, and in the joy of my heart have not only written thus far, but have concluded upon the measures I shall take when admitted to her presence; for well I am aware of the difficulties I shall have to contend with from her perverseness.

Honnored Sur, — This is to sertifie your Honner, as how I am heer at Hamestet, wher I have found out my lady to be in logins at one Mrs. Moore's, near upon Hamestet Hethe. And I have so ordered matters, that her ladiship cannot stur but I must have notice of her goins and comins.

My lady knows nothing of my being hereaway. But I thoute it best not to leve the plase, because she has tacken the logins but fur a fue nites.

I am, may it plese your Honner / WM. SUMMERS.

Now, Jack, will not *her feints* justify *mine?* Does she not invade my province, thinkest thou? And is it not now fairly come to *Who shall most deceive the other*?

This is my dear juggler's letter to me:

Thursday, June 8.

MR. LOVELACE, — Do not give me cause to dread your return. If you would not that I should hate you for ever, send me half a line by the bearer, to assure me that you will not attempt to see me for a week to come. I cannot look you in the face without equal confusion and indignation. The obliging me in this is but a poor atonement for your last night's vile behaviour.

You may pass this time in a journey to Lord M.'s; and I cannot doubt, if the ladies of your family are as favourable to me as you have assured me they are, but that you will have interest enough to prevail with one of them to oblige me with her company. After your baseness of last night, you will not wonder that I insist upon this proof of your future honour. / The unhappy / CL. H.

Now, Belford, what canst thou say in behalf of this sweet rogue of a lady? What *canst* thou say for her? 'Tis apparent that she was fully determined upon an elopement when she wrote it; and thus would she make me of party against myself, by drawing me in to give her a week's time to complete it; and, more wicked still, send me upon a fool's errand to bring up one of my cousins. — When we came, to have the satisfaction of finding her gone off, and me exposed for ever! What punishment can be bad enough for such a little villain of a lady!

.   .   .   .

A gentleman to speak with me, Dorcas? Who can want me thus early?

Captain Tomlinson, sayest thou! Surely he must have travelled all night! Early riser as I am, how could he think to find me up *thus* early?

Let but the chariot come, and he shall accompany me in it to the bottom of the hill (though he return to town on foot; for the captain is all obliging goodness), that I may hear all he has to say, and tell him all my mind, and lose no time.

Dear captain, I rejoice to see you — just in the nick of time. You must accompany me part of the way. I know the delight you take in composing differences.

.   .   .   .

And now (all around me so still and so silent), the rattling of the chariot-wheels at a street's distance do I hear. And to this angel of a woman I fly!

280

MR. LOVELACE TO JOHN BELFORD, ESQ.   *Upper Flask, Hampstead,*
Friday morn. 7 o'clock (June 9).

I AM now here, and here have been this hour and half. What an industrious spirit have I! Nobody can say that I eat the bread of idleness. I take true pains for all the pleasure I enjoy. I cannot but admire myself strangely.

All Will's account, from the lady's flight to his finding her again, all the accounts of the people of the house, the coachman's information to Will, and so forth, collected together, stand thus.

The Hampstead coach, when the dear fugitive came to it, had but two passengers in it. But she made the fellow go off directly, paying for the vacant places.

The two passengers directing the coachman to set them down at the Upper Flask, she bid him set her down there also.

They took leave of her (very respectfully no doubt), and she went into the house and asked if she could not have a dish of tea, and a room to herself for half an hour.

She made no inquiry about a lodging, though by the sequel, thou'lt observe, that she seemed to intend to go no farther that night than Hampstead. But after she had drank two dishes, and put a biscuit in her pocket (sweet soul), to serve for her supper perhaps, she laid down half a crown; and refusing change, sighing, took leave, saying she would proceed towards Hendon, the distance to which had been one of her questions.

They offered to send to know if a Hampstead coach were not to go to Hendon that evening.

No matter, she said — perhaps she might meet the chariot.

Another of her *feints,* I suppose; for how, or with whom, could anything of this sort have been concerted since yesterday morning?

And here, supposing my narrative of the dramatic kind, ends Act the First. And now begins

ACT II

SCENE. — *Hampstead Heath, continued.*

Enter my Rascal.

He had first acquainted me with the accounts he had given them of his lady and me. It is necessary that I give thee the particulars of his tale — and I have a little time upon my hands; for the maid of the house, who had been out of an errand, tells us that she saw Mrs. Moore (with whom must be my first business) go into the house of a young gentleman, within a few doors of her, who has a maiden sister, Miss Rawlins by name, *so notified* for prudence, that none of her acquaintance undertake anything of consequence without consulting her.

Meanwhile my honest coachman is walking about Miss Rawlins's door, in order to bring me notice of Mrs. Moore's return to her own house. I hope her gossip's tale will be as soon told as mine.

Will told them, before I came, that his lady was but lately married to one of the finest gentlemen in the world. But that, he being very gay and lively, she was *mortal* jealous of him; and in a fit of that sort, had eloped from him. For although she loved him dearly, and he doted upon her (as well he might, since, as they had seen, she was the finest creature *that ever the sun shone upon*), yet she was apt to be very wilful and sullen, if he might take the liberty to say so — but truth was truth; — and if she could not have her own way in everything, would be for leaving him.

When I came, my person and dress having answered Will's description, the people were ready to worship me. I now and then sighed, now and then put on a lighter air; which, however, I designed should show more of vexation ill-disguised, than of real cheerfulness.

Here, landlord; one word with you. My servant, I find, has acquainted you with the reason of my coming this way. An unhappy affair, landlord! A very unhappy affair! But never was there a more virtuous woman.

Mother-spoilt, landlord! Mother-spoilt! — that's the thing! But (sighing), I must make the best of it. What I want *you* to do for me, is to lend me a great-coat. I care not what it is. If my spouse should see me at a distance, she would make it very difficult for me to get at her speech. A great-coat with a cape, if you have one. I must come upon her before she is aware. I am afraid, sir, I have none fit for such a gentleman as you. Oh, anything will do! — the worse the better.

Exit Landlord. Re-enter with two great-coats.

Ay, landlord, this will be best; for I can button the cape over the lower part of my face. Don't I look devilishly down and concerned, landlord?

All this time I was adjusting my horseman's coat, and Will was putting in the ties of my wig, and buttoning the cape over my chin.

I asked the gentlewoman for a little powder. She brought me a powder-box, and I lightly shook the puff over my hat, and flapped one side of it, though the lace looked a little too gay for my covering; and slouching it over my eyes, Shall I be known, think you, madam?

The good woman, smiling, wished me success; and so did the landlord. And as thou knowest that I am not a bad mimic, I took a cane, which I borrowed of the landlord, and stooped in the shoulders to a quarter of a foot of less height, and stumped away across to the bowling-green, to practise a little the hobbling gait of a gouty man.

And now I am going to try if I can't agree with goody Moore for lodgings and other conveniences for my sick wife.

"Wife, Lovelace!" methinks thou interrogatest.

Yes, *wife*; for who knows what cautions the dear fugitive may have given in apprehension of me?

Hampstead, Friday Night, June 9.

ALTHOUGH grievously afflicted with the gout, I alighted out of my chariot (leaning very hard on my cane with one hand, and on my new servant's shoulder with the other) the same instant almost that he had knocked at the door, that I might be sure of admission into the house.

The maid came to the door. I asked for her mistress. She showed me into one of the parlours; and I sat down with a gouty Oh!

Enter Goody Moore

Your servant, madam — but you must excuse me; I cannot well stand. I find by the bill at the door, that you have lodgings to let (mumbling my words as if, like my man Will, I had lost some of my fore-teeth); be pleased to inform me what they are; for I like your situation — and I will tell you my family — I have a wife, a good old woman — older than myself, by the way, a pretty deal. She is in a bad state of health, and is advised into the Hampstead air. She will have two maidservants and a footman. The coach or chariot (I shall not have them up both together) we can put up anywhere, and the coachman will be with his horses.

When, sir, shall you want to come in?

I will take them from this very day; and if convenient, will bring my wife in the afternoon.

Perhaps, sir, you would board, as well as lodge?

That as you please. My wife must eat plain food, and I don't love kickshaws.

We have a single lady, who will be gone in two or three days. She has one of the best apartments; that will then be at liberty.

You have one or two good ones meantime, I presume, madam, just to receive my wife; for we have lost time.

You shall see what accommodations I have, if you please, sir. But I doubt you are too lame to walk upstairs.

I can make shift to hobble up now I have rested a little. I'll just look upon the apartment my wife is to have. Anything may do for the servants; and as you seem to be a good sort of gentlewoman, I shan't stand for a price, and will pay well besides for the trouble I shall give.

There were three rooms on a floor; two of them handsome; and the third, she said, still handsomer; but the lady was in it.

I saw, I saw she was! for as I hobbled up, crying out upon my weak ankles, in the hoarse mumbling voice I had assumed, I beheld a little piece of her as she just cast an eye (with the door ajar, as they call it) to observe who was coming up; and seeing such an old clumsy fellow, great-coated in weather so warm, slouched and muffled up, she withdrew, shutting the door without any emotion. But it was not so with me; for thou canst imagine how my heart danced to my mouth at the very glimpse of her, so that I was afraid the thump,

thump, thumping villain, which had so lately thumped as much to no purpose, would have choked me.

I liked the lodgings well; and the more as she said the third room was still handsomer.

But, madam, cannot a body just peep into the other apartment, that I may be more particular to my wife in the furniture of it?

The lady desires to be private, sir — but — and was going to ask her leave.

I caught hold of her hand. However, stay, stay, madam; it mayn't be proper, if the lady loves to be private. Don't let me intrude upon the lady ——

No intrusion, sir, I dare say; the lady is good-humoured. She will be so kind as to step down into the parlour, I dare say. As she stays so little a while, I am sure she will not wish to stand in my way.

No, madam, that's true, if she be good-humoured, as you say, — Has she been with you long, madam?

She came but yesterday, sir ——

I believe I just now saw the glimpse of her. She seems to be an elderly lady.

No, sir; you're mistaken. She's a young lady; and one of the handsomest I ever saw.

There's no casting an eye upon her, is there, without her notice? For in this dress, and thus muffled up about my jaws, I should not care to be seen any more than she, let her love privacy as much as she will.

I appeared, upon the whole, so indifferent about seeing the room, or the lady, that the good woman was the more eager I should see both. And the rather, as I, to stimulate her, declared that there was more required in my eye to merit the character of a handsome woman than most people thought necessary; and that I had never seen six truly lovely women in my life.

To be brief, she went in; and after a little while came out again. The lady, sir, is retired to her closet. So you may go in and look at the room.

Then how my heart began again to play its pug's tricks!

O Belford! to be so near my angel, think what a painful constraint I was under!

I was resolved to fetch her out, if possible: and pretending to be going — You can't agree as to any *time*, Mrs. Moore, when we can have this third room, can you? — Not that (whispered I, loud enough to be heard in the next room; not that) I would incommode the lady: but I would tell my wife *when*-abouts — and women, you know, Mrs. Moore, love to have everything before them of this nature.

Mrs. Moore, says my charmer (and never did her voice sound so harmonious to me. Oh! how my heart bounded again! It even talked to me, in a manner; for I thought I *heard*, as well as felt, its unruly flutters; and every vein about me seemed a pulse; Mrs. Moore), you may acquaint the gentleman that I shall stay here only for two or three days at most, till I receive an answer to a letter I have written into the country; and rather than be your hindrance, I will take up with any apartment a pair of stairs higher.

Not for the world! Not for the world, young lady! cried I. My wife, well as I love her, should lie in a garret, rather than put such a considerate lady, as you seem to be, to the least inconveniency.

She opened not the door yet; and I said, But since you have so much goodness, madam, if I could but just look into the closet as I stand, I could tell my wife whether it is large enough to hold a cabinet she much values, and will have with her wherever she goes.

Then my charmer opened the door, and blazed upon me, as it were, in a flood of light, like what one might imagine would strike a man, who, born blind, had by some propitious power been blessed with his sight, all at once, in a meridian sun.

Upon my soul, I never was so strangely affected before. I had much ado to forbear discovering myself that instant: but hesitatingly, and in great disorder, I said, looking into the closet and around it, There is room, I see, for my wife's cabinet; and it has many jewels in it of high price; but, upon my soul (for I could not forbear swearing, like a puppy: habit is a cursed thing, Jack —), nothing so valuable as the lady I see, can be brought into it.

She started, and looked at me with terror. The truth of the compliment, as far as I know, had taken dissimultation from my accent.

I saw it was impossible to conceal myself longer from her, any more than (from the violent impulses of my passion) to forbear manifesting myself. I unbuttoned therefore my cape, I pulled off my flapped, slouched hat; I threw open my great-coat, and, like the devil in Milton (an odd comparison though!)

> I started up in my own form divine,
> Touch'd by the beam of her celestial eye,
> More potent than Ithuriel's spear! —

She no sooner saw who it was, than she gave three violent screams; and, before I could catch her in my arms (as I was about to do the moment I discovered myself), down she sunk at my feet, in a fit; which made me curse my indiscretion for so suddenly, and with so much emotion, revealing myself.

The gentlewoman, seeing so strange an alteration in my person and features, and voice, and dress, cried out, Murder, help! murder, help! by turns, for half a dozen times running. This alarmed the house, and up ran two servant-maids, and *my* servant after them.

Up then came running a gentleman and his sister, fetched, and brought in by the maid who had run down; and who having let in a cursed crabbed old wretch, hobbling with his gout, and mumbling with his hoarse broken-toothed voice, was metamorphosed all at once into a lively gay young fellow, with a clear accent, and all his teeth; and she would have it, that I was neither more nor less than the devil, and could not keep her eye from my foot; expecting, no doubt, every minute to see it discover itself to be cloven.

For my part, I was so intent upon restoring my angel, that I regarded nobody else. And at last, she slowly recovering motion, with bitter sighs and sobs (only the whites of her eyes however appearing for some moments), I called upon her in the tenderest accent, as I kneeled by her, my arm supporting her head; My angel! My charmer! My Clarissa! Look upon me, my dearest life! I am not angry with you! I will forgive you, my best beloved!

The gentleman and his sister knew not what to make of all this: and the less, when my fair one, recovering her sight, snatched another look at me; and then again groaned, and fainted away.

I threw up the closet sash for air, and then left her to the care of the young gentlewoman, and to that of Mrs. Moore; who by this time had recovered herself; and then retiring to one corner of the room, I made my servant pull off my gouty stockings, brush my hat, and loop it up into the usual smart cock.

I withdrew once more, finding her beginning to recover, lest the sight of me too soon should throw her back again.

The first words she said, looking round her with great emotion, were, Oh! hide me, hide me! Is he gone? Oh! hide me! Is he gone?

Sir, said Miss Rawlins, coming to me with an air both peremptory and assured, this is some surprising case. The lady cannot bear the sight of you. What you have done is best known to yourself. But another such fit will probably be her last. It would be but kind therefore for you to retire.

The dear creature, said I, may *well* be concerned to see me. If *you,* madam, had a husband who loved you as I love her, you would not, I am confident, fly from him, and expose yourself to hazards, as she does whenever she has not all her way — and yet with a mind not capable of intentional evil — but mother-spoilt! This is her fault, and all her fault: and the more inexcusable it is, as I am the man of her choice, and have reason to think she loves me above all the men in the world.

Here, Jack, was a story to support to the lady; face to face too!

You *speak* like a gentleman; you *look* like a gentleman, said Miss Rawlins. But, sir, this is a strange case; the lady seems to dread the sight of you.

No wonder, madam; taking her a little on one side nearer to Mrs. Moore. I have three times already forgiven the dear creature. — But this *jealousy!*

I then made a motion to go to my beloved. But they desired that I would walk into the next room; and they would endeavour to prevail upon her to lie down.

I begged that they would not suffer her to talk; for that she was accustomed to fits, and when in this way, would talk of anything that came uppermost: and the more she was suffered to run on, the worse she was; and if not kept quiet, would fall into ravings; which might possibly hold her a week.

They promised to keep her quiet; and I withdrew into the next room; ordering every one down but Mrs. Moore and Miss Rawlins.

She was full of exclamations. Unhappy creature! miserable! ruined!

286

and undone! she called herself; wrung her hands, and begged they would assist her to escape from the terrible evils she should otherwise be made to suffer.

They preached patience and quietness to her; and would have had her to lie down; but she refused; sinking, however, into an easy chair; for she trembled so, she could not stand.

By this time I hoped that she was enough recovered to bear a presence that it behoved me to make her bear; and fearing she would throw out something in her exclamations that would still more disconcert me, I went into the room again.

Oh! there he is! said she, and threw her apron over her face. I cannot see him! — I cannot look upon him! Begone, begone! touch me not!

For I took her struggling hand, beseeching her to be pacified; and assuring her that I would make all up with her upon her own terms and wishes.

Base man! said the violent lady, I have no wishes, but never to behold you more! Why must I be thus pursued and haunted? Have you not made me miserable enough already? Despoiled of all succour and help, and of every friend, I am contented to be poor, low, and miserable, so I may be free from your persecutions.

My dear creature, how you rave! You will not easily recover from the effects of this violence. Have patience, my love. Be pacified; and we will coolly talk this matter over; for you expose yourself, as well as me; these ladies will certainly think you have fallen among robbers, and that I am the chief of them.

So you are! so you are! stamping, her face still covered (*she thought of Wednesday night, no doubt*); and sighing as if her heart were breaking, she put her hand to her forehead — I shall be quite distracted!

Unhand me, sir, said she. I will not be touched by you. Leave me to my fate. What right, what title, have you to persecute me thus?

What right, what title, my dear? — But this is not a time — I have a letter from Captain Tomlinson — here it is — offering it to her ——

I will receive nothing from your hands — tell me not of Captain Tomlinson — tell me not of anybody — you have no *right* to invade me thus — once more leave me to my fate — have you not made me miserable enough?

But did I ever think I should be so indifferent to you? However, you must permit me to insist on your reading this letter; and on your seeing Captain Tomlinson, and hearing what he has to say from your uncle. He will be here by and by.

Don't trifle with me, said she, in an imperious tone. Do as you offer. I will not receive any letter from your hands. If I see Captain Tomlinson, it shall be on his *own* account; not on *yours*. You tell me you will send me my apparel: if you would have me believe anything you say, let this be the test of your sincerity. Leave me *now*, and send my things.

Nay, hear me out, madam — The captain, you know, has reported our *marriage* to two different persons. It is come to your brother's ears. My own relations have also heard of it. Letters were brought me from town this morning, from Lady Betty Lawrance and Miss Montague. Here they are. Reflect, madam, I beseech you, reflect upon the fatal consequences which this your high resentment may be attended with.

I then put the letters into her lap, and retired into the next apartment with a low bow and a very solemn air.

I was soon followed by the two women. Mrs. Moore withdrew to give the fair perverse time to read them: Miss Rawlins for the same reason; and because she was sent for home. She wished, if there were time for it, and if it were not quite impertinent in her to desire it, that I would give Mrs. Moore and her a brief history of an affair, which, as she said, bore the face of mystery and surprise.

I said that ours was a very particular case: that were I to acquaint them with it, some part of it would hardly appear credible. But, however, as they seemed to be persons of discretion, I would give them a brief account of the whole; and this in so plain and sincere a manner, that it should clear up to their satisfaction everything that had passed, or might hereafter pass between us.

. . . .

I concluded with cautioning them to be guarded against the inquiries of James Harlowe, and of Captain Singleton, or of any sailor-looking men.

This thou wilt see from the letter itself was necessary to be done. Here therefore thou mayest read it. And a charming letter to my purpose wilt thou find it to be:

To Robert Lovelace, Esq.

Wedn. June 7.

DEAR SIR, — Although I am obliged to be in town to-morrow, or next day at farthest, yet I would not dispense with writing to you, by *one of my servants* (whom I send up before me upon a particular occasion), in order to advertise you, *that it is probable you will hear from some of your own relations on your (supposed) nuptials.*

Her ladyship, it seems, has *business that calls her to town* (and you will possibly choose to put her right. If you do, it will, I presume, *be in confidence*; that nothing may transpire from your own family to contradict what I have given out). To make the best of it now, allow me, sir, once more to beg the lady, as soon as possible, to authenticate the report given out. When both you and the lady join in the acknowledgment of your marriage, it will be impertinent in any one to be inquisitive as to the *day* or *week*. And yet it is very probable that minute inquiries will be made.

What makes young Mr. Harlowe the more earnest to find it out is this: Mr. John Harlowe has told the whole family that he will alter and new-settle his will. Mr. Antony Harlowe is resolved to do the same by his; for, it seems, he has now given over all thoughts of changing his condition; *having lately been disappointed in a view he had of that sort with Mrs. Howe.* These two brothers generally *act in concert;* and Mr. James Harlowe dreads that his younger sister will be, at last, more benefited than he wishes. He reminded his uncle of engagements they had all entered into at his sister's going away, *not to be reconciled but by general consent.*

You cannot imagine how dearly my friend still loves this excellent niece of his. I will give you an instance of it, which affected me a good deal: "If once more," said he (the last time but one we were together), "I can but see this sweet child gracing the upper end of my table, as mistress of my house, in my *allotted month;* all the rest of the family present but as her guests; for so I formerly *would* have it; and had her *mother's consent for it*" — There he stopped; for he was forced to turn his reverend face from me. Tears ran down his cheeks. Fain would he have hid them: but he could not — "Yet — yet," said he — "how — how —" (poor gentleman, he perfectly sobbed) — "how shall I be able to bear the first meeting!"

I will put an end to this long epistle. Be pleased to make my compliments acceptable to the most excellent of women; as well as believe me to be, dear sir, / Your faithful friend, and humble servant, / ANTONY TOMLINSON.

I told the women that what I had mentioned to my spouse of Lady Betty's coming to town with her Niece Montague, and of their intention to visit my beloved, whom they had never seen, nor she them, was real; and that I expected news of their arrival every hour. I then showed them copies of the other two letters which I had left with *her;* the one from Lady Betty, the other from my Cousin Montague.

The women having read the copies of these two letters, I thought I might then threaten and swagger. "But very little heart have I," said I "to encourage such a visit from Lady Betty and Miss Montague to my spouse. For after all, I am tired out with her strange ways. She is not what she was, and (as I told her in your hearing, ladies) I will leave this plaguy island, though the place of my birth, and though the stake I have in it is very considerable, and go and reside in France or Italy, and never think of myself as a married man, *nor live like one.*"

O dear, said one.

That would be a sad thing! said the other.

I turned half round; then facing the fan-player, and the matron: You *yourselves,* ladies, knew not what to believe till *now,* that I have told you our story: and I do assure you, that I shall not give myself the same trouble to convince people I hate: people from whom I neither expect nor desire any favour; and who are determined *not* to be convinced. And what, pray, must be the issue, when her uncle's friend comes, although he seems to be a *truly worthy man?* Is it not natural for him to say, "To what purpose, Mr. Lovelace, should I endeavour to bring about a reconciliation between Mrs. Lovelace and her friends, by means of her elder uncle, when a good understanding is wanting between yourselves?" A fair inference, Mrs. Moore! A fair inference, Miss Rawlins! And here is the unhappiness — till she is reconciled to them, this cursed oath, in her notion, is binding.

And here thou mayest read the letter, No. III.

To Robert Lovelace, Esq.

M. Hall, Wedn. June 7.

COUSIN LOVELACE, — I think you might have found time to let us know of your nuptials being actually solemnized. I might have expected this piece of civility from you. But perhaps the ceremony was performed at the very time that you asked me to be your lady's father — but I shall be angry if I proceed in my guesses — and *little said is soon amended.*

Lady Betty and Niece Charlotte will be in town about business *before you know where you are.* They long to pay their compliments to your fair bride. I suppose you will hardly be at the Lawn when they get in town: because Greme informs me you have sent no orders there for your lady's accommodation. / Your truly affectionate uncle, / M.

This letter clenched the nail. Not but that, Miss Rawlins said, she saw I had been a wild gentleman; and, truly, she thought so the moment she beheld me.

I knew no reason, I said, for my wife to object to my lodging in the same house with her here, any more than in town at Mrs. Sinclair's. But were she to make such objection, I would not quit possession; since it was not unlikely that the same freakish disorder which brought her to Hampstead, might carry her absolutely out of my knowledge.

They both seemed embarrassed; and looked upon one another; yet with such an air as if they thought there was reason in what I said. And I declared myself her boarder, as well as lodger; and dinner-time approaching, was not denied to be the former.

MR. LOVELACE TO JOHN BELFORD, ESQ.

I THOUGHT it was now high time to turn my mind to my beloved; who had had full leisure to weigh the contents of the letters I had left with her.

I therefore requested Mrs. Moore to step in, and desire to know whether she would be pleased to admit me to attend her in her apartment, on occasion of the letters I had left with her; or whether she would favour me with her company in the dining-room?

My revenge, my *sworn* revenge, is nevertheless (adore her as I will) uppermost in my heart. Call it an ungenerous pleasure, if thou wilt: softer hearts than mine know it.

[*In his next letter Lovelace records conversations between Miss*

Rawlins, Mrs. Moore, and Clarissa — which he overhears. Finally Clarissa concludes by saying:]

I am greatly distressed! I know not what to do! But Mrs. Moore, be so good as to give him his letters to him — here they are.

Mrs. Moore then came to me; and I, being afraid that something would pass meantime between the other two, which I should not like, took the letters and entered the room, and found them retired into the closet; my beloved whispering with an air of earnestness to Miss Rawlins, who was all attention.

Her back was towards me; and Miss Rawlins, by pulling her sleeve, giving intimation of my being there — Can I have no retirement uninvaded, sir? said she, with indignation, as if she were interrupted in some talk her heart was in. What business have you here, or with me? You have your letters; have you not?

Lovel. I have, my dear; and let me beg of you to consider what you are about. I every moment expect Captain Tomlinson here. Upon my soul, I do. He has promised to keep from your uncle what has happened; but what will he think if he find you hold in this strange humour?

Cl. I will endeavour, sir, to have patience with you for a moment or two, while I ask you a few questions before this lady, and before Mrs. Moore (who just then came in), both of whom you have prejudiced in your favour by your specious stories: — Will you say, sir, that we are married together? Lay your hand upon your heart, and answer me, am I your wedded wife?

Lovel. What *makes a marriage,* we all know. If it be the union of two hearts (there was a turn, Jack!), to my utmost grief, I must say we are *not*; since now I see you hate me. If it be the completion of marriage, to my confusion and regret, I must own we are *not*. But, my dear, will you be pleased to consider what answer half a dozen people whence you came could give to your question?

Well, 'tis a strange case, a very strange one, said Miss Rawlins; and was going to say further, when the angry beauty, coming towards the door, said, Mrs. Moore, I beg a word with you. And they both stepped into the dining-room.

I stepped to the door: I put it to; and setting my back against it, took her struggling hand. — My dearest life! My angel! said I, why will you thus distress me? Is this the forgiveness which you so solemnly promised?

Unhand me, sir! You have no business with me! You have no right over me! You *know* you have not.

She seemed altogether distressed; was ready to sink.

. . . .

I arose, and approached her with reverence. . . . My dearest creature, said I — and was proceeding — but with a face glowing with conscious dignity, she interrupted me — Ungenerous, ungrateful Lovelace! You know not the value of the heart you have insulted! Nor can you conceive how much my soul despises your meanness. But meanness must ever be the portion of the man who can act vilely!

Leave me then, sir, pursue me not! —

Good heaven! interrupting her — and all this, for what? Had I *not* yielded to your entreaties (forgive me, madam), you could not have carried farther your resentments.

She flung from me to the farther end of the room; and just then Mrs. Moore came up, and told her that dinner was ready; and that she had prevailed upon Miss Rawlins to give her her company.

You must excuse me, Mrs. Moore, said she. Miss Rawlins I hope also will — but I cannot eat — I cannot go down. As for *you*, sir, I suppose you will think it right to depart hence; at least till the gentleman comes whom you expect.

I have no objections to his dining with you, madam, added she, in reply, I suppose, to a further question. But I will not stay a night in the house where he lodges.

But let me ask thee, Belford, art thou not solicitous for me in relation to the contents of the letter which the angry beauty has written and dispatched away by man and horse; and for what may be Miss Howe's answer to it? Art thou not ready to inquire, whether it be not likely that Miss Howe, when she knows of her saucy friend's flight, will be concerned about her letter, which she must know could not be at Wilson's till after that flight; and so, probably, would fall into my hands?

All these things, as thou'lt see in the sequel, are provided for with as much contrivance as human foresight can admit.

.   .   .   .

We had at dinner, besides Miss Rawlins, a young widow-niece of Mrs. Moore, who is come to stay a month with her aunt — *Bevis* her name; very forward, very lively, and a great admirer of *me*, I assure you; hanging smirkingly upon all I said; and prepared to approve of every word before I spoke: and who, by the time we had half dined (by the help of what she had collected before), was as much acquainted with our story as either of the other two.

We had hardly dined, when my coachman, who kept a lookout for Captain Tomlinson, as Will did for old Grimes, conducted hither that worthy gentleman. I led him into the parlour and presented him to the women.

Dear captain, I thought you long; for I have had a terrible conflict with my spouse.

.   .   .   .

The captain leered round him; and said, he believed he could guess from the hints I had given him in town (of my *over-love*), and from what had now passed, that we had not consummated our marriage.

O Jack! how sheepishly then looked, or endeavoured to look, thy friend! how primly goody Moore! how affectedly Miss Rawlins! — while the honest widow Bevis gazed around her fearless; and though only simpering with her mouth, her eyes laughed outright, and seemed to challenge a laugh from every eye in the company.

Well, well, captain, no more of this subject before the ladies. *One* feels (shrugging my shoulders in a bashful *try-to-blush* manner) that *one* is *so* ridiculous — I have been punished enough for my tender folly.

Miss Rawlins had taken her fan, and would needs hide her face behind it — I suppose because her blush was not quite ready.

Mrs. Moore hemmed, and looked down, and by that gave hers over. While the jolly widow, laughing out, praised the captain as one of Hudibras's metaphysicians, repeating,

> He knew what's what, and that's as high
> As metaphysic wit can fly.

This made Miss Rawlins blush indeed: — Fie, fie, Mrs. Bevis! cried she, unwilling, I suppose, to be thought absolutely ignorant.

· · · · · · · · ·

It was now high time to acquaint my spouse that Captain Tomlinson was come. And the rather, as the maid told us that the lady had asked her if such a gentleman was not in the parlour?

Mrs. Moore went up, and requested, in my name, that she would give us audience.

But she returned, reporting my beloved's desire that Captain Tomlinson would excuse her for the present. She was very ill. Her spirits were too weak to enter into conversation with him; and she must lie down. She pleaded a violent headache; and Mrs. Moore confirmed the plea to be just.

Accordingly, after I had had a little private conversation with him, he hurried away.

I had hardly taken leave of the captain, and sat down again with the women, when Will came; and calling me out, "Sir, sir," said he, grinning with a familiarity in his looks as if what he had to say entitled him to take liberties; "I have got the fellow down! I have got old Grimes — Hah, hah, hah, hah! — He is at the Lower Flask — almost in the condition of *David's sow*, and please your honour, here is his letter — from — from Miss Howe — Ha, ha, ha, ha!" laughed the varlet; holding it fast, as if to make conditions with me, and to excite my praises as well as my impatience. —

I could have knocked him down; but he would have his *say* out — "Old Grimes knows not that I have the letter — I must get back to him before he misses it — I only made a pretence to go out for a few minutes — but — but" — and then the dog laughed again — "he *must* stay — old Grimes *must* stay — till I go back to pay the reckoning."

I was once thinking to rumple up this billet till I had broken the seal. *Young* families love ostentatious sealings: and it might have been supposed to have been squeezed in pieces in old Grimes's breeches pocket. But I was glad to be *saved* the guilt as well as suspicion of having a hand in so dirty a trick; for thus much of the contents (enough for my purpose) I was enabled to scratch out in character without it; the folds depriving me only of a few connecting words; which I have supplied between hooks:

"I CONGRATULATE you, my dear, with all my heart and soul, upon [your escape] from the villain. [I long] for the particulars of all. [My mother] is out: but, expecting her return every minute, I dispatched [your] messenger instantly. [I will endeavour to come at] Mrs. Townsend without loss of time; and will write at large in a day or two, if in that time I can see her. [Meantime I] am excessively uneasy for a letter I sent you yesterday by Collins, [who must have left it at] Wilson's after you got away. [It is of very] great importance. [I hope the] villain has it not. I would not for the world [that he should.] Immediately send for it, if, by so doing, the place you are at [will not be] discovered. If he has it, let me know it by some way [out of] hand. If not, you need not send. / Ever, ever yours, / A. H. / *June* 9."

O Jack, what heart's-ease does this *interception* give me! I sent the rascal back with the letter to old Grimes, and charged him to drink no deeper. He owned that he was *half-seas over,* as he phrased it.

Dog! said I, are you not to court one of Mrs. Moore's maids to-night?

Cry your mercy, sir! I will be sober. I had forgot that. But old Grimes is plaguy tough — I thought I should never have got him down.

Away, villain! Let old Grimes come; and on horseback, too, to the door ——

He shall, and please your honour, if I can get him on the saddle, and if he can sit ——

And charge him not to have alighted, nor to have seen *any*body ——

Enough, sir! familiarly nodding his head, to show he took me. And away went the villain — into the parlour, to the women, I.

In a quarter of an hour came old Grimes, on horseback, waving to his saddle-bow, now on this side, now on that; his head, at others, joining to that of his more sober beast.

It looked very well to the women, that I made no effort to speak to old Grimes (though I wished *before them,* that I knew the contents of what he brought); but, on the contrary, desired that they would instantly let my spouse know that her messenger was returned.

Down she flew, violently as she had the headache!

Oh, how I prayed for an opportunity to be revenged of her for the ungrateful trouble she had given to her uncle's friend!

She took the letter from old Grimes with her own hands, and retired to an inner parlour to read it.

She presently came out again to the fellow, who had much ado to sit his horse. Here is your money, friend. I thought you long. But what shall I do to get somebody to go to town immediately for me? I see *you* cannot.

The lady applied to Mrs. Moore: she mattered not the price. Could a man and horse be engaged for her? Only to go for a letter left for her, at one Mr. Wilson's in Pall Mall.

A poor neighbour was hired. A horse procured for him. He had his directions.

But yet, is it not taking pains to come at the finest creature in the world, not for a *transitory moment* only, but for one of our lives? The struggle only, Whether I am to have her in *my own way*, or in *hers?*

.   .   .   .

I went up to my new-taken apartment, and fell to writing in character[1] as usual. I thought I had made good my quarters, but the cruel creature, understanding that I intended to take up my lodgings there, declared with so much violence against it, that I was obliged to submit, and to accept of another lodging about twelve doors off, which Mrs. Moore recommended.

The second fellow came back from town about nine o'clock, with Miss Howe's letter of Wednesday last.

She took the letter with great eagerness, opened it in a hurry (I am glad she did: yet, I believe, all was right) before Mrs. Moore and Mrs. Bevis (Miss Rawlins was gone home); and said, She would not for the world that I should have had that letter, for the sake of her dear friend the writer; who had written to her very uneasily about it.

Her *dear friend!* repeated Mrs. Bevis, when she told me this: such mischief-makers are always deemed *dear friends* till they are found out!

The widow says that I am the finest gentleman she ever beheld.

I have found a warm kiss now and then very kindly taken.

See, Belford, how charmingly things work between me and my new acquaintance the widow! Who knows but that she may, after a little farther intimacy (though I am banished the house on nights), contrive a midnight visit for me to my spouse, when all is still and fast asleep?

Where can a woman be safe, who has once entered the lists with a contriving and intrepid lover?

But as to this *letter,* methinks thou sayest, of Miss Howe?

I knew thou wouldst be uneasy for me: but did not I tell thee that I had provided for everything? That I always took care to keep seals entire and to preserve covers? Was it not easy then, thinkest thou, to contrive a shorter letter out of a longer; and to copy the very words?

And now must all my contrivances be set at work, to intercept the expected letter from Miss Howe; which is, as I suppose, to direct her to a place of safety, and out of my knowledge. Mrs. Townsend is, no doubt, in this case, to smuggle her off. I hope the *villain,* as I am so frequently called between these two girls, will be able to manage this point.

[1 That is, in shorthand.]

I am come back from Mrs. Moore's whither, I went in order to attend my charmer's commands. But no admittance — a very bad night.

A visit from the widow Bevis, in my own apartment. She tells me that my spouse had thoughts last night, after I was gone to my lodgings, of removing from Mrs. Moore's.

I almost wish she had attempted to do so.

Miss Rawlins, it seems, who was applied to upon it, dissuaded her from it.

Mrs. Moore also, though she did not own that Will lay in the house (or rather sat up in it, courting), set before her the difficulties, which, in her opinion, she would have to get clear off, without my knowledge; assuring her, that she could be nowhere more safe than with her, till she had fixed whither to go. And the lady herself recollected that if she went, she might miss the expected letter from her dear friend Miss Howe; which, as she owned, was to direct her future steps.

She must also surely have some curiosity to know what her uncle's friend had to say to her from her uncle, contemptuously as she yesterday treated a man of his importance. Nor could she, I should think, be absolutely determined to put herself out of the way of receiving the visits of two of the principal ladies of my family, and to break entirely with me in the face of them all. Besides, whither could she have gone? Moreover, Miss Howe's letter coming (after her elopement) so safely to her hands, must surely put her into a more confiding temper with me and with every one else, though she would not immediately own it.

At four, the appointed hour, I sent up to desire admittance in the captain's name and my own.

She would wait upon the *captain* presently (not upon me!); and in the parlour, if it were not engaged.

[*After a long conference between Captain Tomlinson, Clarissa, and Lovelace, in which the undeviating attitudes of the unmarried couple are exhibited (Clarissa's longing for a reconciliation with her family, her confidence in Tomlinson, her strong conviction of Lovelace's "vileness"; and on the other side, Lovelace's mixture of passion and his proud desire for revenge), a fragile conclusion is reached. Clarissa says:*]

I am a very unhappy creature! I must resign to the will of Providence, and be patient under evils, which *that* will not permit me to shun. But I have taken my measures. Mr. Lovelace can never make *me* happy, nor I *him*. I wait here only for a letter from Miss Howe. That must determine me —

Determine you as to Mr. Lovelace, madam? interrupted the captain.

296

Cl. I am already determined as to him.

Capt. What shall I say to your Uncle Harlowe, madam? Poor gentleman! how will he be surprised! Adieu, Mr. Lovelace.

She started, sighing. Are you going, sir?

She stood up, holding out one hand, with inimitable dignity and sweetness. I am sorry you are going, sir! I can't help it.

Capt. I will *not* go, madam; his eyes twinkling. I will not go, if my longer stay can do you either service or pleasure.

She sighed, and was silent.

REVENGE, *invoked I to myself, keep thy throne in my heart. If the usurper* LOVE *once more drive thee from it, thou wilt never regain possession!*

Lovel. What I had thought of, what I had intended to propose (and I sighed), was this: That the dear creature, if she will not forgive me, as she promised, will suspend the displeasure she has conceived against me, till Lady Betty arrives. That lady may be the mediatrix between us. This dear creature may put herself into *her* protection, and accompany her down to her seat in Oxfordshire. It is one of her ladyship's purposes to prevail on her supposed new niece to go down with her. It may pass to every one but to Lady Betty, and to you, Captain Tomlinson, and to your friend Mr. Harlowe (as he desires), that we have been some time married: and her being with my relations, will amount to a proof to James Harlowe that we *are*; and our nuptials may be privately, and at this beloved creature's pleasure, solemnized; and your report, captain, authenticated.

Capt. Upon my honour, madam, clapping his hand upon his breast, a charming expedient! This will answer every end.

She mused — she was greatly perplexed — at last, God direct me! said she: I know not what to do. A young unfriended creature, whom have I to advise with? Let me retire, if I *can* retire.

[*When Clarissa returns, she is begged to wait for the visit of Lady Betty.*]

I proposed, as on the morrow night, to go to town; and doubted not to bring the licence up with me on Monday morning. Would she be pleased to assure me that she would not depart from Mrs. Moore's?

She should stay at Mrs. Moore's till she had an answer from Miss Howe.

I told her that I hoped I might have her *tacit* consent, at least, to the obtaining of the licence.

I saw by the turn of her countenance that I should not have asked this question. She was so far from *tacitly* consenting, that she declared to the contrary.

As I never intended, I said, to ask her to enter again into a house, with the people of which she was so much offended, would she be pleased to give orders for her clothes to be brought up hither? Or should Dorcas attend her for any of her commands on that head?

She desired not ever more to see anybody belonging to that house. She might perhaps get Mrs. Moore or Mrs. Bevis to go thither for her, and take her keys with them.

I doubted not, I said, that Lady Betty would arrive by that time. I hoped she had no objection to my bringing that lady and my Cousin Montague up with me?

She was silent.

To be sure, Mr. Lovelace, said the captain, the lady can have no objection to this.

She was still silent. So silence in this case was assent.

MR. LOVELACE TO JOHN BELFORD, ESQ.

Sunday Morning.

I HAVE had the honour of my charmer's company for two complete hours. We met before six in Mrs. Moore's garden. A walk on the heath refused me.

She besought me to give over all thoughts of her. Sometimes, she said, she thought herself cruelly treated by her nearest and dearest relations: at *such* times, a spirit of repining, and even of resentment, took place; and the reconciliation, at other times so desirable, was not then so much the favourite wish of her heart, as was the scheme she had formerly planned — of taking her good Norton for her directress and guide, and living upon her own estate in the manner her grandfather had intended she should live.

And now, Belford, thou perceivest that all my reliance is upon the mediation of Lady Betty and Miss Montague; and upon the hope of intercepting Miss Howe's next letter.

MR. LOVELACE TO JOHN BELFORD, ESQ.

Sunday Afternoon.

O BELFORD! what a hair's-breadth escape I had! Such an one, that I tremble between terror and joy at the thoughts of what *might* have happened, and did not.

Not to keep thee in suspense; I have, within this half-hour, obtained possession of the expected letter from Miss Howe — and by *such* an accident! But here, with the former, I dispatch this; thy messenger waiting.

. . . .

My worthy friend Mrs. Bevis thought one sermon a day, *well* observed, enough; so stayed at home to bear me company.

The lady and Mrs. Moore had not been gone a quarter of an hour, when a young country-fellow on horseback came to the door, and inquired for *Mrs. Harriot Lucas.* The widow and I (undetermined how we were to entertain each other) were in the parlour next the door; and hearing the fellow's inquiry, O my dear Mrs. Bevis, said I, I am undone, undone for ever, if you don't help me out! Since here, in all probability, is a messenger from that implacable Miss Howe with a letter; which if delivered to Mrs. Lovelace, may undo all we have been doing.

What, said she, would you have me do?

Call the maid in this moment, that I may give her her lesson; and if it be as I imagine, I'll tell you what you shall do.

Widow. Margaret! Margaret! come in this minute.

Lovel. What answer, Mrs. Margaret, did you give the man, upon his asking for *Mrs. Harriot Lucas?*

Peggy. I only asked, what was his business, and I came at your call, madam, before he answered.

Lovel. Get out of him his message or letter, and bring it to me, and say nothing to Mrs. Lovelace when she comes in; and here is a guinea for you.

Away went Peggy to the fellow at the door.

Peggy. What is your business, friend, with *Mrs. Harriot Lucas?*

Fellow. I must speak to her her own self.

Lovel. My *dearest* widow, do you personate Mrs. Lovelace — for Heaven's sake do you personate Mrs. Lovelace!

Widow. I personate Mrs. Lovelace, sir! How can I do that? She is fair: I am brown. She is slender: I am plump ——

Lovel. No matter, no matter. The fellow may be a new-come servant: he is not in livery, I see. He may not know her person. You can but be bloated, and in a dropsy.

Widow. Dropsical people look not so fresh and ruddy as I do ——

Lovel. True — but the clown may not know that. 'Tis but for a present deception.

Peggy, Peggy, called I, in a female tone, softly at the door. Madam, answered Peggy; and came up to me to the parlour door.

Lovel. Tell him the lady is ill; and has lain down upon the couch. And get his business from him, whatever you do.

Away went Peggy.

Lovel. Now, my dear widow, lie along on the settee, and put your handkerchief over your face, that, if he *will* speak to you himself, he may not see your eyes and your hair. So — that's right. I'll step into the closet by you.

I did so.

Peggy (returning). He won't deliver his business to me. He will speak to Mrs. Harry Lucas for her own self.

Lovel. (holding the door in my hand). Tell him that this is Mrs. Harriot Lucas; and let him come in. Whisper him (if he doubts) that she is bloated, dropsical, and not the woman she was.

And now, my dear widow, let me see what a charming Mrs. Lovelace you'll make.

In came the fellow, bowing and scraping, his hat poked out before him with both his hands.

Fellow. I'm sorry, madam, an't please you, to find you be'n't well.

Widow. What is your business with me, friend?

Fellow. You are Mrs. Harriot Lucas, I suppose, madam?

Widow. Yes. Do you come from Miss Howe?

Fellow. I do, madam.

Widow. My head aches so dreadfully, I cannot hold it up.

Fellow. Nay, my business is soon known. It is but to give this letter into your own *partiklar* hands. Here it is.

Widow (taking it). From my dear friend Miss Howe? — Ah, my head!

He withdrew, bowing and scraping.

Margaret, whispered I, in a female voice (whipping out of the closet), get him out of the house as fast as you can, lest they come from church, and catch him here.

Here read the letter, if thou wilt:

To Mrs. Harriot Lucas, at Mrs. Moore's, at Hampstead

AFTER the discoveries I had made of the villainous machinations of the *most abandoned of men*, particularized in my long letter of Wednesday last, you will believe, my dearest friend, that my surprise upon perusing yours of Thursday evening from Hampstead was not so great as my indignation. Had the *villain* attempted to fire a city instead of a house, I should not have wondered at it. I gave you in my long letter of Wednesday and Thursday last, reasons why you ought to mistrust that specious villain Tomlinson. That man, my dear, must be a solemn villain. Heaven be praised! you have escaped from all their snares.

Sat. Afternoon.

I have just parted with Mrs. Townsend. She has a *manlike spirit*. And her two brothers being in town, she is sure she can engage them in so good a cause, and (if there should be occasion) *both their ship's crews*, in your service.

Give your consent, my dear; and the *horrid villain* shall be repaid with *broken bones*, at least, for all his vileness! Mrs. Townsend cannot be with you till *Thursday next, or Wednesday at soonest*. Are you sure you can be safe where you are till then? If you remove, let me, the very moment, know whither.

In your letter before me, you mention one written to me: I have not received any such. Therefore he must have it. And if he has, it is a wonder that he did not likewise get my long one of the 7th. Heaven be praised that it came safe to your hands!

And now, Jack, I will suppose that thou hast read this cursed letter. As to Mrs. Townsend; her manlike spirit; her two brothers; and their ship's crews: — Let 'em come! But did I want a plot, what a charming new one does this letter of Miss Howe strike me out! How easy would it be for me to assemble a crew of swabbers, and to create a Mrs. Townsend (whose person, thou seest, my beloved knows not) to come, at Miss Howe's repeated solicitations, in order to carry my beloved to a warehouse of my own providing.

This, however, is my triumphant hope, that at the very time that these ragamuffins will be at Hampstead (looking for us), my dear Miss Harlowe and I shall be fast asleep in each other's arms in town.

Sunday Night — Monday Morning.

When we were in the garden, she told me she had formed her scheme for her future life: that, vile as the treatment was which she had received from me, that was not all the reason she had for rejecting my suit: but that, on the maturest deliberation, she was convinced that she could neither be happy with me, nor make me happy.

All the concession I could bring her to in this whole conference, was, that she would wait the arrival and visit of the two ladies, if they came in a day or two, or before she received the expected letter from Miss Howe.

I shall not entirely trust to this. [*And so he leaves his man behind to watch "every step she can take."*]

. . . .

I came to town about seven this morning. All necessary directions and precautions remembered to be given. I had notice from my proctor that I might have the licence for fetching.

MR. LOVELACE TO JOHN BELFORD, ESQ.

WELL, but now my plots thicken; and my employment of writing to thee on this subject will soon come to a conclusion. For now, having got the licence; and Mrs. Townsend with her tars being to come to Hampstead next Wednesday or Thursday; and another letter possibly or message from Miss Howe, to inquire how Miss Harlowe does, upon the rustic's report of her ill health, and to express her wonder that she has not heard from her in answer to hers on her escape; I must soon blow up the lady, or be blown up myself. And so I am preparing, with Lady Betty and my Cousin Montague, to wait upon my beloved with a coach and four, or a set; for Lady Betty will not stir out with a pair for the world; though but for two or three miles. And this is a well-known part of her character.

But as to the arms and crest upon the coach and trappings?

Dost thou not know that a Blunt's must supply her, while her own is new-lining and repairing? An opportunity she is willing to take now she is in town. Nothing of this kind can be done to her mind in the country. Liveries nearly Lady Betty's.

Thou hast seen Lady Betty Lawrance several times, hast thou not, Belford?

No, never in my life.

But thou hast — and lain with her too; or fame does thee more credit than thou deservest. Why, Jack, knowest thou not Lady Betty's other name?

Other name! Has she two?

She has. And what thinkest thou of Lady Bab. Wallis?

Oh, the devil!

Now thou hast it. Lady Barbara, thou knowest, lifted up in circumstances, and by pride, never appears or produces herself, but on occasions special, to pass to men of quality or price, for a duchess, or countess, at least. She has always been admired for a grandeur in her air that few women of quality can come up to: and never was supposed to be other than what she passed for; though often and often a paramour for lords.

And who, thinkest thou, is my Cousin Montague?

Nay, how should I know?

How indeed! Why, my little Johanetta Golding, a lively, yet modest-looking girl, is my Cousin Montague.

There, Belford, is an aunt! There's a cousin! Both have wit at will. Both are accustomed to ape quality.

This sweet girl will half ruin me. But seest thou not by this time that her reign is short? It must be so. And Mrs. Sinclair has already prepared everything for her reception once more.

At Mrs. Sinclair's, Monday Afternoon.

All's right, as heart can wish! In spite of all objection — in spite of a reluctance next to fainting — in spite of all foresight, vigilance, suspicion — once more is the charmer of my soul in her old lodgings!

I have not time for the particulars of our management.

My beloved is now directing some of her clothes to be packed up — never more to enter this house! Nor ever more will she, I dare say, when once again out of it. And yet Lady Betty and Miss Montague (*a man would be tempted to think, Jack, that they wish her to provoke my vengeance*) declare that I ought to be satisfied with such a proud suspension!

They are entirely attached to her. Whatever she says, *is*, *must be*, Gospel! They are guarantees for her return to Hampstead this night. They are to go back with her. A supper bespoken by Lady Betty at Mrs. Moore's. All the vacant apartments there, by my permission (for I had engaged them for a month certain), to be filled with them and their attendants, for a week at least, or till they can prevail upon the dear perverse, as they hope they shall, to restore me to her favour, and to accompany Lady Betty to Oxfordshire.

In short, we are here, as at Hampstead, all joy and rapture; all of us, except my beloved; in whose sweet face (her almost fainting reluctance to re-enter these doors not overcome) reigns a kind of anxious serenity! But how will even that be changed in a few hours!

Is not *this* the crisis for which I have been long waiting? Shall Tomlinson, shall these women, be engaged; shall so many engines be set at work, at an immense expense, with infinite contrivance; and all to no purpose?

Is not *this* the hour of her trial — and in *her*, of the trial of the virtue of her whole sex, so long premeditated, so long threatened?

Whether her frost be frost indeed? Whether her virtue be principle? Whether, if *once subdued, she will not be always subdued*? And will she not want the very crown of her glory, the proof of her till now all-surpassing excellence, if I stopped short of the ultimate trial?

Now is the end of purposes long overawed, often suspended, at hand. And need I to throw the sins of her cursed family into the too weighty scale?

Abhorred be force! — be the thoughts of force! There's no triumph over the will in force! This I know I have said. But would I not have avoided it, if I could? Have I not tried every other method? And have I any other recourse left me? Can she resent the *last outrage* more than she has resented a *fainter effort*? And if her resentments run ever so high, cannot I repair by matrimony? She will not refuse me, I know, Jack; the haughty beauty will not refuse me, when her pride of being corporally inviolate is brought down.

.   .   .   .

What shall we do now! We are immersed in the depth of grief and apprehension! How ill do women bear disappointment! Set upon going to Hampstead, and upon quitting for ever a house she re-entered with infinite reluctance; what things she intended to take with her ready packed up; herself on tiptoe to be gone; and I prepared to attend her thither; she begins to be afraid that she shall not go this night; and in grief and despair has flung herself into her old apartment; locked herself in; and through the keyhole Dorcas sees her on her knees — praying, I suppose, for a safe deliverance.

And from what? And wherefore these agonizing apprehensions?

Why, here, this unkind Lady Betty, *with* the dear creature's knowledge, though to her concern, and this mad-headed Cousin Montague *without* it, while she was employed in directing her package, have hurried away in the coach to their own lodgings (only, indeed, to put up some night-clothes, and so forth, in order to attend their sweet cousin to Hampstead); and, no less to my surprise than hers, are not yet returned.

I have sent to know the meaning of it.

Oh! here's Lady Betty's servant with a billet.

To Robert Lovelace, Esq.

Monday Night.

EXCUSE US, dear nephew, I beseech you, to my dearest kinswoman. One night cannot break squares. For here Miss Montague has been taken violently ill with three fainting fits, one after another.

If she be better, we will certainly go with you to-morrow morning, after we have breakfasted with *her*, at your lodgings. But, whether she be, or not, I will do myself the pleasure to attend your lady to Hampstead: and will be with you for that purpose about nine in the morning. With the compliments to your most worthy beloved, I am / Yours affectionately, / ELIZAB. LAWRANCE.

Faith and troth, Jack, I know not what to do with myself: for here, just now having sent in the above note by Dorcas, out came my beloved with it in her hand: in a fit of frenzy! True, by my soul!

It seems, when she read the billet — Now indeed, said she, am I a lost creature! O the poor Clarissa Harlowe!

Down sunk she at my feet, as soon as she approached me; her charming bosom heaving to her uplifted face; and clasping her arms about my knees, Dear Lovelace, said she, if ever — if ever — and, unable to speak another word, quitting her clasping hold, down prostrate on the floor sunk she neither in a fit nor out of one.

I lifted her into a chair; and in words of disordered passion, told her, all her fears were needless.

At last, with a heart-breaking sob, I see, I see, Mr. Lovelace, in broken sentences she spoke, I see, I see — that at last — at last — I am ruined! Ruined, if *your* pity — let me implore your pity! And down on her bosom, like a half-broken-stalked lily, top-heavy with the overcharging dews of the morning, sunk her head, with a sigh that went to my heart.

All I could think of to reassure her, when a little recovered, I said.

Why did I not send for their coach, as I had intimated? It might return in the morning for the ladies.

Let her go to Lady Betty's lodgings, then; *directly* go; if the person I called Lady Betty was really Lady Betty.

IF, my dear! Good Heaven! What a villain does that IF show you believe me to be!

I cannot help it. I beseech you once more, let me go to Mrs. Leeson's, if *that* IF ought not to be said.

Then assuming a more resolute spirit — I will go! I will inquire my way! I will go by myself! And would have rushed by me.

I folded my arms about her to detain her; pleading the bad way I heard poor Charlotte was in; and what a farther concern her impatience, if she went, would give to poor Charlotte.

She would believe nothing I said, unless I would instantly order a coach (since she was not to have Lady Betty's, nor was permitted to go to Mrs. Leeson's), and let her go in it to Hampstead, late as it was; and all alone; so much the better.

I humoured her, and ordered Will to endeavour to get a coach directly, to carry us to Hampstead; I cared not at what price.

Robbers, with whom I would have terrified her, she feared not — ₁ was all her fear, I found; and this house her terror; for I saw plainly that she now believed that Lady Betty and Miss Montague were both impostors.

O Jack, the rage of love, the rage of revenge, is upon me! By turns they tear me!

.   .   .   .

Will is not yet come back. Near eleven.

.   .   .   .

Will is this moment returned. No coach to be got, either *for love or money*.

Once more she urges — To Mrs. Leeson's let me go, Lovelace! Good Lovelace, let me go to Mrs. Leeson's! What is Miss Montague's illness to my terror? — For the Almighty's sake, Mr. Lovelace! — her hands clasped.

O my angel! What a wildness is this! Do you know, do you see, my dearest life, what appearance your causeless apprehensions have given you? Do you know it is past eleven o'clock?

Twelve, one, two, three, four — any hour — I care not. If you mean me honourably, let me go out of this hated house!

Thou'lt observe, Belford, that though this was written afterwards, yet (as in other places) I write it as it was spoken and happened, as if I had retired to put down every sentence as spoken. I know thou likest this lively *present-tense manner*, as it is one of my peculiars.

Just as she had repeated the last words, *If you mean me honourably, let me go out of this hated house*, in came Mrs. Sinclair, in a great ferment. And what, pray, madam, has *this* house done to you? Mr. Lovelace, you have known me some time; and, if I have not the niceness of this lady, I hope I do not deserve to be treated thus!

I may be to blame, Jack, for suffering this wretch to give herself these airs; but her coming in was without my orders.

The old beldam, throwing herself into a chair, fell a blubbering and exclaiming. And the pacifying of her, and endeavouring to reconcile the lady to her, took up till near one o'clock.

And thus, between terror, and the late hour, and, what followed, she was diverted from the thoughts of getting out of the house to Mrs. Leeson's, or anywhere else.

MR. LOVELACE TO JOHN BELFORD, ESQ.

Tuesday Morn., June 13.

AND now, Belford, I can go no farther. The affair is over. Clarissa lives. And I am / Your humble servant, / R. LOVELACE.

The whole of this black transaction is given by the injured lady to Miss Howe, in her subsequent letters, dated Thursday, July 6.

MR. BELFORD TO ROBERT LOVELACE, ESQ.

Watford, Wedn., June 14.

O THOU savage-hearted monster! What work hast thou made in *one guilty hour*, for a *whole age* of repentance!

Poor, poor lady! It is a pain to me that I ever saw her. Such an adorer of virtue to be sacrificed to the vilest of her sex; and thou their implement in the devil's hands, for a purpose so base, so ungenerous, so inhumane!

I can tell thee, it is well either for thee or for me, that I am not the brother of the lady. Had I been her brother, her violation must have been followed by the blood of one of us.

That thou couldst behold her frenzy on this occasion, and her half-speechless, half-fainting prostration at thy feet, and yet retain thy evil purposes, will hardly be thought credible, even by those who know *thee*, if they have seen *her*.

Poor, poor lady! With such noble qualities as would have adorned the most exalted married life, to fall into the hands of the *only* man in the world who could have treated her as thou hast treated her! And to let loose the old dragon, as thou properly callest her, upon the before-affrighted innocent, what a barbarity was *that*! What a *poor* piece of barbarity! in order to obtain by terror what thou despairedst to gain by love, though supported by stratagems the most insidious!

O LOVELACE! LOVELACE! *had I doubted it before, I should now be convinced that there must be a* WORLD AFTER THIS, *to do justice to injured merit, and to punish barbarous perfidy!* Could the divine SOCRATES, and the divine CLARISSA, otherwise have suffered?

But prithee, dear Lovelace, repair thy sin of ingratitude, by conferring upon thyself the highest honour thou *canst* receive, in making her lawfully thine.

But if thou canst not prevail upon thyself to do her this justice, I think I should not scruple a tilt with thee (an everlasting rupture *at least* must follow) if thou sacrificest her to the accursed women.

Thou art desirous to know what advantage I reap by my uncle's demise. I deem it will be upwards of £5,000 in cash and a clear £1,000 a year.

I wish from my heart thou wert a money-lover! Were the estate to be double the value, thou shouldst have it every shilling; only upon one condition — that thou wouldst permit me the honour of being this fatherless lady's *father*, as it is called, at the altar.

MR. LOVELACE TO JOHN BELFORD, ESQ.

Thursday, June 15.

THY severity — to what purpose, when the mischief is done? when, of consequence, the affair is irretrievable? and when a Clarissa could not move me?

Well, but after all, I must own that there is something very singular in this lady's case.

But people's extravagant notions of things alter not *facts*, Belford: and, when all's done, Miss Clarissa Harlowe has but run the fate of a thousand others of her sex — only that they did not set such a romantic value upon what they call their *honour*; that's all.

Hitherto she is all angel: and was not that the point which at setting out I proposed to try? And was not *cohabitation* ever my darling view? And am I not now, at last, in the high road to it? It is true that I have nothing to boast of as to her will. *The very contrary.* But now are we come to the test, whether she cannot be brought to make the best of an irreparable evil. To thy urgent supplication then, that I will do her grateful justice by marriage, let me answer in Matt Prior's two lines on his hoped-for auditorship; as put into the mouths of his St. John and Harley;

> —— Let that be done, which Matt doth say.
> YEA, quoth the Earl — BUT NOT TO-DAY.

Thou seest, Jack, that I make no resolutions, however, against doing her, one time or other, the wished-for justice, even were I to succeed in my principal view, *cohabitation*. And of this I do assure thee, that, if I ever marry, it must, it shall be Miss Clarissa Harlowe. Nor is her honour at all impaired with *me*, by what she has *so far* suffered: but the contrary. She must only take care, that, if she be at last brought to forgive me, she show me that her Lovelace is the only man on earth whom she could have forgiven on the like occasion.

But, ah, Jack! what, in the meantime, shall I do with this admirable creature? At present (I am loath to say it — but, at present) she is quite stupefied.

I had rather, methinks, she should have retained all her active powers, though I had suffered by her nails and her teeth, than that she should be sunk into such a state of absolute — insensibility (shall I call it?) as she has been in ever since Tuesday morning. She is at present as destitute of will as she always seemed to be of desire. I must not therefore think of leaving her yet for two days together.

. . . .

I have just now had a specimen of what the resentment of this dear creature will be when quite recovered: an affecting one! For, entering her apartment after Dorcas; and endeavouring to sooth and pacify her disordered mind; in the midst of my blandishments, she held up to Heaven, in a speechless agony, the innocent licence (which she has in her own power).

Thou wilt guess, by what I have written, that some *little* art has been made use of: but it was with a *generous* design (if thou'lt allow me the word on such an occasion) in order to lessen the too quick sense she was likely to have of what she was to suffer. A contrivance I never had occasion for before, and had not thought of now, if Mrs. Sinclair had not proposed it to me: to whom I left the management of it: and I have done nothing but curse her ever since, lest the quantity should have for ever damped her charming intellects.

Friday, June 16.

Caesar never knew what it was to be *hipped*, till he arrived at the height of his ambition; nor did thy Lovelace know what it was to be gloomy, till he had completed his wishes upon the most charming creature in the world.

Yet why say I *completed?* when the *will*, the *consent*, is wanting — and I have still views before me of obtaining that? For here the poor lady has run into a contrary extreme to that I told thee of in my last: for now is she as much too lively, as before she was too stupid; and, abating that she has pretty frequent lucid intervals, would be deemed raving mad, and I should be obliged to confine her.

I am most confoundedly disturbed about it: for I begin to fear that her intellects are irreparably hurt. Who the devil could have expected such strange effects from a cause so common and so slight?

Last night, for the first time since Monday last, she got to her pen and ink. I hope this employment will help to calm her spirits.

.   .   .   .

Just now Dorcas tells me that what she writes she tears, and throws the paper in fragments under the table, either as not knowing what she does, or disliking it: then gets up, wrings her hands, weeps, and shifts her seat all round the room: then returns to her table, sits down, and writes again.

.   .   .   .

One odd letter, as I may call it, Dorcas has this moment given me from her. *Carry this*, said she, *to the vilest of men*. Dorcas, a toad, brought it, without any further direction, to *me*. I sat down, intending (though 'tis pretty long) to give thee a copy of it: but, for my life, I cannot; 'tis so extravagant. And the original is too much an original to let it go out of my hands.

But some of the scraps and fragments, as either torn through, or flung aside, I will copy, for the novelty of the thing, and to show thee how her mind works now she is in this whimsical way.

By the first thou'lt guess that I have told her that Miss Howe is very ill, and can't write; that she may account the better for not having received the letter designed for her.

Paper I. *(Torn in two pieces.)*

MY DEAREST MISS HOWE, — O what dreadful, dreadful things have I to tell you! But yet I cannot tell you neither. But say, are you really ill, as a vile, vile creature informs me you are?

But he never yet told me truth, and I hope has not in this: and yet, if it were not true, surely I should have heard from you before now! But what have I to do to upbraid? You may well be tired of me! And if you are, I can forgive you; for I am tired of myself: and all my own relations were tired of me long before you were.

How good you have always been to me, mine own dear Anna Howe! But how I ramble!

Paper II. *(Scratched through, and thrown under the table.)*

— And can you, my dear honoured papa, resolve for ever to reprobate your poor child? But I am sure you would not, if you knew what she has suffered since her unhappy — And will nobody plead for your poor suffering girl? My name is — I don't know what my name is! I never dare to wish to come into your family again! But your heavy curse, my papa — yes, I *will* call you papa, and help yourself as you can — for you are my own dear papa, whether you will or not — and though I am an unworthy child — yet I *am* your child ——

Paper V

Rejoice not now, my Bella, my sister, my friend; but pity the humbled creature, whose foolish heart you used to say you beheld through the thin veil of humility which covered it.

It must have been so! My fall had not else been permitted.

You penetrated my proud heart with the jealousy of an elder sister's searching eye.

You knew me better than I knew myself.

Hence your upbraidings and your chidings, when I began to totter.

Paper VII

Thou pernicious caterpillar, that preyest upon the fair leaf of virgin fame, and poisonest those leaves which thou canst not devour!

Thou fell blight, thou eastern blast, thou overspreading mildew, that destroyest the early promises of the shining year! that mockest the laborious toil, and blastest the joyful hopes, of the painful husbandman!

Thou fretting moth, that corruptest the fairest garment!

Thou eating canker-worm, that preyest upon the opening bud, and turnest the damask rose into livid yellowness!

If, as religion teaches us, God will judge us, in a great measure, by our benevolent or evil actions to one another — O wretch!

Paper VIII

At first, I saw something in your air and person that displeased me not. Your birth and fortunes were no small advantages to you. You acted not ignobly by my passionate brother. Everybody said you were brave: everybody said you were generous. A *brave* man, I thought, could not be a *base* man: a *generous* man could not, I believed, be *ungenerous*, where he acknowledged *obligation*. Thus prepossessed, all the rest that my soul loved and wished for in your reformation, I hoped! I knew not, but by report, any flagrant instances of your vileness.

Yet, God knows my heart, I had no culpable inclinations! I honoured virtue! I hated vice! But I knew not that you were vice itself!

After all, Belford, I have just skimmed over these transcriptions of Dorcas; and I see there are method and good sense in some of them, wild as others of them are; and that her memory, which serves her so well for these poetical flights, is far from being impaired. And this gives me hope that she will soon recover her charming intellects — though I shall be the sufferer by their restoration, I make no doubt.

But, in the letter she wrote to me, there are yet greater extravagances; and though I said it was too affecting to give thee a copy of it, yet, after I have let thee see the loose papers enclosed, I think

309

I may throw in a transcript of that. Dorcas therefore shall here transcribe it. *I* cannot.

To Mr. Lovelace

I NEVER intended to write another line to you. I would not see you, if I could help it. O that I never had!

What you, or Mrs. Sinclair, or somebody (I cannot tell who) have done to my poor head, you best know; but I shall never be what I was. My head is gone. I have wept away all my brain, I believe; for I can weep no more. Indeed I have had my full share; so it is no matter.

But, good now, Lovelace, don't set Mrs. Sinclair upon me again. I never did her any harm. She *so* affrights me, when I see her! Ever since — when was it? I cannot tell. *You* can, I suppose.

I will never be Lovelace — let my uncle take it as he pleases.

Well, but now I remember what I was going to say. It is for *your* good — not *mine* — for nothing can do me good now! O thou villainous man! thou hated Lovelace!

Alas! you have killed my head among you — I don't say who did it! God forgive you all! But had it not been better to have put me out of all your ways at once? You might safely have done it! For nobody would require me at your hands — no, not a soul — except, indeed, Miss Howe would have said, when she should see you, What, Lovelace, have you done with Clarissa Harlowe? And then you could have given any slight gay answer — Sent her beyond sea; or, She has run away from me, as she did from her parents. And this would have been easily credited; for you know, Lovelace, she that could run away from *them*, might very well run away from *you*.

But this is nothing to what I wanted to say. Now I have it!

Then *this* is it — I never shall be myself again: I have been a very wicked creature — a vain, proud, poor creature — full of secret pride — which I carried off under an humble guise, and deceived everybody — my sister says so — and now I am punished. So let me be carried out of this house, and out of your sight; and let me be put into that Bedlam privately, which once I saw: but it was a sad sight to me then! Little as I thought what I should come to *myself*! That is all I would say: this is all I have to wish for — then I shall be out of all your ways; and I shall be taken care of; and bread and water, without your tormentings, will be dainties; and my straw bed the easiest I have lain in — for — I cannot tell how long!

So, suppose, instead of Bedlam, it were a private madhouse, where nobody comes! That will be better a great deal.

But, another thing, Lovelace: don't let them use me cruelly when I am there — *you* have used me cruelly enough, you know!

. . . .

A little interval seems to be lent me. I had begun to look over what I have written. It is not fit for any one to see.

If, therefore, I have not already mentioned my earnest desire, let me tell you, it is *this*: that I be sent out of this abominable house without delay, and locked up in some private madhouse about this town; for such it seems there are; never more to be seen, or to be produced to anybody, except in your own vindication, if you should be charged with the murder of my person; a much lighter crime than that of my honour, which the greatest villain on earth has robbed me of. And deny me not this my last request, I beseech you; and one other, and that is, never to let me see you more! This surely may be granted to / The miserably abused / CLARISSA HARLOWE.

I will not hear thy heavy preachments, Belford, upon this affecting letter. So, not a word of that sort! The paper, thou'lt see, is blistered with the tears even of the hardened transcriber; which has made her ink run here and there.

I know thou wilt blame me for having had recourse to *art*. But do not physicians prescribe opiates in acute cases, where the violence of the disorder would be apt to throw the patient into a fever or delirium? I aver that my motive for this expedient was *mercy*; nor could it be anything else.

If she escape a settled delirium when my plots unravel, I think it is all I ought to be concerned about. What, therefore, I desire of thee is, that if two constructions may be made of my actions, thou wilt afford me the most favourable. For this, not only friendship, but my own ingenuousness, which has furnished thee with the knowledge of the facts against which thou art so ready to inveigh, require of thee.

Meantime, I have a little project come into my head, of a *new* kind — just for amusement-sake, that's all: variety has irresistible charms. I cannot live without intrigue. My charmer has no passions; that is to say, none of the passions that I want her to have. She engages all my reverence. I am at present more inclined to regret what I have done, than to proceed to new offences: and shall regret it till I see how she takes it when recovered.

Shall I tell thee my project? 'Tis not a high one. 'Tis this: to get hither Mrs. Moore, Miss Rawlins, and my widow Bevis; for they are desirous to make a visit to my spouse, now we are so happy together. And, if I can order it right, Belton, Mowbray, Tourville, and I, will show them a little more of the ways of this wicked town than they at present know.

Sunday Afternoon, 6 o'clock (June 18).

I went out early this morning, and returned not till just now; when I was informed that my beloved, in my absence, had taken it into her head to attempt to get away.

[*Mrs. Sinclair stopped her.*]

I will endeavour to see her. It must be in her own chamber, I suppose; for she will hardly meet me in the dining-room. What advantage will the confidence of our sex give me over the modesty of hers, if she be recovered! *I*, the most confident of men: *she*, the most delicate of women. Sweet soul! methinks I have her before me: her face averted: speech lost in sighs — abashed — conscious — what a triumphant aspect will this give me, when I gaze in her downcast countenance!

. . . .

This moment Dorcas tells me she believes she is coming to find me out. She asked her after me: and Dorcas left her, drying her red-swollen eyes at her glass (no design of moving me by her tears!); sighing too sensibly for my courage. But to what purpose have I gone thus far, if I pursue not my principal end? Niceness must be a little abated. She knows the worst. That she cannot fly me; that she must see me; and that I can look her into a sweet confusion; are circumstances greatly in my favour. What can she do but rave and exclaim? I am used to raving and exclaiming — but, if recovered, I shall see how she behaves upon this our first sensible interview after what she has suffered.

Here she comes!

She entered with such dignity in her manner, as struck me with great awe, and prepared me for the poor figure I made in the subsequent conversation.

You see before you, sir, the wretch whose preference of you to all your sex you have rewarded — as it indeed *deserved* to be rewarded. My father's dreadful curse has already operated upon me in the very letter of it, as to this life; and it seems to me too evident that it will not be your fault that it is not entirely completed in the loss of my soul, as well as of my honour.

My dear — my love — I — I — I never — no never — lips trembling, limbs quaking, voice inward, hesitating, broken — never surely did miscreant look so *like* a miscreant! While thus she proceeded, waving her snowy hand, with all the graces of moving oratory:

Tell me (for no doubt thou hast some scheme to pursue), tell me, since I am a prisoner, as I find, in the vilest of houses, and have not a friend to protect or save me, what thou intendest shall become of the remnant of a life not worth the keeping? Tell me, if yet there are more evils reserved for me; and whether thou hast entered into a compact with the grand deceiver, in the person of his horrid agent in this house; and if the ruin of my soul, that my father's curse may be fulfilled, is to complete the triumphs of so vile a confederacy? Answer me! Say, if thou hast courage to speak out to her whom thou hast ruined, tell me what *further* I am to suffer from thy barbarity?

What — what-a — what has been done — I, I, I — cannot but say — must own — must confess — hem — hem —— is not right — is not what should have been — but-a — but — but — I am truly — truly — sorry for it — upon my soul I am — and — and — will do all — do everything — do what — whatever is incumbent upon me — all that you — that you — that you shall require, to make you amends!

O Belford! Belford! whose the triumph now! HERS, or MINE?

Thou wouldst tell me, I suppose — I know what thou wouldst tell me — but thinkest thou that *marriage will satisfy for a guilt like thine?*

Let me therefore know whether I am to be controlled in the future disposal of myself? Whether, in a country of liberty, as *this*, where the *sovereign* of it must not be guilty of *your* wickedness; and where *you* neither durst have attempted it, had I one friend or relation to look upon me; I am to be kept here a prisoner, to sustain fresh injuries? Whether, in a word, you intend to hinder me from going whither my destiny shall lead me?

After a pause; for I was still silent:

Can you not answer me this plain question? I quit all claim, all expectation, upon you — what right have you to detain me here?

I could not speak. What could I say to such a question?

Presume not, interrupted she, base as thou art, to say one word in thine own vindication. I wonder I could not distinguish the behaviour of the unmatronlike jilt, whom thou broughtest to betray me, from the worthy lady whom thou hast the honour to call thy aunt: and that I could not detect the superficial creature whom thou passedst upon me for the virtuous Miss Montague.

That they were, interrupting me, *verily* and *indeed* Lady Betty Lawrance and thy Cousin Montague! O wretch! I see by thy solemn averment (*I had not yet averred it*) what credit ought to be given to all the rest. Had I no other proof —

The two women, she was convinced, were imposters. She knew not but Captain Tomlinson and Mr. Mennell were so too. But whether *they* were so or not, *I* was. And she insisted upon being at her own disposal for the remainder of her short life — for indeed she abhorred me in every light; and more particularly in that in which I offered myself to her acceptance.

And now, Jack, I must address one serious paragraph *particularly* to thee.

I *do* say, if she come *fairly* at her *lights*, at her *clues*, or what shall I call them? her penetration is *wonderful*.

But if she do *not* come at them fairly, *then* is her incredulity, *then* is her antipathy to me evidently accounted for.

I will speak out — Thou couldst not, surely, play me booty, Jack? Surely thou couldst not let thy weak pity for *her* lead thee to an unpardonable breach of trust to thy *friend*, who has been so unreserved in his communications to thee?

I cannot believe thee capable of such a baseness. Satisfy me, however, upon this head.

Monday Morn. 5 o'clock (June 19).

I *must* write on. Nothing else can divert me: and I think thou canst not have been a dog to me. I would fain have closed my eyes; but sleep flies me.

It is now near six. The sun, for two hours past, has been illuminating everything about me: for that impartial orb shines upon mother Sinclair's house, as well as upon any other: but nothing within me can it illuminate.

At day-dawn I looked through the keyhole of my beloved's door. She had declared she would not put off her clothes any more in this house. There I beheld her in a sweet slumber, which I hope will prove refreshing to her disturbed senses; sitting in her elbow-chair, her apron over her head; her head supported by one sweet hand, the other hand hanging down upon her side, in a sleepy lifelessness; half of one pretty foot only visible.

As every vice generally brings on its own punishment, even in *this* life, if anything were to tempt me to doubt of *future* punishment, it would be, that there can hardly be a greater than that which I at this instant experience in my own remorse.

Six o'clock.

Just now Dorcas tells me that her lady is preparing openly, and without disguise, to be gone. Very probable. The humour she flew away from me in last night has given me expectation of such an enterprise.

Now, Jack, to be thus hated and despised! And if I *have* sinned beyond forgiveness ——

.   .   .   .

But she has sent me a message by Dorcas, that she will meet me in the dining-room; and desires (odd enough!) that the wench may be present at the conversation that shall pass between us. This message gives me hope.

Nine o'clock.

Confounded art, cunning villainy! By my soul, she had like to have slipped through my fingers. She meant nothing by her message but to get Dorcas out of the way, and a clear coast. Is a fancied distress sufficient to justify this lady for dispensing with her principles? Does she not show me that she can wilfully deceive, as well as I?

Had she been in the fore-house, and no passage to go through to get at the street door, she had certainly been gone. But her haste betrayed her: for Sally Martin happening to be in the fore-parlour, and hearing a swifter motion than usual, and a rustling of silks, as if from somebody in a hurry, looked out; and seeing who it was, stepped between her and the door, and set her back against it.

You must not go, madam. Indeed you must not.

By what right? And how dare you? And such-like imperious airs the dear creature gave herself. While Sally called out for her aunt; and half a dozen voices joined instantly in the cry, for me to hasten down, to hasten down in a moment.

I was gravely instructing Dorcas abovestairs, and wondering what would be the subject of the conversation to which the wench was to be a witness, when these outcries reached my ears. And down I flew. And there was the charming creature, the sweet deceiver, panting for breath, her back against the partition, a parcel in her hand (women make no excursions without their parcels). Sally, Polly (but Polly obligingly pleading for her), the mother, Mabel, and Peter (the footman of the house) about her; all, however, keeping their distance; the mother and Sally between her and the door — in her soft rage the dear soul repeating, I *will* go! Nobody has a right — I *will* go! If you kill me, women, I won't go up again!

As soon as she saw me, she stepped a pace or two towards me; Mr. Lovelace, I *will* go! said she. Do you authorize these women — What right have they, or *you* either, to stop me?

Is this, my dear, preparative to the conversation you led me to expect in the dining-room? And do you think I can part with you thus? Do you think I will?

And am I, sir, to be thus beset! Surrounded thus? What have these women to do with me?

I desired them to leave us, all but Dorcas, who was down as soon as I. I then thought it right to assume an air of resolution, having found my tameness so greatly triumphed over. And now, my dear, said I (urging her reluctant feet), be pleased to walk into the fore-parlour. Hence, since you will not go upstairs, here we may *hold our parley*; and Dorcas *be witness to it*. And now, madam, seating her, and sticking my hands in my sides, your pleasure!

Insolent villain! said the furious lady. And, rising, ran to the window, and threw up the sash (she knew not, I suppose, that there were iron rails before the windows). And, when she found she could not get out into the street, clasping her uplifted hands together, having dropped her parcel — For the love of God, good honest man! For the love of God, mistress (to two passers-by), a poor, poor creature, said she, ruined ——

I clasped her in my arms, people beginning to gather about the window: and then she cried out, Murder! Help! Help! and carried her up to the dining-room, in spite of her little plotting heart (as I may now call it), although she violently struggled, catching hold of the banisters here and there, as she could. I would have seated her there; but she sunk down half-motionless, pale as ashes. And a violent burst of tears happily relieved her.

Eleven o'clock.

Mrs. Sinclair wishes she never had seen the face of so skittish a lady; and she and Sally are extremely pressing with me, to leave the perverse beauty to their *breaking,* as they call it, for four or five days. But I cursed them into silence; only ordering double precaution for the future.

I thought to have had one trial (having gone so far) for *cohabitation.* But what hope can there be of succeeding? She is invincible! *Against all my notions, against all my conceptions* (thinking of her as a woman, and in the very bloom of her charms), *she is absolutely invincible.* My whole view, at the present, is to do her legal justice, if I can but once more get her out of her altitudes.

᛭ •   •   •   •   •   •   •   •   •   •   •

I have this moment intelligence from Simon Parsons, one of Lord M.'s stewards, that his lordship is very ill. Simon, who is my obsequious servant, in virtue of my presumptive heirship, gives me a hint in his letter that my presence at M. Hall will not be amiss. So I must accelerate, whatever be the course I shall be allowed or compelled to take.

No bad prospects for this charming creature, if the old peer would be so kind as to surrender; and many a summons has his gout given him. A good £8,000 a year, perhaps the title reversionary, or a still higher, would help me up with her.

But now, at last, am I to be admitted to the presence of my angry fair one: after three denials, nevertheless; and a *peremptory* from me, by Dorcas, that I must see her in her chamber, if I cannot see her in the dining-room.

Monday Afternoon.

She began with me like a true woman (*she* in the fault, *I* to be blamed) the moment I entered the dining-room.

I come, said she, into thy detested presence, because I cannot help it. But why am I to be imprisoned here? Although to no purpose, I cannot help ——

Dearest madam, interrupted I, give not way to so much violence. You must know that your detention is entirely owing to the desire I have to make you all the amends that is in my power to make you. And this, as well for *your* sake as *my own*. Surely there is still *one* way left to repair the wrongs you have suffered ——

Canst thou blot out the past week? *Several* weeks past, I should say; ever since I have been with thee? Canst thou call back time? If thou canst ——

Surely, madam, again interrupting her, if I may be permitted to call you *legally* mine, I might have but anticip ——

But thinkest thou that I will give a harlot niece to thy honourable uncle, and to thy *real* aunts; and a cousin to thy cousins from a brothel? For such, in my opinion, is this detested house! Then, lifting up her clasped hands, "Great and good God of Heaven," said she, "give me patience to support myself under the weight of those afflictions, which Thou, for wise and good ends, though at present impenetrable by me, hast permitted!"

Then, turning towards me, who knew neither what to say *to* her, nor *for* myself, I renounce thee for ever, Lovelace! Abhorred of my soul! for ever I renounce thee! Seek thy fortunes wheresoever thou wilt! Only now, that thou hast already ruined me ——

Ruined you, madam — the world need not — I knew not what to say.

Ruined me in my *own* eyes; and that is the same to me as if *all the world* knew it. Hinder me not from going whither my mysterious destiny shall lead me.

I am cut to the heart, madam, with invectives so violent. I am but too sensible of the wrong I have done you, or I could not *bear* your reproaches. The man who perpetrates a villainy, and resolves to go on with it, shows not the compunction I show. Yet, if you think yourself in my power, I would caution you, madam, not to make me desperate. For you *shall* be mine, or my life shall be the forfeit! Nor is life worth having without you!

Be *thine*! I be *thine*! said the passionate beauty. Oh, how lovely in her violence!

I never, never will be yours! said she, clasping her hands together, and lifting up her eyes. I never will be yours!

Hear me out, I beseech you, madam; for she was going to speak with an aspect unpacifically angry: the God, whom you serve, requires but repentance and amendment: imitate *Him*, my dearest love, and bless me with the *means* of reforming a course of life that begins to be hateful to me.

Tell me, then, is there any reality in the treaty thou hast pretended to be on foot between my uncle and Captain Tomlinson and thyself?

This was a cursed thrust. What could I say?

In short, I solemnly averred that there was!

Let me ask thee next, said she, if *really* and *truly*, they were Lady Betty Lawrance and thy Cousin Montague? What sayest thou — hesitate not — what sayest thou to this question?

Astonishing, my dear, that you should suspect them!

Let me, my dearest love, be enabled to-morrow to call you lawfully mine, and we will set out the next day, if you please, to Berkshire, to my Lord M.'s, where they both are at this time; and you shall convince yourself by your own eyes, and by your own ears; which you will believe sooner than all I can say or swear.

Now, Belford, I had really some apprehension of treachery from thee; which made me so miserably evade; for else, I could *as* safely have sworn to the truth of this, as to that of the former; but she pressing me still for a categorical answer, I ventured plumb; and swore to it (*lover's oaths, Jack*) that they were really and truly Lady Betty Lawrance and my Cousin Montague.

She lifted up her hands and eyes — What can I think! — What can I think!

You *think* me a devil, madam; a very devil! or you could not after you have put these questions to me, seem to doubt the truth of answers so solemnly sworn to.

I thought she had now reason to be satisfied; and I begged her to allow me to talk to her of to-morrow, as of the happiest day of my life. We have the licence, madam — and you *must* excuse me, that I cannot let you go hence till I have tried every way I *can* try to obtain your forgiveness.

And am I then (with a kind of frantic wildness) to be detained a prisoner in this horrid house? Am I, sir? Take care! Take care! holding up her hand, menacing, how you make me desperate. If I fall, though by my own hand, inquisition will be made for my blood: and be not out in thy plot, Lovelace, if it *should* be so — make *sure* work, I charge thee: dig a hole deep enough to cram in and conceal this unhappy body; for, depend upon it, that some of those who will not stir to protect me living, will move heaven and earth to avenge me dead!

A horrid dear creature! By my soul, she made me shudder!

Here I was forced to leave off, and sing a song to myself. I aimed at a lively air; but I croaked rather than sung, and fell into the old dismal thirtieth of January strain.

What a-devil ails me! I can neither think nor write!

. . . .

But to proceed with my narrative.

The dear creature resumed the topic her heart was so firmly fixed upon; and insisted upon quitting the *odious house*, and that in very high terms.

I urged her to meet me the next day at the altar in either of the two churches mentioned in the licence. And I besought her, whatever were her resolution, to let me debate this matter calmly with her.

If, she said, I would have her give what I desired the least moment's consideration, I must not hinder her from being her own mistress. To what purpose did I ask her *consent*, if she had not a power over either her own person or actions?

Still she insisted upon being a free agent; of seeing herself in other lodgings before she would give what I urged the *least* consideration. Nor would she promise me favour even then, or to permit my visits. How then, as I asked her, could I comply, without resolving to lose her for ever?

She put her hand to her forehead often as she talked; and at last, pleading disorder in her head, retired; neither of us satisfied with the other. But *she* ten times more dissatisfied with me, than I with her.

Monday Night.

How determined is this lady! Again had she like to have escaped us! What a fixed resentment! She only, I find, assumed a little calm, in order to quiet suspicion. She was got down, and actually had unbolted the street door, before I could get to her, alarmed as I was by Mrs. Sinclair's cookmaid, who was the only one that saw her fly through the passage: yet lightning was not quicker than I.

Again I brought her back to the dining-room, with infinite reluctance on her part. And before her face, ordered a servant to be placed constantly at the bottom of the stairs for the future.

She seemed even choked with grief and disappointment.

Dorcas was exceedingly assiduous about her; and confidently gave it as her own opinion, that the dear lady should be permitted to go to another lodging, since *this* was so disagreeable to her: were she to be killed for saying so, she would say it. And was *good* Dorcas for this afterwards.

But for some time the dear creature was all passion and violence.

I see, I see, said she, when I had brought her up, what I am to expect from your new professions, O vilest of men!

Have I offered to you, my beloved creature, anything that can justify this impatience after a more hopeful calm?

She wrung her hands. She disordered her head-dress. She tore her ruffles. She was in a perfect frenzy.

She arose, Dorcas being about to withdraw; and wildly caught hold of her arm; O Dorcas! If thou art of mine own sex, leave me not, I charge thee! Then quitting Dorcas, down she threw herself upon her knees, in the furthermost corner of the room, clasping a chair with her face laid upon the bottom of it! O where can I be safe? Where, where can I be safe, from this man of violence?

This gave Dorcas an opportunity to confirm herself in her lady's confidence: the wench threw herself at my feet, while I seemed in violent wrath; and, embracing my knees, Kill me, sir, kill me, sir, if you please! I must throw myself in your way, to save my lady. I beg your pardon, sir — but you must be set on! God forgive the mischief-makers! But your own heart, if left to itself, would not permit these things! Spare, however, sir! spare my lady, I beseech you! bustling on her knees about me, as if I were intending to approach her lady, had I not been restrained by her.

. . . .

The lady tells Dorcas that her heart is broken; and that she shall live but a little while. I think nothing of that, if we marry.

And for what should her heart be broken? Her will is unviolated: — at *present,* however, her will is unviolated. The destroying of good habits, and the introducing of bad, to the corrupting of the whole heart, is the violation. That her will is not to be corrupted, that her mind is not to be debased, she has hitherto unquestionably proved.

What nonsense, then, to suppose that such a mere *notional violation* as she has suffered, should be able to cut asunder the strings of life?

To be sure she ought to have forgot it by this time, except the charming, charming consequence happen, that I still am in hopes will happen, were I to proceed no further. And, if she apprehend this herself, then has the dear over-nice soul some reason for taking it so much to heart; and yet would not, I think, refuse to legitimate.

O Jack! had I an imperial diadem, I swear to thee that I would give it up, even to my *enemy,* to have one charming boy by this lady. And should she *escape me,* and no such effect follow, my revenge on her family, and, in *such* case, on herself would be incomplete, and I should reproach myself as long as I lived.

[*Clarissa gives to Dorcas an agreement, written and signed, promising Dorcas a life annuity if she helps Clarissa to escape from Mrs. Sinclair's. Dorcas, double-dealing, agrees with Lovelace to inveigle Clarissa into an escape with a pretended dowager (actually sister to Mrs. Sinclair) and thus to betray Clarissa into Lovelace's arms. The dowager ("Mother H") appears in her coach; but Clarissa, suspicious, declines to go with her, and Lovelace's plot fails. Meanwhile a letter from Tomlinson — left opened where Clarissa will see it — tells her*

*that her Uncle John on his birthday (June 29) will come to London
to see her then married. After a scene of recrimination between
Clarissa and Lovelace, he reflects:*]

Oh, that she would forgive me! Would she but generously forgive
me, and receive my vows at the altar, at the *instant* of her forgiving
me, that I might not have time to relapse into my old prejudices! By
my soul, Belford, this dear girl gives the lie to all our rakish maxims.
There must be something more than a *name* in virtue! I now see that
there is! *Once subdued, always subdued* — 'tis an egregious falsehood! But oh, Jack, she never *was* subdued. What have I obtained
but an increase of shame and confusion! While her glory has been
established by her sufferings!

MR. LOVELACE TO JOHN BELFORD, ESQ.

Wednesday Night.

A MAN is just now arrived from M. Hall, who tells me that
my lord is in a very dangerous way. The gout is in his stomach to an
extreme degree, occasioned by drinking a great quantity of lemonade.

A man of £8,000 a year to prefer his appetite to his health! He
deserves to die! But we have all of us our inordinate passions to
gratify: and they generally bring their punishment along with them
— so witness the nephew, as well as the uncle.

The man says that his lordship was so bad when he came away
that the family began to talk of sending for me in post-haste. As I
know the old peer has a good deal of cash by him, of which he seldom
keeps account, it behoves me to go down as soon as I can. But what
shall I do with this dear creature the while? To-morrow over, I shall,
perhaps, be able to answer my own question. I am afraid she will
make me desperate.

Thursday Noon, June 22.

At my repeated requests, she met me at six this morning. She was
ready dressed; for she has not had her clothes off ever since she
declared that they never more should be off in this house. And
charmingly she looked, with all the disadvantages of a three hours'
violent stomach-ache (for Dorcas told me that she had been really
ill), no rest, and eyes red, and swelled with weeping.

I have been endeavouring, said she, *since I am not permitted to
avoid you,* to obtain a composure which I never more expected to
see you in. How long I may enjoy it, I cannot tell. But I hope I shall
be enabled to speak to you without that vehemence which I expressed yesterday, and could not help it.

After a pause (for I was all attention) thus she proceeded:

It is easy for me, Mr. Lovelace, to see that further violences are
intended me, if I comply not with your purposes; whatever they are,
I will suppose them to be what you so solemnly profess they are. But
I have told you, as solemnly, my mind, that I never *will*, that I never

320

can, be yours; nor, if so, any man's upon earth. All vengeance, nevertheless, for the wrongs you have done me, I disclaim. I want but to slide into some obscure corner, to hide myself from you, and from every one who once loved me. The desire lately so near my heart, of a reconciliation with my friends, is much abated. They shall not receive me *now*, if they *would*. Sunk in mine own eyes, I now think myself unworthy of their favour. In the anguish of my soul, therefore, I conjure you, Lovelace (tears in her eyes), to leave me to my fate. In doing so, you will give me a pleasure the highest I now can know.

Whither, my dearest life ——

No matter whither. I will leave to Providence, when I am out of this house, the direction of my future steps. I am sensible enough of my destitute condition. I know that I have not now a friend in the world. Even Miss Howe has given me up — or you are — but I would fain keep my temper! By your means I have lost them all — and you have been a barbarous enemy to me. You know you have.

She paused.

I could not speak.

The evils I have suffered, proceeded she (turning from me), however irreparable, are but *temporary* evils. Leave me to my hopes of being enabled to obtain the Divine forgiveness for the offence I have been drawn in to give to my parents, and to virtue; that so I may avoid the evils that are *more than temporary*. This is now all I have to wish for. And what is it that I demand, that I have not a right to, and from which it is an illegal violence to withhold me?

It was impossible for me, I told her plainly, to comply. I besought her to give her hand as this very day. I could not live without her. I communicated to her my lord's illness, as a reason why I wished not to stay for her uncle's anniversary. I besought her to bless me with her consent; and, after the ceremony was passed, to accompany me down to Berks. And thus, my dearest life, said I, will you be freed from a house to which you have conceived so great an antipathy.

At last she broke silence. I have no patience, said she, to find myself a slave, a prisoner, in a vile house. Tell me, sir, in so many words tell me, whether it be, or be not, your intention to permit me to quit it? To permit me the freedom which is my birthright as an English subject?

Will not the consequence of your departure hence be, that I shall lose you for ever, madam? And can I bear the thoughts of that?

She flung from me. My soul disdains to hold parley with thee, were her violent words — but I threw myself at her feet, and took hold of her reluctant hand, and began to imprecate, to vow, to promise — but thus the passionate beauty, interrupting me, went on:

I see thy confusion, Lovelace. Or is it thy remorse? I have but one request to make thee — the request so often repeated: that thou wilt this moment permit me to quit this house. Adieu then, let me say, for *ever* adieu! And mayst thou enjoy that happiness in this world, which thou hast robbed me of; as thou hast of every friend I have in it!

And saying this, away she flung, leaving me in a confusion so great, that I knew not what to think, say, or do.

But Dorcas soon roused me. Do you know, sir, running in hastily, that my lady is gone downstairs!

No, sure! And down I flew, and found her once more at the street door, contending with Polly Horton to get out.

She rushed by me into the fore parlour, and flew to the window, and attempted once more to throw up the sash. Good people! Good people! cried she.

I caught her in my arms and lifted her from the window. But being afraid of hurting the charming creature (charming in her very rage), she slid through my arms on the floor: — Let me die here! Let me die here! were her words; remaining jointless and immovable till Sally and Mrs. Sinclair hurried in.

She was visibly terrified at the sight of the old wretch; while I (sincerely affected) appealed, Bear witness, Mrs. Sinclair! Bear witness, Miss Martin! Miss Horton! Every one bear witness, that I offer not violence to this beloved creature!

She then found her feet. O house (looking towards the windows, and all round her, O house) contrived on purpose for my ruin! said she — but let not that woman come into my presence — nor that Miss Horton neither, who would not have dared to control me, had she not been a base one!

She was visibly affrighted: and upstairs she hastened. A bad woman is certainly, Jack, more terrible to her own sex than even a bad man.

Thursday Night.

With great difficulty I prevailed upon her to favour me with her company for one half-hour this evening. The necessity I was under to go down to M. Hall was the subject I wanted to talk upon.

I told her, that as she had been so good as to promise that she would endeavour to make herself easy till she saw the Thursday in next week over, I hoped that she would not scruple to oblige me with her word, that I should find her here at my return from M. Hall.

Indeed she would make me no such promise. Nothing of *this house* was mentioned to me, said she: you know it was not. And do you think that I would have given *my consent to my imprisonment in it?*

I was plaguily nettled, and disappointed too. If I go not down to M. Hall, madam, you'll have no scruple to stay here, I suppose, till Thursday is over?

If I cannot help myself, I must. But I insist upon being permitted to go out of this house whether *you* leave it or not.

Well, madam, then I will comply with your commands. And I will go out this very evening in quest of lodgings that you shall have no objection to.

I will have no lodgings of your providing, sir — I will go to Mrs. Moore's at Hampstead.

Mrs. Moore's, madam? I have no objection to Mrs. Moore's. But will you give me your promise to admit me *there* to your presence?

As I do here — when I cannot help it.

You hate me, madam! You despise me more than you do the most odious of God's creatures!

You ought to despise *me*, if I did not.

You say, madam, you are in a *bad* house. You have *no reliance* upon my honour — you believe you *cannot avoid me* ——

She arose. I beseech you, let me withdraw.

I snatched her hand, rising, and pressed it first to my lips, and then to my heart, in wild disorder. She might have felt the bounding mischief ready to burst its bars. You *shall* go — to your own apartment, if you please — but, by the great God of Heaven, I will accompany you thither!

She trembled. Pray, pray, Mr. Lovelace, don't terrify me so!

Be seated, madam! I beseech you, be seated!

I will sit down ——

Do then, — all my soul in my eyes, and my heart's blood throbbing at my finger-ends.

I will, I will — you hurt me — pray, Mr. Lovelace, don't — don't frighten me so — and down she sat, trembling; my hand still grasping hers.

I hung over her throbbing bosom, and putting my other arm round her waist — And you say you hate me, madam — and you say you despise me — and you say you promised me nothing ——

Yes, yes, I *did* promise you — let me not be held down thus — you see I sat down when you bid me. Why (struggling) need you hold me down thus? I did promise *to endeavour to be easy till Thursday was over!* But you won't let me! How can I be easy? Pray, let me not be thus terrified.

And what, madam, *meant* you by your promise? Did you mean anything in my favour?

Let go my hand, sir — take away your arm from about me (struggling, yet trembling). *Why do you gaze upon me so?*

Answer me, madam. Did you mean anything in my favour by your promise?

Let me not be thus constrained to answer.

Do you intend, madam, to honour me with your hand, in your uncle's presence, or do you not?

My heart and my hand shall never be separated. Why, think you, did I stand in opposition to the will of my best, my natural friends?

Am I then as hateful to you as the vile Solmes?

Let me retire — I ask your *leave* to retire — you really frighten me — yet I give you no hope — from my heart I ab ——

Say not, madam, you *abhor* me. You must, for your own sake, conceal your hatred — at least, not avow it. I seized her hand.

Let me retire — let me retire, said she, in a manner out of breath.

I will only say, madam, that I refer myself to your generosity. My heart is not to be trusted at this instant. As a mark of my submission to your will, you shall, *if you please,* withdraw. But I will not go to M. Hall — live or die my Lord M. I will not go to M. Hall — but will attend the effect of your promise. Remember, madam, you have promised *to endeavour to make yourself easy, till you see the event of next Thursday*. Next Thursday, remember, your uncle comes up to see us married — *that's the event*. You think ill of your Lovelace — do not, madam, suffer your own morals to be degraded by the *infection*, as you called it, of his example.

Away flew the charmer with this half-permission — and no doubt thought that she had an escape — nor without reason.

I knew not for half an hour what to do with myself. Vexed at the heart, nevertheless (now she was from me, and when I reflected upon her hatred of me, and her defiances), that I suffered myself to be so overawed, checked, restrained.

And now I have written thus far (having, of course, recollected the whole of our conversation) I am more and more incensed against myself.

June 23, Friday Morning.

Nothing will do, Jack! I can procure no favour from her, though she has obtained from me the point which she had set her heart upon.

I first proposed instant marriage; and this in the most fervent manner: but was denied as fervently.

'Tis well, madam! But ask me anything I can do to oblige you, though in nothing will you oblige *me*.

Then I ask you, then I request of you, to let me go to Hampstead.

I paused — and at last: By my soul you shall. You know the condition, madam — next Thursday.

You dare not trust —

I *ought* not. Nevertheless I *will* confide in your generosity. Tomorrow morning (no *new cause* arising) you may go to Hampstead.

.   .   .   .

Dost thou ask, what I meant by this promise?

No *new cause* arising, was the proviso on my side, thou'lt remember. But there *will be* a new cause.

Suppose Dorcas should drop the promissory note given her by her lady? Suppose I take it up? — at a time, too, that I was determined that the dear creature should be her own mistress? Will not this detection be a *new cause*?

.   .   .   .

Just come from my charmer. She claimed the performance of my promise, the moment she saw me, of *permitting* her (haughtily she spoke the word) to go to Hampstead as soon as I was gone to Berks.

Most cheerfully I renewed it. One favour, however, I would not be denied; to be admitted to pass the evening with her.

All sweetness and obsequiousness will I be on this occasion. My soul shall be poured out to move her to forgive me. If she will not, and if the promissory note should fall in my way, my revenge will doubtless take total possession of me. A few hours will decide all.

I had agreed with the women, that if I could not find a pretence in her presence to begin my operations, the note should lie in my way, and I was to pick it up soon after her retiring from me. But I began to doubt at near ten-o'clock (so earnest was she to leave me, suspecting my over-warm behaviour to her, and eager grasping of her hand two or three times, with eyestrings, as I felt, on the strain, while her eyes showed uneasiness and apprehension) that if she actually retired for the night, it might be a chance whether it would be easy to come at her again. Loath therefore to run such a risk, I stepped out at a little after ten, with intent to alter the preconcerted disposition a little; saying I would attend her again instantly. But as I returned, I met her at the door, intending to withdraw for the night. I could not persuade her to go back: nor had I presence of mind (so full of complaisancy as I was to her just before) to stay her by force: so she slid through my hands into her own apartment. I had nothing to do, therefore, but to let my former concert take place.

She had hardly got into her chamber, but I found a little paper, as I was going into mine; which I took up; and, opening it (for it was carefully pinned in another paper), what should it be but a promissory note, given as a bribe, with a further promise of a diamond ring, to induce Dorcas to favour her mistress's escape?

How my temper changed in a moment! Ring, ring, ring, ring I my bell, with a violence enough to break the string, and as if the house were on fire.

Up ran two or three of the sisterhood: What's the matter! What's the matter!

The matter! (for still my beloved opened not her door; on the contrary, drew another bolt). This *abominable* Dorcas! — (Call her aunt up! Let her see what a traitress she has placed about me! And let her bring the toad to answer for herself) — has taken a bribe, a provision for life, to betray her trust; by that means to perpetuate a quarrel between a man and his wife, and frustrate for ever all hopes of reconciliation between us!

Let me perish, Belford, if I have patience to proceed with the farce!

.   .   .   .

If I must resume, I must ——

Up came the aunt puffing and blowing. As she hoped for mercy, *she* was not privy to it! She never knew such a plotting perverse lady in her life! Well might servants be at the pass they were, when such ladies as Mrs. Lovelace made no conscience of corrupting them. For *her* part, she desired no mercy for the wretch: no niece of hers, if she were not faithful to her trust! But what was the proof?

She was shown the paper ——

But too evident! Cursed, cursed toad, devil, jade, passed from each mouth: and the vileness of the *corrupted*, and the unworthiness of the *corruptress*, were inveighed against.

Up we all went, passing the lady's door into the dining-room, to proceed to trial ——

Stamp, stamp, stamp up, each on her heels; rave, rave, rave, every tongue ——

Bring up the creature before us all, this instant ——

And would she have got out of the house, say you?

These the noises and the speeches as we clattered by the door of the fair briberess.

Up was brought Dorcas (whimpering).

Come up and be damned. Bring her forward, her imperial judge. What a plague, is it the *detection*, not the *crime*, that confounds you. You could be quiet enough for days together, as I see by the date, under the villainy. Tell me, ungrateful devil, tell me, who made the first advances?

Tell all you know. Tell the whole truth, Dorcas, cried Polly Horton. His honour loves his lady too well to make her suffer *much*; little as she requites his love!

But suppose, sir, said Sally, you have my lady and the wench face to face? You see she cares not to confess. Your lady won't, she *dare* not come out to save you; though it is more his honour's mercy, than your desert, if he does not cut your throat this instant.

Just then, we heard the lady's door unbar, unlock, unbolt —

Now, sir!

Now, Mr. Lovelace!

Now, sir, from every encouraging mouth!

But O Jack, Jack, Jack! I can write no more!

.   .   .   .

If you must have it all, you must!

Now, Belford, see us all sitting in judgment, resolved to punish the fair briberess — I, and the mother, the hitherto *dreaded* mother, the nieces Sally, Polly, the traitress Dorcas, and Mabel, a guard, as it were, over Dorcas, that she might not run away and hide herself: all predetermined and of *necessity* predetermined, from the journey I was going to take, and my precarious situation with her — and hear her *unbolt, unlock, unbar* the door; then, as it proved afterwards, put the key into the lock on the outside, lock the door, and put it in her pocket — Will, I knew, below, who would give me notice, if, while we were all above, she would mistake her way, and go downstairs instead of coming into the dining-room: the street doors also doubly secured, and every shutter to the windows round the house fastened, that no noise or screaming should be heard (such was the brutal preparation) — and then *hear* her step towards us, and instantly *see* her enter among us, confiding in her own innocence; and with a majesty in her person and manner, that is *natural* to her; but which then shone out in all its glory! She passed backwards and forwards, now towards me, now towards the door several times, before speech could get the better of indignation; and at last, after twice or thrice hemming, to recover her articulate voice: "O thou contemptible and abandoned Lovelace, thinkest thou that I see not through this poor villainous plot of thine, and of these thy wicked accomplices?

"Thou, woman (looking at the mother), once my terror! always my dislike! but now my detestation! shouldst once more (for thine perhaps was the preparation) have provided for me intoxicating potions, to rob me of my senses ——

"And then (*turning to me*), thou, wretch, mightest more securely have depended upon such a low contrivance as this!

"And ye, vile women, who perhaps have been the ruin, body and soul, of hundreds of innocents (you show me *how*, in full assembly), know that I am not married — ruined as I am, by your help, I bless God, I am *not* married to this miscreant. And I have friends that will demand my honour at your hands!

"And as for thee, thou vile Dorcas! Thou *double* deceiver! whining out thy pretended love for me! Begone, wretch! Nobody will hurt thee! Begone, I say! Thou hast too well acted thy part to be blamed by *any* here but myself — thou art safe: thy guilt is thy security in such a house as this!"

And, as I hope to live, the wench, confoundedly frightened, slunk away; so did her sentinel Mabel; though I, endeavouring to rally, cried out for Dorcas to stay — but I believe the devil could not have stopped her, when an angel bid her begone.

Madam, said I, let me tell you; and was advancing towards her, with a fierce aspect, most cursedly vexed, and ashamed too.

But she turned to me; "Stop where thou art, O vilest and most abandoned of men! Stop where thou art! Nor, with that determined face, offer to touch me, if thou wouldst not that I should be a corpse at thy feet!"

To my astonishment, she held forth a penknife in her hand, the point to her own bosom, grasping resolutely the whole handle, so that there was no offering to take it from her.

"I offer not mischief to anybody but myself. You, sir, and ye women, are safe from every violence of mine. The LAW shall be all my resource: the LAW," and she spoke the word with emphasis, that to such people carries natural terror with it, and now struck a panic into them.

"The LAW only shall be my refuge!" ——

The infamous mother whispered me that it were better to *make terms* with this *strange* lady, and let her go.

Sally, notwithstanding all her impudent bravery at other times, said, *If* Mr. Lovelace had told *them* what was *not true* of her being his wife ——

And Polly Horton, That she must *needs* say, the lady, if she were *not* my wife, had been very much injured; that was all.

That is not now a matter to be disputed, cried I: you and I know, madam. ——

"We do," said she; "and I thank God, I am *not* thine — *once more*, I thank God for it — I have no doubt of the further baseness that thou hadst intended me, by this vile and low trick: but I have my

327

SENSES, Lovelace: and from my heart I despise thee, thou very poor Lovelace! How canst thou stand in my presence! Thou, that ——"

Madam, madam, madam — these are insults not to be borne — and was approaching her.

She withdrew to the door, and set her back against it, holding the pointed knife to her heaving bosom; while the women held me, beseeching me not to provoke the violent lady — for their *house's* sake, and be cursed to them, they besought me — and all three hung upon me — while the truly heroic lady braved me at that distance:

"Approach me, Lovelace, with resentment, if thou wilt. I dare die. It is in defence of my honour. God will be merciful to my poor soul! I expect no mercy from thee! I have gained this distance, and two steps nearer me, and thou shalt see what I dare do!"

Leave me, women, to myself, and to my angel! They retired at a distance. O my beloved creature, how you terrify me! Holding out my arms, and kneeling on one knee — Not a step, not a step farther, except to receive my death at that injured hand which is thus held up against a life far dearer to me than my own. I am a villain! the blackest of villains! Say you will sheathe your knife in the injurer's, not the injured's, heart; and then will I indeed approach you, but not else.

The mother twanged her damned nose; and Sally and Polly pulled out their handkerchiefs, and turned from us. They never in their lives, they told me afterwards, beheld such a scene. ——

Innocence so triumphant; villainy so debased, they must mean!

Unawares to myself, I had moved onward to my angel. "And dost thou, dost thou, *still* disclaiming, *still* advancing, dost thou, dost thou, *still* insidiously move towards me?" (and her hand was extended). "I dare — I dare — not rashly neither — my heart from *principle* abhors the act, which *thou* makest *necessary*! God, in Thy mercy! (lifting up her eyes and hands) God, in Thy mercy!"

I threw myself to the further end of the room. An ejaculation, a silent ejaculation, employing her thoughts that moment; Polly says the whites of her lovely eyes were only visible: and, in the instant that she extended her hand, *assuredly* to strike the fatal blow (how the very recital terrifies me!), she cast her eye towards me, and saw me at the utmost distance the room would allow, and heard my broken voice — my voice was utterly broken; nor knew I what I said, or whether to the purpose or not — and her charming cheeks, that were all in a glow before, turned pale, as if terrified at her own purpose; and lifting up her eyes — "Thank God! — Thank God!" said the angel — "delivered *for the present*; for the *present* delivered — from myself! Keep, sir, keep that distance" (looking down towards me, who was prostrate on the floor, my heart pierced as with a hundred daggers!). "That distance has saved a life; to what reserved, the Almighty only knows!"

To *be* happy, madam; and to *make* happy! And oh, let me but hope for your favour for to-morrow — I will put off my journey till then — and may God ——

If not to-morrow, madam, say but next Thursday, your uncle's birthday; say but next Thursday!

"This I say, of this you may assure yourself, I never, never *will* be yours. And let me hope that I may be entitled to the performance of your promise, to be permitted to leave this *innocent* house, as one called it (but long have my ears been accustomed to such inversions of words), as soon as the day breaks."

Did my perdition depend upon it, that you cannot, madam, but upon terms. And I hope you will not terrify me — still dreading the accursed knife.

"Nothing less than an attempt upon my honour shall make me desperate. I have no view, but to defend my honour: with such a view only I entered into treaty with your infamous agent below. The resolution you have seen, I trust, God will give me again, upon the same occasion. But for a *less*, I wish not for it. Only take notice, women, that I am no wife of *this man*: basely as he has used me, I am not his wife. He has no authority over me. If he go away by and by, and you act by his authority to detain me, look to it."

Then, taking one of the lights, she turned from us; and away she went, unmolested. Not a soul was *able* to molest her.

Mabel saw her, tremblingly, and in a hurry, take the key of her chamber door out of her pocket, and unlock it; and, as soon as she entered, heard her double lock, bar, and bolt it.

By her taking out her key, when she came out of her chamber to us, she no doubt suspected my design: which was, to have carried her in my arms thither, if she made such force necessary, after I had intimidated her; and to have been her companion for that night.

She was to have had several bedchamber women to assist to undress her upon occasion: but, from the moment she entered the dining-room with so much intrepidity, it was absolutely impossible to think of prosecuting my villainous designs against her.

. . . .

This, this, Belford, was the hand I made of a contrivance from which I expected so much! And now am I ten times worse off than before.

And now it is time to set out: all I have gained, detection, disgrace, fresh guilt by repeated perjuries, and to be despised by her I *dote upon*; and, what is still worse to a proud heart, by *myself*.

Success, success in projects, is everything. What an admirable contriver did I think myself till now! Even for *this* scheme among the rest! But how pitifully foolish does it now appear to me! Scratch out, erase, never to be read, every part of my preceding letters where I have boastingly mentioned it. And never presume to rally me upon the cursed subject: for I cannot bear it.

But for the lady, by my soul I love her, I admire her, more than ever! I *must* have her. I *will* have her still — *with* honour, or *without,* as I have often vowed. Had she threatened ME, I should soon have been master of *one* arm, and in *both*! But for so sincere a virtue to threaten *herself*, and not offer to intimidate *any other*, and with so much presence of mind, as to distinguish, in the very passionate intention, the necessity of the act, in defence of her *honour*, and so *fairly* to disavow *lesser* occasions; showed such a deliberation, such a choice, such a principle; and then keeping me so watchfully at a distance, that I could not seize her hand so soon as she could have given the fatal blow; how impossible not to be subdued by so *true* and so *discreet* a magnanimity!

But she is not *gone*. She shall not go. I will press her with letters for the Thursday. She shall yet be mine, legally mine. For, as to cohabitation, there is now no such thing to be thought of.

The captain shall give her away, as proxy for her uncle. My lord will die. My fortune will help my *will*, and set me above everything and everybody.

But here is the curse — she despises me, Jack! What man, as I have heretofore said, can bear to be despised, especially by his wife? O Lord! O Lord! What a hand, what a cursed hand, have I made of this plot! And here ends

The History of the Lady and the Penknife! The devil take the penknife! — It goes against me to say, God bless the lady!

Near 5, Sat. Morn.

Mr. Lovelace to Miss Clarissa Harlowe

(*Superscribed to Mrs. Lovelace*)   *M. Hall, Sat. Night, June 24.*

My dearest Life, — If you do not impute to love, and to terror raised by love, the poor figure I made before you last night, you will not do me justice. I thought I would try to the very last moment, if, by complying with you in *everything*, I could prevail upon you to promise to be mine on Thursday next, since you refused me an earlier day. Could I have been so happy, you had not been hindered going to Hampstead, or wherever else you pleased. But when I could not prevail upon you to give me this assurance, what room had I (my demerit so great) to suppose that your going thither would not be to lose you for ever?

The orders I have given to the people of the house are: that you shall be obeyed in every particular that is consistent with my expectations of finding you there on my return to town on Wednesday next: that Mrs. Sinclair, and her nieces, having incurred your just displeasure, shall not, without your orders, come into your presence: that neither shall Dorcas, till she has fully cleared her conduct to your satisfaction, be permitted to attend you: but Mabel, in her place; of whom you seemed some time ago to express some liking. Will I have left behind me to attend your commands. If he be either negligent or impertinent, *your* dismission shall be a dismission of him from my service for ever. But, as to letters which may be sent you, or any which you may have to send, I must humbly entreat that none such pass *from* or to *you*, for the few days that I shall be absent. But I do assure you, madam, that the seals of both sorts shall be sacred: and the letters, if such be sent, shall be given into your own hands the moment the ceremony is performed, or before, if you require it.

Meantime I will inquire, and send you word, how Miss Howe does; and to what, if I can be informed, her long silence is owing.

His lordship is exceeding ill. Dr. S. has no hopes of him. The only consolation I can have for the death of a relation who loves me so well, if he *do* die, must arise from the additional power it will put into my hands of showing how much I am, / My dearest life, / Your ever affectionate and faithful / LOVELACE.

MR. LOVELACE TO MISS CLARISSA HARLOWE
(*Superscribed to Mrs. Lovelace*)   *M. Hall, Sunday Night, June 25.*

MY DEAREST LOVE, — I cannot find words to express how much I am mortified at the return of my messenger without a line from you.

Thursday is so near, that I will send messenger after messenger every four hours, till I have a favourable answer; the one to meet the other, till its eve arrives, to know if I may venture to appear in your presence with the hope of having my wishes answered on that day.

Let me, therefore, propose an expedient, in order to spare my own confusion; and to spare you the necessity for that soul-harrowing recrimination, which I cannot stand, and which must be disagreeable to yourself — to name the church, and I will have everything in readiness; so that our next interview will be, in a manner, at the very altar; and then you will have the kind husband to forgive for the faults of the ungrateful lover.

MR. LOVELACE TO MISS CLARISSA HARLOWE
(*Superscribed to Mrs. Lovelace*)   *M. Hall, Monday, June 26.*

IF WE are married, all the disgrace you imagine you have suffered while a single lady, will be my own, and known only to ourselves. Consider well the situation we are both in, and remember, my dearest life, that Thursday will soon be here.

In a letter sent by the messenger whom I dispatch with this, I have desired that my friend, Mr. Belford, will wait upon you, to know what I am to depend upon as to the chosen day.

MR. LOVELACE TO JOHN BELFORD, ESQ.
Monday, June 26.

THOU wilt see the situation I am in with Miss Harlowe by the enclosed copies of letters.

One would imagine (so long used to constraint too as she has been) that she might have been satisfied with the triumph she had over us all on Friday night: a triumph that to this hour has sunk my pride and my vanity so much, that I almost hate the words *plot, contrivance, scheme*; and shall mistrust myself in future for every one that rises to my inventive head.

But seest thou not that I am under a necessity to continue her at Sinclair's, and to prohibit all her correspondence?

Now, Belford, as I really, in my present mood, think of nothing less than marrying her, if she let not Thursday slip; I would have thee attend her, in pursuance of the intimation I have given her in my letter of this date; and vow for me, swear for me, bind thy soul to her for my honour, and use what arguments thy friendly heart can suggest, in order to procure me an answer from her; which, as thou wilt see, she may give in four words only. And then I purpose to leave Lord M. (dangerously ill as he is) and meet her at her appointed church, in order to solemnize: if she will sign but *Cl. H.* to *thy* writing the four words, that shall do; for I would not come up to be made a fool of in the face of all my family and friends.

If she should let the day go off, I shall be desperate. I am entangled in my own devices, and cannot bear that she should detect me.

[*Belford declines the suggested office for Lovelace unless completely assured that he intends to marry Clarissa on Thursday. So from M. Hall late on Tuesday Lovelace sends the scornful word: "Let it alone, and be cursed." Then on Wednesday Tomlinson–M'Donald sends the bad news to Lovelace:*]

To Mr. Lovelace
Wedn. June 28, near 12 o'clock.

HONOURED SIR, — I received yours by ten this morning. I instantly equipped myself as if come off from a journey, and posted away to the lady; but, upon my entering Mrs. Sinclair's house, I found all in the greatest consternation.

It is a trouble to me to be the relater of the bad news: but so it is — The lady is gone off. She was missed but half an hour before I came.

Her waiting-maid is run away, or hitherto is not to be found: so that they conclude it was by her connivance.

They had sent, before I came, to my honoured masters, Mr. Belton, Mr. Mowbray, and Mr. Belford. Mr. Tourville is out of town.

High words are passing between Madam Sinclair, and Madam Horton, and Madam Martin; as also with Dorcas. And your servant William threatens to hang or drown himself.

They have sent to know if they can hear of Mabel, the waiting-maid, at her mother's, who it seems lives in Chick Lane, West Smithfield; and to an uncle of hers also, who keeps an alehouse at Cowcross, hard by, and with whom she lived last.

Your messenger, having just changed his horse, is come back: so I will not detain him longer than to add, that I am, with great concern for this misfortune, and thanks for your seasonable favour and kind intentions towards me (I am sure this was not my fault), / Honoured sir, / Your most obliged, humble servant, / PATRICK M'DONALD.

MR. MOWBRAY TO ROBERT LOVELACE, ESQ.

Wednesday, 12 o'clock.

DEAR LOVELACE, — I have plaguy news to acquaint thee with. Miss Harlowe is gone off! Quite gone, by my soul! I have not time for particulars, your servant being going off. But if I had, we are not yet come to the bottom of the matter. The ladies here are all blubbering like devils, accusing one another most confoundedly: whilst Belton and I damn them all together in thy name.

If thou shouldst hear that thy fellow Will is taken dead out of some horse-pond, and Dorcas cut down from her bed's tester from dangling in her own garters, be not surprised. Here's the devil to pay. Nobody serene but Jack Belford, who is taking minutes of examinations, accusations, and confessions, with the significant air of a Middlesex justice; and intends to write at large all particulars, I suppose.

MR. BELFORD TO ROBERT LOVELACE, ESQ.

Thursday, June 29.

THOU hast heard the news.

I came to town purely to serve thee with her, expecting that thy next would satisfy me that I might endeavour it without dishonour: and at first when I found her gone, I half pitied thee; for now wilt thou be inevitably blown up: and in what an execrable light wilt thou appear to all the world! Poor Lovelace! Caught in thy own snares! Thy punishment is but beginning!

But to my narrative; for I suppose thou expectest all particulars from me.

The noble exertion of spirit she had made on Friday night, had, it seems, greatly disordered her; insomuch that she was not visible till Saturday evening; when Mabel saw her; and she seemed to be very ill: but on Sunday morning, having dressed herself, as if designing to go to church, she ordered Mabel to get her a coach to the door.

The wench told her she was to obey her in everything but the calling of a coach or chair, or in relation to letters.

She sent for Will, and give him the same command.

He pleaded his master's orders to the contrary, and desired to be excused.

Upon this, down she went herself, and would have gone out without observation: but finding the street door double locked, and the key not in the lock, she stepped into the street parlour, and would have thrown up the sash to call out to the people passing by, as they doubted not: but that, since her last attempt of the same nature, had been fastened down.

Hereupon she resolutely stepped into Mrs. Sinclair's parlour in the back house; where were the old devil and her two partners; and demanded the key of the street door, or to have it opened for her.

They were all surprised; but desired to be excused, and pleaded your orders.

She asserted that you had no authority over her; and never should have any: that their present refusal was their own act and deed: she saw the intent of their back house, and the reason of putting her there: she pleaded her condition and fortune; and said they had no way to avoid utter ruin, but by opening their doors to her, or by murdering her, and burying her in their garden or cellar, too deep for detection: that already what had been done to her was punishable by death: and bid them at their peril detain her.

She made no other attempt till the effectual one. Your letters and messages, they supposed, coming so fast upon one another (though she would not answer one of them), gave *her* some amusement, and an assurance to *them* that she would at last forgive you: and that then all would end as you wished.

'Tis probable she might have been contriving something all this time; but saw no room for perfecting any scheme: the contrivance by which she effected her escape seems to me not to have been fallen upon till the very day: since it depended partly upon the *weather*, as it proved. But it is evident she hoped something from Mabel's simplicity, or gratitude, or compassion, by cultivating all the time her civility to her.

Polly waited on her early on Wednesday morning; and met with a better reception than she had *reason* to expect. She complained however with warmth of her confinement. Polly said there would be a happy end to it (if it *were* a confinement) next day, she presumed. She absolutely declared to the contrary, in the way Polly meant it; and said, That Mr. Lovelace on his *return (which looked as if she intended to wait for it)*, should have reason to repent the orders he had given, *as they all should* their observance of them: let him send twenty letters, she would not answer one, be the consequence what it would; nor give him hope of the least favour, while she was in that house. She had given Mrs. Sinclair and themselves fair warning, she said: no orders of another ought to make them detain a free person: but having made an open attempt to *go*, and been detained by them, she was the calmer, she told Polly; let *them* look to the consequence.

But yet she spoke this with temper; and Polly gave it as her opinion (with apprehension for their own safety) that, having so good a handle to punish them all, she would not go away if she might. And what, inferred Polly, is the indemnity of a man who has committed the vilest of rapes on a person of condition; and must himself, if prosecuted for it, either fly or be hanged?

Sinclair (so I will still call her), upon this representation of Polly, foresaw, she said, *the ruin of her poor house* in the issue of this *strange* business; and the infamous Sally and Dorcas bore their parts in the apprehension: and this put them upon thinking it advisable for the future, that the street door should generally in the daytime be only left upon a bolt-latch, as they called it, which anybody might open on the inside; and that the key should be kept in the door; that their numerous *comers* and *goers*, as they called their guests, should be able to give evidence *that she might have gone out if she would*: not forgetting, however, to renew their orders to Will, to Dorcas, to Mabel, and the rest, to redouble their vigilance on this occasion, to prevent her escape; none of them doubting, at the same time, that her love of a man so considerable in *their* eyes, and the prospect of what was to happen, as she had reason to believe, on Thursday, her uncle's birthday, would (though perhaps not till the *last hour*, for her *pride's sake*, was their word) engage her to change her temper.

They believe that she discovered the key to be left in the door; for she was down more than once to walk in the little garden, and seemed to cast her eye each time to the street door.

About eight yesterday morning, an hour after Polly had left her, she told Mabel she was sure she should not live long; and having a good many suits of apparel, which after her death would be of no use to anybody she valued, she would give her a brown lustring gown, which, with some alterations, to make it more suitable to her degree, would a great while serve her for a Sunday wear; for that she (Mabel) was the only person in that house of whom she could think without terror or antipathy.

Mabel expressing her gratitude upon the occasion, the lady said she had nothing to employ herself about; and if she could get a workwoman directly, she would look over her things then, and give her what she intended for her.

Her mistress's mantua-maker, the maid replied, lived but a little way off; and she doubted not that she could procure *her*, or one of her journey-women, to alter the gown out of hand.

I will give you also, said she, a quilted coat, which will require but little alteration, if any; for you are much about my stature: but the gown I will give directions about, because the sleeves and the robings and facings must be altered for your wear, being, I believe, above your station: and try, said she, if you can get the workwoman, and we'll advise about it. If she cannot come now, let her come in the afternoon; but I had rather now, because it will amuse me to give you a lift.

Then stepping to the window, It rains, said she (and so it had done all the morning): slip on the hood and short cloak I have seen you wear, and come to me when you are ready to go out, because you shall bring me in something that I want.

Mabel equipped herself accordingly, and received her commands to buy her some trifles, and then left her; but, in her way out, stepped into the back parlour, where Dorcas was with Mrs. Sinclair, telling her where she was going, and on what account, bidding Dorcas look out till she came back. So faithful was the wench to the trust reposed in her, and so little had the lady's generosity wrought upon her.

Mrs. Sinclair commended her; Dorcas envied her, and took her cue: and Mabel soon returned with the mantua-maker's journey-woman (she was resolved, she said, she would not come without her); and then Dorcas went off guard.

The lady looked out the gown and petticoat, and before the workwoman caused Mabel to try it on; and, that it might fit the better, made the willing wench pull off her upper petticoat, and put on that she gave her. Then she bid them go into Mr. Lovelace's apartment, and contrive about it before the pier-glass there, and stay till she came to them, to give them her opinion.

Mabel would have taken her own clothes, and hood, and short cloak with her: but her lady said, No matter; you may put them on again here, when we have considered about the alterations: there's no occasion to litter the other room.

They went; and instantly, as it is supposed, she slipped on Mabel's gown and petticoat over her own, which was white damask, and put on the wench's hood, short cloak, and ordinary apron, and down she went.

Hearing somebody tripping along the passage, both Will and Dorcas whipped to the inner hall door, and saw her; but, taking her for Mabel, Are you going far, Mabel, cried Will?

Without turning her face, or answering, she held out her hand, pointing to the stairs; which they construed as a caution for them to look out in her absence; and supposing she would not be long gone, as she had not in form repeated her caution to them, up went Will, tarrying at the stairs-head in expectation of the supposed Mabel's return.

Mabel and the workwoman waited a good while, amusing themselves not disagreeably, the one with contriving in the way of her business, the other delighting herself with her fine gown and coat: but at last, wondering the lady did not come in to them, Mabel tiptoed it to her door, and tapping, and not being answered, stepped into the chamber.

Will at that instant, from his station at the stairs-head, seeing Mabel in her *lady's* clothes; for he had been told of the present (gifts to servants fly from servant to servant in a minute), was very much surprised, having, as he thought, just seen her go out in *her own*; and stepping up, met her at the door. How the devil can this be? he said. Just now you went out in your own dress! How came you here in this? And how could you pass me unseen? But nevertheless, kissing her, said he would now brag he had kissed his lady, or one in her clothes.

I am glad, Mr. William, cried Mabel, to see you here so diligently. But know you where my lady is?

In my master's apartment, answered Will. Is she not? Was she not talking with you this moment?

No, that's Mrs. Dolins's journey-woman.

They both stood aghast, as they said; Will again recollecting he had seen Mabel, as he thought, go out in her own clothes. And while they were debating and wondering, up comes Dorcas with your fourth letter, just then brought for her lady; and seeing Mabel dressed out (whom she had likewise beheld a little before, as she supposed, in her common clothes) she joined in the wonder; till Mabel, re-entering the lady's apartment, missed her own clothes; and then suspecting what had happened, and letting the others into the ground of her suspicion, they all agreed that she had certainly escaped. And then followed such an uproar of mutual accusation, and *You should have done this*, and *You should have done that*, as alarmed the whole house; every apartment in both houses giving up its devil, to the number of fourteen or fifteen, including the mother and her partners.

Will told them *his* story; and then ran out, as on the like occasion formerly, to make inquiry whether the lady was seen by any of the coachmen, chairmen, or porters, plying in that neighbourhood.

The poor Mabel, frightened out of her wits, expected every moment to be torn in pieces, having half a score open-clawed paws upon her all at once. She promised to confess all. But that all, when she had obtained a hearing, was nothing; for *nothing* had she to confess.

The wench, glad of this reprieve, went upstairs; and while Sally was laying out the law, and prating away in her usual dictatorial manner, whipped on another gown, and sliding downstairs, escaped to her relations. And this flight, which was certainly more owing to *terror* than *guilt*, was, in the true Old Bailey construction, made a confirmation of the latter.

These are the particulars of Miss Harlowe's flight. Thou'lt hardly think me too minute. How I long to triumph over thy impatience and fury on the occasion!

Let me beseech thee, my dear Lovelace, in thy next letter, to rave most gloriously! I shall be grievously disappointed if thou dost not.

Where, Lovelace, can the poor lady be gone? And who can describe the distress she must be in?

By thy former letters, it may be supposed that she can have very little money; nor, by the suddenness of her flight, more clothes than those she has on. And thou knowest who once said, "Her parents will not receive her. Her uncles will not entertain her. Her Norton is in their direction, and cannot. Miss Howe dare not. She has not one friend or intimate in town; entirely a stranger to it." And, let me add, has been despoiled of her honour by the man for whom she made all these sacrifices; and who stood bound to her by a thousand oaths and vows, to be her husband, her protector, and friend!

P.S. Mabel's clothes were thrown into the passage this morning; nobody knows by whom.

MR. LOVELACE TO JOHN BELFORD, ESQ.

Friday, June 30.

I AM ruined, undone, blown up, destroyed, and worse than annihilated, that's certain!

It is as much my misfortune to have fallen in with Miss Clarissa Harlowe, were I to have valued my reputation or ease, as it is that of Miss Harlowe to have been acquainted with me. And, after all, what have I done more than prosecute the maxims by which thou and I and every rake are governed, and which, before I knew this lady, we have pursued from pretty girl to pretty girl, as fast as we had set one down, taking another up; just as the fellows do with the flying coaches and flying horses at a country fair, with a *Who rides next! Who rides next!*

.   .   .   .

One thing I will nevertheless add, to show the sincerity of my contrition: 'Tis this, that if thou canst by any means find her out within these three days, or any time before she has discovered the stories relating to Captain Tomlinson and her uncle to be what they are; and if thou canst prevail upon her to consent; I will actually, in thy presence and his (he to represent her uncle), marry her.

I am still in hopes it may be so — she cannot be long concealed — I have already set all engines at work to find her out; and if I do, what *indifferent* persons (and no one of her *friends*, as thou observest, will look upon her) will care to embroil themselves with a man of my figure, fortune, and resolution? Show her this part then, or any other part, of this letter, at thy own discretion, if thou *canst* find her.

MISS CLARISSA HARLOWE TO MISS HOWE

Wednesday Night, June 28.

O MY DEAREST Miss Howe! — Once more have I escaped — but, alas! *I*, my *best self*, have *not* escaped! Oh, your poor Clarissa Harlowe! *You* also will hate me, I fear! Yet you won't when you know all.

.   .   .   .

Forgive my rambling. My peace is destroyed. My intellects are touched. And what flighty nonsense must you read, if now you will vouchsafe to correspond with me, as formerly!

O my best, my dearest, my *only* friend! What a tale have I to unfold! But still upon *self*, this vile, this hated *self*! I will shake it off, if possible; and why should I not, since I think, except one wretch, I hate nothing so much? Self, then, be banished from *self* one moment (for I doubt it *will* for no longer), to inquire after a *dearer* object, my beloved Anna Howe! — whose mind, all robed in spotless white, charms and irradiates — but what would I say? ——

.   .   .   .

And how, my dearest friend, after this rhapsody, which, on re-perusal, I would not let go, but to show you what a distracted mind dictates to my trembling pen; *how do you?* You have been very ill, it seems. That you are *recovered*, my dear, let me hear.

．　．　．　．　．　．　．　．　．　．

And what is all this wild incoherence for? It is only to beg to know how you have been, and how you now do, by a line directed for Mrs. Rachel Clark, at Mr. Smith's, a glove shop in King Street, Covent Garden; which (although my abode is a secret to everybody else) will reach the hands of — *your unhappy* — but that's not enough —— / Your miserable / CLARISSA HARLOWE.

MRS. HOWE TO MISS CLARISSA HARLOWE

(Superscribed as directed in the preceding.)   *Friday, June 30.*

MISS CLARISSA HARLOWE, — You will wonder to receive a letter from me. I am sorry for the great distress you seem to be in. Such a hopeful young lady as you were! But see what comes of disobedience to parents!

But pray, miss, don't make my Nancy guilty of your fault; which is that of disobedience. I have charged her over and over not to correspond with one who has made such a giddy step. It is not to her reputation, I am sure. You *knew* that I so charged her; yet you go on corresponding together, to my very great vexation; for she has been very perverse upon it more than once. *Evil communication*, miss — you know the rest.

If people, who seek their own ruin, could be the only sufferers by their headstrong doings, it were something: but, O miss, miss, what have *you* to answer for, who have made as many grieved hearts as have known you? The whole sex is indeed wounded by you: for who but Miss Clarissa Harlowe was proposed by every father and mother for a pattern for their daughters?

I write a long letter, where I proposed to say but a few words; and those to forbid you writing to my Nancy: and this as well because of the false step you have made, as because it will grieve her poor heart, and do you no good. If you love her, therefore, write not to her. Your sad letter came into my hands, Nancy being abroad, and I shall not show it her: for there would be no comfort for her, if she saw it, nor for me whose delight she is — as you once was to your parents.

MISS CLARISSA HARLOWE TO MRS. HOWE

         Saturday, July 1.

PERMIT me, madam, to trouble you with a few lines, were it only to thank you for your reproofs; which have, nevertheless, drawn fresh streams of blood from a bleeding heart.

My story is a dismal story. It has circumstances in it that would engage pity, and possibly a judgment not altogether unfavourable, were those circumstances known. But it is my business, and shall be *all* my business, to repent of my failings, and not endeavour to extenuate them.

Nor will I seek to distress your worthy mind. If *I cannot suffer alone*, I will make as few parties as I can in my sufferings. And indeed, I took up my pen with this resolution when I wrote the letter which has fallen into your hands. It was only to know, and that for a very particular reason, as well as for affection unbounded, if my dear Miss Howe, from whom I had not heard of a long time, were ill; as I had been told she was; and if so, how she now does.

Miss Howe being abroad when my letter came, I flatter myself that she is recovered. But it would be some satisfaction to me to be informed if she *has been ill*. Another line from *your* hand would be too great a favour; but, if you will be pleased to direct any servant to answer *yes*, or *no*, to that question, I will not be further troublesome.

Nevertheless, I must declare that my Miss Howe's friendship was all the comfort I had or expected to have in this world; and a line from her would have been a cordial to my fainting heart. Judge then, dearest madam, how reluctantly I must obey your prohibition — but yet I will endeavour to obey it; although I should have hoped, as well from the tenor of all that has passed between Miss Howe and me, as from *her* established virtue, that she could not be tainted by *evil communication*, had one or two letters been permitted. This, however, I ask not for, since I think I have nothing to do, but to beg of God (who, I hope, has not yet withdrawn His grace from me, although He is pleased to let loose His justice upon my faults) to give me a truly broken spirit, if it be not already broken enough, and then to take to His mercy / The unhappy / CLARISSA HARLOWE.

Two favours, good madam, I have to beg of you. The first that you will not let any of my relations know that you have heard from me. The other, that no living creature be apprised where I am to be heard of, or directed to. This is a point that concerns me more than I can express. In short, my preservation from further evils may depend upon it.

MISS CLARISSA HARLOWE TO HANNAH BURTON
Thursday, June 29.

MY GOOD HANNAH, — Strange things have happened to me since you were dismissed my service (so sorely against my will) and your pert fellow-servant set over me. But that must be all forgotten now.

How do you, my Hannah? Are you recovered of your illness? If you are, do you choose to come and be with me? Or *can* you conveniently?

I am a very unhappy creature, and, being among all strangers, should be glad to have *you* with me, of whose fidelity and love I have had so many acceptable instances.

Living or dying, I will endeavour to make it worth your while, my Hannah.

Don't let any of my friends know of this my desire; whether you can come or not.

I am at Mr. Smith's, a hosier's and glove shop, in King Street, Covent Garden.

You must direct to me by the name of Rachel Clark.

Do, my good Hannah, come if you can, to your poor young mistress, who always valued you, and always will, whether you come or not.

HANNAH BURTON (IN ANSWER)

Monday, July 3.

HONORED MADDAM, — I have not forgot to write, and never will forget anything you, my dear young lady, was so good as to larn me. I am very sorrowfull for your misfortens, my dearest young lady; so sorrowfull, I do not know what to do. Gladd at harte would I be to be able to come to you. But indeed I have not been able to stir out of my rome here at my mother's, ever since I was forsed to leave my plase with a roomatise, which has made me quite and clene helpless. I will pray for you night and day, my dearest, my kindest, my goodest young lady, who have been so badly used; and I am very sorry I cannot come to do you love and sarvice; which will ever be in the harte of mee to do, if it was in my power: who am / Your most dewtifull sarvant to command, / HANNAH BURTON.

MISS CLARISSA HARLOWE TO MRS. JUDITH NORTON

Thursday, June 29.

MY DEAR MRS. NORTON, — I address myself to you after a very long silence (which, however, was not owing either to want of love or duty), principally to desire you to satisfy me in two or three points, which it behoves me to know.

My father, and all the family, I am informed, are to be at my Uncle Harlowe's this day, as usual. Pray acquaint me, if they *have* been there? And if they were cheerful on the anniversary occasion? And also, if you have heard of any journey, or intended journey, of my brother, in company with Captain Singleton and Mr. Solmes.

Strange things have happened to me, my dear worthy and maternal friend — very strange things! Mr. Lovelace has proved a very barbarous and ungrateful man to me. But, God be praised, I have escaped from him.

Say nothing to any of my friends that you have heard from me.

Pray, do you think my father would be prevailed upon, if I were to supplicate him by letter, to take off the heavy curse he laid upon me at my going from Harlowe Place? I can expect no other favour from him: but that being literally fulfilled as to my prospects in this life, I hope it will be thought to have operated far enough: and my heart is *so* weak! — it is *very* weak! But for my father's *own* sake — what *should* I say? Indeed, I hardly know how I *ought* to express myself on this sad subject! But it will give ease to my mind to be released from it.

Be pleased to direct for Rachel Clark, at Mr. Smith's in King Street, Covent Garden. But keep the direction an absolute secret.

MRS. NORTON. (IN ANSWER)

Saturday, July 1.

YOUR letter, my dearest young lady, cuts me to the heart! Why will you not let me know all your distresses! Yet you have said enough!

My son is very good to me. A few hours ago he was taken with a feverish disorder. But I hope it will go off happily, if his ardour for business will give him the recess from it which his good master is willing to allow him. He presents his duty to you, and shed tears at hearing your sad letter read.

You have been misinformed as to your family's being at your Uncle Harlowe's. They did not intend to be there. Nor was the day kept at all. Indeed, they have not stirred out, but to church (and that but three times), ever since the day you went away. Unhappy day for them, and for all who know you! To me, I am sure, most particularly so! My heart now bleeds more and more for you.

I have not heard a syllable of such a journey as you mention, of your brother, Captain Singleton, and Mr. Solmes. There has been some talk indeed of your brother's setting out for his northern estates: but I have not heard of it lately.

I am afraid no letter will be received from you. It grieves me to tell you so, my dearest young lady. No evil can have happened to you, which they do not *expect* to hear of; so great is their antipathy to the wicked man, and so bad is his character.

I cannot but think hardly of their unforgivingness: but there is no judging for others by one's self.

You are escaped, my dearest miss,— happily, I hope — that is to say, with your honour — else how great must be your distress! Yet from your letter I dread the worst.

I am very seldom at Harlowe Place. The house is not the house it used to be, since you went from it. Then they are *so* relentless!

I have a little money by me. You say you *are poor yourself.* How grievous are those words from one entitled and accustomed to affluence!

Nevertheless, you know not what God has in store for you yet! But if you are to be punished all your days here, for example's sake, in a case of such importance, for your one false step, be pleased to consider that this life is but a state of probation; and if you have your purification in it, you will be the more happy. Nor doubt I that you will have the higher reward *hereafter* for submitting to the will of Providence *here* with patience and resignation.

I cannot conclude without asking for your leave to attend you, and that in a very earnest manner. And I beg of you not to deny me, on any consideration relating to *myself*, or even to the indisposition of my *other* beloved child; if I can be either of use or comfort to you.

[*On June 29 Clarissa addresses a letter to Lady Betty Lawrance asking formally if her ladyship had written to Lovelace on June 7 congratulating him on his supposed nuptials, and whether on Sunday June 11 she had attended him to Hampstead, etc. Her ladyship replies in kindly distress that she neither wrote such a letter nor visited London in June; nor does she know one Tomlinson. Clarissa later explains the impersonations, forgeries, and perjuries that Lovelace used against herself and the members of his family. — Mrs. Hodges (housekeeper to Uncle John Harlowe), similarly approached, replies that neither she nor "her Master" knows any Tomlinson.*]

MISS CLARISSA HARLOWE TO MRS. NORTON
Sunday Evening, July 2.

IT IS kind in you to endeavour to extenuate the fault of one so greatly sensible of it; but that I may not make you think me more guilty than I am, give me leave briefly to assure you, that when my story is known I shall be entitled to more compassion than blame, even on the score of going away with Mr. Lovelace.

As to all that happened afterwards, let me only say that although I must call myself a lost creature as to this world, yet have I this consolation left me, that I have not suffered either for want of circumspection, or through credulity or weakness. Not one moment was I off my guard, or unmindful of your early precepts. But (having been enabled to baffle many base contrivances) I was at last ruined by arts the most inhuman. But had I not been rejected by every friend, this low-hearted man had not dared, nor would have had opportunity, to treat me as he has treated me.

But although your son should recover, I charge you, my dear Mrs. Norton, that you do not think of coming to me. I don't know still, but your mediation with my mother (although at present your interposition would be so little attended to) may be of use to procure me the revocation of that most dreadful part of my father's curse, which only remains to be fulfilled.

Let me briefly say that it is necessary to my present and future hopes that you keep well with my family.

Then the people I am now with seem to be both honest and humane; and there is in the same house a widow lodger, of low fortunes, but of great merit — almost such another serious and good woman as the dear one to whom I am now writing; who has, as she says, given over all other thoughts of the world but such as shall assist her to leave it happily. How suitable to my own views!

You are very obliging in your offer of money. But although I was forced to leave my clothes behind me, yet I took several things of value with me, which will keep me from present want. You'll say I have made a miserable hand of it. So indeed I have — and to look backwards, in a very little while too.

You must not be angry with me that I wrote not to you before. I was very desirous for your sake, as well as for my own, that you should have it to say that we did not correspond: had they thought we did, every word you could have dropped in my favour would have been rejected; and my mother would have been forbid to see you, or to pay any regard to what you should say.

MRS. NORTON TO MISS CLARISSA HARLOWE

Monday Night, July 3.

OH, the barbarous villainy of this detestable man!

And is there a man in the world who could offer violence to so sweet a creature!

And are you sure you are now out of his reach?

You command me to keep secret the particulars of the vile treatment you have met with; or else, upon an unexpected visit which Miss Harlowe favoured me with, soon after I had received your melancholy letter, I should have been tempted to own I had heard from you, and to have communicated to her such parts of your two letters as would have demonstrated your penitence, and your earnestness to obtain the revocation of your father's malediction, as well as his protection from outrages that may still be offered to you. But then your sister would probably have expected a sight of the letters, and even to have been permitted to take them with her to the family.

The wicked man gives it out at Lord M.'s, as Miss Harlowe tells me, that he is actually married to you: yet she believes it not; nor had I the heart to let her know the truth.

She put it close to me, whether I had not corresponded with you from the time of your going away? I could safely tell her (as I did) that I had not: but I said, that I was well informed that you took extremely to heart your father's imprecation; and that, if she would excuse me, I would say it would be a kind and sisterly part, if she would use her interest to get you discharged from it.

Among other severe things, she told me that my partial fondness for you made me very little consider the honour of the rest of the family: but, if I had not heard this from you, she supposed I was set on by Miss Howe.

She expressed herself with a good deal of bitterness against that young lady: who, it seems, everywhere, and to everybody (for you must think that your story is the subject of all conversations), rails against your family; treating them, as your sister says, with contempt and even with ridicule.

MISS CL. HARLOWE TO MRS. JUDITH NORTON

Thursday, July 6.

I AM very sorry Miss Howe is so lively in her resentments on my account. I have always blamed her very freely for her liberties of this sort with my friends.

You need not, you say, exhort me to despise such a man as him by whom I have suffered — indeed you need not: for I would choose the cruellest death rather than to be his. And yet, my dear Mrs. Norton, I will own to you, *that once I could have loved him — ungrateful man! had he permitted me to love him, I* once *could have loved him.* Yet he never deserved my love. And was not this a fault? But now, if I can but keep out of his hands, and obtain a last forgiveness, and that as well for the sake of my dear friends' future reflections, as for my own present comfort, it is all I wish for.

Reconciliation with my friends I do not expect; nor pardon from them, till in extremity, and as a *viaticum.*

I will write. But to *whom* is my doubt. Calamity has not yet given me the assurance to address myself to my FATHER. My UNCLES (well as they once loved me) are hard-hearted. They never had their masculine passions humanized by the tender name of FATHER. Of my BROTHER I have no hope. I have then but my MOTHER, and my SISTER, to whom I can apply.

And may I not, my dearest mamma, be permitted to lift up my trembling eye to your all-cheering, and your once *more* than indulgent, your *fond* eye, in hopes of seasonable mercy to the poor sick heart that yet beats with life drawn from your own dearer heart? Especially when pardon only, and not restoration, is implored?

Yet were I able to engage my mother's pity, would it not be a means to make *her* still more unhappy than I have already made her, by the opposition she would meet with, were she to try to give force to that pity?

To my SISTER then, I think, I will apply — yet how hard-hearted has my sister been! But I will not ask for protection; and yet I am in hourly dread that I shall want protection. All I will ask for at present (preparative to the last forgiveness I will implore) shall be only to be freed from the heavy curse that seems to have operated as far as it *can* operate as to *this* life. And surely it was passion, and not intention, that carried it so very far as to the *other!*

MISS HOWE TO MISS CLARISSA HARLOWE

(*Superscribed for Mrs. Rachel Clark, etc.*)   *Wednesday, July 5.*

MY DEAR CLARISSA, — I have at last heard from you from a quarter I little expected.

From my mother.

She had for some time seen me uneasy and grieving; and justly supposed it was about you. And this morning dropped a hint, which made me conjecture that she must have heard something of you more than I knew. And when she found that this added to my uneasiness, she owned she had a letter in her hands of yours, dated the 29th of June, directed for me.

You may guess that this occasioned a little warmth that could not be wished for by either.

Need I to remind you, Miss Clarissa Harlowe, of *three* letters I wrote to you, to none of which I had any answer; except to the *first*, and that a few lines only, promising a letter at large; though you were well enough, the day after you received my *second*, to go joyfully back again with him to the vile house? But more of these by and by. I must hasten to take notice of your letter of Wednesday last week; which you could *contrive* should fall into my mother's hands.

Let me tell you that that letter has almost broken my heart. Good God! what have you brought yourself to, Miss Clarissa Harlowe? Could I have believed, that after you had escaped from the miscreant (with such mighty pains and earnestness escaped), and after such an attempt as he had made, you would have been prevailed upon not only to forgive him, but (without being married too) to return with him to that horrid house! — A house I had given you such an account of! — Surprising! What an intoxicating thing is *this love*? I *always* feared that you, even you, were not proof against its *inconsistent* effects.

Your peace is destroyed! I wonder not at it: since now you must reproach yourself for a credulity so ill-placed.

Your intellect is touched! I am sure my heart bleeds for you: but, excuse me, my dear, I doubt your intellect was touched before you left Hampstead; or you would never have let him find you out there; or, when he did, suffer him to prevail upon you to return to the horrid brothel.

I tell you, I sent you *three letters*: the *first* of which, dated the 7th and 8th of June (for it was written at twice), came safe to your hands, as you sent me word by a few lines dated the 9th: had it not, I should have doubted my own safety; since in it I gave you such an account of the abominable house, and threw such cautions in your way in relation to that Tomlinson, as the more surprised me that you could think of going back to it again, after you had escaped from it, and from Lovelace — O my dear! But nothing now will I ever wonder at!

The *second*, dated June 10, was given into your own hand at Hampstead, on Sunday the 11th, as you was lying upon a couch, in a strange way, according to my messenger's account of you, bloated, and flush-coloured; I don't know how.

The *third* was dated the 20th of June. Having not heard one word from you since the promising billet of the 9th, I own I did not spare you in it. I ventured it by the usual conveyance, by that Wilson's, having no other: so cannot be sure you received it.

My love for you, and my concern for your honour, may possibly have made me a little of the severest: if you think so, place it to its proper account; to *that* love, and to *that* concern: which will but do justice to / Your afflicted and faithful / A. H.

P.S. My mother would not be satisfied without reading my letter herself; and that before I had fixed all my proposed hooks. She knows, by this means, and has excused, our former correspondence.

She indeed suspected it before: and so she very well might; knowing me, and knowing my love of you.

She has so much real concern for your misfortunes, that, thinking it will be a consolation to *you*, and that it will oblige *me*, she consents that you shall write to me the *particulars at large of your sad story*: but it is on condition that I show her all that has passed between us, relating to yourself and the vilest of men. I have the more cheerfully complied, as the communication cannot be to your disadvantage.

You may therefore write freely, and direct to our own house.

MISS CLARISSA HARLOWE TO MISS HOWE

Thursday, July 6.

How to defend myself in everything that has happened, I cannot tell: since in some part of the time, in which my conduct appears to have been censurable, I was not myself; and to this hour know not all the methods taken to deceive and ruin me.

Alas, my dear! I was tricked, most vilely tricked back, as you shall hear in its place.

Without *knowing* the house was so very *vile* a house from your *intended* information, I disliked the people too much, ever *voluntarily* to have returned to it. But had you really written such cautions about Tomlinson, and the house, as you seem to have *purposed* to do, they must, had they come in time, have been of infinite service to me. But not one word of either, whatever was your *intention*, did you mention to me, in that *first* of the *three* letters you so warmly TELL ME you *did* send me. *I will enclose it to convince you.*[1]

But your account of your messenger's delivering to me your second letter, and the description he gives of me, *as lying upon a couch, in a strange way, bloated and flush-coloured, you don't know how*, absolutely puzzles and confounds me.

Lord have mercy upon the poor Clarissa Harlowe! What can this mean! *Who* was the messenger you sent? Was *he* one of Lovelace's creatures too! Could nobody come near me but that man's confederates, either *setting out so*, or *made so*? I know not what to make of any one syllable of this! Indeed I don't.

Let me see. You say this was *before* I went from Hampstead! My intellects had not then been touched — nor had I ever been surprised

1 The letter she encloses was Mr. Lovelace's forged one.

by wine (strange if I had!): how then could I be found in such a *strange way, bloated, and flush-coloured; you don't know how!* Yet what a vile, what a hateful figure has your messenger represented me to have made!

But indeed, I know nothing of ANY messenger from you.

Believing myself secure at Hampstead, I stayed longer there than I would have done, in hopes of the letter promised me in your short one of the 9th, brought me by my own messenger, in which you undertake to send for and engage Mrs. Townsend in my favour.

As I shall not be able, perhaps, to conclude what I have to write in even two or three letters, I will begin a new one with my story; and send the whole of it together, although written at different periods, as I am able.

Allow me a little pause, my dear, at this place; and to subscribe myself / Your ever affectionate and obliged, / CLARISSA HARLOWE.

MISS CLARISSA HARLOWE TO MISS HOWE

Thursday Night.

HE had found me out at Hampstead: strangely found me out; for I am still at a loss to know by what means.

I was loath, in my billet of the 9th, to tell you so, for fear of giving you apprehensions for me; and besides, I hoped then to have a shorter and happier issue to account to you for, through your assistance, than I met with.

She then gives a narrative of all that passed at Hampstead between herself, Mr. Lovelace, Captain Tomlinson, and the women there, to the same effect with that so amply given by Mr. Lovelace.

Mr. Lovelace, finding all he could say, and all Captain Tomlinson could urge, ineffectual, to prevail upon me to forgive an outrage so flagrantly premeditated, rested all his hopes on a visit which was to be paid me by Lady Betty Lawrance and Miss Montague.

On Monday, the 12th of June, these pretended ladies came to Hampstead; and I was presented to them, and they to me, by their kinsman.

They were richly dressed, and stuck out with jewels; the pretended Lady Betty's were particularly very fine.

They came in a coach and four, hired, as was confessed, while their own was repairing in town: a pretence made, I now perceive, that I should not guess at the imposture by the want of the real lady's arms upon it. Lady Betty was attended by her woman, whom she called Morrison; a modest country-looking person.

I had heard that Lady Betty was a fine woman, and that Miss Montague was a beautiful young lady, genteel, and graceful, and full of vivacity — such were these imposters; and having never seen either of them, I had not the least suspicion that they were not the ladies they personated; and being put a little out of countenance by the richness of their dresses, I could not help (fool that I was!) to apologize for my own.

Could I help, my dear, being pleased with them?

Permit me here to break off. The task grows too heavy at present.

. . . .

The pretended ladies, the more we talked, the fonder seemed to be of me. And *the* Lady Betty had Mrs. Moore called up; and asked her if she had accommodations for her niece and self, her woman, and two menservants, for three or four days?

Mr. Lovelace answered for her that she had.

The Lady Betty liked the place, she said. Her Cousin Leeson would excuse her. The air, and my company, would do her good. She never chose to lie in the smoky town, if she could help it. In short, my dear, said she to me, I will stay till you hear from Miss Howe; and till I have your consent to go with me to Glenham Hall. Not one moment will I be out of your company, when I can have it. Stedman, my solicitor, as the distance from town is so small, may attend me here for instructions. Niece Charlotte, one word with you, child.

They retired to the farther end of the room, and talked about their night-dresses.

The Miss Charlotte said, Morrison might be dispatched for them.

True, said the other; but I have some letters in my private box which I must have up. And you know, Charlotte, that I trust nobody with the keys of that.

Could not Morrison bring up that box?

No. She thought it safest where it was. She had heard of a robbery committed but two days ago at the foot of Hampstead Hill; and she should be ruined if she lost her box.

Well, then, it was but going to town to undress, and she would leave her jewels behind her, and return; and should be easier a great deal on all accounts.

For my part, I wondered they came up with them. But that was to be taken as a respect paid to me. And then they hinted at another visit of ceremony which they had thought to make, had they not found me so inexpressibly engaging.

They talked loud enough for me to hear them; on purpose, no doubt, though in affected whispers; and concluded with high praises of me.

. . . .

But amidst all these delightful prospects, I must not, said *the* Lady Betty, forget that I am to go to town.

She then ordered her coach to be got to the door. We will all go to town together, said she, and return together. Morrison shall stay here, and see everything as I am used to have it, in relation to my apartment, and my bed; for I am very particular in some respects. My Cousin Leeson's servants can do all I want to be done with regard to my night-dresses, and the like. And it will be a little airing for you, my dear, and a good opportunity for Mr. Lovelace to order what you want of your apparel to be sent from your former lodgings to Mrs. Leeson's; and we can bring it up with us from thence.

I had not intention to comply. But as I did not imagine that she would insist upon my going to town with them, I made no answer to that part of her speech.

I must here lay down my tired pen!

Recollection! Heart-affecting recollection! How it pains me!

.   .   .   .

In the midst of these agreeablenesses, the coach came to the door. The pretended Lady Betty besought me to give them my company to their Cousin Leeson's. I desired to be excused: yet suspected nothing. She would not be denied. How happy would a visit so condescending make her Cousin Leeson! Her Cousin Leeson was not unworthy of my acquaintance: and would take it for the greatest favour in the world.

I objected my dress. But the objection was not admitted. She bespoke a supper of Mrs. Moore to be ready at nine.

Mr. Lovelace, vile hypocrite, and wicked deceiver! seeing, as he said, my dislike to go, desired her ladyship not to insist upon it.

Fondness for my company was pleaded. She begged me to oblige her: made a motion to help me to my fan herself: and, in short, was so very urgent, that my feet complied against my speech and my mind: and being, in a manner, led to the coach by her, and made to step in first, she followed me; and her pretended niece, and the wretch, followed her: and away it drove.

But think, my dear, what a dreadful turn all had upon me; when, through several streets and ways I knew nothing of, the coach slackening its pace, came within sight of the dreadful house of the dreadfullest woman in the world, as she proved to me.

Lord be good unto me! cried the poor fool, looking out of the coach. Mr. Lovelace! — Madam! turning to the pretended Lady Betty — Madam! turning to the niece, my hands and eyes lifted up — Lord be good unto me!

What! What! What, my dear!

He pulled the string. What need to have come this way? said he. But since we are, I will but ask a question. My dearest life, *why* this apprehension?

The coachman stopped: *his* servant, who, with one of hers, was behind, alighted. Ask, said he, if I have any letters? Who knows, my dearest creature, turning to me, but we may already have one from the captain? We will not go out of the coach! Fear nothing — why so apprehensive? Oh! these fine spirits! cried the execrable insulter.

Dreadfully did my heart then misgive me: I was ready to faint. Why this terror, my life? You shall not stir out of the coach — but one question, now the fellow has drove us this way.

Your lady will faint, cried the execrable Lady Betty, turning to him. My dearest niece! (niece I *will* call you, taking my hand) we must alight, if you are so ill. Let us alight — only for a glass of water and hartshorn — indeed we must alight.

No, no, no — I am well — quite well. Won't the man drive on? I am well — quite well — indeed I am. *Man*, drive on, putting my head out of the coach. *Man*, drive on! though my voice was too low to be heard.

The coach stopped at the door. How I trembled!

Dorcas came to the door, on its stopping.

My dearest creature, said the vile man, gasping, as it were for breath, you shall *not* alight. Any letters for me, Dorcas?

There are two, sir. And here is a gentleman, Mr. Belton, sir, waits for your honour; and has done so above an hour.

I'll just speak to him. Open the door. You shan't step out, my dear. A letter perhaps from the captain already! You shan't step out, my dear.

I sighed as if my heart would burst.

But we *must* step out, nephew: your lady will faint. Maid, a glass of hartshorn and water! My dear, you *must* step out. You will faint, child — we must cut your laces. (I believe my complexion was all manner of colours by turns). Indeed, you must step out, my dear.

He knew, he said, I should be well, the moment the coach drove from the door. I should *not* alight. By his soul, I should not.

Lord, Lord, nephew, Lord, Lord, cousin, both women in a breath, what ado you make about nothing! You *persuade* your lady to be afraid of alighting! See you not that she is just fainting?

Indeed madam, said the vile seducer, my dearest love must not be moved in this point against her will. I beg it may not be insisted upon.

Fiddle-faddle, foolish man! What a pother is here! I guess how it is: you are ashamed to let us see, what sort of people you carried your lady among but do you go out, and speak to your friend, and take your letters.

He stepped out; but shut the coach door after him, to oblige me.

The coach may go on, madam, said I.

The coach *shall* go on, my dear life, said he — but he gave not, nor intended to give, orders that it should.

Immediately came the old creature to the door. A thousand pardons, dear madam, stepping to the coach-side, if we have any way offended you. Be pleased, ladies (to the other two), to alight.

Well, my dear, whispered *the* Lady Betty, I now find that a hideous description of a person we never saw, is an advantage to them. I thought the woman was a monster — but, really, she seems tolerable.

I was afraid I should have fallen into fits: but still refused to go out. Man! — Man! — Man! cried I, gaspingly, my head out of the coach and in, by turns, half a dozen times running, drive on! — Let us go!

My heart misgave me beyond the power of my own accounting for it; for still I did not suspect these women. But the antipathy I had taken to the vile house, and to find myself so near it, when I expected no such matter, with the sight of the old creature, made me behave like a distracted person.

The hartshorn and water was brought. The pretended Lady Betty made me drink it. Heaven knows if there were anything else in it!

Besides, said she, whisperingly, I must see what sort of creatures the *nieces* are. Want of delicacy cannot be hid from me. You could not surely, my dear, have this aversion to re-enter a house, for a few minutes, in our company, in which you lodged and boarded several weeks, unless these women could be so presumptuously vile, as my nephew ought not to know.

Out stepped the pretended lady; the servant, at her command, having opened the door.

Dearest madam, said the other to me, let me follow you (for I was next the door). Fear nothing: I will not stir from your presence.

Come, my dear, said the pretended lady: give me your hand; holding out hers. Oblige me this once.

We shall stay but a few minutes, my dear! — but a few minutes! said the same specious jilt — out of breath with her joy, as I have since thought, that they had thus triumphed over the unhappy victim!

Come, Mrs. Sinclair, I think your name is, show us the way — following her, and leading me. I am very thirsty. You have frighted me, my dear, with your strange fears. I must have tea made, if it can be done in a moment. We have further to go, Mrs. Sinclair, and must return to Hampstead this night.

It shall be ready in a moment, cried the wretch. We have water boiling.

Hasten, then. Come, my dear, to me, as she led me through the passage to the fatal inner house. Lean upon me — how you tremble! how you falter in your steps! Dearest Niece Lovelace (the old wretch being in hearing), why these hurries upon your spirits? We'll be gone in a minute.

And thus she led the poor sacrifice into the old wretch's too well-known parlour.

The called-for tea was ready presently.

I was made to drink two dishes, with milk, complaisantly urged by the pretended ladies helping me each to one. I was stupid to their hands; and, when I took the tea, almost choked with vapours; and could hardly swallow.

I thought, *transiently* thought, that the tea, the last dish particularly, had an odd taste.

At the pretended lady's motion, I went upstairs, attended by Dorcas; who affected to weep for joy that once more she saw my *blessed* face, that was the vile creature's word; and immediately I set about taking out some of my clothes, ordering what should be put up, and what sent after me.

While I was thus employed, up came the pretended Lady Betty, in a hurrying way. My dear, you won't be long before you are ready. My nephew is very busy in writing answers to his letters: so, I'll just whip away, and change my dress, and call upon you in an instant.

O madam! I *am* ready! I am *now* ready! You must not leave me here: and down I sunk, affrighted, into a chair.

This instant, this instant, I will return — before you can be ready. — before you can have packed up your things — we would not be late — the robbers we have heard of may be out — don't let us be late.

And away she hurried before I could say another word. Her pretended niece went with her, without taking notice to me of her going.

I had no suspicion yet that these women were not indeed the ladies they personated; and I blamed myself for my weak fears. It cannot *be*, thought I, that *such* ladies will abet treachery against a poor creature they are so fond of. They must undoubtedly *be* the persons they *appear* to be — what folly to doubt it! The air, the dress, the dignity of women of quality. How unworthy of them, and of my charity, concluded I, is this ungenerous shadow of suspicion!

So, recovering my stupefied spirits, as well as they could be recovered (for I was heavier and heavier; and wondered to Dorcas what ailed me; rubbing my eyes, and taking some of her snuff, pinch after pinch, to very little purpose), I pursued my employment: but when that was over, all packed up that I designed to be packed up; and I had nothing to do but to *think*; and found them tarry so long; I thought I should have gone distracted. I shut myself into the chamber that had been mine; I kneeled, I prayed; yet knew not what I prayed for: then ran out again: It was almost dark night, I said: where, where was Mr. Lovelace?

I *demanded* his aunt! I *demanded* his cousin! The evening, I said, was closing! My head was very, *very* bad, I remember I said — and it grew worse and worse.

Terror, however, as yet kept up my spirits; and I insisted upon his going himself to hasten them.

He called his servant. He raved at the *sex* for *their* delay: 'twas well that business of consequence seldom depended upon such parading, unpunctual triflers!

But now, indifferent as my head was, I had a little time to consider the man and his behaviour. He terrified me with his looks, and with his violent emotions, as he gazed upon me. Evident *joy-suppressed* emotions, as I have since recollected. O my dear, What mischiefs was he not then meditating!

I complained once or twice of thirst. My mouth seemed parched. At the time, I supposed that it was my terror (gasping often as I did for breath) that parched up the roof of my mouth. I called for water: some table-beer was brought me: beer, I suppose, was a better vehicle (if I were not dosed enough before) for their potions. I told the maid that she knew I seldom tasted malt-liquor: yet, suspecting nothing of this nature, being extremely thirsty, I drank it, as what came next: and instantly, as it were, found myself much worse than before; as if inebriated, I should fancy: I know not how.

His servant was gone twice as long as he needed: and just before his return, came one of the pretended Lady Betty's with a letter for Mr. Lovelace.

He sent it up to me. I read it: and then it was that I thought myself a lost creature; it being to put off her going to Hampstead that night, on account of violent fits which Miss Montague was pretended to be seized with; for then immediately came into my head his vile attempt upon me in this house; the revenge that my flight might too probably inspire him with on that occasion, and because of the difficulty I made to forgive him, and to be reconciled to him; his very looks wild and dreadful to me; and the women of the house such as I had more reason than ever, even from the pretended Lady Betty's hint, to be afraid of: all these crowding together in my apprehensive mind, I fell into a kind of frenzy.

I have not remembrance how I was for the time it lasted: but I know that, in my first agitations, I pulled off my head-dress, and tore my ruffles in twenty tatters, and ran to find him out.

When a little recovered, I insisted upon the hint he had given of their coach. But the messenger, he said, had told him that it was sent to fetch a physician, lest his chariot should be put up, or not ready.

I then insisted upon going directly to Lady Betty's lodgings.

Mrs. Leeson's was now a crowded house, he said: and as my earnestness could be owing to nothing but groundless apprehension (and O what vows, what protestations of his honour did he then make!), he hoped I would not add to their present concern.

All impatient with grief and apprehension, I still declared myself resolved not to stay in that house till morning. All I had in the world, my rings, my watch, my little money, for a coach; or, if one were not to be got, I would go on foot to Hampstead that night, though I walked it by myself.

A coach was hereupon sent for, or pretended to be sent for. Any price, he said, he would give to oblige me, late as it was; and he would attend me with all his soul. But no coach was to be got.

Let me cut short the rest. I grew worse and worse in my head; now stupid, now raving, now senseless. The vilest of vile women was brought to frighten me. Never was there so horrible a creature as she appeared to me at the time.

I remember I pleaded for mercy. I remember that I said *I would be his — indeed I would be his* — to obtain his mercy. But no mercy found I! My strength, my intellects, failed me — and then such scenes followed — O my dear, such dreadful scenes! — fits upon fits (faintly indeed and imperfectly remembered) procuring me no compassion — but death was withheld from me. That would have been too great a mercy!

. . . .

Thus was I tricked and deluded back by blacker hearts of my own sex than I thought there were in the world. I was so senseless, that I dare not aver that the horrible creatures of the house were personally aiding; but some visionary remembrances I have of female figures flitting before my sight, the wretched woman's particularly.

[*Events between the time of "her recovery from her delirium and sleepy disorder" and the time of Lovelace's departure for M. Hall and Clarissa's subsequent escape are summarized (by Richardson); and then Clarissa continues:*]

The very hour that I found myself in a place of safety, I took pen to write to you. When I began, I designed only to write six or eight lines, to inquire after your health: for, having heard nothing from you, I feared *indeed* that you *had been*, and *still were*, too ill to write. But no sooner did my pen begin to blot the paper, but my sad heart hurried it into length.

I doubt not that the stories of Mrs. Fretchville, and her house, would be found as vile impostures as any of the rest, were I to inquire; and had I not enough, and too much, already against the perjured man.

And now, honoured madam, and my dearest Miss Howe, who are to sit in judgment upon my case, permit me to lay down my pen with one request, which, with the greatest earnestness, I make to you both: and that is, That you will neither of you open your lips in relation to the potions and the violences I have hinted at. Not that I am solicitous that my disgrace should be hidden from the world, or that it should not be generally known that the man has proved a villain to me: for this, it seems, everybody but myself expected from his character. But suppose, as his actions by me are really of a *capital nature*, it were insisted upon that I should appear to prosecute him and his accomplices in a court of justice, how do you think I could bear that?

But since my character, *before* the capital enormity, was lost in the eye of the world; and that from the very hour I left my father's house; and since all my own hopes of worldly happiness are entirely over; let me slide quietly into my grave; and let it not be remembered, except by one friendly tear, and no more, dropped from your gentle eye, mine own dear Anna Howe, on the happy day that shall shut up all my sorrows, that there was such a creature as / CLARISSA HARLOWE. / *Saturday, July 8.*

MISS HOWE TO MISS CLARISSA HARLOWE

Sunday, July 9.

MAY Heaven signalize its vengeance, in the face of all the world, upon the most abandoned and profligate of men! And in its own time, I doubt not but it will. And we must look to a WORLD BEYOND THIS for the reward of your sufferings!

Another shocking detection, my dear! How have you been deluded! Very watchful I have thought you; very sagacious: but, alas! not watchful, not sagacious enough, for the horrid villain you have had to deal with!

The letter you sent me enclosed as mine, of the 7th of June, is a villainous forgery. The hand, indeed, is astonishingly like mine; and the cover, I see, is actually my cover: but yet the letter is not so exactly imitated, but that (had you had any suspicions about his vileness at the time) you, who so well know my hand, might have detected it.

He has omitted everything, I see, in it that could have shown you what a detestable house the house is; and have given you suspicions of the vile Tomlinson.

Apprehensive for *both* our safeties from the villainy of such a daring and profligate contriver, I must call upon you, my dear, to resolve upon taking legal vengeance of the infernal wretch. And this not only for our own sakes, but for the sakes of innocents who otherwise may yet be deluded and outraged by him.

She then gives the particulars of the report made by the young fellow whom she sent to Hampstead with her letter; and who supposed he had delivered it into her own hand; and then proceeds:

I am astonished that the vile wretch, who could know nothing of the time my messenger (whose honesty I can vouch for) would come, could have a creature ready to personate you! Strange, that the man should happen to arrive just as you were gone to church (as I find was the fact, on comparing what he says with your hint that you were at church twice that day), when he might have got to Mrs. Moore's two hours before!

'Tis my opinion, my dear, that you will be no longer safe where you are, than while the V. is in the country. Words are poor! or how could I execrate him! I have hardly any doubt that he has sold himself for a time. Oh, may the time be short! Or may his infernal prompter no more keep convenant with him than he does with others!

I enclose not only the rough draft of my long letter mentioned above; but the heads of that which the young fellow thought he delivered into your own hands at Hampstead. And when you have perused them, I will leave you to judge how much reason I had to be surprised that you wrote me not an answer to either of those letters; one of which you owned you had received (though it proved to be his forged one); the other delivered into your own hands, as I was assured; and both of them of so much concern to your honour; and still how much more surprised I must be, when I received a letter from Mrs. Townsend, dated June 15, from Hampstead, importing, that Mr. Lovelace, who had been with you several days, had, on the Monday before, brought Lady Betty and his cousin, richly dressed, and in a coach and four, to visit you: who, with your own consent, had carried you to town with them — to your former lodgings; where you still were: that the Hampstead women believed you to be married; and reflected upon me as a fomenter of differences between man and wife: that he himself was at Hampstead the day before; viz. Wednesday the 14th; and boasted of his happiness with you; inviting Mrs. Moore, Mrs. Bevis, and Miss Rawlins, to go to town to visit his spouse; which they promised to do: that he declared that you were entirely reconciled to your former lodgings: and that, finally, the women at Hampstead told Mrs. Townsend, that he had very handsomely discharged theirs.

I own to you, my dear, that I was so much surprised and disgusted at these appearances against a conduct till then unexceptionable that I was resolved to make myself as easy as I could, and wait till you should think fit to write to me. But I could rein in my impatience but for a few days; and on the 20th of June I wrote a sharp letter to you; which I find you did not receive.

Miss Howe to Miss Clarissa Harlowe
Monday, July 10.

I now resume my pen, to obey my mother in giving you her opinion upon your unhappy story.

She says that the good of society requires that such a beast of prey should be hunted out of it: and, if you do not prosecute him, she thinks you will be answerable for all the mischiefs he may do in the course of his future villainous life.

Then she thinks, and so do I, that the vile creatures, his accomplices, ought by all means to be brought to condign punishment, as they must and will be, upon bringing him to his trial: and this may be a means to blow up and root out a whole nest of vipers, and save many innocent creatures.

She added that if Miss Clarissa Harlowe could be so indifferent about having this public justice done upon such a wretch for her *own* sake, she ought to overcome her scruples out of regard to her family, her acquaintance, and her sex, which are all highly injured and scandalized by his villainy to her.

I long for the full particulars of your story.

Miss Clarissa Harlowe to Miss Howe
Tuesday, July 11.

As you are so earnest to have all the particulars of my sad story before you, I will, if life and spirits be lent me, give you an ample account of all that has befallen me, from the time you mention. But this, it is very probable, you will not see, till after the close of my last scene: and as I shall write with a view to that, I hope no other voucher will be wanted for the veracity of the writer, be who will the reader.

I am far from thinking myself out of the reach of this man's further violence. But what can I do? Whither can I fly? Perhaps my bad state of health (which must grow worse, as recollection of the past evils, and reflections upon them, grow heavier and heavier upon me) may be my protection. Once, indeed, I thought of going abroad; and had I the prospect of many years before me, I would go. But, my dear, the blow is given. Nor have you reason now, circumstanced as

I am, to be concerned that it is. What a heart must I have, if it be not broken! And indeed, my *dear* friend, I do so earnestly wish for the last closing scene, and with so much comfort find myself in a declining way, that I even sometimes ungratefully regret that naturally healthy constitution, which used to double upon me all my enjoyments.

As to the earnestly recommended prosecution, I may possibly touch upon it more largely hereafter, if ever I shall have better spirits; for they are at present extremely sunk and low. But, just now, I will only say that I would sooner suffer every evil (the repetition of the capital one excepted) than appear publicly in a court to do myself justice.

MISS HOWE TO MISS CLARISSA HARLOWE

Wedn. Night, July 12.

I WRITE, my dearest creature, I cannot *but* write, to express my concern on your dejection. Let me beseech you, my charming excellence, let me beseech you, not to give way to it.

Comfort yourself, on the contrary, in the triumphs of a virtue unsullied; a will wholly faultless. Who could have withstood the trials that you have surmounted? Your Cousin Morden will soon come. He will see justice done you, I make no doubt, as well with regard to what concerns your person as your estate. And many happy days may you yet see; and much good may you still do, if you will not heighten unavoidable accidents into guilty despondency.

But why, my dear, this pining solicitude continued after a reconciliation with relations as unworthy as implacable; whose wills are governed by an all-grasping brother, who finds his account in keeping the breach open? On this over-solicitude it is now plain to me that the vilest of men built all his schemes.

I shall send this short letter (I am obliged to make it a short one) by *young* Rogers, as we call him; the fellow I sent to you to Hampstead; an innocent, though pragmatical rustic. Admit him, I pray you, into your presence, that he may report to me how you look, and how you are.

Mr. Hickman should attend you; but I apprehend that all his motions, and mine own too, are watched by the execrable wretch: as indeed his are by an agent of mine; for I own that I am apprehensive of his plots and revenge, now I know that he has intercepted my vehement letters against him, that he is the subject of my dreams, as well as of my waking fears.

· · · · · · · · · · ·

My mother, at my earnest importunity, has just given me leave to write, and to receive your letters — but fastened this condition upon the concession, that yours must be under cover to Mr. Hickman (this with a view, I suppose, to give him consideration with me); and upon this further condition, that she is to see all we write. "When girls are set upon a point," she told one who told me again, "it is better for a mother, if possible, to make herself of their party, than to oppose them; since there will be then hopes that she will still hold the reins in her own hands."

Pray let me know what the people are with whom you lodge? Shall I send Mrs. Townsend to direct you to lodgings either more safe or more convenient for you?

Adieu, my dearest creature. Comfort *yourself*, as you would in the like unhappy circumstances comfort / Your own / ANNA HOWE.

MISS CLARISSA HARLOWE TO MISS HOWE

Thursday, July 13.

I AM extremely concerned, my dear Miss Howe, for being primarily the occasion of the apprehensions you have of this wicked man's vindictive attempts. What a wide-spreading error is mine!

If I find that he sets on foot any machination against you, or against Mr. Hickman. I do assure you I will consent to prosecute him, although I were sure I should not survive my first appearance at the bar he should be arraigned at.

I own the justice of your mother's arguments on that subject; but must say that I think there are circumstances in my particular case which will excuse me.

Your messenger has now *indeed* seen me. I talked with him on the cheat put upon him at Hampstead: and am sorry to have reason to say, that had not the poor young man been very *simple* and very *self-sufficient*, he had not been so grossly deluded.

I think I cannot be more private than where I am. I hope I am safe. All the risk I run, is in going out and returning from morning prayers; which I have two or three times ventured to do; once at Lincoln's Inn Chapel, at eleven; once at St. Dunstan's, Fleet Street, at seven in the morning, in a chair both times; and twice, at six in the morning, at the neighbouring church in Covent Garden.

The man's name at whose house I lodge is Smith — a glove-*maker*, as well as *seller*. His wife is the shopkeeper. A dealer also in stockings, ribbands, snuff, and perfumes. A matron-like woman, plain-hearted, and prudent. The husband an honest, industrious man.

Two neat rooms, with plain, but clean furniture, on the first floor, are mine; one they call the dining-room.

There is, up another pair of stairs, a very worthy widow lodger, Mrs. Lovick by name; who, although of low fortunes, is much respected, as Mrs, Smith assures me, by people of condition of her acquaintance, for her piety, prudence, and understanding. With her I propose to be well acquainted.

At present my head is much disordered. I have not indeed enjoyed it with any degree of clearness since the violence done to that, and to my heart too, by the wicked arts of the abandoned creatures I was cast among.

Friday, July 7.

WHAT heart, thinkest thou, can I have to write, when I have lost the only subject worth writing upon?

Well, but, Jack, 'tis a surprising thing to me that the dear fugitive cannot be met with; cannot be heard of. She is so poor a plotter (for plotting is not her talent) that I am confident, had I been at liberty, I should have found her out before now; although the different emissaries I have employed about town, round the adjacent villages, and in Miss Howe's vicinage, have hitherto failed of success. But my lord continues so weak and low-spirited, that there is no getting from him. I would not disoblige a man whom I think in danger still: for would his gout, now it has got him down, but give him, like a fair boxer, the rising blow, all would be over with him. And here (pox of his fondness for me! it happens at a very bad time) he makes me sit hours together entertaining him with my rogueries (a pretty amusement for a sick man!): and yet, whenever he has the gout, he prays night and morning with his chaplain. But what must *his* notions of religion be, who, after he has nosed and mumbled over his responses, can give a sigh or groan of satisfaction, as if he thought he had made up with Heaven; and return with a new appetite to my stories? — encouraging them, by shaking his sides with laughing at them, and calling me a sad fellow, in such an accent as shows he takes no small delight in his kinsman.

My two cousins are generally present when I *entertain*, as the old peer calls it. Those stories must drag horribly, that have not more hearers and applauders than relaters.

These are smart girls; they have life and wit; and yesterday, upon Charlotte's raving against me upon a related enterprise, I told her that I had had it in debate several times, whether she were or were not too near to kin to me: and that it was once a moot point with me, whether I could not love her dearly for a month or so: and perhaps it was well for her that another pretty little puss started up and diverted me just as I was entering the course.

They all three held up their hands and eyes at once. But I observed, that though the girls exclaimed against me, they were not so angry at this plain speaking, as I have found my beloved upon hints so dark that I have wondered at her quick apprehension.

MR. LOVELACE TO JOHN BELFORD, ESQ.

Sunday Night, July 9.

Now, Jack, have I a subject with a vengeance. I am in the very height of my trial for all my sins to my beloved fugitive. For here, to-day, at about five o'clock, arrived Lady Sarah Sadleir and Lady Betty Lawrance, each in her chariot and six. Dowagers love equipage; and these cannot travel ten miles without a set, and half a dozen horsemen.

And now I enter upon my TRIAL

With horrible grave faces was I received. The two antiques only bowed their tabby heads; making longer faces than ordinary; and all the old lines appearing strong in their furrowed foreheads and fallen cheeks. How do you, cousin? and, How do you, Mr. Lovelace? looking all round at one another, as who should say, Do you speak first; and, Do you: for they seemed resolved to lose no time.

I had nothing for it but an air as manly as theirs was womanly. Your servant, madam, to Lady Betty; and, Your servant, madam, I am glad to see you abroad, to Lady Sarah.

I took my seat. Lord M. looked horribly glum; his fingers clasped, and turning round and round, under and over, his but just disgouted thumbs; his sallow face, and goggling eyes, cast upon the floor, on the fireplace, on his two sisters, on his two kinswomen, by turns: but not once deigning to look upon me.

I am sorry, very sorry, hesitated Lady Sarah, that there is no hope of your ever taking up —

What's the matter *now*, madam?

The matter now! — Why, Lady Betty has two letters from Miss Harlowe which have told us what's the matter.

Then they all chorused upon me. Such a character as Miss Harlowe's cried one — A lady of so much generosity and good sense! Another: How charmingly she writes! the two maiden monkeys, looking at her fine handwriting: her perfections my crimes. What can you expect will be the end of these things?

[In a sequence of four vivid letters Lovelace tells Belford how he met charges made by his family of dishonourable treatment of Clarissa as well as his forgery of letters supposedly by the family. He is urged to offer marriage, and agrees to marry Clarissa if she will have him. His two Cousins Montague will wait upon Miss Howe and beg her aid in furthering the match.]

Thus, Jack, have I at once reconciled myself to all my relations — and, if the lady refuses me, thrown the fault upon her. This, I knew, would be in my power to do at any time: and I was the more arrogant to them, in order to heighten the merit of my compliance.

But, after all, it would be very whimsical, would it not, if all my plots and contrivances should end in wedlock? What a punishment would this come out to be, upon myself too, that all this while I have been plundering my own treasury?

MISS HOWE TO MISS CLARISSA HARLOWE

Thursday Night, July 13.

I AM to acquaint you, that I have been favoured with a visit from Miss Montague and her sister, in Lord M.'s chariot and six.

They came in the name of Lord M. and Lady Sarah and Lady Betty, his two sisters, to desire my interest to engage you to put yourself into the protection of Lady Betty; who will not part with you till she sees all the justice done you that can now be done.

Their joint strength, united with Lord M.'s, has so far succeeded, that the wretch has bound himself to them, and to these young ladies, in the solemnest manner, to wed you in their presence, if they can prevail upon you to give him your hand.

He promises by them to make the best of husbands; and my lord, and Lady Sarah, and Lady Betty, are all three to be guarantees that he will be so. Noble settlements, noble presents, they talked of: they say they left Lord M. and his two sisters talking of nothing else but of those presents and settlements, how most to do you honour.

I made a great many objections for you — all, I believe, that you could have made yourself had you been present. But I have no doubt to advise you, my dear (and so does my mother), instantly to put yourself into Lady Betty's protection, with a resolution to take the wretch for your husband.

Your melancholy letter, brought by Rogers, with his account of your indifferent health, confirmed to him by the woman of the house, as well as by your looks, and by your faintness while you talked with him, would have given me inexpressible affliction, had I not been cheered by this agreeable visit from the young ladies. I hope you will be equally so on my imparting the subject of it to you.

Indeed, my dear, you must not hesitate. You *must* oblige them. The alliance is splendid and honourable. Very few will know anything of his brutal baseness to you. All must end, in a little while, in a general reconciliation; and you will be able to resume your course of doing the good to every deserving object, which procured you blessings wherever you set your foot.

Your prudence, your piety, will crown all. You will reclaim a wretch that, for a hundred more sakes than for his own, one would wish to be reclaimed.

MISS HOWE TO MISS CHARLOTTE MONTAGUE

Tuesday Morning, July 18.

IN THE frenzy of my soul I write to you, to demand of you, and of any of your family who can tell, news of my beloved friend; who, I doubt, has been spirited away by the base arts of one of the blackest — oh, help me to a name bad enough to call him by! Her piety is proof against self-attempts. It must, it must be he, the only wretch who could injure such an innocent; and now — who knows what he has done with her!

I wrote to her the very moment you and your sister left me. Judge my astonishment, my distraction, when last night the messenger, returning post-haste, brought me word that she had not been heard of since Friday morning! And that a letter lay for her at her lodgings which came by post, and must be mine!

She went out about six that morning; only intending, as they believe, to go to morning prayers at Covent Garden Church, just by her
lodgings, as she had done divers times before. Went on foot! Left
word she should be back in an hour. Very poorly in health!

Lord, have mercy upon me! What shall I do! I was a distracted
creature all last night!

Surely, my good ladies, you were well authorized in the proposals
you made in presence of my mother! Surely he dare not abuse your
confidence, and the confidence of your noble relations! I make no
apology for giving you this trouble, nor for desiring you to favour
with a line by this messenger.

MR. LOVELACE TO JOHN BELFORD, ESQ.

M. Hall, Sat. Night, July 15.

ALL undone, by Jupiter! Zounds, Jack, what shall I do now!
A curse upon all my plots and contrivances!

Thy assistance I bespeak. This messenger rides for life and death
— and I hope he'll find you at your town lodgings; if he meet not
with you at Edgware; where, being Sunday, he will call first.

This cursed, cursed woman, on Friday dispatched man and horse
with the joyful news (as she thought it would be to me) in an exulting letter from Sally Martin, that she had found out my angel as on
Wednesday last; and on Friday morning, after she had been at prayers
at Covent Garden Church — praying for my reformation perhaps
— got her arrested by two sheriff's officers, as she was returning to her
lodgings, who (villains!) put her into a chair they had in readiness,
and carried her to one of the cursed fellow's houses.

She has arrested her for £150, pretendedly due for board and
lodgings: a sum (besides the low villainy of the proceeding) which
the dear soul could not possibly raise; all her clothes and effects, except what she had on and with her when she went away, being at the
old devil's.

And here, for an aggravation, has the dear creature lain already
two days; for I must be gallanting my two aunts and my two cousins,
and giving Lord M. an airing after his lying-in — pox upon the whole
family of us! — and returned not till within this hour: and now returned to my distraction, on receiving the cursed tidings and the
exulting letter.

Hasten, hasten, dear Jack; for the love of God, hasten to the injured charmer! My heart bleeds for her. She deserved not this! I
dare not stir. It will be thought done by my contrivance — and if I
am absent from this place, that will confirm the suspicion.

Set her free the moment you see her: without conditioning, free!
On your knees, for me, beg her pardon: and assure her that, wherever
she goes, I will not molest her: no, nor come near her, without her
leave: and be sure allow not any of the damned crew to go near her.
Only let her permit *you* to receive her commands from time to time.

You have always been her friend and advocate. What would I now give had I permitted you to have been a successful one!

Let her have all her clothes and effects sent her instantly, as a small proof of my sincerity. And force upon the dear creature, who must be moneyless, what sums you can get her to take. Let me know how she has been treated. If roughly, woe be to the guilty!

A line! a line! a kingdom for a line! with tolerable news, the first moment thou canst write! This fellow waits to bring it.

Miss Charlotte Montague to Miss Howe

M. Hall, Tuesday Afternoon.

Dear Miss Howe, — Your letter has infinitely disturbed us all. This wretched man has been half distracted ever since Saturday night.

We knew not what ailed him till your letter was brought.

Vile wretch as he is, he is, however, innocent of this new evil.

A horrid mistake of his general orders has subjected her to the terror and disgrace of an arrest.

But she must be now quite at liberty.

He has been a distracted man ever since the news was brought him; and we knew not what ailed him.

Miss Montague to Miss Howe

M. Hall, July 18.

Dear Madam, — We resolved upon a little tour of two days, the Friday and Saturday, in order to give an airing to my lord and Lady Sarah. We returned not till Saturday night, all in as good humour with one another as we went out. We never had such pleasure in his company before. If he would be good, and as he ought to be, no man would be better beloved by relations than he. But never was there a greater alteration in man when he came home, and received a letter from a messenger, who, it seems, had been flattering himself in hopes of a reward, and had been waiting for his return from the night before. In *such* a fury! The man fared but badly. He instantly shut himself up to write, and ordered man and horse to be ready to set out before daylight the next morning, to carry the letter to a friend in London.

He would not see us all that night; neither breakfast nor dine with us next day. He ought, he said, never to see the light; and bid my sister, whom he called an *innocent* (and who was very desirous to know the occasion of all this), shun him; saying, he was a wretch, and made so by his own inventions and the consequences of them.

Late on Monday night he received a letter from Mr. Belford, his most favoured friend, by his own messenger; who came back in a foam, man and horse. Whatever were the contents, he was not easier, but like a madman rather: but still would not let us know the occasion. But to my sister he said, Nobody, my dear Patsey, who can think but of half the plagues that pursue an intriguing spirit, would ever quit the right path.

He was out when your messenger came: but soon came in; and bad enough was his reception from us all. And he said that his own torments were greater than ours, than Miss Harlowe's, or yours, madam, all put together. He would see your letter. He always carries everything before him: and said, when he had read it, that he thanked God he was not such a villain as you, with too great an appearance of reason, thought him.

Thus then he owned the matter to be:

He had left general directions to the people of the lodgings the dear lady went from, to find out where she was gone to, if possible, that he might have an opportunity to importune her to be his, before their difference was public. The wicked people (*officious* at least, if not wicked) discovered where she was on Wednesday; and, for fear she should remove before they could have his orders, they put her under a *gentle restraint*, as they call it; and dispatched away a messenger to acquaint him with it; and to take his orders.

This messenger arrived on Friday afternoon; and stayed here till we returned on Saturday night: and when he read the letter he brought — I have told you, madam, what a fury he was in.

The letter he retired to write, and which he dispatched away so early on Sunday morning, was to conjure his friend Mr. Belford, on receipt of it, to fly to the lady, and set her free; and to order all her things to be sent her; and to clear him of so *black* and *villainous* a fact, as he justly called it.

And by this time he doubts not that all is happily over; and the beloved of his soul (as he calls her at every word) in an easier and happier way than she was before the horrid fact.

He declares, and we can vouch for him, that he has been, ever since last Saturday night, the most miserable of men.

We are, dear madam, / Your obliged and faithful servants,

CHARLOTTE } MONTAGUE.
MARTHA }

DEAR MISS HOWE, — We join in the above request of Miss Charlotte and Miss Patty Montague, for your favour and interest; being convinced that the accident was an accident; and no plot or contrivance of a wretch too full of them. We are, madam, / Your most obedient humble servants,

M.
SARAH SADLEIR.
ELIZ. LAWRANCE.

DEAR MISS HOWE, — After what is written above, by names and characters of such unquestionable honour, I might have been excused signing a name almost as hateful to myself, as I KNOW it is to you.

365

But the *above* will have it so. Since, therefore, I *must* write, it shall be the truth; which is, that if I may be once more admitted to pay my duty to the most deserving and most injured of her sex, I will be content to do it with a halter about my neck; and attended by a parson on my right hand, and the hangman on my left, be doomed, at her will, either to the church or the gallows. / Your most humble servant, / ROBERT LOVELACE.

MR. BELFORD TO ROBERT LOVELACE, ESQ.

Sunday Night, July 16.

WHAT a cursed piece of work hast thou made of it, with the most excellent of women! Thou mayest be in earnest, or in jest, as thou wilt; but the poor lady will not be long either thy sport, or the sport of fortune!

This last act, however unintended by thee, yet a consequence of thy general orders, and too likely to be thought agreeable to thee, by those who know thy other villainies by her, has finished thy barbarous work. And I advise thee to trumpet forth everywhere, how much in earnest thou art to marry her, whether true or not.

Thou mayest *safely* do it. She will not live to put thee to the trial; and it will a little palliate for thy enormous usage of her, and be a means to make mankind, who know not what I know of the matter, herd a little longer with thee, and forbear to hunt thee to thy fellow-savages in the Libyan wilds and deserts.

Your messenger found me at Edgware, expecting to dinner with me several friends, whom I had invited three days before. I sent apologies to them, as in a case of life and death; and speeded to town to the wicked woman's.

Finding the lady not there, I posted away to the officer's, although Sally told me that she had been just come from thence; and that she had refused to see her, or (as she sent down word) anybody else; being resolved to have the remainder of that Sunday to herself, as it might, perhaps, be the last she should ever see.

I had the same thing told me, when I got thither.

I sent up to let her know that I came with a commission to set her at liberty. I was afraid of sending up the name of a man known to be your friend. She absolutely refused to see *any man*, however, for that day, or to answer further to anything said from me.

Having, therefore, informed myself of all that the officer, and his wife, and servant, could acquaint me with, as well in relation to the horrid arrest, as to her behaviour, and the women's to her; and her ill state of health; I went back to Sinclair's, as I will still call her, and heard the three women's story: from all which I am enabled to give you the following shocking particulars; which may serve till I can see the unhappy lady herself to-morrow, if then I can gain admittance to her. You will find that I have been very minute in my inquiries.

Your villain it was that *set* the poor lady, and had the impudence to appear, and abet the sheriff's officers in the cursed transaction. He thought, no doubt, that he was doing the most acceptable service to his blessed master. They had got a chair; the head ready up, as soon as service was over. And as she came out of the church, at the door fronting Bedford Street, the officers, stepping to her, whispered that they had an action against her.

She was terrified, trembled, and turned pale.

Action! said she. What is that? I have committed *no bad action!* Lord bless me! Men, what mean you?

That you are our prisoner, madam.

Prisoner, sirs! What — How — Why — What have I done?

You must go with us. Be pleased, madam, to step into this chair.

With *you!* With *men!* Must go with *men!* I am not used to go with *strange men!* Indeed you must excuse me!

We can't excuse you: we are sheriff's officers. We have a writ against you. You *must* go with us, and you shall know at whose suit.

She then spied thy villain. O thou wretch, said she, where is thy vile master? Am I again to be *his prisoner?* Help, good people!

A crowd had before begun to gather.

My master is in the country, madam, many miles off. If you please to go with these men, they will treat you civilly.

The people were most of them struck with compassion. A fine young creature! A thousand pities! cried some. While some few threw out vile and shocking reflections! But a gentleman interposed, and demanded to see the fellows' authority.

They showed it. Is your name Clarissa Harlowe, madam? said he.

Yes, yes, indeed, ready to sink, my name *was* Clarissa Harlowe: but it is now *Wretchedness!* Lord, be merciful to me! what is to come next?

You *must* go with these men, madam, said the gentleman: they have authority for what they do.

He pitied her, and retired.

Indeed you must, said one chairman.

Indeed you must, said the other.

She said, Well, if I must go, I must — I cannot resist — but I will not be carried to the woman's! I will rather die at your feet than be carried to the woman's!

You won't be carried there, madam, cried thy fellow.

Only to *my* house, madam, said one of the officers.

Where is that?

In High Holborn, madam.

I know not where High Holborn is: but anywhere, except to the woman's. — But am I to go with *men* only?

. . . .

The unhappy lady fainted away when she was taken out of the chair at the officer's house.

Several people followed the chair to the very house, which is in a wretched court. Sally was there; and satisfied some of the inquirers that the young gentlewoman would be exceedingly well used: and they soon dispersed.

Sally, as a favour, offered to carry her to her former lodgings: but she declared they should carry her hither a corpse, if they did.

What is to be the end of this disgraceful violence?

The end, said the vile Sally Martin, is, for honest people to come into their own. Who do you think, *Miss Harlowe*, for I understand you are not married; who do you think is to pay for your board and your lodgings; such handsome lodgings! for so long a time as you were at Mrs. Sinclair's?

Lord have mercy upon me! Miss Martin (I think you are Miss Martin!) — and is this the cause of such a disgraceful insult upon me in the open streets?

And cause enough, *Miss Harlowe* (fond of gratifying her jealous revenge, by calling her *Miss*) — one hundred and fifty guineas, or pounds, is no small sum to lose — and by a young creature who would have bilked her lodgings.

You amaze me, Miss Martin! What language do you talk in? — *Bilk my lodgings!* What is that?

She stood astonished and silent for a few moments.

Rowland, for that is the officer's name, told her she had friends enough to pay the debt, if she would write.

She would trouble nobody; she had no friends; was all they could get from her, while Sally stayed: but yet spoken with a patience of spirit, as if she enjoyed her griefs.

Again they asked her if they should send any word to her lodgings?

These are my lodgings now, are they not? was all her answer.

She sat up in a chair all night, the back against the door; having, it seems, thrust a broken piece of a poker through the staples where a bolt had been on the inside.

. . . .

Next morning, Sally and Polly both went to visit her.

They asked if she had any commands? If she *had*, she need only mention what they were, and she should be obeyed.

None at all, she said.

Will you not send to your new lodgings? The people will be frighted.

So they will, if I send. So they will, if they know where I am.

But have you no things to send for from thence?

There is what will pay for their lodgings and trouble: I shall not lessen their security.

But perhaps letters or messages may be left for you there.

I have very few friends; and to those I *have*, I will spare the mortification of knowing what has befallen me.

We are surprised at your indifference, *Miss Harlowe*. Will you not write to any of your friends?

No.

Why, you don't think of tarrying *here* always?

I shall not *live* always.

Do you think you are to stay here as long as you live?

That's as it shall please God, and those who have brought me hither.

What we came for, was to know if you had any proposals to make for your enlargement?

Then, it seems, the officer put in, you have very good friends, madam, I understand. Is it not better that you make it up? Charges will run high. A hundred and fifty guineas are easier paid than two hundred. Let these ladies bail you, and go along with them; or write to your friends to make it up.

Sir, said she, with high indignation, to the officer, did not you say last night that it was as much your business to protect me from the insults of others as from escaping? Cannot I be permitted to see whom I please; and to refuse admittance to those I like not?

Your creditors, madam, will expect to see you.

Not if I declare I will not treat with them.

Then, madam, you will be sent to prison.

Prison, friend! What dost thou call thy house?

Not a prison, madam.

Why these iron-barred windows, then? Why these double locks and bolts all on the outside, none on the in?

And down she dropped into her chair, and they could not get another word from her. She threw her handkerchief over her face, as once before, which was soon wet with tears; and grievously, they own, she sobbed.

Gentle treatment, Lovelace! — Perhaps thou, as well as these wretches, will think it so!

. . . .

'Tis twelve of the clock, Sunday night. I can think of nothing but of this excellent creature.

After the women had left her, she complained of her head and her heart; and seemed terrified with apprehensions of being carried once more to Sinclair's.

Refusing anything for breakfast, Mrs. Rowland came up to her and told her (as these wretches owned they had ordered her, for fear she should starve herself) that she *must* and *should* have tea and bread and butter.

If it be for *your own sakes*, said she, that is another thing: let coffee, or tea, or chocolate, or what you will, be got: and put down a chicken to my account every day, if you please, and eat it yourselves. I will taste it, if I can. I would do nothing to hinder you. I have friends will pay you liberally, when they know I am gone.

They wondered, they told her, at her strange composure in such distresses.

The ladies might possibly dispense with her going back to the house to which she had such an antipathy. Then the compassionate gentleman, who was inclined to make it up with her creditors on her own

369

bond — it was strange to them she hearkened not to so generous a proposal.

I charge you, said she, as you will answer to it one day to my friends, that you bring no gentleman into my company. I charge you don't. If you do, you know not what may be the consequence.

They apprehended no bad consequence, they said, in doing their duty: and if she knew not her own good, her friends would thank them for taking any innocent steps to serve her, though against her will.

Don't push me upon extremities, man! Don't make me desperate, woman! I have no small difficulty, notwithstanding the seeming composure you just now took notice of, to bear, as I ought to bear, the evils I suffer. But if you bring a man or men to me, be the pretence *what* it will ——

Sally came again at dinner-time *to see how she fared,* as she told her; and that she did not starve herself: and, as she wanted to have some talk with her, if she gave her leave, she would dine with her.

I cannot eat.

You must try, *Miss Harlowe.*

She turned from them, and, to herself, said, *Too much! Too much!* She tossed her handkerchief, wet before with her tears, from her, and held her apron to her eyes.

Don't weep, Miss! said the vile Polly.

Yet *do*, cried the viler Sally, if it be a relief. Nothing, as Mr. Lovelace once told *me*, dries sooner than tears.

They advised her to write out of hand.

But how much must I write for? What is the sum? Should I not have had a bill delivered me? God knows, I took not your lodgings. But he that could treat me as he has done could do this!

Don't speak against Mr. Lovelace, *Miss Harlowe*. He is a man I greatly esteem (cursed toad!). And, 'bating that he will take his advantage where he can, of *us* silly credulous women, he is a man of honour.

She lifted up her hands and eyes instead of speaking: and well she might! For any words she could have used could not have expressed the anguish she must feel on being comprehended in the *us*.

She must write for one hundred and fifty guineas, at least: two hundred, if she were short of money, might as well be written for.

Will not Mrs. Sinclair think my clothes a security till they can be sold? They are very good clothes. A suit or two but just put on, as it were; never worn. They cost much more than is demanded of me. *My father loved to see me fine.* All shall go. But let me have the particulars of her demand. I suppose I must pay for my *destroyer* (that was her well-adapted word!) and his servants, as well as for myself. I am content to do so. Indeed, I am content to do so — I am above wishing that anybody who could *thus* act should be so much as expostulated with, as to the justice and equity of this payment. If I have but enough to pay the demand, I shall be satisfied;

and will leave the baseness of such an action as this, as an aggravation of a guilt which I thought could *not* be aggravated.

I own, Lovelace, I have malice in this particularity, in order to sting thee to the heart. And, let me ask thee, what now thou canst think of thy barbarity, thy unprecedented barbarity, in having reduced a person of her rank, fortune, talents, and virtue, so low?

At twelve, Saturday night, Rowland sent to tell them that she was so ill that he knew not what might be the issue; and wished her out of his house.

And this made them as heartily wish to hear from you. For their messenger, to their great surprise, was not then returned from M. Hall. And they were sure he must have reached that place by Friday night.

Early on Sunday morning both devils went to see how she did. They had such an account of her weakness, lowness, and anguish, that they forbore (out of compassion, they said, finding their visits so disagreeable to her) to see her. But their apprehension of what might be the issue was, no doubt, their principal consideration: nothing else could have softened such flinty bosoms.

They sent for the apothecary Rowland had had to her, and gave him, and Rowland, and his wife, and maid, strict orders, many times repeated, for the utmost care to be taken of her — no doubt, with an Old Bailey forecast. And they sent up to let her know what orders they had given: but that, understanding she had taken something to compose herself, they would not disturb her.

She had scrupled, it seems, to admit the apothecary's visit overnight, because he was a MAN. Nor could she be prevailed upon to see him till they pleaded *their own safety* to her.

When I first came, and told them of thy execrations for what they had done, and joined my own to them, they were astonished. The mother said she had thought she had known Mr. Lovelace better; and expected thanks, and not curses.

Under what shocking disadvantages, and with this addition to them, that I am thy friend and intimate, am I to make a visit to this unhappy lady to-morrow morning! In thy name too! Enough to be refused, that I am of a *sex* to which, for *thy* sake, she has so justifiable an aversion: nor, having such a tyrant of a father, and such an implacable brother, has she reason to make an exception in favour of *any* of it on *their* accounts.

It is three o'clock. I will close here; and take a little rest: what I have written will be a proper preparative for what shall offer by and by.

Monday, July 17.

ABOUT six this morning I went to Rowland's. Mrs. Sinclair was to follow me, in order to dismiss the action; but not to come in sight.

Rowland, upon inquiry, told me that the lady was extremely ill; and that she had desired that no one but his wife or maid should come near her.

I said I *must* see her. I had told him my business overnight; and I *must* see her.

His wife went up: but returned presently, saying she could not get her to speak to her; yet that her eyelids moved; though she either would not, or could not, open them to look up at her.

Oons, woman, said I, the lady may be in a fit: the lady may be dying. Let me go up. Show me the way.

A horrid hole of a house, in an alley they call a court; stairs wretchedly narrow, even to the first-floor rooms: and into a den they led me, with broken walls, which had been papered, as I saw by a multitude of tacks, and some torn bits held on by the rusty heads.

The floor indeed was clean, but the ceiling was smoked with variety of figures, and initials of names, that had been the woeful employment of wretches who had no other way to amuse themselves.

A bed at one corner, with coarse curtains tacked up at the feet to the ceiling. The windows dark and double-barred; and only a little four-paned eyelet-hole of a casement to let in air; more, however, coming in at broken panes than could come in at that.

. . . .

To finish the shocking description, in a dark nook stood an old broken-bottomed cane-couch, sunk at one corner, and unmortised by the failing of one of its worm-eaten legs.

And this, thou horrid Lovelace, was the bedchamber of the divine Clarissa!!!

I had leisure to cast my eye on these things: for, going up softly, the poor lady turned not about at our entrance; nor, till I spoke, moved her head.

She was kneeling in a corner of the room, near the dismal window, against the table, on an old bolster (as it seemed to be) of the cane couch, half-covered with her handkerchief; her back to the door; which was only shut to (no need of fastenings!); her arms crossed upon the table, the forefinger of her right hand in her Bible. She had perhaps been reading in it, and could read no longer. Paper, pens, ink, lay by her book on the table. Her dress was white damask, exceeding neat; but her stays seemed not tight-laced. I was told afterwards that her laces had been cut when she fainted away at her entrance into this cursed place; and she had not been solicitous enough about her dress to send for others. Her head-dress was a little discomposed; her charming hair, in natural ringlets, as you have heretofore described it, but a little tangled, as if not lately combed, irregularly shading one side of the loveliest neck in the world; as her disordered, rumpled handkerchief did the other. Her face (oh, how altered from what I had seen it! Yet lovely in spite of all her griefs and sufferings!) was reclined, when we entered, upon her crossed arms; but so as not more than one side of it to be hid.

I thought my concern would have choked me. Something rose in my throat, I know not what, which made me, for a moment, guggle, as it were, for speech: which, at last, forcing its way. Con — con —

confound you both, said I to the man and woman, is this an apartment for such a lady? And could the cursed devils of her own sex, who visited this suffering angel, see her, and leave her, in so damned a nook?

Sir, we would have had the lady to accept of our own bedchamber; but she refused it. We are poor people — and we expect nobody will stay with us longer than they can help it.

You are people chosen purposely, I doubt not, by the damned woman who has employed you: and if your usage of this lady has been but half as bad as your house, you had better never to have seen the light.

Up then raised the charming sufferer her lovely face; but with such a significance of woe overspreading it that I could not, for the soul of me, help being visibly affected.

She waved her hand two or three times towards the door, as if commanding me to withdraw; and displeased at my intrusion; but did not speak.

Permit me, madam — I will not approach one step farther without your leave — permit me, for one moment, the favour of your ear!

No — no — go, go, MAN! with an emphasis — and would have said more; but, as if struggling in vain for words, she seemed to give up speech for lost, and dropped her head down once more, with a deep sigh, upon her left arm; her right, as if she had not the use of it (numbed, I suppose), self-moved, dropping down on her side.

Oh, that thou hadst been there! and in my place!

.   .   .   .

I dare not approach you, dearest lady, without your leave: but on my knees I beseech you to permit me to release you from this damned house, and out of the power of the accursed woman who was the occasion of your being here!

She lifted up her sweet face once more, and beheld me on my knees. Never knew I before what it was to pray so heartily.

Are you not — are you not Mr. Belford, sir? I think your name is Belford?

It is, madam, and I ever was a worshipper of your virtues, and an advocate for you; and I come to release you from the hands you are in.

And in whose to place me? Oh, leave me, leave me! Let me never rise from this spot! Let me never, never believe in man!

This moment, dearest lady, this very moment, if you please, you may depart whithersoever you think fit. You are absolutely free, and your own mistress.

I had now as lief die here in this place as anywhere. I will owe no obligation to any friend of *him* in whose company you have seen me. So, pray, sir, withdraw.

Then turning to the officer, Mr. Rowland I think your name is? I am better reconciled to your house than I was at first. If you can but engage that I shall have nobody come near me but your wife (no *man!*), and neither of those women who have sported with my calamities, I will die with you, and in this very corner. And you shall be well satisfied for the trouble you have had with me. I have value enough for that — for, see, I have a diamond ring; taking it out of her bosom; and I have friends will redeem it at a high price, when I am gone.

But for *you*, sir, looking at me, I beg you to withdraw. If you mean me well, God, I hope, will reward you for your good meaning; but to the friend of my *destroyer* will I not owe an obligation.

You will owe no obligation to me, nor to anybody. You have been detained for a debt you do not owe. The action is dismissed; and you will only be so good as to give me your hand into the coach, which stands as near to this house as it could draw up. And I will either leave you at the coach door, or attend you whithersoever you please, till I see you safe where you would wish to be.

Will you then, sir, *compel* me to be beholden to you?

You will inexpressibly oblige me, madam, to command me to do you either service or pleasure.

Why then, sir (looking at me) — but why do you mock me in that humble posture! Rise, sir! I cannot speak to you else.

I arose.

Only, sir, take this ring. I have a sister, who will be glad to have it at the price it shall be valued at, for the *former* owner's sake! Out of the money she gives, let this man be paid; handsomely paid.

I approached her, and was going to speak ——

Don't speak, sir: here's the ring.

I stood off.

And won't you take it? Won't you do this last office for me? I have no other person to ask of it; else, believe me, I would not request it of *you*. But take it or not, laying it upon the table — you must withdraw, sir: I am very ill. I would fain get a little rest, if I could. I find I am going to be bad again.

And offering to rise, she sunk down through excess of weakness and grief, in a fainting fit.

The maid coming in just then, the woman and she lifted her up on the decrepit couch; and I withdrew with this Rowland.

I went down meanwhile; for the detestable woman had been below some time. Oh, how I did curse her. I never before was so fluent in curses.

She tried to wheedle me; but I renounced her; and, after she had dismissed the action, sent her away crying, or pretending to cry, because of my behaviour to her.

You will observe that I did not mention one word to the lady about *you*. I was afraid to do it. For 'twas plain that she could not bear your name: your *friend*, and the *company* you have seen me in, were the words nearest to naming you she could speak: and yet I wanted to clear your intention of this brutal, this sordid-looking villainy.

I sent up again, by Rowland's wife, when I heard that the lady was recovered, beseeching her to quit that devilish place; and the woman assured her that she was at full liberty to do so; for that the action was dismissed.

But she cared not to answer her: and was so weak and low that it was almost as much out of her power as inclination, the woman told me, to speak.

Being told that she desired not to be disturbed, and seemed inclined to doze, I took this opportunity to go to her lodgings in Covent Garden; to which Dorcas (who first discovered her there, as Will was the setter from church) had before given me a direction.

The man's name is Smith, a dealer in gloves, snuff, and such petty merchandise: his wife the shopkeeper: he a maker of the gloves they sell. Honest people, it seems.

I thought to have got the woman with me to the lady; but she was not within.

He told me that a letter was left for her there on Saturday; and, about half an hour before I came, another, superscribed by the same hand; the first, by the post; the other, by a countryman;

I thought it right to take the two letters back with me; and, dismissing my coach, took a chair, as a more proper vehicle for the lady, if I (the friend of her *destroyer*) could prevail upon her to leave Rowland's.

MR. LOVELACE TO JOHN BELFORD, ESQ.

Monday, July 17, Eleven at Night.

CURSE upon thy hard heart, thou caitiff! How hast thou tortured me by thy designed *abruption*! 'Tis impossible that Miss Harlowe should have ever suffered as thou hast made me suffer, and as I now suffer!

Give this fellow the sequel of thy tormenting scribble.

Dispatch him away with it. Thou hast promised it shall be ready. Every cushion or chair I shall sit upon, the bed I shall lie down upon (if I go to bed) till he return, will be stuffed with bolt-upright awls, bodkins, corking-pins, and packing-needles: already I can fancy that, to pink my body like my mind, I need only to be put into a hogshead stuck full of steel-pointed spikes, and rolled down a hill three times as high as the Monument.

But I lose time; yet know not how to employ it till this fellow returns with the sequel of thy soul-harrowing intelligence!

MR. BELFORD TO ROBERT LOVELACE, ESQ.

Monday Night, July 17.

ON my return to Rowland's, I found that the apothecary was just gone up. Mrs. Rowland being above with him, I made the less scruple to go up too, as it was probable that to ask for leave would be to ask to be denied; hoping also that the letters I had with me would be a good excuse.

I besought her excuse; and, winking for the apothecary to withdraw (which he did), told her that I had been at her new lodgings, to order everything to be got ready for her reception, presuming she would choose to go thither: that I had a chair at the door: that Mr. Smith and his wife (I named their names, that she should not have room for the least fear of Sinclair's) had been full of apprehensions for her safety: that I had brought two letters, which were left there for her; one by the post, the other that very morning.

I besought her to think of quitting that wretched hole.

I gave her the solemnest assurances that she should not be invaded in her new lodgings by anybody; and said that I would particularly engage my honour, that *the person who had most offended her should not come near her without her own consent.*

Your honour, sir! Are you not that man's friend!

I am not a friend, madam, to his vile actions to the *most excellent of women.*

Do you flatter me, sir? Then are you a MAN. But oh, sir, your friend, holding her face forward with great earnestness, your *barbarous* friend, what has he not to answer for!

There she stopped: her heart full; and putting her hand over her eyes and forehead, the tears trickled through her fingers: resenting thy barbarity, it seemed, as Cæsar did the stab from his distinguished Brutus!

Though she was so very much disordered, I thought I would not lose this opportunity to assert your innocence of this villainous arrest.

There is no defending the unhappy man in any of his vile actions by you, madam; but of this last outrage, by all that's good and sacred, he is innocent.

O wretches! what a sex is yours! Have you all one dialect? *Good and sacred!* If, sir, you can find an oath, or a vow, or an adjuration, that my ears have not been twenty times a day wounded with, then speak it, and I may again believe a MAN.

I was excessively touched at these words, knowing thy baseness, and the reason she had for them.

But say you, sir; for I would not, methinks, have the wretch capable of this sordid baseness! — Say you that he is innocent of this *last* wickedness? Can you *truly* say that he is?

Madam, said I, I have a regard, a regard a gentleman *ought* to have, to my word; and whenever I forfeit it to you ——

Nay, sir, don't be angry with me. It is grievous to me to question a gentleman's veracity. But your friend calls himself a *gentleman.* You know not what I have suffered by a *gentleman!* And then again she wept.

I would give you, madam, demonstration, if your grief and your weakness would permit it, that he has no hand in this barbarous baseness: and that he resents it as it ought to be resented.

Well, well, sir (with quickness), he will have his account to make up somewhere else; not to me. I should not be sorry to find him able to acquit his intention on this occasion. Let him know, sir, only one thing, that when you heard me, in the bitterness of my spirit, most vehemently exclaim against the undeserved usage I have met with from him, that even *then*, in *that* passionate moment, I was able to say (and never did I see such an earnest and affecting exaltation of hands and eyes), "Give him, good God! repentance and amendment; that I may be the last poor creature who shall be ruined by him! And, in Thine own good time, receive to *Thy* mercy the poor wretch who had *none* on me!"

By my soul, I could not speak. She had not her Bible before her for nothing.

I was forced to turn my head away, and to take out my handkerchief.

I assured her, in the strongest terms (*but swore not*), that you were resolved not to molest her: and, as a proof of the sincerity of my professions, besought her to give me directions (in pursuance of my friend's express desire) about sending all her apparel, and whatever belonged to her, to her new lodgings.

She seemed pleased; and gave me instantly out of her pocket her keys; asking me if Mrs. Smith, whom I had named, might not attend me; and she would give *her* further directions? To which I cheerfully assented; and then she told me that she would accept of the chair I had offered her.

She gave the maid something; probably the only half-guinea she had: and then with difficulty, her limbs trembling under her, and supported by Mrs. Rowland, got downstairs.

I offered my arm: she was pleased to lean upon it. I doubt, sir, said she, as she moved, I have behaved rudely to you: but, if you knew all, you would forgive me.

I ordered my servant (whose mourning made him less observable as such, and who had not been in the lady's eye) to keep the chair in view; and to bring me word how she did when set down. The fellow had the thought to step into the shop just before the chair entered it, under pretence of buying snuff; and so enabled himself to give me an account that she was received with great joy by the good woman of the house; who told her she was but just come in; and was preparing to attend her in High Holborn. O Mrs. Smith, said she, as soon as she saw her, did you not think I was run away? You don't know what I have suffered since I saw you. I have been in a prison! — Arrested for debts I owe not! But, thank God, I am here!

Will you let Catharine assist me to bed? I have not had my clothes off since Thursday night.

What she further said the fellow heard not, she leaning upon the maid, and going upstairs.

But dost thou not observe what a strange, what an uncommon openness of heart reigns in this lady? *She had been in a prison*, she said, before a stranger in the shop, and before the maid-servant: and so, probably, she would have said had there been twenty people in the shop.

The disgrace she cannot hide from *herself*, as she says in her letter to Lady Betty, she is not solicitous to conceal from the *world!*

But this makes it evident to me that she is resolved to keep no terms with thee. And yet to be able to put up such a prayer for thee, as she did in her prison (I will often mention the *prison-room*, to tease thee!); does not this show that revenge has very little sway in her mind; though she can retain so much proper resentment?

Mrs. Smith, whom I took with me to Sinclair's, saw everything looked out, and put into the trunks and boxes they were first brought in, and carried away in two coaches.

Had I not been there, Sally and Polly would each of them have taken to herself something of the poor lady's spoils. This they declared: and I had some difficulty to get from Sally a fine Brussels lace head, which she had the confidence to say she would wear for *Miss Harlowe's* sake. Nor should either I or Mrs. Smith have known she had got it, had she not been in search after the ruffles belonging to it.

My resentment on this occasion, and the conversation which Mrs. Smith and I had (in which I not only expatiated on the merits of a lady, but expressed my concern for her sufferings; though I left her room to suppose her married, yet without averring it), gave me high credit with the good woman: so that we are perfectly well acquainted already: by which means I shall be enabled to give you accounts from time to time of all that passes; and which I will be very industrious to do, provided I may depend upon the solemn promises I have given the lady, in your name, as well as in my own, that she shall be free from all personal molestation from you. And thus shall I have it in my power to return *in kind* your writing favours; and preserve my shorthand besides: which, till this correspondence was opened, I had pretty much neglected.

I ordered the abandoned women to make out your account. They answered, *that* they would do with a *vengeance*. Indeed they breathe nothing but revenge. For now, they say, you will assuredly marry; and your example will be followed by all your friends and companions — as the old one says, to the utter ruin of her poor house.

MR. BELFORD TO ROBERT LOVELACE, ESQ.

Tuesday, July 18. Afternoon.

I RENEWED my inquiries after the lady's health, in the morning, by my servant: and, as soon as I had dined, I went myself.

She returned me thanks for all my good offices; and her excuses, that they could not be *personal* just then, being very low and faint: but if I gave myself the trouble of coming about six this evening, she should be able, she hoped, to drink a dish of tea with me, and would then thank me herself.

She has two handsome apartments, a bedchamber and dining-room, with light closets in each. She has already a nurse (the people of the house having but one maid); a woman whose care, diligence, and honesty, Mrs. Smith highly commends. She has likewise the benefit of the voluntary attendance, and *love*, as it seems, of a widow gentle-woman, Mrs. Lovick her name, who lodges over her apartment, and of whom she seems very fond, having found something in her, she thinks, resembling the qualities of her worthy Mrs. Norton.

About seven o'clock this morning, it seems, the lady was so ill that she yielded to their desires to have an apothecary sent for. Not the fellow she had had at Rowland's; but one Mr. Goddard, a man of skill and eminence; and of conscience too; demonstrated as well by general character, as by his prescriptions to this lady: for, pronouncing her case to be grief, he ordered for the present, only innocent juleps and light kitchen diet; telling Mrs. Lovick that that, with air, moderate exercise, and cheerful company, would do her more good than all the medicines in his shop.

Mrs. Lovick gratified me with an account of a letter she had written from the lady's mouth to Miss Howe; she being unable to write herself with steadiness.

It was to this effect; in answer, it seems, to her two letters, whatever were the contents of them:

That she had been involved in a dreadful calamity, which she was sure, when known, would exempt her from the effects of her friendly displeasure, for not answering her first; having been put under an arrest. — Could she have believed it? — That she was released but the day before: and was now so weak, and so low, that she was obliged to get a widow gentlewoman in the same house to account thus for her silence to her (Miss Howe's) two letters of the 13th and 16th: that she would, as soon as able, answer them — begged of her, mean-time, not to be uneasy for her; since (only that this was a calamity which came upon her when she was far from being well; a load laid upon the shoulders of a poor wretch, ready before to sink under too heavy a burden) *it was nothing to the evil she had before suffered*: and one felicity seemed likely to issue from it; which was, that she should be at rest, in an honest house, with considerate and kind-hearted people; having assurance given her that she should not be molested by the wretch, whom it would be death for her to see: so that now she (Miss Howe) needed not to send to her by private and expensive conveyances: nor need Collins to take precautions for fear of being dogged to her lodgings; nor she to write by a fictitious name to her, but by her own.

Tuesday Night, July 18.

I am just come from the lady. I was admitted to the dining-room, where she was sitting in an elbow-chair, in a very weak and low way.

You'll excuse me, Mr. Belford: I ought to rise to thank you for all your kindness to me. I was to blame to be so loath to leave that sad place; for I am in Heaven here, to what I was there: and good people about me too! I have not had good people about me for a long, long time before; so that (with a half smile) I had begun to wonder whither they were all gone.

I told her I knew enough to be convinced that she had the merit of a saint, and the purity of an angel: and was proceeding, when she said, No flighty compliments! No undue attributes, sir!

I disclaimed all intention of compliment: all I *had* said, and what I *should* say was, and should be, the effect of sincere veneration. My unhappy friend's account of her had entitled her to that.

I then mentioned your grief, your penitence, your resolutions of making her all the amends that were possible now to be made her: and, in the most earnest manner, I asserted your innocence as to the last villainous outrage.

Her answer was to this effect: It is painful to me to think of him. The amends you talk of cannot be made. This last violence you speak of *is nothing to what preceded it.*

Having mentioned the outrageous letter you had written to me on this occasion, she asked if I had that letter about me?

I owned I had.

She wished to see it.

This puzzled me horribly: for you must needs think that most of the free things which, among us rakes, pass for wit and spirit, must be shocking stuff to to the ears or eyes of persons of delicacy of that sex: and then such an air of levity runs through thy most serious letters; such a false bravery, endeavouring to carry off ludicrously the subjects that most affect thee; that those letters are generally the least fit to be seen, which ought to be most to thy credit.

Something like this I observed to her; and would fain have excused myself from showing it: but she was so earnest, that I undertook to read some parts of it, resolving to omit the most exceptionable.

I know thou'lt curse me for that; but I thought it better to oblige her than to be suspected myself; and so not have it in my power to serve thee with her, when so good a foundation was laid for it; and when she knows as bad of thee as I can tell her.

Thou rememberest the contents, I suppose, of thy furious letter. Her remarks upon the different parts of it which I read to her, were to the following effect:

Upon thy first two lines, *All undone! undone, by Jupiter! Zounds, Jack, what shall I do now! A curse upon all my plots and contrivances!* thus she expressed herself:

"Oh, how light, how unaffected with the sense of its own crimes, is the heart that could dictate to the pen this libertine froth!"

The paragraph which mentions the vile arrest affected her a good deal.

She desired me to proceed.

I did; but fared not much better afterwards: for on that passage where you say, *I had always been her friend and advocate,* this was her unanswerable remark: I find, sir, by this expression, that he had always designs against me; and that you all along *knew* that he had: would to Heaven you had had the goodness to have contrived some way, that might not have endangered your own safety, to give me notice of his baseness, since you approved not of it! But you gentlemen, I suppose, had rather see an innocent fellow-creature ruined, than be thought capable of an action which, however generous, might be likely to loosen the bands of a wicked friendship.

You have read enough, said she. He is a wicked, wicked man! I see he intended to have me in his power at any rate; and I have no doubt of what his purposes were, by what his actions have been. You know his vile Tomlinson, I suppose. You know — But what signifies talking? Never was there such a premeditately false heart in man (*nothing can be truer, thought I!*). What has he not vowed! What has he not invented! And all for what? — Only to ruin a poor young creature, whom he ought to have protected; and whom he had first deprived of all other protection!

She arose, and turned from me, her handkerchief at her eyes: and, after a pause, came towards me again. I hope, said she, I talk to a man who has a better heart: and I thank you, sir, for all your kind, though ineffectual, pleas in my favour formerly, whether the motives for them were compassion, or principle, or both.

I was afraid, for thy sake, to let her know how *very* earnest I had been: but assured her that I had been her zealous friend; and that my motives were founded upon a merit that, I believed, was never equalled; that, however indefensible Mr. Lovelace was, he had always done justice to her virtue: that to a full conviction of her untainted honour it was owing that he so earnestly desired to call so inestimable a jewel his — and was proceeding when she again cut me short ——

Enough, and too much, of this subject, sir! If he will never more let me behold his face, that is all I have now to ask of him. Indeed, indeed, clasping her hands, *I never will,* if I can, by any means not criminally desperate, avoid it.

What could I say for thee? There was no room, however, *at that time,* to touch this string again, for fear of bringing upon myself a prohibition, not only of the subject, but of ever attending her again.

. . . .

Wednesday, July 19.

This morning I took chair to Smith's; and, being told that the lady had a very bad night, but was up, I sent for her worthy apothecary; who, in his coming to me, approving of my proposal of calling in Dr. H.; I bid the women acquaint her with the designed visit.

It seems she was at first displeased; yet withdrew her objection: but, after a pause, asked them what she should do? She had effects of value, some of which she intended, as soon as she *could,* to turn into money; but, till then, had not a single guinea to give the doctor for his fee.

Mrs. Lovick said she had five guineas by her: they were at her service.

She would accept of three, she said, if she would take *that* (pulling a diamond ring from her finger) till she repaid her; but on no other terms.

Having been told I was below with Mr. Goddard, she desired to speak one word with me, before she saw the doctor.

She was sitting in an elbow-chair, leaning her head on a pillow;

Mrs. Smith and the widow on each side her chair; her nurse, with a phial of hartshorn, behind her; in her own hand her salts.

Raising her head at my entrance, she inquired if the doctor knew Mr. Lovelace?

I told her no; and that I believed you never saw him in your life.

Was the doctor my friend?

He was; and a very worthy and skilful man. I named him for his eminence in his profession: and Mr. Goddard said he knew not a better physician.

The doctor paid his respects to her with the gentlemanly address for which he is noted: and she cast up her sweet eyes to him with that benignity which accompanies her every graceful look.

I would have retired; but she forbid it.

He took her hand, the lily not so beautiful a white; Indeed, madam, you are very low, said he: but, give me leave to say, that you can do more for yourself than all the faculty can do for you.

He then withdrew to the window. And, after a short conference with the women, he turned to me, and to Mr. Goddard, at the other window: We can do nothing here, speaking low, but by cordials and nourishment. What friends has the lady? She seems to be a person of condition; and ill as she is, a very fine woman. — A single lady, I presume?

I knew I was right, said the doctor. A love case, Mr. Goddard! A love case, Mr. Belford! There is one person in the world who can do her more service, than all the faculty.

Mr. Goddard said he had apprehended her disorder was in her mind; and had treated her accordingly: and then told the doctor what he had done; which he approving of, again taking her charming hand, said, My good young lady, you will require very little of our assistance. You must, in a great measure, be your own doctress. Come, *dear* madam (forgive me the familiar tenderness; your aspect commands love, as well as reverence; and a father of children, some of them older than yourself, may be excused for his familiar address), cheer up your spirits. Resolve to do all in your power to be well; and you'll soon grow better.

You are very kind, sir, said she. I will take whatever you direct. My spirits have been hurried. I shall be better, I believe, before I am worse. The care of my good friends here, looking at the women, shall not meet an ungrateful return.

We all withdrew together; and the doctor and Mr. Goddard having a great curiosity to know something more of her story, at the motion of the latter we went into a neighbouring coffee-house, and I gave them, in confidence, a brief relation of it; making all as light for you as I could; and yet you'll suppose, that, in order to do but common justice to the lady's character, heavy must be that light.

Three o'clock, Afternoon.

I just now called again at Smith's; and am told she is somewhat better; which she attributed to the soothings of her doctor. She expressed herself highly pleased with both gentlemen; and said that their behaviour to her was perfectly *paternal*.

Paternal, poor lady! — Never having been, till very lately, from under her parents' wings, and now abandoned by all her friends, she is for finding out something *paternal* and *maternal* in every one (the latter qualities in Mrs. Lovick and Mrs. Smith) to supply to herself the father and mother her dutiful heart pants after.

Mrs. Smith told me that after we were gone, she gave the keys of her trunks and drawers to her and the widow Lovick, and desired them to take an inventory of them; which they did in her presence.

They also informed me that she had requested them to find her a purchaser for two rich dressed suits; one never worn, the other not above once or twice.

This shocked me exceedingly — *perhaps it may thee a little!!!* Her reason for so doing, she told them, was that she should never live to wear them: that her sister, and other relations, were above wearing them: that her mother would not endure in her sight anything that was hers: that she wanted the money: that she would not be obliged to anybody, when she had effects by her for which she had no occasion: and yet, said she, I expect not that they will fetch a price answerable to their value.

They were both very much concerned, as they owned; and asked my advice upon it: and the richness of her apparel having given them a still higher notion of her rank than they had before, they supposed she must be of quality; and again wanted to know her story.

I told them that she was indeed a woman of family and fortune: I still gave them room to suppose her married: but left it to her to tell them all in her own time and manner: all I would say was, that she had been very vilely treated; deserved it not; and was all innocence and purity.

You may suppose that they both expressed their astonishment, that there could be a man in the world who could ill-treat so fine a creature.

As to disposing of the two suits of apparel, I told Mrs. Smith, that she should pretend that, upon inquiry, she had found a friend who would purchase the richest of them; but (*that she might not mistrust*) would stand upon a good bargain. And having twenty guineas about me, I left them with her, in part of payment; and bid her *pretend* to get her to part with it for as little more as she could induce her to take.

Mr. Lovelace to John Belford, Esq.

M. Hall, Wedn. Night, July 19.

You might well apprehend that I should think you were playing me booty in communicating my letter to the lady.

You ask, who would think you might not read to her the least exceptionable parts of a letter written in my own defence? *I'll tell you who* — the man who, in the same letter that he asks this question, tells the friend whom he exposes to her resentment, that there is such an air of levity runs through his most serious letters, that those of his are *least fit to be seen,* which ought to be *most to his credit.* And now what thinkest thou of thy self-condemned folly? Be, however, I charge thee, more circumspect for the future, that so this clumsy error may stand singly by itself.

But as to thy opinion, and the two women's at Smith's, that her heart is broken; that is the true women's language: I wonder how *thou* camest into it: thou who has seen and heard of so many *female deaths* and *revivals.*

I'll tell thee what makes *against* this notion of theirs.

Her time of life and charming constitution: the good she ever delighted to do, and fancied she was born to do; and which she may still continue to do, to as high a degree as ever; nay, higher; since I am no sordid varlet, thou knowest: her religious turn; a turn that will always teach her to bear *inevitable* evils with patience: the contemplation upon her last noble triumph over me, and over the whole crew; and upon her succeeding escape from us all: her will unviolated: and the inward pride of having *not deserved* the treatment she has met with.

How is it possible to imagine that a woman who has all these *consolations* to reflect upon, will die of a broken heart?

On the contrary, I make no doubt but that, as she recovers from the dejection into which this last scurvy villainy (which none but wretches of her own sex *could* have been guilty of) has thrown her, returning love will re-enter her *time-pacified* mind: her thoughts will then turn once more on the *conjugal pivot.*

And, after all (methinks thou askest), art thou still resolved to repair, if reparation be put into thy power?

Why, Jack, I must needs own that my heart has now and then some retrograde motions, upon thinking seriously of the irrevocable ceremony. We do not easily give up the desire of our hearts, and what we imagine essential to our happiness, let the expectation or hope of compassing it be ever so unreasonable or absurd in the opinion of others. *Recurrings* there will be; hankerings that will, on every but remotely favourable incident (however before discouraged and beaten back by ill-success), pop up, and abate the satisfaction we should otherwise take in *contrariant* overtures.

'Tis ungentlemanly, Jack, *man to man,* to lie. — But matrimony I do not *heartily* love — although with a CLARISSA — yet I am in earnest to marry her.

Of this I am absolutely convinced, that if a man ever intends to marry, and to enjoy in peace his own reflections; and not be afraid of retribution, or of the consequences of his own example; he should never be a rake.

This looks like conscience; don't it, Belford?

But, being in earnest still, as I have said, all I have to do, in my present uncertainty, is to brighten up my faculties, by filing off the rust they have contracted by the town smoke, a long imprisonment in my close attendance to so little purpose on my fair perverse; and to brace up, if I can, the relaxed fibres of my mind.

I am not discouraged by the difficulties I have met with from this sweet individual, from endeavouring to make myself acceptable to them [the ladies] as before.

If she reject me, one tour to France and Italy, I dare say, will do the business. Miss Harlowe will by that time have forgotten all she has suffered from her ungrateful Lovelace: though it will be impossible that her Lovelace should ever forget a woman whose equal he despairs to meet with, were he to travel from one end of the world to the other.

Tourville, Mowbray, and myself, pass away our time as pleasantly as possibly we can without thee.

This is one advantage, as I believe I have elsewhere observed, that we male delinquents in love matters have of the other sex: for while they, poor things! sit sighing in holes and corners, or run to woods and groves to bemoan themselves for their baffled hopes, we can rant and roar, hunt, and hawk; and, by new loves, banish from our hearts all remembrance of the old ones.

Merrily, however, as we pass our time, my reflections upon the injuries done to this noble creature bring a qualm upon my heart very often. But I know she will permit me to make her amends, after she has plagued me heartily; and that's my consolation.

An honest fellow still! Clap thy wings, and crow, Jack!

MISS HOWE TO MISS CLARISSA HARLOWE

Thursday Morn. July 20.

WHAT, my dearest creature, have been your sufferings! What must have been your anguish on so disgraceful an insult, committed in the open streets, and in the broad day!

But whatever you do, my dear, you must not despond! Indeed you must not despond! Hitherto you have been in no fault: but despair would be all your own; and the worst fault you can be guilty of.

I cannot bear to look upon another hand instead of yours. My dear creature, send me a few lines, though *ever so few,* in your own hand, if possible. For they will revive my heart; especially if they can acquaint me of your amended health.

His relations are persons of *so much* honour — they are so *very* earnest to rank you among them — the wretch is so *very* penitent: *every one* of *his* family says he is — *your own* are so implacable — your last distress, though the consequence of his former villainy, yet neither brought on by his direction, nor with his knowledge; and so much resented by him — that my mother is absolutely of opinion that *you should be his* — especially if, yielding to my wishes, as expressed in my letter, and those of all his friends, you *would* have complied, had it not been for this horrid arrest.

385

I will enclose the copy of the letter I wrote to Miss Montague last Tuesday, on hearing that nobody knew what was become of you; and the answer to it, underwritten and signed by Lord M., Lady Sarah Sadleir, and Lady Betty Lawrance, as well as by the young ladies; and also by the wretch himself.

I am obliged to accompany my mother soon to the Isle of Wight. My Aunt Harman is in a declining way, and insists upon seeing us both — and Mr. Hickman too, I think.

It would be the death of me to set out for the little island, and not see you first: and yet my mother (fond of exerting an authority that she herself, by that exertion, often brings into question) insists that my next visit to you *must* be a congratulatory one as Mrs. Lovelace.

MISS CLARISSA HARLOWE TO MISS HOWE

Thursday Afternoon.

YOU pain me, my dearest Miss Howe, by the ardour of your noble friendship. I will be very brief, because I am not well; yet a good deal better than I was; and because I am preparing an answer to yours of the 13th. But, beforehand, I must tell you, my dear, I will *not* have that man. Don't be angry with me. But indeed I won't. So let him be asked no questions about me, I beseech you.

I do *not* despond, my dear. I hope I may say, *I will not* despond. Is not my condition greatly mended? I thank Heaven it is!

I am no prisoner now in a vile house. I am not now in the power of that man's devices. I am not now obliged to hide myself in corners for fear of him. One of his intimate companions is become my warm friend, and engages to keep him from me, and that by his own consent. I am among honest people. I have all my clothes and effects restored to me. The wretch himself bears testimony to my honour.

Indeed, I am very weak and ill: but I have an excellent physician, Dr. H., and as worthy an apothecary, Mr. Goddard. Their treatment of me, my dear, is perfectly *paternal!* My mind, too, I can find, begins to strengthen: and methinks, at times, I find myself superior to my calamities.

MR. BELFORD TO ROBERT LOVELACE, ESQ.

Friday Noon, July 21.

THIS morning I was admitted, as soon as I sent up my name, into the presence of the divine lady. Such I may call her; as what I have to relate will fully prove.

She had had a tolerable night, and was much better in spirits; though weak in person; and visibly declining in looks.

Mrs. Lovick and Mrs. Smith were with her; and accused her, in a gentle manner, of having applied herself too assiduously to her pen for her strength, having been up ever since five. She said she had rested better than she had done for many nights: she had found her spirits free, and her mind tolerably easy: and having, as she had reason to think, but a short time, and much to do in it, she must be a good housewife of her hours.

She had been writing, she said, a letter to her sister: but had not pleased herself in it; though she had made two or three essays: but that the last must go.

By hints I had dropped from time to time, she had reason, she said, to think that I knew everything that concerned her and her family; and, if so, must be acquainted with the heavy curse her father had laid upon her; which had been dreadfully fulfilled in one part, as to her prospects in this life, and that in a very short time; which gave her great apprehensions of the other part. She had been applying herself to her sister, to obtain a revocation of it. I hope my father will revoke it, said she, or I shall be very miserable. Yet (and she gasped as she spoke, with apprehension) I am ready to tremble at what the answer may be; for my sister is hard-hearted.

I said something reflecting upon her friends; as to what they would deserve to be thought of, if the unmerited imprecation were not withdrawn. Upon which she took me up, and talked in such a dutiful manner of her parents, as must doubly condemn them (if they remain implacable) for their inhuman treatment of such a daughter.

I then besought her, while she was capable of such glorious instances of generosity and forgiveness, to extend her goodness to a man whose heart bled in every vein of it for the injuries he had done her; and who would make it the study of his whole life to repair them.

The women would have withdrawn when the subject became so particular. But she would not permit them to go. She told me, that if after this time I was for entering with so much earnestness into a subject so very disagreeable to *her*, my visits must not be repeated.

Meantime, you may let him know, said she, that I reject him with my whole heart — yet that, although I say this with such a determination as shall leave no room for doubt, I say it not however with passion. On the contrary, tell him that I am trying to bring my mind into such a frame, as to be able to *pity* him (poor perjured wretch! what has he not to answer for!); and that I shall not think myself qualified for the state I am aspiring to, if, after a few struggles more, I cannot *forgive* him too: and I hope, clasping her hands together, uplifted, as were her eyes, my dear *earthly* father will set me the example my *heavenly* one has already set us all; and, by forgiving his fallen daughter, teach her to forgive the man, who then, I hope, will not have destroyed my eternal prospects, as he has my temporal!

[*In his next letter, a continuation, Belford tries, in a moving scene, to persuade Clarissa to accept from him as banker £100 — which she refuses. She thereafter proceeds to tell the women of the house the true and entire story of her sufferings.*]

Sat. July 22.

WELL, but after all, what need of her history to these women? She will certainly repent, some time hence, that she has thus needlessly exposed us both.

Strange, confoundedly strange, and as perverse (that is to say, as *womanly*) as strange, that she should refuse, and sooner choose to die (O the obscene word! and yet how free does thy pen make with it to me!) than be mine, who offended her by acting *in* character, while her parents acted shamefully *out of theirs,* and when I am now willing to act *out of my own* to oblige her: yet *I* not to be forgiven! *They* to be faultless with her! And marriage the only medium to repair all breaches, and to salve her own honour! Surely thou must see the inconsistence of her *forgiving* unforgivingness, as I may call it! Yet, heavy varlet as thou art, thou wantest to be drawn up after her!

Can she be any man's but mine? Will I be any woman's but hers? I never will! I never can! And I tell thee, that I am every day, every hour, more and more in love with her: and at this instant have a more vehement passion for her than ever I had in my life! — and that with views absolutely honourable, in *her own sense* of the word: nor have I varied, so much as in wish, for this week past.

I shall go on Monday morning to a kind of ball, to which Colonel Ambrose has invited me. It is given on a family account. I care not on what: for all that delights me in the thing is, that Mrs. and Miss Howe are to be there; Hickman, of course; for the old lady will not stir abroad without him. The colonel is in hopes that Miss Arabella Harlowe will be there likewise; for all the men and women of fashion round him are invited.

I fell in by accident with the colonel, who, I believe, hardly thought I would accept of the invitation. But he knows me not, if he thinks I am ashamed to appear at any place where women dare show their faces. Yet he hinted to me that my name *was up,* on Miss Harlowe's account. But, to allude to one of Lord M.'s phrases, if it be, I will not *lie abed* when anything joyous is going forward.

As I shall go in my lord's chariot, I would have had one of my Cousins Montague to go with me; but they both refused: and I shall not choose to take either of thy brethren. It would look as if I thought I wanted a bodyguard: besides, one of them is too rough, the other too smooth, and too great a fop for some of the staid company that will be there; and for *me* in particular. Men are known by their companions; and a fop (as Tourville, for example) takes great pains to hang out a sign by his dress of what he has in his shop. Thou, indeed, art an exception; dressing like a coxcomb, yet a very clever fellow. Nevertheless so clumsy a beau, that thou seemest to me to owe thyself a double spite, making thy ungracefulness appear the *more* ungraceful, by thy remarkable tawdriness, when thou are out of mourning.

But, although I put on these lively airs, I am sick at my soul! My whole heart is with my charmer! With what indifference shall I look upon all the assembly at the colonel's, my beloved in my ideal eye, and engrossing my whole heart?

MISS HOWE TO MISS ARABELLA HARLOWE

Thursday, July 20.

MISS HARLOWE, — I cannot help acquainting you (however **it** may be received, coming from *me*) that your poor sister is dangerously ill, at the house of one Smith, who keeps a glover's and perfume shop in King Street, Covent Garden. She knows not that I write. Some violent words, in the nature of an imprecation, from her father, afflict her greatly in her weak state. I presume not to direct you what to do in this case. You are her sister. I therefore could not help writing to you, not only for her sake, but for your own. I am, madam, / Your humble servant, / ANNA HOWE.

MISS ARABELLA HARLOWE. (IN ANSWER)

Thursday, July 20.

MISS HOWE, — I have yours of this morning. All that has happened to the unhappy body you mention is what we foretold and expected. Let *him*, for whose sake she abandoned us, be her comfort. We are told he has remorse, and would marry her. We don't **believe** it, indeed. She *may* be very ill. Her disappointment may make her so, or ought. Yet is she the only one I know who is disappointed.

I cannot say, miss, that the notification from you is the *more* welcome for the liberties you have been pleased to take with our whole family, for resenting a conduct that it is a shame any young lady should justify. Excuse this freedom, occasioned by greater. I am, miss, / Your humble servant, / ARABELLA HARLOWE.

MISS HOWE. (IN REPLY)

Friday, July 21.

MISS ARABELLA HARLOWE, — If you had half as much sense as you have ill-nature, you would (notwithstanding the exuberance of the latter) have been able to distinguish between a kind intention to you all (that you might have the less to reproach yourselves with, if a deplorable case should happen), and an officiousness I owed you not, by reason of freedoms at least reciprocal. I will not, for the *unhappy body's* sake, as you call a sister you have helped to make so, say all that I *could* say. If what I fear happen, you shall hear (whether desired or not) all the mind of / ANNA HOWE.

MISS ARABELLA HARLOWE TO MISS HOWE

Friday, July 21.

MISS ANN HOWE, — Your pert letter I have received. You, that spare nobody, I cannot expect should spare me. You are very happy in a prudent and watchful mother — but else mine cannot be exceeded in prudence: but we had all too good an opinion of somebody, to think watchfulness needful. There may possibly be some reason why *you* are so much attached to her in an error of this flagrant nature.

I help to make a sister unhappy! It is false, miss! It is all her own doings! — except, indeed, what she may owe to somebody's advice — you know who can best answer for that.

Let us *know your mind* as soon as you please: as we shall know it to be *your* mind, we shall judge what attention to give it. That's all, from, etc. / AR. H.

MISS HOWE TO MISS ARABELLA HARLOWE

Sat. July 22.

I OWN to you, that had it not been for the prudent advice of that admirable somebody (whose principal fault is the superiority of her talents, and whose misfortune to be brothered and sistered by a couple of creatures who are not able to comprehend her excellences), I might at one time have been plunged into difficulties. But, pert as the superlatively pert may think me, I thought not myself *wiser*, because I was *older*; nor for that *poor* reason qualified to prescribe to, much less to maltreat, a genius so superior.

But why run I into length to such a poor thing? Why push I so weak an adversary? whose first letter is all low malice, and whose next is made up of falsehood and inconsistence, as well as spite and ill-manners! Yet I was willing to give you a *part* of my mind. Call for more of it; it shall be at your service: from one who, though she thanks God she is not your sister, is not your *enemy*: but that she is *not* the latter, is withheld but by two considerations; one, that you bear, though unworthily, a relation to a sister so excellent; the other, that you are not of consequence enough to engage anything but the pity and contempt of / A. H.

MRS. HARLOWE TO MRS. HOWE

Sat. July 22.

DEAR MADAM, — I send you, enclosed, copies of five letters that have passed between Miss Howe and my Arabella. You are a person of so much prudence and good sense, and (being a mother yourself) can so well enter into the distress of all our family, upon the rashness and ingratitude of a child we once doted upon, that I dare say you will not countenance the strange freedoms your daughter has taken with us all. These are not the only ones we have to complain of;

but we were silent on the others, as they did not, as these have done, spread themselves out upon paper. We only beg that we may not be reflected upon by a young lady who knows not what we have suffered, and do suffer, by the rashness of a naughty creature who has brought ruin upon herself, and disgrace upon a family which she has robbed of all comfort. I offer not to prescribe to your known wisdom in this case; but leave it to you to do as you think most proper. I am, madam, / Your most humble servant, / CHARL. HARLOWE.

MRS. HOWE. (IN ANSWER)

Sat. July 22.

DEAR MADAM, — I am highly offended with my daughter's letters to Miss Harlowe. I knew nothing at all of her having taken such a liberty. These young creatures have such romantic notions, some of *love*, some of *friendship*, that there is no governing them in either. Nothing but time, and dear exeprience, will convince them of their absurdities in both. I have chidden Miss Howe very severely. I had before so just a notion of what your whole family's distress must be, that, as I told your brother, Mr. Antony Harlowe, I had often forbid her corresponding with the poor fallen angel — for surely never did young lady more resemble what we imagine of angels, both in person and mind. But, tired out with her headstrong ways (I am sorry to say this of my own child), I was forced to give way to it again. And, indeed, so sturdy was she in her will that I was afraid it would end in a fit of sickness, as too often it did in fits of sullens.

I believe, however, you will have no more such letters from my Nancy. I have been forced to use compulsion with her upon Miss Clary's illness (and it seems she is very bad), or she would have run away to London, to attend upon her: and this she calls doing the duty of a friend; forgetting that she sacrifices to her romantic friendship her duty to her fond indulgent mother.

There are a thousand excellences in the poor sufferer, notwithstanding her fault: and, if the hints she has given to my daughter be true, she has been most grievously abused. But I think your forgiveness and her father's forgiveness of her ought to be all at your own choice; and nobody should intermeddle in that, for the sake of due authority in parents.

I am, madam, with compliments to good Mr. Harlowe, and all your afflicted family, / Your most humble servant, / ANNABELLA HOWE.

MISS HOWE TO MISS CLARISSA HARLOWE

Sat. July 22.

MY DEAREST FRIEND, — We are busy in preparing for our little journey and voyage: but I will be ill, I will be very ill, if I cannot hear you are better before I go.

Rogers greatly afflicted me by telling me the bad way you are in. But now you have been able to hold a pen, and as your sense is strong and clear, I hope that the amusement you will receive from writing will make you better.

I dispatch this by an extraordinary way, that it may reach you time enough to move you to *consider well* before you absolutely decide upon the contents of mine of the 13th, on the subject of the two Misses Montague's visit to me; since, according to what you write, must I answer them.

In your last you conclude very positively that you will not be his. To be sure, he rather deserves an infamous death than such a wife. But, as I really believe him innocent of the arrest, and as all his family are such earnest pleaders, and will be guarantees for him, I think the compliance with *their* entreaties, and *his own*, will be now the best step you can take; your own family remaining implacable, as I *can assure you they do.* He is a man of sense; and it is not impossible but he may make you a good husband, and in time may become no bad man.

I long to have your answer to mine of the 13th. Pray keep the messenger till it be ready. If he return on Monday night it will be time enough for his affairs, and to find me come back from Colonel Ambrose's; who gives a ball on the anniversary of Mrs. Ambrose's birth and marriage both in one. The gentry all round the neighbourhood are invited this time, on some good news they have received from Mrs. Ambrose's brother, the Governor.

My mother promised the colonel for me and herself, in my absence. I would fain have excused myself to her; and the rather, as I had exceptions on account of the day:[1] but she is almost as young as her daughter; and thinking it not so well to go without me, she told me, She could propose *nothing* that was agreeable to me. And having had a *few sparring blows* with each other very lately, I think I must comply. For I don't love jangling when I can help it; though I seldom make it my study to avoid the occasion, when it offers of itself. I don't know, if either were not a little afraid of the other, whether it would be possible that we could live together: — I, *all my father!* My mamma — What? — *All my mother* — What else should I say?

MISS CLARISSA HARLOWE TO MISS HOWE

Sunday, July 23.

You set before me your reasons, enforced by the opinion of your honoured mother, why I should think of Mr. Lovelace for a husband.

I am willing to believe, not only from your own opinion, but from the assurances of one of Mr. Lovelace's friends, Mr. Belford, a good-natured and humane man, who spares not to censure the author of my calamities (*I think*, with undissembled and undesigning sincerity), that that man is innocent of the disgraceful arrest.

And even, if you please, in sincere compliment to your opinion, and

[1] The 24th of July, Miss Clarissa's birthday.

to that of Mr. Hickman, that (over-persuaded by his friends, and ashamed of his unmerited baseness to me) he would in earnest marry *me*, if I would have him.

"[1] Well, and now, what is the result of all? It is this: that I must abide by what I have already declared — and that is (don't be angry at me, my best friend), that I have much more pleasure in thinking of death than of such a husband. In short, as I declared in my last, that I cannot (forgive me, if I say, I *will* not) ever be his.

"My pride, then, my dearest friend, although a great deal mortified, is not *sufficiently* mortified, if it be necessary for me to submit to make that man my choice, whose actions are, and ought to be, my abhorrence! What! shall I, who have been treated with such premeditated and perfidious barbarity, as is painful to be thought of, and cannot with modesty be described, think of taking the violator to my heart? Can I vow duty to one so wicked, and hazard my salvation by joining myself to so great a profligate, now I *know* him to be so? Do you think your Clarissa Harlowe so lost, so *sunk*, at least, as that she could, for the sake of patching up, in the world's eye, a broken reputation, meanly appear indebted to the generosity, or perhaps *compassion*, of a man who has, by means so inhuman, robbed her of it? Indeed, my dear, I should not think my penitence for the rash step I took, anything better than a specious delusion, if I had not got above the least wish to have Mr. Lovelace for my husband.

"Let me then repeat, that I truly despise this man! If I know my own heart, indeed I do! I pity him! *Beneath* my very pity as he is, I nevertheless pity him! But this I could not do, if I still loved him: for, my dear, one must be greatly sensible of the baseness and ingratitude of those we love. I love him not, therefore! My soul disdains communion with him.

"The single life, at such times, has offered to me, as the life, the *only* life, to be chosen. But in *that*, must I not *now* sit brooding over my past afflictions, and mourning my faults till the hour of my release? And would not every one be able to assign the reason why Clarissa Harlowe chose solitude, and to sequester herself from the world?

"What then, my dear and only friend, can I wish for but death? And what, after all, *is* death? 'Tis but a cessation from mortal life; 'tis but the finishing of an appointed course: the refreshing inn after a fatiguing journey: the end of a life of cares and troubles; and, if happy, the beginning of a life of immortal happiness.

"If I die not now, it may possibly happen that I may be taken when I am less prepared. Had I escaped the evils I labour under, it might have been in the midst of some gay promising hope; when my heart had beat high with the desire of life; and when the vanity of this earth had taken hold of me.

"But now, my dear, for *your* satisfaction let me say that, although

[1] Those parts of this letter which are marked with inverted commas (thus ") were transcribed afterwards by Miss Howe, in her letter of July 29, written to the ladies of Mr. Lovelace's family; and are thus distinguished to avoid the necessity of repeating them in that letter.

I wish not for life, yet would I not, like a poor coward, desert my post when I *can* maintain it, and when it is my *duty* to maintain it.

"More than once, indeed, was I urged by thoughts so sinful: but then it was in the height of my distress: and once, particularly, I have reason to believe, I saved myself by my *desperation* from the most shocking personal insults; from a repetition, as far as I know, of his vileness; the base women (with so much reason dreaded by me) present, to intimidate *me*, if not to assist *him*!"

O my dear, you know not what I suffered on that occasion! Nor do I what I *escaped* at the time, if the wicked man had approached me to execute the horrid purposes of his vile heart."

As I am of opinion, that it would have manifested more of revenge and despair than of principle, had I committed a violence upon myself, when the villainy was *perpetrated*; so I should think it equally criminal, were I now *wilfully* to neglect myself; were I *purposely* to run into the arms of death (*as that man supposes I shall do*), when I might avoid it.

Nor, my dear, whatever are the suppositions of such a short-sighted, such a low-souled man, must you impute to gloom, to melancholy, to despondency, nor yet to a spirit of faulty pride, or still *more* faulty revenge, the resolution I have taken never to marry *this*; and if not *this*, *any* man. So far from deserving this imputation, I do assure you (my dear and *only* love) that I will do everything I can to prolong my life, till God, in mercy to me, shall be pleased to call for it. I have reason to think my punishment is but the due consequence of my fault, and I will not run away from it; but beg of Heaven to sanctify it to me. When appetite serves, I will eat and drink what is sufficient to support nature. A very little, you know, will do for that. And whatever my physicians shall think fit to prescribe, I will take, though ever so disagreeable. In short, I will do everything I can do to convince all my friends, who hereafter may think it worth their while to inquire after my last behaviour, that I possessed my soul with tolerable patience; and endeavoured to bear with a lot of my own drawing.

"But here, my dear, is another reason; a reason that will convince you yourself that I ought not to think of wedlock; but of a preparation for a quite different event. I am persuaded, as much as that I am now alive, that I shall not long live.

"I am sure, if I may say it with as little presumption as grief, That God will soon *dissolve my substance; and bring me to death, and to the house appointed for all living.*"

And now, my dearest friend, you know all my mind. And you will be pleased to write to the ladies of Mr. Lovelace's family that I think myself infinitely obliged to them for their good opinion of me; and that it has given me greater pleasure than I thought I had to come in this life, that, upon the little knowledge they have of me, and that not personal, I was thought worthy (after the ill-usage I have received) of an alliance with their honourable family: but that I can by no means think of their kinsman for a husband: and do you, my dear, extract from the above such reasons as you think have any weight in them.

MISS CLARISSA HARLOWE TO MISS HOWE

Sunday, July 23.

MY good Mrs. Norton, so long ago as in a letter dated the 3rd of this month, hinted to me that my relations took amiss some severe things you were pleased, in love to me, to say of them. And soon afterwards, I was put under that barbarous arrest; so that I could not well touch upon that subject till now.

Now, my dearest Miss Howe, let me *repeat* my earnest request (for this is not the first time by several that I have been obliged to chide you on this occasion), that you will spare my parents, and other relations, in all your conversations about me. Indeed, I wish they had thought fit to take other measures with me but who shall judge for them? The event has justified them, and condemned me.

You give me hope of a visit from Mr. Hickman: let him *expect* to see me greatly altered. I know he loves me: for he loves every one whom you love. A painful interview, I doubt! But I shall be glad to see a man whom *you* will one day, and that on an *early* day, I hope, make happy; and whose gentle manners, and unbounded love for you, will make *you* so, if it be not your own fault.

MRS. NORTON TO MISS CLARISSA HARLOWE

Monday, July 24.

EXCUSE, my dearest young lady, my long silence. I have been extremely ill. My poor boy has also been at death's door; and, when I hoped that he was better, he has relapsed. Alas! my dear, he is very dangerously ill. Let us both have your prayers!

Very angry letters have passed between your sister and Miss Howe. Every one of your family is incensed against that young lady. I wish you would remonstrate against her warmth; since it can do no good; for they will not believe but that her interposition has your connivance; nor that you are so ill as Miss Howe assures them you are.

Before she wrote, they were going to send up young Mr. Brand, the clergyman, to make private inquiries of your health, and way of life. But now they are so exasperated that they have laid aside their intention.

We have flying reports here, and at Harlowe Place, of some fresh insults which you have undergone: and that you are about to put yourself into Lady Betty Lawrance's protection. I believe they would now be glad (as I should be) that you would do so; and this, perhaps, will make them suspend for the present any determination in your favour.

How unhappy am I, that the dangerous way my son is in prevents my attendance on you! Let me beg of you to write me word how you are, both as to person and mind.

395

Monday Night, July 24.

MY DEAR MRS. NORTON, — I am exceedingly concerned at Miss Howe's writing about me to my friends. I do assure you, that I was as ignorant of her intention so to do, as of the contents of her letters. I am sure that nothing but my own application to my friends will procure me favour. Least of all can I expect that either your mediation or hers will avail me.

She then gives a brief account of the arrest: of her dejection under it: of Mr. Lovelace's promise not to molest her: of the earnest desire of all his friends, and of himself, to marry her: and of her declared resolution rather to die than be his, sent to Miss Howe, to be given to his relations. After which she thus proceeds:

Now, my dear Mrs. Norton, you will be surprised, perhaps, that I should have returned such an answer; but, when you have everything before you, you, who know me so well, will not think me wrong. And, besides, I am upon a *better preparation* than for an earthly husband.

Nor let it be imagined, my dear and ever-venerable friend, that my present turn of mind proceeds from gloominess or melancholy: for although it was *brought on* by disappointment (the world showing me early, even at my first *rushing* into it, its true and ugly face), yet I hope that it has obtained a better root, and will every day more and more, by its fruits, demonstrate to me, and to all my friends, that it has.

I have written to my sister. Last Friday I wrote. So the die is thrown. I hope for a gentle answer.

Don't be uneasy you cannot answer your wishes to be with me. I am happier than I could have expected to be among mere strangers. It was grievous at first; but use reconciles everything to us. The people of the house where I am are courteous and honest. There is a widow who lodges in it (have I not said so formerly?), a good woman; who is the better for having been a proficient in the school of affliction.

So you see, my venerable and dear friend, that I am not always turning the dark side of my prospects, in order to move compassion; a trick imputed to me, too often, by my hard-hearted sister; when, if I know my own heart, it is above all trick or artifice. Yet I hope at last I shall be so happy as to receive *benefit* rather than *reproach* from this talent, if it *be* my talent. At *last*, I say; for whose heart have I *hitherto* moved? Not one, I am sure, that was not *predetermined* in my favour.

As to the day[1] — I have passed it, as I ought to pass it. It has been a very heavy day to me! More for my friends' sake, too, than for my own! How did *they* use to pass it! What a festivity! How have they now passed it! To *imagine* it, how grievous!

[1 The day was her nineteenth birthday.]

Friday, July 21.

If, my dearest sister, I did not think the state of my health very precarious, and that it was my duty to take this step, I should hardly have dared to approach you, although but with my pen, after having found your censures so dreadfully justified as they have been.

I have not the courage to write to my father himself; nor yet to my mother. And it is with trembling that I address myself to you, to beg of you to intercede for me, that my father will have the goodness to revoke that heaviest part of the very heavy curse he laid upon me, which relates to HEREAFTER: for, as to the HERE, *I have* indeed *met with my punishment from the very wretch in whom I was supposed to place my confidence.*

As I hope not for restoration to favour, I may be allowed to be very earnest on this head: yet will I not use any arguments in support of my request, because I am sure my father, were it in his power, would not have his poor child miserable for ever. / My dear and happy sister, / Your afflicted servant.

A letter directed for me, at Mr. Smith's, a glover, in King Street, Covent Garden, will come to hand.

Mr. Belford to Robert Lovelace, Esq.

Edgware, Monday, July 24.

In vain dost thou impute to pride or wilfulness the necessity to which thou hast reduced this lady of parting with her clothes: for can she do otherwise, and be the noble-minded creature she is?

Her implacable friends have refused her the current cash she left behind her; and wished, as her sister wrote to her, to see her reduced to want: probably, therefore, they will not be sorry that she is reduced to such straits; and will take it for a justification from Heaven of their wicked hard-heartedness. Thou canst not suppose she would take supplies from thee: to take them from me would, in her opinion, be taking them from thee.

The lady shut herself up at six o'clock yesterday afternoon; and intends not to see company till seven or eight this; not even her nurse — imposing upon herself a severe fast. And why? *It is her* BIRTHDAY!

Wednesday, July 26.

I came not to town till this morning early. I hastened to Smith's; and had but a very indifferent account of the lady's health. I sent up my compliments; and she desired to see me in the afternoon.

About three o'clock I went again to Smith's. The lady was writing when I sent up my name; but admitted of my visit. I saw a visible alteration in her countenance for the worse; and Mrs. Lovick, respectfully accusing her of too great assiduity to her pen, early and late, and of her abstinence the day before, I took notice of the alteration; and told her that her physician had greater hopes of her than she had of herself; and I would take the liberty to say that despair of recovery allowed not room for cure.

She said she neither despaired nor hoped. Then stepping to the glass, with great composure, My countenance, said she, is indeed an honest picture of my heart. But the mind will run away with the body at any time.

She then stepped to her closet, and brought to me a parcel sealed up with three seals: Be so kind, said she, as to give this to your friend. A very grateful present it ought to be to him: for, sir, this packet contains all his letters to me. Such letters they are, as compared with his actions, would reflect dishonour upon all his sex, were they to fall into other hands.

As to my letters to him, they are not many. He may either keep or destroy them, as he pleases.

I thought, Lovelace, I ought not to forego this opportunity to plead for you: I therefore, with the packet in my hand, urged all the arguments I could think of in your favour.

I would not interrupt you, Mr. Belford, said she, though I am far from being pleased with the subject of your discourse. The motives for your pleas in his favour are generous. I love to see instances of generous friendship in either sex. But I have written my full mind on this subject to Miss Howe, who will communicate it to the ladies of his family.

Her apothecary came in. He advised her to the air, and blamed her for so great an application, as he was told she made, to her pen; and he gave it as the doctor's opinion, as well as his own, that she would recover, if she herself desired to recover, and would use the means.

Mr. Goddard took his leave; and I was going to do so too, when the maid came up, and told her a gentleman was below, who very earnestly inquired after her health, and desired to see her: his name Hickman.

She was overjoyed; and bid the maid desire the gentleman to walk up.

I would have withdrawn; but I suppose she thought it was likely I should have met him upon the stairs; and so she forbid it.

She shot to the stairs-head to receive him, and, taking his hand, asked half a dozen questions (without waiting for any answers) in relation to Miss Howe's health; acknowledging, in high terms, her goodness in sending him to see her, before she set out upon her little journey.

He gave her a letter from that lady, which she put into her bosom, saying she would read it by and by.

He was visibly shocked to see how ill she looked.

You look at me with concern, Mr. Hickman, she said. O sir! times are strangely altered with me since I saw you last at my dear Miss Howe's! What a cheerful creature was I then! — my heart at rest!

my prospects charming! and beloved by everybody! — but I will not pain you!

Indeed, madam, said he, I am grieved for you at my soul.

He turned away his face with visible grief in it.

Her own eyes glistened: but she turned to each of us, presenting one to the other — him to me, as a gentleman *truly* deserving to be *called so* — me to him, as *your* friend, indeed (how was I, at that instant, ashamed of myself!); but, nevertheless, as a man of humanity; detesting my friend's baseness; and desirous of doing her all manner of good offices.

MR. BELFORD TO ROBERT LOVELACE, ESQ.

Thursday, July 27.

I WENT this morning, according to the lady's invitation, to breakfast, and found Mr. Hickman with her.

Mr. Hickman and I went afterwards to a neighbouring coffee-house; and he gave me some account of your behaviour at the ball on Monday night, and of your treatment of him in the conference he had with you before that; which he represented in a more favourable light than you had done yourself: and yet he gave his sentiments of you with great freedom, but with the politeness of a gentleman.

He told me how very determined the lady was against marrying you; that she had, early this morning, set herself to write a letter to Miss Howe, in answer to one he brought her, which he was to call for at twelve, it being almost finished before he saw her at breakfast; and that at three he proposed to set out on his return.

.   .   .   .

I threw myself in Mr. Hickmans' way, on his return from the lady.

He was excessively moved at taking leave of her; being afraid, as he said to me (though he would not tell her so), that he should never see her again. She charged him to represent everything to Miss Howe in the most favourable light that the truth would bear.

He told me of a tender passage at parting; which was, that having saluted her at her closet door, he could not help once more taking the same liberty, in a more fervent manner, at the stairs-head, whither she accompanied him; and this in the thought, that it was the last time he should ever have that honour; and offering to apologize for his freedom (for he had pressed her to his heart with a vehemence that he could neither account for nor resist.) Excuse you, Mr. Hickman! that I will: you are my brother, and my friend: and to show you that the good man, who is to be happy with my beloved Miss Howe, is very dear to me, you shall carry to her this token of my love (offering her sweet face to his salute, and pressing his hand between hers): and perhaps her love of *me* will make it more agreeable to her, than her punctilio would otherwise allow it to be: and tell her, said she, dropping on one knee, with clasped hands, and uplifted eyes, that in this posture you see me, in the last moment of our parting, begging a blessing upon you both, and that you may be the delight and comfort of each other, for many, very many, happy years!

Tears, said he, fell from my eyes.

I went into the back shop, continued the worthy man, and recommended the angelic lady to the best care of Mrs. Smith; and, when I was in the street, cast my eye up at her window: there, for the last time, I doubt, said he, that I shall ever behold her, I saw her; and she waved her charming hand to me, and with such a look of smiling goodness, and mingled concern, as I cannot describe.

Miss Howe to Miss Clarissa Harlowe

Tuesday, July 25.

I AM yet excessively fluttered. The occasion I will communicate to you by and by: for nothing but the flutters given by the stroke of death could divert my *first* attention from the sad and solemn contents of your last favour. These therefore I must begin with.

How can I bear the thoughts of losing so dear a friend! I will not so much as suppose it. Indeed I *cannot!* Such a mind as yours was not vested in humanity to be snatched away from us so soon. There must be still a great deal for you to do for the good of all who have the happiness to know you.

You chide me in yours of Sunday on the freedom I take with your friends.

I *may* be warm. I know I *am* — too warm. Yet warmth in friendship, surely, cannot be a crime; especially when our friend has great merit, labours under oppression, and is struggling with undeserved calamity.

You leave it to me to give a negative to the hopes of the noble family, whose only disgrace is that so very vile a man is so nearly related to them. But yet — alas! my dear, I am so fearful of consequences, so *selfishly* fearful, if this negative must be given — I don't know what I should say — but give me leave to suspend, however, this negative, till I hear from you again.

. . . .

Know then, my dear, that I accompanied my mother to Colonel Ambrose's, on the occasion I mentioned to you in my former. Many ladies and gentlemen were there whom you know; particularly Miss Kitty D'Oily, Miss Lloyd, Miss Biddy D'Ollyffe, Miss Biddulph, and their respective admirers, with the colonel's two nieces, fine women both; besides many whom you know not; for they were strangers to me but by name. A splendid company, and all pleased with one another, till Colonel Ambrose introduced one who, the moment he was brought into the great hall, set the whole assembly into a kind of agitation.

It was your villain.

I thought I should have sunk as soon as I set my eyes upon him. My mother was also affected; and, coming to me, Nancy, whispered she, can you bear the sight of that wretch without too much emotion? If not, withdraw into the next apartment.

I could not remove. Everybody's eyes were glanced from him to me. I sat down, and fanned myself, and was forced to order a glass of water. Oh, that I had the eye the basilisk is reported to have, thought I, and that his life were within the power of it! — directly would I kill him.

He entered with an air so hateful to me, but so agreeable to every other eye, that I could have looked him dead for that too.

Miss D'Oily, upon his complimenting her, among a knot of ladies, asked him, in their hearing, how Miss Clarissa Harlowe did?

He heard, he said, you were not so well as he wished you to be, and as you deserved to be.

O Mr. Lovelace, said she, what have you to answer for on that young lady's account, if all be true that I have heard?

I have a great deal to answer for, said the unblushing villain: but that dear lady has so many excellences, and so much delicacy, that little sins are great ones in her eye.

Little sins! replied Miss D'Oily: Mr. Lovelace's character is so well known that nobody believes he can commit *little* sins.

You are very good to me, Miss D'Oily.

Indeed I am not.

Then I am the only person to whom you are *not* very good: and so I am the less obliged to you.

He turned, with an unconcerned air, to Miss Playford, and made her some genteel compliments. I believe you know her not. She visits his Cousins Montague. Indeed, he had something in his specious manner to say to everybody: and this too soon quieted the disgust each person had at his entrance.

I still kept my seat, and he either saw me not or would not yet see me; and addressing himself to my mother, taking her unwilling hand, with an air of high assurance, I am glad to see you here, madam. I hope Miss Howe is well. I have reason to complain greatly of her: but hope to owe to her the highest obligation that can be laid on man.

It is not every one who has a soul capable of friendship: and what a heart must that be, which can be insensible to the interests of a suffering friend?

This sentiment from Mr. Lovelace's mouth! said my mother. Forgive me, sir; but you can have no end, surely, in endeavouring to make *me* think as well of you as some innocent creatures have thought of you, to their cost.

But, dearest madam, permit me to say, that I hope for your interest with your *charming* daughter (was his sycophant word) to have it put into my power to convince all the world that there never was a truer penitent. And why, why this anger, dear madam (for she struggled to get her hand out of his), these violent airs — so *maidenly!* (impudent fellow!) — May I not ask if Miss Howe be here?

She would not have been here, replied my mother, had she known whom she had been to see.

And is she here, then? Thank Heaven! He disengaged her hand, and stepped forward into company.

Dear Miss Lloyd, said he, with an air (taking her hand as he quitted my mother's), tell me, is Miss Arabella Harlowe here? Or will she be here? I was informed she would — and this, and the opportunity of paying my compliments to your friend Miss Howe, were great inducements with me to attend the colonel.

Superlative assurance! Was it not, my dear?

Miss Arabella Harlowe, excuse me, sir, said Miss Lloyd, would be very little inclined to meet you here, or anywhere else.

Perhaps so, my dear Miss Lloyd: but, perhaps, for that very reason, I am desirous to see *her*.

Miss Harlowe sir, said Miss Biddulph, with a threatening air, will hardly be here without her *brother*. I imagine, if one come, both will come.

Heaven grant they both may! said the wretch. Nothing, Miss Biddulph, shall *begin* from me to disturb this assembly, I assure you, if they do. One calm half-hour's conversation with that brother and sister would be a most fortunate opportunity to me, in presence of the colonel and his lady, or whom else they should choose.

Then turning round, as if desirous to find out the one or the other, or both, he 'spied me, and, with a very low bow, approached me.

I was all in a flutter, you may suppose. He would have taken my hand. I refused it, all glowing with indignation: everybody's eyes upon us.

I went from him to the other end of the room, and sat down, as I thought, out of his hated sight: but presently I heard his odious voice, whispering, behind my chair (he leaning upon the back of it, with impudent unconcern).

We are so much observed — else on my knees, my dear Miss Howe, would I beg your interest with your charming friend.

She'll have nothing to say to you.

I had not then your letters, my dear.

Killing words! But indeed I have deserved them, and a dagger in my heart besides. I am so conscious of my demerits, that I have no hope but in *your* interposition. Could I owe that favour to Miss Howe's mediation which I cannot hope for on any other account ——

My mediation, vilest of men! — *my* mediation! — I abhor you! — from my *soul*, I abhor you, vilest of men! Three or four times I repeated these words, stammering too. I was excessively fluttered.

You can call me nothing, madam, so bad as I will call myself. I *have* been, indeed, the vilest of men: but now I am not so. Permit me — everybody's eyes are upon us! — but one moment's audience -- to exchange but ten words with you, dearest Miss Howe — in whose presence you please — for your dear friend's sake — but ten words with you in the next apartment.

It is an insult upon me, to presume that I would exchange *one* with you, if I could help it! Out of my way! Out of my sight — fellow!

And away I would have flung: but he took my hand. I was excessively disordered — everybody's eyes more and more intent upon us.

Mr. Hickman, whom my mother had drawn on one side, to enjoin him a patience which perhaps needed not to have been enforced, came up just then with my mother, who had him by his leading-strings — by his sleeve, I should say.

Mr. Hickman, said the bold wretch, be my advocate but for ten words in the next apartment with Miss Howe, in your presence, and in yours, madam, to my mother.

Hear, Nancy, what he has to say to you. To get rid of him, hear his *ten words*.

Excuse me, madam! his very breath — Unhand me, sir!

He sighed, and looked — Oh, how the practised villain sighed and looked! He then let go my hand, with such a reverence in his manner, as brought blame upon me from some, that I would not hear him. And this incensed me the more. O my dear, this man is a devil! This man is *indeed* a devil! So much patience when he pleases! So much gentleness! Yet so resolute, so persisting, so audacious!

I was going out of the assembly in great disorder. He was at the door as soon as I.

How kind this is! said the wretch; and, ready to follow me, opened the door for me.

I turned back upon this, and, not knowing what I did, snapped my fan just in his face, as he turned short upon me; and the powder flew from his wig.

Everybody seemed as much pleased as I was vexed.

He then turned to my mother, resolved to be even with *her* too: Where, good madam, could miss get all this spirit?

The company round smiled; for I need not tell you that my mother's high-spiritedness is pretty well known.

When the wretch saw how industriously I avoided him (shifting from one part of the hall to another), he at last boldly stepped up to me, as my mother and Mr. Hickman were talking to me; and thus before them accosted me:

I beg your pardon, madam; but, by your mother's leave, I must have a few moments' conversation with you, either here, or at your own house; and I beg you will give me the opportunity.

Nancy, said my mother, hear what he has to say to you. In my presence you may: and better in the adjoining apartment, if it must be, than to come to you at our own house.

I retired to one corner of the hall, my mother following me, and he, taking Mr. Hickman under the arm, following her — Well, sir, said I, what have you to say? Tell me *here*.

I have been telling Mr. Hickman, said he, how much I am concerned for the injuries I have done to the most excellent woman in the world: and yet, that she obtained such a glorious triumph over me the last time I had the honour to see her, as, with my penitence, ought to have qualified her former resentments: but that I will, with all my soul, enter into any measures to obtain her forgiveness of me. My Cousins Montague have told you this. Lady Betty, and Lady Sarah, and my Lord M. are engaged for my honour. I know your power with the dear creature. My cousins told me you gave them hopes you would use it in my behalf. My Lord M. and his two sisters are impatiently expecting the fruits of it. You must have heard from her before now: I hope you have. And will you be so good as to tell me, if I may have any hopes?

If I must speak on this subject, let me tell you that you have broken her heart. You know not the value of the lady you have injured. You deserve her not. And she despises you as she ought.

Dear Miss Howe, mingle not passion with denunciations so severe. I must know my fate. I will go abroad once more, if I find her absolutely irreconcilable. But I hope she will give me leave to attend upon her, to know my doom from her own mouth.

It would be death immediate for her to see you. And what must *you* be, to be able to look her in the face?

. . . .

You will let Mr. Hickman know your whole mind; and when he acquaints me with it, I will tell you all my own.

Meantime, may the news he will bring me of the state of your health be favourable! prays, with the utmost fervency, / Your ever faithful and affectionate / ANNA HOWE.

MISS CLARISSA HARLOWE TO MISS HOWE

Thursday, July 27.

MY DEAREST MISS HOWE, — After I have thankfully acknowledged your favour in sending Mr. Hickman to visit me before you set out upon your intended journey, I must chide you (in the sincerity of that faithful love, which could not be the love it is if it would not admit of that *cementing* freedom) for suspending the decisive negative, which, upon such full deliberation, I had entreated you to give to Mr. Lovelace's relations.

I am sorry that I am obliged to *repeat* to you, my dear, who know me so well, that, were I sure I should live *many years*, I would not have Mr. Lovelace: much less can I think of him, as it is probable I may not live *one*.

I send you enclosed the copy of my letter to my sister. I hope it will be thought to be written with a true penitent spirit; for indeed it is. I desire that you will not think I stoop too low in it; since there can be no such thing as *that* in a child to parents whom she has unhappily offended.

And after all, what can they do for me? They can only pity me: and what will that do, but augment their own *grief*; to which at present their *resentment* is an alleviation? For can they by their pity restore to me my lost reputation? Can they by it purchase a sponge that will wipe out from the year past the fatal five months of my life?

Your account of the gay unconcerned behaviour of Mr. Lovelace at the colonel's, does not surprise me at all, after I am told that he had the intrepidity to go thither, knowing who were *invited* and *expected*. Only this, my dear, I really wonder at, that Miss Howe could imagine that I could have a thought of such a man for a husband.

Since you are so loath, my dear, to send the desired negative to the ladies of his family, I will only trouble you to transmit the letter I shall enclose for that purpose; directed indeed to yourself, because it was to you that those ladies applied themselves on this occasion; but to be sent by you to any one of the ladies at your own choice.

MISS CLARISSA HARLOWE TO MISS HOWE
(*Enclosed in the preceding*) Thursday, July 27.

MY DEAREST MISS HOWE, — Since you seem loath to acquiesce in my determined resolution, signified to you as soon as I was able to hold a pen, I beg the favour of you, by this, or by any other way you think most proper, to acquaint the worthy ladies who have applied to you in behalf of their relation, that, although I am infinitely obliged to their generous opinion of me, yet I cannot consent to *sanctify*, as I may say, Mr. Lovelace's repeated breaches of all moral sanctions, and hazard my *future* happiness by an union with a man, through whose premeditated injuries, in a long train of the basest contrivances, I have forfeited my *temporal* hopes.

He himself, when he reflects upon his own actions, must surely bear testimony to the justice as well as fitness of my determination. The ladies, I dare say, would, were they to know the whole of my unhappy story.

Be pleased to acquaint them that I deceive myself, if my resolution on this head (however ungratefully, and even inhumanly, he has treated me) be not owing more to *principle* than *passion*. Nor can I give a stronger proof of the truth of this assurance, than by declaring that I *can* and *will* forgive him, on this one easy condition, *that he will never molest me more*.

In whatever way you choose to make this declaration, be pleased to let my most respectful compliments to the ladies of the noble family, and to my Lord M., accompany it. And do you, my dear, believe that I shall be, to the last moment of my life, / Your ever obliged and affectionate / CLARISSA HARLOWE.

MR. LOVELACE TO JOHN BELFORD, ESQ.
Friday, July 28.

I CAN tell thee that, if nothing else will do, I am determined, in spite of thy buskin-airs, and of thy engagements for me to the contrary, to see her myself.

I cannot bear the thought that a woman whom once I had bound to me in the silken cords of love, should slip through my fingers, and be able, while *my* heart flames out with a violent passion for her, to despise me, and to set both love and me at defiance. Thou canst not imagine how much I envy *thee*, and her *doctor*, and her *apothecary*, and every one who I hear are admitted to her presence and conversation; and wish to be the *one* or the *other* in turn.

Wherefore, if nothing else will do, I *will* see her. I'll tell thee of an admirable expedient, just come across me, to save *thy* promise, and *my own*.

Mrs. Lovick, you say, is a good woman: if the lady be worse, she shall advise her to send for a parson to pray by her: unknown to her, unknown to the lady, unknown to *thee* (for so it may pass), I will contrive to be the man, *petticoated out*, and vested in a gown and cassock. I once, for a certain purpose, did assume the canonicals; and I was thought to make a fine sleek appearance; my broad rose-bound beaver became me *mightily*; and I was much admired upon the whole by all who saw me.

Methinks it must be charmingly apropos to see me kneeling down by her bedside (I am sure I shall pray heartily), beginning out of the Common Prayer Book the Sick Office for the restoration of the languishing lady, and concluding with an exhortation to charity and forgiveness for myself.

.   .   .   .

I am encouraged to hope, what it will be very surprising to me if it do not happen; that is, in plain English, that the dear creature is in the way to become a mamma.

This cursed arrest, because of the ill effects the terror might have upon her, in the hoped-for circumstances, has concerned me more than on any other account. It would be the pride of my life to prove, in this charming frost-piece, the triumph of nature over principle, and to have a young Lovelace by such an angel; and then, for its sake, I am confident that she will live and will legitimate it.

.   .   .   .

The dear extravagant takes a delight in oddnesses, choosing to part with her clothes, though for a song. Dost think she is not a little touched at times? I am afraid she is. A little spice of that insanity, I doubt, runs through her, that she had a stronger degree in the first week of my operations. Her contempt of life; her proclamations; her refusal of matrimony; and now of money from her most intimate friends, are sprinklings of this kind, and no other way, I think, to be accounted for.

Her apothecary is a good honest fellow. I like him much. But the silly dear's harping so continually upon one string, dying, dying, dying, is what I have no patience with. I hope all this melancholy jargon is owing entirely to the way I would have her to be in

MISS HOWE TO MISS CLARISSA HARLOWE

Friday Night, July 28.

I WILL now, my dearest friend, write to you all my mind, without reserve, on your resolution not to have this vilest of men. You gave me, in yours of Sunday the 23rd, reasons so worthy of the pure mind of my Clarissa, in support of this your resolution, that nothing but self-love, lest I should lose my ever-amiable friend, could have prevailed upon me to wish you to alter it.

For Heaven's sake, then, for the world's sake, for the honour of our sex, and for *my* sake, once more I beseech you, try to overcome this shock; and if you *can* overcome it, I shall then be as happy as I wish to be; for I cannot, indeed I cannot, think of parting with you for many, many years to come.

You wish I had not mediated for you to your friends. I wish so too; because my mediation was ineffectual!

You are for excusing them beforehand for their expected cruelty, as not knowing what you have suffered, nor how ill you are: they have *heard* of the former, and are not sorry for it: of the latter they have been *told*, and *I* have most reason to know how they have taken it — but I shall be far from avoiding the *fault*, and as surely shall incur the *rebuke*, if I say any more upon this subject.

I send this day, by a particular hand, to the Misses Montague, your letter of just reprobation of the greatest profligate in the kingdom; and hope I shall not have done amiss that I transcribe some of the paragraphs of your letter of the 23rd, and send them with it, as you at first intended should be done.

You are, it seems (and that too much for your health), employed in writing. I hope it is in penning down the particulars of your tragical story. And my mother has put me in mind to press you to it, with a view that one day, if it might be published under feigned names, it would be of as much use as honour to the sex. My mother says she cannot help admiring you for the propriety of your resentment in your refusal of the wretch; and she would be extremely glad to have her advice of penning your sad story complied with.

MISS HOWE TO THE TWO MISSES MONTAGUE

Sat., July 29.

DEAR LADIES, — I have not been wanting to use all my interest with my beloved friend, to induce her to forgive and be reconciled to your kinsman (though he has so ill deserved it); and have even *repeated* my earnest advice to her on this head. This repetition, and the waiting for her answer, having taken up time, have been the cause that I could not sooner do myself the honour of writing to you on this subject.

You will see, by the enclosed, her immovable resolution, grounded on noble and high-souled motives, which I cannot but *regret* and *applaud* at the same time: *applaud*, for the justice of her determination, which will confirm all your worthy house in the opinion you had conceived of her unequalled merit; and *regret,* because I have but too much reason to apprehend, as well by that, as by the report of a gentleman just come from her, that she is in such a declining way as to her health, that her thoughts are very differently employed than on a continuance here.

The enclosed letter she thought fit to send to me unsealed, that, after I had perused it, I might forward it to you: and this is the reason it is superscribed by myself and sealed with my seal.

MRS. NORTON TO MISS CLARISSA HARLOWE

Friday, July 28.

YOUR letter to your sister is received and answered. You have the answer by this time, I suppose. I wish it may be to your satisfaction: but am afraid it will not: for, by Betty Barnes, I find they were in a great ferment on receiving yours, and much divided whether it should be answered or not. They will not yet believe that you are so ill as (to my infinite concern) I find you are. What passed between Miss Harlowe and Miss Howe has been, as I feared it would be, an aggravation.

I showed Betty two or three passages in your letter to me; and she seemed moved, and said she would report them favourably, and would procure me a visit from Miss Harlowe, if I would promise to show the same to *her.* But I have heard no more of that.

I am glad you are with such honest people; and that you have all your effects restored. How dreadfully have you been used, that one should be glad of such a poor piece of justice as that!

Your talent at moving the passions is always hinted at; and this Betty of your sister's never comes near me that she is not full of it. But as you say, whom has it moved that you *wished* to move? Yet were it not for this unhappy notion, I am sure your mother would relent. Forgive me, my dear Miss Clary; for I must try one way to be convinced if my opinion be not just. But I will not tell you what that is, unless it succeeds. I will try, in pure duty and love to *them,* as well as to *you.*

May Heaven be your support in all your trials, is the constant prayer, my dearest young lady, of / Your ever affectionate friend and servant, / JUDITH NORTON.

MRS. NORTON TO MRS. HARLOWE

Friday, July 28.

HONOURED MADAM, — Being forbidden (without leave) to send you anything I might happen to receive from my beloved Miss Clary, and so ill, that I cannot attend to *ask* your leave, I give you this trouble, to let you know that I have received a letter from her, which,

I think, I should hereafter be held inexcusable, as things may happen, if I did not desire permission to communicate to you, and that as soon as possible.

Applications have been made to the dear young lady from Lord M., from the two ladies his sisters, and from both his nieces, and from the wicked man himself, to forgive and marry him. This, in noble indignation for the usage she has received from him, she has absolutely refused.

The letter I have received will show how truly penitent the dear creature is; and if I have your permission, I will send it sealed up, with a copy of mine, to which it is an answer. But as I resolve upon this step without her knowledge (and indeed I do), I will not acquaint her with it unless it be attended with desirable effects: because, otherwise, besides making me incur her displeasure, it might quite break her already half-broken heart.

MRS. HARLOWE TO MRS. JUDITH NORTON

Sunday, July 30.

WE all know your virtuous prudence, worthy woman: we all do. But your partiality to this your rash favourite is likewise known. And we are no less acquainted with the unhappy body's power of painting her distresses so as to pierce a stone.

Every one is of opinion that the dear naughty creature is working about to be forgiven and received; and for this reason it is that Betty has been forbidden (not by *me*, you may be sure!) to mention any more of her letters; for she did speak to my Bella of some moving passages you read to her.

This will convince you that nothing will be heard in her favour. To what purpose, then, should I mention anything about her? But you may be sure that I *will*, if I can have but one second. However, that is not at all likely, until we see what the *consequences* of her crime will be: and who can tell that? — She may — How can I speak it, and my once darling daughter unmarried! — She may be with child! This would perpetuate her stain. Her brother may come to some harm; which God forbid! One child's ruin, I hope, will not be followed by another's murder!

That *he* would now marry her, or that *she* would refuse him, if she believed him in earnest, as she has circumstanced herself, is not at all probable; and were *I* inclined to believe it, *nobody else* here would.

All I can expect to prevail for her is, that in a week or so Mr. Brand may be sent up to inquire privately about her present state and way of life, and to see she is not altogether destitute: for nothing she writes herself will be regarded.

Her father indeed has, at her earnest request, withdrawn the curse, which, in a passion, he laid upon her, at her first wicked flight from us.

These liberties of Miss Howe with us; the general cry against us abroad wherever we are spoken of; and the *visible*, and not seldom *audible*, disrespectfulness which high and low treat us with to our faces, as we go to and from church, and even *at* church (for nowhere else have we the heart to go), as if none of us had been regarded but upon her account; and as if she were innocent, we all in fault; are constant aggravations, you must needs think, to the whole family.

She has made my lot heavy, I am sure, that was far from being light before! To tell you truth, I am enjoined not to receive anything of hers, from any hand, without leave. Should I therefore gratify my yearnings after her, so far as to receive privately the letter you mention, what would the case be, but to torment myself, without being able to do her good?

And is she *really* ill? — so *very* ill? — But she *ought* to sorrow. She has given a double measure of it.

But does she *really* believe she shall not *long* trouble us? — But O my Norton! — she must, she *will* long trouble us — for can she think her death, if we should be deprived of her, will put an end to our afflictions? Can it be thought that the fall of such a child will not be regretted by us to the last hour of our lives?

Perhaps I may find an opportunity to pay you a visit, as in your illness, and then may weep over the letter you mention, with you. But, for the future, write nothing to me about the poor girl that you think may not be communicated to us all.

MISS CLARISSA HARLOWE TO MRS. NORTON

Sat., July 29.

I WRITE in some hurry, being apprehensive of the consequence of the hints you give of some method you propose to try in my favour (with my relations, I presume you mean): but you will not tell me what, you say, if it prove unsuccessful.

Now I must beg you that you will not take any step in my favour with which you do not first acquaint me.

I have reason to be very thankful that my father has withdrawn that heavy malediction which affected me so much — a parent's curse, my dear Mrs. Norton! What child could die in peace under a parent's curse? so literally fulfilled too as this has been in what relates to this life!

But I can write nothing but what must give you trouble. I will therefore, after repeating my desire that you will not intercede for me but with my previous consent, conclude. . . .

MISS ARAB. HARLOWE TO MISS CL. HARLOWE

Thursday, July 27.

O MY UNHAPPY LOST SISTER! — What a miserable hand have you made of your romantic and giddy expedition! — I pity you at my heart.

You may *well* grieve and repent! Lovelace has left you! — In what way or circumstances you know best.

I wish your conduct had made your case more pitiable. But 'tis your own seeking!

God help you! — for you have not a friend will look upon you! Poor, wicked, undone creature! — fallen, as you are, against warning, against expostulation, against duty!

But it signifies nothing to reproach you. I weep over you.

My poor mother! — your rashness and folly have made *her* more miserable than *you* can be. Yet she has besought my father to grant your request.

My uncles joined with her; for they thought there was a little more modesty in your letter than in the letters of your pert advocate: and my father is pleased to give me leave to write; but only these words for *him*, and no more: That he withdraws the curse he laid upon you, at the first hearing of your wicked flight, so far as it is in his power to do it; and hopes that your present punishment may be all that you will meet with. For the rest, he will never own you, nor forgive you; and grieves he has such a daughter in the world.

My brother is now at Edinburgh, sent thither by my father (though he knows not this to be the motive), that he may not meet your triumphant deluder.

We are told he would be glad to marry you: but why then did he abandon you? He had kept you till he was tired of you, no question; and it is not likely he would wish to have you but upon the terms you have already without doubt been *his*.

You ought to advise your friend Miss Howe to concern herself less in your matters than she does, except she could do it with more decency. She has written three letters to me: very insolent ones.

Your Cousin Morden is every day expected in England. He as well as others of the family, when he comes to hear what a blessed piece of work you have made of it, will wish you never had had a being.

Miss Clarissa Harlowe to Miss Howe

Sunday, July 30.

You have given me great pleasure, my dearest friend, by your approbation of my reasonings, and of my resolution founded upon them, never to have Mr. Lovelace. This approbation is so *right* a thing, give me leave to say, from the nature of the case, and from the strict honour and true dignity of mind, which I always admired in my Anna Howe, that I could hardly tell to what, but to my evil destiny, which of late would not let me please anybody, to attribute the advice you gave me to the contrary.

I am more grieved (at times, however) for *others*, than for *myself*. And so I *ought*. For as to *myself*, I cannot but reflect that I have had an escape, rather than a loss, in missing Mr. Lovelace for a husband — even had he *not* committed the vilest of all outrages.

411

Let any one, who knows my story, collect his character from his behaviour to *me before* that outrage; and then judge whether it was in the least probable that such a man should make me happy. But to collect his character from his principles with regard to the *sex in general*, and from his enterprises upon many of them, and to consider the *cruelty of his nature*, and the *sportiveness of his invention*, together with the *high opinion he has of himself*, it will be not be doubted that a wife of his must have been miserable; and more miserable if she loved him, than she could have been were she to be indifferent to him.

.   .   .   .

You are very obliging to me, *intentionally*, I know, when you tell me it is in my power to hasten the day of Mr. Hickman's happiness. But you know it is *not* in my power to say *when* I can dismiss my physician; and you should not put the celebration of a marriage *intended* by *yourself*, and so desirable to your mother, upon so precarious an issue.

I am glad you have sent my letter to Miss Montague. I hope I shall hear no more of this unhappy man.

I had begun the particulars of my tragical story: but it is so painful a task, and I have so many more important things to do, and, as I apprehend, so little time to do them in, that could I avoid it, I would go no further in it.

Mr. Lovelace, it seems, has communicated to his friend Mr. Belford all that has passed between himself and me, as he went on. Mr. Belford has not been able to deny it. So that (as we may observe by the way) a poor young creature, whose indiscretion has given a libertine power over her, has a reason *she little thinks of*, to regret her folly; since these wretches, who have no more honour in one point than in another, scruple not to make her weakness a part of their triumph to their brother-libertines.

I have nothing to apprehend of this sort, if I have the justice done me in his letters which Mr. Belford assures me I have: and therefore the particulars of my story, and the base arts of this vile man, will, I think, be best collected from those very letters of his (if Mr. Belford can be prevailed upon to communicate them); to which I dare appeal.

There is one way which may be fallen upon to induce Mr. Belford to communicate these letters. It is no other than this:

I think to make Mr. Belford the executor of my last will (don't be surprised): and with this view I permit his visits with the less scruple: and every time I see him, from his concern for me, am more and more inclined to do so. If I hold in the same mind, and if he accept the trust, and will communicate the materials in his power, those, joined with what you can furnish, will answer the whole end.

I know you will start at my notion of such an executor: but pray, my dear, consider, in my present circumstances, what I can do better, as I am empowered to make a will, and have considerable matters in my own disposal.

If indeed my *Cousin Morden* were to come in time, and would undertake this trust — but even *him* it might subject to hazards; and the more, as he is a man of great spirit; and as the other man (of *as* great) looks upon me (unprotected as I have long been) as his property.

Now Mr. Belford, as I have already mentioned, knows everything that has passed. He is a man of spirit, and, it seems, as fearless as the other, with more humane qualities. You don't know, my dear, what instances of sincere humanity this Mr. Belford has shown, not only on occasion of the cruel arrest, but on several occasions since.

All these reasons have already in a manner *determined* me to ask this favour of him; although it will have an odd sound with it to make an intimate friend of Mr. Lovelace my executor.

Miss Clarissa Harlowe to Miss Harlowe
Saturday, July 29.

I repine not, my dear sister, at the severity you have been pleased to express in the letter you favourd me with; because that severity was accompanied with the grace I had petitioned for; and because the reproaches of mine own heart are stronger than any other person's reproaches can be and yet I am not half so culpable as I am imagined to be: as would be allowed, if all the circumstances of my unhappy story were known; and which I shall be ready to communicate to Mrs. Norton, if she be commissioned to inquire into them; or to you, my sister, if you can have patience to hear them.

Believe me, my dear sister, I say not this merely to move compassion; but from the *best* grounds. And as, on that account, I think it of the highest importance to my peace of mind to obtain one further favour, I would choose to owe to your intercession, *as my sister*, the leave I beg, to address half a dozen lines (with the hope of having them answered as I wish) to either or to both my honoured parents, to beg their *last blessing*.

This blessing is all the favour I have now to ask: it is all I *dare* to ask: yet am afraid to rush at once, though by *letter*, into the presence of either. And if I did not ask it, it might seem to be owing to stubbornness and want of duty, when my heart is all humility and penitence. Only, be so good as to embolden me to attempt this task — write but this one line, "Clary Harlowe, you are at liberty to write as you desire." This will be enough — and shall to my last hour be acknowledged as the greater favour by / Your truly penitent sister, / Clarissa Harlowe.

Mrs. Norton to Miss Clarissa Harlowe
Monday, July 31.

My dearest Young Lady, — I must indeed own that I took the liberty to write to your mother, offering to enclose to her, if she gave me leave, yours of the 24th. I am glad the letter was *not required of me* — and indeed it may be better that the matter lie wholly between you and them; since my affection for you is thought to proceed from partiality.

Mr. Brand has business in town; to solicit for a benefice which it is expected the incumbent will be obliged to quit for a better preferment and when there, he is to inquire privately after your way of life, and of your health.

He is a very officious young man; and, but that your Uncle Harlowe (who has chosen him for this errand) regards him as an oracle, your mother had rather anybody else had been sent.

I know not the day he is to set out: and as his inquiries are to be private, be pleased to take no notice of this intelligence. I have no doubt that your life and conversation are such as may defy the scrutinies of the most officious inquirer.

I am just now told that you have written a second letter to your sister: but am afraid they will wait for Mr. Brand's report before further favour will be obtained from them; for they will not yet believe you are so ill as I fear you are.

MISS CLARISSA HARLOWE TO MRS. NORTON

Wednesday, Aug. 2.

You tell me that you did actually write to my mother, *offering* to enclose to her mine of the 24th past: and you say it was not *required* of you. That is to say, although you cover it over as gently as you could, that your offer was rejected; which makes it evident that no plea will be heard for me. Yet you bid me hope that the grace I sued for would, *in time*, be granted.

The grace I then sued for was indeed granted: but you are afraid, you say, that they will wait for Mr. Brand's report before favour will be obtained in return to the second letter which I wrote to my sister.

But what, my dear Mrs. Norton, what is the grace I sue for in my second letter? It is not that they will receive me into favour — if they think it is, they are mistaken. I do not, I cannot expect that: nor, as I have often said, should I, if they *would* receive me, bear to live in the eye of those dear friends whom I have so grievously offended. 'Tis only, simply, a blessing I ask: a blessing to *die* with; not to *live* with. Do they know that? And do they know that their unkindness will perhaps shorten my date? So that their favour, if ever they intend to grant it, may come too late?

MR. LOVELACE TO JOHN BELFORD, ESQ.

Tuesday, Aug. 1.

I AM most confoundedly chagrined and disappointed: for here, on Saturday, arrived a messenger from Miss Howe with a letter to my cousins; which I knew nothing of till yesterday; when Lady Sarah and Lady Betty were procured to be here, to sit in judgment upon it with the old peer and my two kinswomen. And never was bear so miserably baited as thy poor friend! — And for what? — Why, for the cruelty of Miss Harlowe: for have I committed any *new* offence? And would I not have succeeded in her favour upon her own terms, if I could? And is it fair to punish me for what is my misfortune, and not my fault? Such *event-judging* fools as I have for my relations! I am ashamed of them all.

In that of Miss Howe was enclosed one to *her* from Miss Harlowe, to be transmitted to my cousins, containing a final rejection of me; and that in very vehement and positive terms; yet she pretends that in this rejection she is governed more by *principle* than *passion* (damned lie, as ever was told!). And, as a proof that she is, says that she *can* forgive me, and does, on this one condition, That I will never molest her more — the whole letter so written as to make *herself* more admired, *me* more detested.

What we have been told of the agitations and workings, and sighings and sobbings, of the French prophets among us formerly, was nothing at all to the scene exhibited by these maudlin souls, at the reading of these letters; and of some affecting passages extracted from another of my fair implacable's to Miss Howe. Such lamentations for the loss of so charming a relation! Such applaudings of her virtue, of her exaltedness of soul and sentiment! Such menaces of disinherisons! I, not needing *their* reproaches to be stung to the heart with my own reflections, and with the rage of disappointment; and as sincerely as any of them admiring her — "What the devil," cried I, "is all this for? Is it not enough to be despised and rejected? Can I help her implacable spirit? Would I not repair the evils I have made her suffer?" Then was I ready to curse them all, herself and Miss Howe for company: and heartily I swore that she should yet be mine.

I now swear it over again to thee. "Were her death to follow in a week after the knot is tied, by the Lord of Heaven, it *shall* be tied, and she shall die a Lovelace." Tell her so, if thou wilt: but at the same time, tell her that I have no *view of her fortune*; and that I will solemnly resign that, and all pretensions to it, in whose favour she pleases, if she resign life issueless.

I will go to town in a few days, in order to throw myself at her feet; and I will carry with me, or have at hand, a *resolute, well-prepared* parson; and the ceremony shall be performed, let what will be the consequence.

But if she will permit me to attend her for this purpose at either of the churches mentioned in the licence (which she has by her, and, thank Heaven! has not returned me with my letters), then will I not disturb her; but meet her at the altar in either church, and will engage to bring my two cousins to attend her, and even Lady Sarah and Lady Betty; and my Lord M. in person shall give her to me.

.   .   .   .

My Cousin Charlotte, finding me writing on with too much earnestness to have any regard for politeness to her, and guessing at my subject, besought me to let her see what I had written.

I obliged her. And she was so highly pleased on seeing me so much in earnest, that *she* offered, and I accepted her offer, to write a letter to Miss Harlowe; with permission to treat me in it as she thought fit.

I shall enclose a copy of her letter.

If it do not succeed, all the blame will be thrown upon the dear creature's perverseness: her charitable or forgiving disposition, about which she makes such a parade, will be justly questioned; and the pity of which she is now in full possession, will be transferred to me.

Putting, therefore, my whole confidence in this letter, I postpone all my other alternatives, as also my going to town, till my empress send an answer to my Cousin Montague.

Miss Montague to Miss Clarissa Harlowe

Tuesday, Aug. 1.

Dearest Madam, — All our family is deeply sensible of the injuries you have received at the hands of one of it, whom you only can render in any manner worthy of the relation he stands in to us all and if, as an act of mercy and charity, the greatest your pious heart can show, you will be pleased to look over his past wickedness and ingratitude, and suffer yourself to be our kinswoman, you will make us the happiest family in the world. This, madam, we should not, however, dare to petition for, were we not assured that Mr. Lovelace is most sincerely sorry for his past vileness to you; and that he will, on his knees, beg your pardon, and vow eternal love and honour to you.

If, by way of encouragement, you will but say you will be glad to see, and to be as much known personally as you are by fame to Charlotte Montague, I will, in two days' time from the receipt of your permission, wait upon you, *with* or *without* my sister, and receive your further commands.

Let me, *our dearest cousin* (we cannot deny ourselves the pleasure of calling you so; let me) entreat you to give me your permission for my journey to London; and put it in the power of Lord M., and of the ladies of the family, to make you what reparation they *can* make you, for the injuries which a person of the greatest merit in the world has received from one of the most audacious men in it; and you will infinitely oblige us all; and particularly her who repeatedly presumes to style herself / Your affectionate cousin and obliged servant, / Charlotte Montague.

Mr. Belford to Robert Lovelace, Esq.

Thursday Morning, Aug. 3, Six o'clock.

I was admitted to her presence last night; and found her visibly altered for the worse. When I went home, I had your letter of

Tuesday last put into my hands. Let me tell thee, Lovelace, that I insist upon the performance of thy engagement to me that thou wilt not personally molest her.

Mr. Belford dates again on Thursday morning ten o'clock; and gives an account of a conversation which he had just held with the lady upon the subject of Miss Montague's letter to her, preceding.

MISS CLARISSA HARLOWE TO MISS MONTAGUE

Thursday, Aug. 3.

DEAR MADAM, — I am infinitely obliged to you for your kind and condescending letter. A letter, however, which heightens my regrets, as it gives me a new instance of what a happy creature I might have been in an alliance so much approved of by such worthy ladies; and which, on their accounts, and on that of Lord M., would have been so reputable to myself, and was once so desirable.

Allow me then, dear madam, to declare with fervour that I think I never could deserve to be ranked with the ladies of a family so splendid and so noble, if, by vowing love and honour at the altar to such a violator, I could *sanctify*, as I may say, his unprecedented and elaborate wickedness.

Permit me, however, to make one request to my good Lord M., and to Lady Betty and Lady Sarah, and to your kind self and your sister. It is, that you will all be pleased to join your authority and interests to prevail upon Mr. Lovelace not to molest me further.

If I am, on the other hand, destined for *death*, it will be no less cruel, if he will not permit me to die in peace — since a peaceable and happy end I wish him. Indeed I do.

Every worldly good attend you, dear madam, and every branch of the honourable family, is the wish of one whose misfortune it is, that she is obliged to disclaim any other title than that of, dear madam, / Your and their obliged and faithful servant, / CLARISSA HARLOWE.

MR. BELFORD TO ROBERT LOVELACE, ESQ.

Thursday Afternoon, Aug. 3.

I AM just now agreeably surprised by the following letter, delivered into my hands by a messenger from the lady. The letter she mentions, as enclosed, I have returned, without taking a copy of it. The contents of it will soon be communicated to you, I presume, by other hands. They are an absolute rejection of thee — *Poor Lovelace!*

To John Belford, Esq.

Aug. 3.

SIR, — You have frequently offered to oblige me in anything that shall be within your power: and I have such an opinion of you, as to be willing to hope that at the times you made these offers you meant more than mere compliment.

417

I have, therefore, two requests to make to you: the first I will now mention; the other, if this shall be complied with, otherwise not.

It behoves me to leave behind me such an account as may clear up my conduct to several of my friends who will not at present concern themselves about me: and Miss Howe, and her mother, are very solicitous that I will do so.

I am apprehensive that I shall not have time to do this; and you will not wonder that I have less and less inclination to set about such a painful task; especially as I find myself unable to look back with patience on what I have suffered; and shall be too much discomposed by the retrospection.

Now, sir, if I may have a fair, a faithful specimen from his letters or accounts to you, written upon some of the most interesting occasions, I shall be able to judge whether there will or will not be a necessity for me, for my honour's sake, to enter upon the solicited task.

If, sir, you think fit to comply with my request, the passages I would wish to be transcribed (making neither better nor worse of the matter) are those which he has written to you on or about the 7th and 8th of June, when I was alarmed by the wicked pretence of a fire; and what he has written from Sunday, June 11, to the 19th. And in doing this you will oblige. . . .

Now, Lovelace, I see not why I may not oblige her, upon her honour, and under the restrictions, and for the reasons she has given. But, be this as it may, she *will* be obliged before thy remonstrances or clamours against it can come; so, prithee now, make the best of it, and rave not.

I long to know what the second request is: but this I know, that if it be anything less than cutting *thy* throat, or endangering *my* own neck, I will certainly comply; and be proud of having it in my power to oblige her.

MR. BELFORD TO MISS CLARISSA HARLOWE

Aug. 3, 4.

MADAM, — You have engaged me to communicate to you, upon honour (making neither better nor worse of the matter), what Mr. Lovelace has written to me in relation to yourself, in the period preceding your going to Hampstead, and in that between the 11th and 19th of June: and you assure me you have no view in this request but to see if it be necessary for you, from the account he gives, to touch the painful subjects yourself, for the sake of your own character.

Your commands, madam, are of a very delicate nature, as they may seem to affect the *secrets of private friendship*: but as I know you are not capable of a view, the motives to which you will not own; and as I think the communication may do some credit to my unhappy friend's character, as an *ingenuous* man; though his actions by the most excellent woman in the world have lost him all title to that of an *honourable* one; I obey you with the greater cheerfulness.

MISS CLARISSA HARLOWE TO JOHN BELFORD, ESQ.

Friday, Aug. 4.

SIR, — I hold myself extremely obliged to you for your communications. I will make no use of them that you shall have reason to reproach either yourself or me with.

. . . .

And now, sir, acknowledging gratefully your favour in the extracts, I come to the second request I had to make you; which requires a great deal of courage to mention. Thus, then, I preface it:

You see, sir, that I am thrown absolutely into the hands of strangers, who, although as kind and compassionate as strangers can be wished to be, are nevertheless persons from whom I cannot expect anything more than pity and good wishes; nor can my memory receive from them any more protection than my person, if either should need it.

If then I request it of the *only* person possessed of materials that will enable him to do my character justice;

And who has courage, independence, and ability to oblige me;

To be the protector of my memory, as I may say;

And to be my *executor*; and to see some of my dying requests performed;

And if I leave it to him to do the whole in his own way, manner, and time; consulting, however, in requisite cases, my dear Miss Howe; I presume to hope that this my second request may be granted.

Who knows, but that Mr. Belford, who already, from a principle of humanity, is touched at my misfortunes, when he comes to revolve the whole story, placed before him in one strong light, and when he shall have the catastrophe likewise before him; and shall become in a manner interested in it: who knows but that, *from a still higher principle,* he may so regulate his future actions as to find his own reward in the everlasting welfare which is wished him by his / Obliged servant, / CLARISSA HARLOWE?

MR. BELFORD TO MISS CLARISSA HARLOWE

Friday, August 4.

MADAM, — I am so sensible of the honour done me in yours of this day, that I would not delay for one moment the answering of it. I hope you will live to see many happy years; and to be your own executrix in those points which your heart is most set upon. But, in case of survivorship, I most cheerfully accept of the sacred office you are pleased to offer me; and you may absolutely rely upon my fidelity, and, if possible, upon the literal performance of every article you shall enjoin me.

The effect of the kind wish you conclude with has been my concern ever since I have been admitted to the honour of your conversation. It shall be my whole endeavour that it be not vain.

MR. BELFORD TO ROBERT LOVELACE, ESQ.

Friday Night, Aug. 4.

I HAVE actually delivered to the lady the extracts she requested me to give her from your letters. I do assure you that I have made the very best of the matter for you, *not* that conscience, but that friendship, could oblige me to make.

The lady is extremely uneasy at the thoughts of your attempting to visit her. For Heaven's sake (your word being given), and for pity's sake (for she is really in a very weak and languishing way), let me beg of you not to think of it.

But what thinkest thou is the second request she had to make to me? No other than that I would be her *executor*! Her motives will appear before thee in proper time; and then, I dare to answer, will be satisfactory.

You cannot imagine how proud I am of this trust. I am afraid I shall too soon come into the execution of it.

Saturday Morning, Aug. 5.

I am just returned from visiting the lady, and thanking her in person for the honour she has done me; and assuring her, if called to the sacred trust, of the utmost fidelity and exactness.

I found her very ill. I took notice of it. She said she had received a second hard-hearted letter from her sister; and she had been writing a letter (and that on her knees) directly to her mother; which, *before,* she had not had the courage to do. It was for a last blessing and forgiveness.

MISS ARAB. HARLOWE TO MISS CL. HARLOWE

(*In answer to hers of July* 29.)   *Thursday Morn., Aug. 3.*

SISTER CLARY, — I wish you would not trouble me with any more of your letters. You had always a knack at writing; and depended upon making every one do what you would when you wrote. But your wit and your folly have undone you. And now, as all naughty creatures do, when they can't help themselves, you come begging and praying, and make others as uneasy as yourself.

And so you'd creep on, by little and little, till you'll want to be received again.

But you only hope for *forgiveness* and a *blessing,* you say. A blessing for what, Sister Clary? Think for what! However, I read your letter to my father and mother.

I won't tell you what my father said — one who has the true sense you boast to have of your misdeeds may guess, without my telling you, what a justly incensed father would say on such an occasion.

My poor mother — O wretch! what has not your ungrateful folly cost my poor mother! Had you been less a darling, you would not, perhaps, have been so graceless: but I never in my life saw a cockered favourite come to good.

420

Upon the whole, I am sorry I have no more comfort to send you: but I find nobody willing to forgive you.

I don't know what *time* may do for you; and when it is seen that your penitence is not owing more to disappointment than to true conviction: for it is too probable, Miss Clary, that, had you gone on as swimmingly as you expected, and had not your feather-headed villain abandoned you, we should have heard nothing of these moving supplications; nor of anything but defiances from *him*, and a guilt gloried in from you. And this is every one's opinion, as well as that of / Your grieved sister, / ARABELLA HARLOWE.

MISS CLARISSA HARLOWE TO HER MOTHER

Sat. Aug. 5.

HONOURED MADAM, — No self-convicted criminal ever approached her angry and just judge with greater awe, nor with a truer contrition, than I do you by these lines.

Indeed I must say, that if the matter of my humble prayer had not respected my future welfare, I had not dared to take this liberty. But my heart is set upon it, as upon a thing next to God Almighty's forgiveness necessary for me.

My humble prayer is founded upon a true and unfeigned repentance: and this you will the readier believe, if the creature who never, to the best of her remembrance, told her mamma a wilful falsehood, may be credited, when she declares, as she does, in the most solemn manner, that she met the seducer with a determination not to go off with him: that the rash step was owing more to compulsion than to infatuation: and that her heart was so little in it, that she repented and grieved from the moment she found herself in his power; and for every moment after, for several weeks *before* she had any cause from him to apprehend the usage she met with.

Wherefore, on my knees, my ever-honoured mamma (for on my knees I write this letter), I do most humbly beg your blessing; say but, in so many words (I ask you not, madam, to call me your daughter): *Lost, unhappy wretch, I forgive you! and may God bless you!* This is all!

I can conjure you, madam, by no subject of motherly tenderness, that will not, in the opinion of my severe censurers (before whom this humble address must appear), add to my reproach: let me therefore, for God's sake, prevail upon you to pronounce me blest and forgiven, since you will thereby sprinkle comfort through the last hours of / Your / CLARISSA HARLOWE.

MR. LOVELACE TO JOHN BELFORD, ESQ.

Sat. Aug. 5.

I AM so excessively disturbed at the contents of Miss Harlowe's answer to my Cousin Charlotte's letter of Tuesday last (which was given her by the same fellow that gave me yours), that I have hardly patience or consideration enough to weigh what you write.

She had need indeed to cry out for mercy herself from *her* friends, who knows not how to show any! She is a true daughter of the Harlowes — by my soul, Jack, she is a true daughter of the Harlowes! Yet has she so many excellences that I must love her; and, fool that I am, love her the more for her despising me.

But no more of thy cursed knell; thy changes upon death's candlestick turned bottom upwards: she'll live to bury me; I see that: for, by my soul, I can neither eat, drink, nor sleep; nor, what is still worse, love any woman in the world but her. Nor care I to look upon a woman now: on the contrary, I turn my head from every one I meet; except by chance an eye, an air, a feature, strikes me resembling hers in some glancing-by face, and then I cannot forbear looking again; though the second look recovers me; for there can be nobody like her.

And here, while I am thus worthily waging war with beetles, drones, wasps, and hornets, and am all on fire with the rage of slighted love, thou art regaling thyself with phlegm and rock-water, and art going on with thy reformation scheme, and thy exultations in my misfortunes!

And thou art a pretty fellow, art thou not? to engage to transcribe for her some parts of my letters written to thee in confidence? Letters that thou shouldst sooner have parted with thy cursed tongue, than have owned thou ever hadst received such: yet these are now to be communicated to *her*! But I charge thee, and woe be to thee if it be too late! that thou do not oblige her with a line of mine.

If thou *hast* done it, the least vengeance I will take is to break through *my* honour given to thee not to visit her, as thou wilt have broken through *thine* to me in communicating letters written under the seal of friendship.

I am now convinced, too sadly for my hopes, by her letter to my Cousin Charlotte, that she is determined never to have me.

I will venture one more letter to her, however; and if that don't do, or procure me an answer, then will I endeavour to see her, let what *will* be the consequence. If she go out of my way, I will do some noble mischief to the vixen girl whom she most loves and then quit the kingdom for ever.

MR. LOVELACE TO JOHN BELFORD, ESQ.

Monday, Aug. 7.

AND so you have actually delivered to the fair implacable extracts of letters written in the confidence of friendship! Take care — take care, Belford — I do indeed love you better than I love any man in the world: but this is a very delicate point. The matter is grown very serious to me. My heart is bent upon having her. And have her I will, though I marry her in the agonies of death.

She is very earnest, you say, that I will not offer to molest her. *That*, let me tell her, will absolutely depend upon herself, and the answer she returns, whether by pen and ink, or the contemptuous one of silence, which she bestowed upon my last four to her: and I will write it in such humble, and in such reasonable terms, that, if she be not a true Harlowe, she *shall* forgive me. But as to the *executorship* which she is for conferring upon thee — thou shalt not be her *executor*: let me perish if thou shalt. Nor shall she die. Nobody shall be anything, nobody shall *dare* to be anything to her but I — thy happiness is already too great, to be admitted daily to her presence; to look upon her, to talk to her, to hear her talk, while I am forbid to come within view of her window.

Mr. Lovelace to Miss Clarissa Harlowe

Monday, Aug. 7.

YOUR angelic purity, and my awakened conscience, are standing records of your exalted merit and of my detestable baseness: but your forgiveness will lay me under an eternal obligation to you — forgive me, then, my dearest life, my earthly good, the visible anchor of my future hope! As you (who believe you have something to be forgiven for) hope for pardon yourself, forgive me, and consent to meet me, upon your own conditions, and in whose company you please, at the holy altar, and to give yourself a title to the most repentant and affectionate heart that ever beat in a human bosom.

But perhaps a time of probation may be required. It may be impossible for you, as well from *indisposition* as *doubt*, so soon to receive me to absolute favour as my heart wishes to be received.

If you refuse me this, you will make me desperate. But even then I must, at all events, throw myself at your feet, that I may not charge myself with the omission of any earnest, any humble effort, to move you in my favour: for in YOU, madam, in YOUR *forgiveness*, are centered my hopes as to *both worlds*: since to be reprobated finally by *you* will leave me without expectation of mercy from *above*!

Your whole conduct, madam, has been so nobly principled, and your resentments are so admirably just, that you appear to me even in a divine light; and in an infinitely more amiable one at the same time, than you could have appeared in, had you not suffered the barbarous wrongs that now fill my mind with anguish and horror at my own recollected villainy to the most excellent of women.

I *repeat* that all I beg for the present is a few lines, to guide my doubtful steps; and (if possible for you so far to condescend) to encourage me to hope that, if I can justify my present vows by my future conduct, I may be permitted the honour to style myself / Eternally yours, / R. LOVELACE.

Miss Clarissa Harlowe to Lord M. and to the Ladies of his House

Tuesday, Aug. 8.

EXCUSE me, my good lord, and my ever-honoured ladies, from accepting of your noble quarterly bounty; and allow me to return, with all grateful acknowledgment and true humility, the enclosed earnest of your goodness to me. Indeed I have no need of the one, and cannot possibly want the other: but, nevertheless, have such a sense of your generous favour that, to my last hour, I shall have pleasure in contemplating upon it, and be proud of the place I hold in the esteem of such venerable personages, to whom I once had the ambition to hope to be related.

MR. BELFORD TO ROBERT LOVELACE, ESQ.

Thursday Night, Aug. 10.

I CALLED at Smith's on Monday, in my way to Epsom. The lady was gone to chapel: but I had the satisfaction to hear she was not worse; and left my compliments, and an intimation that I should be out of town for three or four days.

. . . .

She had received several letters in my absence, as Mrs. Lovick acquainted me, besides yours. Yours, it seems, much distressed her; but she ordered the messenger, who pressed for an answer, to be told that it did not require an immediate one.

On Wednesday she received a letter from her Uncle Harlowe, in answer to one she had written to her mother on Saturday on her knees. It must be a very cruel one, Mrs. Lovick says, by the effects it had upon her: for, when she received it, she was intending to take an afternoon airing in a coach; but was thrown into so violent a fit of hysterics upon it, that she was forced to lie down; and (being not recovered by it) to go to bed about eight o'clock.

On Thursday morning she was up very early; and had recourse to the Scriptures to calm her mind, as she told Mrs. Lovick: and, weak as she was, would go in a chair to Lincoln's Inn Chapel, about eleven. She was brought home a little better; and then sat down to write to her uncle. But was obliged to leave off several times — to struggle, as she told Mrs. Lovick, for a humble temper. "My heart," said she to the good woman, "is a proud heart, and not yet, I find, enough mortified to my condition; but, do what I can, will be for prescribing resenting things to my pen."

I arrived in town from Belton's this Thursday evening; and went directly to Smith's. She was too ill to receive my visit.

Mrs. Smith gave me the following particulars of a conversation that passed between herself and a young clergyman on Tuesday afternoon, who, as it appears, was employed to make inquiries about the lady by her friends.

He came into the shop in a riding-habit, and asked for some Spanish snuff; and finding only Mrs. Smith there, he desired to have a little talk with her in the back shop.

[*The little talk shows the Rev. Mr. Brand's complete lack of sympathy with regard to Clarissa's distresses.*]

424

When Mrs. Smith told him that the lady was in a very bad state of health, he gave a careless shrug. She may be very ill, says he, her disappointments must have touched her to the quick: but she is not bad enough, I dare say, yet to atone for her very great lapse, and to expect to be forgiven by those whom she has so much disgraced.

He departed highly satisfied with himself, no doubt, and assured of Mrs. Smith's great opinion of his sagacity and learning: but bid her not say anything to the lady about him or his inquiries. And I, for very different reasons, enjoined the same thing.

I am glad, however, for her peace of mind's sake, that they begin to think it behoves them to inquire about her.

Miss Clarissa Harlowe to Robert Lovelace, Esq.

Friday, Aug. 11.

It is a cruel alternative to be either forced to see you or to write to you but to avoid a greater evil, nay, now I may say, the greatest, I write.

Were I capable of disguising or concealing my real sentiments, I might safely, I dare say, give you the remote hope you request, and yet keep all my resolutions. But I must tell you, sir (it becomes my character to tell you), that were I to live more years than perhaps I may weeks, and there were not another man in the world, I could not, I would not, be yours.

Religion enjoins me not only to forgive injuries, but to return good for evil. And accordingly I tell you that, wherever you go, I wish you happy. And now having, with great reluctance I own, complied with one of your compulsatory alternatives, I expect the fruits of it.

Mr. John Harlowe to Miss Clarissa Harlowe
(*In answer to hers to her mother.*)   *Monday, Aug. 7.*

Poor ungrateful, naughty Kinswoman, — Your mother neither caring, nor being *permitted* to write, I am desired to set pen to paper, though I had resolved against it.

And so I am to tell you that your letters, joined to the occasion of them, almost break the hearts of us all.

Were we sure you had seen your folly, and were *truly* penitent, and, at the same time, that you were so very ill as you pretend, I know not what might be done for you. But we are all acquainted with your moving ways when you want to carry a point.

Your mother *can't* ask, and your sister knows not in modesty *how* to ask; and so *I* ask you, If you have any reason to think yourself with child by this villain? You *must* answer this, and answer it truly, before anything can be resolved upon about you.

425

MISS CLARISSA HARLOWE TO JOHN HARLOWE, ESQ.

Thursday, Aug. 10.

HONOURED SIR, — It was an act of charity I begged: only for a last blessing, that I might die in peace. I ask not to be received again, as my severe sister (O that I had not written to her!) is pleased to say is my view.

I could not look forward to my last scene with comfort, without seeking at least to obtain the blessing I petitioned for; and that with a contrition so deep, that I deserved not, were it known, to be turned over from the tender nature of a mother to the upbraiding pen of an uncle; and to be wounded by a cruel question, put by him in a shocking manner; and which a little, a very little time, will better answer than I can: for I am not either a hardened or shameless creature.

And permit me to say that I asked it as well for my father and mother's sake as for my own; for I am sure *they* at least will be uneasy, after I am gone, that they refused it to me.

I should still be glad to have theirs, and yours, sir, and all your blessings and your prayers; but, denied in such a manner, I will not presume again to ask it: relying entirely on the Almighty's; which is never denied when supplicated for with such true penitence as I hope mine is.

MR. ANTONY HARLOWE TO MISS CL. HARLOWE

(*In reply to hers to her Uncle Harlowe of Thursday, Aug. 10*)

Aug. 12.

UNHAPPY GIRL! — Brother John has hurt your niceness, it seems, by asking a plain question, which your mother's heart is too full of grief to let her ask; and modesty will not let your sister ask, though but the consequence of your actions. And yet it *must* be answered before you'll obtain from your father and mother, and us, the notice you hope for, I can tell you that.

You lived several guilty weeks with one of the vilest fellows that ever drew breath, at bed as well as board, no doubt (for is not his character known?); and pray don't be ashamed to be asked after what may naturally come of such free living. We hope all is not true *that we hear of you*. Only take care that, bad as you have acted, you act not still worse, if it be possible.

Sunday, Aug. 13.

MISS CLARISSA HARLOWE TO ANTONY HARLOWE, ESQ.

HONOURED SIR, — I am very sorry for my pert letter to my Uncle Harlowe. Yet I did not intend it to be pert. People *new* to misfortune may be too easily moved to impatience.

The fall of a regular person, no doubt, is dreadful. Would to Heaven, however, that I had had the circumstances of mine inquired into! If, sir, I make myself worse than I am in my health, and better than I am in my penitence, it is fit I should be punished for my double dissimulation. My sincerity in both respects will, however, be best justified by the event.

Why, why, sir, were not *other* inquiries made of me, as well as this shocking one? — Inquiries that modesty *would* have permitted a mother or a sister to make; and which, if I may be excused to say so, would have been still *less* improper, and *more* charitable, to have been made by *uncles* (were the mother *forbidden*, or the sister *not inclined* to make them) than those they have made.

God Almighty bless, preserve, and comfort my dear sorrowing and grievously offended father and mother! — And continue in honour, favour, and merit, my happy sister! May God forgive my brother, and protect him from the violence of his own temper, as well as from the destroyer of his sister's honour! And may you, my dear uncle, and your no less now than ever dear brother, and my second papa, as he used to bid me call him, be blessed and happy in them, and in each other! And, in order to this, may you all speedily banish from your remembrance for ever / The unhappy / CLARISSA HARLOWE.

MRS. NORTON TO MISS CLARISSA HARLOWE

Monday, Aug. 14.

ALL your friends here, my dear young lady, now seem set upon proposing to you to go to one of the plantations. This, I believe, is owing to some misrepresentations of Mr. Brand; from whom they have received a letter.

Let me advise you, my dear Miss Clary, to discountenance any visits which, with the censorious, may affect your character.

·　·　·　·　·　·　·　·　·　·

I am just informed that your Cousin Morden is arrived in England. He is at Canterbury, it seems, looking after some concerns he has there; and is soon expected in these parts. Who knows what may arise from his arrival? God be with you, my dearest Miss Clary, and be your comforter and sustainer. And never fear but He will; for I am sure, I am very sure, that you put your whole trust in Him.

MISS CLARISSA HARLOWE TO MRS. NORTON

Thursday, Aug. 17.

WHAT Mr. Brand, or anybody, can have written or said to my prejudice I cannot imagine; and yet some evil reports have gone out against me; as I find by some hints in a very severe letter written to me by my Uncle Antony. Such a letter as I believe was never written to any poor creature who, by ill-health of body as well as of mind, was before tottering on the brink of the grave. But my friends may possibly be better justified than the reporters — for who knows what they may have heard?

I am glad to hear of my Cousin Morden's safe arrival. I should wish to see him, methinks: but I am afraid that he will sail with the stream; as it must be expected that he will hear what they have to say first. But what I most fear is that he will take upon himself to avenge me. Rather than he should do so, I would have him look upon me as a creature utterly unworthy of his concern; at least of his *vindictive concern.*

MR. LOVELACE TO JOHN BELFORD, ESQ.
Sunday, Aug. 13.

I DON'T know what a devil ails me; but I never was so much indisposed in my life. Neither eat, drink, nor sleep! A piteous case, Jack! If I should die like a fool now, people would say Miss Harlowe had broken my heart. That she *vexes* me to the heart is certain.

Confounded squeamish! I would fain write it off. But must lay down my pen again. It won't do. Poor Lovelace! What a devil ails thee?

.   .   .   .

But I can tell thee, for all this, I will never suffer thee to expose my letters. They are too ingenuous by half to be seen. And I absolutely insist it, that on receipt of this thou burn them all.

My beloved mistakes me if she thinks I proposed her writing to me as an alternative that should dispense with my attendance upon her. That it shall *not* do, nor did I intend it should, unless she had pleased me better in the contents of her letter than she has done. Bid her read again. I gave no such hopes. I would have been with her, in spite of you both, by to-morrow at furthest, had I not been laid by the heels thus, like a helpless miscreant.

But I grow better and better every hour, *I* say: the *doctor* says not: but I am sure I know best: and I will soon be in London, depend on't. But say nothing of this to my dear, cruel, and implacable Miss Harlowe.

MR. BELFORD TO MISS CLARISSA HARLOWE
Sat. Morn. Aug. 19.

MADAM, — I think myself obliged in honour to acquaint you that I am afraid Mr. Lovelace will try his fate by an interview with you.

I wish to Heaven you could prevail upon yourself to receive his visit. All that is respectful, even to veneration, and all that is penitent, will you see in his behaviour, if you can admit of it.

He flatters himself that you are not so ill as I represent you to be. When he sees you, he will be convinced.

I beg you will not too much hurry and discompose yourself. It is impossible he can be in town till Monday at soonest. And if he resolve to come, I hope to be at Mr. Smith's before him.

MR. LOVELACE TO JOHN BELFORD, ESQ.

London, Aug. 21, Monday.

THAT thou mightest have as little notice as possible of the time I was resolved to be in town, I set out in my lord's chariot and six yesterday, as soon as I had dispatched my letter to thee, and arrived in town last night: for I knew I could have no dependence on thy friendship where Miss Harlowe's humour was concerned.

I took a chair to Smith's, my heart bounding in almost audible thumps to my throat, with the assured expectation of seeing my beloved. I clasped my fingers, as I was danced along, till I arrived at Smith's, and there the fellows set down their gay burden. Off went their hats; Will ready at hand in a new livery; up went the head; out rushed my honour; the woman behind the counter all in flutters; respect and fear giving due solemnity to the features; and her knees, I doubt not, knocking against the inside of her wainscot fence.

Your servant, madam. — Will, let the fellows move to some distance, and wait.

You have a young lady lodges here; Miss Harlowe, madam: is she above?

Sir, sir, and please your honour (the woman is struck with my figure, thought I): Miss Harlowe, sir! There is, indeed, such a young lady lodges here — but, but ——

But what, madam? I must see her. One pair of stairs, is it not? Don't trouble yourself — I shall find her apartment. And was making towards the stairs.

Sir, sir, the lady — the lady is not at home. She is abroad — she is in the country ——

In the country! Not at home! Impossible! You will not pass this story upon me, good woman. I *must* see her. I have business of life and death with her.

Indeed, sir, the lady is not at home! Indeed, sir, she is abroad! ——

She then rung a bell: John, cried she, pray step down! — Indeed, sir, the lady is not at home.

Down came John, the good man of the house, when I expected one of his journeymen, by her saucy familiarity.

My dear, said she, the gentleman will not believe Miss Harlowe is abroad.

John bowed to my fine clothes: Your servant, sir. Indeed the lady is abroad. She went out of town this morning by six o'clock — into the country — by the doctor's advice.

Still I would not believe either John or his wife. I am sure, said I, she cannot be abroad. I heard she was very ill.

O sir, she is very ill very ill, indeed — she could hardly walk to the coach.

429

Well, friend, I must not believe you. You'll excuse me; but I must go upstairs myself. And was stepping up.

John hereupon put on a serious and a less respectful face: Sir, this house is mine; and —

And what, friend? not doubting then but she was above. I must and will see her. I have authority for it. I am a justice of peace. I have a search-warrant.

And up I went; they following me, muttering, and in a plaguy flutter.

The first door I came to was locked. I tapped at it.

The lady, sir, has the key of her own apartment.

On the inside, I question not, my honest friend; tapping again. And being assured, if she heard my voice, that her timorous and soft temper would make her betray herself, by some flutters, to my listening ear, I said aloud, I am confident Miss Harlowe is here. Dearest madam, open the door: admit me but for one moment to your presence.

But neither answer nor fluttering saluted my ear; and, the people being very quiet, I led on to the next apartment; and, the key being on the outside, I opened it, and looked all round it and into the closet.

The man said he never saw so uncivil a gentleman in his life.

Hark thee, friend, said I; let me advise thee to be a little decent; or I shall teach thee a lesson thou never learnedst in all thy life.

Sir, said he, 'tis not like a gentleman to affront a man in his own house.

Then prithee, man, replied I, don't crow upon thine own dunghill.

I stepped back to the locked door: My dear Miss Harlowe, I beg of you to open the door, or I'll break it open; pushing hard against it, that it cracked again.

The man looked pale; and, trembling with his fright, made a plaguy long face; and called to one of his bodice-makers above: *Joseph, come down quickly.*

Joseph came down: a lion's-face, grinning fellow; thick, and short, and bushy-headed, like an old oak pollard. Then did Master John put on a sturdier look. But I only hummed a tune, traversed all the other apartments, sounded the passages with my knuckles, to find whether there were private doors, and walked up the next pair of stairs, singing all the way; John, and Joseph, and Mrs. Smith, following me trembling.

[*Lovelace searches the house insolently, but finds no Clarissa. He facetiously scorns Mrs. Smith and her husband, who are amazed and somewhat fearful of his arrogance. A crowd gathers, and he goes away, but sends Will back to watch the house. He is skeptical of Clarissa's illness.*]

August 22.

Here this moment is Will, come running hither to tell me that his lady actually returned to her lodgings last night between eleven and twelve; and is now there, though very ill.

I hasten to her. But that I may not add to her indisposition by any rough or boisterous behaviour, I will be as soft and gentle as the dove herself in my addresses to her.

.   .   .   .

Curse upon my stars! Disappointed again! It was about eight when I arrived at Smith's. The woman was in the shop.

So, old acquaintance, how do you now? I know my love is above. Let her be acquainted that I am here, waiting for admission to her presence, and can take no denial. Tell her that I will approach her with the most respectful duty, and in whose company she pleases; and I will not touch the hem of her garment without her leave.

Indeed, sir, you are mistaken. The lady is not in this house, nor near it.

I'll see that.

I went into each apartment, except that which was locked before, and was now also locked: and I called to my Clarissa in the voice of love: but by the still silence was convinced she was not there. Yet, on the strength of my intelligence, I doubted not but she was in the house.

I then went up two pair of stairs, and looked round the first room: but no Miss Harlowe.

And who, pray, is in this room? stopping at the door of another.

A widow gentlewoman, sir — Mrs. Lovick.

Oh, my dear Mrs. Lovick! said I. I am intimately acquainted with Mrs. Lovick's character from my cousin John Belford. I must see Mrs. Lovick by all means. Good Mrs. Lovick, open the door.

She did.

Your servant, madam. Be so good as to excuse me. You have heard my story. You are an admirer of the most excellent woman in the world. Dear Mrs. Lovick, tell me what is become of her?

The poor lady, sir, went out yesterday on purpose to avoid you.

How so? She knew not that I would be here.

She was afraid you would come, when she heard you were recovered from your illness. Ah! sir, what pity it is that so fine a gentleman should make such ill returns for God's goodness to him!

You are an excellent woman, Mrs. Lovick; and Miss Clarissa Harlowe is an angel.

Miss Harlowe is indeed an angel, replied she; and soon will be company for angels.

No jesting with such a woman as this, Jack.

Sir, said the widow, it would be death for her to see you. She was at home last night; I'll tell you truth: but fitter to be in bed all day. She came home, she said, to die; and, if she could not avoid your visit, she was unable to fly from you; and believed she should die in your presence.

And yet go out again this morning early? How can that be, widow?

Why, sir, she rested not two hours, for fear of you. Her fear gave her strength, which she'll suffer for when that fear is over. And finding herself, the more she thought of your visit, the less able to stay to receive it, she took chair, and is gone nobody knows whither.

I am told she is actually in the house.

Indeed, sir, she is *not*. You may satisfy yourself, if you please: but Mrs. Smith and I waited on her to her chair. We were forced to support her, she was so weak. She said: Whither *can* I go, Mrs. Lovick? Whither *can* I go, Mrs. Smith? Cruel, cruel man! Tell him I called him so, if he come again! God give him that peace which he denies me!

Sweet creature! cried I, and looked down, and took out my handkerchief.

The widow wept. I wish, said she, I had never known so excellent a lady, and so great a sufferer! I love her as my own child!

Mrs. Smith wept.

I then gave over the hope of seeing her for this time. I was extremely chagrined at my disappointment, and at the account they gave of her ill-health.

In short, I told them I *must* and *would* see her: but that it should be with all the respect and veneration that heart could pay to excellence like hers. This I bid them tell her. And thus ended our serious conversation.

While I was there, a letter was brought by a particular hand. They seemed very solicitous to hide it from me; which made me suspect it was for her. I desired to be suffered to cast my eye upon the seal and the superscription; promising to give it back to them unopened.

Looking upon it, I told them I knew the hand and seal. It was from her sister. And I hoped it would bring her news that she would be pleased with. They joined most heartily in the same hope. I civilly took my leave, and went away.

Mr. Belford to Robert Lovelace, Esq.

Tuesday, Aug. 22.

I am extremely concerned for the poor unprotected lady; she was so excessively low and weak on Saturday that I could not be admitted to her speech: and to be driven out of her lodgings, when it was fitter for her to be in bed, is such a piece of cruelty as he only could be guilty of, who could act as thou hast done by such an angel.

Canst thou thyself say, on reflection, that it has not the look of a wicked and hardened sportiveness in thee, for the sake of a wanton humour only (since it can answer no end that thou proposest to thyself, but the direct contrary), to hunt from place to place a poor lady, who like a harmless deer that has already a barbed shaft in her breast, seeks only a refuge from thee, in the shades of death?

But I will leave this matter upon thy own conscience.

Mr. Lovelace to John Belford, Esq.

Wednesday Morn. Aug 23.

All alive, dear Jack, and in ecstasy! Likely to be once more a happy man! For I have received a letter from my beloved Miss HAR-LOWE; in consequence, I suppose, of that which I mentioned in my last to be left for her from her sister. And I am setting out for Berks directly, to show the contents to my Lord M., and to receive the congratulations of all my kindred upon it.

I went last night, as I intended, to Smith's: but the dear creature was not returned at near ten o'clock. At eight this morning, as I was dressing, to be in readiness against the return of my fellow, who I had sent to inquire after the lady, I had this letter brought me by a chairman.

To Robert Lovelace, Esq.

Tuseday Night, 11 o'clock (Aug. 22).

SIR, — I have good news to tell you. I am setting out with all dili-- gence for my Father's House. I am bid to hope that he will receive his poor penitent with a goodness peculiar to himself; for I am over-joyed with the assurance of a thorough reconciliation, through the interposition of a dear, blessed friend whom I always loved and honoured. I am so taken up with my preparation for this joyful and long-wished-for journey that I cannot spare one moment for any other business, having several matters of the last importance to settle first. So pray, sir, don't disturb or interrupt me — I beseech you, don't. You may possibly in time see me at my Father's; at least, if it be not your own fault.

I will write a letter, which shall be sent you when I am got thither and received: till when, I am, etc. / CLARISSA HARLOWE.

I dispatched instantly a letter to the dear creature, assuring her, with the most thankful joy, that I would directly set out for Berks, and wait the issue of the happy reconciliation and the charming hopes she had filled me with. I poured out upon her a thousand blessings.

I hurried it away without taking a copy of it; and I have ordered the chariot and six to be got ready; and hey for M. Hall!

I knew they loved her (the pride and glory of their family) too well to hold out long!

There is a solemnity, however, I think, in the style of her letter, which pleases and affects me at the same time. But as it is evident she loves me still, and hopes soon to see me at her father's, she could not help being a little solemn, and half-ashamed (dear blushing, pretty rogue!) to own her love, after my usage of her.

. . . .

Although I have the highest opinion that man can have of the generosity of my dear Miss Harlowe, yet I cannot for the heart of me account for this agreeable change in her temper, but one way. Faith and troth, Belford, I verily believe, laying all circumstances together, that the dear creature unexpectedly finds herself in the way I have so ardently wished her to be in; and that this makes her, at last, incline to favour me, that she may set the better face upon her gestation when at her father's.

[For at least a week (August 19–25) Belford has been at Epsom, performing "the last friendly offices for poor Mr. Belton." At this time it helps to have Belford "off-stage;" and besides for Richardson there is a powerful moral lesson — portrayed at length — in the fate of this hapless rake, Belton. The whole episode is here omitted.]

MR. BELFORD TO ROBERT LOVELACE, ESQ.

Sat. Aug. 26.

IT IS impossible to account for the contents of her letter to you; or to reconcile those contents to the facts I have to communicate.

I was at Smith's by seven yesterday (Friday) morning; and found that the lady was just gone in a chair to St. Dunstan's to prayers: she was too ill to get out by six to Covent Garden Church; and was forced to be supported to her chair by Mrs. Lovick. They would have persuaded her against going; but she said she knew not but it would be her last opportunity. Mrs. Lovick, dreading that she would be taken worse at church, walked thither before her.

Mrs. Smith told me she was so ill on Wednesday night, that she had desired to receive the Sacrament; and accordingly it was administered to her by the parson of the parish: whom she besought to take all opportunities of assisting her in solemn preparation.

This the gentleman promised: and called in the morning to inquire after her health; and was admitted at the first word. He stayed with her about half an hour; and when he came down, with his face turned aside, and a faltering accent: "Mrs. Smith, said he, you have an angel in your house. I will attend her again in the evening, as she desires, and as often as I think it will be agreeable to her."

Her increased weakness she attributed to the fatigues she had undergone by your means; and to a letter she had received from her sister, which she answered the same day.

Mrs. Smith told me that two different persons had called there, one on Thursday morning, one in the evening, to inquire after her state of health; and seemed as if commissioned from her relations for that purpose; but asked not to see her, only were very inquisitive after her visitors (particularly, it seems, after *me*: what could they mean by that?), after her way of life, and expenses; and one of them inquired after her manner of supporting them; to the latter of which Mrs. Smith said she had answered, as the truth was, that she had been obliged to sell some of her clothes, and was actually about parting with more; at which the inquirist (a grave old farmer-looking man) held up his hands, and said: Good God! this will be sad, sad news to somebody! I believe I must not mention it. But Mrs. Smith says she desired he *would*, let him come from whom he would. He shook his head, and said, if she died, the flower of the world would be gone, and the family she belonged to would be no more than a common family.[1] I was pleased with the man's expression.

On Wednesday morning, when she received your letter in answer

[1] This man came from her Cousin Morden; as will be seen hereafter.

434

to hers, she said: Necessity may well be called the mother of invention — but calamity is the test of integrity. I hope I have not taken an inexcusable step —— And there she stopped a minute or two; and then said: I shall now, perhaps, be allowed to die in peace.

I stayed till she came in. She was glad to see me; but, being very weak, said she must sit down before she could go upstairs; and so went into the back shop; leaning upon Mrs. Lovick: and when she had sat down, I am glad to see you, Mr. Belford, said she; I *must* say so — let misreporters say what they will.

I wondered at this expression; but would not interrupt her.

Oh! sir, said she, I have been grievously harassed. Your friend, who would not let me live with reputation, will not permit me to die in peace. You see how I am. Is there not a great alteration in me within this week? But 'tis all for the better. Yet were I to wish for life, I must say that your friend, your barbarous friend, has *hurt* me greatly.

. . . .

We had hardly recovered ourselves when she, quite easy, cheerful, and smiling returned to us. Doctor, said she (seeing we had been moved), you will excuse me for the concern I give you; and so will you, Mr. Goddard, and you, Mr. Belford; for 'tis a concern that only generous natures can show; and to such natures *sweet* is the pain, if I may so say, that attends such a concern. But as I have some few preparations still to make, and would not (though in ease of Mr. Belford's future cares, which is, and ought to be, part of my study) undertake more than it is likely I shall have time lent me to perform, I would beg of you to give me your opinions (you see my way of living; and you may be assured that I will do nothing wilfully to shorten life) how long it may possibly be before I may hope to be released from all my troubles.

They both hesitated, and looked upon each other. Don't be afraid to answer me, said she, and with a look serenely earnest, Tell me how long you think I may hold it? And believe me, gentlemen, the shorter you tell me my time is likely to be, the more comfort you will give me.

How long, doctor? I believe I *shall* have a little more ruffling — I am afraid I shall — but there can happen only one thing that I shall not be tolerably easy under —— How long then, sir?

He was silent.

A fortnight, sir?

He was still silent.

Ten days? A week? How long, sir? with smiling earnestness.

If I *must* speak, madam: if you have not better treatment than you have lately met with, I am afraid —— There again he stopped.

Afraid of what, doctor? Don't be afraid. How long, sir?

That a fortnight or three weeks may deprive the world of the finest flower in it.

A fortnight or three weeks yet, doctor? But God's will be done! I shall, however, by this means, have full time, if I have but strength and intellect, to do all that is now upon my mind to do.

She then retired, with a cheerful and serene air. The two gentlemen went away together. I went down to the women, and, inquiring, found that Mrs. Lovick was this day to bring her twenty guineas more, for some other of her apparel.

The widow told me that she had taken the liberty to expostulate with her upon the *occasion* she had for raising this money to such great disadvantage; and it produced the following short and affecting conversation between them.

None of my friends will wear anything of mine, said she. I shall leave a great many good things behind me. And as to what I want the money for — don't be surprised: but suppose I want it to purchase a house?

You are all mystery, madam. I don't comprehend you.

Why then, Mrs. Lovick, I will explain myself. I have a man, not a woman, for my executor: and think you that I will leave to his care anything that concerns my own person? Now, Mrs. Lovick, smiling, do you comprehend me?

Mrs. Lovick wept.

I should have mentioned that the lady explained to me what the *one thing* was that she was afraid might happen to ruffle her. It was the apprehension of what may result from a visit which Col. Morden, as she is informed, designs to make *you*.

THE REV. DR. LEWEN TO MISS CLARISSA HARLOWE

Friday, Aug. 18.

PRESUMING, dearest and ever-respectable young lady, upon your former favour, and upon your opinion of my judgment and sincerity, I cannot help addressing you by a few lines, on your present unhappy situation.

What I principally write for now is, to put you upon doing a piece of justice to yourself, and to your sex, in the prosecuting for his life (I am assured his life is in your power) the most profligate and abandoned of men, as *he* must be who could act so basely as I understand Mr. Lovelace has acted by you.

In a word, the reparation of your family dishonour now rests in your own bosom: and which only one of these two alternatives *can* repair; to wit, either to marry the offender, or to prosecute him at law. Bitter expedients for a soul so delicate as yours! It is a terrible circumstance to be under the obligation of telling so shocking a story in public court: but it is still a worse imputation that she should pass over so mortal an injury unresented. / Your sincere admirer and humble servant, / ARTHUR LEWEN.

I just now understand that your sister will, by proper authority, propose this prosecution to you. I humbly presume that the reason why you resolved not upon this step *from the first*, was that you did not know that it would have the *countenance and support of your relations*.

Reverend and dear Sir, — I thought, till I received your affectionate and welcome letter, that I had neither father, uncle, brother left; nor hardly a friend among my former favourers of your sex. Yet, knowing *you* so well, and having no reason to upbraid myself with a faulty will, I was to blame (even although I had doubted the continuance of your good opinion) to decline the trial whether I had forfeited it or not; and if I had, whether I could not *honourably* reinstate myself in it.

Permit me, then, to say that I believe your arguments would have been unanswerable in almost every *other* case of this nature but in that of the unhappy *Clarissa Harlowe*.

It is certain that creatures who cannot stand the shock of *public shame* should be doubly careful how they expose themselves to the danger of incurring *private guilt*, which may possibly bring them to it. But as to *myself*, suppose there were no objections from the declining way I am in as to my health; and supposing I could have prevailed upon myself to appear against this man; were there not room to apprehend that the end so much wished for by my friends (to wit, his condign punishment) would not have been obtained?

Had the prosecution been carried on to *effect*, and had he even been *sentenced to death*, can it be thought that his family would not have had interest enough to obtain his pardon? And had he been *pardoned*, would he not then have been at liberty to do as much mischief as ever?

The injury I have received from him is indeed of the highest nature, and it was attended with circumstances of unmanly baseness and premeditation; yet, I bless God, it has not tainted my mind; it has not hurt my morals.

I have *another* plea to make, which alone would have been enough (as I presume) to answer the contents of your very kind and friendly letter.

I know that you will allow of my endeavour to bring myself to this charitable disposition, when I tell you how near I think myself to that great and awful moment *in* which, and even in the ardent preparation *to* which every sense of indignity or injury that concerns not the immortal soul ought to be absorbed in higher and more important contemplations.

Thus much for *myself*.

And for the satisfaction of my *friends* and *favourers,* Miss Howe is solicitous to have all those letters and materials preserved which will set my whole story on a true light. The good Dr. Lewen is one of the principal of those friends and favourers.

The warning that may be given from those papers to all such young creatures as may have known or heard of me, may be of more efficacy to the end wished for, as I humbly presume to think, than my appearance could have been in a court of justice, pursuing a doubtful event under the disadvantages I have mentioned.

MISS ARAB. HARLOWE TO MISS CL. HARLOWE
(*In answer to hers to her Uncle Antony*)   *Monday, Aug. 21.*

I FIND by your letters to my uncles, that they, as well as I, are in great disgrace with you for writing our minds to you.

We can't help it, Sister Clary.

Well, then, since this is the case, Sister Clary, let me, *with all humility,* address myself with a proposal or two to you, to which you will be *graciously* pleased to give an answer.

Now you must know that we have had hints given us from several quarters, that you have been used in such a manner by the villain you ran away with, that his life would be answerable for his crime if it were fairly to be proved. And, by your own hints, something like it appears to us.

Let me, therefore, know (*if you please*) whether you are willing to appear to do *yourself*, and *us*, and your *sex*, this justice? If *not,* Sister Clary, we shall know what to think of you; for neither *you* nor *we* can suffer more than we have done from the scandal of your fall.

One word only more as to the above proposal: your admirer, Dr. Lewen, is clear in his opinion that you should prosecute the villain.

But if you will not agree to this, I have another proposal to make to you, and that in the name of every one in the family; which is, that you will think of going to Pennsylvania to reside there for some few years till all is blown over; and, if it please God to spare you, and your unhappy parents, till they can be satisfied that you behave like a true and uniform penitent; at least till you are one-and-twenty: you may then come back to your own estate, or have the produce of it sent you thither, as you shall choose. A period which my father fixes, because it is the *custom*; and because he thinks your *grandfather* should have fixed it; and because, let *me* add, you have fully proved by your fine conduct, that you were not at years of discretion at *eighteen.*

These are what I had to communicate to you; and if you'll oblige me with an answer (which the hand that conveys this will call for on Wednesday morning), it will be very condescending.

Miss Cl. Harlowe to Miss Arab. Harlowe

Tuesday, Aug. 22.

I KNOW Dr. Lewen's opinion. He has been so good as to enforce it in a kind letter to me. I have answered his letter; and given such reasons as I hope will satisfy *him*.[1]

To your other proposal, of going to Pennsylvania, this is my answer: If nothing happen within a month which may full as effectually rid my parents and friends of that world of cares, and fears, and scandals, which you mention, and if I am *then* able to be carried on board of ship, I will cheerfully obey my father and mother, although I were sure to die in the passage.

I am equally surprised and concerned at the hints which both you and my Uncle Antony give of *new* points of misbehaviour in me! What can be meant by them?

I will not tell you, Miss Harlowe, how much I am afflicted at your severity, and how much I suffer by it, and by your hard-hearted levity of style, because what I shall say may be construed into *jingle* and *period*, and because I know it is *intended*, very possibly for *kind* ends, to mortify me. All I will therefore say is, that it does not lose its end, if that be it.

Mrs. Norton to Miss Clarissa Harlowe

Tuesday, Aug. 22.

MY DEAREST YOUNG LADY, — The letters you sent me I now return by the hand that brings you this.

It is impossible for me to express how much I have been affected by them, and by your last of the 17th. Indeed, my dear Miss Clary, you are very harshly used; indeed you are!

The motives which incline them all to this severity, if well grounded, would authorize any severity they could express, and which, while they believe them to be so, both they and you are to be equally pitied.

They are owing to the information of that officious Mr. Brand, who has acquainted them (from some enemy of yours in the neighbourhood about you) that visits are made you, highly censurable, by a man of a free character, and an intimate of Mr. Lovelace; who is often in private with you; sometimes twice or thrice a day.

Something of this nature was hinted at by Betty to me before, but so darkly that I could not tell what to make of it; and this made me mention it to you so *generally* as I did in my last.

Your Cousin Morden has been among them. He is exceedingly concerned for your misfortunes; and as they will not believe Mr. Lovelace would marry you, he is determined to go to Lord M.'s, in

[1] Her letter containing the reasons she refers to, was not asked for; and Dr. Lewen's death, which fell out soon after he had received it, was the reason that it was not communicated to the family till it was too late to do the service that might have been hoped for from it.

order to inform himself from Mr. Lovelace's own mouth whether he intends to do you that justice or not.

MR. LOVELACE TO JOHN BELFORD, ESQ.

Monday Noon, Aug. 28.

WHAT is the meaning I hear nothing from thee? And why dost thou not let me into the grounds of the sudden reconciliation between my beloved and her friends, and the cause of the generous invitation which she gives me of attending her at her father's some time hence?

Thou must certainly have been let into the secret by this time; and I can tell thee I shall be plaguy jealous if there be any one thing pass between my angel and thee that is to be concealed from me. For either I am a principal in this cause, or I am nothing.

But let me whisper a word or two in thy ear. I begin to be afraid, after all, that this letter was a stratagem to get me out of town, and for nothing else.

My lord and I expect this very afternoon a visit from Colonel Morden; who undertakes, it seems, to question me as to my intention with regard to his cousin.

But Colonel Morden is come, and I must break off.

MR. BELFORD TO ROBERT LOVELACE, ESQ.

Monday Night, Aug. 28.

I GOT to town in the evening, and went directly to Smith's. I sent up my compliments; and she returned that she would take it for a favour if I would call upon her in the morning, by eight o'clock. Mrs. Lovick told me that she had fainted away on Saturday, while she was writing, as she had done likewise the day before.

. . . .

She had a pretty good night, it seems; and this morning went in a chair to St. Dunstan's Church.

The chairmen told Mrs. Smith that after prayers (for she did not return till between nine and ten) they carried her to a house in Fleet Street, whither they never waited on her before. And where dost think this was? Why, to an undertaker's! Good Heaven! what a woman is this! She went into the back shop, and talked with the master of it about half an hour, and came from him with great serenity; he waiting upon her to her chair with a respectful countenance, but full of curiosity and seriousness.

'Tis evident that she then went to bespeak her *house* that she talked of. *As soon as you can, sir,* were her words to him as she got into the chair. Mrs. Smith told me this with the same surprise and grief that I heard it.

She was very ill in the afternoon, having got cold either at St.

Dunstan's or at chapel, and sent for the clergyman to pray by her; and the women, unknown to her, sent both for Dr. H. and Mr. Goddard: who were just gone, as I told you, when I came to pay my respects to her this evening.

Tuesday, Aug. 29.

I was at Smith's at half an hour after seven. They told me that the lady was gone in a chair to St. Dunstan's.

She returned immediately after prayers.

The good people retiring after breakfast, the following conversation passed between us.

Pray, sir, let me ask you, said she, if you think I may promise myself that I shall be no more molested by your friend?

I hesitated; for how could I answer for such a man?

I hope not, madam; I have not heard from him since Thursday last, that he went out of town, rejoicing in the hopes your letter gave him of a reconciliation between your friends and you, and that he might in good time see you at your father's; and he is gone down to give all his friends joy of the news, and is in high spirits upon it.

Alas for me! I shall then surely have him come up to persecute me again! As soon as he discovers that that was only a stratagem to keep him away, he will come up; and who knows but even *now* he is upon the road.

I believe I looked surprised to hear her confess that her letter was a stratagem only; for she said: You wonder, Mr. Belford, I observe, that I could be *guilty of such an artifice. I doubt it is not right*: it was done in a hurry of spirits. Yet, 'tis strange too, that neither you nor he found out my meaning on perusal of my letter. You have seen what I wrote, no doubt?

I have madam. And then I began to account for it as an *innocent* artifice.

Thus far indeed, sir, it is *innocent,* that I meant him not hurt, and had a *right* to the effect I hoped for from it; and he had *none* to invade me. But have you, sir, that letter of his in which he gives you (as I suppose he does) the copy of mine?

I have, madam. And pulled it out of my letter-case: but hesitating, Nay, sir, said she, be pleased to read my letter to yourself — I desire not to see *his* — and see if you can be longer a stranger to a meaning so obvious.

I read it to myself. Indeed, madam, I can find nothing but that you are going down to Harlowe Place to be reconciled to your father and other friends: and Mr. Lovelace presumed that a letter from your sister, which he saw brought when he was at Mr. Smith's, gave you the welcome news of it.

She then explained all to me, and that, as I may say, in six words. A *religious* meaning is couched under it, and that's the reason that neither you nor I could find it out.

Read but for my *father's house, heaven,* said she, and for the interposition of my dear blessed friend, suppose the *mediation* of my

441

Saviour (which I humbly rely upon); and all the rest of the letter will be accounted for. I hope (repeated she) that it is a pardonable artifice. But I am afraid it is not strictly right.

I read it so, and stood astonished for a minute at her invention, her piety, her charity, and at thine and mine own stupidity, to be thus taken in.

And for this reason, Lovelace, do I lay the whole matter before you, and desire you will authorize me, as soon as this and mine of Saturday last come to your hands, to dissipate her fears.

MR. BELFORD TO ROBERT LOVELACE, ESQ.

Wednesday, Aug. 30.

I HAVE a conversation to give you that passed between this admirable lady and Dr. H. which will furnish a new instance of the calmness and serenity with which she can talk of death and prepare for it.

After inquiring how she did, and hearing her complaints of short-ness of breath (which she attributed to inward decay, precipitated by her late harasses, as well from her friends as from you), he was for advising her to go into the air.

Doctor, tell me truly, may I stay here, and be clear of any imputa-tions of curtailing, through wilfulness or impatience, or through resentments which I hope I have got above, a life that might other-wise be prolonged? Tell me, sir, you are not talking to a coward in this respect; indeed you are not! — unaffectedly smiling.

The doctor, turning to me, was at a loss what to say, lifting up his eyes only in admiration of her.

I must tell you, madam, that, understanding how much you suffer by the displeasure of your friends; and having no doubt but that if they knew the way you are in, they would alter their conduct to you; and believing it must cut them to the heart when, too late, they shall be informed of everything; I have resolved to appraise them by letter (stranger as I am to their persons) how necessary it is for some of them to attend you very speedily. For *their* sakes, madam, let me press for your approbation of this measure.

She paused, and at last said: This is kind, very kind in you, sir. But I hope that you do not think me so perverse, and so obstinate, as to have left till now any means unessayed which I thought likely to move my friends in my favour. But now, doctor, said she, I should be too much disturbed at their grief, if they were any of them to come or to send to me; and perhaps, if I found they still loved me, wish to live; and so should quit unwillingly that life which I am now really fond of quitting, and hope to quit, as becomes a person who has had such a weaning-time as I have been favoured with.

It is very kindly, very humanely considered, said she. But, if you think me not so *very* near my last hour, let me desire this may be postponed till I see what effect my Cousin Morden's mediation may have. Perhaps he may vouchsafe to make me a visit yet, after his intended interview with Mr. Lovelace is over; of which, who knows, Mr. Belford, but your next letters may give an account?

MR. LOVELACE TO JOHN BELFORD, ESQ.

Tuesday Morn. Aug. 29.

Now, Jack, will I give thee an account of what passed on occasion of the visit made us by Colonel Morden.

He came on horseback, attended by one servant; and Lord M. received him as a relation of Miss Harlowe's, with the highest marks of civility and respect.

After some general talk of the times, and of the weather, and such nonsense as Englishmen generally make their introductory topics to conversation, the colonel addressed himself to Lord M. and to me, as follows:

I need not, my lord, and Mr. Lovelace, as you know the relation I bear to the Harlowe family, make any apology for entering upon a subject which, on account of that relation, you must think is the principal reason of the honour I have done myself in this visit.

Miss Harlowe, Miss Clarissa Harlowe's affair, said Lord M., with his usual forward bluntness. That, sir, is what you mean. She is, by all accounts, the most excellent woman in the world.

I am glad to hear that is your lordship's opinion of her. It is every one's.

It is not only my opinion, Colonel Morden (proceeded the prating peer), but it is the opinion of all my family. Of my sisters, of my nieces, and of Mr. Lovelace himself.

Col. Would to Heaven it had been always Mr. Lovelace's opinion of her!

Lovel. You have been out of England, colonel, a good many years. Perhaps you are not yet fully apprised of all the particulars of this case.

Col. I have been out of England, sir, about seven years. My Cousin Clary was then about *twelve* years of age: but never was there at *twenty* so discreet, so prudent, and so excellent a creature. All that knew her, or saw her, admired her. Mind and person, never did I see such promises of perfection in any young lady: and I am told, nor is it to be wondered at, that as she advanced to maturity, she more than justified and made good those promises. Then, as to fortune — what her father, what her uncles, and what I myself intended to do for her, besides what her grandfather had done — there is not a finer fortune in the county.

Lovel. All this, colonel, and more than this, is Miss Clarissa Harlowe; and had it not been for the implacableness and violence of her family (all resolved to push her upon a match as unworthy *of* her as hateful *to* her), she had still been happy.

Col. I own, Mr. Lovelace, the truth of what you observed just now, that I am not thoroughly acquainted with all that has passed between you and my cousin. But permit me to say that when I first heard that you made your addresses to her, I knew but of one objection against you. That, indeed, a very great one: and upon a letter sent me, I gave her my free opinion upon the subject. Your education has given you great advantages; your manners are engaging, and you have travelled; and I know, if you'll excuse me, you make better observations than you are governed by. All these qualifications make it not at all surprising that a young lady should love you.

[Hereafter for almost ten pages Lovelace and Morden tread back and forth along the very verge of "honour" and near-insult. Throughout the interview the colonel is allowed to think that Lovelace seduced Clarissa, persuasively, by a promise of marriage. To the colonel a promise is a sacred engagement, and so to the suspectedly neglectful Lovelace the colonel's crucial question, "Is it true that you would marry my cousin if she would have you?" is infuriating. "High language," though toned down more than once by Lord M., makes swords restless in their scabbards. The whole dialogue is Richardson's concept of the decorum and rhetoric that may hardly control "men of honour." An amicable pause leads to more burgundy and champagne. In a continuing narrative Lovelace recounts to the colonel his own efforts and those of the ladies of his family to win Clarissa's consent. The colonel is impressed.]

This made him ready to think that his fair cousin carried her resentment against me too far. He did not imagine, he said, that either myself or our family had been so much in earnest.

So thou seest, Belford, that it is but glossing over *one* part of a story, and omitting *another*, that will make a bad cause a good one at any time. What an admirable lawyer should I have made!

[Here Lovelace reads to the colonel his letter to Clarissa dated August 7.]

This letter gave him high satisfaction. You write here, Mr. Lovelace, from your heart. 'Tis a letter full of penitence and acknowledgment. Your request is reasonable — to be forgiven only as you shall appear to deserve it after a time of probation, which you leave to her to fix. Pray, sir, did she return an answer to this letter?

She did, but with *reluctance*, I own, and not till I had declared by my friend, that if I could not procure one, I would go up to town and throw myself at her feet.

I wish I might be permitted to see it, sir, or to hear such parts of it read as you shall think proper.

Turning over my papers, Here it is, sir. I will make no scruple to put it into your hands.

This is very obliging, Mr. Lovelace.

He read it. My charming cousin! How strong her resentments!

Yet how charitable her wishes! Good Heaven! that such an excellent creature —— But, Mr. Lovelace, it is to your regret, as much as to mine, I doubt not ——

Interrupting him, I swore that it was.

So it ought, said he.

But, sir, will you permit me to take with me these two letters? I shall make use of them to the advantage of you both.

I told him I would oblige him with all my heart. And this he took very kindly (as he had reason) and put them in his pocket-book, promising to return them in a few days.

I then told him that upon this her refusal, I took upon myself to go to town, in hopes to move her in my favour; and at last, when she found I was fully determined at all events to see her, before I went abroad (which I *shall* do, said I, if I cannot prevail upon her), she sent me the letter I have already mentioned to you, desiring me to suspend my purposed visit: and that for a reason which amazes and confounds me, because I don't find there is anything in it: and yet I never knew her once dispense with her word; for she always made it a maxim, that *it was not lawful to do evil, that good might come of it*: and yet in this letter, for no reason in the world but to avoid seeing me to gratify a humour only), has she sent me out of town depending upon the assurance she had given me.

Col. This is indeed surprising. But I cannot believe that my cousin, for such an end *only*, or indeed for *any* end, according to the character I hear of her, should stoop to make use of such an artifice.

Lovel. This, colonel, is the thing that astonishes me; and yet, see here! This is the letter she wrote me — nay, sir, 'tis her own hand.

Col. I see it is; and a charming hand it is.

Lovel. You observe, colonel, that all her hopes of reconciliation with her parents are from you. You are her *dear blessed friend*! She always talked of you with delight.

The colonel read the letter twice over, and then returned it to me. 'Tis all a mystery, said he. I can make nothing of it. For, alas! her friends are as averse to reconciliation as ever.

But I shall know better how to judge of this when my Cousin James comes from Edinburgh; and he is every hour expected.

But let me ask you, Mr. Lovelace, What is the name of your friend, who is admitted so easily into my cousin's presence! Is it not Belford, pray?

Lóvel. It is, sir; and Mr. Belford's a man of honour, and a great admirer of your fair cousin.

Col. Are you sure, sir, that Mr. Belford is a man of honour?

Lovel. I can swear for him, colonel. What makes you put this question?

Col. Only this: that an officious pragmatical novice has been sent up to inquire into my cousin's life and conversation: and, would you believe it? the frequent visits of this gentleman have been interpreted basely to her disreputation. Read that letter, Mr. Lovelace, and you will be shocked at every part of it.

This cursed letter, no doubt, is from the young Levite whom thou, Jack, describedst as making inquiry of Mrs. Smith about Miss Harlowe's character and visitors.

I believe I was a quarter of an hour in reading it: for I made it, though not a short one, six times as long as it is, by the additions of oaths and curses to every pedantic line. Lord M. too helped to lengthen it by the like execrations. And thou, Jack, wilt have as much reason to curse it as we.

. . . .

Col. Well, my lord, I can only say that I will make some use of the letters Mr. Lovelace has obliged me with: and after I have had some talk with my Cousin James, who is hourly expected; and when I have dispatched two or three affairs that press upon me, I will pay my respects to my dear cousin; and shall then be able to form a better judgment of things. Meantime I will write to her; for I have sent to inquire about her, and find she wants consolation.

Thus ended this doughty conference.

I cannot say, Jack, but I am greatly taken with Colonel Morden. He is brave and generous, and knows the world; and then his contempt of the parsons is a certain sign that he is one of *us*.

We parted with great civility .

Mr. Belford to Robert Lovelace, Esq.

Thursday,
Three o'clock, Aug. 31.

On my revisit to the lady I found her almost as much a sufferer from joy as she had sometimes been from grief: for she had just received a very kind letter from her Cousin Morden, which she was so good as to communicate to me. As she had already begun to answer it, I begged leave to attend her in the evening, that I might not interrupt her in it.

The letter is a very tender one. But all will now be too late. The decree is certainly gone out. The world is unworthy of her.

Colonel Morden to Miss Clarissa Harlowe

Tuesday, Aug. 29.

I should not, my dearest cousin, have been a fortnight in England, without either doing myself the honour of waiting upon you in person, or of writing to you, if I had not been busying myself almost all the time in your service, in the hopes of making my visit or letter still more acceptable to you.

I was yesterday with Mr. Lovelace and Lord M. I need not tell *you*, it seems, how very desirous the whole family and all the relations of that nobleman are of the honour of an alliance with you; nor how exceedingly earnest the ungrateful man is to make you all the reparation in his power.

446

I think, my dear cousin, that you cannot now do better than to give him the honour of your hand. He says such just and great things of your virtue, and so heartily condemns himself, that I think there is honourable room for you to forgive him: and the more room, as it seems you are determined against a legal prosecution.

Your effectual forgiveness of Mr. Lovelace, it is evident to me, will accelerate a general reconciliation: for, at present, my other cousins cannot persuade themselves that he is in earnest to do you justice; or that you would refuse him, if you believed he was.

But, my dear cousin, there may possibly be something in this affair to which I may be a stranger. If there be, and you will acquaint me with it, all that a *naturally* warm heart can do in your behalf shall be done.

Meanwhile I beg the favour of a few lines, to know if you have reason to doubt Mr. Lovelace's sincerity. For my part, I can have none, if I am to judge from the conversation that passed between us yesterday, in the presence of Lord M.

MISS CL. HARLOWE TO WM. MORDEN, ESQ.

Thursday, Aug. 31.

I MOST heartily congratulate you, dear sir, on your return to your native country.

I heard with much pleasure that you were come; but I was both afraid and ashamed, till you encouraged me by a first notice, to address myself to you.

I have not the least reason to doubt Mr. Lovelace's sincerity in his offers of marriage: nor that all his relations are heartily desirous of ranking me among them. I have had noble instances of their esteem for me, on their apprehending that my father's displeasure must have subjected me to difficulties: and this, after I had absolutely refused *their* pressing solicitations in their kinsman's favour, as well as *his own.*

I can indeed forgive him. But that is because I think his crimes have set me above him. Can I be above the man, sir, to whom I shall give my hand and my vows, and with them a sanction to the most premeditated baseness? No, sir, let me say that your Cousin Clarissa, were she likely to live many years, and *that* (if she married not this man) in penury or want, despised and forsaken by all her friends, puts not so high a value upon the conveniences of life, nor upon life itself, as to seek to re-obtain the one, or to preserve the other, by giving *such* a sanction: a sanction which (*were she to perform her duty*) would reward the violator.

Nor is it so much from pride, as from principle, that I say this. What, sir! when virtue, when chastity, is the crown of a woman, and particularly of a wife, shall your cousin stoop to marry the man who could not form an attempt upon *hers* but upon a presumption that she was capable of receiving his offered hand, when he had found himself mistaken in the vile opinion he had conceived of her?

One day, sir, you will perhaps know all my story. But, whenever it is known, I beg that the author of my calamities may not be vindictively sought after. As the law will not be able to reach him when I am gone, the apprehension of any other sort of vengeance terrifies me. Since, in such a case, should my friends be *safe*, what honour would his death bring to my memory? If any of them should come to misfortune, how would my fault be aggravated!

MR. LOVELACE TO JOHN BELFORD, ESQ.

Thursday, Aug. 31.

I CANNOT but own that I am cut to the heart by *this* Miss Harlowe's interpretation of her letter. She ought never to be forgiven. *She*, a meek person, and a penitent, and innocent, and pious, and I know not what, who can deceive with a foot in the grave!

'Tis evident that she sat down to write this letter with a design to mislead and deceive. And if she be capable of that, at such a crisis, she has as much need of *Heaven's* forgiveness as I have of *hers*: and, with all her cant of *charity* and *charity*, if she be not more sure of it than I am of her *real pardon*, and if she take the thing in the light she ought to take it in, she will have a few darker moments yet to come than she seems to expect.

She is to send me a letter after she is in heaven, is she? The devil take such *allegories*; and the devil take thee for calling this absurdity an innocent artifice!

But, notwithstanding all, you may let her know from me that I will *not* molest her, since my visits would be so shocking to her: and I hope she will take this into her consideration as a piece of generosity which she could hardly expect after the deception she has put upon me. And let her further know, that if there be anything in my power, that will contribute either to her ease or honour, I will obey her, at the very first intimation, however disgraceful or detrimental to myself. All this to make her unapprehensive, and that she may have nothing to pull her back.

If her cursed relations could be brought as cheerfully to perform *their* parts, I'd answer life for life for her recovery.

I am now so impatient to hear oftener of her, that I take the hint accidentally given me by our two fellows meeting at Slough, and resolve to go to our friend Doleman's at Uxbridge; whose wife and sister, as well as he, have so frequently pressed me to give them my company for a week or two. There shall I be within two hours' ride, if anything should happen to induce her to see me.

I shall accordingly be at Doleman's to-morrow morning, by eleven at furthest. My fellow will find me there at his return from you (with a letter, I hope). I shall have Joel with me likewise, that I may send the oftener, as matters fall out. Were I to be *still nearer*, or in town, it would be impossible to withhold myself from seeing her.

But, if the worst happen! — as, by your continual knelling, I know not what to think of it! — (Yet, once more, Heaven avert that worst!

How natural is it to pray, when one cannot help oneself!) — THEN say not, in so many dreadful words, what the event is — only, that you advise me to take a trip to Paris — and that will stab me to the heart.

MR. BELFORD TO ROBERT LOVELACE, ESQ.

Thursday Night, Aug. 31.

WHEN I attended her about seven in the evening, she told me that she found herself in a very petulant way after I had left her, Strange, said she, that the pleasure I received from my cousin's letter should have such an effect upon me!

She had hardly said this, when she started, and a blush overspread her sweet face, on hearing, as I also did, a sort of lumbering noise upon the stairs, as if a large trunk were bringing up between two people: and, looking upon me with an eye of concern, Blunderers! said she, they have brought in *something* two hours before the time. Don't be surprised, sir — it is all to save *you* trouble.

Before I could speak, in came Mrs. Smith: O madam, said she, what have you done? Mrs. Lovick, entering, made the same exclamation. Lord have mercy upon me, madam, cried I, what have you done! For, she stepping at the instant to the door, the women told me it was a coffin.

With an intrepidity of a piece with the preparation, having directed them to carry it into her bedchamber, she returned to us: They were not to have brought it in till after dark, said she. Pray excuse me, Mr. Belford: and don't you, Mrs. Lovick, be concerned: nor you, Mrs. Smith. Why should you? There is nothing more in it than the unusualness of the thing. I love to do everything for myself that I can do. I ever did. Every other material point is so far done and taken care of, that I have had *leisure* for things of lesser moment. Some of you must have seen *this* in a few days, if not now; perhaps have had the friendly trouble of directing it.

We were all silent still, the women in grief, I in a manner stunned. I took my leave; telling her she had done wrong, very wrong; and ought not, by any means, to have such an object before her.

Down I posted; got a chair; and was carried home, extremely shocked and discomposed; yet, weighing the lady's arguments, I know not why I was so affected — except, as she said, at the unusualness of the thing.

While I waited for a chair, Mrs. Smith came down, and told me that there were devices and inscriptions upon the lid. Lord bless me! Is a coffin a proper subject to display fancy upon? But these great minds cannot avoid doing extraordinary things!

MR. BELFORD TO ROBERT LOVELACE, ESQ.

Friday Morn. Sept. 1.

I REALLY was ill and restless all night. Thou wert the subject of my execration, as she of my admiration, all the time I was quite awake: and, when I dozed, I dreamt of nothing but of flying hour-glasses, death's-heads, spades, mattocks, and eternity; the hint of her devices (as given me by Mrs. Smith) running in my head.

However, not being able to keep away from Smith's, I went thither about seven. The lady was just gone out: she had slept better, I found, than I, though her solemn repository was under her window not far from her bedside.

I was prevailed upon by Mrs. Smith and her nurse Shelburne (Mrs. Lovick being abroad with her) to go up and look at the devices.

The principal device, neatly etched on a plate of white metal, is a crowned serpent, with its tail in its mouth, forming a ring, the emblem of eternity; and in the circle made by it is this inscription:

CLARISSA HARLOWE
April x
[Then the year]
ÆTAT. XIX.

For ornaments: at top, an hour-glass winged. At bottom, an urn. Under the hour-glass, on another plate, this inscription:

HERE the wicked cease from troubling: and HERE the weary be at rest. Job. iii, 17.

Over the urn, near the bottom:

Turn again unto thy rest, O my soul! for the Lord hath rewarded thee. And why? Thou hast delivered my soul from death; mine eyes from tears; and my feet from falling. Ps. cxvi, 7, 8.

Over this text is the head of a white lily snapped short off, and just falling from the stalk; and this inscription over that, between the principal plate and the lily:

The days of man are but as grass. For he flourisheth as a flower of the field: for, as soon as the wind goeth over it, it is gone; and the place thereof shall know it no more. Ps. ciii, 15, 16.

The date, April 10, she accounted for, as not being able to tell what her *closing-day* would be; and as that was the fatal day of her leaving her father's house.

She discharged the undertaker's bill after I went away, with as much cheerfulness as she could ever have paid for the clothes she sold to purchase this her *palace*: for such she called it; reflecting upon herself for the expensiveness of it, saying that they might observe in *her* that pride left not poor mortals to the last: but indeed she did not know but her father would permit it, *when furnished*, to be carried down to be deposited with her ancestors; and, in that case, she ought not to discredit those ancestors in her *appearance amongst them*.

Mrs. Lovick said she took the liberty to blame her; and wished the removal of such an object — from her *bedchamber* at least: and was so affected with the noble answer she made upon it, that she entered it down the moment she left her.

To persons in health, said she, this sight may be shocking; and the preparation, and my unconcernedness in it, may appear affected: but to me, who have had so gradual a weaning-time from the world, and so much reason not to love it, I must say I dwell on, I indulge (and, strictly speaking, I enjoy) the thoughts of death. Believe me, my good friends, it does what nothing else can do: it teaches me, by strengthening in me the force of the divinest example, to forgive the injuries I have received; and shuts out the remembrance of past evils from my soul.

Friday, Sept. 1, Two o'clock, at Smith's.

You have, on several occasions, convinced me that the suspense you love to *give* would be the greatest torment to you that you could *receive*. A common case with all aggressive and violent spirits, I believe. I will just mention then (your servant waiting till I have written) that the lady has had two very severe fits; in the last of which, whilst she lay, they sent for the doctor and Mr. Goddard, who both advised that a messenger should be dispatched for me, as her executor; being doubtful whether, if she had a third, it would not carry her off.

She was tolerably recovered by the time I came; and the doctor made her promise before me, that, while she was so weak, she would not attempt any more to go abroad; for, by Mrs. Lovick's description, who attended her, the shortness of her breath, her extreme weakness, and the fervour of her devotions when at church, were contraries which, pulling different ways (the soul aspiring, the body sinking), tore her tender frame in pieces.

MR. LOVELACE TO JOHN BELFORD, ESQ.   *Uxbridge, Sept. 1,*
Twelve o'clock at Night.

DON'T let the wonderful creature leave us! Set before her the sin of her preparation, as if she thought she could depart when she pleased. She'll persuade herself, at this rate, that she has nothing to do, when all is ready, but to lie down and go to sleep: and such a lively fancy as hers will make a reality of a jest at any time.

A *jest*, I call all that has passed between her and me; a mere jest to die for — for has not her triumph over me, from first to last, been infinitely greater than her sufferings from me?

But *nineteen*, Belford! — *nineteen* cannot so soon die of grief, if the doctor deserve that name; and so blooming and so fine a constitution as she had but three or four months ago!

.   .   .   .

But this I mention as an answer to thy reproaches, that I could be so little edified by perfections to which, thou supposest, I was for so

451

long together daily and hourly a personal witness — when, admirable as she was in all she said, and in all she did, occasion had not at that time ripened, and called forth, those amazing perfections which now astonish and confound me.

Hence it is that I admire her more than ever; and that my love for her is less *personal*, as I may say, more *intellectual*, than ever I thought it could be to woman.

.   .   .   .

After all, as I am so little distant from the dear creature, and as she is so very ill, I think I cannot excuse myself from making her *one* visit. Nevertheless, if I thought her so near — (what word shall I use that my soul is not shocked at!), and that she would be *too much discomposed* by a visit, I would not think of it. Yet how can I bear the recollection, that when she last went from me (her innocence so triumphant over my premeditated guilt, as was enough to reconcile her to life, and set her above the sense of injuries so nobly sustained, that) she should then depart with an incurable fracture in her heart; and that *that* should be the last time I should ever see her! How, how, can I bear this reflection!

O Jack! how my conscience, that gives edge even to thy blunt reflections, tears me! Even this moment would I give the world to push the cruel reproacher from me by one ray of my usual gaiety! Sick of myself! Sick of the remembrance of my vile plots; and of my *light*, my momentary ecstasy (villainous burglar, felon, thief, that I was!), which has brought upon me such *durable* and such *heavy* remorse! what would I give that I had not been guilty of such barbarous and ungrateful perfidy to the most excellent of God's creatures!

I would end, methinks, with one sprightlier line! But it will not be. Let me tell thee then, and rejoice at it if thou wilt, that I am / *Inexpressibly miserable!*

MR. BELFORD TO ROBERT LOVELACE, ESQ.

Sat. Morning, Sept. 2.

THE lady is alive, and serene, and calm, and has all her noble intellects clear and strong: but *nineteen* will not, however, save her. She says she will now content herself with her closet duties and the visits of the parish minister; and will not attempt to go out. Nor, indeed, will she, I am afraid, ever walk up or down a pair of stairs again.

I am sorry at my soul to have this to say: but it would be a folly to flatter thee.

As to thy seeing her, I believe the least hint of that sort, now, would cut off some hours of her life.

What has contributed to her serenity, it seems, is that, taking the alarm her fits gave her, she has entirely finished, and signed and sealed, her last will: which she had deferred doing till this time, in hopes, as she said, of some good news from Harlowe Place; which would have induced her to alter some passages in it.

I called just now, and found the lady writing to Miss Howe. She made me a melancholy compliment, that she showed me not Miss Howe's letter, because I should soon have that and all her papers before me. But she told me that Miss Howe had very considerately obviated to Colonel Morden several things which might have occasioned misapprehensions between him and me; and had likewise put a lighter construction, for the sake of peace, on some of your actions than they deserved.

She added that her Cousin Morden was warmly engaged in her favour with her friends: and one good piece of news Miss Howe's letter contained; that her father would give up some matters, which (appertaining to her of right) would make my executorship the easier in some particulars that had given her a little pain.

She owned she had been obliged to leave off (in the letter she was writing) through weakness.

MISS HOWE TO MISS CLARISSA HARLOWE

Tuesday, Aug. 29.

MY DEAREST FRIEND, — We are at length returned to our own home. I had intended to wait on you in London: but my mother is very ill. Alas! my dear, she is very ill indeed. And you are likewise very ill — I see *that* by yours of the 25th. What shall I do if I lose two such near, and dear, and tender friends?

I see, I see, my dear, you are very bad — and I cannot bear it. Do, my beloved Miss Harlowe, if you *can* be better, do, for *my* sake, *be* better; and send me word of it. Let the bearer bring me a line. Be sure you send me a line. If I lose you, my more than sister, and lose my mother, I shall distrust my own conduct, and will not marry.

Wednesday, Aug. 30.

My mother, Heaven be praised! has had a fine night, and is much better. Her fever has yielded to medicine! And now I can write once more with freedom and ease to you, in hopes that *you* also are better.

You must know then, my dear, that your Cousin Morden has been here with me. He told me of an interview he had on Monday at Lord M.'s with Lovelace; and asked me abundance of questions about you, and about that villainous man.

I could have raised a fine flame between them if I would: but, observing that he is a man of very lively passions, and believing you would be miserable if anything should happen to him from a quarrel with a man who is known to have so many advantages at his sword, I made not the worst of the subjects we talked of. But, as I could

453

not tell untruths in his favour, you must think I said enough to make him curse the wretch.

He says that none of your friends think you so ill as you are; nor will believe it. He is sure they all love you, and that dearly too.

If they do, their present hardness of heart will be the subject of everlasting remorse to them should you be taken from us. But now it seems (barbarous wretches!) you are to *suffer within an inch of your life.*

He asked me questions about Mr. Belford: and when he had heard what I had to say of that gentleman, and his disinterested services to you, he raved at some villainous surmises thrown out against you by that officious pedant, Brand: who, but for his gown, I find, would come off poorly enough between your cousin and Lovelace.

He was so uneasy about you himself, that on Thursday the 24th he sent up an honest serious man, one Alston, a gentleman farmer, to inquire of your condition, your visitors, and the like, who brought him word that you was very ill, and was put to great straits to support yourself: but as this was told him by the gentlewoman of the house where you lodge, who it seems mingled with it some tart, though deserved, reflections upon your relations' cruelty, it was not credited by them: and I myself hope it cannot be true; for surely you could not be so *unjust*, I will say, to my friendship, as to suffer any inconveniences for want of money. I think I could not forgive you if it were so.

Your cousin imagines that, before a reconciliation takes place, they will insist that you shall make such a will as to that estate as they shall approve of: but he declares he will not go out of England till he has seen justice done you by *everybody*; and that you shall not be imposed on either by friend or foe ——

So, my dear, you are to *buy your peace*, if some people are to have their wills!

Your cousin (not *I*, my dear, though it was always my opinion) says that the whole family is *too rich* to be either *humble, considerate,* or *contented.* And as for himself, he has an ample fortune, he says, and thinks of leaving it wholly to you

MISS HOWE TO MISS CLARISSA HARLOWE

Thursday, Aug. 31.

THE colonel thought fit, in praise of Lovelace's *generosity*, to say, that (*as a man of honour ought*) he took to himself all the blame, and acquitted you of the consequences of the precipitate step you had taken; since, he said, as you loved him, and was in his power, he *must* have had advantages, which he would *not* have had, if you had continued at your father's, or at any friend's.

Mighty generous, I said (were it as he *supposed*), in such insolent reflectors, the best of them; who pretend to *clear* reputations which never had been *sullied* but by falling into their dirty acquaintance!

But in this case, I averred that there was no need of anything but the strictest truth to demonstrate Lovelace to be the blackest of villains, you the brightest of innocents.

This he catched at; and swore that if anything uncommon or barbarous in the seduction were to come out, as indeed one of the letters you had written to your friends, and which had been shown him, very strongly implied; that is to say, my dear, if anything *worse* than perjury, breach of faith, and abuse of a generous confidence were to appear! (sorry fellows!) he would avenge his cousin to the utmost.

I urged your apprehensions on this head from your last letter to me: but he seemed capable of taking what I know to be real greatness of soul in an unworthy sense: for he mentioned directly upon it the expectation your friends had that you should (previous to any reconciliation with them) appear in a court of justice against the villain — IF you could do it with the advantage to yourself that I hinted might be done.

And truly, if I would have heard him, he had indelicacy enough to have gone into the nature of the proof of the crime upon which they wanted to have Lovelace arraigned. Yet this is a man improved by travel and learning! Upon my word, my dear, I, who have been accustomed to the most delicate conversation ever since I had the honour to know you, despise this sex from the gentleman down to the peasant.

I prepared Mr. Morden to expect your appointment of Mr. Belford for an office that we both hope he will have no occasion to act in (nor anybody else) for many, very many years to come. He was at first startled at it: but, upon hearing such of your reasons as had satisfied me, he only said that such an appointment, were it to take place, would exceedingly affect his other cousins.

I find he is willing to hope that a marriage between you may still take place; which, he says, will heal up all breaches.

I cannot express how much your staggering lines, and your conclusion, affect me!

MR. BELFORD TO ROBERT LOVELACE, ESQ.

Sunday Evening, Sept. 3.

THEY had sent for Mr. Goddard when she was so ill last night; and not being able to see him out of her own chamber, he, for the first time, saw her *house*, as she calls it. He was extremely shocked and concerned at it; and chid Mrs. Smith and Mrs. Lovick for not persuading her to have such an object removed from her bedchamber: and when they excused themselves on the *little authority* it was reasonable to suppose they must have with a lady so much their superior, he reflected warmly on those who had *more* authority, and who left her to proceed with such a shocking and solemn whimsy, as he called it.

It is placed near the window, like a harpsichord, though covered over to the ground: and when she is so ill that she cannot well go to her closet, she writes and reads upon it, as others would upon a desk or table. But (only as she was so ill last night) she chooses not to see anybody in that apartment.

The doctor told Mrs. Smith that he believed she would hold out long enough for any of her friends to have notice of her state, and to see her, and hardly longer; and since he could not find that she had any certainty of seeing her Cousin Morden (which made it plain that her relations continued inflexible), he would go home and write a letter to her father, take it as she would.

MISS CLARISSA HARLOWE TO MISS HOWE

Saturday, Sept. 2.

I RESUME my trembling pen. Excuse the unsteady writing. It *will* be so —

In the disposition of what belongs to me, I have endeavoured to do everything in the justest and best manner I could think of. I hope they will not think much of some bequests where wanted, and where due from my gratitude but if they should, what is done, is done; and I cannot now help it. Yet I must repeat that I *hope* I have pleased every one of them. For I would not, on any account, have it thought that, in my last disposition, anything undaughterly, unsisterly, or unlike a kinswoman, should have had place.

My cousin, you tell me, thinks I was off my guard, and that I was taken at some advantage. Indeed, my dear, I was not. Indeed I gave no room for advantage to be taken of me. I hope, one day, that will be seen, if I have the justice done me which Mr. Belford assures me of.

I am glad you so considerately gave my Cousin Morden favourable impressions of Mr. Belford; since, otherwise, some misunderstandings might have happened between them.

When I began this letter, I did not think I could have run to such a length. But 'tis to YOU, my dearest friend, and *you* have a title to the spirits you raise and support; for they are no longer mine, and will subside the moment I cease writing to you.

I must conclude —

God for ever bless you, and all you love and honour, and reward you here and hereafter.

MRS. NORTON TO MISS CLARISSA HARLOWE

Thursday, Aug. 31.

I HAD written sooner, my dearest young lady, but that I have been endeavoring ever since the receipt of your last letter to obtain a private audience of your mother, in hopes of leave to communicate it to her. But last night I was surprised by an invitation to breakfast at Harlowe Place this morning: and the chariot came early to fetch me: an honour I did not expect.

When I came, I found there was to be a meeting of all your family with Colonel Morden at Harlowe Place; and it was proposed by your mother, and consented to, that I should be present. Your cousin, I understand, had with difficulty brought this meeting to bear; for your brother had before industriously avoided all conversation with him on the affecting subject;

I was ordered in just before Mr. Morden came; and was bid to sit down — which I did by the window.

The colonel, when he came, began the discourse by *renewing*, as he called it, his solicitations in your favour. He set before them your penitence; your ill-health; your virtue, though once betrayed and basely used: he then read to them Mr. Lovelace's letter, a most contrite one indeed; and your *high-souled* answer; for that was what he justly called it; and he treated as it deserved Mr. Brand's officious information (of which I had before heard he had made them ashamed), by representations founded upon inquiries made by Mr. Alston, whom he had procured to go up on purpose to acquaint himself with your manner of life, and what was meant by the visits of that Mr. Belford.

He then told them that he had the day before waited upon Miss Howe, and had been shown a letter from you to her, and permitted to take some memorandums from it, in which you appeared, both by handwriting and the contents, to be so very ill that it seemed doubtful to him if it were possible for you to get over it. And when he read to them that passage where you ask Miss Howe, "What can be done for you now, were your friends to be ever so favourable? and wish, for *their* sakes more than for your *own*, that they would still relent"; and then say, "You are very ill — you must drop your pen — and ask excuse for your crooked writing; and take, as it were, a last farewell of Miss Howe: *Adieu, my dear, adieu*," are your words —

O my child! my child! said your mamma, weeping, and clasping her hands.

Dear madam, said your brother, be so good as to think you have more children than this ungrateful one.

Yet your sister seemed affected.

Your Uncle Harlowe, wiping his eyes, O cousin, said he, if one thought the poor girl was really so ill ——

She *must*, said your Uncle Antony. This is written to her private friend. God forbid she should be quite lost!

Your Uncle Harlowe wished they did not carry their resentments too far.

I begged for God's sake, wringing my hands, and with a bended knee, that they would permit me to go up to you; engaging to give them a faithful account of the way you were in. But I was chidden by your brother; and this occasioned some angry words between him and Mr. Morden.

I believe, sir, I believe, madam, said your sister to her father and mother, we need not trouble my cousin to read any more. It does but grieve and disturb you. My sister Clary seems to be ill: I think, if Mrs. Norton were permitted to go up to her, it would be right. Wickedly as she has acted, if she be truly penitent ——

Here she stopped; and every one being silent, I stood up once more, and besought them to let me go: and then I offered to read a passage or two in your letter to me of the 24th. But I was taken up again by your brother; and this occasioned still higher words between the colonel and him.

Your mother, hoping to gain upon your inflexible brother, and to divert the anger of the two gentlemen from each other, proposed that the colonel should proceed in reading the minutes he had taken from your letter.

Your uncles were also both affected: but your brother went round to each; and again reminded your mother that she had other children: What was there, he said, in what was read, but the result of the talent you had of moving the passions? And he blamed them for choosing to hear read what they knew their abused indulgence could not be proof against.

This set Mr. Morden up again: Fie upon you, Cousin Harlowe! said he, I see plainly to whom it is owing that all relationship and ties of blood with regard to this sweet sufferer are laid aside. Such rigours as these make it difficult for a sliding virtue ever to recover itself.

But, sir, and ladies, said I, rising from my seat in the window, and humbly turning round to each, if I may be permitted to speak, my dear miss asks only for a blessing. She does not beg to be received to favour: she is very ill, and asks only for a last blessing.

Come, come, goody Norton (I need not tell you who said this), you are up again with your lamentables! A good woman, as you are, to forgive so readily a crime that has been as disgraceful to your part in her education as to her family, is a weakness that would induce one to suspect your virtue if you were to be encountered by a temptation *properly adapted.*

By some such charitable logic, said Mr. Morden, as this is my Cousin Arabella captivated, I doubt not. If to be uncharitable and unforgiving is to give a proof of virtue, you, Mr. James Harlowe, are the most virtuous young man in the world.

I knew how it would be, replied your brother in a passion, if I met Mr. Morden upon this business. I would have declined it: but you, sir, to his father, would not permit me so to do.

Miss Harlowe was apprehensive, she said, that you would leave all you *could* leave to that pert creature Miss Howe (so she called her) if you should die.

Oh, do not, do not suppose *that*, my Bella, said your poor mother. I cannot think of parting with my Clary. With all her faults, she is my child. Her reasons for her conduct are not heard. It would break my heart to lose her. I think, my dear, to your father, none so fit as I to go up, if you will give me leave: and Mrs. Norton shall accompany me.

This was a sweet motion; and your father paused upon it. Mr. Morden offered his service to escort her. Your uncles seemed to approve of it. But your brother dashed all. I hope, sir, said he to his father; I hope, madam, to his mother, that you will not endeavour to recover a faulty daughter by losing an inculpable son. I do declare, that if ever my Sister Clary darkens these doors again, I never will. I will set out, madam, the same hour you go to London (on such an errand), to Edinburgh; and there I will reside; and try to forget that I have relations in England so near and so dear as you are now all to me.

Good God! said the colonel, what a declaration is this! And suppose, sir, and suppose, madam (turning to your father and mother), this *should* be the case, whether is it better, think you, that you should lose for ever such a daughter as my Cousin Clary, or that your son should go to Edinburgh, and reside there upon an estate which will be the better for his residence upon it?

Your brother's passionate behaviour hereupon is hardly to be described. He resented it, as prompting an alienation of the affection of the family to him. And to such a height were resentments carried, every one siding with him, that the colonel, with hands and eyes lifted up, cried out: What hearts of flint am I related to!

The colonel turned from them to draw out his handkerchief, and could not a minute speak. The eyes of every one but the hard-hearted brother caught tears from his.

But then turning to them (with the more indignation, as it seemed, as he had been obliged to show a humanity which, however, no brave heart should be ashamed of), I leave ye all, said he, fit company for one another. I will never open my lips to any of you more upon this subject. I will instantly make my will, and in me shall the dear creature have the father, uncle, brother she has lost. I will prevail upon her to take the tour of France and Italy with me; nor shall she return till ye know the value of *such* a daughter.

And saying this he hurried out of the room, went into the courtyard, and ordered his horse.

·   ·   ·   ·   ·   ·   ·   ·   ·   ·

Your mother led me to her chamber; and there we sat and wept together for several minutes without being able to speak either of us one word to the other. At last she broke silence; asking me if you were really and indeed so ill as it was said you were?

I answered in the affirmative; and would have shown her your last letter; but she declined seeing it.

To my plea of your illness: She could not flatter herself, she answered, that it was from lowness of spirits and temporary dejection. A young creature, she said, so very considerate as you naturally were, and fallen so low, must have enough of that. Should they lose you, which God forbid! the scene would then indeed be sadly changed; for then those who now most resented would be most grieved; all your fine qualities would rise to their remembrance, and your unhappy error would be quite forgotten.

She wished you would put yourself into your cousin's protection entirely, and have nothing more to say to Mr. Belford.

Friday Morning.

Betty was with me just now. She tells me that your Cousin Morden is so much displeased with them all that he has refused to lodge any more at your Uncle Antony's; and has even taken up with inconvenient lodgings till he is provided with others to his mind. This very much concerns them; and they repent their violent treatment of him: and the more as he is resolved, he says, to make you his sole executrix and heir to all his fortune.

Your mother wished me not to attend you as yet, because she hopes that I may give myself that pleasure soon with everybody's good liking, and even at their desire.

MR. BELFORD TO ROBERT LOVELACE, ESQ.

Monday, Sept. 4.

THE lady would not read the letter she had from Mrs. Norton till she had received the Communion, for fear it should contain anything that might disturb that happy calm which she had been endeavouring to obtain for it. And when that solemn office was over, she was so composed, she said, that she thought she could receive any news, however affecting, with tranquility.

When I was admitted to her presence, I have received, said she, a long and not very pleasing letter from my dear Mrs. Norton. It will soon be in your hands. I am advised against appointing you to the office you have so kindly accepted of: but you must resent nothing of these things. My choice will have an odd appearance to them: but it is now too late to alter it if I would.

I would fain write an answer to it, continued she: but I have no distinct sight, Mr. Belford, no steadiness of fingers. This mistiness, however, will perhaps be gone by and by.

While were were solemnly engaged, a servant came with a letter from her Cousin Morden: Then, said she, he is not come *himself!*

She broke it open; but every line, she said, appeared two to her: so that, being unable to read it herself, she desired I would read it to her. I did so; and wished it were more consolatory to her: but she was all patient attention; tears, however, often trickling down her cheeks. By the date it was written yesterday; and this is the substance of it:

He tells her that the Thursday before he had procured a general meeting of her principal relations at her father's; though not without difficulty, her haughty brother opposing it, and, when met, rendering all his endeavours to reconcile them to her ineffectual.

But that her noble letter, as he calls it, of Aug. 31, being brought him about an hour after their departure, he thought it might affect them as much as it did him; and give them the exalted opinion of her virtue which was so well deserved; he therefore turned his horse's head back to her Uncle Antony's instead of forward towards London.

If she be so absolutely determined against marrying you, as she declares she is, he hopes, he says, to prevail upon her to take (as soon as her health will permit) a little tour abroad with him, as what will probably establish it; since travelling is certainly the best physic for all those disorders which owe their rise to grief or disappointment. An absence of two or three years will endear her to every one on her return, and every one to her.

He expresses his impatience to see her. He will set out, he says, the moment he knows the result of her family's determination; which, he doubts not, will be favourable. Nor will he wait long for that.

I asked if I should write to her cousin, as he knew not how ill she was, to hasten up.

By no means, she said; since, if he were not already set out, she was persuaded that she should be so low by the time he could receive my letter and come, that his presence would but discompose and hurry *her*, and afflict *him*.

I hope, however, she is not so very near her end. And without saying any more to her, when I retired I wrote to Colonel Morden that, if he expects to see his beloved cousin alive, he must lose no time in setting out. I sent this letter by his own servant.

Dr. H. sent away *his* letter to her father by a particular hand this morning.

And as all these, and the copy of the lady's letter to Col. Morden, will be with them pretty much at a time, the devil's in the family if they are not struck with a remorse that shall burst open the double-barred doors of their hearts.

DR. H. TO JAMES HARLOWE, SENIOR, ESQ.

London, Sept. 4.

SIR, — If I may judge of the hearts of other parents by my own, I cannot doubt but you will take it well to be informed that you have yet an opportunity to save yourself and family great future regret, by dispatching hither some one of it, with your last blessing and your lady's, to the most excellent of her sex.

She knows not that I write. I hope I shall not be thought an officious man on this occasion: but if I am, I cannot help it; being driven to write by a kind of *parental* and irresistible impulse.

But, sir, whatever you think fit to do, or permit to be done, must be speedily done; for she cannot, I verily think, live a week: and how long of that short space she may enjoy her admirable intellects to take comfort in the favours you may think proper to confer upon her, cannot be said. I am, sir, / Your most humble servant, / R. H.

MR. BELFORD TO WILLIAM MORDEN, ESQ.

London, Sept. 4.

SIR, — The urgency of the case, and the opportunity by your servant, will sufficiently apologize for this trouble from a stranger to your person; who, however, is not a stranger to your merit.

I understand you are employing your good offices with the parents of Miss Clarissa Harlowe, and other relations, to reconcile them to the most meritorious daughter and kinswoman that ever family had to boast of.

Generously as this is intended by you, we *here* have too much reason to think all your solicitudes on this head will be unnecessary: for it is the opinion of every one who has the honour of being admitted to her presence, that she cannot live over three days: so that if you wish to see her alive you must lose no time to come up.

She knows not that I write.

MISS CLARISSA HARLOWE TO MRS. NORTON[1]

MY DEAREST MRS. NORTON, — I am afraid I shall not be able to write all that is upon my mind to say to you upon the subject of your last. Yet I will try.

The granting of one request only now remains as a desirable one from them; which nevertheless, when granted, I shall not be sensible of. It is that they will be pleased to permit my remains to be laid with those of my ancestors — placed at the feet of my dear grandfather — as I have mentioned in my will. This, however, as they please. For, after all, this vile body ought not so much to engage my cares. It is a weakness — but let it be called a *natural* weakness, and I shall be excused; especially when a reverential gratitude shall be known to be the foundation of it. You know, my dear woman, how my grandfather loved me. And you know how much I honoured him, and that from my very infancy to the hour of his death. How often since have I wished that he had not loved *me* so well!

I wish not now, at the writing of this, to see even my Cousin Morden. O my blessed woman! My dear maternal friend! I am entering upon a better tour than to France or Italy either! or even than to settle at my once beloved Dairy-house! All these prospects and pleasures, which used to be so agreeable to me in health, how poor seem they to me now!

Let me tell you for your comfort that I have not left undone anything that ought to be done, either respecting *mind* or *person*; no, not to the minutest preparation: so that nothing is left for *you* to do for me. Every one has her direction as to the last offices. And my desk,

1 Begun on Monday, Sept. 4, and by piecemeal finished on Tuesday; but not sent till the Thursday following.

that I now write upon — O my dearest Mrs. Norton, all is provided! All is ready! And all will be as decent as it should be!

. . . .

As for me, never bride was so ready as I am. My wedding garments are bought. And though not fine or gaudy to the sight, yet will they be the easiest, the *happiest* suit, that ever bridal maiden wore, for they are such as carry with them a security against all those anxieties, pains, and pertubations which sometimes succeed to the most promising outsettings.

Oh, hasten, good God, if it be Thy blessed will, the happy moment that I am to be decked out in this all-quieting garb! And sustain, comfort, bless, and protect with the all-shadowing wing of Thy mercy, my dear parents, my uncles, my brother, my sister, my Cousin Morden, my ever dear and ever kind Miss Howe, my good Mrs. Norton, and every deserving person to whom *they* wish well! is the ardent prayer, first and last, of every beginning hour, as the clock tells me (hours now are days, nay years) of / Your now not sorrowing or afflicted, / but happy / Clarissa Harlowe.

Mr. Lovelace to John Belford, Esq.   *Wedn. Morn, Sept. 6,*
                                          half an hour after Three.

I am not the savage which you and my worst enemies think me. My soul is *too much* penetrated by the contents of the letter which you enclosed in your last to say one word more to it than that my heart has bled over it from every vein! I will fly from the subject — but what other can I choose that will not be as grievous, and lead into the same?

Surely it will be better when *all is over* — when I know the *worst* the Fates can do against me. Yet how shall I bear that *worst*? O Belford, Belford! write it not to me; but, if it *must* happen, get somebody else to write; for I shall curse the pen, the hand, the head, and the heart employed in communicating to me the fatal tidings. But what is this saying, when already I curse the whole world except her — myself most?

I must after my messenger. I have told the varlet I will meet him, perhaps at Knightsbridge, perhaps in Piccadilly; and I trust not myself with pistols, not only on his account, but my own: for pistols are *too ready* a mischief.

Mr. Belford to Robert Lovelace, Esq.
                        Tuesday, Sept. 5, Eight o'clock.

She is somewhat better than she was. The doctor has been here, and thinks she will hold out yet a day or two. He has ordered her, as for some time past, only some little cordials to take when ready to faint. She seemed disappointed when he told her she might yet live two or three days; and said she longed for dismission! Life was not so easily extinguished, she saw, as some imagine. *Death from grief* was, she believed, *the slowest of deaths*. But God's will must be done! Her only prayer was now for submission to it: for she doubted not but by the Divine goodness she should be a happy creature as soon as she could be divested of these *rags of mortality*.

Of her own accord she mentioned you; which, till then, she had avoided to do. She asked, with great serenity, where you were?

I told her where; and your motives for being so near; and read to her a few lines of yours of this morning, in which you mention your wishes to see her, your sincere affliction, and your resolution not to approach her without her consent.

I would have read more; but she said: Enough, Mr. Belford; enough! Poor man! Does his conscience begin to find him! Then need not anybody to wish him a greater punishment! May it work upon him to a happy purpose!

The divine creature then turning aside her head: Poor man, said she! I once could have loved him. This is saying more than ever I could say of any other man out of my own family! Would he have permitted me to have been a humble instrument to have made him good, I think I could have made him happy! But tell him not this if he be *really* penitent — it may too much affect him! — There she paused.

Then resuming: But pray tell him that if I could know that my death might be a means to reclaim and save him, it would be an inexpressible satisfaction to me!

But let me not, however, be made uneasy with the apprehension of seeing him. I cannot *bear* to see him!

You see, Lovelace, that I did not forget the office of a friend, in endeavouring to prevail upon her to give you her last forgiveness personally. And I hope, as she is so near her end, you will not invade her in her last hours; since she must be extremely discomposed at such an interview; and it might make her leave the world the sooner for it.

This reminds me of an expression which she used on your barbarous hunting her at Smith's, on her return to her lodgings; and that with a serenity unexampled (as Mrs. Lovick told me, considering the occasion, and the trouble given her by it, and her indisposition at the time): He will not let me die decently, said the angelic sufferer! He will not let me enter into my Maker's presence with the composure that is required in entering into the drawing-room of an earthly prince!

MR. LOVELACE TO JOHN BELFORD, ESQ.

Wedn. Morn. Sept. 6.

AND is she somewhat better? Blessings upon thee without number or measure! Let her be better and better!

464

What she bid, and what she *forbid* you, to tell me (the latter for *tender* considerations); that she forgives me; and that, could she have made me a *good* man, she could have made me a *happy* one! That she even *loved me*! At such a moment to own that *she once loved me*! Never *before* loved any man! That she prays for me! That her last tear should be shed for me, could she by it save a soul doomed, without *her*, to perdition! O Belford, Belford! I cannot bear it!

Curse upon my *intriguing head* and upon my *seconding heart*! To sport with the fame, with the honour, with the *life* of such an angel. Oh, my damned incredulity! that, believing her to *be* a woman, I must hope to *find* her a woman! On my incredulity that there could be such virtue in the sex.

But say not, Jack, that she must leave us yet. If she recover, and I can but re-obtain her favour, then indeed will life be life to me. I will have no will but hers. She shall conduct me in all my steps. Confirm the hopes, I beseech thee —

MR. BELFORD TO ROBERT LOVELACE, ESQ.

Wedn. Morn. Eight o'clock (6 Sept.).

YOUR servant arrived here before I was stirring. I sent him to Smith's to inquire how the lady was; and ordered him to call upon me when he came back. I was pleased to hear she had had tolerable rest. As soon as I had dispatched him with the letter I had written overnight, I went to attend her.

I found her up and dressed; in a white satin night-gown. Ever elegant; but now more so than I had seen her for a week past: her aspect serenely cheerful.

She mentioned the increased dimness of her eyes, and the tremor which had invaded her limbs. If this be dying, said she, there is nothing at all shocking in it. My body hardly sensible of pain, my mind at ease, my intellects clear and perfect as ever. What a good and gracious God have I! For this is what I always prayed for.

I told her it was not so serene with you.

There is not the same reason for it, replied she. 'Tis a choice comfort, Mr. Belford, at the winding-up of our short story, to be able to say I have rather *suffered* injuries *myself* than *offered* them to *others*. I bless God, though I have been unhappy, as the *world* deems it, and once I thought more so than at present I think I ought to have done; since my calamities were to work out for me my everlasting happiness; yet have I not wilfully made any one creature so. I have no reason to grieve for anything but for the sorrow I have given my friends.

Wednesday Morning, 10 o'clock.

The poor lady is just recovered from a fainting fit, which has left her at death's door. Her late tranquillity and freedom from pain seemed but a *lightening*, as Mrs. Lovick and Mrs. Smith call it.

She has sent for the divine who visited her before, to pray with her.

MR. LOVELACE TO JOHN BELFORD, ESQ.

Kensington, Wednesday Noon.

IF SHE live but one year, that I may acquit myself *to* myself (no matter for the world!) that her death is not owing to me, I will compound for the rest.

Will neither vows nor prayers save her? I never prayed in my life. put all the years of it together, as I have done for this fortnight past: and I have most sincerely repented of all my baseness to her — and will nothing do?

But after all, if she recover not, *this* reflection must be my comfort; and it is *truth*: that her *departure* will be owing rather to wilfulness, to downright *female* wilfulness, than to any other cause.

But I'll have none of her forgiveness! My own heart tells me I do not deserve it; and I cannot bear it! And what is it but a mere *verbal* forgiveness, as ostentatiously as cruelly given, with a view to magnify herself and wound me deeper? A little, dear, specious — but let me stop, lest I blaspheme!

.   .   .   .

Reading over the above, I am ashamed of my ramblings: but what wouldst have me do? Seest thou not that I am but seeking to run out of myself, in hope to lose myself; yet that I am unable to do either?

MR. BELFORD TO ROBERT LOVELACE, ESQ.

Wednesday, 11 o'clock.

DR. H. has just been here. He tarried with me till the minister had done praying by the lady; and then we were both admitted. Mr. Goddard, who came while the doctor and the clergyman were with her, went away with them when they went. They took a solemn and everlasting leave of her, as I have no scruple to say; blessing her, and being blessed by her; and wishing (when it came to be their lot) for an exit as happy as hers is likely to be.

She had again earnestly requested of the doctor his opinion how long it was *now* probable that she could continue: and he told her that he apprehended she would hardly see to-morrow night. She said she should number the hours with greater pleasure than ever she numbered any in her life on the most joyful occasion.

This moment a man is come from Miss Howe with a letter. Perhaps I shall be able to send you the contents.

.   .   .   .

She endeavoured several times with earnestness, but in vain, to read the letter of her dear friend. The writing, she said, was too fine for her grosser sight, and the lines staggered under her eyes. And, indeed, she trembled so she could not hold the paper: and at last desired Mrs. Lovick to read it to her, the messenger waiting for an answer.

Mrs. Lovick will transcribe it; and I shall send it — to be read in this place, if thou wilt.

Miss Howe to Miss Clarissa Harlowe

O MY DEAREST FRIEND, — What will become of your poor Anna Howe! I see by your writing, as well as read by your own account (which, were you not very, *very* ill, you would have touched more tenderly), how it is with you! Why have I thus long delayed to attend you! Could I think that the comfortings of a faithful friend were as nothing to a gentle mind in distress, that I could be prevailed upon to forbear visiting you so much as *once* in all this time! I, as well as everybody else, to desert and abandon my dear creature to strangers! What will become of me if you be as bad as my apprehensions make you!

I will set out this moment, little as the encouragement is that you give me to do so! My mother is willing I should! Why, oh, why, was she not before willing!

Yet she persuades me too (lest I should be fatally affected were I to find my fears too well justified) to wait the return of this messenger, who rides our swiftest horse. God speed him with good news to me — else — but, O my dearest, dearest friend, what else? One line from your hand by him! Send me but *one* line to bid me attend you! I will set out the moment, the very moment I receive it.

The effect this letter had on the lady, who is so near the end which the fair writer so much apprehends and deplores, obliged Mrs. Lovick to make many breaks in reading it, and many changes of voice.

She said her dear friend was so earnest for a line or two that she would fain write, if she could: and she tried; but to no purpose. She could dictate, however, she believed; and desired Mrs. Lovick would take pen and paper. Which she did, and then she dictated to *her*. I would have withdrawn; but at her desire stayed.

She wandered a good deal at first. She took notice that she did. You will find the sense surprisingly entire, her weakness considered. I made the messenger wait while I transcribed it:

Wedn. near 3 o'clock.

MY DEAREST MISS HOWE, — You must not be surprised — nor grieved — that Mrs. Lovick writes for me. Although I cannot obey you, and write with my *pen*, yet my *heart* writes by hers — accept it so — it is the nearest to obedience I can!

And now, what *ought* I to say? What *can* I say? — But why should you not know the truth? since soon you must — very soon.

Know then, and let your tears be those, if of pity, of *joyful* pity! for I permit you to shed a few, to embalm, as I may say, a fallen blossom — know then, that the good doctor, and the pious clergyman, and the worthy apothecary, have just now — with joint benedictions

— taken their last leave of me: and the former bids me hope — do, my dearest, let me say *hope* — hope for my enlargement before to-morrow sunset.

Adieu, therefore, my dearest friend! — Be this *your* consolation, as it is *mine*, that in God's good time we shall meet in a blessed eternity, never more to part! — Once more, then, adieu — and be happy! — which a generous nature cannot be, unless — to its power — it makes others so too.

What a letter hast thou sent me! Poor Lovelace!
Five o'clock. Colonel Morden is this moment arrived.

Eight in the Evening.

The colonel, as Mrs. Smith told me afterwards asked with great impatience, the moment he alighted, How Miss Harlowe was? She answered, Alive, but, she feared, drawing on apace. Good God! said he, with his hands and eyes lifted up. Can I see her? My name is Morden. I have the honour to be nearly related to her. Step up, pray; and let her know (she is sensible, I hope) that I am here. Who is with her?

Nobody but her nurse, and Mrs. Lovick, a widow gentlewoman, who is as careful of her as if she were her mother.

And *more* careful too, interrupted he, or she is not careful at all ——

Except a gentleman be with her, one Mr. Belford, continued Mrs. Smith, who has been the best friend she has had.

If Mr. Belford be with her, surely I may — but, pray step up and let Mr. Belford know that I shall take it for a favour to speak with him first.

Mrs. Smith came up to me in my new apartment.

The colonel, who is really a fine gentleman, received me with great politeness. After the first compliments, My kinswoman, sir, said he, is more obliged to you than to any of her own family. For my part, I have been endeavouring to move so many rocks in her favour; and, little thinking the dear creature so very bad, have neglected to attend her, as I ought to have done the moment I arrived; and *would*, had I known how ill she was, and what a task I should have had with the family. But, sir, your friend has been excessively to blame; and you being so *intimately* his friend has made her fare the worse for your civilities to her. But are there no hopes of her recovery?

The doctors have left her, with the melancholy declaration that there are none.

I satisfied him about the care that had been taken of her; and told him of the friendly and even *paternal* attendance she had had from Dr. H. and Mr. Goddard.

He was impatient to attend her, having not seen her, as he said, since she was twelve years old; and that then she gave promises of being one of the finest women in England.

Mrs. Smith, at his request, stepped up, and brought us down word that Mrs. Lovick and her nurse were with her; and that she was in so sound a sleep, leaning upon the former in her elbow-chair, that she neither heard her enter the room nor go out. The colonel begged, if not improper, that he might see her, though sleeping. He said that his impatience would not let him stay till she awaked. Yet he would not have her disturbed; and should be glad to contemplate her sweet features, when she saw not him; and asked if she thought he could not go in and come out without disturbing her?

She believed he might, she answered; for her chair's back was towards the door.

He said he would take care to withdraw if she awoke, that his sudden appearance might not surprise her.

Mrs. Smith, stepping up before us, bid Mrs. Lovick and the nurse not stir when we entered: and then we went up softly together.

We beheld the lady in a charming attitude. Dressed, as I told you before, in her virgin white, she was sitting in her elbow-chair, Mrs. Lovick close by her in another chair, with her left arm round her neck, supporting it, as it were; for, it seems, the lady had bid her do so, saying she had been a mother to her, and she would delight herself in thinking she was in her mamma's arms; for she found herself drowsy; perhaps, she said, for the last time she should ever be so.

One faded cheek rested upon the good woman's bosom, the kindly warmth of which had overspread it with a faint, but charming flush; the other paler and hollow, as if already iced over by death. Her hands, white as the lily, with her meandering veins more transparently blue than ever I had seen even hers.

In this heart-moving attitude she appeared to us when we approached her, and came to have her lovely face before us.

The colonel, sighing often, gazed upon her with his arms folded, and with the most profound and affectionate attention; till at last, on her starting, and fetching her breath with greater difficulty than before, he retired to a screen that was drawn before her *house*, as she calls it, which, as I have heretofore observed, stands under one of the windows. This screen was placed there at the time she found herself obliged to take to her chamber; and in the depth of our concern, and the fullness of other discourse at our first interview, I had forgotten to apprise the colonel of what he would probably see.

Retiring thither, he drew out his handkerchief, and, overwhelmed with grief, seemed unable to speak: but, on casting his eye behind the screen, he soon broke silence; for, struck with the shape of the coffin, he lifted up a purplish-coloured cloth that was spread over it, and, starting back, Good God! said he, what's here!

Mrs. Smith standing next him: Why, said he, with great emotion, is my cousin suffered to indulge her sad reflections with such an object before her?

Alas! sir, replied the good woman, who should control her? We are all strangers about her, in a manner: and yet we have expostulated with her upon this sad occasion.

Curse upon the hard-heartedness of those, said he, who occasioned her to make so sad a provision for herself!

The lady fetched a profound sigh, and, starting, it broke off our talk; and the colonel then withdrew farther behind the screen, that his sudden appearance might not surprise her.

Where am I? said she. How drowsy I am! How long have I dozed? Don't go, sir (for I was retiring). I am very stupid, and shall be more and more so, I suppose.

She then offered to raise herself; but, being ready to faint through weakness, was forced to sit down again, reclining her head on her chair-back; and, after a few moments: I believe now, my good friends, said she, all your kind trouble will soon be over. I have slept, but am not refreshed, and my fingers' ends seem numbed — have no feeling! (holding them up). 'Tis time to send the letter to my good Norton.

Shall I, madam, send my servant post with it?

Oh, no, sir, I thank you. It will reach the dear woman too soon (as she will think) by the post.

If, madam, your Cousin Morden should come, you would be glad to see him, I presume?

I am too weak to wish to see my cousin now. It would but discompose me, and him too. Yet, if he come while I *can* see, I *will* see him, were it but to thank him for former favours, and for his present kind intentions to me. Has anybody been here from him?

He has called, and will be here, madam, in half an hour; but he feared to surprise you.

Nothing can surprise me now, except my mamma were to favour me with her last blessing in person. That would be a welcome surprise to me, even yet. But did my cousin come purposely to town to see me?

Yes, madam. I took the liberty to let him know, by a line last Monday, how ill you were.

You are very kind, sir. I am and have been greatly obliged to you. But I think I shall be pained to see him now, because he will be concerned to see me. And yet, as I am not so ill as I shall presently be, the sooner he comes the better. But if he come, what shall I do about that screen? He will chide me, very probably; and I cannot bear chiding now. Perhaps (leaning upon Mrs. Lovick and Mrs. Smith) I can walk into the next apartment to receive him.

She motioned to rise; but was ready to faint again, and forced to sit still.

The colonel was in a perfect agitation behind the screen to hear this discourse; and twice, unseen by his cousin, was coming from it towards her; but retreated, for fear of surprising her too much.

I stepped to him and favoured his retreat; she only saying: Are you going, Mr. Belford? Are you sent for down? Is my cousin come? For she heard somebody step softly across the room, and thought it to be me; her hearing being more perfect than her sight.

I told her I believed he was; and she said: We must make the best of it, Mrs. Lovick and Mrs. Smith. I shall otherwise most grievously shock my poor cousin: for he loved me dearly once. Pray give me a few of the doctor's last drops in water, to keep up my spirits for this one interview; and that is all, I believe, that can concern me now.

The colonel (who heard all this) sent in his name; and I, pretending to go down to him, introduced the afflicted gentleman; she having first ordered the screen to be put as close to the window as possible, that he might not see what was behind it; while he, having heard what she had said about it, was determined to take no notice of it.

He folded the angel in his arms as she sat, dropping down on one knee; for, supporting herself upon the two elbows of the chair, she attempted to rise, but could not. Excuse, my dear cousin, said she, excuse me, that I cannot stand up. I did not expect this favour now. But I am glad of this opportunity to thank you for all your generous goodness to me.

I never, my best-beloved and dearest cousin, said he (with eyes running over), shall forgive myself that I did not attend you sooner. Little did I think you were so ill; nor do any of your friends believe it. If they did ——

If they did, repeated she, interrupting him, I should have had more compassion from them. I am sure I should. But pray, sir, how did you leave them? Are *you* reocnciled to them? If you are not, I beg, if you love your poor Clarissa, that you will: for every widened differ- ence augments but my fault, since that is the foundation of all.

I only beg, sir, that you and *this* gentleman — to whom I am ex- ceedingly obliged — will adjust those matters — according to the will I have written. Mr. Belford will excuse me; but it was in truth more necessity than choice that made me think of giving him the trouble he so kindly accepts. Had I had the happiness to see you, my cousin, sooner — or to know that you still honoured me with your regard — I should not have had the assurance to ask this favour of *him*. But, though the friend of Mr. Lovelace, he is a man of honour, and he will make peace rather than break it. And, my dear cousin, let me beg of you to contribute your part to it — and remember that, while I have nearer relations than my Cousin Morden, dear as you are, and always were to me, you have no title to avenge my wrongs upon him who has been the occasion of them. But I wrote to you my mind on this subject, and my reasons; and hope I need not further urge them. And saying this, she sunk down in her chair, and was silent.

Hereupon we both withdrew, leaving word that we would be at the Bedford Head, if anything extraordinary happened.

We procured Mr. Goddard (Dr. H. not being at home) once more to visit her, and to call upon us in his return. He was so good as to do so; but he tarried with her not five minutes; and told us that she was drawing on apace; that he feared she would not live till morning; and she wished to see Colonel Morden directly.

The colonel made excuses where none were needed; and though our little refection was just brought in, he went away immediately.

Ten o'clock.

The colonel sent to me afterwards, to tell me that the lady having been in convulsions, he was so much disordered that he could not possibly attend me.

I have sent every half-hour to know how she does: and just now I have the pleasure to hear that her convulsions have left her; and that she is gone to rest in a much quieter way than could be expected.

Soho, Six o'clock, Sept 7.

The lady is still alive. The colonel having just sent his servant to let me know that she inquired after me about an hour ago, I am dressing to attend her. Joel begs of me to dispatch him back, though but with one line to gratify your present impatience. He expects, he says, to find you at Knightsbridge, let him make what haste he can back; and if he has not a line or two to pacify you, he is afraid you will pistol him; for he apprehends that you are hardly yourself.

Ten o'clock.

The colonel being earnest to see his cousin as soon as she awoke, we were both admitted. We observed in her, as soon as we entered, strong symptoms of her approaching dissolution, notwithstanding what the women had flattered us with from her last night's tranquility. The colonel and I, each loath to say what we thought, looked upon one another with melancholy countenances.

Her breath being very short, she desired another pillow. Having two before, this made her in a manner sit up in her bed; and she spoke then with more distinctness; and seeing us greatly concerned, forgot her own stutterings to comfort us.

I beseech ye, my good friends, proceeded she, mourn not for one who mourns not, nor has cause to mourn, for herself. On the contrary, rejoice with me, that all my worldly troubles are so near their end. Believe me, sirs, that I would not, if I might, choose to live, although the pleasantest part of my life were to come over again: and yet *eighteen years of it*, out of *nineteen*, have been *very* pleasant. To be so much exposed to temptation, and to be so liable to fail in the trial, who would not rejoice that all her dangers are over! All I wished was pardon and blessing from my dear parents. Easy as my departure seems to promise to be, it would have been still easier had I had that pleasure. BUT GOD ALMIGHTY WOULD NOT LET ME DEPEND FOR COMFORT UPON ANY BUT HIMSELF.

She then repeated her request, in the most earnest manner, to her *cousin*, that he would not *heighten* her fault by seeking to avenge her death; to *me*, that I would endeavour to make up all breaches, and use the power I had with my friend to prevent all future mischiefs *from* him, as well as that which this trust might give me to prevent any *to* him.

She made some excuses to her *cousin*, for having not been able to alter her will, to join him in the executorship with me; and to *me*, for the trouble she had given, and yet should give me.

She had fatigued herself so much (growing sensibly weaker) that she sunk her head upon her pillows, ready to faint; and we withdrew to the window.

. . . .

THE colonel tells me that he has written to Mr. John Harlowe, by his servant, that they might spare themselves the trouble of debating about a reconciliation; for that his dear cousin would probably be no more before they could resolve.

He asked me after his cousin's means of subsisting; and whether she had accepted of any favour from *me*: he was sure, he said, she would not from *you*.

I acquainted him with the truth of her parting with some of her apparel.

This wrung his heart; and bitterly did he exclaim as well against you as against her implacable relations.

He wished he had not come to England at all, or had come sooner; and hoped I would apprise him of the whole mournful story at a proper season. He added that he had thoughts, when he came over, of fixing here for the remainder of his days: but now, as it was impossible his cousin could recover, he would go abroad again, and resettle himself at Florence or Leghorn.

. . . .

The lady has been giving orders, with great presence of mind, about her body; directing her nurse and the maid of the house to put her into her coffin as soon as she is cold. Mr. Belford, she said, would know the rest by her will.

. . . .

She has just now given from her bosom, where she always wore it, a miniature picture set in gold of Miss Howe: she gave it to Mrs. Lovick, desiring her to fold it up in white paper, and direct it, *To Charles Hickman, Esq.*, and to give it to me, when she was departed, for that gentleman.

She looked upon the picture before she gave it her. *Sweet and ever-amiable friend — companion — sister — lover!* said she — and kissed it four several times, once at each tender appellation.

Thursday Afternoon, 4 o'clock.

MR. BELFORD TO RICHARD MOWBRAY, ESQ.

Thursday Afternoon.

DEAR MOWBRAY, — I am glad to hear you are in town. Throw yourself the moment this comes to your hand (if possible with Tourville) in the way of a man who least of all men deserves the love of the worthy heart; but most that of thine and Tourville: else the news I shall most probably send him within an hour or two will make annihilation the greatest blessing he has to wish for.

You will find him between Piccadilly and Kensington, most probably on horseback, riding backwards and forwards in a crazy way; or put up, perhaps, at some Inn or Tavern in the way; a waiter possibly, if so, watching for his servant's return to him from me.

.   .   .   .

His man Will is just come to me. He will carry this to you in his way back, and be your director. Hie away in a coach or anyhow. Your being with him may save either his or a servant's life. See the blessed effects of triumphant libertinism! Sooner or later it comes home to us, and all concludes in gall and bitterness.

MR. LOVELACE TO JOHN BELFORD, ESQ.

LIVING or dying, she is mine — and only mine. Have I not earned her dearly? Is not damnation likely to be the purchase to me, though a happy eternity will be hers?

An eternal separation! O God! O God! How can I bear that thought! But yet there is life! Yet, therefore, hope — enlarge my hope, and thou shalt be my good genius, and I will forgive thee everything.

For this last time — but it must not, shall not be the *last* — let me hear, the moment thou receivest this — what I *am* to be — for at present I am / The most miserable of men.

Rose, at Knightsbridge, 5 o'clock.

My fellow tells me that thou art sending Mowbray and Tourville to me. I want them not. My soul's sick of them, and of all the world; but most of myself. Yet, as they send me word they will come to me immediately, I will wait for them, and for thy next. O Belford let it not be ——— But hasten it, hasten it, be it what it may!

MR. BELFORD TO ROBERT LOVELACE, ESQ.

Seven o'clock, Thursday Evening, Sept. 7.

I HAVE only to say at present: Thou wilt do well to take a tour to Paris; or wherever else thy destiny shall lead thee!!! ——— / JOHN BELFORD.

MR. MOWBRAY TO JOHN BELFORD, ESQ.

Uxbridge, Sept. 7, between 11 and 12 at Night.

DEAR JACK, — I send, by poor Lovelace's desire, for *particulars* of the fatal breviate thou sentest him this night. He cannot bear to set pen to paper; yet wants to know every minute passage of Miss Harlowe's departure.

I never heard of such a woman in my life. What great matters has she suffered, that grief should kill her thus?

It was well we were with him when your note came. You showed your true friendship in your foresight. Why, Jack, the poor fellow was quite beside himself — mad as any man ever was in Bedlam.

Will brought him the letter just after we had joined him at the Bohemia Head; where he had left word at the Rose at Knightsbridge he should be; for he had been sauntering up and down, backwards and forwards, expecting us and his fellow. Will, as soon as he delivered it, got out of his way; and when he opened it, never was such a piece of scenery. He trembled like a devil at receiving it: fumbled at the seal, his fingers in a palsy, like Tom Doleman's; his hand shake, shake, shake, that he tore the letter in two before he could come at the contents: and, when he had read them, off went his hat to one corner of the room, his wig to the other. Damnation seize the world! and a whole volley of such-like *execratious* wishes; running up and down the room, and throwing up the sash, and pulling it down, and smiting his forehead with his double fist with such force as would have felled an ox, and stamping and tearing, that the landlord ran in, and faster out again. And this was the *distraction scene* for some time.

By degrees we brought him a little to his reason, and he promised to behave more like a man.

And you know, Jack (as we told him, moreover), that it was a shame to manhood, for a man who had served twenty and twenty women as bad or worse, let him have served Miss Harlowe never so bad, should give himself such *obstropulous* airs because she would die: and we advised him never to attempt a woman proud of her character and *virtue*, as they call it, any more: for why? The conquest did not pay trouble; and what was there in one woman more than another? Hey, you know, Jack! And thus we comforted him and advised him.

But he must and shall go abroad: and in a month or two Jemmy, and you, and I will join him, and he'll soon get the better of this chicken-hearted folly.

MR. BELFORD TO ROBERT LOVELACE, ESQ.

Thursday Night.

I MAY as well try to write; since, were I to go to bed, I shall not sleep. I never had such a weight of grief upon my mind in my life as upon the demise of this admirable woman; whose soul is now rejoicing in the regions of light.

You may be glad to know the particulars of her happy exit. I will try to proceed; for all is hush and still; the family retired; but not one of them, and least of all her poor cousin, I dare say, to rest.

At four o'clock, as I mentioned in my last, I was sent for down; and, as thou usedst to like my descriptions, I will give thee the woeful scene that presented itself to me as I approached the bed.

The colonel was the first that took my attention, kneeling on the side of the bed, the lady's right hand in both his.

On the other side of the bed sat the good widow; her face overwhelmed with tears, leaning her head against the bed's head in a most disconsolate manner.

Mrs. Smith, with clasped fingers and uplifted eyes, as if imploring help from the only Power which could give it, was kneeling down at the bed's feet, tears in large drops trickling down her cheeks.

Her nurse was kneeling between the widow and Mrs. Smith, her arms extended. The maid of the house, with her face upon her folded arms, as she stood leaning against the wainscot, more audibly expressed her grief than any of the others.

The lady had been silent a few minutes, and speechless, as they thought, moving her lips without uttering a word; one hand, as I have said, in her cousin's. But when Mrs. Lovick on my approach pronounced my name, O Mr. Belford, said she, with a faint inward voice, but very distinct nevertheless — Now! — Now! (in broken periods she spoke) — I bless God for His mercies to His poor creature — all will soon be over — a few — a very few moments — will end this strife — and I shall be happy!

Comfort here, sir — turning her head to the colonel — comfort my cousin — see! — the blam — able kindness — he would not wish me to be happy — so *soon*!

She *looked* what she said, a sweet smile beaming over her countenance.

After a short silence: Once more, my dear cousin, said she, but still in broken accents, commend me most dutifully to my father and mother —— There she stopped. And then proceeding: To my sister, to my brother, to my uncles — and tell them I bless them with my parting breath — for all their goodness to me — even for their displeasure I bless them — most happy has been to me my punishment *here!* Happy indeed!

She was silent for a few moments, lifting up her eyes, and the hand her cousin held not between his. Then: *O Death!* said she, *where is thy sting?* (the words I remember to have heard in the Burial Service read over my uncle and poor Belton.) And after a pause: *It is good for me that I was afflicted!* Words of Scripture, I suppose.

Then turning her head towards me: Do *you*, sir, tell your friend that I forgive him! — And I pray to God to forgive him! Again pausing, and lifting up her eyes, as if praying that He would: Let him know how happily I die. — And that such as my own, I wish to be his last hour.

She was again silent for a few moments: and then resuming: My sight fails me! Is not this Mr. Morden's hand? pressing one of his with that he had just let go. Which is Mr. Belford's? holding out the other. I gave her mine. God Almighty bless you both, said she, and make you both — in your last hour — for you *must* come to this — happy as I am.

We thought she was then gone; and gave way to a violent burst of grief.

But soon showing signs of returning life, our attention was again engaged; and I besought her, when a little recovered, to complete in my favour her half-pronounced blessing. She waved her hand to us both, and bowed her head six several times, as we have since recollected, as if distinguishing every person present; not forgetting the nurse and the maid-servant; the latter having approached the bed, weeping, as if crowding in for the divine lady's last blessing; and she spoke faltering and inwardly: Bless — bless — bless — you all — and now — and now (holding up her almost lifeless hands for the last time) — come — O come — blessed Lord — Jesus!

And with these words, the last but half-pronounced, expired: such a smile, such a charming serenity overspreading her sweet face at the instant, as seemed to manifest her eternal happiness already begun.

O Lovelace! ——— But I can write no more!

.   .   .   .

I resume my pen to add a few lines.

While warm, though pulseless, we pressed each her hand with our lips; and then retired into the next room.

We looked at each other with intent to speak: but, as if one motion governed, as one cause affected both, we turned away silent.

The colonel sighed, — My blessed, blessed cousin! uttering some other words, and then recollecting himself, Excuse me, Mr. Belford. And downstairs he went, and out of the house, leaving me a statue.

When I recovered I was ready to repine at what I *then* called an unequal dispensation; forgetting her happy preparation, and still happier departure; and that she had but drawn a common lot; triumphing in it.

She departed exactly at 40 minutes after 6 o'clock, as by her watch on the table.

One o'clock Friday Morning.

Mr. Belford to Robert Lovelace, Esq.

Nine, Friday Morn.

I HAVE no opportunity to write at length, having necessary orders to give on the melancholy occasion.

Three letters are just brought by a servant in livery, directed *To Miss Clarissa Harlowe.* I will send copies of them to you. The contents are enough to make one mad. How would this poor lady have rejoiced to receive them.

Mrs. Norton to Miss Clarissa Harlowe

AT LENGTH, my best-beloved Miss Clary, everything is in the wished train: for all your relations are unanimous in your favour. Even your brother and sister are with the foremost to be reconciled to you.

I knew it must end thus! By patience and persevering sweetness, what a triumph have you gained!

The happy change is owing to letters received from your physician, from your Cousin Morden, and from Mr. Brand.

Colonel Morden will be with you no doubt before this can reach you, with his pocket-book filled with money-bills, that nothing may be wanting to make you easy.

And *now*, all our hopes, all our prayers are that this good news may restore you to spirits and health; and that (so long withheld) it may not come too late.

For this day, being sent for by the general voice, I was received by every one with great goodness and condescension, and *entreated* (for that was the word they were pleased to use, when I needed *no* entreaty, I am sure) to hasten up to you, and to assure you of all their affectionate regards to you: and your father bid me say all the kind things that were in my *heart* to say, in order to comfort and raise you up; and they would hold themselves bound to make them good.

I am to bring you down with me as soon as your health and inclination will permit. You will be received with open arms.

An unhappy delay as to the chaise will make it Saturday morning before I can fold you to my fond heart.

Miss Arab. Harlowe to Miss Cl. Harlowe

DEAR SISTER, — We have heard that you are exceedingly ill. We all loved you as never young creature was loved: you are sensible of that, Sister Clary. And you have been very naughty — but we could not be angry always.

We are indeed more afflicted with the news of your being so very ill than I can express: for I see not but, after this separation (as we understand that your misfortune has been greater than your fault, and that, however unhappy, you have demeaned yourself like the good young creature you used to be), we shall love you better, if possible, than ever.

Take comfort, therefore, Sister Clary; and don't be too much cast down — whatever your mortifications may be from such noble prospects overclouded, and from the reflections you will have from *within*, on your faulty step, and from the sullying of such a charming character by it, you will receive none from *any of us*: and, as an earnest of your papa's and mamma's favour and reconciliation, they assure you by me of their blessing and hourly prayers.

Adieu, my dear Clary! I am / Your loving sister, and true friend, / ARABELLA HARLOWE.

To his dear Niece Miss Clarissa Harlowe

Wedn. Sept. 6.

WE WERE greatly grieved, my beloved Miss Clary, at your fault; but we are still more, if possible, to hear you are so very ill; and we are sorry things have been carried so far. Forgive my part in it, my dearest Clary. I am your *second papa*, you know. And you *used* to love me.

I hope you'll soon be able to come down, and, after a while, when your indulgent parents can spare you, that you will come to me for a whole month, and rejoice my heart, as you used to do. But if, through illness, you cannot so soon come down as we wish, I will go up to you: for I hope to see you. I never more longed to see you in my life; and you was always the darling of my heart, you know.

My brother Antony desires his hearty commendations to you, and joins with me in the tenderest assurance, that all shall be well, and, if possible, better than ever; for we now have been so long without you that we know the miss of you, and even hunger and thirst, as I may say, to see you, and to take you once more to our hearts: whence indeed you was never banished so far as our concern for the unhappy step made *us* think and *you* believe you were. Your sister and brother both talk of seeing you in town: so does my dear sister, your indulgent mother.

God restore your health, if it be His will: else I know not what will become of / Your truly loving uncle, and second papa, / JOHN HARLOWE.

MR. BELFORD TO ROBERT LOVELACE, ESQ.

Friday Night, Sept. 8, past Ten.

I WILL now take up the account of our proceedings from my letter of last night, which contained the dying words of this incomparable lady.

In the morning, between seven and eight o'clock, according to appointment, the colonel came to me here.

I unlocked the drawer, in which she had deposited her papers. I told you in mine of Monday last that she had the night before sealed up with three black seals a parcel inscribed, *As soon as I am certainly dead, this to be broke open by Mr. Belford.* I accused myself for not having done it overnight. But really I was then incapable of anything.

I broke it open accordingly, and found in it no less than eleven letters, each sealed with her own seal and black wax, one of which was directed to me.

I will enclose a copy of it.

To John Belford, Esq.

Sunday Evening, Sept. 3.

SIR, — I take this last and solemn occasion to repeat to you my thanks

479

for all your kindness to me at a time when I most needed countenance and protection.

A few considerations I beg leave, as *now* at your perusal of this from the dead, to press upon you, with all the warmth of a sincere friendship.

By the time you will see this, you will have had an instance, I humbly trust, of the comfortable importance of a pacified conscience, in the last hours of one who, *to* the last hour, will wish your eternal welfare.

Sir, let me beg of you, for *my sake*, who AM, or as *now* you will best read it, *have been*, driven to the necessity of applying to you to be the executor of my will, that you will bear, according to that generosity which I think to be in you, with all my friends, and particularly with my brother (who is really a worthy young man, but perhaps a little too headstrong in his first resentments and conceptions of things), if anything, by reason of this trust, should fall out disagreeably; and that you will study to make peace, and to reconcile all parties; and more especially that you, who seem to have a great influence upon your *still more* headstrong friend, will interpose, if occasion be, to prevent *further* mischief — for surely, sir, that violent spirit may sit down satisfied with the evils he has already wrought; and, particularly, with the wrongs, the heinous and ignoble wrongs, he has in me done to my family, wounded in the tenderest part of its honour.

I have another request to make of you: it is that you will be pleased, by a particular messenger, to forward the enclosed letters as directed. / Your obliged servant / CLARISSA HARLOWE.

The other letters are directed to her father, to her mother, one to her two uncles, to her brother, to her sister, to her Aunt Hervey, to her Cousin Morden, to Miss Howe, to Mrs. Norton, and lastly to you, in performance of her promise *that a letter should be sent you when she arrived at her father's house!* —— I will withhold this last till I can be assured that you will be fitter to receive it than Tourville tells me you are at present.

I gave the colonel his letter, and ordered Harry instantly to get ready to carry the others.

Meantime (retiring into the next apartment) we opened the will. We were both so much affected in perusing it, that at one time the colonel, breaking off, gave it to me to read on; at another, I gave it back to him to proceed with; neither of us being able to read it through without such tokens of sensibility as affected the voice of each.

The colonel told me he was ready to account with me for the money and bills he had brought up from Harlowe Place; which would enable me, as he said, directly to execute the legacy parts of the will; and he would needs at that instant force into my hands a paper relating to that subject. I put it in my pocket-book without looking into it; telling him that, as I hoped he would do all in his power to promote a literal performance of the will, I must beg his advice and assistance in the execution of it.

Her request to be buried with her ancestors made a letter of the following import necessary, which I prevailed upon the colonel to write.

To James Harlowe, jun., Esq.

SIR, — The letter which the bearer of this brings with him will, I presume, make it unnecessary to acquaint you and my cousins with the death of the most excellent of women. But I am requested by her executor, who will soon send you a copy of her last will, to acquaint her father (which I choose to do by your means) that in it she earnestly desires to be laid in the family vault, at the feet of her grandfather.

If her father will not admit of it, she has directed her body to be buried in the churchyard of the parish where she died.

I need not tell you that a speedy answer to this is necessary.

Her beatification commenced yesterday afternoon, exactly at forty minutes after six.

I can write no more, than that I am / Yours, etc. / WM. MORDEN. / *Friday Morn. Sept 8.*

By the time this was written, and by the colonel's leave transcribed, Harry came booted and spurred, his horse at the door; and I delivered him the letters to the family, with those to Mrs. Norton and Miss Howe (eight in all) together with the above of the colonel to Mr. James Harlowe; and gave him orders to make the utmost dispatch with them.

MR. BELFORD TO ROBERT LOVELACE, ESQ.

Sat. Ten o'clock.

POOR Mrs. Norton is come. She was set down at the door; and would have gone upstairs directly. But Mrs. Smith and Mrs. Lovick being together and in tears, and the former hinting too suddenly to the truly venerable woman the fatal news, she sunk down at her feet in fits; so that they were forced to breathe a vein to bring her to herself.

She was impatient to see the corpse. The women went up with her. But they owned that they were too much affected themselves on this occasion to describe her extremely affecting behaviour.

I thought it would divert the poor gentlewoman, and not altogether unsuitably, if I were to put her upon furnishing mourning for herself; as it would rouse her, by a seasonable and necessary employment, from the dismal lethargy of grief which generally succeeds the too violent anguish with which a gentle nature is accustomed to be torn upon the first communication of the unexpected loss of a dear friend. I gave her therefore the thirty guineas bequeathed to her and to her son for mourning; the only mourning which the testatrix has mentioned; and desired her to lose no time in preparing her own, as I doubted not that she would accompany the corpse, if it were permitted to be carried down.

The colonel proposes to attend the hearse, if his kindred give him not fresh cause of displeasure; and will take with him a copy of the will. And being intent to give the family some favourable impressions of me, he desired me to permit him to take with him the copy of the posthumous letter to me: which I readily granted.

I could have shown to Mrs. Norton the copies of the two letters which she missed by coming up. But her grief wants not the heightenings which the reading of them would have given her.

. . . .

I have been dipping into the copies of the posthumous letters to the family, which Harry has carried down. I will enclose some of them, which I desire you to return as soon as you can.

[*Of the eleven posthumous letters Richardson printed those to Clarissa's mother, father, brother, sister, uncles; he "abstracted" those to her Aunt Hervey, Mrs. Norton, and Miss Howe. He professes that "although every letter varies in style as well as matter . . . yet as they are written on the same subject, and are pretty long, it is thought proper to abstract them." In the present text all the letters of the group, except those to her father, to Lovelace, and to Morden, are omitted.*]

To the Ever-honoured Jas. Harlowe, sen., Esq.

MOST DEAR SIR! — With exulting confidence now does your emboldened daughter come into your awful presence by these lines, who dared not but upon this occasion to look up to you with hopes of favour and forgiveness; since, when this comes to your hands, it will be out of her power ever to offend you more.

And now let me bless you, my honoured papa, and bless you, as I write, upon my knees, for all the benefits I have received from your indulgence: for your fond love to me in the days of my prattling innocence: for the virtuous education you gave me: and, for the crown of all, the happy end, which, through Divine grace, by means of that virtuous education, I hope, by the time you will receive this, I shall have made. And let me beg of you, dear venerable sir, to blot from your remembrance, if possible, the last unhappy eight months; and then I shall hope to be remembered with advantage for the pleasure you had the goodness to take in your Clarissa.

Still on her knees, let your poor penitent implore your forgiveness of all her faults and follies; more especially of that fatal error which threw her out of your protection.

That the Almighty, in His own good time, will bring you, sir, and my ever-honoured mother, after a series of earthly felicities, of which may my unhappy fault be the only interruption (and very grievous I

482

know that must have been), to rejoice in the same blessed state, is the repeated prayer of, sir, / Your now happy daughter. / CLARISSA HARLOWE.

MR. BELFORD TO ROBERT LOVELACE, ESQ.

Sat. Night.

YOUR servant gives me a dreadful account of your raving unmanageableness. I wonder not at it. But as nothing violent is lasting, I dare say that your habitual gaiety of heart will quickly get the better of your frenzy: and the rather do I judge so, as your fits are of the raving kind (suitable to your natural impetuosity), and not of that melancholy species which seizes slower souls.

Harry is returned from carrying the posthumous letters to the family and to Miss Howe; and that of the colonel which acquaints James Harlowe with his sister's death, and with her desire to be interred near her grandfather.

It is easy then to judge what must be their grief and surprise on receiving the fatal news which the letters Harry sent in to them communicated.

He stayed there long enough to find the whole house in confusion; and he went to an inn; and pursued on foot his way to Mrs. Norton's; and finding her come to town, left the letter with her son.

He proceeded to Miss Howe's with the letter for her. That lady had just given orders for a young man to post to London to bring her news of the dear friend's condition, and Harry was just in time to prevent the man's setting out.

He had the precaution to desire to speak with Miss Howe's woman or maid, and communicated to her the fatal tidings. The maid was herself so affected that her old lady (who, Harry said, seemed to be *everywhere at once*) came to see what ailed her; and was herself so struck with the communication that she was forced to sit down in a chair: O the sweet creature! said she. And is it come to this!

She took the letter, and her salts in her hand. And they had occasion for the latter. For the housekeeper soon came hurrying down to the kitchen. Her young mistress had fainted away, she said. Nor did she wonder at it. Never did there live a lady more deserving of general admiration and lamentation than Miss Clarissa Harlowe!

The answer which James Harlowe returned to Colonel Morden's letter of notification of his sister's death, and to her request as to interment, will give a faint idea of what their concern must be. Here follows a copy of it.

To William Morden, Esq.

Saturday, Sept. 9.

DEAR COUSIN, — I cannot find words to express what we all suffer on the most mournful news that ever was communicated to us.

483

God be merciful to us all! To what purpose did the doctor write if she was so near her end? Why, as everybody says, did he not send sooner? or why at all?

Alas! sir, I fear my mother will never get over this shock — she has been in hourly fits ever since she received the fatal news. My poor father has the gout thrown into his stomach; and Heaven knows — O cousin, O sir! — I meant nothing but the honour of the family; yet I have all the weight thrown upon me (O this cursed Lovelace! may I perish if he escape the deserved vengeance!).[1]

We can have nothing to do with her executor (another strange step of the dear creature's!) — he cannot expect we will — nor, if he be a gentleman, will he think of acting. Do you, therefore, be pleased, sir, to order an undertaker to convey the body down to us.

If we know her will in relation to the funeral, it shall be punctually complied with: as shall everything in it that is fit or reasonable to be performed; and this without the intervention of strangers.

Will you not, dear sir, favour us with your presence at this melancholy time? Pray do, and pity and excuse, with the generosity which is natural to the brave and wise, what passed at our last meeting. / Ja. Harlowe, jun.

Everything that is fit or reasonable to be performed (repeated I to the colonel, from the above letter, on his reading it to me): that is everything which she has directed, that *can* be performed. I hope, colonel, that I shall have no contention with them. I wish no more for *their* acquaintance than they do for *mine*. But you, sir, must be the mediator between them and me; for I shall insist upon a literal performance in every article.

The colonel was so kind as to declare that he would support me in my resolution.

Mr. Belford to Robert Lovelace, Esq.

Sunday Morn. 8 o'clock, Sept. 10.

I stayed at Smith's till I saw the last of all that is mortal of the divine lady.

As she has directed rings by her will to several persons, with her hair to be set in crystal, the afflicted Mrs. Norton cut off, before the coffin was closed, four charming ringlets; one of which the colonel took for a locket, which, he says, he will cause to be made, and wear next his heart in memory of his beloved cousin.

Between four and five in the morning the corpse was put into the hearse; the coffin before being filled, as intended, with flowers and aromatic herbs, and proper care taken to prevent the corpse suffering (to the eye) from the jolting of the hearse.

When the hearse moved off, and was out of sight, I locked up the

---

1 The words thus enclosed ( ) were omitted in the transcript to Mr. Lovelace.

lady's chamber, into which all that had belonged to her was removed.

I expect to hear from the colonel as soon as he is got down, by a servant of his own.

MR. MOWBRAY TO JOHN BELFORD, ESQ.

Uxbridge, Sunday Morn. 9 o'clock.

DEAR JACK, — I send you enclosed a letter from Mr. Lovelace; which, though written in the cursed algebra, I know to be such a one as will show what a *queer* way he is in; for he read it to us with the air of a tragedian.

But he has had no rest for these ten days: that's the thing! You must write to him; and prithee coax him, Jack, and send him what he writes for, and give him all his way: there will be no bearing him else. And get the lady buried as fast as you can; and don't let him know where.

This letter should have gone yesterday. We told him it did. But were in hopes he would not have inquired after it again. But he raves *as he has not* any answer.

MR. LOVELACE TO JOHN BELFORD, ESQ.

Uxbridge, Sat. Sept. 9.

JACK, — I think it absolutely right that my ever-dear and beloved lady should be opened and embalmed. It must be done out of hand — this very afternoon.

I will see everything done with that decorum which the case, and the sacred person of my beloved, require.

Everything that can be done to preserve the charmer from decay shall also be done. And when she *will* descend to her original dust, or cannot be kept longer, I will then have her laid in my family vault, between my own father and mother. Myself, as I am in my *soul*, so in *person*, chief mourner. But her *heart*, to which I have such unquestionable pretensions, in which once I had so large a share, and which I will prize above my own, I *will* have. I will keep it in spirits. It shall never be out of my sight. And all the charges of *sepulture* too shall be mine.

I will free you from your executorship and all your cares.

Take notice, Belford, that I do hereby actually discharge you, and everybody, from all cares and troubles relating to her. And as to her last testament, I will execute it mself.

I send in the meantime for a lock of her hair.

I charge you stir not any part of her will but by my express direction. I will order everything myself. For am I not her husband? And being forgiven by her, am I not the chosen of her heart? What else signifies her forgiveness?

I will take her papers. And as no one can do her memory justice

485

equal to myself, and I will not spare myself, who can better show the world what she was, and what a villain he that could use her ill? And the world shall also see what implicable and unworthy parents she had.

All shall be set forth in words at length. No mincing of the matter. Names undisguised as well as facts. For as I shall make the worst figure in it myself, and have a right to treat myself as nobody else shall, who will control me? Who dare call me to account?

Adieu, Jack! I am preparing to be with you. I charge you, as you value my life or your own, do not oppose me in anything relating to my Clarissa Lovelace.

In a separate paper enclosed in the above

I know not what I have written. But her dear heart and a lock of her hair I will have, let who will be the gainsayers!

MR. BELFORD TO RICHARD MOWBRAY, ESQ.
Sunday, Sept. 10, 4 in the Afternoon.

I HAVE yours, with our unhappy friend's enclosed. I am glad my lord is with him. As I presume that his frenzy will be but of short continuance, I most earnestly wish that on his recovery he could be prevailed upon to go abroad. Mr. Morden, who is inconsolable, has seen by the will (as indeed he suspected before he read it) that the case is more than a common seduction; and has dropped hints already that he looks upon himself, on that account, as freed from his promises made to the dying lady, which were that he could not seek to avenge her death.

You must make the recovery of his health the motive for urging him on this head; for if you hint at his own safety, he will not stir, but rather seek the colonel.

As to the lock of hair, you may easily pacify him (as you once saw the angel) with hair near the colour, if he be intent upon it.

[*Belford sends Lovelace a long and gruesome account (here omitted) of the death of Mrs. Sinclair. Intoxicated, she had fallen down stairs, had broken a leg, and gangrene set in. She died in frantic terror and fear of eternal punishment.*]

COLONEL MORDEN TO JOHN BELFORD, ESQ.
Sunday Night, Sept. 10.

DEAR SIR, — According to my promise, I send you an account of matters here. Poor Mrs. Norton was so very ill upon the road, that, slowly as the hearse moved, and the chariot followed, I was afraid we should not have got her to St. Albans. We put up there as I had intended.

When we were within five miles of Harlowe Place, I put on a hand-gallop. I ordered the hearse to proceed more slowly still, the cross-road we were in being rough; and having more time before us than I wanted; for I wished not the hearse to be in till near dusk.

I got to Harlowe Place about four o'clock. You may believe I found a mournful house. You desire me to be very minute.

At my entrance into the court, they were all in motion. Every servant whom I saw had swelled eyes, and looked with so much concern, that at first I apprehended some new disaster had happened in the family.

Mr. John and Mr. Antony Harlowe and Mrs. Hervey were there. They all helped on one another's grief, as they had before done each other's hardness of heart.

My Cousin James met me at the entrance of the hall. His countenance expressed a fixed concern; and he desired me to excuse his behaviour the last time I was there.

My Cousin Arabella came to me full of tears and grief.

O cousin! said she, hanging upon my arm, I dare not ask you any questions!

Mr. Antony Harlowe came to me soon after. His face was overspread with all the appearance of woe. He requested me to walk into the parlour; where, as he said, were all his fellow-mourners.

My Cousin Harlowe, the dear creature's father, as soon as he saw me, said: O cousin, cousin, of all our family, you are the only one who have nothing to reproach yourself with! *You* are a happy man!

The poor mother, bowing her head to me in speechless grief, sat with her handkerchief held to her eyes with one hand. The other hand was held by her Sister Hervey between both hers; Mrs. Hervey weeping upon it.

Near the window sat Mr. John Harlowe, his face and his body turned from the sorrowing company; his eyes red and swelled.

My Cousin Antony, at his re-entering the parlour, went towards Mrs. Harlowe: Don't — dear sister! said he. Then towards my Cousin Harlowe: Don't — dear brother! Don't thus give way. And without being able to say another word, went to a corner of the parlour, and, wanting himself the comfort he would fain have given, sunk into a chair, and audibly sobbed.

Miss Arabella followed her Uncle Antony, as he walked in before me; and seemed as if she would have spoken to the pierced mother some words of comfort.

Young Mr. Harlowe, with all his vehemence of spirit, was now subdued.

O cousin, cousin! cried the unhappy mother, withdrawing her hand from that of her Sister Hervey, and pressing mine with it, you know not what a child I have lost! Then in a lower voice, And *how* lost! — That it is that makes the loss unsupportable.

They all joined in a kind of melancholy chorus, and each accused him and herself, and some of them one another. But the eyes of all, in turn, were cast upon my Cousin James as the person who had kept up the general resentment.

O brother, brother! but for you! — but for you —!

Double not upon me, said he, my own woes! I have everything before me that passed! I thought only to reclaim a dear creature that had erred! I intended not to break her tender heart! But it was the villainous Lovelace who did that — not any of us! Yet, cousin, did she not attribute all to *me*? I fear she did! Tell me only, did she name *me*, did she *speak* of me, in her last hours? I hope she, who could forgive the greatest villain on earth, and plead that he may be safe from our vengeance, I *hope* she could forgive *me*.

She died blessing you all; and justified rather than condemned your severity to her.

Then they set up another general lamentation.

We see, said her father, in her heart-piercing letters what a happy frame she was in a few days before her death. But did it hold to the last? Had she no repinings?

None at all! I never saw, and never shall see, so blessed a *departure*: and no wonder; for I never heard of such a *preparation*. Every hour for weeks together was taken up in it. Let this be our comfort; we need only to wish for so happy an end for ourselves, and for those who are nearest to our hearts. We may any of us be grieved for acts of unkindness to her: but had all happened that once she wished for, she could not have made a happier, perhaps not so happy, an end.

Dear soul! and Dear sweet soul! the father, uncles, sister, my Cousin Hervey, cried out all at once in accents of anguish inexpressibly affecting.

O this cursed friend of yours, Mr. Belford! This detested Lovelace! To him, to him is owing ——

Pardon me, sir. I will lay down my pen till I have recovered my temper.

One in the morning.

In vain, sir, I endeavoured to compose myself to rest. You wished me to be very particular, and I cannot help it. This melancholy subject fills my whole mind. I will proceed, though it be midnight.

About six o'clock the hearse came to the outward gate. The parish church is at some distance; but the wind setting fair, the afflicted family were struck, just before it came, into a fresh fit of grief, on hearing the funeral bell tolled in a very solemn manner. A respect, as it proved, and as they all guessed, paid to the memory of the dear deceased out of officious love, as the hearse passed near the church.

Judge, when their grief was so great in expectation of it, what it must be when it arrived.

A servant came in to acquaint us with what its lumbering heavy noise up the paved inner courtyard apprised us of before.

He spoke not. He could not speak. He looked, bowed, and withdrew.

I stepped out. No one else could then stir. Her brother, however, soon followed me.

When I came to the door I beheld a sight very affecting.

You have heard, sir, how universally my dear cousin was beloved. By the poor and middling sort especially, no young lady was ever so much beloved. And with reason; she was the common patroness of all the honest poor in her neighbourhood.

It is natural for us in every deep and sincere grief to interest all we know in what is so concerning to ourselves. The servants of the family, it seems, had told *their* friends, and those *theirs*, that though, living, their dear young lady could not be received nor looked upon, her body was permitted to be brought home.

These, when the coffin was taken out of the hearse, crowding about it, hindered, for a few moments, its being carried in; the young people, struggling who should bear it and yet with respectful *whisperings*, rather than clamorous *contention*.

At last six maidens were permitted to carry it in by the six handles. The corpse was thus borne, with the most solemn respect, into the hall, and placed for the present upon two stools there. The plates, and emblems, and inscription, set every one gazing upon it and admiring it. The more, when they were told that all was of her own ordering.

As for Mr. James Harlowe (who accompanied me, but withdrew when he saw the crowd), he stood looking upon the lid, when the people had left it, with a fixed attention: yet, I dare say, knew not a symbol or letter upon it at that moment, had the quesion been asked him. In a profound reverie he stood, his arms folded, his head on one side, and marks of stupefaction imprinted upon every feature.

But when the corpse was carried into the lesser parlour, adjoining to the hall, which she used to call *her* parlour, and put upon a table in the middle of the room, and the father and mother, the two uncles, her Aunt Hervey, and her sister came in, joining her brother and me, with trembling feet, and eager woe, the scene was still more affecting.

They would have withheld the mother, it seems, from coming in: but when they could not, though undetermined before, they all bore her company, led on by an impulse they could not resist. The poor lady but just cast her eye upon the coffin, and then snatched it away, retiring with passionate grief towards the window.

Her son (his heart then softened, as his eyes showed) besought her to withdraw: and her woman looking in at that moment, he called her to assist him in conducting her lady into the middle parlour: and then returning, met his father going out at the door, who also had but just cast his eye on the coffin, and yielded to my entreaties to withdraw.

His grief was too deep for utterance, till he saw his son coming in; and then, fetching a heavy groan, Never, said he, was sorrow like my sorrow! O son! son! in a reproaching accent, his face turned from him.

I attended him through the middle parlour, endeavouring to console him. His lady was there in agonies. She took his eye. He made a motion towards her: O my dear, said he — but turning short, his eyes as full as his heart, he hastened through to the great parlour: and when there he desired me to leave him to himself.

The uncles and the sister looked and turned away, looked and turned away, very often, upon the emblems, in silent sorrow. Mrs. Hervey would have read to them the inscription. These words she did read: *Here the wicked cease from troubling* —— but could read no further.

. . . .

When the unhappy mourners were all retired, I directed the lid of the coffin to be unscrewed, and caused some fresh aromatics and flowers to be put into it.

The corpse was very little altered, notwithstanding the journey. The sweet smile remained.

When my cousins were told that the lid was unscrewed, they pressed in again, all but the mournful father and mother, as if by consent. Mrs. Hervey kissed her pale lips. Flower of the world! was all she could say; and gave place to Miss Arabella; who, kissing the forehead of *her* whom she had so cruelly treated, could only say to my Cousin James (looking upon the corpse, and upon him): O brother! While he, taking the fair lifeless hand, kissed it, and retreated with precipitation.

Her two uncles were speechless. They seemed to wait each other's example, whether to look upon the corpse or not. I ordered the lid to be replaced; and then they pressed forward, as the others again did, to take a last farewell of the casket which so lately contained so rich a jewel.

The unhappy parents proposed to take one last view and farewell of their once darling daughter. The father was got to the parlour door, after the inconsolable mother: but neither of them were able to enter it. The mother said she must once more see the child of her heart, or she should never enjoy herself. But they both agreed to refer their melancholy curiosity till the next day; and hand in hand retired inconsolable, and speechless.

When all were withdrawn I retired, and sent for my Cousin James, and acquainted him with his sister's request in relation to the discourse to be pronounced at her interment; telling him how necessary it was that the minister, whoever he were, should have the earliest notice given him that the case would admit.

Mr. Melvill, Doctor Lewen's assistant, must, he said, be the man.

He called out his sister, and she was of his opinion. So I left this upon them.

They both, with no little warmth, hinted their disapprobation of you, sir, for their sister's executor, on the score of your intimate friendship with the author of her ruin.

You must not resent anything I shall communicate to you of what they say on this occasion: depending that you will not, I shall write with the greater freedom.

They said there was no need of an executor out of their family; and they hoped that you would relinquish so *unnecessary* a trust, as they called it. My Cousin James declared that he would write to you as soon as the funeral was over, to desire that you would do so, upon proper assurances that all that the will prescribed should be performed.

I said you were a man of resolution: that I thought he would hardly succeed; for that you made a point of honour of it.

I then showed them their sister's posthumous letter to you; in which she confesses her obligations to you, and regard for you, and for your future welfare. You may believe, sir, they were extremely affected with the perusal of it.

They were surprised that I had given up to you the produce of her grandfather's estate since his death. I told them plainly that they must thank themselves if anything disagreeable to them occurred from their sister's devise; deserted, and thrown into the hands of strangers, as she had been.

Monday Morning, between Eight and Nine.

The unhappy family are preparing for a mournful meeting at breakfast. Mr. James Harlowe, who has had as little rest as I, has written to Mr. Melvill, who has promised to draw up a brief eulogium on the deceased. Miss Howe is expected here by and by, to see, for the last time, her beloved friend.

Miss Howe, by her messenger, desires she may not be taken any notice of. She shall not tarry six minutes, was the word. Her desire will be easily granted her.

Her servant, who brought the request, if it were denied, was to return and meet her; for she was ready to set out in her chariot when he got on horseback.

If he met her not with the refusal, he was to stay here till she came.

Monday Afternoon, Sept. 11.

I was summoned to breakfast about half an hour after nine. Slowly did the mournful congress meet.

By the time we were well seated, the bell ringing, the outward gate opening, a chariot rattling over the pavement, of the courtyard, put them into motion.

I left them; and was just time enough to give Miss Howe my hand, as she alighted: her maid in tears remaining in the chariot.

Never did I think, said she, as she gave me her hand, to enter more these doors: but, living or dead, my *Clarissa* brings me after her anywhither!

She entered with me the little parlour; and seeing the coffin, withdrew her hand from mine, and with impatience pushed aside the lid. As impatiently she removed the face-cloth.

O my blessed friend! said she — my sweet companion! — my lovely monitress! — kissing her lips at every tender appellation. And is this all! — is it all of my CLARISSA's story!

But why, sir, why, Mr. Morden, was she sent *hither*? Why not to *me*? She has no father, no mother, no relations; no, not *one*! They had all renounced her. I was her sympathizing friend — and had not *l* the best right to my dear creature's remains? And must names, without nature, be preferred to such a love as mine?

Then surveying the lid, she seemed to take in at once the meaning of the emblem: and this gave her so much fresh grief, that though she several times wiped her eyes, she was unable to read the inscription and texts: turning therefore to me; Favour me, sir, I pray you, by a line, with the description of these emblems, and with these texts: and if I might be allowed a lock of the dear creature's hair ——

I told her that her executor would order both; and would also send her a copy of her last will; in which she would find the most grateful remembrances of her love for her, whom she calls *the sister of her heart.*

Justly, said she, does she call me so: for we had but one heart, but one soul, between us: and now my better half is torn from me, — *what shall I do?*

But looking round her, on a servant's stepping by the door, as if again she had apprehended it was some of the family: Once more, said she, a solemn, an everlasting adieu! Alas! for *me*, a solemn, an everlasting adieu!

Then again embracing her face with both her hands, and kissing it, and afterwards the hands of the dear deceased, first one, then the other, she gave me her hand; and, quitting the room with precipitation, rushed into her chariot; and, when there, with profound sighs, and a fresh burst of tears, unable to speak, she bowed her head to me, and was driven away.

Thursday Night, Sept. 14.

We were just returned from the solemnization of the last mournful rite. My Cousin James and his sister, Mr. and Mrs. Hervey, and *their* daughter, a young lady whose affection for my departed cousin shall ever bind me to her, my Cousin John and Antony Harlowe, myself, and some other more distant relations of the names of Fuller and Allinson (who, to testify their respect to the memory of the dear deceased, had put themselves in mourning), self-invited, attended it.

The father and mother would have joined in these last honours, had they been able: but they were both very much indisposed, and continue to be so.

The inconsolable mother told Mrs. Norton that the two mothers of the sweetest child in the world ought not, on this occasion, to be separated. She therefore desired her to stay with *her*.

The whole solemnity was performed with great decency and order. The distance from Harlowe Place to the church is about half a mile. All the way the corpse was attended by great numbers of people of all conditions.

It was nine when it entered the church; every corner of which was crowded. Such a profound, such a silent respect did I never see paid at the funeral of princes. An attentive sadness overspread the face of all.

The eulogy pronounced by Mr. Melvill was a very pathetic one.

He wiped his own eyes often, and made everybody present still oftener wipe theirs.

What he most insisted upon was the happy end she made; and thence drew consolation to her relations, and instruction to the auditory.

When the corpse was to be carried down into the vault (a very spacious one, within the church) there was great crowding to see the coffin-lid, and the devices upon it.

Miss Harlowe was extremely affected: her overwhelmed eye pursued the coffin till she could see no more of it: and then she threw herself on the seat, and was near fainting away.

I accompanied it down, that I might not only satisfy myself, but you, sir, her executor, that it was deposited, as she had directed, at the feet of her grandfather.

And here I left the remains of my beloved cousin; having bespoken my own place by the side of her coffin.

P.S. You will have a letter from my Cousin James, who hopes to prevail upon you to relinquish the executorship. It has not my encouragement.

MR. JAMES HARLOWE TO JOHN BELFORD, ESQ.

Harlowe Place, Friday Night, Sept. 15.

SIR, — I hope from the character my worthy Cousin Morden gives you, that you will excuse the application I make to you, to oblige a whole family in an affair that much concerns their peace, and cannot equally concern anybody else. You will immediately judge, sir, that this is the executorship of which my sister has given you the trouble by her last will.

We shall all think ourselves extremely obliged to you, if you please to relinquish this trust to our family.

We are the more concerned, sir, to wish you to decline this office, because of your short and accidental knowledge of the dear testatrix, and long and intimate acquaintance with the man to whom *she* owed her ruin, and *we* the greatest loss and disappointment (her manifold excellences considered) that ever befell a family.

You will allow due weight, I dare say, to this plea, if you make our case your own: and so much the readier, when I assure you that your interfering in this matter so much against our inclinations (excuse, sir, my plain-dealing) will very probably occasion an opposition in some points, where otherwise there might be none.

What, therefore, I propose is, not that my father should assume this trust: he is too much afflicted to undertake it — nor yet myself — I might be thought too much concerned in interest; but that it may be allowed to devolve upon my two uncles; whose known honour, and whose affection to the dear deceased, nobody ever doubted: and they will treat with you, sir, through my Cousin Morden, as to the points they will undertake to perform.

Your compliance, sir, will oblige a family (who have already distress enough upon them) in the circumstance that occasions this application to you; and more particularly, sir, / Your most humble servant, / JAMES HARLOWE, jun.

I send this by one of my servants, who will attend your dispatch.

MR. BELFORD TO JAMES HARLOWE, JUN., ESQ.

Saturday, Sept. 16.

SIR, — You will excuse my plain dealing in turn: for I must observe that if I had *not* the just opinion I have of the sacred nature of the office I have undertaken, some passages in the letter you have favoured me with convince me that I ought not to excuse myself from acting in it.

I need name only one of them. You are pleased to say that your uncles, if the trust be relinquished to them, will *treat with me*, through colonel Morden, *as to the points they will undertake to perform.*

Permit me, sir, to say that it is the *duty* of an executor to see *every point* performed that *can* be performed. Nor will I leave the performance of mine to any other persons, especially where a qualifying is so directly intimated, and where all the branches of your family have shown themselves, with respect to the incomparable lady, to have but one mind.

Occasions of litigation or offence shall not proceed from me. You need only apply to Colonel Morden, who shall command me in everything that the will allows me to oblige your family in. I do assure you that I am as unwilling to obtrude myself upon it, as any of it can wish.

I own that I have not yet proved the will; nor shall I do it till next week at soonest, that you may have time for amicable objections, if such you think fit to make through the colonel's mediation.

Permit me to add, that when you have perused the will, and coolly considered everything, it is my hope that you will yourself be of opinion that there can be no room for dispute or opposition: and that if your family will join to expedite the execution, it will be the most natural and easy way of shutting up the whole affair, and to have done with a man so causelessly, as to his *own* particular, the object of your dislike, as is, sir, / Your very humble servant (notwithstanding), / JOHN BELFORD.

THE WILL

[*Gentlefolk of the eighteenth century found wills especially fascinating. Thus Richardson naturally printed entire Clarissa's will, which ran to fourteen pages of print and which is here omitted. Her bequests, naturally, are altogether fitting. All her real estate goes to her father, with the proviso that Mrs. Norton is to occupy for the rest of her life the apartments at The Grove used by Clarissa in her grandfather's time. Income that has accrued from her grandfather's estate (now Clarissa's) is to be devoted to a fund for "her poor." Members of the family, all servants, all her friends in London as well as those living near Harlowe Place are tactfully and generously remembered — and there are appropriate reflections from time to time of a sound moral nature.]*

COLONEL MORDEN TO JOHN BELFORD, ESQ.

Sat. Sept. 10.

I HAVE been employed in a most melancholy task: in reading the will of the dear deceased.

When I read the direction, "That her body was not to be viewed, except any of her relations should *vouchsafe for the last time to look upon her;*" they turned away, and turned to me, three or four times alternately. Mrs. Hervey and Miss Arabella sobbed; the uncles wiped their eyes; the brother looked down; the father wrung his hands.

I was obliged to stop at the words "That she was nobody's."

When the article was read which bequeathed to the father the grandfather's estate, and the reason assigned for it (so generous and so dutiful), the father could sit no longer; but withdrew, wiping his eyes, and lifting up his spread hands at Mr. James Harlowe; who arose to attend him to the door, as Arabella likewise did — all he could say: O son! son! — O girl! girl! as if he reproached them for the parts they had acted, and put him upon acting.

But yet, on some occasions, this brother and sister showed themselves to be true will-disputants.

The clothes, the thirty guineas for mourning to Mrs. Norton, with the recommendation of the good woman for housekeeper at *The Grove,* were thought sufficient, had the article of £600, which was called monstrous, been omitted. Some other passages in the will were called *flights, and such whimsies as distinguish people of imagination from those of judgment.*

My Cousin Dolly Hervey was grudged the library. Miss Harlowe said that as she and her sister never bought the same books, she would take that to herself, and would *make it up* to her Cousin Dolly *one way or other.*

I intend, Mr. Belford, to save you the trouble of interposing — the library *shall* be my Cousin Dolly's.

Mrs. Hervey could hardly keep her seat. On *this* occasion, however, she only said that her late dear and *ever* dear niece was *too good* to her and *hers.*

How wounding a thing, Mr. Belford, is a generous and well-distinguished forgiveness! What revenge can be more effectual, and more noble, were revenge intended, and were it wished to strike remorse into a guilty or ungrateful heart! But my dear cousin's motives were all duty and love.

495

The £600 bequeathed to Mrs. Norton, the library to Miss Hervey, and the remembrances to Miss Howe, were not the only articles grudged. Yet to what purpose did they regret the pecuniary bequests, when the poor's fund, and not themselves, would have had the benefit, had not those legacies been bequeathed?

I will only add, that they could not bear to hear read the concluding part, so solemnly addressed to her Redeemer. They all arose from their seats, and crowded out of the apartment we were in: and then, as I afterwards found, separated, in order to seek that consolation in solitary retirement which, though they could not hope for from their own reflections, yet, at the time, they had less reasons to expect in each other's company. I am, / Sir, / Your faithful and obedient servant, / WM. MORDEN.

MR. BELFORD TO THE RIGHT HONOURABLE LORD M.

London, Sept. 14.

MY LORD, — I am very apprehensive that the affair between Mr. Lovelace and the late excellent Miss Clarissa Harlowe will be attended with further bad consequences, notwithstanding her dying injunctions to the contrary. I would therefore humbly propose that your lordship and his other relations will forward the purpose your kinsman lately had to go abroad; where I hope he will stay till all is blown over. But as he will not stir, if he know the true motives of your wishes, the avowed inducement, as I hinted once to Mr. Mowbray, may be such as respects his own health both of person and mind. To Mr. Mowbray and Mr. Tourville all countries are alike; and they perhaps will accompany him.

I am glad to hear that he is in a way of recovery: but this the rather induces me to press the matter. And I think no time should be lost.

[*Here, struck with the need for concision, Richardson inserts a summary narrative section chiefly concerned with the success Belford meets as executor of Clarissa's will.*]

This collection having run into a much greater length than was wished, it is thought proper to omit several letters that passed between Colonel Morden, Miss Howe, Mr. Belford, and Mr. Hickman, in relation to the execution of the lady's will, etc.

It is, however, necessary to observe on this subject, that the unhappy mother, being supported by the two uncles, influenced the afflicted father to overrule all his son's objections, and to direct a literal observation of the will; and at the same time to give up all the sums which he was empowered by it to reimburse himself; as also to take upon himself to defray the funeral expenses.

Mr. Belford sends to Miss Howe the lady's memorandum-book; and promises to send her copies of the several posthumous letters. He tells her that Mr. Lovelace being upon the recovery, he had enclosed the posthumous letter directed for him to Lord M., that his lordship might give it to him, or not, as he should find he could bear it. The following is a copy of that letter:

To Mr. Lovelace

Thursday, Aug. 24.

I TOLD you, in the letter I wrote to you on *Tuesday* last, that you should have another sent you when I had got to *my father's house.*

I presume to say that I am *now*, at your receiving of this, arrived there; and I invite you to follow me, as soon as you can be *prepared* for so great a journey.

Not to allegorize further — my fate is *now*, at your perusal of this, accomplished. My doom is unalterably fixed: and I am either a miserable or a happy being to all eternity. If *happy*, I owe it solely to the Divine mercy: if *miserable*, to your undeserved cruelty.

How poor a triumph will you then find it, to have been able, by a series of black perjuries, and studied baseness, under the name of gallantry or intrigue, to betray poor inexperienced young creatures, who perhaps knew nothing but their duty till they knew you! — Not one good action in the hour of languishing to recollect, not one worthy intention to revolve, it will be all reproach and horror; and you will wish to have it in your power to compound for annihilation.

To say I once respected you with a preference, is what I ought to blush to own, since, at the very time, I was far from thinking you even a moral man; though I little thought that you, or indeed that any man breathing, could be — what you have proved yourself to be. But indeed, sir, I have long been greatly above you: for from my heart I have despised you, and all your ways, ever since I saw what manner of man you were.

Hear me, therefore, O Lovelace! as one speaking from the dead — Lose no time. Set about your repentance instantly. Be no longer the instrument of Satan, to draw poor souls into those subtile snares, which at last shall entangle your own feet. Seek not to multiply your offences, till they become beyond the *power*, as I may say, of the Divine mercy to forgive; since *justice*, no less than *mercy*, is an attribute of the Almighty.

Tremble and reform, when you read what is *the portion of the wicked man from God.* May you be enabled to escape the fate denounced against the abandoned man, and be entitled to the mercies of a long-suffering and gracious God, is the sincere prayer of / CLARISSA HARLOWE.

MR. LOVELACE TO JOHN BELFORD, ESQ.

M. Hall, Thursday, Sept. 14.

EVER since the fatal seventh of this month, I have been lost to myself, and to all the joys of life. I might have gone farther back than that fatal seventh; which, for the future, I will never see anniversarily revolve but in sables; only till that cursed day I had some gleams of hope now and then darting in upon me.

I have been in a cursed way. Methinks something has been working strangely retributive. I never was such a fool as to disbelieve a Providence: yet I am not for resolving into judgments everything that seems to wear an avenging face. Yet if we must be punished either here or hereafter for our misdeeds, better *here*, say I, than *hereafter*. Have I not then an interest to think my punishment already not only begun, but completed; since what I have suffered, and do suffer, passes all description?

Monday, Sept. 18.

Heavy, damnably heavy, and sick at soul, by Jupiter! I must come into their expedient. I must see what change of climate will do.

"To say I once respected you with a preference." — In what stiff language does maidenly modesty on these nice occasions express itself! — *To say I once loved you*, is the English; and there is truth and ease in the expression. "To say I once loved you," then let it be, "is what I ought to blush to own."

And dost thou own it, excellent creature? and dost thou then own it? — What music in these words from such an angel! What would I give that my Clarissa were in being, and *could* and *would* own that she loved me?

"But indeed, sir, I have long been greatly above you."

Long, my blessed charmer! — Long indeed, for you have been *ever* greatly above me, and above your sex, and above all the world.

"That preference was not grounded on ignoble motives."

What a wretch was I, to be so distinguished by her, and yet to be so unworthy of her hope to reclaim me!

"Consider my ways." — Dear life of my life! Of what avail is consideration now, when I have lost the dear creature for whose sake alone it was worth while to *have* consideration? Lost her beyond retrieving — swallowed up by the greedy grave — for *ever* lost her — that, *that's* the sting — matchless woman! how does this reflection wound me!

"Your golden dream cannot long last." — Divine prophetess! my golden dream is *already* over. "Thought and reflection *are* no longer to be kept off." — No *longer continues* that "hardened insensibility" thou chargest upon me. "Remorse *has* broken in upon me." "Dreadful *is* my condition!" It *is* all reproach and horror with me!" — A thousand virtues in turn are preying upon my heart!

Acquaint me, then, with all thou knowest which I do *not* know: how her relations, her cruel relations, take it; and whether, now, the barbed dart of after-reflection sticks not in their hearts, as in mine, up to the very feathers.

. . . .

I will soon quit this kingdom. For now my Clarissa is no more, what is there in it (in the world indeed) worth living for? But should I not first, by some masterly mischief, avenge her and myself upon her cursed family?

MR. LOVELACE TO JOHN BELFORD, ESQ.

Wedn. Sept. 20.

BELFORD ('tis a folly to deny it), I have been, to use an old word, quite *bestrought*.

Why, why did my mother bring me up to bear no control? Why was I so educated, *as that to my very tutors it was a request that I should not know what contradiction or disappointment was?* Ought she not to have known what cruelty there was in her kinaness?

What a punishment, to have my first very great disappointment touch my intellect! And intellects once touched — but that I cannot bear to think of — only thus far; the very repentance and amendment wished me so heartily by my kind and cross dear have been invalidated and postponed, who knows for how long? — the *amendment* at least: — can a madman be capable of either?

Once touched, therefore, I must endeavour to banish those gloomy reflections, which might *otherwise* have brought on the right turn of mind; and this, to express myself in Lord M.'s style, that my wits may not be sent a *wool-gathering*.

How my heart sickens at looking back upon what I was! Denied the sun, and all comfort: *all* my visitors low-born, tiptoe attendants: even those tiptoe slaves never approaching me but periodically, armed with gallipots, boluses, and cephalic draughts; delivering their orders to me in hated whispers; and answering other curtain-holding impertinents, inquiring how I was, and how I took their execrable potions, whisperingly too! What a cursed still-life was this! Nothing active in me, or about me, but the worm that never dies.

Again I hasten from the recollection of scenes which *will*, at times, obtrude themselves upon me.

Adieu, Belford!

MR. LOVELACE TO JOHN BELFORD, ESQ.

I AM preparing to leave this kingdom. Mowbray and Tourville promise to give me their company in a month or two.

I'll give thee my route.

I shall first to Paris; and, for amusement and diversion's sake, try to renew some of my old friendships: thence to some of the German courts: thence, perhaps, to Vienna: thence descend through Bavaria and the Tyrol to Venice, where I shall keep the carnival: thence to

Florence and Turin: thence again over Mount Cenis to France: and, when I return again to Paris, shall expect to see my friend Belford.

I am mad again, by Jupiter! But, thank my stars, not gloomily so! Farewell, farewell, farewell, for the third or fourth time, concludes / Thy LOVELACE.

MR. BELFORD TO ROBERT LOVELACE, ESQ.

Friday, Sept. 22.

Mr. Belford gives an account of the wretched Sinclair's terrible exit, which he had just then received.

If this move thee not, I have news to acquaint thee with, of another dismal catastrophe that is but within this hour come to my ear, of another of thy blessed agents. Thy TOMLINSON! — Dying, and, in all probability, before this can reach thee, dead, in Maidstone Jail. As thou sayest in thy first letter, *something strangely retributive seems to be working.*

Let me consider, Lovelace — *Whose turn can be next*? I wish it may not be thine. But since thou givest me one piece of advice, I will give thee another: and that is, *prosecute, as fast as thou canst, thy intended tour.* Change of scene, and of climate, may establish thy health: while this gross air, and the approach of winter, may thicken thy blood; and, with the help of a conscience that is upon the struggle with thee, and like a cunning wrestler watches its opportunity to give thee another fall, may make thee miserable for thy life.

And so much for this subject at present.

I should be glad to know when you intend to set out. I have too much concern for your welfare, not to wish you in a thinner air and more certain climate.

MR. BELFORD TO COLONEL MORDEN

Thursday, Sept. 21.

GIVE me leave, dear sir, to address myself to you in a very serious and solemn manner on a subject that I must not, cannot, dispense with; as I promised the divine lady that I would do everything in my power to prevent that further mischief of which she was so very apprehensive.

I will not content myself with distant hints. It is with very great concern that I have just now heard of a declaration which you are said to have made to your relations at Harlowe Place, that you will not rest till you have avenged your cousin's wrongs upon Mr. Lovelace.

Far be it from me to offer to defend the unhappy man, or even *unduly* to extenuate his crime: but yet I must say that the family, by their persecutions of the dear lady at first, and by their implacableness afterwards, ought, *at least*, to *share* the blame with him.

I have just now read over the *copies* of the dear lady's posthumous letters. I send them all to you, except that directed for Mr. Lovelace; which I reserve till I have the pleasure of seeing you. Let me entreat you to read once more that written to yourself, and that to her brother; which latter I now send you, as they are in point to the present subject.

Let me also (though I presume to hope there is no need, when you coolly consider everything) remind you of your own promise to your departing cousin; relying upon which, her last moments were the easier.

Reflect, my dear Colonel Morden, that the highest injury was to *her*: her family all have a share in the *cause*: *she* forgives it: why should we not endeavour to imitate what we admire?

The following is the posthumous letter to Colonel Morden, referred to in the above.

Superscribed: *To my beloved Cousin, William Morden, Esq.*
To be delivered after my death.

One principal end of my writing to you in this solemn manner, is to beg of you, which I do with the utmost earnestness, that when you come to hear the particulars of my story, you will not suffer *active* resentment to take place in your generous breast on my account.

Remember, my dear cousin, that vengeance is God's province, and He has undertaken to repay it; nor will you, I hope, invade that province: — especially as there is no necessity for you to attempt to vindicate my fame; since the offender himself (before he is called upon) has stood forth, and offered to do me all the justice that you could have extorted from him, had I lived: and when your own person may be endangered by running an *equal* risk with a *guilty man*.

Seek not then, I beseech you, sir, to aggravate my fault by a pursuit of blood, which must necessarily be deemed a consequence of that fault. Give not the unhappy man the merit (were you assuredly to be the victor) of falling by your hand. At present he is the perfidious, the ungrateful deceiver; but will not the forfeiture of his life, and the probable loss of his soul, be a dreadful expiation for having made me miserable for a *few months* only, and through that misery, by the Divine favour, happy to all eternity?

In such a case, my cousin, where shall the evil stop? And who shall avenge on you? And who on your avenger?

So prays, and to her latest hour will pray, my dear Cousin Morden, my friend, my guardian, but *not* my avenger — (dear sir! remember that!) / Your ever affectionate and obliged / CLARISSA HARLOWE.

COLONEL MORDEN TO JOHN BELFORD, ESQ.

Sat. Sept. 23.

DEAR SIR, — I am very sorry that anything you have heard I have said should give you uneasiness.

501

Yet I do assure you that I have not made any resolutions that will be a tie upon me.

I have indeed expressed myself with vehemence upon the occasion. Who could forbear to do so? But it is not my way to resolve in matters of moment, till opportunity brings the execution of my purposes within my reach. We shall see by what manner of spirit this young man will be acted, on his recovery. If he continue to brave and defy a family, which he has so irreparably injured — if — But resolutions depending upon future contingencies are best left to future determination, as I just now hinted.

Meantime, I will own that I think my cousin's arguments unanswerable. No *good* man but must be influenced by them. But, alas! sir, who *is* good?

The author of this diffusive mischief perpetrated it premeditatedly, wantonly, in the gaiety of his heart. To *try* my cousin, say you, sir? To try the virtue of a Clarissa, sir? Had she then given him any cause to doubt her virtue? It could *not* be. If he avers that she did, I am indeed called upon —— But I will have patience.

That he carried her, as now it appears, to a vile brothel, purposely to put her out of all human resource; himself out of the reach of all humane remorse: and that, finding her proof against all the common arts of delusion, base and unmanly arts were there used to effect his wicked purposes. *Once dead*, the injured saint, in her will, says, *he has seen her*.

That I could not know this when I saw him at M. Hall: that, the object of his attempts considered, I could not suppose there was such a monster breathing as he.

That the injured family has a son who, however unworthy of such a sister, is of a temper vehement, unbridled, fierce; unequal, therefore (as he has once indeed been found), to a contention with this man: and who, nevertheless, resolves to call him to account, if I do not: his very *misbehaviour* perhaps to such a sister stimulating his perverse heart to do her memory the *more signal* justice; though the attempt might be fatal to himself.

But I will force myself from the subject, after I have repeated that I have not yet made any resolutions that can bind me. Whenever I do, I shall be glad they may be such as may merit the honour of your approbation.

.   .   .   .

Mr. Belford, in his answer to this letter, further enforces the lady's dying injunctions; and rejoices that the colonel has made no vindictive resolutions; and hopes everything from his prudence and consideration, and from his promise given to the dying lady.

He desires the colonel will give him a day's notice of his coming to town, lest otherwise he may be absent at the time.

This he does, though he tells him not the reason, with a view to prevent a meeting between him and Mr. Lovelace; who might be in town (as he apprehends) about the same time, in his way to go abroad.

COLONEL MORDEN TO JOHN BELFORD, ESQ.

Tuesday, Sept. 26.

DEAR SIR, — I cannot help congratulating myself, as well as you, that we have already got through with the family every article of the will, where *they* have any concern.

You left me a discretional power in many instances; and, in pursuance of it, I have had my dear cousin's personal jewels valued; and will account to you for them, at the highest price, when I come to town, as well as for other matters that you were pleased to entrust to my management.

These jewels I have presented to my Cousin Dolly Hervey, in acknowledgment of her love to the dear departed. I have told Miss Howe of this; and she is as well pleased with what I have done as if she had been the purchaser of them herself. As that young lady has jewels of her own, she could only have wished to purchase these because they were her beloved friend's.

The grandmother's jewels also are valued; and the money will be paid me for you, to be carried to the uses of the will.

Mrs. Norton is preparing, by general consent, to enter upon her office as housekeeper at *The Grove.* But it is my opinion that she will not be long on this side heaven.

Having now seen everything that relates to the will of my dear cousin brought to a desirable issue, I will set about making my own.

I hope soon to pay my respects to you in town.

LORD M. TO JOHN BELFORD, ESQ.

M. Hall, Friday, Sept. 29.

DEAR SIR, — My kinsman Lovelace is now setting out for London; proposing to see you, and then to go to Dover, and so embark. God send him well out of the kingdom!

On Monday he will be with you, I believe. Pray let me be favoured with an account of all your conversations; for Mr. Mowbray and Mr. Tourville are to be there too; and whether you think he is grown quite his own man again. What I mostly write for is to wish you to keep Colonel Morden and him asunder; and so I give you notice of his going to town.

We shall all here miss the wild fellow. To be sure, there is no man better company when he pleases.

Pray, do you never travel thirty or forty mile? I should be glad to see you here at M. Hall. It will be charity when my kinsman is gone; for we suppose you will be his chief correspondent: although he has promised to write to my nieces often. But he is very apt to forget his promises; to us his relations particularly. God preserve us all; Amen! prays / Your very humble servant, / M.

MR. BELFORD TO LORD M.

London, Tuesday Night, Oct. 3.

MY LORD, — I obey your lordship's commands with great pleasure.

Yesterday in the afternoon Mr. Lovelace made me a visit at my lodgings. As I was in expectation of one from Colonel Morden about the same time, I thought proper to carry him to a tavern which neither of us frequented (on pretence of a half-appointment); ordering notice to be sent me thither, if the colonel came: and Mr. Lovelace sent to Mowbray, and Tourville, and Mr. Doleman of Uxbridge (who came to town to take leave of him), to let them know where to find us.

Mr. Lovelace is *too well recovered*, I was going to say. I never saw him more gay, lively, and handsome. We had a good deal of bluster about some parts of the trust I have engaged in; and upon freedoms I had treated him with; in which he would have it that I had exceeded our agreed-on limits; but on the arrival of our three old companions, and a nephew of Mr. Doleman's (who had a good while been desirous to pass an hour with Mr. Lovelace), it blew off for the present.

We parted about four; he not a little dissatisfied with me; for we had some talk about subjects which, he said, he loved not to think of; to wit, Miss Harlowe's will; my executorship; papers I had in confidence communicated to that admirable lady (with no unfriendly design, I assure your lordship); and he insisting upon, and I refusing, the return of the letters he had written to me, from the time that he had made his first addresses to her.

He would see me once again, he said; and it would be upon very ill terms if I complied not with his request. Which I bid him not expect. But, that I might not deny him everything, I told him that I would give him a copy of the will; though I was sure, I said, when he read it, he would wish he had never seen it.

I had a message from him about eleven this morning, desiring me to name a place at which to dine with him, and Mowbray, and Tourville, for the last time: and soon after, another from Colonel Morden, inviting me to pass the evening with him at the Bedford Head in Covent Garden. And, that I might keep them at distance from one another, I appointed Mr. Lovelace at the Eagle in Suffolk Street.

I give your lordship this account, in answer to your desire to know if I think him the man he was?

In our conversation at dinner, he was balancing whether he should set out the next morning, or the morning after. But finding he had nothing to do, and Colonel Morden being in town (which, however, I told him not of), I turned the scale; and he agreed upon setting out to-morrow morning; they to see him embark; and I promised to accompany them for a morning's ride (as they proposed their horses); but said that I must return in the afternoon.

With much reluctance they let me go to my evening's appointment: they little thought with whom: for Mr. Lovelace had put it as a case of humour to all of us, whether, as he had been told that Mr. Morden and Mr. James Harlowe had thrown out menaces against him, he ought to leave the kingdom till he had thrown himself in their way.

Mowbray gave his opinion that he ought to leave it like a man of honour, as he was; and if he did not take those gentlemen to task for their opprobrious speeches, that, at least, he should be seen by them in public before he went away; else they might give themselves airs, as if he had left the kingdom in fear of them.

To this he himself so much inclined, that it was with difficulty I persuaded him that, as they had neither of them proceeded to a *direct* and *formal challenge*; as they knew he had not made himself difficult of access; and as he had already done the family injury enough; and it was Miss Harlowe's earnest desire that he would be content with that; he had no reason, from any point of honour, to delay his journey; especially as he had so just a motive for his going as the establishment of his health; and as he might return the sooner, if he saw occasion for it.

I wish Mr. Lovelace could have been prevailed upon to take any other tour than that of France and Italy. I did propose Madrid to him; but he laughed at me, and told me that the proposal was in character from a *mule*; and from one who was become as grave as a Spaniard of the *old cut*, at *ninety*.

I expressed to the colonel my apprehensions that his cousin's dying injunctions would not have the force upon him that were to be wished.

They have *great force* upon me, Mr. Belford, said he; or *one world* would not have held Mr. Lovelace and me thus long. But my intention is to go to Florence; not to lay my bones there, as upon my cousin's death I told you I thought to do; but to settle all my affairs in those parts, and then to come over, and reside upon a little paternal estate in Kent, which is strangely gone to ruin in my absence. Indeed, were I to meet Mr. Lovelace, either here or abroad, I might not be answerable for the consequence.

MR. BELFORD TO LORD M.

Wedn. Night, Oct. 4.

MY LORD, — I am just returned from attending Mr. Lovelace as far as Gad's Hill, near Rochester. He was exceedingly gay all the way. Mowbray and Tourville are gone on with him. They will see him embark, and under sail; and promise to follow him in a month or two; for they say there is no living without him, now he is once more himself.

He and I parted with great and even solemn tokens of affection;

but yet not without gay intermixtures, as I will acquaint your lordship.

Taking me aside, and clasping his arms about me, "Adieu, dear Belford! (said he). May you proceed in the course you have entered upon! — Whatever airs I give myself, this charming creature has fast hold of me *here* (clapping his hand upon his heart); and I must either appear what you see me, or be what I so lately was. O the divine creature!" (lifting up his eyes) ——

"But if I live to come to England, and you remain fixed in your present way, and can give me encouragement, I hope rather to follow your *example*, than to ridicule you for it. This will (for I had given him a copy of it) I will make the companion of my solitary hours. You have told me part of its melancholy contents; and that, and her posthumous letter, shall be my study; and they will prepare me for being your disciple, if you hold on.

"*You*, Jack, may marry (continued he); and I have a wife in my eye for you. Only thou'rt such an awkward mortal" (he saw me affected, and thought to make me smile): "but we don't make ourselves, except it be worse by our dress. Thou art in mourning now, as well as I: but if ever thy ridiculous turn lead thee again to be beau-brocade, I will *bedizen* thee, as the girls say, on my return, to my own fancy, and according to thy own *natural appearance* — thou shalt doctor my soul, and I will doctor thy body: thou shalt see what a clever fellow I will make of thee.

"As for *me*, I never *will*, I never *can*, marry. That I will not take a few liberties, and that I will not try to start some of my former game, I won't promise — habits are not easily shaken off — but they shall be by way of weaning. So *return* and *reform* shall go together."

I hope, my lord, for all your noble family's sake, that we shall see him soon return, and reform, as he promises.

I return your lordship my humble thanks for the honour of your invitation to M. Hall. The first letter I receive from Mr. Lovelace shall give me the opportunity of embracing it. I am, my lord, / Your most faithful and obedient servant, / J. BELFORD.

MR. LOVELACE TO JOHN BELFORD, ESQ.

Paris, Octob. 14.

I OUGHT to have written to you sooner. But I loitered two days at Calais, for an answer to a letter I wrote to engage my former travelling valet, De la Tour; an ingenious, ready fellow, as you have heard me say. I *have* engaged him, and he is now with me.

I shall make no stay here; but intend for some of the Electoral Courts. That of Bavaria, I think, will engage me longest. Perhaps I may step out of my way (if I can be out of my way anywhere) to those of Dresden and Berlin: and it is not impossible that you may have one letter from me at Vienna. And then perhaps I may fall down into Italy by the Tyrol; and so, taking Turin in my way, return to Paris; where I hope to see Mowbray and Tourville: nor do I despair of you.

I have my former lodgings in the Rue St. Antoine: which I shall hold, notwithstanding my tour: so they will be ready to accommodate any two of you, if you come hither before my return: and for this I have conditioned.

I write to Charlotte; and that is writing to all my relations at once.

MR. BELFORD TO ROBERT LOVELACE, ESQ.

London, Oct. 25.

I WRITE to show you that I am incapable of slighting even the minutest requests of an absent and distant friend. Yet you may believe that there cannot be any great alterations in the little time that you have been out of England, with respect to the subjects of your inquiry.

I am very earnest in my wishes to be admitted into the nuptial state. But I think I ought to pass some time as a probationary.

The Harlowes continue inconsolable; and I dare say will to the end of their lives.

Miss Howe is not yet married; but I have reason to think will soon. I have the honour of corresponding with her; and the more I know of her, the more I admire the nobleness of her mind.

As to Mowbray and Tourville, I see them but seldom. I suppose they'll be at Paris before you can return from Germany; for they cannot live without you: and you gave them such a specimen of your recovered volatility, in the last evening's conversation, as equally delighted *them*, and concerned *me*.

I wish, with all my heart, that thou wouldst bend thy course towards the Pyrenean. I wonder thou wilt not, since then thy subjects would be as new to thyself as to / Thy BELFORD.

MR. LOVELACE TO JOHN BELFORD, ESQ.

Paris, Oct. 16/27.

I FOLLOW my last on occasion of a letter just now come to hand from Joseph Leman. The fellow is conscience-ridden, Jack, and tells me that he cannot rest either day nor night for the mischiefs which he fears he has been, and may still further be the means of doing. He wishes, if it please God, and if it please me, that he had never seen my Honour's face.

But the chief occasion of troubling my Honour now is to prevent future mischiefs to me: for he can assure me that Colonel Morden has set out from them all, with a full resolution to *have his will of me*: and he is well assured that he said, and swore to it, *as how* he was resolved that he would either have my Honour's heart's blood, or I should have his; or *some such-like sad threatenings*: and that all the family rejoice in it, and hope I shall *come short home*.

As soon as I can inform myself where to direct to him, [Colonel Morden] I will write to know his purpose; for I cannot bear suspense in such a case as this: that solemn act, were it even to be marriage or hanging, which must be done tomorrow, I had rather should be done today.

I cannot get off my regrets on account of this dear lady for the blood of me. If the colonel and I are to meet, as he has done me no injury, and loves the memory of his cousin, we shall engage with the same sentiments as to the object of our dispute: and that, you know, is no very common case.

In short, I am as much convinced that I have done wrong as he can be; and regret it as much. But I will not bear to be threatened by any man in the world, however conscious I may be of having deserved blame.

Adieu, Belford! be sincere with me. No palliation, as thou valuest /
Thy LOVELACE.

MR. BELFORD TO ROBERT LOVELACE, ESQ.

London, Oct. 26.

I CANNOT think, my dear Lovelace, that Colonel Morden has either threatened you in those gross terms mentioned by the vile, hypocritical, and ignorant Joseph Leman, or intends to follow you. They are the words of people of that fellow's class, and not of a gentleman: not of Colonel Morden, I am sure. You'll observe that Joseph pretends not to say that he heard him speak them.

I have been very solicitous to sound the colonel, for your sake, and for his own, and for the sake of the injunctions of the excellent lady to me, as well as to him, on that subject. He is (and you will not wonder that he should be) extremely affected; and owns that he has expressed himself in terms of resentment on the occasion. Once he said to me, that had his beloved cousin's case been that of a *common seduction*, her own credulity or weakness contributing to her fall, he could have forgiven you. But, in so many words, he assured me that he had not taken any resolutions; nor had he declared himself to the family in such a way as should bind him to resent; on the contrary, he has owned that his cousin's injunctions have hitherto had the force upon him which I could wish they should have.

He went abroad in a week after you. When he took his leave of me, he told me that his design was to go to Florence; and that he would settle his affairs there; and then return to England, and here pass the remainder of his days.

I was indeed apprehensive that if you and he were to meet, something unhappy might fall out: and as I knew that you proposed to take Italy, and very likely Florence, in your return to France, I was very solicitous to prevail upon you to take the Court of Spain into your plan. I am still so. And if you are not to be prevailed upon to do that, let me entreat you to avoid Florence or Leghorn in your

508

return, since you have visited both heretofore. At least, let not the proposal of a meeting come from you.

It would be matter of serious reflection to me, if the *very fellow*, this *Joseph Leman*, who gave you such an opportunity to turn all the artillery of his masters against themselves, and to play them upon one another to favour your plotting purposes, should be the instrument in the devil's hand (unwittingly too) to avenge them all upon *you*: for should you even get the better of the colonel, would the mischief end there? It would but add remorse to your present remorse; since the interview *must* end in death; for he would not, I am confident, take his life at your hand. The Harlowes would, moreover, prosecute you in a legal way. You hate *them*; and *they* would be gainers by *his* death: rejoicers in *yours* — and have you not done mischief enough already?

Let *me*, therefore (and through me all your friends), have the satisfaction to hear that you are resolved to avoid this gentleman. Time will subdue all things. Nobody doubts your bravery. Nor will it be known that your plan is changed through persuasion.

Young Harlowe talks of calling you to account. This is a plain evidence that Mr. Morden has not taken the quarrel upon himself for their family.

I am in no apprehension of anybody but Colonel Morden. I know it will not be a means to prevail upon you to oblige me, if I say that I am well assured that this gentleman is a skilful swordsman; and that he is as cool and sedate as skilful. But yet I will add, that if I had a value for my life, he should be the last man, except yourself, with whom I would choose to have a contention.

Moreover, seest thou not, in the deaths of two of thy principal agents, *the handwriting upon the wall against thee*?

Mr. Lovelace to John Belford, Esq.
Munich, Nov. 11–22.

I received yours this moment, just as I was setting out for Vienna.

As to going to Madrid, or one single step out of the way, to avoid Colonel Morden, let me perish if I do! You cannot think me so mean a wretch.

And so you own that he *has* threatened me; but not in gross and ungentlemanly terms, you say. If he has threatened me like a gentleman, I will resent his threats like a gentleman. But he has not done as a man of honour, if he has threatened me at all behind my back. I would scorn to threaten any man to whom I *knew* how to address myself either personally, or by pen and ink.

He had not taken any resolutions, you say, when you saw him. He *must* and *will* take resolutions, one way or other, very quickly; for I wrote to him yesterday, without waiting for this or your answer to my last. I could not avoid it. I could not (as I told you in that) live in suspense. I have directed my letter to Florence.

509

It would be sweet revenge to him, were I to fall by his hand. But what should I be the better for killing him?

I will enclose the copy of the letter I sent him.

. . . .

Thou art really an honest fellow, and a sincere and warm friend. I could almost wish I had not written to Florence till I had received thy letter now before me. But it is gone. Let it go. If he wish peace, and to avoid violence, he will have a fair opportunity to embrace the one, and shun the other. If not — he must take his fate.

But be this as it may, you may contrive to let young Harlowe know (he is a menacer too!) that I shall be in England in March next at farthest.

Mr. Lovelace to William Morden, Esq.
(Enclosed in the above)

Munich, Nov. 10/21

SIR, — I have heard, with a great deal of surprise, that you have thought fit to throw out some menacing expressions against me.

I should have been very glad that you had thought I had punishment enough in my own mind, for the wrongs I have done to the most excellent of women; and that it had been possible for two persons, so ardently joining in one love (especially as I was desirous, to the utmost of my power, to repair those wrongs), to have lived, if not on amicable terms, in such a way, as not to put either to the pain of hearing of threatenings thrown out in absence, which either ought to be despised for, if he had not spirit to take notice of them.

Being uncertain when this letter may meet you, I shall set out to-morrow for Vienna; where any letter directed to the post-house in that city, or to Baron Windisgratz's (at the Favorita), to whom I have commendations, will come to hand.

Meantime, believing you to be a man too generous to make a wrong construction of what I am going to declare, and knowing the value which the dearest of all creatures had for you, and your relation to her, I will not scruple to assure you that the most acceptable return will be, that Colonel Morden chooses to be upon an amicable, rather than upon any other footing, with / His sincere admirer, and humble servant, / R. LOVELACE.

MR. LOVELACE TO JOHN BELFORD, ESQ.

Lintz, { *Nov. 28.* / *Dec. 9.*

I AM now on my way to Trent, in order to meet Colonel Morden, in pursuance of his answer to my letter enclosed in my last. I had been at Pressburgh, and had intended to visit some other cities of Hungary: but having obliged myself to return first to Vienna, I there met with his letter: which follows:

510

SIR, — Your letter was at Florence four days before I arrived there.

That I might not appear unworthy of your favour, I set out for this city the very next morning.

I own, sir, that I have, on all occasions, spoken of your treatment of my ever dear cousin as it deserved. It would have been very surprising if I had not. And it behoves me (now you have given me so noble an opportunity of explaining myself) to convince you, that no words fell from my lips, of you, merely because you were absent. I acquaint you, therefore, that I will attend your appointment; and would, were it to the farthest part of the globe.

I shall stay some days at this court; and if you please to direct for me at M. Klienfurt's in this city, whether I remain here or not, your commands will come safely and speedily to the hands of, sir, / Your most humble servant, / WM. MORDEN.

So you see, Belford, that the colonel, by his ready, his even eagerly expressed acceptance of the offered interview, *was determined*. And is it not much better to bring such a point as this to an issue, than to give pain to friends for my safety, or continue in suspense myself; as I must do, if I imagined that another had aught against me?

This was my reply:

SIR, — I have this moment the favour of yours. I will suspend a tour I was going to take into Hungary, and instantly set out for Munich: and, if I find you not there, will proceed to Trent. This city, being on the confines of Italy, will be most convenient, as I presume, to you, in your return to Tuscany; and I shall hope to meet you in it on the 3/14th of December.

I shall bring with me only a French valet and an English footman. Other particulars may be adjusted when I have the honour to see you. Till when, I am, sir, / Your most obedient servant, / R. LOVELACE.

Now, Jack, I have no manner of apprehension of the event of this meeting. And I think I may say he seeks me; not I him. And so let him take the consequence.

What is infinitely nearer to my heart is my ingratitude to the most excellent of women — my *premeditated* ingratitude!

I will aggravate to myself this aggravation of the colonel's pretending to call me to account for my treatment of a lady so much *my own*, lest, in the approaching interview, my heart should relent for one so nearly related to her, and who means honour and justice to her memory; and I should thereby give him advantages which otherwise he cannot have. For I know that I shall be inclined to trust to my skill, to save a man who was so much and so justly valued by

511

her; and shall be loath to give way to my resentment, as a threatened man. And in this respect only am I sorry for his skill, and his courage, lest I should be obliged, in my own defence, to add a chalk to a score that is already too long.

. . . .

Indeed, indeed, Belford, I am, and shall be, to my latest hour, the most miserable of beings Such exalted generosity! — Why didst thou put into my craving hands the copy of her will? Why sentest thou to me the posthumous letter? What though I was earnest to see the will? Thou knewest what they *both* were (*I* did not); and that it would be cruel to oblige me.

The meeting of twenty Colonel Mordens, were there twenty to meet in turn, would be nothing to me; would not give me a moment's concern, as to my own safety: but my reflections upon my vile ingratitude to so superior an excellence will ever be my curse.

If any mishap should befall me, you'll have the particulars of it from De la Tour. He indeed knows but little of English: but every modern tongue is yours. He is a trusty and ingenious fellow: and, if anything happens, will have some other papers, which I shall have ready sealed up, for you to transmit to Lord M. And since thou art so expert and so ready at executorships, prithee, Belford, accept of the office for me, as well as for my Clarissa — Clarissa Lovelace let me call her.

By all that's good, I am bewitched to her memory. Her very name, with mine joined to it, ravishes my soul, and is more delightful to me than the sweetest music.

Thus much only I know, that if I should kill him (which I will not do if I can help it), I shall be far from being easy in my mind; *that* shall I never more be. But as the meeting is evidently of his own seeking, against an option fairly given to the contrary, and I cannot avoid it, I'll think of that hereafter. It is but repenting and mortifying for all at once: for I am as sure of victory as I am that I now live, let him be ever so skilful a swordsman; since, besides that I am no unfleshed novice, this is a sport that, when provoked to it, I love as well as my food. And, moreover, I shall be *as calm and undisturbed* as the bishop at his prayers: while he, as is evident by his letter, must be actuated by revenge and passion.

Doubt not, therefore, Jack, that I shall give a good account of this affair. Meantime, I remain / Yours most affectionately, etc. / Lovelace.

Mr. Lovelace to John Belford, Esq.

Trent, Dec. 3–14.

To-morrow is to be the day that will, in all probability, send either one or two ghosts to attend the manes of my Clarissa.

I arrived here yesterday; and inquiring for an English gentleman of the name of Morden, soon found out the colonel's lodgings. He had been in town two days; and left his name at every probable place.

He was gone to ride out; and I left *my* name, and where to be found: and in the evening he made me a visit.

He was plaguy gloomy. That was not I. But yet he told me that I had acted like a man of true spirit in my first letter; and with honour, in giving him so readily this meeting. He wished I had in other respects; and then we might have seen each other upon better terms than now we did.

I said there was no recalling what was passed; and that I wished some things had not been done, as well as he.

To recriminate now, he said, would be as exasperating as unavailable. And as I had so cheerfully given him this opportunity, words should give place to business. *Your* choice, Mr. Lovelace, of time, of place, of weapon, shall be *my* choice.

The two latter be yours, Mr. Morden. The time to-morrow, or next day, as you please.

Next day, then, Mr. Lovelace; and we'll ride out to-morrow to fix the place.

Agreed, sir.

Well, now, Mr. Lovelace, do you choose the weapon.

I said I believed we might be upon an equal foot with the single rapier; but, if he thought otherwise, I had no objection to a pistol.

They may both be of use to you, sir, at the sword, as well as at the pistol: the sword, therefore, be the thing, if you please.

With all my heart.

We parted with a solemn sort of ceremonious civility: and this day I called upon him; and we rode out together to fix upon the place: and both being of one mind, and hating to put off for the morrow what could be done to-day, would have decided it then: but De la Tour, and the colonel's valet, who attended us, being unavoidably let into the secret, joined to beg we would have with us a surgeon from Brixen, whom La Tour had fallen in with there, and who had told him he was to ride next morning to bleed a person in a fever, at a lone cottage, which, by the surgeon's description, was not far from the place where we then were, if it were not that very cottage within sight of us.

We fixed upon a little lone valley for the spot — ten to-morrow morning the time — and single rapier the sword. Yet I repeatedly told him that I valued myself so much upon my skill in that weapon that I would wish him to choose any other.

He said it was a gentleman's weapon; and he who understood it not, wanted a qualification that he ought to suffer for not having; but that, as to him, one weapon was as good as another throughout all the instruments of offence.

So, Jack, you see I take no advantage of him: but my devil must deceive me if he take not his life or his death at my hands before eleven to-morrow morning.

His valet and mine are to be present; but both strictly enjoined to be impartial and inactive: and, in return for my civility of the like nature, he commanded *his* to be assisting to me, if he fell.

We are to ride thither, and to dismount when at the place; and his footman and mine are to wait at an appointed distance, with a chaise to carry off to the borders of the Venetian territories the survivor, if one drop; or to assist either or both, as occasion may demand.

And thus, Belford, is the matter settled.

A shower of rain has left me nothing else to do: and therefore I write this letter; though I might as well have deferred it till to-morrow twelve o'clock, when I doubt not to be able to write again, to assure you how much I am / Yours, etc. / LOVELACE.

TRANSLATION OF A LETTER FROM F. J. DE LA TOUR TO
JOHN BELFORD, ESQ., NEAR SOHO SQUARE, LONDON
Trent, Dec. 18. N.S.

SIR, — I have melancholy news to inform you of, by order of the Chevalier Lovelace. He showed me his letter to you before he sealed it; signifying that he was to meet the Chevalier Morden on the 15th. Wherefore, as the occasion of the meeting is so well known to you, I shall say nothing of it here.

I had taken care to have ready, within a little distance, a surgeon and his assistant, to whom, under an oath of secrecy, I had revealed the matter (though I did not own it to the two gentlemen); so that they were prepared with bandages, and all things proper. For well was I acquainted with the bravery and skill of my chevalier; and had heard the character of the other; and knew the animosity of both. A post-chaise was ready, with each of their footmen, at a little distance.

The two chevaliers came exactly at their time: they were attended by Monsieur Margate (the colonel's gentleman) and myself. They had given orders overnight, and now repeated them in each other's presence, that we should observe a strict impartiality between them: and that, if one fell, each of us should look upon himself, as to any needful help or retreat, as the servant of the survivor, and take his commands accordingly.

After a few compliments, both the gentlemen, with the greatest presence of mind that I ever beheld in men, stripped to their shirts, and drew.

They parried with equal judgment several passes. My chevalier drew the first blood, making a desperate push, which, by a sudden turn of his antagonist, missed going clear through him, and wounded him on the fleshy part of his ribs of his right side; which part the sword tore out, being on the extremity of the body: but, before my chevalier could recover himself, the colonel, in return, pushed him into the inside of the left arm, near the shoulder: and the sword (raking his breast as it passed), being followed by a great effusion of blood, the colonel said, Sir, I believe you have enough.

My chevalier swore by G—d he was not hurt: 'twas a pin's point: and so made another pass at his antagonist; which he, with a surprising dexterity, received under his arm, and run my dear chevalier into the body; who immediately fell, saying, The luck is yours, sir — Oh, my beloved Clarissa! — Now art thou —— Inwardly he spoke three or four words more. His sword dropped from his hand. Mr. Morden threw his down, and ran to him, saying in French, Ah, monsieur, you are a dead man! — Call to God for mercy!

We gave the signal agreed upon to the footmen; and they to the surgeons; who instantly came up.

Colonel Morden, I found, was too well used to the bloody work; for he was as cool as if nothing so extraordinary had happened, assisting the surgeons, though his own wound bled much. But my dear chevalier fainted away two or three times running, and vomited blood besides.

However, they stopped the bleeding for the present; and we helped him into the voiture; and then the colonel suffered his own wound to be dressed; and appeared concerned that my chevalier was between whiles (when he could speak and struggle) extremely outrageous. Poor gentleman! he had made quite sure of victory!

The colonel, against the surgeons' advice, would mount on horseback to pass into the Venetian territories; and generously gave me a purse of gold to pay the surgeons; desiring me to make a present to the footman; and to accept of the remainder as a mark of his satisfaction in my conduct; and in my care and tenderness of my master.

The surgeons told him that my chevalier could not live over the day.

When the colonel took leave of him, Mr. Lovelace said, You have well revenged the dear creature.

I have, sir, said Mr. Morden: and perhaps shall be sorry that you called upon me to this work, while I was balancing whether to obey or disobey the dear angel.

There is a fate in it! replied my chevalier — a cursed fate! — or this could not have been! But be ye all witnesses that I have provoked my destiny, and acknowledge that I fall by a man of honour.

Sir, said the colonel, with the piety of a confessor (wringing Mr. Lovelace's hand), snatch these few fleeting moments, and commend yourself to God.

And so he rode off.

The voiture proceeded slowly with my chevalier; yet the motion set both his wounds bleeding afresh; and it was with difficulty they again stopped the blood.

We brought him alive to the nearest cottage; and he gave orders to me to dispatch to you the packet I herewith send sealed up; and bid me write to you the particulars of this most unhappy affair: and give you thanks, in his name, for all your favours and friendship to him.

Contrary to all expectation, he lived over the night: but *suffered much*, as well from his *impatience* and *disappointment* as from his *wounds*; for he seemed *very unwilling to die*.

He was delirious at times in the two last hours; and then several times cried out, as if he had seen some frightful spectre, Take her away! take her away! but named nobody. And sometimes praised some lady (that Clarissa, I suppose, whom he had invoked when he received his death's wound), calling her, Sweet Excellence! Divine Creature! Fair Sufferer! And once he said, Look down, Blessed Spirit, look down! —— And there stopped; his lips, however, moving.

At nine in the morning he was seized with convulsions, and fainted away; and it was a quarter of an hour before he came out of them.

His last words I must not omit, as they show an ultimate composure; which may administer some consolation to his honourable friends.

Blessed — said he, addressing himself no doubt to Heaven; for his dying eyes were lifted up. A strong convulsion prevented him for a few moments saying more, but recovering, he again, with great fervour (lifting up his eyes and his spread hands), pronounced the word *blessed*. Then, in a seeming ejaculation, he spoke inwardly, so as not to be understood: at last, he distinctly pronounced these three words,

LET THIS EXPIATE!

And then, his head sinking on his pillow, he expired, at about half an hour after ten.

He little thought, poor gentleman! his end so near: so had given no direction about his body. I have caused it to be embowelled, and deposited in a vault, till I have orders from England.

This is a favour that was procured with difficulty; and would have been refused, had he not been an Englishman of rank: a nation with reason respected in every Austrian Government. For he had refused ghostly attendance, and the Sacraments in the Catholic way. May his soul be happy, I pray God!

I have had some trouble also, on account of the manner of his death, from the magistry here: who have taken the requisite informations in the affair. And it has cost me some money. Of which, and of my dear chevalier's effects, I will give you a faithful account in my next. And so, waiting at this place your commands, I am, sir / Your most faithful and obedient servant, / F. J. DE LA TOUR.

CONCLUSION

[*At the end of the story Richardson appended a Conclusion (here omitted), "Supposed to be written by Mr. Belford." It told in somewhat less than ten thousand words the fates of some of the remaining characters. At the end of her six months mourning Miss Howe "made Mr. Hickman one of the happiest men in the world," and after his period of probation Belford married Miss Charlotte Montague. Colonel*

Morden decided to settle in Italy. Doubtless because of moral lessons, inferred or explicit, about half the space in this Conclusion summarizes the careers of Mrs. Sinclair's "nieces," Sally Martin and Polly Horton.

[This Conclusion is followed by a shorter Postscript that deals with poetical justice, the doctrine of rewards and punishments, and the theory of tragedy. The ideas are conventional of their time.]

YZ—A—8987654